The Book of Watford

R. W. Billings, del.

J. Wright, sc.

ENTRANCE LODGE.

The Book of Watford
J B Nunn A.R.P.S.
First Published October 1987, reprinted 1988
Hard-cover, ISBN 0 9511777 1 0

Reprinted, Soft-cover, 1992
ISBN 0 9511777 4 5

Published by

J B NUNN (trading as PAGEPRINT)

Watford, Herts

1992

The Book of Watford

A *portrait of our town, c1800-1987*

Contributors

Ted Parrish
Edgar Chapman B.A. (Hons)
George Lorimer

Main Photographs by

Frederick Downer
William Coles
Whitford Anderson A.R.I.B.A.
Albert Warren
George Bolton F.L.A., M.B.E.
Greville Studios
Harry Williamson
Bob Nunn A.R.P.S.

Text Excerpts from

The West Herts & Watford Observer
The West Herts Post
Watford Newsletter
Watford Illustrated
Evening Echo
Watford Our Town

Design Consultant

Larry Noades

Compiled and Edited by

Bob Nunn A.R.P.S.

J.W.M.Turner Esq.ʳ R.A.   Hill aqu

View at South West Angle.
CASSIOBURY.

IV

Contents

Excerpts from contemporary newspapers, documents, etc, are headed as closely to the style of original as space permits and carry a reference name or title of publication, and the publication date.

Editorial comment relevant to a photograph, particular time, or a story, is typeset in *italics*. Dates in brackets, e.g., *WHP (July 1950)* indicate related subject or interest but included out of time context.

Where street numbers have been given they relate to the numbers in use during the years c1935-1950, in particular, as listed in Kelly's Directories of Watford.

A great number of photographs carry a further reference in addition to the caption, e.g., *p.277 t, 291 b*. This is a short-cut locator to identify pictures, on other pages, of the same place or subject, but of a different time scale.

The abbreviations are: *tl* – top left; *tr* – top right; *cl* – and *cr* – centre left and centre right; *bl* – and *br* – bottom left and bottom right; and *s* – additional story.

Newspaper references to the cuttings are: *WO* – Watford Observer; *WHP* – West Herts Post; *WI* – Watford Illustrated; *WN* – Watford Newsletter; *EE* – Evening Echo and *WOT* – Watford Our Town.

Albert G. Dillingham, J.P., Freeman of the Borough of Watford.

During the year of the Coronation riots in Watford's Market Place, Albert Dillingham was born 'within the sound of Bow Bells'. As did so many others, in 1910 his parents came to Watford.

His working life started in the manner of many North Watford men, of work on the railway. In the troubled time of depression he became involved in Union activities and in 1940 was co-opted to serve as a member of Watford Borough Council, being elected to the Aldermanic Bench in 1951. He was later elected to the County Council where he similarly served as Councillor and then as Alderman. He was made Justice of the Peace, for life, in 1943. He served as Borough Councillor and Alderman, County Councillor and Alderman, and J.P. each for 30 years.

He was Watford's Mayor during Coronation Year (1953).

For his outstanding services to the Town he was created Freeman of the Borough in 1976.

Preface

by

A. G. Dillingham, J.P.

As a boy I well remember walking the roads and knowing the shops of the time. That was in 1910 when I came to live in Watford. My life's work has been involved in and with Watford and Watford's people; my wife and I have memories stretching back and reaching to us from every turn.

The changes which span the past 80 years have been vast; places I knew well are, to others, just names. One day the younger readers too will be faced with youngsters asking about the past.

This book chronicles the happenings of the town, not for 50 or 80 years, but essentially for the 150 years since the coming of the railway. It succeeds admirably; it was with considerable pleasure that I was able to browse through it in advance of publication.

Watford is a fine town in which to live, work and play; it has achieved its present status through hardship and hard work and the town's popularity is a measure of that success.

For me the book captures the flavour and anxieties, hopes, joys, and, yes, some disappointments of the times. I know that every reader fortunate enough to own a copy will feel the same; for every Watfordian, young or old, "The Book of Watford" will become an ever more valued and priceless possession.

Albert Dillingham

June, 1987

THE BOROUGH ARMS

In the top third of the shield are the Arms of St. Albans to commemorate the long association between that city and Watford. The "harts" represent the Herts in Hertfordshire.

In the lower part of the shield occur two escallop shells taken from the Arms of the Earl of Clarendon, Charter Mayor. The wavy blue and white lines represent the ford in Watford.

The fasces in the centre denote magisterial authority.

The motto "*Audentior*" is a quotation from Virgil's *Aeneid* VI, 95: "tu ne cede malis, sed contra *audentior* ito, quam tua te Fortuna sinet". (Yield not thou to ills, but go forth to face them *more boldly* than thy Fortune shall allow thee.)

Introduction

Like so many others I have been astonished at the speed with which the town has changed. Some of the changes are recorded in my own collection of photographs which spans 40 years and in the Reference Library's collection which goes back a further 84 years to 1863. Of the latter only a scant few hundred have been published (and inevitably some of the oldest are fading with age); I thought it was time to include them in a book.

I had envisaged text being written to accompany the photographs; this proved impractical and I decided that the original text and comment of the period would provide a satisfactory alternative. In the event the 'original extracts' provide far more detail and fact than could ever be written from a modern stance. Some of the original excerpts may be quite terse and so there are some 'explanations' typeset in italics, but for those readers who enjoy a good detective story there will be found any number of clues to link one story with another way beyond the scope of the index.

The book was planned to run to about 200 pages with perhaps some 300 photographs but as I found more and more interesting photographs I was so often asked 'where was it' that I decided I must provide answers.

There have been previous histories, perhaps the most popular being the oldest, by Henry Williams (1884), published before it was practical to provide illustrations. Next came that of W R Saunders; researched in the years following the first war the author was unable, during the depression, to find a publisher until the Watford Observer serialised it in 1931, and then produced it in book form. It remains an interesting factual account of the town's early history and formed the basis for the 1951 Festival of Britain 'Pictorial Record' which, in 100 pages presented about 150 photographs of bygone Watford. This was followed, in 1972, by the Borough's 'Watford, 1922-72' which presented a pictorial record of 50 years since incorporation as a Borough.

None, I felt, attempted to detail the tremendous growth of the town, or explain some of the happenings of this century. From the planned 200 pages my book began to grow.

A number of subjects, for instance, sports, Cassiobury, brewing, buses, railways and canals have been well covered in books which are still available. Many aspects of local industry are well documented as, for example, De Havillands and Scammell's, and consequently they are remarked upon only as they fit within a particular period of time.

The photographs are presented to show the town's history and the text selected to cover a wide range of social activities and town development.

I am only too well aware that readers will know infinitely more about their own particular subject than I could ever hope to cover and so, whilst every effort has been made to achieve a high degree of accuracy, I hope the interest value will pardon any shortcomings.

Dates are a thorny subject; I have taken many founding dates from various adverts of the firms concerned but even these sometimes disagree. An advert by Frederick Downer, and a price list of his, give a founding date two years apart. Some buildings are put into use a year or more before being 'officially' opened, thus giving two dates. Many photographs are undated but these have been included within the time span of the accompanying text.

Without the skill and dedication of the early photographers we would not have the splendid collection of photographs we now have. As many readers are also camera users they will find, here and there, brief comments on the progress of cameras and how the advent of the Leica, indirectly, had such an effect upon the fortunes of the 'Sun'.

In retrospect the text does not necessarily record the activities of the many old and new charitable and non-profit-making organisations which contribute to the social fabric of Watford's community. The town owes much to the voluntary workers whose presence in all facets of local activities has been a constant factor in an ever-changing society.

I am indebted to many people for help and encouragement (they are listed among the acknowledgements on page 372) and in particular to Ted Parrish for his help, knowledge and advice in writing captions and other text, without which this work would have been incomplete, and especially to George Lorrimer for casting a critical eye over, and proof-reading the whole.

Finally, after two years of intensive preparation, I have to thank those people who matter most; those who have lived their lives in the town and seen the vast changes, and those who are newcomers and who want to know more. They have one interest in common; it is that many were pleased to become subscribers to this book and so made its eventual production possible.

There is a postscript to this soft-cover edition (1992) inasmuch the end of 1990 saw the early termination of our lease on part of the premises at New Hertford House, in St Albans Road, as New Hertford House and the entire Fishburn Ink site was acquired by Hunting Gate for redevelopment . . .

*This book is dedicated to the memory of
the late
Sqdn. Ldr. Cyril G. Pascoe, DFC*

I

Early History

"I saw Watford and Rickmansworth, two market towns, touching which we have no account, until we find that King Offa bestowed them upon St. Albans, as also he did Caishobery that lies next to Watford.

Camden's Brittania 1586

After the Ice Ages had passed and our local landscape had settled into its present shape, the clay-capped Chiltern plateau with its forests, and the Colne and Gade valleys with their marshes, offered poor sites for human habitation at a time when men had scarcely begun to scratch the soil.

Analysis of finds of artefacts reported to, and by, the Watford and South West Herts Archaeological Society in recent years suggests that Croxley, Moor Park, Tolpits, Oxhey and Abbots Langley were populated, albeit sparsely, from Mesolithic (Middle Stone) times. Stone arrowheads were found in Eastbury Road in 1930, during clearance and preparation for the building of houses in Thorpe Crescent, and in 1960 a large hoard of late Bronze Age tools were found on the Holywell Industrial Estate and exhibited at the Ashmolean Museum, Oxford.

The artefacts so far recovered as evidence of the presence of prehistoric man may have been left or lost by hunting parties, marauders, feuding families, or as the result of tribal conflicts. Some were smiths' hoards. These earliest inhabitants seem to have been nomadic as no dwellings have been found.

In the Celtic Iron Age the district came under the sway of the Belgic Catuvellauni, who had their centre at Prae Wood, near St. Albans. In Watford Parish they had a small settlement at Hamper Mill, now alas covered by the lake. Their Roman conquerors built a walled city at Verulam for their new cantonal capital, and several Roman villas (farmhouses) have been discovered and excavated in the district: Kings Langley, Munden, Sarratt and Moor Park are all sites where the long arm of Rome once reached. The Belgic settlement at Hamper Mill was succeeded by some Roman buildings, discovered by Dr. Norman Davey, and evaluated carefully by Martin Biddle. They too are now under the water. The Romans wisely adapted some existing trackways to their use, but their own roads were built long and straight for their armies and merchants to travel. The nearest certain Roman roads were the Watling Street at Radlett, and Akeman Street at Two Waters; a road from Verulam to Silchester via Buck's Hill has also been described.

By 410 AD the majority of Rome's soldiers and administrators had been withdrawn, leaving the locals to their own devices. Mr. Rutherford Davis has argued that a Catuvellaunian remnant population held out against the incoming Anglo-Saxons in the Chiltern forests. He adduced, to support his argument, evidence from place-names; lack of pagan burial sites; and the dark hair and eyes of our nineteenth century villagers. Christianity, widespread in the Roman Empire by the 4th century, may have persisted, so that King Offa, much later, was able to identify the site of Alban's martyrdom.

Be that as it may, the popular belief that the early English invaded and conquered South East England has now been discounted in favour of long term immigration and integration. The late arrival of Anglo-Saxons in the Watford area may be due, as Davis has suggested, to local Celtic resistance, but is just as likely to have been the result of avoiding terrain unwelcome to far

mers. When they did arrive our English ancestors settled along the valley sides above the flood levels at Berkhamsted (Birch Farm), Hemel Hempstead (Farm in the twisting valley), and Aldenham (Old Farm). They had already been Christianised and probably moved in when King Wulfhere of Mercia extended his realm southwards in 660 AD.

As the population grew it expanded into less agreeable sites, such as Rickmansworth (Ricimer's Paddock) a marshy spot; or up on the Chilterns at Chipperfield (Forest clearing used by traders). Prominent landmarks were names, such as Cassio (Cay's Hoe or promontory hill) now the West Herts Golf Course. This hill would in time give name to: a) a nearby farm; b) the district or 'manor'; and c) as an alternative name to the administrative hundred of Albanstow.

A successor of King Wulfhere, the great Offa, King of Mercia, friend of Charlemagne, founded an abbey in the 8th century on the site of the reputed tomb of the martyred Christian Roman soldier Alban. He endowed it with lands stretching south-west to Rickmansworth, including Cassio and Oxhey (Ox enclosure). The Anglo-Saxon Oxhey Charter of 1007 AD is the first mention of our Watford by name, but only as a boundary ford. Despite recent suggestions that the first element is 'Wath' meaning hunting, this seems unlikely for two reasons: the Anglo-Saxon spelling ends in 't' not in 'th'; and all fords were used for hunting. Because this particular ford and another of the same name in Northants, were notoriously liable to flood in winter it seems more likely that the first element is 'Waet' meaning full of water. Watford is again mentioned just before the Norman Conquest in the will of Edwin of Caddington who owned Watford and regranted it to St. Albans Abbey, so by then it must have been a territorial name, although no house foundations older than the 12th century have been found.

The abbey lands in Cassio and Oxhey were let to tenants on various leases. The idea that monks did the farming of these outlying estates is due to a popular misconception. Monks were confined to the immediate environs of the abbey. The farms in Watford 'parish' were at Cassio Hall or Bury, and at Oxhey Hall.

The primitive Saxon huts were often sunk into the ground for warmth, but the larger 'halls' were built of logs. As time went on the standard of housing slowly improved, but there are no known Saxon buildings or artefacts in the Watford area.

The Battle of Hastings in 1066 changed the course of our history yet again, and a French-speaking aristocracy was imposed upon an English population. William and his forces headed north to Berkhamsted where a castle was erected.

Twenty years later, by which time the English had been subjugated, commissioners were appointed to tour the country and survey it. 'Not even an ox, nor one cow, nor one pig, escaped notice...' The tremendous undertaking was completed within a year and, written in Latin, the clerkly tongue, was called Domesday Book, (Law-Day Book). All available rural statistics were

... Domesday ... the Wat-ford village ...

included for calculating feudal dues. Watford was included, together with Oxhey and Sarrett, in the land or 'manor' of Cassio, and this in turn formed part of the Hundred of Albanstow or Cassio (originally an Anglo-Saxon district of 100 families). The abbots and their chief tenants were now Frenchmen. There were four watermills in 'Cassio'. They may have been Sarratt Mill, Grove Mill, Tolpits Mill and Oxhey Mill (later Rookery). In these, tenants had to have their corn ground into flour and pay the abbey for the privilege. 'Free' tenants held their lands by either military service (Oxhey Hall), or socage, which meant paying a rent or providing certain amenities or produce. Unfree tenants or 'villeins' were tied to their pieces of land. When they died, or their children married, dues had to be paid to the abbey. Villeins were not allowed to leave the manors they lived on without the lord's permission, and they had to do compulsory unpaid work on the abbey's private estates or 'demesnes'.

By the 12th century a village had grown up along the highway from Aylesbury to Stanmore, where the old Roman Watling Street was joined. The village was a little north of the Wat-ford and clear of the floodable area. Henry I granted to the Abbots of St. Albans a Charter enabling Watford to enjoy the rights and privileges of weekly markets — a privilege which in no small part contributed to Watford's present-day position of eminence — and a church was built for their worship. Sarratt also received a church as it was remote. (The name Sarratt is of French origin and may mean terraced). Watford villagers had two open arable fields in furlong strips; Westfield from Colney Butts to the Colne; and Powfield from St. Albans Road to Loates Lane. The demesne farm of Cassio was held either by stewards, or by farmers on short leases. Oxhey Hall was held by military service on an inheritable tenancy. Its holders made a moat around their house. In addition to the common fields there were patches of manorial waste where the land was unfavourable for agriculture, such as Watford Heath, Commonwood, and Penmans Green. On these geese or cattle could be grazed.

Long distance roads or army paths grew up. On the Ayles

bury road was our original Wat-ford, by now slowly growing in size and importance. Another road linked St.Albans to Rickmansworth via Cassio Ford (later Bridge). A third linked Watford to Pinner and Harrow (Eastbury Road). Tolpits Mill became disused, after adapting to fulling or cloth-cleaning. New mills were made at Watford High Street and Hamper Mill (Waterhen Pool).

Though some feudal rigidities were gradually loosened, life stayed the same for most folk until 1349 when the Black Death, a bubonic plague carried by black rats, struck. At Oxhey the old military family was replaced by Roger Louth, a Royal official, who made a park or warren on his estate. From now on Oxhey was held by rent instead of by military assistance. Due to labour shortage villeins began to work for wages and to wander from manor to manor seeking more reward. Lords converted tillage to sheep-runs to save labour and some Watford villagers grew rich by trading in wool and leather. More and more neglected their land and became traders in the markets. It was men like these who marched on St. Albans Abbey in 1381 to extort freedoms from the Abbot. The so-called Peasants' Revolt was instigated by a government Poll Tax, but the Watford men sought liberty to fish in the Colne and Gade, snare rabbits, and for the cessation of 'alepenny', a tax paid to the Abbey. They also wanted to grind their own corn. But the local leaders were executed and the new freedoms soon retracted.

Watford had its importance recognized by the institution under Richard II of a Court Leet which met in the town under the Abbey Steward as judge, and with a jury of free tenants. It settled disputes between landholders and fined people who had offended against the common good. It appointed constables to keep the King's Peace in the 'hamlets' or 'tithings' of Watford, Cassio, Grove, Sarratt, Oxhey, Garston and Munden. In Watford town aletasters and leathersealers were created. Richer townsfolk left wills recorded by the Abbey clerks or at Canterbury; such as Sir Hugh Holes of Oxhey Hall who died in 1415 and has a memorial brass in our church. Feudal dues were

THE COLNE AT WIGGENHALL, WHICH CLEARLY SHOWS THE MARSHY NATURE
OF THE GROUND. THIS WAS PROBABLY THE BOUNDARY AND PROTECTION
ON THE SOUTH SIDE OF THE "VILL OF WATAFORD."

ignored or forgotten. Copyholders (villeins) began to consolidate their open field strips and enclose them with hedges. Tithes on crops supported the clergy.

Houses were of timber, mud and straw. Smoke from open hearths escaped through the thatch, often catching it alight. Stone didn't exist locally and bricks were confined to the continent until c1500. Only our church, built of flint and freestone, survives from the Middle Ages. Our present language, Anglo-Saxon at base but with French and Latin additives, had evolved by c1400 to provide a vehicle for Chaucer's poetry. Food was monotonous, even for the wealthy, and consisted principally of bread, beans, cabbage, cheese, eggs and meat. Meat was salted, as cattle were slaughtered for lack of winter keep, and was eaten mainly by the wealthier folk.

National events passed us by, but Walkelin of Oxhey fought at St. Albans in the civil war of Stephen's reign, and William Troutbeck of Oxhey died at Blore Heath in the War of the Roses in 1459 fighting for Henry VI.

Modern times begin with Henry VIII's Protestant Reformation. The dissolution of the St. Albans Abbey in 1539 rang the death knell of feudalism. Those estates (demesnes) which had been under the direct control of the abbey were sold by the king as separate manors. They included part of Oxhey, called Oxhey Walrond or Wiggenhall, sold to a Londoner, James Joskins; and Cassiobury, sold in 1545 to a royal servant, Richard Morrison. Former villein holdings were now called copyholds as they were freed from all feudal dues except for payments which had to be 'copied' into the manorial books when a tenant died or sold his estate.

King Henry divided Watford Town from Cassio Manor and made it a separate manor of which he was the direct lord. In 1607 it was granted by James I to Lord Chancellor Egerton, and continued with his successors the Earls and Dukes of Bridgewater, who sold it in the late 18th century to the Earl of Essex. Watford now had the Court Leet for the entire former manor of Cassio and also a Court Baron for the copyholds within the town.

Lawyers did well under the Tudors. One such, William Heydon, grandson of a Leavesden farmer, was of Lincolns Inn which he partly built, and Clerk to the Duchy of Lancaster. In Watford he built, on land acquired by his father in New Street, a mansion partly of the new brick. It became known as Watford Place and later as the Lecture House. Heydon's father and grandmother had built the south chapel of St. Mary's Church by 1505. Watford Place had two new features, chimneys and a porch.

Our parish register begins in 1539 and in it we can trace most of Watford's inhabitants up to the present. The Protestant Reformation, which started as a gesture by an aggrieved monarch against a pope who would not allow him to divorce, took on a special shape by Elizabeth's reign. The Morrisons and Heydons chose Watford's vicars and lecturers. Under their aegis the parish vestry began to exercise local government powers, and in particular was responsible for poor relief, and later for highway maintenance. The local gentry, as Justices of the Peace, took much of the work from the Royal judges. Within the Hundred or Liberty of St. Albans they kept the jail for minor malefactors. They controlled the village constables, and raised rates for administration. But all J.P.s, vestrymen and constables were unpaid except for necessary expenses.

From the late Middle Ages onwards into the 18th century the tenor of life scarcely varied. Watford was an agricultural market with a radius of from three to five miles and it contained a fair number of rural processors; tanners, millers, bakers, maltsters, brewers and butchers. The richest townsfolk were mealmen (corn-dealers). The first brewer of note was Nicholas Colbourn in Elizabeth's reign. He died in 1630.

The Great Civil War had little impact on our life. The gentry supported Parliament, and except for small scuffles there was no fighting in the district. The strict hand of Cromwellian control gave way to the more liberal sway of the Merry Monarch. In 1683 the Earl of Essex was arrested at Cassiobury and charged with

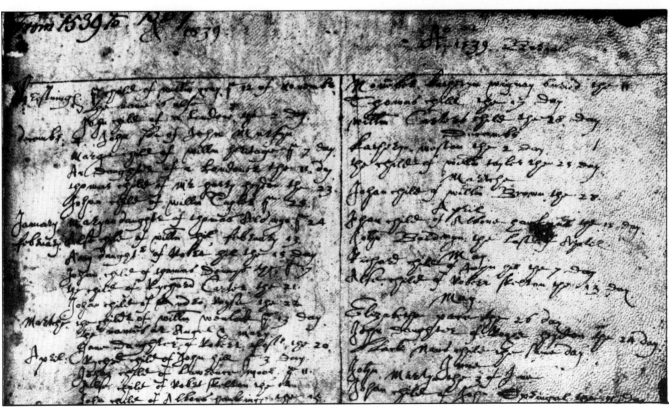

Copy of a page of the parish register started in 1539

... travel was slow and cumbersome ...

complicity to kidnap the king for Whiggish purposes. He committed suicide in the Tower to save his family's property. His friend Monmouth, from Moor Park, was executed in 1685.

Some London citizens came to Watford to escape the epidemics of that crowded and insanitary city. Lawyers and government officials also settled here. Thomas Hobson, Bushey born, a government lawyer, built his new Watford Place south of the churchyard. His widow Elizabeth (nee Chilcott) remarried a Mr. Fuller, and in 1704 built and endowed Watford's second 'free' school. The children had to wear uniforms and attend the parish church. They were taught to read and do useful tasks. Nearby, at the vicarage gate, an older 'free' school functioned, founded in the mid 17th century by Francis Combe of Hemel Hempstead.

Local gentry were educated by private tutors in their own homes or at the 'grammar' schools at Berkhamsted, St. Albans, or Aldenham. A few would proceed to Oxford or Cambridge, and more to the London Inns of Court and Chancery to become lawyers, a suitable preparation for J.P.s. But most Watfordians would remain unlettered except for a few days at a dame school. Most marriage contracts were signed by 'marks', especially by the females. Baptists, who did a deal of Bible study in their private houses, (and after 1721 in their new meeting house), were somewhat more literate. Shops were often distinguished by signs, like public houses.

In 1721 the parish built a workhouse near the church to house the increasing numbers of the poor and provide them with work. The building was enlarged in 1772. Various laws attempted to stop the increase in vagrancy by returning 'sturdy' beggars to their parishes of origin, after whipping them.

Houses in Watford, by 1760, were much improved. Thatch had often been replaced by clay tiles. Most houses had strong timber frames, proper fireplaces and chimneys. The richer folk built in brick, though sometimes they merely refronted timber houses. Drainage services, despite the Court Leet and their fines, were almost non-existent. Offal from tanyards and butchers polluted the streets and alleys. The town pump by the Market Hall and wells in the yards were the only source of water except for the river and the millstream. Disease was rife, though the town had its apothecaries and even medical doctors. Life expectancy was short and infantile mortality high, not least in the crowded courts which were springing up behind the High Street to house the growing population. The town had about 2,000 people in 1760. They now had more varied food, including potatoes since 1600, turnips since 1660, and, from Elizabeth's reign, the comfort of tobacco in clay pipes. Travel was slow and cumbersome over rutted roads. So it was in Watford when the Rookery Silk Mill opened in 1770, to begin our Industrial Age.

HOUSES IN HIGH STREET, OPPOSITE SEDGWICK'S OLD BREWERY.

The Poor Law ... whipped and sent on her way ...

As the Elizabethan era ended the essence of a poor law emerged when national legislation required local magistrates to relieve the plight of the poor, under the jurisdiction of the Privy Council, with modest funds to be provided by a compulsory poor rate system. For many years bands of 'sturdy beggars' had been terrorising the countryside and something had to be done to curtail if not control their activities.

The course of history would have been so different if Henry VIII had invested even a small proportion of the spoils acquired at the time of the Dissolution in the care and education of the common people. The long-term beneficiaries proved to be the gentry and not the crown. They were given the opportunity of buying monastic land with manorial rights at prices they could not refuse. The Morrisons and the Russells are local examples.

Tudor England came to realise that the presence of so many vagrants and beggars constituted a threat to the country, a threat which whipping would not cure. In the interests of the state and the church they should be gainfully employed and to that end the local Overseer of the Poor was directed to purchase a working stock of "flax, hemp, wool, thread, iron and other stuff to set the poor to work" by the Statute of 1601.

In 1535 Henry VIII had ordered all parish churches to keep registers of christenings, marriages and burials. Watford's earliest register covers the period 1539-1557. Between the years 1540-1541 fifty four deaths from the plague are recorded. The second register spans the years 1558-1666. The leaves of both registers are made of parchment and most of the entries are still legible. In the early years the entries were generally of an informal nature with marginal notes reflecting the personal touches of the recorder, a source of useful information to the researcher.

Contrary to the practice of many parish churches, the Churchwarden's Accounts were not maintained in a separate ledger but included with the reports of business conducted by the Vestry which acted in the capacity of a local governing body. Members included the Lord of the Manor, the Vicar, Churchwardens, Overseer of the Poor as well as the Parish Clerk. Their interests were many and varied but their main preoccupation was concerned with the Church and the role it played within the community. The bells and the bell-ringers assumed great importance. The condition of the structure, inside and out, concerned the churchwardens.

The conduct of their parishioners also received the attention of the Vestry along with the apprenticing of children, the care of the poor and the infirm. Each meeting was reported to the Archdeaconry Court where the submission was examined in detail and the accounts checked. Occasional surprise visits were made by the Archdeacon to see for himself that all was well.

In the Vestry Records of 1681 is an entry reporting the fate of Richard Man who was whipped and with his wife and two children was sent by pass to Bishop Auckland for which journey 60 days was allowed. Another entry, two years later, tells of a similar incident in the following words:

"Jane Joyner, wife of Wm. Joyner, a sturdy vagrant beggar whipped according to the law, sent with her two children under 7 years by a pass, the nearest way to Taunton Dean in Somerset, where she confessed she was born."

The manner in which the Vestry administered the Poor Law was absolute. In 1696 an entry reveals that those receiving Parish Relief "shall wear on the right shoulder of their uppermost garment a brass badge with the letters W.P. on it denoting them to be Watford Poor".

In the year of the Revolution (1688) roughly twenty per cent of the population (over one million souls) received at some time public relief through parish authorities. At the end of the seventeenth century the claim was made that the parish dole sometimes exceeded current wages and was sometimes so generous as to encourage people not to work, to drink the best ale and eat the 'finest wheat flour'. None complained more bitterly than the ratepayers.

This state of affairs, if correctly reported, came to an end with the Act of Settlement passed by Charles II's Cavalier Parliament. The Act, a reactionary piece of legislation, gave the parish and authorities the necessary power to evict a non-resident and send him back to the parish of which he was native so that he may not become a charge on the rates. Technically, few people were safe from arrest whether or not they were law-abiding or of excellent character. The Act, as well as causing untold distress, completely upset the mobility of labour to meet the needs of seasonal employment, as well as the peace of mind of many whose employment took them outside their native parish. In addition hostility was generated between local authorities, none of whom were adequately briefed, directed or controlled by a central organisation or body. Another factor to be taken into account was the resentment expressed by local tax payers at having to pay for the maintenance of roads and sanitation as required by the local magistrate. The Poor Rate was yet another burden levied without reasonable justification!

In the Justice of the Peace was vested the necessary authority to determine the amount of the local rate to be raised and the purpose for which the revenue would be spent. In earlier times their appointment had been the prerogataive of the Privy Council but now the Lord Lieutenant appointed them in the name of the Crown. Without a central control the J.P.s were relatively free agents inasmuch as they had local control over county life. Their functions included the administration of justice, the licensing of public houses, the maintenance of roads, bridges, workhouses and prisons to name but a few duties. Without a staff

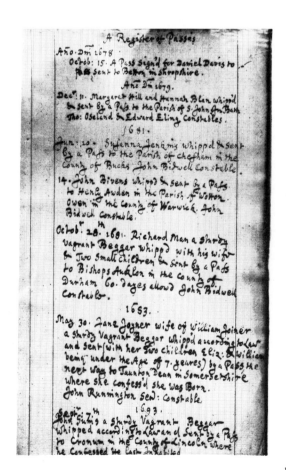

... *Clothing of coarse material was supplied* ...

or adequate premises the J.P. went about his business as best he could without sympathy from the ratepayers who were content to encourage inefficient local government if the cost of efficiency represented a further charge against the rates!

The surprise was that corruption was not rife although acts of favouritism and prejudice were not unknown. There was no remuneration for the post so Justices of the Peace were invariably landowners and of substantial independent means.

In common with most other towns in England, Watford had its workhouse, a purpose-built, three storey brick edifice of barrack proportions relieved only by a series of small windows at each floor level. For good reason the communal workhouse was erected, in juxtaposition to the Parish Church, in Church Street in 1721. Here the inmates, a motley mix of young and old, healthy and sick, law-abiding and law-breakers, were given shelter at the expense of the ratepayers. However, this captive workforce had a revenue-producing potential and it was accordingly exploited to the full by the Master and his subordinates by directing some of the inmates to provide the services with which to maintain the workhouse. Alternatively, children and adults were hired out to factory owners or households who utilised their services in menial tasks for long hours. The inmates enjoyed at least one good meal a day, a bed and, if they were lucky, some heating. Clothing of coarse materials was also supplied. When they were not gainfully employed they were allowed to spend their time in the town, much to the annoyance of the residents.

The opportunities open to workhouse staff to line their own pockets were regarded as the perquisites of the job and as a result the wrong types achieved management and support status, the consequence being that priority of care was forsaken for personal gain. The inmates became tools of the Master and the workhouse, as a provident institution, went into a temporary decline.

Provision was made for the sick and an infirmary became an essential adjunct of the workhouse. When isolation of a patient suffering from an infectious disease, such as smallpox, was required, the pesthouse, as its name implies, served to accommodate him.

By the end of the eighteenth century signs of improvement in the care of inmates became apparent. The feudal outlook of the latter day yeoman farmers, however, was still in evidence. The lot of the farm labourer was never a happy one. His staple diet was bread and cheese. Meat was a luxury he or his family seldom enjoyed. His diet was no better than his low wages permitted, hovering at starvation level. In 1795 the magistrates of Berkshire, conscious of the conditions prevailing, called a meeting at Speenhamland near Newbury at which it was hoped to devise a sliding wage-scale based on the cost of bread at a time of widely-fluctuating prices. The J.P.s decided against such measures and opted for a sliding scale subsidy from the parish rates. The scheme was readily adopted by local county authorities who ignored its inherent dangers. In theory the labourer should have benefited by the move but in practice the employer paid him less the amount he would receive from the parish. He no longer earned even a living wage. Although fully employed he was still forced to become a pauper

The Speenhamland Act brought ruin to the labourer and ratepayer alike and it was succeeded by the new Poor Act of 1834, which made conditions so unattractive in the workhouse

that it was argued that none would wish to avail themselves of its facilities. The Act ignored the plight of the aged, children and the infirm who, as inmates, would suffer the same indignities as adults. The conditions of the workhouse were intentionally reduced to an intolerable low. At the other end of the scale three Commissioners were appointed at national level to represent central government and made responsible for the creation of rules for administering the Poor Law and the means by which they were enforced.

The physical application of the Act through the Commissioners at local level was through a "board of guardians of the poor" democratically elected through the ratepayers. The Justices of the Peace were no longer involved with the parish poor and despite their reputation their withdrawal from the scene was deplored by those who appreciated the personal touch.

Four years after the enactment, in 1838, the complex of workhouse buildings in Church Street was sold and towards the end of the century was occupied by the Watford and West Herts Co-operative Society, the Parish Clerk and others. In its place was built a brand new Union Workhouse —representing a union of local parishes — in Vicarage Road and later an Infirmary and Chapel, which together, through the Local Board of Guardians, continued to care for the poor and under-privileged. Half a century later the Workhouse was claimed to be the only non-growth area in an expanding Watford. Not that the problem of the poor had been solved so much as contained within reasonable limits.

A Statement of Accounts for the year ending Lady Day 1883 revealed that the average cost per head of indoor (resident) paupers for food, clothing and burial per week was 3s 7d. (18p). The 'average contract prices of provisions' include 'Table ale at £1 7s. 0d. per barrel, beef 7d. per lb. and flour at £1 11s. 6d. a sack.'

The complex was a self-contained operation administering not only to the needy but also the sick, with schooling for the children and a convalescent home at St. Leonards on Sea. It was, in effect, a sort of welfare and education centre where active assistance was given as opposed to discharging the duty of the state with largess in the form of monetary hand-outs.

The Union served a large area encompassing the parishes of Watford, Abbots Langley, Aldenham, Bushey, Rickmansworth and Sarratt. Each parish was represented by ex-officio and elected members on the Board of Guardians. Officers of the Union included the Medical Officer, Relieving Officer and, as residents of the Workhouse, the Governor, Matron, two nurses, two teachers and the porter.

After World War I and during the post-war days of unemployment and recession the Union Workhouse still had a role to fulfil by offering overnight accommodation to unemployed who walked from town to town in search of work. By 1939 the roving unemployed had become a token force although the traditional tramp to whom conformity was anathema still used the facilities available at Watford in the course of his perigrinations. After the second World War the birth of the Welfare State contributed to the dissolution of the Union Workhouse for which there was no place in an emerging new society. The Union Workhouse was, in the early 1930's, renamed 'Shrodells', and the title 'Workhouse' went out of use but the name 'Infirmary' persisted for very many more years.

... *Richard Morrison, new owner of Watford* ...

When, for a token sum, Henry VIII conveyed, together with other estates, the manor of Cayshobury on August 29th, 1545 from the Monastery of St. Alban to a grateful Richard Morrison, he acquired himself a dependable ally. Sir Richard became the owner of a large wooded estate. John Russell had been the steward in 1540 just one year after the Dissolution.

Watford was an adjunct of Cashio at the time of the Domesday survey so it is not beyond the realms of possibility that on the Normans' arrival there was a manor house occupied by bailiffs or agents of the Abbot at the abbey church of St. Alban. Sir Richard chose virgin land on which to build a 'fair and large house, situated on a dry hill, not far from a pleasant river park . . .'

Morrison chose to live in London during the period of construction of his new house but before its completion he was forced to flee the country because of protestant leanings on the accession of Queen Mary. He died in voluntary exile in 1556 and his son Charles was left to complete the 'sturdy structure' in the contemporary style. Its size may be judged by the number of rooms, quoted as fifty six, including outbuildings as assorted as stables, dairy and brewhouse. Charles was not a militant protestant like his father.

His mother, Bridget, Dowager Countess of Bedford had survived three husbands when she died in 1601 at the age of seventy-five, the widow of Francis Russell, 2nd Earl of Bedford. Although resident at Woburn she still retained her own suite of rooms at Cassiobury House. Evidence of her generosity to the widows of Watford, Langley and Chenies may still be seen in the form of the Bedford or Essex Almshouses built in Church Street, which then connected the High Street with what was later to become Vicarage Road.

Knighted in 1588, Sir Charles, and his mother, followed the fashion of the times by providing for themselves a chapel in advance of their demise as an extension to the Parish Church. Unexpectedly Charles predeceased his mother and died in 1599. In accordance with their own provision they were buried in what is still called the Essex Chapel. Then, as recently as 1907, the monument to her, along with accoutrements of a military nature, was removed to Chenies while monuments to Sir Charles, his wife and sons, remain.

Dame Dorothy Morrison assumed control of Cassiobury until her son reached his majority. In 1606 young Charles married the daughter of Sir Baptist Hicks, a rich mercer, who helped his son-in-law to increase the size of the estate by acquiring peripheral farms and woods. He was made Deputy Lieutenant by the Earl of Salisbury and a baronet in 1625. Following the accession of James to the throne he was made a Knight of the Bath at his coronation in 1625. In 1628, representing the Shire of Hertford, he died after a short illness.

The Morrison ladies also left their spiritual mark on Watford. His step-daughter, Dame Elizabeth Russell, set up a trust to provide for a lecturer to regularly preach at the Parish Church. She died before the appointment could be made and her mother Mary Morrison not only arranged the appointment of Thomas Valentine in 1613 but also generously provided the new incumbent with a Lecturer's House.

Both infant sons of Sir Charles, named after their grandfather, Baptist and Hicks, died leaving a surviving daughter, Elizabeth. She married Arthur Capel of Little Hadham Hall in 1627, thereby introducing the family name to Cassiobury with which it is now synonymous. The family seat stayed at Hadham.

As Lieutenant-General of Shropshire, Cheshire and North Wales he left for Shrewsbury ostensibly to prevent Parliamentarian General Sir William Brereton from joining the forces already besieging Chester, with reasonable success. His popularity and his future seemed assured in his task to protect the Prince of Wales, which duty should have divorced him from further military exposure to the Royalist/ Parliamentarian conflict. When everything appeared to be resolving itself he involved himself again in 1648, this time at Colchester, but his luck ran out. He surrendered to Fairfax, who already held his son, Arthur, captive. The son survived but the father was beheaded at the Tower in 1649, and his heart, after his execution, was placed in a silver casket at the feet of his dead King.

The casket was kept at Hadham and not placed in the family vault until 1703. As a further penalty the Cassiobury estate was sequestrated. Lady Capel stayed at Kings Langley or Little

A. Pugin, del.

RIDGE LANE COTTAGE.

... Arthur Capel was created Earl of Essex ...

Hadham until the restoration of Charles II.

Arthur Capel was created Earl of Essex by Charles II and as Viscount Malden and Earl of Essex, was appointed Lord Lieutenant of Hertfordshire. By 1670 he was again in residence at Cassiobury. Seven years later Arthur became leader in the House of Lords and a member of the Privy Council under Shaftesbury. Unhappily he was exposed to the hatred and prejudice generated by a protestant parliament and a catholic James. He aligned himself with Monmouth and was promptly expelled from the Privy Council. Disillusioned, he returned to Cassiobury and transferred his attention to it. Lord Arthur had married Elizabeth Percy, daughter of the Earl of Northumberland. Of a family of seven sons, only two boys reached maturity. He spent his time studying English history and involving himself in the reconstruction of the house, except for one wing which was retained. Hugh May was entrusted with the work and his head gardener, based at Hadham, laid out the Versailles-inspired gardens.

In the prime of his life, although not a totally happy man, but fully occupied by the house and estate, he was accused in 1683 of involvement in the Rye House plot to kidnap King Charles on his way from Newmarket races and force him to disinherit his heir, brother James (a catholic). Ironically, when awaiting trial, he was lodged in the same room in the Tower in which his father had been prior to his execution, thirty four years before. He was found dead, his throat cut. It was said by Whig propagandists that he had been murdered.

The second Earl, Algernon, born in 1657, served William of Orange in many capacities and Queen Anne as Lieutenant General of her army in Spain. He married Mary, daughter of William Bentinck, Duke of Portland, in 1692. She bore him two sons and one daughter. He died in 1710 *and was succeeded by thirteen-year old William* who also became a member of the Privy Council. His first marriage brought no male heirs. His wife Jane, daughter of Henry Hyde, Earl of Clarendon, died in 1724. He then married Elizabeth, daughter of the second Duke of Bedford. Their second son succeeded to the title as *William Anne, fourth Earl of Essex.* Algernon died in 1743 and was interred at Watford. William served George II and followed in the family tradition as Lord Lieutenant of Hertfordshire, and married twice. His first wife gave him a son and two daughters and the second, four sons.

The fifth Earl, George Capel Coningsby (family name of his maternal grandmother) was born in 1757 and for two decades served as a member of Parliament. A patron of the arts he commissioned James Wyatt to remodel the house and Humphry Repton to put romance into the eighteenth-century garden and estate. Ornamental lodges and cottages were carefully sited at points of access to the estate including Swiss Cottage and the celebrated Cassiobury Park Gates, all attributed to members of the Wyatt family. By the beginning of the nineteenth-century the work had been largely completed.

His marriage to Sarah, daughter of Henry Bazet of St. Helena

was less than successful and after her death in 1838, George, at the age of eighty two, married Kitty Stephens, the toast of the aristocracy, a well-known singer and actress of her day as well as being an acknowledged beauty. She gave him a year's happiness; he died in 1839. *Arthur Algernon Capel* the eldest son of George's half brother, assumed the title of the *Sixth Earl of Essex* at the age of thirty six. He was married three times, to Lady Caroline Beauclerk, Lady Caroline Boyle and widow Louisa Heneage.

He found time to involve himself in local affairs as a Lay Rector, President of the Watford and Bushey Volunteer Fire Brigade and the West Hertfordshire Agriculture Society. In 1880 he changed his name to the original version of 'Capell' by Royal Licence. Eton-educated Arthur died in 1892, having brought to Cassiobury a new outlook and new interests which included involvement in the manufacture of croquet sets and the popularising of the game on a national basis.

Towards the end of the nineteenth century the old aristocratic families felt the pressures of a changing social and economic order. In 1846 Cassiobury House had been rented to Queen Adelaide, widow of William IV, who came to Watford to recuperate from an illness. Some weeks later Queen Victoria and Prince Albert travelled from Windsor to see her. Prince Albert took the opportunity of joining a shooting party bound for Callowland. After two years Queen Adelaide moved to Bentley Priory where she died in 1849.

George Devereux succeeded to the title in 1892. He served as *seventh Earl* with the Imperial Yeomanry in South Africa at the turn of the century. He married twice. His only son of the first marriage, Algernon, was destined to become the *eighth Earl.*

Cassiobury was famous for its parties, balls and entertainment generally. They were both lavish and costly. The aristocracy in general and chosen guests, such as Churchill, Henry James and John Sargent, in particular, were just some of the distinguished visitors who enjoyed the hospitality of the fun-loving Essex family.

On George's succession he instructed Christies to sell a number of paintings and other pieces which realised in all over £40,000, which sum was said to be required to meet the cost of repairing the neglected fabric of the house. A year before King Edward VII paid an official visit to the house in 1909, 184 acres of parkland were sold to Robert Ashby and Charles Brightman. The family had moved out of Cassiobury at the beginning of the century to live in London. A staff of servants was left to care for paying guests and short-term visitors. It was the beginning of the end as the estate was sold off on a piecemeal basis. The long association of the Essex family with Watford was about to come to an end but few could foresee that in just a few years the severence would be so irrevocable and so utterly final.

The 7th Earl died in London in September, 1916, seven months after receiving minor injuries and shock caused by being knocked down by a taxi-cab. The family line continues but has no connection with Watford.

. . . the new Endowed Schools in Derby Road . . .

The picturesque Queen Anne building, which is still called the Free School, sited in the south-west corner of St. Mary's Churchyard, has close associations with Dame Elizabeth Fuller, one of Watford's many past benefactors. The School is now a Grade II listed building, which gives it special protection, in recognition of its architectural merit and unique historial association. For many years it was a popular meeting place for many local organizations with direct access to St. Mary's Church Hall (demolished only a few years ago). Concurrently the Free School was converted to offices. In this newly-designated capacity the fabric of the building neatly dovetails into the environs of the Church at the same time serving the needs of Watford's commercial growth.

A clue to the building's past role in the town's history may be found in the following inscription on the stone lintel above the main door:

> *"Anno Dni 1704. This Free School was built*
> *and endowed for the teaching of poor children*
> *at the proper cost of Mrs. Elizabeth Fuller*
> *of Watford Place."*

To trace the grass roots relationship of the School with the Watford Grammar Schools it is necessary to go back as far as the late seventeenth-century when religious conventions subscribed to propriety rather than piety. In those remote pre-evangelistic days the plight of the poor was not considered to be a moral issue except to an enlightened minority who believed that poverty was neither a natural phenomenon nor God's will. To combat this problem in practical terms the Society for Promoting Christian Knowledge initiated the 1699 'Charity School'.

Mrs. Elizabeth Fuller found herself wholly in accord with the ideals of the movement as it conformed with her own interpretation of the Christian faith. Moved by the ignorance of the poor and in empathy with this wind of change she acquired part of the Vicarage garden and graveyard on which to build her new school for Watford's deprived children. By 1704 the building was completed, endowed and occupied. Forty boys and fourteen girls were initially accommodated in large and light classrooms. There they received a basic education and religious instruction. Children were accepted from the age of seven and required to leave on reaching fourteen.

In 1709 at the age of sixty-five, Dame Elizabeth Fuller, who had survived three husbands, died. She was buried in the

Churchyard of St. James' Parish Church, Bushey, but even in death she had provided for the financing of her Free School. Notwithstanding her generosity, changing circumstances in later years only served to increase operating costs, forcing the Trustees to appeal for financial assistance. Many local people responded, not least Queen Adelaide, who was familiar with the town as a resident of Cassiobury House as well as Bentley Priory.

The Trustees monitored the progress of the pupils for over one hundred and fifty years, until 1870, when examinations were introduced in conformity with the requirements of the Education Act of the same year. The problem of funding the School from its own resources increased each year. The endowments and gifts could no longer sustain its operation as a Free School and although strict economies were applied there was no way in which it could be made viable unless fundamental changes were made.

At that time Dr. Brett, who was a Trustee, in searching for a solution to this apparently insurmountable problem, discovered that the school may qualify for a grant from the Platt's Charity of Aldenham. Application was made, and the Trustees were informed that Consols to the value of £13,333 6s. 8d. would be conditionally assigned to Watford when 'a scheme for the management of Watford Charities should be found'.

After considerable research a scheme was duly presented to the Charity Commission in 1881 in which scholarships would be offered to a certain number of boys and girls. The package was well prepared, researched and presented. The application could not fail!

A Board of Governors was appointed and then a search made for a suitable site. A consensus supported the Derby Road location where a single building would be erected. Although under the one roof each school would have its own entrance.

The new Derby Road School for Boys was opened by the Earl of Clarendon on April 21st 1884, and on the next day he opened the Girls' School. On the occasion of his second speech he apologised for having omitted to give credit to Dr. Brett in his first speech for having initiated the project and bringing it to a successful conclusion. The new-look Endowed Schools were regarded as a highly successful venture and in 1903 the names were changed to the Watford Grammar Schools, thus diminishing the connection with Dame Elizabeth Fuller and the old Free School of 1704. The euphoria was short-lived as success brought its own problems.

The Education Act of 1902, amongst other things, specified a space of not less than 18sq. foot per pupil excluding hall or assembly areas, a requirement that could not be met because of the ever-increasing number of pupils. A proposal to place an extra storey on top of the existing building was considered only to be rejected. An alternative proposal was adopted in which the Girls' School moved to new premises and the Boys' School took possession of the building. In theory this was an ideal solution but unfortunately the necessary funds were not available to the Trustees. They were obliged to go cap-in-hand to the local and county authorities for financial assistance. As soon as the appeal became public knowledge there was an immediate adverse reaction. The question was asked whether public funds should be used to support the historically sectarian nature of the Schools' curriculum.

The reconstitution of the Board of Governors to include representatives of local authorities and the introduction of denomination safeguards appeared to placate if not wholly satisfy a very sensitive public. A site was found not far from the Watford District Hospital in Vicarage Road and St. Mary's Church which enjoyed a panoramic view of the Colne Valley and the wooded hill beyond. C. Brightman of Watford was appointed general contractor and by 1907 a two storey building designed to accommodate two hundred and fifty girls had been

... there was no ceremony ...

completed. Because feelings were still running high the new accommodation was quietly occupied without being officially opened. There was no ceremony and as little as possible attendant publicity. The move was deliberately planned as a low-key exercise that would not further exacerbate the feelings of the protesters.

Ironically within five years of the departure of the Girls' School, the Derby Road premises could no longer house the ever-increasing number of boys. The inconvenience of using 'Mr. Fisher's Field' for sports activities ended when the School Governors secured a long lease on five acres of land at Bushey Hall Farm. By 1908 there were 267 boys attending school with classroom space for only 240 pupils. Inspectors of the Board of Education recommended a new building on a larger site. The

Governors lost no time in negotiating with the Earl of Essex and acquired a little over twelve acres. Included in the deal was Shepherds Lodge, which for many years had guarded a minor entrance to Cassiobury House from Rickmansworth Road. The new school premises were completed in 1912. The official opening was arranged for the 20th March with Lord Clarendon again presiding. On this occasion the Headmaster, W. R. Carter, is reported as saying "My greatest ambition is to make the School a great and important institution of the town and I hope all the boys here now will be proud some day to say they were among the first to be educated within its walls." That his dream was realised there is no doubt, although sadly in the space of two years both the Earl of Clarendon and Mr. Carter died.

OLD HOUSES, LOATES LANE.
THIS WAS THE ORIGINAL LANE TO ALDENHAM.

... the British and the National Schools ...

Ambitious parents in the middle ages sent their sons to the Abbey of St. Alban to be educated. If their social status or economic circumstances did not permit such indulgence the local Parish priests were asked to undertake a form of tuition. The first intimation of a school in Watford is to be found in an entry for the year 1595, making reference to "George Redhead schoolmaster" and to Nicholas Hall who was "licenced to keep a Grammar School". This school may have been located on the upper floors of two cottages, close to the Vicarage, which were demolished in 1821. The location to which the school was transferred is not known although records indicated that it was still in existence in 1832.

The foundation of the London University in 1827 was the materialistic inspiration of secularists and non-conformists for whom there was no place at Oxford or Cambridge where traditionally a classical curriculum offered a ticket to ride to the establishment of the Church of State. The 'cockney college' was the first straw in the wind to give an indication of a switch from theology to science which was achieved despite inter-denomination rivalry and enmity.

Numerically the Dissenters were in a minority but their militant voices were nevertheless heard in matters of education. Public money was available to promote education facilities but only, claimed the Church, if grants and disbursements were deployed under the protection of the State religion; terms which were abhorrent to all Dissenters. In defiance they raised money by voluntary contribution to finance the building and running of their own day schools and Sunday schools. Under the patronage of the Whigs the British and Foreign School Society was formed as a viable alternative to the Church School.

In response the Church founded the National Society for the Education of the Poor according to the principles of the Church of England. In deference to the proper title the name 'National School' was adopted and by the same token the Dissenters' Schools were called 'British Schools'. The National Schools dominated the scene in cities, towns, villages and hamlets aided by a modest grant that was made available from 1833.

Perhaps as a result of the grant some of the members of the Parish Church decided to raise by subscription an amount sufficient to acquire the site of the notorious 'Nag's Head' beerhouse in the High Street — notorious because it became the meeting place of the body snatchers — and build there a new infants' school.

At the time the Earl of Essex maintained what became known as "My Lord's Schools" in Rickmansworth Road, at his own expense, for children of the working classes in Watford of any denomination. The school closed on his death. Then there was the private sector ranging from 'minders' of children on a daily basis to reputable establishments attracting the children of local tradespeople, merchants and others of adequate means.

In 1841 members of the Parish Church subscribed towards a new National School in Church Street for boys and girls which served in that capacity for the next eighty one years until it was closed in 1922 when it became better known as Almond Wick.

One of the first areas to receive the attention of the developer as a direct result of the arrival of the London and Birmingham Railway, and because of its convenience to the main station, included Church Road. There, in 1860, a Church School was erected to accommodate boys and infants. The school for girls was in Sotheron Road. In common with other Church and National Schools religious instruction was in accord with the doctrines of the Church of England.

The Dissenters (noncomformists) taught their first pupils in cottages near the old Baptist Chapel in Beechen Grove until the accommodation proved inadequate for an ever- increasing number of children. A larger custom-built school was erected in 1859 for boys and girls but even these premises proved unsuitable after a very short time and the boys were transferred to the old Baptist church premises.

Victorian politicians disagreed about most things but on one aspect they were unanimous, that it was in the national interest to provide education facilities for the masses; a matter so important as to override religious intolerance and allied issues. In a climate of sectarian zeal and religious ardour the reconciliation of all these factors to achieve a kind of unity presented a problem so imponderable as to defy an acceptable solution. W. E. Foster of Quaker origin, against all odds, cut the Gordian knot without compromising Gladstone.

The immediate impact of the Education Bill of 1870 was to double State grants to all church schools, including those of the Roman Catholics, and so bring them into line within a common system. Any shortfall in the educational cover was to be made good by introducing a new Board School, each governed by a locally elected board and funded by a direct charge on the rates.

FOX ALLEY, HIGH STREET.
LEADING TO WATFORD FIELDS RECREATION GROUND.

. . . formation of a School Board . . .

was to be religious teaching but only in general and not specific terms. The Act avoided the major pitfalls and created some degree of parity between Church and Board schools. Long overdue, a primary education system had been created, at least in principle. In practice, hamlets and villages, the population of which could only sustain one school, were obliged to stay with the old established Church School. The National School serving the hamlet at Watford Heath is a prime example.

There were other problems, some incidental to the enactment. In twenty years the number of children attending school increased nationally by one hundred per cent and costs in the same proportion. The new schools' prescribed function confined their curriculum strictly to a primary level. The School Board was, by its very nature, parochial in outlook, having little regard for events and developments beyond its influence. The induced pact between Church and Dissenter was sometimes infringed and occasionally broken but, undeniably, tremendous progress had been made in bringing together those of different persuasions.

The implementation of the 1870 Act was not effected in Watford until 1883. For thirteen years those eligible to pay rates had enjoyed the doubtful benefit of the local schools having to operate without a School Board and so saved on the expenses they would have otherwise incurred.

The long period of grace may have suited the pockets of the town's rate-paying citizens but the School Authorities, without additional State aid, had difficulty in collecting sufficient subscriptions to meet the cost of teaching ever more children. The British (Dissenting) Schools ran into debt. To place so many infants was beyond the financial means of all school managers and so they called a meeting of all ratepayers. Mr. C. E. Humbert, Chairman of the Local Board of Health and the Hon. Richard Capel, one of the managers at St. Mary's School, explained to a

disinterested audience the statistics and the facts pertinent to the problem of providing schooling for local children. Of 1,724 parish ratepayers only 250 helped maintain the schools by voluntary subscription. The meeting agreed to circularise all ratepayers recommending a voluntary increase of 6d. in the £. Not unexpectedly there was so little response that the matter was shelved.

To avoid a stalemate and provoke action the Education Department was requested to order the formation of a School Board. The outcome, in the pursuit of efficiency and economy, was the uncontested election of the original school managers of the National, Church and British Schools who duly formed the first Watford School Board. After its formation the boys of Beechen Grove Baptist School were transferred to the Victoria Senior Boys' School. Other schools built in this era included Watford Field, Chater, Callow Land, Parkgate, Alexandra and Oxhey.

The shortcomings in the 1870 Act were largely remedied in Balfour's Act of 1902. The era of the School Boards ended with the transfer of their near absolute power to County Councils at both primary and secondary levels, through the media of Education Committees.

For two decades the schools founded or acquired by the Board and the Council served the ever-growing population until the development of farmland still surrounding the town, which forced the South West Herts Divisional Executive to provide a series of new schools conforming to an enlightened design concept and which included Leggatt's Way in 1934 followed by Kingswood, Knutsford and Oaklands. These new schools in turn coped with the ever-changing, but always increasing population during the town's phenominal expansion during the inter-war years including the development of the Tudor, Bradshaw, Kingswood, Leavesden Green and Harebreaks estates.

CHURCH STREET (LOOKING TOWARDS HIGH STREET).

II
Growing Pains

Even the quietest hamlets face problems of space. In 1771, Watford, with a population of just over 2,000, had a very pressing problem — the graveyard was overcrowded and it was becoming increasingly difficult to deal decently with burials.

The Vestry reckoned that if the road past the Churchyard was moved nearer to the Almshouses the size of the Churchyard would be almost doubled.

Accordingly application was made for an Act of Parliament allowing re-alignment of the road. This was duly passed and the road was moved to the line we know today. A further enlargement was made in 1843 and the enlarged Churchyard sufficed until the laying out in 1858 of a new burial ground in Vicarage Road.

(A map drawn to support the application for road re-alignment, and which also serves as a plan of the church area, is reproduced overleaf.)

In 1771 the Workhouse had been established for some fifty years and Mrs. Fuller's Free School for nearly seventy years. The Town's growth was static. The Canal was some twenty or so years away, gas, about fifty years, and the railway was sixty-six years in the future.

The canal, when built, made little impact, except to bring coal into the district — this paved the way for the founding of the gas works. The canal later gave impetus to the paper-making mills of Apsley, Nash, Home Park and Croxley

Far over the horizon, in the north of England, successful experiments with steam locomotives were taking place and in 1830 it was decided to build a railway line between Birmingham and London. Taking several years to plan and survey, the line was projected to run in the Gade valley, almost alongside the canal.

Whilst the Earl of Clarendon and the 5th Earl of Essex were tolerant of the canal, and canal traffic travelling at a speed of three or four miles per hour through their parks, they were less inclined to tolerate the rush, noise and smell of the new-fangled steam train. The projected line

had to be resurveyed, and was moved somewhat to the north, necessitating the construction of a mile-long tunnel.

The coming of a railway, in itself, would naturally bring a degree of growth, as happened to many other towns and villages countrywide.

Watford, however, had three other contributory factors which greatly enhanced the impetus of the railway.

Firstly, the town had a degree of prominence resulting from the crossing of two turnpike roads and being sited on the main track from London to Aylesbury. Secondly, it had a considerable degree of importance by virtue of the grant and right to hold weekly markets and thirdly, not long after the coming of the railway, when Arthur Algernon Capel was thirty-six, he inherited the title of Earl of Essex and as Lord of the Manor he became involved in local activities. It was not long before he realised the cash advantage of the land he owned and started to sell parcels of it, a trend that other landowners followed. He had sufficient virgin land to keep pace with demand and its release enabled Watford to grow without the excesses of industrial connurbations.

Not that Watford was without problems. The town's growth, when it started, was beyond the power of the Vestry to deal with.

Our story starts a little before the coming of the railway, but is principally of the 150 years since 1837.

In 1861 Frederick Downer started in business as a photographer at No. 97 High Street, and two years later, in the then new Queens Road, Samuel Peacock started 1863 well by presenting Watford with a weekly newspaper. Each recorded facts and facets of the town but not for more than 30 years could their efforts be combined . . .

For the first time ever this book puts some of the early photographs together with the original text of the day. When, later in the 1880's, Dr. Brett complains of the 'pools of urine' and 'the stench they leave', the photographs of the old cattle market take on a new meaning.

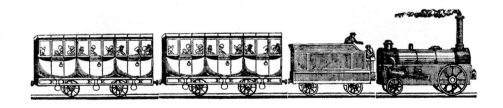

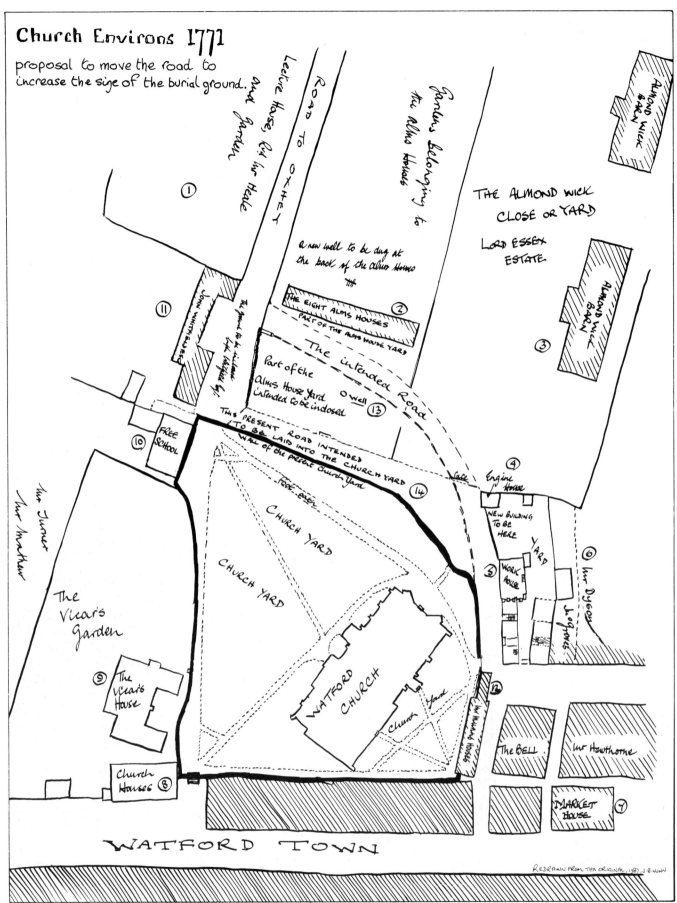

Church Environs 1771

proposal to move the road to
increase the size of the burial ground.

ALMOND WICK BARN

Lecture House, Rd for Heale and Garden

ROAD TO OXHEY

Gardens belonging to the Alms Houses

THE ALMOND WICK CLOSE OR YARD

LORD ESSEX ESTATE

①

a new well to be dug at the back of the alms Houses

ALMOND WICK BARN

⑪

JOHN WHITFIELD Es?

THE EIGHT ALMS HOUSES ②

PART OF THE ALMS HOUSE YARD

③

The intended Road

Part of the Alms House Yard intended to be inclosed

O well ⑬

THIS PRESENT ROAD INTENDED TO BE LAID INTO THE CHURCH YARD

WALL OF the present Church Yard

④

Engine House

Mr Turner

Mr Matthew

FREE SCHOOL ⑩

Foot path

CHURCH YARD

CHURCH YARD

⑭

Sale

NEW BUILDING TO BE HERE

YARD

Mr Dyson

The Vicar's Garden

⑨ The Vicar's House

WATFORD CHURCH

WORK HOUSE ⑤

Ja Jones

Mr Dyson ⑥

Church Yard

Mr Williams Houses ⑫

Church Houses ⑧

The BELL

Mr Hawthorn

MARKET HOUSE ⑦

WATFORD TOWN

REDRAWN FROM THE ORIGINAL, 1981 J.B.NUNN

In 1771 a map was drawn to support a proposal to re-align the road (New Street) to increase the size of the burial ground. The original map still exists but in a condition not conducive to acceptable standards of reproduction. The above illustration is redrawn from the original. The Vicarage, which in 1771 was the second, survived until 1915 (the first, demolished in 1914) was located on the site now occupied by Woolworth's. The 'Church Houses' were demolished in 1822 and the grounds became part of the Vicarage garden. After 1916 a new (third) vicarage was built, set back a little further and to the left of that shown in this drawing. At the time of writing (1987) the present (third) Vicarage has been vacated and awaits demolition after which the site will be redeveloped for residential accommodation.

Enlarging the Churchyard . . .

In 1771, a plan was prepared for "enclosing part of a certain yard called Almond Wick yard and part of a court or yard belonging to the eight almshouses, standing west of the Church, and also the road between Almond Wick and the said court or yard, by way of enlargement of the present churchyard and to make a new road near the said Almshouses. 5s. to be paid yearly, out of the poor rates to each of the persons placed in the Almshouses, or to be paid in lieu of the use of the courtyard to be closed, and for the well therein and the way to it and other privileges they claim thereout."

On 21st January 1771, Parliament passed "An Act to enlarge the cemetary or church yard of the Parish of Watford in the County of Hertford, and to make an additional building to the present workhouse for the reception of the poor of the said Parish; and for other purposes therein mentioned."

The 'other purposes' were financial. A rate of up to 6d. in the £ was to be raised on the rental values of all properties in the parish, and collected with the Land Tax. Most of the proceeds would be used to enlarge the church yard and workhouse but part would be used for the creation of a fund, administered by Trustees, to sell annuities at £10 per annum.

The work was carried out and the line of the road taken past the 'engine house' to curve round and in front of the Almshouses to the line we know today.

The plan opposite shows several interesting places around the church:

1) The Lecturer's House, where a kind of parish curate lived provided he gave periodic lectures on the Protestant faith. In the same building lived the Morrison Trust Almswomen. The building was erected by William Heydon of Lincolns Inn (died 1545), enlarged by his grandson Francis (died 1606), when it was known as 'Watford Place'.

2) The Bedford Almshouses built by Bridget Lady Bedford, widow of Sir Richard Morrison, in 1580. (p.355)

3) The Almond Wick Barns, used to store the tithe corn from the Earl of Essex's estates. (The name was originally Nambourne Wick.)

4) The engine house for the parish manual firepump. (p.87 c)

5) The workhouse, built in 1721, to keep the poor together in one place and make their relief easier to administer.

6) Mr. Dyson's Yard, in which Dyson's brewery was established in 1750. The yard was later known as Ballard's Buildings. (p.160)

7) The Market House, open underneath to give shelter on wet days. (p.29)

8) The Church Houses where Francis Combe's Free School was housed. They were demolished in 1822 and ground added to the Vicarage garden.

9) The new vicarage, built about 1630 and demolished in 1915. (p.135 b)

10) The Free School built by Dame Fuller in 1704. (p.355)

11) Mr. Whitfield's House. This was built in 1668-70 by Thomas Hobson, Dame Fuller's first husband, on the site of two previous buildings. It was called 'Watford Place'.

12) Mr. Munn's houses, the old cottages shown on p.74.

13) One of the wells remarked upon in 'water supply', p.22.

14) The existing road which was to be incorporated in the extended church yard.

The two small cottages on the extreme right were demolished in 1888 to make way for new buildings erected by Mr.Francis Fisher, including a butcher's shop with generous living accommodation above. The shop premises, as well as the adjacent lane (New Street) leading to St. Mary's Church, still exist. The building on the opposite corner, considerably altered, is currently (1987) occupied by the 'Body Shop' following its long occupation by Bewlay's. The 'Spread Eagle' was rebuilt c1958 as a block of shops; the 'King's Head' and adjoining butcher's shop was burned down in 1828 and after rebuilding survived until 1961. The distant trees on the extreme left are in the grounds of the Vicarage.

Copyholds

'Copyholds' in the Manor of Watford were those properties once held by mediaeval villeins from the Abbey of St. Albans. In more modern times the Lord of the Manor was the Earl of Essex and his steward, a local solicitor, had to enter in the Manor Books all changes in copyhold ownership, whether caused by sale to another, death and inheritance, or regranting to the Lord if no heir was found.

It was also possible for a copyholder to sell to somebody for a term of years only, at the end of of which it would revert to the proper copyholder, in this case John Finch who wished to pass its ownership to another for 21 years. There was a sitting tenant, Elizabeth Browning. Transactions of this nature needed a 'licence' from the steward and a 'fine' was payable. This deed is copied from the Manor Books and given to the copyholder to retain as his right to the property. By the early 20th century, all copyholds were converted to freeholds.

Two early printers

From Herts Sessions Books (Liberty Sessions) the following entries are of interest:
a) an application from James Perry, lately of Uxbridge, for a licence to print. 1816.
b) a refusal by Perry to re-accept an apprentice. 1827.
c) John Peacock applies for licence. 1827.

In the 1841 Census, John Peacock, then aged 60, lived one house above Chater the chemist, near Carey Place (Chater was No. 129). In 1851 he was in the 'Manor House' between Local Board Road and Farthing Lane. His son, Samuel, established the Watford Observer in 1863.

Copy of a typical document relating to copyhold ownership changes, 11th March, 1795.

Henry Williams

To Richard Williams, Beadle at the Parish Church, and his wife, was born a son, on 17th August, 1828. He was named Henry, later to become Sanitary Inspector, Inspector of Nuisances, and author of the 'History of Watford' (1884).

A Water Supply

Prior to the early part of the present century the quantity of water obtainable at Watford for domestic purposes was small and of very doubtful purity. The supply was obtained from two or three wells, and the River Colne. One of these wells was close to the old churchyard, and another very near to an old-established slaughterhouse. Men, and even women, might be seen with yokes and pails, fetching water from the Colne at the bottom of Water Lane, and not unfrequently this heavy work was assigned to children. A circular, of which the following is a copy, was issued on the 26th May, 1819, showing that a committee of the inhabitants had been formed for the purpose of erecting a public pump in the High Street, from which a better and more ready supply could be obtained:–

"VESTRY ROOM, WATFORD,
"May 26th, 1819.

"At a meeting of the subscribers to the fund for sinking a well and putting down an engine for public use, convened by notice given in the church on Sunday last, to examine the treasurer's accounts, it appears that the total amount of subscriptions is £312 16s., and the total amount of expenditure is £310 19s. 1d., leaving a balance in the hands of the treasurer of £1 16s. 11d., which accounts have been examined and approved.

"It was resolved that it will be expedient to raise a fund to keep the engine in repair, and that the amount thereof be placed in the Watford Savings Bank."

Henry William's "History of Watford"

● *The well was built and the old pump (engine) stood in the market place until the formation of the Local Board (1850) when it was later removed, having become much delapidated from constant use, and a drinking fountain, purchased by subscription, raised on the site. (It was 'an unsightly piece of architecture' and soon removed).*

The pump had been used to draw water to fight a fire (c1828) in a butcher's shop next to the 'King's Head' when fat used in candle-making boiled over, destroying the house and the 'King's Head'; and later (1853) in an attempt to save the Market Hall from being destroyed by fire.

The well was forgotten until 1931 when it was rediscovered by workmen digging a trench for Post Office telephone works.

Discovered in Market Place

Brick-lined and four or five feet across, the well had a depth to the water-line of about 75 feet. There was about ten feet of water at the bottom. Apparently, when the well was built-in the brickwork was dome-shaped at the top, the top of the dome being only 12 inches below the street level. For years this brickwork, under the thin layer of cobble and concrete, has withstood the weight of the market stalls and the cattle in the old days, political and religious meetings, and in more recent times the cars and lorries that have been parked above it. WO (May, 1931)

This illustration was drawn by P. Heseltine in March 1880, and captures the cold stark days of early spring. The tow line is hardly visible attached to a horse out of the picture. Although the print illustrates a working boat some 90 years after the canal's opening, the scene changed little in the ensuing years. Compare with the illustration of another working boat on page 104.

The canal . . .

The Grand Junction Canal was the name of the Company that gave its name to the waterway connecting London with Birmingham. The total length of the canal was one hundred and thirty seven miles. It was built, without mechanical aids, by gangs of navigators (navvies) under the supervision and direction of some of the best civil engineers of the day. The section between Brentford and Berkhamsted opened in 1798 and the extension to Braunston in 1805.

The canal passed through the estates of the Earl of Essex and the Earl of Clarendon, the tow paths in each place being built on the side furthest from the stately homes. The Company was soon operating in a profit situation using pairs of narrow boats pulled by horses. The cargoes carried by the working boats included corn, coal, bricks and allied building products. The carriage of coal beyond Lady Capel's Wharf was at first prohibited but the order was relaxed in 1805 when a resident tax collector permitted passage of the coal to all points south of Watford on payment of Coal Tax.

By 1890 the duty was abolished by which time the railway was successfully competing for the cargoes traditionally carried by boats of the Canal Company. As bulk carriers the Company survived until 1920 when business had declined to the extent that a merger was forced on the controlling company. Under the new title Grand Union Canal Company, long-overdue improvements were made to the canal. To this end Lady Capel's Wharf was entirely removed. Only the name has survived to the present.

The Grand Union was nationalised in 1948 and two decades later its commercial status ended when the canal was reserved for those who like messing about in boats, for anglers and for those who treasure one of the unique legacies of the Industrial Revolution.

CUSTOMS

OF THE

MANOR

OF

WATFORD.

Fences in the Common Fields .. — ALL those that have Lands in Watford Field, or Land in any of the Common Fields in or about Watford, shall make up their Fences belonging to their several Lands lying against the Lands adjoining, for their winter crop before Michaelmas; and for their *Court 9th. April, 1624. ......* summer crop before Lady-Day in every year, on pain of forfeiting to the Lord of the Manor twelve-pence per pole.

Gate and Fence against Wiggen-hall Mead — The Occupiers of Church-Acre shall keep a sufficient Fence and Gate, at the end of Church-Acre, between Watford Field and Wiggenhall Mead, all the year long, (ex- *Courts 1621 and 1624. ......* cept between All-hallowed Tide and Candlemas; upon pain of forfeiting twelve-pence per week to the Lord of the Manor.

Sheep .... — No Man shall put any Sheep in Common Meads, Wiggen-hall Mead, or Middle-more, before the first day of November, nor after Candlemas-Day following, on pain of forfeiting for every Sheep six-pence; half to the Lord of the Manor, and the other half *1624. ....* to the Meadow Drivers.

1631. .... — No Man not holding Land in the Common Field, shall at any time put upon, or into, the Common Fields and Meadows above the number of Ten Sheep, on pain of forfeiting for every Sheep twelve-pence, so often as they shall be taken; half to the Lord and half to the Finder.

Batchelors. ...... — No Batchelor (unless he be a Householder) shall put any Sheep in the Commons on the same forfeiture.

Foreigners. ...... — No foreigners have any Right of Commoning in Wiggen-hall Meadow, Middle-more, or Bushey Mead, except they have Land in the Meadow, and in their own pos- session at the same time. And also, that none but Housekeepers have a Right of Com- *5th. April, 1709.* moning, except they have Land in the Meadow.

Also that the ANCIENT CUSTOM is, that all Cattle that are put in con- trary to the Custom of the Manor, shall pay FOUR-PENCE per foot to the Meadow Driver.

Cattle in the Highways or Lanes. — No Inhabitant within the Town or Parish of Watford, shall keep above Two Beasts in the Highways nor then either, unless they have a Follower to keep them from breaking or hurting the Fences, upon pain of forfeiting twelve-pence to the Lord of the Manor, by them that shall keep above Two; or any Beast there at all, without a Keeper.— ☞ The fine twelve-pence each, half to the Lord and half to him that poundeth them.

Mares. .... — No Man shall put any Mare to feed in the Common Meadows, or Highways, or Lanes, in the Parish of Watford, upon pain of forfeiting twenty shillings for every Mare so found; half to the Lord of the Manor, and the other half to the Meadow Driver.

Diseased Horses .. — No Man shall put any Horse or Gelding that hath the Fashions (Farcy) or Mange into any of the Common Meadows, upon pain of forfeiting ten shillings for every such Beast so put in; half to the Lord and half to the Finder.

River Cleansing .. — The Landholders on both sides the River between the Town Mill and Hamper Mill, to clear the River 5 Feet Wide; on pain of forfeiting two shillings and six-pence per pole.

Shutting up the Meadows .... — Common Meadows to be shut up at Candlemas-Day; and any putting Cattle therein between that Day and Lammas forfeit three shillings and four-pence; half to the Lord, and the other to him who receives the Damage.

Geese, &c. ...... — Neither Cattle or Geese to be put in the Common Mead before the Crop be off; but shall keep them from thence from Candlemas-Day until Lammas-Day.

Hogs. .... — Whoever have any Hogs go into the Common Fields and Meadows unrunged, shall pay for every Hog one shilling.

Passages into Wat- ford Field .. — Dagnall's Alley and Moody's Alley, a Passage for foot Passengers into Watford Field, and a stile or Fence to be maintained by the Persons who own the Houses.

Extract of Court Roll. { EDWARD BOODLE, Chief Steward.
{ PHILIP COWLEY, Deputy Steward of the said Manor.

PERRY, Printer, Engraver, Bookbinder, Librarian, &c. Market-Place, WATFORD.
[Printer to THE EARL OF ESSEX, THE EARL OF CLARENDON, &c. &c.]

A unique poster (original size 10¾" x 17½") detailing the 'country rules' of 1820. The arrival of gas and the railway was still awaited. Many place-names are still familiar, but Watford Field perpetuates one of the few direct links with the town's agrarian past. The map on the facing page includes the area covered by the Court Roll.

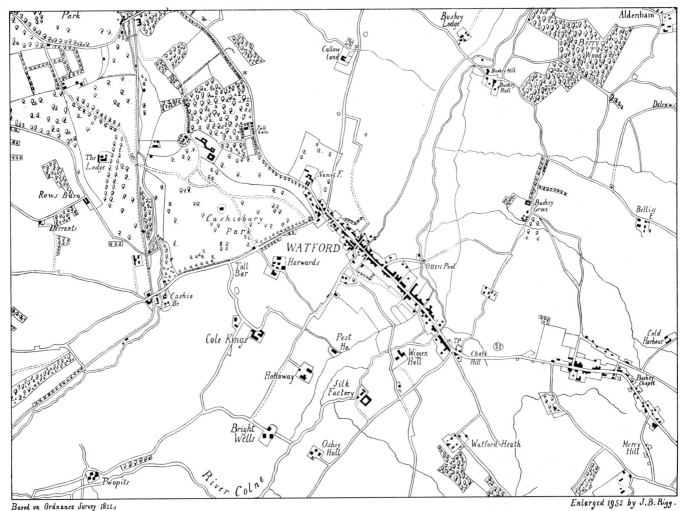

WATFORD IN 1822.

Monmouth House, the Poa Fields and the Lammas Lands

From the early 18th century the principal owners of Watford land were the Earls of Essex, Fellows of the Merton College, Oxford, and the Church.

Between our now Clarendon Road and the Pond were two large estates, that of Watford House, notable as the home of the County Historian, Clutterbuck (of which part is now the site of Clements) and Monmouth House. Monmouth House was built in 1610 by Sir Robert Carey, Earl of Monmouth, as a dower house. Named the 'Mansion House', it had all the land called Great and Little Poa Fields which extended from the High Street to beyond where the railway was built.

Upon the death of Sir Robert's widow, in 1640, the house and grounds passed into the ownership of William Carpender, of Coleford, Gloucester and upon grandson John's death in 1771 the house was divided into two and the land belonging to the property was sold, the Great and Little Poa Fields being bought by Mr. Clutterbuck.

The two houses stayed within the Carpender/Cox family, and in 1865 the south house was named 'The Platts', the north 'Monmouth'. The houses were finally sold in 1927, a little later the north house was almost entirely rebuilt, using bricks from the demolished Cassiobury House, the south much altered, and the whole converted into the shop premises we know today.

The extensive grounds of Watford House included the area later known as Dudley's Corner which at that time (c1800), accommodated maltings. The maltings were removed to the rear of 66 High Street, cottages built in their stead, and the gates to the grounds removed and Clarendon Road cut through in 1864. This development heralded the end of Poa Fields.

The town's people used the Common Fields and Lammas lands which were small tracts of ground spreading to the rear of the Church, towards Colney Butts, southwards towards our present Watford Fields (which perpetuates the name) and, in part, bounded by the river Colne before the advent of both the Rickmansworth Railway and Electric Railway to London.

Countrywide, between 1750 and 1820, 'enclosure' of open fields was carried out to improve farming methods although, of course, many ancient rights were lost in the process. The enclosure of the Watford fields—which at that time was grazing and arable land behind the Crown Passage in the High Street—seemed more in the nature of acquisition for development. The ancient rights were sold in 1855 for compensation of £1698. A further £159 was received for two crops of grass and a further £507 17s. in 1862 when the Rickmansworth railway company put their line through the fields. Of the resultant £2991 7s., £161 12s. was later granted to the Library committee. The remaining £2,828 was invested and the income was, until the advent of the National Health Service, devoted to help the upkeep of the Peace Memorial Hospital.

Upon the implementation of the Enclosure Act part of the land was retained for public recreation ground—our present Watford Fields.

25

...being rarely more than the loss of the end of a finger, or fingers...

Extracts from a

REPORT

from the Committee on the

"BILL to regulate the LABOUR of CHILDREN in the MILLS and "FACTORIES of the United Kingdom"

Ordered, by The House of Commons, *to be Printed,*
8 August 1832

---

10 July, 1832
MICHAEL THOMAS SADLER, ESQUIRE, in the Chair.

Mr. *Thomas Daniel,* (Rookery Mill) called in; and further Examined.

HAVE you been employed in any other business in mills and factories besides cotton?—*In the silk mills I have been employed.*

Where both silk throwing and silk spinning have been conducted?—*Yes.*

In what departments were you in any such mills?—*I was a superintendent in throwing and spinning the silk.*

In both instances, therefore, you are competent to speak as to questions relating to that branch of business?—*I am.*

Is a great proportion of children employed in that manufacture?—*There is a great number.*

Does the proportion of boys or girls preponderate?—*They are girls principally.*

Do you think that girls are as well capable of sustaining long-continued exertion as boys?—*By no means.*

You have already mentioned that the labour of the children in the cotton factories has been considerably increased of late years?—*It has been very considerably increased.*

Will you state whether that is the fact in regard to the labour of children in silk mills?—*It is; their labour has been increased very much.*

Has the number of spindles that they have to attend to been considerably increased by recent alterations in the machinery?—*They have, more than one-half, I should think.*

Do you consider that those improvements of alterations in the machinery have materially lessened their labour with respect to the same number of spindles that children had previously to endure?—*No, it has increased their labour very materially; they have as much labour again, thereabouts now, as they have to perform before.*

Have not the children in silk mills also to regulate, in some measure, their own labour, so as to be often in a state of considerable anxiety regarding the quantity of work that they produce?—*They have to be answerable for all the work that goes through their fingers, have the children in silk mills.*

So that they have a kind of responsibility upon them, as well as actual labour, to endure?—*They are responsible for all work that goes through their fingers.*

Does the mill system, as at present pursued, occasion many accidents among the hands employed?—*I know that it does produce those accidents inseparable from machinery. It is possible that, at a late period of the day, a state of languor and lassitude may be brought on, whereby they would be less able to guard against the accidents which would naturally occur in such large establishments, and with such machinery.*

It is sometimes said, that those accidents occur often at the termination of the day's labour, but generally at the termination of a week's labour, when the person becomes fatigued; does that consist with your experience?—*Yes, the latter part of it does; for on*

Saturday there was always a number of accidents, but generally trifling, being rarely more than the loss of the end of a finger or fingers; that is as far as relates to the cleaning of the machinery at the time specified; but I cannot say that these ever appeared to me to be connected with or produced by reason of the languor to which the question refers; although, as I have already observed, I can conceive that listlessness might deprive them of that caution which, with their full energies, they would exercise.

Daniel Fraser, called in; and further Examined.

DID you bear a summons to George Montagu, of Watford?—*Yes, I did.*

To appear before this Committee to give evidence touching an inquiry respecting a Bill for limiting the hours of children employed in mills and factories?—*Yes, I did.*

Are you aware that an answer has been returned to that summons, stating that he is too unwell to attend?—*Yes.*

Do you know that, nevertheless, he worked on the day on which you delivered the summons to him?—*Yes; and I found him coming out of the mill when I delivered the summons.*

Where you desired to summon others also?—*Yes, I was.*

Have you not found much disinclination to attend as witnesses on the part of those that would have been brought before this Committee, had it not been for their expressing their apprehension, that if they appeared they should endanger their interests, and, perhaps, lose their situations? —*Yes; I am sorry to see that this feeling is very deeply impressed upon the minds of the operatives in connexion with the factories; otherwise they said they would give evidence with cheerfulness; it is my deep impression, that though very favourable to the passing of a Bill to limit the hours of labour to ten hours a day, they are afraid to express their sentiments upon this subject, lest it should affect their interests.*

What, speaking from your own knowledge, is the state of employment in the silk mills which you have recently visited, in respect of the number of hours; state, also, whether they work several of them by night, and the general condition and appearance of the hands employed, specifying the particular places that you have visited, with a view to collect information upon the subject, and to select witnesses to appear before this Committee?—*As far as I have had an opportunity of knowing, I find that there is very little difference between the number of hours that the children work in those various places which I have visited in Essex, Suffolk, and elsewhere, from those which I have already stated to the Committee, viz. twelve hours' actual labour per day. They work from half-past 5 in the morning, at Braintree, in Essex, till half-past 6 in the evening, and with the intermission for meals of one hour, half an hour for breakfast, and half an hour for dinner; and the children there are fined a penny per hour for being absent. I am quite confident that they would be glad of a regulation of the hours of labour, even if it was attended with diminished wages. One woman, in particular, said, "She would "far rather have less wages, than see her children so tired at night;" and another thus*

... from 6 in the morning till 7 at night, half an hour breakfast, half an hour dinner, but no tea time ...

remarked, relative to the health and morals of the children employed in factories, "That if a jolly girl goes into a mill, her countenance soon alters, and they "become more unruly than they were before." And another trait of the factory system is, that women and children do the work of men and grown-up people. I observed one man kept to attend to the engine and to the repair of the mill, and females performed the rest of the labour along with children.

Have you inquired whether the children employed that length of time are beaten and chastised at the silk-mills as well as at the cotton and other factories?—*Yes, they are chastised; and it is found necessary, under this system, to keep driving them on; and the children are taken into this mill at any age, if tall enough.*

The children are taken much earlier to the silk-mill than to any other mill, are they not?—*Yes; and when they are not tall enough, they find them little stools to stand upon, to reach their work.*

How old are some of them?—*Some of them turned 5, and at 6 years of age.*

...At Watford, in Hertfordshire, the mill is worked both day and night. In Hertfordshire, the children go at 6 in the morning, and work till 7 at night, and they have one hour and twenty minutes intermission.

Then the night hands go on at 7, and work till 6 in the ensuing morning?—*Yes, The Committee most likely will have some further evidence upon that subject, which will be able to state that more particularly. In this mill, children were going in at 5 years of age, and those children have worked the usual hours. At this mill, if the children are not tall enough, stools are got for the infants; they have no Sunday-school, nor week-day evening-school at this village; it is a little village where this mill is. I found that one of the children, Elizabeth Taylor, went to the mill at between 7 and 8 years old, for 1s. a week at first; she is now nearly 15 years old, and has 3s. 6d. a week. There are instances there, where the wife is working during the night, and the husband working during the day; the amount of their wages is 20s. a week, both their wages united, for working night and day.*

Do you know whether the children are beaten up to their work there also?—*Yes; they are regularly urged to their work by beating; they use canes in that mill to beat the children.*

Have you seen any instances, in going round, of those children being chastised?—*Yes; I saw a boy of the name of Richard Love, for making a waste with a peg, which is a thing that will very frequently occur in the silk business, by being thrown off the bobbin; I saw him standing in the midst of a group of little children; he had received a bleeding wound in the right side of his face, in consequence of making this peg waste.*

Are you able to say, whether that fault might not have been unavoidable, and whether it might not have been an accident?—*From the number of pegs they have to keep up, it is a thing that might occur with older ones than this Richard Love. I dare say he might be from 12 to 15 years of age.*

This was not inside the mill, was it?—*No.*

Is there not considerable objection made to yourself and other persons, that wish to observe upon the system of examining those mills?—*Yes, they do not allow any person to examine those mills except they have business; they fine the children at this mill: there is James Naylor, who has 2s. a week, he lost two hours one morning, and he was fined for that 7d.; his mother asked the reason of this deduction, and Mr. Rodduck, the overlooker, simply replied, "That this was the "rule." I found there was one female doing the work of three or four men in the throwing department, in taking charge of the silk which they wound. Thirty or forty children are the usual charge for a man. This young woman had nearly 100 under her care, and the amount of her wages was 10s. a week, for which, as I calculate, she was doing the work of three men; and if the children had been properly attended to, they would have required more than three.*

Had not several of the hands in those mills previously petitioned *against* the Bill now under the consideration of Parliament?—*Yes, all the hands in this mill had signed a petition, but neither old nor young, parents nor children, knew anything of the matter; all the infants signed with a cross. I am fully prepared to mention names, but refrain solely from a fear of injuring individuals. That petition was signed by the orders of their employer.*

Did they sign it?—*Yes.*

And they told you that they knew nothing about it?—*They did; neither parents nor children, nor up-growing operatives in the mill, could give any proper account what it was, or for what purpose it was done, the masters possess so much power, I would almost say unconstitutional power, over the operatives.*

William Rastrick, called in; and Examined.

WHERE do you reside?—*At Watford.*

What age are you?—*Thirty-four.*

Have you ever been in a silk-mill? *Yes.*

At what age did you go into one?—*At 11 years of age. (1809)*

Are there not many children that go at a much earlier period than that?—*Yes, considerably younger.*

How young have you known children go into silk-mills?—*I have known three at 6; but very few at that age.*

In whose mill did you work at that period?—*Mr. Shute's, at Watford.*

What were your hours of labour?—*From 6 in the morning till 7 at night.*

What time had you allowed for breakfast, for dinner and for tea?—*Half an hour breakfast, half an hour dinner, but no tea time; at least not at that time.*

Was the mill worked at night?—*No, not then.*

Have you found that employment to be hard and laborious?—*Yes, at times.*

Was it fatiguing?—*Yes.*

Had you, or any of the hands, any opportunity of going to an evening-school, or of learning anything during that time?—*No, it was too far from the town; a mile from the town.*

Was there a Sunday-school in the town?—*Yes, two or three.*

Did those afford the hands, generally, the only opportunities they possessed of getting a little learning?—*The only opportunity.*

Were not the children very much disinclined to attend the Sunday-schools after having been thus employed during the week?—*Yes; in a great many instances they would absent themselves from the school and ramble in the fields, instead of going.*

Were the children beaten up to their labour, so as to be compelled to do it?—*Yes, at times.*

What did you become afterwards?—*At that time I worked at the spinning-mills; and from them I went to what are called the throwing-mills.*

What age were you when you went to the throwing mills?—*About 11.*

Were you a throwster?—*Yes; I began learning the throwing department at that time.*

Is not that an employment which requires very close attention?—*Yes.*

What hours did you labour there?—*The same.*

Has not the silk-throwing business to be performed in a standing position?—*Yes, the whole of it.*

Did you not find that to stand that length of time, to say nothing whatever about the employment itself, was very fatiguing?—*Certainly.*

Did it ever produce pain in your limbs?—*Pain in my legs and my back.*

When did you leave that mill?—*About the year 1821; I went from there to Mitcham, and was in Mitcham seven months.*

In what capacity were you there?—*As a throwster, at first, and then I looked over a room.*

What were your hours of labour there?—*Six in the morning to 7 at night; half an hour for breakfast, an hour dinner, and a quarter of an hour for tea.*

Did you find the children were much fatigued?—*Yes.*

... they twist themselves about on their legs and stand on the sides of their feet ...

High Street, drawing by Buckler 1832. Modern numbers 114-104.

Did you find them particularly fatigued towards the evening?—*Yes, excepting some of them; there are some of stronger constitutions whom the labour does not affect so much.*

Have the children to stand at that employment?—*Yes.*

Was it not found necessary to beat children at that age, so as to keep them up to their employment?—*Certainly.*

Did the beating increase towards evening?—*Their strength relaxes more towards the evening, they get tired, and they twist themselves about on their legs, and stand on the sides of their feet.*

They begin then to neglect their work, being in a state, perhaps, of exhaustion?—*Yes.*

So that they have to be occasionally beaten to induce them to perform it?—*Yes.*

And in some cases with considerable severity?—*In some cases they are.*

Are those children under the control of the overlookers, or are they under the master?—*Under the control of the overlookers. The master comes in perhaps three or four times in the course of the day; he merely comes up and down the room a time or two.*

Does the overlooker hire or pay them?—*The master in that mill hires them and pays them.*

Is it the case in all other mills?—*No, it is not.*

Have the children often to work over-time in those mills?—*Yes.*

How much over-time?—*Two hours.*

Making altogether fifteen hours of confinement?—*Yes.*

You state that during the time you were in those mills, you had no opportunity during the week to obtain instruction?—*None whatever; it is always the rule in those mills, if we find children with books, to take them from them.*

And the only opportunity you had for obtaining instruction was in the Sunday-schools?—*Yes.*

Do they teach writing in those schools?—*No.*

There is no opportunity therefore for the children to learn to write?—*No; unless the parents can write, and set them to it of an evening.*

Do you think that many children can write?—*Very few.*

The system, then, has the direct tendency to deprive them of what may be now justly denominated a necessary part of education for a working person?—*Yes, it has.*

Have you observed whether there are a large proportion of males or females engaged in silk-mills?—*Females.*

Do you think that they can bear labour so well as boys or men?—*No; I do not think they can.*

Has it not a visible effect upon their health, their growth, and their strength?—*There is not the least doubt of it.*

From your experience in mills, do not you think that a limitation of the hours of labour would be a great benefit to those employed at present in the silk-mills, especially if connected with an opportunity of giving them an education?—*Certainly it would.*

And that it would, notwithstanding the apparent opposition that may be offered to such a legislative measure, meet with the ready concurrence, and gratify the earnest wishes of those who may be engaged in such pursuits?—*Yes, I am confident it would.*

Do you think that the children, and workmen generally, that work in those mills, are worse off than the agricultural labourers?—*Yes, they are, considerably.*

●*The Enquiry led to the Factory Act of 1833 in which children under nine years of age were barred from all textile factories; hours for 9-13 years were limited to forty-eight; young persons of 13-18 years, sixty-nine hours. It was also laid down that every factory child should receive two hours schooling per day — a part of the Act usually ignored!*

A further Factory Act of 1844 reduced Children's hours still more, and controlled womens' hours to the same as a 'young person', and stipulated that all dangerous machinery had to be fenced.

The Rookery Mill was built by Thomas Deacon of Wiggenhall c1770 and leased to Edward Crutchley. Later it was bought by Mr. Paumier and by the 1820's it had passed to Thomas Rock Shute in whose ownership it was at the time of the Silk Mill Enquiry Report.

The name 'Rookery' was acquired from a rookery in nearby elms — the site is shown on the map on page 52 and in an aerial view on page 158.

The building on the right is the 'Spread Eagle'; the 'King's Head' and the 'Bell' are behind the Market Hall and are not visible. The premises behind the wagon survived until 1959 (No2. 92 & 94). Until some 30 or 40 years on from the drawing premises were not numbered and the houses were known by the names of the owners or occupiers. The site of the houses behind the wagon, Mr. Allway's houses, is better known today as 'Ratner's'. *Buckler 1832*

The Watford Gas and Coke Company

THE Watford Gas and Coke Company was formed on the 2nd January, 1834, by a Deed of Partnership made between the subscribers for the total capital of £2,500, and Richard Pugh, the elder, Gentlemen, Philip Cowley, the younger, Gentleman, and George Dracott, Maltster, all of Watford. All the members agreed "to be firmly bound unto one another in Co-partnership, and as members of an undertaking for supplying the town of Watford with Inflammable Air or Gas and for the making and sale of Coke."

The control of the undertaking was in the hands of the following gentlemen: *Directors:* William Frederick Brown; Daniel Adcock; James Child; William Hollingsworth; John Fowler; Henry Lomas; John Mitchell; Sampson Wright; The Rev. James Cauldfield Browne. *Treasurer:* George Reeve. *Trustees:* Philip Cowley; Richard Pugh; George Dracott. *Secretary:* Robert F. Howard.

The first recorded directors' meeting was held at the Essex Arms Inn in August, 1834, when twelve gentlemen attended, the business consisting of:
- (a) Instructing the Secretary to know the price of the coals which had *already* been sent to the coal-shed.
- (b) The purchase of 25 bushels of lime.
- (c) Ordering of 250 price cards.

Like many other new things, gas did not become suddenly popular, but by dint of long and amicable arrangements with the lighting inspectors, lamp columns were erected to light the streets and also to serve as a reminder to the public that their premises could be lighted by gas. The agreement for the public lighting contained a clause that the lamps were not to be lighted when there was a full moon or on the the night prior to or the night following a full moon. Argand burners with fifteen holes or large Bats Wing were originally supplied to private consumers, and, as the consumption of gas was not metered in the first case, rates were levied according to the hour the lights were left on, with an extra charge of one-sixth for Sundays.

The coal used was, until the advent of the railway, delivered by canal to Cassiobridge, and thence by road to the present Works at the lower end of the High Street. The coal carbonized in the first years amounted to 200 tons per annum.

Towards the end of 1835 a request was made by the Lessee of the Tolls, (Mr. Carver), for lights to be supplied to the Toll-gate House at the bottom of the town, in place of the little oil lantern which used to hang on the wall, but as the expense of carrying the main there was £20, it was deemed necessary for the Commissioners of the Sparrows Herne Trust to bear half the expense involved.

In 1835 the monthly coal bill for the Company reached the sum of £19

11s. 11d. (16½ tons), and the monthly receipts for the 50 public lamps were £22 10s. 0d. Private accounts to the extent of £27 13s. 3d. were recorded and the residual products sold for the month totalled £16 11s. 4d.

In 1838, it was agreed to lease the Works to Mr. J. P. Taylor of Watford, for one year for the sum of £200 plus 5s. for each additional light fixed during the period of the lease. Unfortunately, Mr. J. P. Taylor sustained a loss of £50 on his year's working!

In the fifties and sixties, the Directors held their meetings at various inns in the town the Chairman no doubt having first choice with his favourite place and the other directors choosing in turn. The Essex Arms is again mentioned, and the Eight Bells, and "Mr. John Kilby's house at the sign of the Queen's Arms."

The accounts for 1855 make interesting reading, and it is to be noted that four directors have audited the accounts and certified them as correct! It will be seen that the Works were still being leased in this year, the lessee collecting all accounts for gas and coke himself, and paying to the Company the sum of £50 per quarter.

The affairs of the Company by 1867 were, at any rate, to the Directors, such as to necessitate the appointment of three Managing Directors; Messrs. Charles William Moore, John Kilby and Joseph Hill, who were awarded £5 each per annum for their extra services. At this time the need for expert engineering advice was realized and a most important step was taken when Mr. Henry E. Jones was made Consulting Engineer to the Company. For the first time the local control was supplemented by the advice of this Engineer who was connected with London Gas Companies, and the productive side of the Company soon began to show the results of this wise step. Problems of distribution also were given attention and mains were laid to the new estates which were beginning to spring up in the locality. The increased loads on the new mains soon required much larger quantities of gas being made, thus requiring more storage room, and in turn more capital from the shareholders. Apparently by the seventies the faith of the Watford public in gas was growing, as the issue of £2,000 shares was over-subscribed by quite a number of the local people. With this new capital the Works were improved and a Gasholder built. It is recorded that Mr. George Allen of Watford successfully tendered for the building of the Gasholder tank, his price being £589 13s. 0d. The holder itself was built by Messrs. H. Balfour and Co. at a cost of £633.

Watford & St. Albans Gas Company (1934)

29

'The first railway trials'; from a painting by Alan Fearnley.

The London and Birmingham Railway

On September 28, 1829, George and Robert Stephenson's locomotive "Rocket", fitted with Henry Booth's patent multi-tubular boiler, arrived at Liverpool and on October 6 it drew the Liverpool & Manchester Railway directors' carriages from the crossing of the Huyton Turnpike to Rainhill where, from October 6 to 14, it competed for the premium of £500 offered by the directors of the L & M R for the best locomotive power and won outright, against competition from three other steam locomotives and a horse-powered machine. Huge crowds gathered to witness the competition.

The trial had proved successful; within two years the Liverpool to Manchester line was carrying upwards of 1000 passengers a day—profitably. In many other parts of the country, businessmen made haste to promote their own railway and a free-for-all system was the result. George and Robert Stephenson engineered the London to Birmingham line and the following excerpts (from The Railway Worker *and* The London and Birmingham Railway*) describe its initial effect upon Watford.*

The first section, Euston to Boxmoor, was opened on July 20th, 1837.

Population 1838, 2,960

Preparations . . .

Through this tranquil and old-fashioned spot, rumour spread the intelligence that a railway was about to be constructed from London to Birmingham. What a railway was, and by what new and unheard-of evils it would destroy the repose of the country, no resident had any distinct idea. Some of the readers of the two or three copies of the *Times* that passed through the post-office were aware, rather as a matter of abstract historic announcement than of local interest, that in the preceding year a bill for this purpose had been thrown out in the House of Lords, in consequence of the opposition of a noble Earl, (the fifth Earl of Essex) half-brother to the vicar, through whose park Robert Stephenson, following the line selected by Telford for the Grand Junction Canal, had proposed to lead the railway. A second bill had been brought forward by which, at the expense of heavy works, the park and ornamental grounds of the Earl had been avoided, the line crossing the valley of the Colne by an embankment of what was, in those days, unprecedented magnitude, and thus boring beneath the woods, at a distance from the mansion, by an equally unprecedented tunnel of nearly a mile in length.

At last one or two strange faces appeared in the town, and men in leathern leggings, dragging a long chain, and attended by one or two country labourers armed with bill-hooks, were remarked as trespassing in the most unwarrantable manner over pasture land, standing crops, copse and cover; actually cutting gaps in the hedges, through which they climbed and dragged the land-chain. Then would follow another intruder, bearing a telescope set on three legs, which he erected with the most perfect coolness wherever he thought fit, peering through it at a long white staff, marked with unintelligible hieroglyphics, which was borne by another labourer, and moved or held stationary in accordance with a mysterious code of telegraphic signals made by the hand.

The farmers, naturally indignant, ordered these intruders from their fields. The engineers, for such they were, took but little notice.

The next step in the the invasion proved a yet further aggrava-

"The Tring Excavation is about two miles and a half long. It was executed by means of a number of "horse runs," so called by excavators, from the men being drawn up planks nearly in a perpendicular position, by horses. A rope is attached to the front of the barrow containing the soil, while the excavator takes firm hold of the handles, and both barrow and man are drawn up the plank,—the latter having his body nearly horizontal during the ascent. It is a fearful practice; and should any accident occur, by the break of the rope or restiveness of the horse, the workman is precipitated to the bottom in an instant."

tion to the farmers, although it was one which, for the first time in the course of the contest, afforded them the pleasure of retaliation. Loads of oak pegs, accurately squared, planed, and pointed, were driven to the fields, and the course of the intended railway was marked out by driving two of these pegs, one left standing about four inches above the surface to indicate position, and a smaller one driven lower to the ground a few inches off on which to take the level, at every interval of twenty-two yards. It is obvious that the operations of farming afforded many an opportunity for an unfriendly blow at these pegs. Ploughs and harrows had a remarkable tendency to become entangled in them; cart wheels ran foul of them; sometimes they disappeared altogether. A mute and irregular warfare on the subject of the pegs was generally protracted until the last outrage was perpetrated by the agents of the company; the land was purchased for the railway.

The Railway Worker

The achievement . . .

The primary object in the application of steam to Railroad travelling being the *economizing of time*, the inhabitants of Watford cannot be congratulated on enjoying the advantages of the discoverey to its fullest extent, for the "line" here, after intersecting the houses at the *eastern end of the town*, proceeds onwards for nearly two miles, before it reaches the Watford "station," which is at a point where the western extremity of the town is one mile distant. Without dwelling on the causes which have rendered it expedient to fix the resting-place here, we may remark that it has afforded an opportunity to compare Railway with Omnibus speed, and to call into action the rivalry of inn-keepers, and accordingly a choice of vehicles, from the "Essex Arms" and the "Rose and Crown" is offered to carry passengers into the town. This journey of a mile is not uninteresting. There is a small portion of the high road from Watford to St. Albans' (which crosses the Railway) leading South, lined with elms, at the end of which, turning East, lies the town, ranging on both sides of the road for about a mile in length.

(Railroadiana, 1838)

In 1830 two lines were proposed; one by Sir John Rennie, taking the Banbury and Oxford line of road, and the other by Mr. Giles, taking its course by the way of Coventry.

George Stephenson had, a little prior to this, been engaged by the parties who had chosen the Coventry line for the Railway, and as he also gave his opinion in favour of that route, it was finally decided that the London and Birmingham Railway should go *via* Coventry, and George Stephenson and his Son were appointed engineers to the now united 'London and Birmingham Railway Company.'

The country between London and Birmingham is a series of basins or low districts separated from each other by considerable ridges of hills; the object to be gained was, therefore, to cross the valleys at as high a point as possible, and the hills at as low an one. The low districts are the London basin—the valley of the Colne, extending from Brentford by Watford, to St. Alban's,—the lowland in the neighbourhood of Leighton Buzzard, on the Stoke Bruern,— the valley of the Nen, in which is Northampton,—and the basin of the Avon; which last, from its great depth, low level, and abrupt termination on the south, by the high ridge of hills on which Daventry, Kilsby, and Crick are situated, and on the north side by the Meriden ridge, required particular attention.

The high grounds which bound these districts are the county boundary between the London basin and valley of the Colne,—the Chalk ridge, at Ivinghoe, which rises between the Colne valley and the Leighton Buzzard district,—the Blisworth ridge, which forms the southern side of the valley of the Nen,—and the Kilsby and Meriden ridges, forming the abrupt sides of the valley of the Avon.

Bushey Arches (in foreground) and bridge at Watford Heath (in background). The road to Pinner begins on the left of the Arches and takes a route at approximately 45° up the dell formed by the 'fold' in the undulating country to Watford Heath (top left). "The bridge which conveys Oxhey-lane over the Railway is formed of three fine segmental arches, the centre one springing from two very lofty piers at an elevation of twenty-five feet, and the two side arches abutting upon the slopes of the excavation; the parapets are about thirty-five feet above the level of the Railway."

From this sketch of the nature of the ground it is evident what care was required in searching for the best line of road. Mr. Robert Stephenson examined the country in the Autumn of 1830, and was ordered to prepare the necessary plans and sections to deposit with Parliament in the November of that year. The time, however, was much too short; and it was only by great haste and force of numbers that the preliminary step of depositing these plans was accomplished.

It may be safely said that no private bill was ever more strictly scrutinized than was that of the London and Birmingham Railway; the opposition to it being confined more to the cross examination of the witnesses in its favour than in producing any direct evidence against it, which, it must be confessed, would have been rather a difficult task. There was not a single fact proved against the great utility of the measure, while its advocates clearly established in its support the following important points,—viz., that the exporting of goods suffered material loss and great inconvenience by the present slow mode of traffic,—that goods for the Baltic trade were often delayed by the frost for the whole winter, through a very short delay in shipping them,—that considerable orders were frequently lost from the impossibility of completing them in time,—that in fancy articles it is almost indispensable, orders being frequently sent subject to the condition of their being shipped in a particular vessel,—that returns of money were sometimes made in eighteen months instead of nine, through this delay in the shipment of the goods ordered,—that farmers would be able to send to London a different kind of produce altogether, and a much better one, particularly lambs, calves, dairy produce, &c., saving also a great expense in their carriage;—besides which, cattle were often driven till their feet were sore, and they could go no further, they were then sold on the road for what they would fetch.

At about eleven and a half miles from the Euston Station, and immediately on the other side of the bridge which carries the road from Harrow to Harrow Weald over the Railway, we reach the HARROW STATION, being the first from London. It might be well here to notice that the stations are classified into two kinds: the first class and mail trains stopping for passengers only at certain stations, called *principal stations*; whilst the second class, or mixed trains, take up and set down passengers at *all the stations*. This arrangement is common to all the railways yet open to the public, and affords those who require expeditious travelling to make choice of the particular train which will convey them soonest to their destination; whilst those who merely propose to view the surrounding country, and those to whom economy is an object, will perhaps choose a second class train for their trip.

The London and Birmingham Railway Act passed the Commons' Committee March the 15th, 1833, and the Lords, April the 22nd, 1833, receiving the Royal assent May the 6th; and the means which the directors were obliged to resort to must be left to the imagination of the reader; suffice it to say, that no variation sufficient to account for the different features of the case took place in the numerical value of the assenting or dissenting landowners, between the time of the first application being thrown out by the Lord's Committee and the time when the bill was passed by them.

Further along the line we enter the excavation through the first ridge which this Railway crosses; it varies from thirty to forty feet deep, and is composed of plastic clay and sand, which appears in some parts to be very loose. There are two or three bridges in this cutting which present a bold appearance, and are exceedingly elegant in their proportions; that, for instance which conveys Oxhey-lane over the Railway is formed of three fine segmental arches, the centre one springing from two very lofty piers at an elevation of twenty-five feet, and the two side arches abutting upon the slopes of the excavation; the parapets are about thirty-five feet above the level of the Railway, and the whole is composed of brickwork of a very superior description. The trains as they pass through this bridge present a remarkably picturesque object. It was originally intended to have had a short tunnel through this ridge, but

Bushey Arches before the building of Bushey Station. The road to Oxhey is in foreground. The Railway "goes over the London Road by a brick viaduct of five arches of forty-three feet span each; they are composed of ellipses, having voissoirs at the intrados; the centre arch is in an oblique form, in order that the course of the old road should be preserved as heretofore."

the soil was found of such a nature that a saving of expense was effected in adopting an open cutting. From the summit of the ridge a most extensive and delightful view is obtained of the surrounding country, more especially in the direction of Watford and the valley of the Colne, in which the course of the Railway may be traced for several miles in advance, and being on a curve, the trains are seen winding along for some time before they approach this spot. The soil taken from this excavation amounted to about 372,000 cubic yards, and was conveyed partly to a spoil bank, and partly to form an embankment towards the town of Watford, of about three quarters of a mile long.

Soon after entering upon it the Railway goes over the London road, by a brick viaduct of five arches, of forty-three feet span each; they are composed of ellipses, having voissoirs at the intrados; the centre arch is of an oblique form, in order that the course of the road should be preserved as heretofore. This may be thought a bad feature in a design of this kind, but it was unavoidable, the trustees having compulsory clauses in the Act of Parliament to compel the Company to adopt this form of arch. The manner in which the engineer has overcome the defect in the design is admirable, and it is scarcely perceptible to the observer: it is a very massiv structure, and cost in its erection £9,700. The other arches are square with the line of the Railway; and at either end are retaining walls built into the embankment, making the total length of the viaduct three hundred and seventy feet.

The next bridge conveys the Railway over the river Colne. It consists of five semicircular brick arches, of thirty feet span each, with side walls, and having a stone cornice its whole length,—the total length of the parapet walls being 312 feet. It has a light appearance; and viewed from the meadows appears very lofty, being fifty feet high. The construction of the bridge was a work of considerable skill and labour, the foundations being of the loosest material possible; in fact, it may almost be called a floating bridge— for it rests entirely on platforms of wood, having sheet piling to protect them. The cost of its construction was little less than £10,000. The whole of the land in this spot is most precarious in stability; and the effects are clearly visible in the amazing "slips" which have taken place in the embankment across the valley. Oftentimes, in a very few hours, the level of the newly-formed ground has sunk several feet, while the base of the embankment has

Watford Station on the St. Albans Road. The building from which the chimney appears is the pumping house, in which a 10hp steam engine was used for pumping water. The small building in front of the tree, and from which steps led down to the tracks, is the Station proper. The building still exists at time of writing. *p.343 b.* **1839**

widened out to an enormous extent, causing infinite labour to bring the level of the Railway back again to its original state, and to make it solid enough for the passage of the trains; this has caused many a sleepless night to the workmen and engineers. The length of this embankment is about a mile and a half, and is composed entirely of

'Five Arches' bridge over the River Colne at Water Fields. "The next bridge conveys the Railway over the river Colne. It consists of five semicircular brick arches, of thirty feet span each, with side walls, and having a stone cornice its whole length,—the total length of the parapet walls being 312 feet. It has a light appearance; and viewed from the meadows appears very lofty, being fifty feet high." *p.345 t*

the finest materials for such a purpose—chalk and gravel.

On arrival at a very elegant skew bridge, which carries the road from Watford to St. Albans over the Railway, and at about seventeen miles and a half from London, we enter the WATFORD STATION: and here, as we before observed, every arrangement is made for the comfort and convenience of passengers. The first and second class waiting rooms are very commodious, and so is the departure yard, which is sheltered from rain by an elegant corrugated iron roof. This is the first principal station, and where the engineers supply their tenders with water after leaving London; for which purpose a ten-horse steam engine is provided with suitable pumps and machinery. There is also an engine house for locomotives, and a carriage shed; in fact the arrangements of the whole are

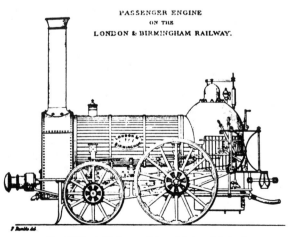

PASSENGER ENGINE
ON THE
LONDON & BIRMINGHAM RAILWAY.

From Wishaw's 'Railways of Great Britain and Ireland'

of the most perfect description, and no expense appears to have been spared in their construction.

The entrance of the Watford Tunnel is composed of an arch, nearly semicircular, twenty-five feet high and twenty-four feet wide, with retaining walls on either side, extending to the slopes of the cutting; a blocking and cornice runs through the whole length of the front, and the arch is surmounted by a pediment. The Tunnel is one mile and a tenth in length, and is excavated entirely from chalk and loose gravel, the treacherous nature of which rendered it a work of great difficulty. It was first formed by sinking six shafts to a certain depth, and then excavated horizontally in what is called by miners a "drift," which is a small aperture just large to admit a man to walk in. The use of these drifts are, that greater accuracy in setting out the line is obtained, through which a communication is formed to the several working shafts, as also a free ventilation of air for the men during the progress of their work, which in many instances had to be conveyed to them by side shafts. An idea may be formed of the treacherous nature of this soil, when it is known that a certain part of the tunnel was found to consist of such firm and solid material, that the invert, which supports the upper structure of the brick arch and sides, was not introduced, but that the side walls rest upon the chalk; yet other parts were so mixed with gravel and sand, that, when in the course of the operation a fissure was made, a stream of it poured in like water.

In passing through the tunnel, and near the centre, travellers will not fail to observe a wide opening or shaft; this was formed through an unfortunate accident which occurred here during the formation of the tunnel. At this spot one of the six working shafts was sunk, of about eight or nine feet diameter, and it had been nearly finished, when the whole mass of soil surrounding it gave way, completely burying ten men who were at work below. They were engaged in fixing one of the iron rings, which are built into the top of the tunnel to support the brickwork of this shaft; and from all that could be learned by observation,—for not one was spared to tell the tale,—it

Watford Station from the south. The building shown is the pumping house; the steps down from the station can be seen. In the middle distance is Mr. Moore's accommodation bridge and beyond that the mouth of the tunnel. Mr. C. W. Moore, prominent resident, farmed land on what was Callowland farm on the north side of the railway and when the railway was put through it left him with one field on the Nascot Wood side of the railway. In the same manner as 'accommodation' bridges may be built across new motorways to connect farmland, etc., so an accommodation bridge was built for Mr. Moore. This remained until the second widening of the railway (at the first widening the third line was laid in the original tunnel). The cutting was considerably widened for the addition of the fourth line, at which stage a new tunnel was made and the bridge removed.

appeared that one of the men had cut away some of the chalk to obtain more room to fix the iron-work, and by so doing had penetrated so near the gravel that it broke through in an instant, and entirely filled up the space, leaving them not a moment's time to save themselves.

So instantaneous was the accident, that one poor fellow was found, three weeks afterwards, standing perfectly upright, with his trowel in his hand. It was nearly a month before the soil that had given way around the shaft could be cleared out; when the opening was found to be so extensive, and the material so loose, that the idea of making a large ventilating shaft at once occurred, and it was immediately executed.

Mr. Stephenson originally projected the Railway considerably more to the west of the present line, by which the Watford tunnel would have been entirely avoided, and a considerable saving in the cost of this portion of the line effected; but the very powerful opposition which the Earl of Essex (whose park is not far distant,) gave to this plan, compelled the projectors of the Railway to acquiesce in the present course, and to submit to a much heavier expenditure.

At every three miles will be observed a policeman and each man has his beat and duties defined, and is provided with two signal flags, one of which is red and the other white; the white flag is held out when no obstruction exists; and, on the contrary, the red flag indicates that there is danger, and that the train must not pass the signal till it is ascertained that the cause of danger is removed.

Each policeman, also, is furnished with a revolving lamp, to be used after dark, which shows, at the will of the holder, a white light when the line is clear, a green one when it is necessary to use caution, and the speed of the train to be diminished; and a red light, to intimate the necessity of immediately stopping. The whole of the police department is under the able control and superintendence of Captain C. R. Moorsam, R.N., a gentleman who has been connected with the Company since its formation, as one of the the

Line engraving showing Berkhamsted Station during the first year of operation.

Secretaries. It is but justice to add, that the police arrangements on the London and Birmingham Railway are more complete than on any other line.

Every station is furnished with an alarum, to give notice of the approach of each train, and to summon the whole of the men to their appointed places. These alarums are so constructed, that a weight is wound up after they have performed their office which prepares them to perform it again. On seeing the forthcoming train has reached the proper spot, the policeman stationed at them pulls a trigger, and the weight begins to descend, ringing a loud gong-shaped bell by means of internal machinery. Bells are also hung so as, in a few seconds, to collect together the whole of the men belonging to the station for any required purpose.

Roscoe, The London and Birmingham Railway. c1840

35

Defective state of drainage in the town . . .

In Clutterbuck's county history the population is given as 'Watford Town', 3,530 for 1801; which includes Leavesden, Oxhey and Cassio Hamlets. The population of Watford Hamlet would be about 2,300.

By 1838 the Town Hamlet is recorded as 2,960, but by 1851 this had more than doubled, to 6,546 and, by surmise, an increase to around 6,000 in 1848 would be appropriate.

For countless generations the Town Hamlet, the area around the Market Place and stretching down the street towards the Colne river, would have been static, or at best, very slow in growth.

The railway was to change all this.

The town's growth came about in three ways; small cottages to house railway employees were built in the vicinity of the station (described in a later Rates Book as 'houses beyond the station', but which would later be named as Church Road and Bedford Street), rather larger houses were built to accommodate a new class of resident who saw the desirability of a new part of the county in which to live—i.e. Nascot (or, later, Watford New Town), and, in the Hamlet, an increase in population was the result of the extra trade and business which came with the railway.

An influx of people over-crowded the tiny houses in the narrow courtyards of Watford Hamlet and combined with rudimentary forms of sanitation, dating back to the middle ages, to create an ideal breeding place for the plague. The system which had previously sufficed for a smaller population had totally broken down.

In 1831 an outbreak of cholera in Sunderland spread quickly and claimed the lives of thousands (including a maid in service to Lord Clarendon. "She sat down to gooseberry fool in the evening and was carried out in a coffin in the morning.") But it struck hardest in overcrowded slum areas where insanitary conditions were common. The Government was forced to act in this crisis situation but it did so slowly and reluctantly in deference to the hitherto sacrosanct rights of the property owners.

A report in 1842 revealed a grim state of affairs nationwide; without 'local government' there could be no improvement in conditions, and many land-owners would be against such improvements, believing they would be involved in heavy expense and increased rates.

Six years later conditions were so bad that the Vestry was obliged to take action . . .

An enquiry into the state of drainage

At a Vestry held on the 6th of October 1848 for the purpose of taking into consideration the defective state of the drainage of the town of Watford, it was moved by Mr. Moore, and seconded by Mr. Vaughan, that a Committee be appointed forthwith to inquire into the defective state of the drainage of this parish, and the various nuisances which exist in it, and to report the same at the next Vestry.

A Committee was accordingly appointed, consisting of the following gentlemen:—
R. Clutterbuck, Esq., Mr. Young, Mr. F. Dyson, Mr. Lavender, Mr. C. Lewin, Mr. Capell, Mr. Catlin, Mr. Chater, The Surveyors, ex-officio.

The Committee appointed to inquire into the defective state of the drainage of the parish, and the various nuisances which exist in it, proceeded on the 9th instant, in accordance with their instructions, to inspect the sanitary condition of the town. After a careful examination of the present means of drainage in the main street, and the various courts and alleys leading into it, they have to report that they found both in a very unsatisfactory condition. In a large proportion of the yards, the privies and pigsties are most offensive; whilst the open cesspools and manure heaps, loaded with decaying vegetable and animal matter, infected the atmosphere to such an extent as to be in many cases almost intolerable, and do more than justify the very general complaint made by the inhabitants of the prejudicial effect of these accumulated nuisances on their comfort and general health. The few drains carried under ground in the main street were choked at the different gratings and gully-holes, and appeared in a very filthy condition. The Committee would particularly call the attention of the Vestry to a cesspool placed in the footpath in the High-street, which receives the drainage from Wells's-yard: it is in a very filthy state, and is merely covered with wooden flaps which are not air tight.

With regard to the condition of the courts and alleys, it is worthy of consideration, that the houses they contain have, with hardly an exception, no means of disposing of the refuse matter, whether liquid or solid, except by throwing it either into open cesspools, on the manure heaps, or at once into the surface-drains, which lead into the open side-channels in the main street: so long, therefore, as no efficient and permanent means are taken to remedy these serious defects, accumulations of filth and manure are indispensable evils. These various receptacles may in future be emptied more frequently, at more regular intervals, but under existing arrangements the accumulation of the nuisances described cannot possibly be entirely obviated. The Old Yard may be quoted as an instance of the injurious effect of an open cesspool, from which the inhabitants suffer severely. The cottages there command an increased rent in proportion as they are removed from the cesspool; that nearest pays 1s. 6d. per week, the next 2s., and those beyond 2s. 6d.

In conclusion, the Committee beg to remark that the sanitary condition of the town, as detailed in this Report, appears to be so unsatisfactory as to have demanded immediate attention under ordinary circumstances. But at this moment, when the cholera is almost at our own doors, they would impress upon the attention of the rate-payers that they are now especially called upon to act cordially together, not merely for the purpose of abating existing nuisances, but to devise and adopt without delay such measures as may secure the permanent improvement of the town, and thus advance the real interests of its inhabitants.

> Robert Clutterbuck
> Thomas Young
> James Capell
> C. W. Moore
> F. Dyson
> Thomas Lavender
> John Sedgwick, Hon. Sec.

Moved by Mr. Cotton, and seconded by Mr. Vaughan,—
    That the above Report be adopted, and entered upon the minutes of the Vestry.
Agreed to *nem. con.*

Moved by Mr. Clutterbuck, seconded by Mr. Sedgwick, and carried unanimously,—
    That the Report presented to the Vestry this day be printed, and a copy sent to every rate-payer of the town and Cashio hamlet; and that at the same time notice be given them that a vestry meeting will be held on the 3rd of November next, at 11 o'clock in the forenoon, for the purpose of taking into consideration what measure it may be desirable to adopt for the purpose of improving effectually the present imperfect drainage of the town.

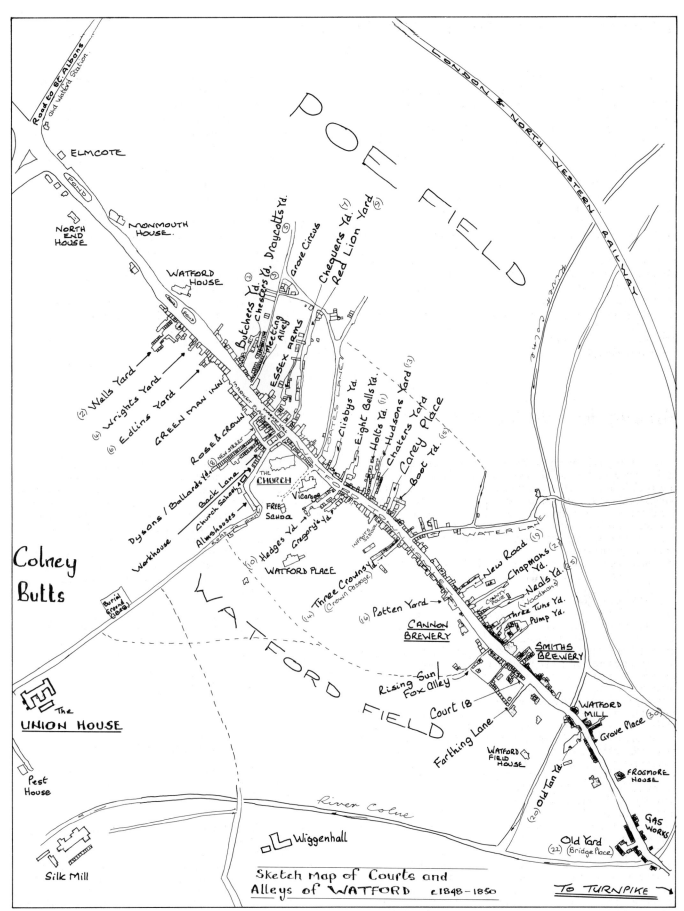

POE FIELD

LONDON & NORTH WESTERN RAILWAY

Road to St. Albans
Old Watford Station

ELMCOTE

NORTH END HOUSE

MONMOUTH HOUSE.

WATFORD HOUSE

River Colne

Butchers Yd.
Chesters Yd. Draycotts Yd.
Grove Circus
Chequers Yd. (7)
Red Lion Yard (5)
Meeting Alley
ESSEX ARMS

(3) Walls Yard
(4) Wrights Yard
(6) Edlins Yard
GREEN MAN INN

LOATES LANE
Clisbys Yd.
Eight Bells Yd.
Holts Yd. (1)
Hudsons Yard (13)
Chaters Yard
Carey Place
Boot Yd. (15)

ROSE & CROWN
(8) NEW STREET
Dysons/Ballards Yd.
Back Lane
THE CHURCH
Vicarage
Church School
Workhouse
Almshouses
FREE SCHOOL

(10) Hedges Yd.
Gregory's Yd.
WATFORD PLACE
INFANTS SCHOOL

WATER LANE

New Road (19)
Chapmans Yd. (21)
COUNTY POLICE
Neals Yd. (25)
Woodman
Three Tuns Yd.
Pump Yd.

Colney Butts

Burial Ground (clear)

WATFORD FIELD

(14) Three Crowns Yd. (Crown Passage)
(16) Potten Yard
CANNON BREWERY

SMITHS BREWERY

The UNION HOUSE

Rising Sun/ Fox Alley
Court 18
Farthing Lane

WATFORD FIELD HOUSE

WATFORD MILL
Grove Place (30)

FROGMORE HOUSE

Pest House

(20) Old Tan Yd.

River Colne

Wiggenhall

Old Yard (22) (Bridge Place)

GAS WORKS

Silk Mill

Sketch Map of Courts and Alleys of WATFORD c.1848-1850

TO TURNPIKE

By 1849 the railway had been established some twelve years. House construction in the 'Nascot' area signalled the beginning of a growth in population. Houses were still not numbered as everyone knew everyone else. The exception was of a handful of houses "beyond the station". Numbers (e.g. 13) refer to William's 'Court Numbers' of a later date. p.56

At the time of this map two turnpike roads crossed, and four lanes joined the High Street. Of the latter one by the Parish Church led to Watford Field and then by path to Wiggenhall; another lower down the High Street, Farthing Lane, also gave access to Watford Field. On the opposite side were the other two lanes, Water Lane and Loates Lane leading to Aldenham, Radlett and St. Albans. At the Bushey end were turnings to Pinner and Oxhey.

The Parish Church 1856. Building in distance, left-hand side, is the National School, built in 1842.

Public Health Act

Report to the General Board of Health, on a Preliminary Inquiry into the Sewerage, Drainage, and Supply of Water, and the Sanitary Condition of the Inhabitants of the Town of WATFORD. By GEORGE THOMAS CLARK, Superintending Inspector, 1849.

MY LORDS AND GENTLEMEN, *London, 25th April, 1849*

In obedience to your instructions I proceeded, on the 26th of February last, to inspect the town hamlet of Watford, and so much of the contiguous district as it seemed necessary to include within one administrative area. I held public sittings at the Rose and Crown inn, on the mornings of the 26th and 27th, and employed the rest of those days and the 28th in carrying on the inquiry, and in framing this Report.

Plans of the town were produced by Mr. Humbert, and part of a section by the Rev. J. C. Clutterbuck.

Although the petition proceeded only from the town hamlet, which forms, though by much the chief part, yet but a part of the town of Watford, I found it necessary to include the whole town in my examination.

The subject of drainage has been frequently brought forward in Watford during the last five or six years, and various meetings thereupon have been held, at which the Earl of Essex, Mr. Clutterbuck, and other gentlemen largely interested in the place, have taken a leading part. The existing evils have been fully admitted, but the want of legislative power has always prevented the application of an effectual remedy. After the passing of the Public Health Act, a meeting was called to consider the propriety of putting in force the "Nuisances Removal Act," but such was the effect produced by a clear statement of the bad condition of the town, and of the want of the necessary powers in the Nuisances Act to carry out permanent remedies, that, after a long discussion, and two adjourned meetings, the petition upon which my inquiry proceeded was determined upon.

Watford is composed of a principal street, about 1½ mile long, built along a sort of ridge sloping southwards to the river. On either side, and communicating with this street, are numerous courts and alleys, composed of small tenements, in which the bulk of the population is lodged. There are scarcely any cross streets, and the town is nowhere above 440 yards, and seldom above 200 yards broad. The London and Birmingham Railway passes about a mile from the top of the town. About the station, and along the road leading to it from Watford, houses have recently been built, and are still in progress.

GOVERNMENT.—Watford has grown up gradually into a town, and still retains its old village and manorial institutions. The parish is composed of the hamlets of Watford Town, (the hamlet petitioning,) Cashio, Oxhey, and Levesden, the three former of which enter into the composition of the town, of which, however, the first constitutes by much the chief part. The northern extremity of the town, in Cashio, is known as Nascott. The lord of the manor levies market tolls, and holds manor courts. The rate-payers in vestry annually elect parish officers, including two surveyors of highways, for the town hamlet, and one for each of the other hamlets, five in all; they also elect inspectors under the General Gas Act.

The rates annually levied, besides poor and church-rates, are a highway-rate of 6d. in the pound, and a gas-rate of about 6d. on houses and 2d. on land, producing severally about £800 and £214.

The above government, if such it can be called, is miserably unfit for the wants of the town. The expenditure is in consequence high in proportion to the quantity or quality of the work done. Persons ignorant of road-making are appointed surveyors of highways, and there is fostered a strong party spirit fatal to all improvement.

MORTALITY.—Mr. Ward, surgeon to the Union, produced a list of 62 fever cases attended by him in the town between April, 1848, and February, 1849. Out of these there were 13 deaths; 23, or above 37 per cent. of the cases were children, of whom 8, or nearly 35 per cent. of those attacked died. It appears from a statement from the Registrar-General, that the current mortality of Watford is 23.33 in the 1,000; that of the surrounding rural districts being 20 in the 1,000.

. . . three houses without a privy and with an open dungheap and a slaughter house . . .

Here I may quote an extract from a Report made to the Board of Guardians by the Messrs. Pidcock, as medical officers to the Union, in 1838, upon the state of Watford, and which has been put into my hands by Mr. Clutterbuck:—*"The most unhealthy localities in the town are found to be Meeting-alley, Dyson's (now Ballard's) buildings, Red Lion, Chequers, and Old-yards. The confined position of the former, and the open drains and deposit of ordure in the latter, at once account for this unhealthy condition. Few dwellings in these yards have escaped the visitation of disease, and but few of the inhabitants of them can be said ever to enjoy robust health. Those yards, which have blind extremities, such as Dyson's, are in the worst condition; having no thoroughfares, little publicity is given to the habits of the cottagers, and thus a principal stimulus to cleanliness is wanting."* This was in 1838, and it will be seen that the 10 or 11 years which have elapsed have produced no improvement, nor indeed, under the existing system of government by vestry officers, is any likely to be produced.

Commencing at the top of the town, the houses below the Dog public-house have privies with open cesspools, pigsties, dung-heaps, and are without drains. The house slops are for the most part thrown into the main road and public footway, which, at the time of my visit, was in a state very offensive to passers by. This is a fever locality.

At the hand-post, just below, is a large pond. A few surface drains run into it, but nevertheless, the water being moderately soft, is much in request for washing. Near it, also upon the high road, is a smaller pond, in a dirty state at all times, and the condition of which in summer is much complained of.

Proceeding down the street on the west side is Wells-yard, a fever locality with an overflowing cesspool, the filth from which passes down the court into another cesspool, covered with trap-doors in the open footway of the main street of the town. In Stones-yard, a slaughter-house and divers nuisances open upon a public footpath. Around the Market-place, the oldest part of the town, the nuisances are very numerous. In the words of the Report (already cited), as applied to the town generally, *"the privies and pigsties are most offensive, whilst the open cesspools and manure heaps, loaded with decaying vegetable and animal matter, infected the atmosphere to such an extent as to be in many cases almost intolerable, and do more than justify the very general complaints made by the inhabitants of the prejudicial effect of these accumulated nuisances on their comforts and general health."*

Ballard's-buildings, otherwise in a creditable state, has a very narrow passage on its south side, blocked with privies, open cesspools, and night soil, upon an unpaved surface. On the north side of the churchyard, a block of poor houses is closely shut up between the churchyard and the narrow street, with no back yard or privies whatever. Close by, against the churchyard wall, is a heap upon which the refuse of these houses is thrown.

In Hedge's-yard are three boarded hovels, of which two contain one room each, with unceiled roofs open to the weather, and floors below the level of the undrained ground. These are the worst dwellings in the town. Saunder's-yard has a large slaughter-house and pigsties, besides privies and cess-pools. It contains several tenements, and is undrained and badly paved. Clarke's-buildings, Crown-yard, Farthing-lane, Swan-alley, all leading from the main street into Watford Common-field, are without drainage save a few open gutters, and have all open cesspools and ill-conditioned privies. Along the edge of the Common-field, bordering a much frequented public walk, are heaps of filfth thrown out from these houses.

In the main street, opposite to one of the best houses in the town, is a pond, dry in summer, and which when cleaned out, as is the case annually, is a very great nuisance. This pond should be filled up. Butcher's-yard, a seat of fever, Hollingsworth-yard, and Meeting-House-alley, a place in which the fever cases were very numerous, form a cluster of houses set close together, badly built, and approached through very narrow passages. The privies are very offensive, and in one part is a slaughter-house.

At the back of these is Grove-circus, the refuse from which is led through iron piping under the road in front of the houses into an open stagnant ditch, running alongside a thoroughfare which is much frequented. In Chequer's-yard are three houses, without a privy, and with an open dung-heap and a slaughter-house.

At the Post-office, a newly-erected building, the garden slopes towards and drains upon the house. The drainage of the back yard is led into the street by an iron pipe, laid between the ceiling of the kitchen and the floor of the room above. In this house last year seven children were all attacked with fever, and three died. Mr. Smith, surgeon, states, *"I am of opinion the disease was produced, and the symptoms rendered more severe in consequence of bad drainage, so that the filth was coming into the cellar through the wall."* Red Lion-yard, Boot and Pump-yard (both fever localities), and Water-lane, contain pigsties, dung-heaps, privies, overflowing cesspools, dirty gardens, and badly paved passages. Since this Report was drawn up the following extract from the district medical-relief-book has been transmitted to me:—*"There have been four cases of fever at Brown's, in the Red Lion-yard, and two have died. The drainage is most defective, and cannot be otherwise than extremely prejudicial to the health of the inhabitants residing in the cottages in the neighbourhood."*—THOS A. WARD.*"*

At the lower end of the town the main street is crossed by the tail-race of the Town-mill, and afterwards by the main stream of the Colne. The land on each of these water-courses, including the island between them, is very low and swampy, and though thickly built over, utterly undrained. On the island may be mentioned the Old Tan-yard, as occasionally flooded. Old-yard lies near the Colne. Here a cesspool in the corner, though much improved, is still a considerable nuisance. Fever was recently prevalent here.

Cottage property in the town appears in various cases to have become depreciated by the want of cleanliness.

SEWERS AND DRAINS.—There are no efficient sewers in the town. Down the main street on either side of the road is an open gutter, which at one or two points is exchanged for a small 9-inch culvert, with frequent and foul catch-pits, and large open gutter-grates, complained of as frequently stopped up. Into this, whether open gutter or close culvert, a number of side gutters usually open, and uncovered drains cross the footway, and flowing down from the side courts, convey the overflow of cesspools and the offal of slaughter-houses where present.

Along the margins of the town are a number of stagnant ditches and catch-pits, producing a great nuisance near the various public walks. Among these, below Mr. King's garden in Watford-field, are two ponds receiving the drainage of a considerable portion of the town, surcharged with filth and much complained of. This is on the southern and best side of the town. There is no regular system of house drainage.

WATER SUPPLY.—Watford is supplied with water chiefly from wells worked with buckets, varying from 10 to 60 feet deep. There is a public well in the main street fitted with Braithwaite's pump. Samples of this water shewed 60° of hardness, and of another well 26½°.

Besides these waters, which are much too hard to be used for washing, rain water is largely collected from the roofs, and stored in butts and tanks or pans. It appears that the rain water storage of a cottage lasts from one to three weeks, seldom longer. When the butts run dry, the people either purchase water from a neighbour, or fetch it from the river. In the former case the price is about 1d. for seven gallons, in the latter it varies according to the distance, but is not less than 1d. per week on an average per family of those using it. The consumption of soap and soda is unusually great; 6d. or 7d. per week does not appear an extraordinay payment per family for these articles, and it is stated by several poor persons engaged in washing that the use even of river water adds about one-fourth to their consumption as compared with rain water. In rainy weather, when the waters of the Colne, though turbid, are much softer, the water is not needed by the people.

All the town wells reach the chalk, and most of them penetrate 6 to 10 feet into it. The cost of an average well, steyned with brick to the chalk, is about £10 to £14, exclusive of tackle.

A corner of Market Place. The prominent three-storey building was once a Royal Mail coaching inn until Mr. Rogers acquired the premises for his corn, timber and salt business in 1771. Later becoming Rogers & Gowlett it was sold in 1938 and Findlaters, wine merchants, who were then on the other side of the Market Place, became the next occupiers, with part premises sold to Maypole grocers. This building featured as a landmark and was last occupied by Gough Brothers, also wine merchants. It was recently rebuilt and is now Burtons's, menswear; Mr. Roger's original Coal office which stood between the shop and Meeting Alley, was demolished c1960 and the space thus released is now an entrance to our present-day Charter Place.

At the time of this photograph Queens Road had yet to be built; and when it was, Cordery, the baker, would move. Although the photograph was taken in the same period as that of the procession on p.45, and somewhat later than Mr. Clarke's report, it gives a fair idea, unembellished by artistic licence, of this part of the town, c1863.　　　　　　　　　　　　　　*p.177, 251 t, br.*

The expenses incurred in well-sinking appear to have been very considerable. Almost every house of £20 to £30 rental has its well, the original cost of which is equal to a 30 years' rent charge of 10s. to 15s. per annum.

Also, unless expensive gearing be used, the women can only draw the water in small buckets, so that as much time is spent in drawing water as in washing the room when it is drawn; and the inconvenience of this system in wet weather, and the sickness ascribed to it, appear to be considerable. It has been mentioned that the water of the Upper Pond, though dirty and but moderately soft, is used by the neighbours for washing. This pond, above the town, and the river below it, are the only resources in case of fire.

From various statements made to me on the spot, it appears that the want of soft water is severely felt by the poor. One woman, though so poor as to receive relief from the parish, yet finds it worth while to pay a boy 2d. weekly to fetch river-water when her rain-water store fails, as it does for nine months in the year. Others complained of the increased consumption of soda and soap caused even by the river water, and all said that 2d. a-week would be less than they at present paid directly in one shape or another either for soft water or for the means of making hard water usable.

HIGHWAYS, PAVING, SCAVENGING, AND WATERING.—The turnpike-roads in the whole parish are in the hands of the Turnpike Trustees, excepting those within the town, which are now, with the highways generally, under the parish surveyors. These officers are not surveyors by profession, and are usually changed every two years; they are independent of each other, and proceed each on his own system, and in no case do they repair by contract, using day-work only.

The expenses appear, on an average of eight years, to have been something under £360 per annum, but since the maintenance of the turnpike-roads within the town has been thrown upon the highway rate, at least another £100 has been expended. The roads are unscientifically formed, and suffered to remain unscavenged, and thus to become rotten from wet. They are not drained. In the town they are in many places hollow, so as to receive the kennel water in rain.

The state of the footways is very bad, the courts are usually pitched with flints with little care, and on an undrained bed; they work into holes and collect dirt. The street paths are sometimes pitched with a white and very hard silicious sandstone, known as Denner Hill stone, and laid in small blocks 6 inches by 4. A part of the footway is flagged, part only gravelled. Each inhabitant usually, when new paving is laid down, pays the surveyor, for the part in front of his own door, the difference between Denner stone and flagging. The street watering for the Town hamlet costs about £80 per annum, and is stated to be very imperfectly performed.

On the whole, this system of managing the parish highways seems to be exceedingly ill-devised. The officers are set over a department of the details of which they have no technical knowledge, and the check upon the accounts is applied annually, at a vestry meeting, in which party feeling often runs high. The system also affords very great opportunities for jobbing.

Sir James M'Adam, in a report upon the main road or street of Watford, in 1843, comments upon the want of system in proceedings of the way-wardens:—"*The paved water channels in many parts being higher than the centre of the turnpike-road, and* the outer paving-stone, forming a shoulder, so as effectually to prevent the surface water finding its way into the water channel." In 1845, upon the renewal of the Sparrow's-Hearn Turnpike Trust, £400 was laid out upon the turnpike-road in the town, under Sir. James M'Adam. The road was left in good repair, and a comparatively small sum judiciously spent from time to time, would have sufficed to keep it so. The road has, however, been neglected, and has now fallen into nearly the same condition as that described by Sir James five years ago. It was pointed out to me that the highway in front of the surveyors' houses was in far better order than elsewhere, and it seems to be admitted on all hands that this was a sort of legitimate perquisite of office.

GAS.—The town is lighted with gas supplied by a private Company, and contracted for by the town through inspectors elected under the Lighting Act, 3 & 4 Wm IV., cap. 90. The works are on the margin of the town, and as they are the only works near, the form of requiring public tenders, as laid down by the Act, is productive of no competition. There are 55 street lamps lighted for 8 and a half months in the year, for which the town pays £4 per lamp. The private supply by meter is charged at 8s. 6d. per 1000 cubic feet. The gas rate is about £214 per annum, and the cost being £245, the arrear is made up by an augmented rate every third year. The tax thus laid upon the town by the bad management of its surveyors of highways, and the determination of the Gas Company to keep up their prices, is very severe, and would be materially lightened under a proper system of management.

The Company supply the railway station. There is a great want of some power of reducing the price paid for gas, and it is highly desirable that the town, through the local Board, should possess a power of purchasing the works, or of establishing others, and letting them by contract. The gas shares pay about 6 per cent.

PUBLIC NUISANCES.—There are six principal slaughter-houses, for the most part in the most crowded and filthiest alleys in the town. It is also a common custom with those who keep pigs to kill the animals in the stye. These pig-styes are very numerous, and are chiefly found in the worst parts of the town.

In the public street are several offensive cesspools covered over with wooden trap-doors, which permit stench to ascend. The house cesspools are emptied at night by buckets carried across the footway into a cart in the main street. This practice is much complained of. Also the dirty kennel water is occasionally employed to lay the dust of the high road opposite.

It is very much the practice in the town to expose wares in front of the shops in the street. This is particularly the case with butchers, who thus suspend carcases on each side of the footway.

POLICE.—An inspector and two men reside in the town and attend to the district. They belong to the county police. This force, or that of its attention that falls to the town, seems to be insufficient for its protection, since some few of the inhabitants contribute as much as £2 annually for private watching.

BURIAL-GROUNDS.—A new burial-ground has recently been opened upon the margin of the town.

CONSTITUTION OF THE LOCAL BOARD.—Under the Act as it now stands, the efficiency of the works will depend on the Local Board, and I have seen quite enough of the spirit of dissention which prevails in this small town, to apprehend some difficulties in the formation of a Board determined to carry out the provisions of the Act without fear or favour.

It is absolutely necessary in the discharge of my duty, to speak very plainly upon this important point. The town of Watford is admitted by all to need drainage, and it does need, still more, water supply. These two wants, if attended to together, may be supplied very cheaply; but to secure cheapness and efficiency, in either or both, it is absolutely necessary that the members of the executive Board should draw cordially together.

Those who are most largely interested in cottage property of the worst description, and who are enabled by the imperfection of the existing law, to take advantage of the poverty of their tenants, to escape poor's rates, *and who do not possess foresight sufficient to see that economical sanitary reforms will augment the value of their property*, are precisely the class of persons who are generally opposed to any attempt to better the condition of the poor. With them, or among them, are others who have an interest in keeping up the present high price of gas, which be done by influence in vestry. It is not surprising that where abuses are so great, and some of them of so long standing, the outcry should be loud against any remedial measure, however efficient or however economical.

Under these circumstances, which though present in a greater or less degree every where, are unusually prominent at Watford, I conceive that the General Board should use great caution in the exercise of their discretionary power of permitting loans to be raised, and the charges to be distributed over long periods of time. It will be necessary that they be satisfied that the plans upon which the public money is proposed to be spent, be complete and economical, and that advantage be taken of all the improvements now coming into use in the arrangements for house drainage. The Local Board will be directly responsible for the cost, management, and efficiency of whatever they take upon themselves.

REMEDIES

WATER SUPPLY.—The existing pumps are quite inadequate to supply Watford with a proper quantity of water, and the quality is much too hard to allow of its general use. The latter objection applies to all the springs which rise out of the chalk near the town, such, for example, as Otters-pool, which though very abundant, is very hard.

There are several southern streams, but the most considerable, and nearest to the town, is the Oxhey Brook, which drains about 2½ square miles of area, chiefly gravel and shingle upon clay, as high up as Bushey Heath. Passing under the railway, it falls into the Colne, below the silk mill, and at no great distance from the proposed outfall well of the sewage. Its quantity is sufficient for the wants, present and prospective, of both town and railway. Two samples of this water, taken during the inquiry, one from the principal tributary, and one from the channel common to all, showed each, 10° of hardness. This, therefore, which is also capable of being improved by tile drainage, is by far the softest water within reach of the town.

In order to employ it, a reservoir holding 120 days' supply should be formed at a natural gorge about a mile from Watford Bridge, where the water will be husbanded and filtered. From thence it will be led by a clay main to the river bank, and by an iron pipe across to the engine, placed in the meads below Watford Field. From thence it will be forced through a main into a small service reservoir at the top of the town, by the pressure from which, or direct from the engine, the water will be distributed throughout the town, and to the railway station, and surrounding houses. The engine will be sufficiently near to the Colne to allow of its waters being pumped up in case of any accident to or failure of the storage reservoir.

SEWAGE DISTRIBUTION.—Watford is in an excellent position for the employment of its sewage as liquid manure, owing to the great extent of meadow land upon the Colne banks. There are various points on the rising ground above the river well suited, in respect of moderate elevation, and distance from houses, for the position of a reservoir, into which the sewage would be pumped from the main outfall, and whence it would be distributed by main pipes skirting the edge of the valley and commanding a considerable area of both arable and meadow land. It is highly desirable that powers should be taken to employ the sewage-manure, in the first instance, upon the common or lammas lands already referred to.

With respect to the amount of the private improvement rate, it is difficult to speak with equal certainty; because there is no detailed survey of the properties. Judging, however, from similar expenses elsewhere, and from my personal knowledge of this place, I see no reason to suppose that these expenses will be heavy. Suppose, for example, that upon a court of 12 houses, such as may be seen in Watford, the outlay for water, service pipes, house drainage, conversion of privies into water closets, and making the surface good, should amount to £48. This, at the rate of £4 per house, and, supposing the interest of money to be 5 per cent., will amount to an annual rate per house for 30 years of 4s. 10d., or, making the

... the town of Watford is in a very filthy condition indeed ...

necessary deduction for interest, about 1d. per week. I am inclined to think that the owners of cottage property, who, at present, oppose the measure, will see that in so doing *they consult their own pecuniary interests as little as the comfort, health, and life of their tenants.*

The house-owner or private improvement rate, then, must not be confounded with the *general rates* of 8d. and 5d. For the general-rates, when the house-owner has done his part, there will be supplied to each house, always laid on at a pressure commanding the whole town, a supply of soft filtered water, and each privy, converted into a water closet, will be supplied with water. The streets will be regularly watered, and the supply will be always ready in case of fire.

SUMMARY.—In conclusion I have to state,—

1. That it appears by the appended statement of the Vestry Committee, as well as from what is advanced in this Report, that the town of Watford is in a very filthy condition indeed; and that existing arrangements are quite insufficient to remedy the evils.

2. That the mortality of the town is considerably above that of the surrounding district; that epidemics and febrile diseases have recently prevailed extensively in the worst drained and filthiest quarters; and that such diseases are mainly attributable to a want of drainage and of the means of cleanliness.

3. That cottage property in the town has suffered depreciation in great part from the want of proper drainage; that the highway rates are high, and the roads ill kept; and that the direct expenses incurred by the poor in the use of hard water, or the purchase of soft water, far exceed the whole probable cost of the remedies.

4. That the requisite remedies, that is to say, a proper water supply and drainage, the removal and filling up of all cesspools, and the construction of a proper surface in the courts, can be supplied for a very moderate expense, or for a general rate of 13d. in the pound, and a special private improvement rate upon cottage property, according to its need of the remedies.

5. That the proposed rates will be in reduction of existing charges.

6. That the circumstances of the town admit of its sewage being employed profitably as a source of revenue, under the form of fluid manure, and that, with this view, it is desirable that special powers should be given to commence the application of it upon the common lands below the town upon the river.

7. That in the case of Watford, it is in a peculiar degree essential to the cheap and effectual execution of the sanitary works recommended, that the General Board should be fully convinced that the plans finally agreed upon provide for the *complete* removal of the evils, that they are extended over the whole of the town, and that they embody all the various improvements and economies in house drainage which are now carrying out by the Metropolitan Board of Sewers.

GEO. T. CLARK.
The General Board of Health.

●*Arising from the town's disquiet was the formation of the Watford Local Board of Health, with Mr. C. W. Moore elected as Chairman, a post he held for 22 years. The first rate raised, in July 1851, was of 6 pence in the pound.*

From being founded to deal with improvements to water supply and sanitary conditions, as well as paving, road-making and lighting, the Local Board of Health was set upon a course to become the future local government.

In 1854 the rate income of the Local Board of Health was £603. This was budgeted for in the following manner:

Clerk	£30
Surveyor and Inspector of nuisances, and collector	£100
Road Officer	£25
Rental of Board Room	£8
Stationery & adverts	£25
Labour for roads	£100
Materials for roads	£100
Repairs of pavements	£25
Watering street	£50
Incidental expenses	£80

Rookery Mill rateable value was £288 10s. 0d.; One Bell £13; the Brewery £287; Gas Light Co £100; and the railway (for 1 mile 6 furlongs) £41 13s. 6d.

At the time of the opening of the London and Birmingham Railway, Watford's population was around 2000. 18 years later, in 1855, it had grown to 3800.

By comparison:- (1855)

Bushey	2675
St. Albans	7000
Kings Langley	1600
Berkhamsted	2943
Tring	3218
Aylesbury	26794

Watford's first new street

The first Watford Place was build c1540 by William Heydon and became known as such after it was enlarged by his grandson. It was demolished in 1824 and replaced by almshouses in which lived the Morrison Trust Almswomen. (This is No.1 on p.20 plan.) The second Watford Place (No. 11 on plan) was built 1668-70 by Thomas Hobson and became the home of his widow Elizabeth (nee Chilcott) who later married Edward Fuller. She built, next door, the Free School. The second Watford Place survived until 1790.

The third Watford Place (in what we know as King Street), was built c1790; it passed into ownership of Jonathan King in 1826 and in 1851 he sold it after the death of his first wife. The purchaser subsequently cut the estate into building plots and formed the streets. The stable block (and vacant land beside), was bought by Charles Healey upon which he built the 'New Inn', and converted the stables into a brewery. (At time of writing the old brewery site is that of Pickford's repository).

King Street was formed on what was the carriage drive from the High Street to Watford Place house and the Lodge which stood in the High Street was converted into a public house to be called the 'King's Arms'; this was demolished in 1961. (p.276)

King Street was advertised as an intended road to Rickmansworth via Colney Butts but the plan did not materialise; the development of the road, together with Smith and George Streets, took place slowly during the mid-1850's.

Drawn to illustrate W. R. Saunder's 'History of Watford', this picture shows the auction rooms and, on the left, part of the 'King's Arms', on the corner of King Street. Incorrectly included in the drawing is 'Boot's'. This was not built until 1914 by which time the auction rooms had become a butcher's shop. The courtyard entrance to the right is Gregory's Yard in which could be found the first vicarage early tithe barn. *p.135 tr, cr, 249 bl, 276 cr, 325 b*

... two fire engines sent by train from Euston ...

When the Market Hall Was Destroyed

On Thursday (last week) a fire broke out in the town of Watford, which reduced to a heap of ruins the old building used as the Corn exchange and Market-house.

On the alarm being given, it was recollected that about 23 years since, every house opposite the premises on fire was destroyed by a similar misfortune; and the Market-house was then partially destroyed.

The authorities, fearing the recurrence of a like calamity, and profiting by proximity to the L. and N.W. Railway, sent an electric telegraph message to London for the aid of the Fire Brigade engines. Two engines were, by order of Mr. Braidwood, the superintendent, despatched to Euston-square, for the purpose of proceeding by a special train to the scene of the conflagration.

Notwithstanding this precaution, at noon next day, the ruins were still emitting sheets of fire, and some hours elapsed before the fire was wholly extinguished.

The damage done may be thus described: The Market-house burnt down; the contents, consisting of 90 quarters of wheat, 100 quarters of oats, and a considerable quantity of barley and other produce, destroyed. The premises of Mrs. Taylor, the "King's Head" Hotel, much damaged by fire and water. "The Spread Eagle," kept by Mr. Coulson, had the windows demolished and the shutters burnt. The premises of Mr. Hollingworth, a butcher, were also much burnt; as were those belonging to Mr. Brent, also a butcher; Mr. Flaxman, a corn-dealer, and Mr. Tirzon, are likewise considerable losers.

The origin of the fire is not precisely known, but there is strong ground for supposing that it was the work of incendiarism.

The illustration sketched by Mr. Henshew from a window of the "King's Head" Hotel, shows the Market-house, a low-pitched building of considerable age, now a mass of black ruins.

Illustrated London News, June 4th, 1853

More Details of the Fire

"This building, which was about 100ft. long by 24ft. wide, was built principally of wood, and had lofts and corn stores standing on numerous strong wooden columns about 18ins. or 2ft. square; it was open at the bottom, and round the columns were shambles and stalls, on which goods were exposed for sale at the annual fairs and on market days; corn was also pitched in the open space on market days.

Two or three days after one of the fairs the fire broke out, and it was thought a spark from one of the lights used at that fair having settled in some crevice, set the wood on fire, which smouldered, until obtaining vent, it burst into a flame. Shortly after the fire was discovered, the parish engine was brought round, and plenty of willing hands being present, it was speedily set to work, and water thrown onto the burning building; but it was soon found that from the inflammable nature of the material of which the building was composed, it would be labour in vain to try to save it with the small quantity of water available, so attention was given to "The Kings Head" public house and other houses on that side. Several times the window sashes caught fire, but it was extinguished by the water thrown from the engine, which was worked willingly by the inhabitants in relays.

In the exigency, a number of men and lads were called together and placed at intervals from the Market House to a pump in the "Essex Arms" Hotel yard, from which water was supplied and handed from one to the other in the parish leather buckets and several pails lent by the inhabitants, and the engine thereby kept at work.

The Market House, left a prey to the fire, soon became a vast body of flame, and great was the excitement of the thousands of persons present when the bell-turret, with tinkling bell that had been rung at the opening of the corn market each week for years previously fell with a loud crash on the road, together with the machinery that had denoted the changes of the wind. Shortly after, the roof fell in and forced out one of the ends of the building, which, burning fiercely, fell in a piece, against the house then occupied by Mr. Taylor, a bootmaker, but now a wine merchant's establishment. This would undoubtedly have set fire to the house had not a number of men at great personal risk pushed it back on to the burning mass.

Through the burning floor of the lofts corn ran freely to the ground, the greater quantity of which, it was stated, had been deposited there some years previously by a dealer who had bought it at a high price, and had declared it should not be moved until it sold at a profit; but never having had offered him the price he required, the corn remained in the lofts until it was destroyed by the fire.

The surrounding property ran a great risk during the conflagration—even the houses on the opposite side of the street; one of them, occupied by Mr. Wise, a grocer, was made so hot by the fire that the window shutters, frames and doors were stripped of their paint, and when water was poured over the walls, which it was found necessary to do frequently, steam was emitted in dense clouds. The Market House was entirely destroyed.

WHP (July, 1928)

St. Andrews

The ecclesiastical district of St. Andrews, an area of 1200 acres which included Callowland, was formed in February 1855 and a temporary church built. Building of the present church was started in 1857.

Literary Institute

A library was opened in 1854 in Carey Place. The Literary Institute had a library, a reading room and also accommodation for classes and lectures.

In 1855 the Public Library Act allowed a 1d. in the pound rate to be collected, once per year, which the Local Board added to a general and water rate.

Drawing by a correspondent of the Illustrated London News of the scene the morning after the fire. The bow-fronted window across the street is part of Henry Kingham's shop (established c1790) and is now the site of 'Mothercare' and 'Pearl Assurance' Chambers. Kingham's premises, at a later date, were located a little further south. That site is now occupied by British Home Stores.

A proposal to move the station from Watford to Bushey . . .

Letter to London and North Western Railway Company

Watford, Herts
11th February, 1857

Chas. E. Steward Esq.

Sir,

As the agent to Lord Essex, in charge of his Estates (his Lordship being ill in Scotland) and as the agent for Mr. Wm. Jones Loyd's Langley Bury Estate & knowing intimately the property in this neighbourhood, the rumour which some ten days since reached me, respecting the probable removal of the Watford Station to Bushey, seemed an event so unlikely to take place, that I perhaps paid less attention to it than a proper consideration of the interests of my employers required of me.

To remove the Watford Station, as proposed, would cause such a serious depreciation in the value of houses & land immediately connected to it, and would entail so much inconvenience and such pecuniary loss, that I hesitated to believe the question was ever seriously entertained by the directors of the London and North Western Railway Company.

I have reason to fear that I have been mistaken & that, as the project has been seriously discussed, it may eventually be carried out.

I think it my duty briefly and without loss of time to point out to you, for the information of the directors, some of the inconveniences which would arise to proprietors in this neighbourhood from the course proposed, hoping at all events I may be enabled to induce the directors to defer the discussion of the question until fuller evidence can be brought before them.

Strong objections may be taken to Bushey as the site of your station. First, because between it and the town is a turnpike with a toll of 4½d. for a vehicle with a single horse, & secondly because all the residents west of Bushey can only reach the station by the main street of Watford, some portion of which is narrow & much encumbered with vehicles.

I will endeavour to give a few instances of the injury that would be effected to some of the most important proprietors in the neighbourhood by the increase of the distance to the station.

	Distance to present Station	Distance to Bushey Station
The Earl of Essex, Cassiobury	1½ miles	2¼ miles
The Earl of Clarendon, The Grove	2½ miles	3¼ miles
Lord Rokeby, Hazlewood	3½ miles	4¼ miles
Chas. Pearser Esq. Russell Farm	2¼ miles	3¼ miles
George Roper Esq. Nascott	¾ mile	1¼ miles
Arthur Currie Esq. High Elms	2⅞ miles	3½ miles
J. Cobb Esq. Garston	1⅞ miles	2⅝ miles
N. Hibbert Esq. Mundon	3¼ miles	3¼ miles
Wm. Stuart Esq, Aldenham Abbey	3½ miles	3½ miles
J. Currie Esq. Hill Side	3½ miles	4¼ miles
Wm. Jones Loyd Esq. Langley Bury	3¾ miles	4½ miles

But Lord Essex is deeply interested in another respect—

He is the owner in fee of the Nascott Estate, a fine tract of land comprising about one hundred & fifty acres, lying between the Railway & the high road to Hemel Hempstead, on which it has a frontage of about 1600 yards. Its nearest point to the Watford Station is 1/5 of a mile & its most distant is 1 mile.

Upon my strong recommendation Lord Essex has consented to allow me to dispose of this for building purposes, for which it is in all respects most eligible.

I have made the ground plans & am about to lay out the streets with the view of immediately bringing the matter before the public. As there is ample space for some hundreds of good houses, I need hardly remark that the land is now very valuable; but if the Watford Station is moved as proposed I shall abandon the idea of selling it for building purposes. The nearest point to the Bushey Station being within a fraction of a mile & three quarters, whilst the farthest is two miles & a half.

If time be given me I shall be enabled to lay before you very full evidence on the subject & I hope I have said enough to induce the directors to pause in the matter. If this is the only application made to the Board on the subject, I beg to assure you that the cause is that the landowners & residents have not thought seriously upon it, even if the report has reached them.

I have the honour to be Sir
Your most obedient servant

C. F. Humbert

Train derailed at Watford!

"The train passed Watford Station, and, on looking out of the window, I saw we were on the Watford embankment, which is at least from fifty to sixty feet high. All of a sudden the carriage seemed to sink under us, and then followed a series of the most violent oscillations and bumping of the carriage for a period of ten or fifteen seconds; the speed of the carriage became less and less, and all at once it turned over flat on its side, myself undermost, and the whole of the passengers on me. While all was in confusion, some persons made their appearance on the topside of the carriage, and drew us out one by one. The first inquiry naturally was 'Is any-body killed or hurt?' and we were pleased to find, beyond a few scratches with glass, and a few shakes, no personal damage was done.

"I was the first passenger who ran back to look at the road, when the cause of the accident was at once apparent. A gang of workmen were employed in repairing the permanent way, putting new sleepers, and doing general repairs. On looking at the work only one chair out of every two was spiked to the sleeper, and those which were fastened, were fastened with wooden pegs about one inch in diameter. In one place no chair had been placed on the sleeper to support the rail, but the rail was left to a distance of six feet six inches without any support whatever. A greater act of negligence can scarcely be conceived. The result was, as soon as the train came on the unsupported part of the rail, the rail bent outwards, the chair on the next sleeper broke in two, and at the second sleeper the engine ran off the rails. From the impression of the wheel, made on the rail, it was quite evident, the engine commenced to leave the rails at the spot where the rail gave way for the want of a chair to support it. When the engine got off the rails it ploughed up the road for fifty or seventy yards, dashing everything to atoms.

"The chief cause of our preservation undoubtedly was the sand ballast, which was put fresh on the road, and which checked the force of the train as it ploughed through the sand after the engine and train got off the rails. The next cause which prevented us from being hurled over the embankment was, the Company are widening their road for three lines of rails, and our train happened to be on the middle line.

Illustrated News of the World, 27th March 1858

The newly-opened Watford Junction station   1860

Extra track, branch line and new station

Within just a few years travel by the iron-road—smooth and very fast—created demands for greater passenger-carrying capacity.

The Watford Station, by the road to St. Albans, was not well-sited for expansion. With an embankment on one side and pumping house and machinery on the other there was no space for extra platforms. In 1858 the addition of a third track was nearing completion, as was the branch line to St. Albans. Laid out upon open land, the site of the new Watford Junction was such as to admit of ample expansion, as well as industrial development between branch line and the road. In 1862 another branch line was opened. This went to Rickmansworth and crossed Loates Lane and Wiggenhall Road by level-crossings.

Celebrations upon the wedding of Prince of Wales (later Edward VII) and Princess Alexandra of Denmark.   *p.40, 61, 189, 323 b.*   10th March 1863

The St. Albans Branch Line

The opening of the new branch in May 1858, was celebrated as follows:—
"The festivity was inaugurated at 1 p.m. by a procession from the Town Hall, 'headed by 30 navvies in white smocks, wearing bunches of pink and white ribbons upon their caps,' accompanied by the 'St. Albans Original' Brass Band, in caps of crimson and gold, with massive gold tassels." Then followed the Beadle, holding the Staff of Office, officers of the Borough police, the Mayor, George Debenham, Esq., in robes; Aldermen and Town Councillors; also the gentlemen and traders, marching four abreast. The Town brass band likewise attended, arrayed in new caps of blue and gold. The procession passed through the Market-place and High-street, thence down Holywell-hill to the new station; 8,000 people are stated to have been present. " The expected train arrived 'with the engine and tender decked in flags and evergreens.'

WO (May, 1958)

Caractacus

On Thursday, the 9th October, 1862, Mr. Charles Snewing, of Holywell Farm, gave a dinner to five hundred of the working people of Watford, to celebrate the event of his horse Caractacus winning the Derby that year. A large marquee was erected in front of his residence, and the place was gaily decorated with flags, the word "Welcome" being on the largest. The fife and drum band of the Watford Rifle Volunteers performed a variety of music in the grounds, and Mr. Snewing gave a ball in the evening to a number of his friends and acquaintances.

William's, 'History of Watford'

Watford in the Sixties

Early memories are my being taken to a dame's school nearby, and watching the removal of Mr. John Peacock's printing office from the site of the present High-street Station to new premises in Queen-street, wherein, subsequently, Mr. Samuel Peacock, his son, first published "The Watford Observer." Queen-street was one of the new roads marking the early development of Watford. This "street" had but few houses then, and it terminated at a pathway which led one way to Otterspool and the other to Beechen Grove, across the site of the present Clarendon-road, and out by the Verulam Arms to the Railway Station. A portion of this pathway can still be traced. The vacant site of the London and County Bank had evidently been cleared when Queen-street was first opened out. The Eight Bells Inn was near to it, with Mr. S. Peck's grocer's shop on the opposite corner. The Queen's Arms was comparatively new, and the site of the first Public Library was a cabbage patch. King-street was much as it is now, except that a furniture warehouse and a Police Station occupy the site of Mr. Flaxman's hay and corn stores. Mr. Armstrong, the tailor, had the corner shop on Smith-street, now Mr. Longman's, and there was an inn at the High-street corner, once the lodge to Watford Place (the residence of Mr. J. R. Tivaz, a retired Indian judge). The New Inn was in being and also the County Court, in charge of the polite Mr. Belliss. Lady's Close consisted of two or three imposing private residences. Mr. John James lived at Southfield House, his father residing in High-street nearby. Other members of this well-known family of papermakers lived in other parts of the town, and at Hamper Mills, where handmade paper was still made. Mr. Jonathan King was living at Wiggen Hall, and the Silk Mills were in work for

a firm named Shute, I think.

Beyond was Oxhey-place, with its park and the famous Grimston oak, and the little private chapel, the property of the Blackwell family. Approached over the Little Bridges was Tommy Deacon's-hill, now no more, a well-frequented walk which led from Wiggen Hall to the Green-lane, and there, too was a pleasant pathway alongside the river Colne to the bottom of the town.

T. J. Peacock   WO (October, 1933)

●*John Peacock was the founder of the printing business which later played a prominent part in the town's history; T. J. Peacock was his grandson.*

'T. J.' was the elder son of the founder of the 'Watford Observer', Samuel Peacock, (son of John Peacock). Upon Samuel's death in 1880 the business was carried on by T. J. on behalf of his widowed mother and the family. Upon Mrs. Peacock's death in 1893 T. J. Peacock gave his brother, Charles Herbert, the option to purchase, the option being accepted. C. H. Peacock ran the business until his death in 1930.

●*Frederick Downer was born in Watford in 1841. He left school at an early age to work for a solicitor; he then worked for his father but in 1860 realised that the rewards of working 12 hours a day in a stationer's shop would not suffice; for a summer season he caught the 4.50 a.m. train to Euston where he took an art course at Newman Street, and would be back in Watford by 10 o'clock for a day's work at his father's shop.*

The following year, 1861, he started a studio at the rear of his father's shop, then 97 High Street.

NEW ALMSHOUSES AT WATFORD ERECTED BY THE SALTERS' COMPANY OF LONDON.

New Almshouses

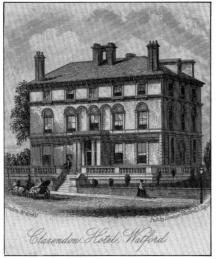

An engraving of the 'Clarendon Hotel' published by David Downer, in 1862.

The rebuilding of the almshouses of the civic companies in the environs of the Metropolis instead of the densely-crowded City, as occasion requires, is a sanitary change much to be commended.

The wealthy Company of Salters—one of twelve great companies–has just followed this good example. More than four centuries ago (1454) Thomas Beaumont Esq. gave to the company a hall, in Bread-street, and six almshouses adjoining. And, in 1578, Sir Ambrose Nicholas, Lord Mayor in 1576, gave an almshouse, in Monkwell-street, for twelve women. The original premises were burnt down in the Great Fire of 1666, after which the company rebuilt the almshouses which had become so delapidated as to require reconstruction; when the Master, and Wardens, and Assistants—trustees for all time—instead of rebuilding the refuge for their decayed brethren in Monkwell-street, chose the neighbourhood of Watford for their new location. The new almshouses, a view of which is engraved from a photograph by Mr. F. Downer of Watford, have been erected at a cost of £8000 exclusive of the expense of the site

and adjoining grounds in a pleasant part of Watford about ten minutes' walk from the railway station.

The buildings present three sides of a square, or a centre and two wings, the principal portion resting on a raised terrace. The interiors are planned with careful regard to sanitary considerations and the domestic accommodation of the inmates—the Almswomen from Monkwell-street and the almsmen from Salters'-rents, Bow-lane. The architect is Mr. John Collier of Putney and the builder Mr. King of Shefford, Bedfordshire. The grounds are tastefully laid out for the recreaion of the almsfolk.

The Salters flourished in the times when salt fish formed part of every meal, and the use and consumption of salt fish in the ancient Catholic periods was amazing. In short, it formed part of the allowance of the King and nobility, of monastic establishments and of all ranks of society; and the custom is even commemorated in modern times, in the 'King's Maundy', which was, in great part, composed of salt fish.

Illustrated London News, July 30th, 1864

Watford Volunteer Rifle Brigade. Drs. Iles and Brett on the left. Photograph taken on a piece of land next to where the Baptist Church stands in Clarendon Road, and showing the (then) new Estcourt Road in the background.

The Police . . .

Police were established on a village basis of Parish Constable, appointed annually at the Watford Manorial Court Leet, without regular pay, but being paid by result. For each prisoner brought to quarter sessions a fee could be charged. Early constables had various duties ranging from suppression of drunkenness to checking weights and measures. Over and above the Parish constables were 'head' or 'chief' constables responsible for an area of a 'hundred'.

Robert Peel, made Home Secretary in 1822, was dissatisfied with the public's confusion of the roles of 'police' and 'military' particularly after the military, in trying to suppress a meeting at Manchester, charged the crowd, killing eleven and injuring hundreds. Peel's early action was to dress the police in a manner totally unlike the army—and so we have the dress of the Peelers, with top hat and frock coat.

Watford's early Parish Constable (from 1832 until the coming of the County Police in 1841) was James West. In addition the Watford Subscription Police force was founded in 1829, this costing a few inhabitants £1 annually for private watching (Clarke's report, 1849).

In 1841 a County Police presence was established at 193 High Street with Superintendant Captain Kelly and a constable. Premises were later obtained in the then new Estcourt Road.

In William's 'History of Watford' is a long account of a 'murder at Aldenham', and the solving of this crime and apprehending of the suspect, involved local magistrates Clutterbuck and Finch in journeys to Bow Street to liaise with a Constable. (1823)

Arising from the early duty of checking weights and measures it was perhaps appropriate that the Estcourt Road premises would become the local office of the Inspector of Weights and Measures, food and drugs, petroleum and explosives, and fertilisers and feeding-stuffs for the county of Hertfordshire (Western Division), until well past the 1939-45 war.

Red Flag Act 1865

A steam locomotive or steam carriage, when driven upon the highway, must be preceded by a man walking and carrying a red flag.

Population 1871, 7,461

Watford Police of 1863, the County Police had a station at 193 High Street (approx. opposite present museum, for many years prior to demolition, H. A. Swann, leather merchant) and later moved to another Station in the then new Estcourt Road. Photograph taken in Mr. Downer's Loates Lane outdoor studio.

Meeting of the Hunt at the Cross Road outside the 'Elms', High Street in the foreground, Hempstead Road to the right c1870.   p.185 b, 337 b.

Post Office staff of c1870. Mr. Morley's shop of No. 5 Queens Road.

Bushey Station

The original Bushey Station, on the down line and next to the bridge; date given as c1867, but may be earlier.

The area around the River Colne where it crosses the High Street is low-lying marshy ground. In the very early days, probably long before Domesday, it would be recognised as an extremely unpleasant and wide ford to cross, especially after heavy rains, hence the derivation of 'Wet' ford from which Watford gets its name.

We know the area today as a busy road junction and a one-way system with the traffic flow constrained by the arches of the viaduct.

In the 1830's there was a small thriving community centred around the ironworks and the trades catering for travellers who perforce had to halt for a while before or after going through the toll.

The view from Watford towards Bushey was uninterrupted except for tree-clad slopes. This changed quite dramatically when the railway builders took over.

From the north, a massive embankment and from the south, a huge bridge; wonders of engineering the like of which was unknown to Watfordians.

But, at one stroke, Watford was enclosed with a physical wall which one entered or left via the toll. From that day to this the 'Bushey Arches' marks a tangible boundary between the town and all to the south.

Four years after the Watford station was opened in the fields adjacent to the road to St. Albans, a station was built at Bushey. This was on the Kingsfield side of the track with entrance from what we know as Eastbury Road. As at Watford, roads were soon laid out and houses built, and the area called 'New Bushey', but which we know as Oxhey.

The drawing on page 33 shows the area soon after the construction of the railway. The details appear accurate when compared with later photographs—even if the perspective is fanciful (our modern illustrators of town planning developments are little better in this respect!)

The date suggested for the Bushey Station photograph is 1869. This is after the construction of the third track on the embankment and through the single Watford Tunnel. The points on the track, in the top photograph, are shown on the map on page 52 and this indicates that there were, in 1871, four lines into Bushey from the south, and which were reduced to three carrying on northwards, at least, until the bridge was widened and a new tunnel, north of Watford, was built.

The Tollgate across the Turnpike Road through Bushey and Watford. Date of photograph possibly c1860-1867.

p.331 rc

Later view of the tollgate; the iron girder bridge was started in 1871 and when finished served until 1963. This photograph may have been of one of the last tolls, or a 'posed' picture later after completion of the new bridge.

p.332 tl

● 1852 Sanitary arrangements comprised cesspools
1852-75 Sewer system without ventilation
1875-87 Incomplete system of chiefly road ventilation
1871 Storm water partly diverted from the sewer system.

The Turnpike Trusts

There were two turnpikes passing through Watford. The first was the Hatfield Trust which set up Toll Houses in North Watford and Hagden Lane. Collection of tolls started in 1757 and ended in 1881. The second, the Aylesbury to Bushey Heath turnpike, was operated by the Sparrow's Herne Trust with local Toll Houses at Bushey Arches and near Ridge Lane on the road to Hemel Hempstead. Opened in 1762, the turnpike tolls were last collected in 1872. These trusts repaired the roads they controlled by collecting tolls from road users and so maintained them as 'long-distance' routes in a better state than when they had been repaired by parish labour. Milestones were set up by these Trusts.

From 1770 onwards, coaches were able to travel at faster speeds on these roads and after 1800 they were further improved by engineers such as McAdam, employed by the Trustees. The two roads crossed by the 'Elms', or Pond Cross Roads.

Before 1757 Rickmansworth Road was called New Mill Lane, and afterwards often called Coach Lane. In 1887, at the time of the tree-planting ceremony outside the 'Elms', it was called the 'Park Road'.

It was said that the Hatfield Trust was set up by the Earl of Salisbury to give the family a good road to Bath and their west country properties.

The Bushey Lime Kilns were located adjacent to Bushey Arches on the north side of Chalk Hill. The chalk used in the kilns was obtained locally. The process of burning converted the chalk to quicklime which was spread on fields as a fertiliser, especially on acid and clay soils. It could also be used for making lime-based mortars for bonding bricks or for plastering walls. Thinner solutions provided whitewash.

The new estates . . .

The laying out of an estate or the making of a road was a process which spread over a long period of time. There was rarely a start or finish date. In the early days of the building of Watford no planning permission was needed. The only public announcements would be those of the Auctioneer announcing the sale of the plots (as for Market Street, seen later). In any event such happenings could be seen daily by the town's inhabitants and in the 1860's and 70's would not be news to the Watford Observer.

The role of a newspaper in this period can be defined as 'having ears with which to report' but, lacking means to print photographs, had no 'eyes'.

(Reports of learned society's meetings, Literary and Local Board, Flower Shows, Music and Drama meetings, Yeomanry, etc., were. at extreme length as befitted a journal tailored exactly to the readers who in most part would be the gentry, businessmen and farming community spread over a wide area which included that from St. Albans to Hendon and Edgware.)

King Street was opened just after 1851 and Queens Road was started in 1860. Also at the start of the 1860's, land owned by Thomas Henry Sutton Sotheron Estcourt between Clarendon Road and the railway was developed, resulting in Estcourt and Sutton Roads, etc, followed a little later by Derby Road. The Clarendon Road was laid out in 1864.

The Estcourt Road estate ran off Beechen Grove, in which a Meeting House had been since 1707, and which in turn was connected to the High Street by narrow 'Meeting Alley'.

Near the Railway Station, Church Road and Bedford Street had been in existence since soon after the coming of the railway, although un-named for many years.

From the letter of Mr. Humbert in 1857 (p.44) will be seen the intention to develop the Nascott area; this eventually included Denmark Street and Alexander Road, so named because of the feeling of affection and respect following the wedding of the Prince of Wales to Princess Alexandra of Denmark, in 1863.

George Street and Smith Street were established soon after 1851.

Before these streets had been built in the now 'central area' of Watford, a compact development had already taken place at 'New Bushey' (Oxhey) and which consisted of Villiers and Capel Roads.

The workhouse opposite the church was in disuse of its original purpose, a new workhouse having been built in 1838 at Colney Butts (Vicarage Road). The cemetery was started in 1858.

From the Mother Church, St. Mary's, had grown St. Andrews in Church Road (1855); the Baptist Church was still in Beechen Grove and other places of worship included the Town Mission at Farthing Lane, a Primitive Methodist Chapel in Carey Place and Wesleyan and Beulah Chapels in Queens Road.

Watford, to the north along the road to St. Albans, did not exist. There was a lane (later Leavesden Road) which led to Leavesden, further along still was the lane to Bushey Mill and beyond that were fields to St. Albans.

The roads, such as they were, were still 'turnpike tolls', at least until 1872.

Steam engines had been developed to power road wagons, but unlike the Continent where new transport was welcomed, they were virtually stifled at birth by the 1865 'Red Flag' act, which had the effect of limiting speed to about 4 miles per hour.

Watford had the paradox of the swiftness of rail-travel and the slowness of the lumbering horse and cart; the roads were problems which constantly occupied the minds of the members of the Local Board.

The map which follows shows the extent of Watford by 1871.

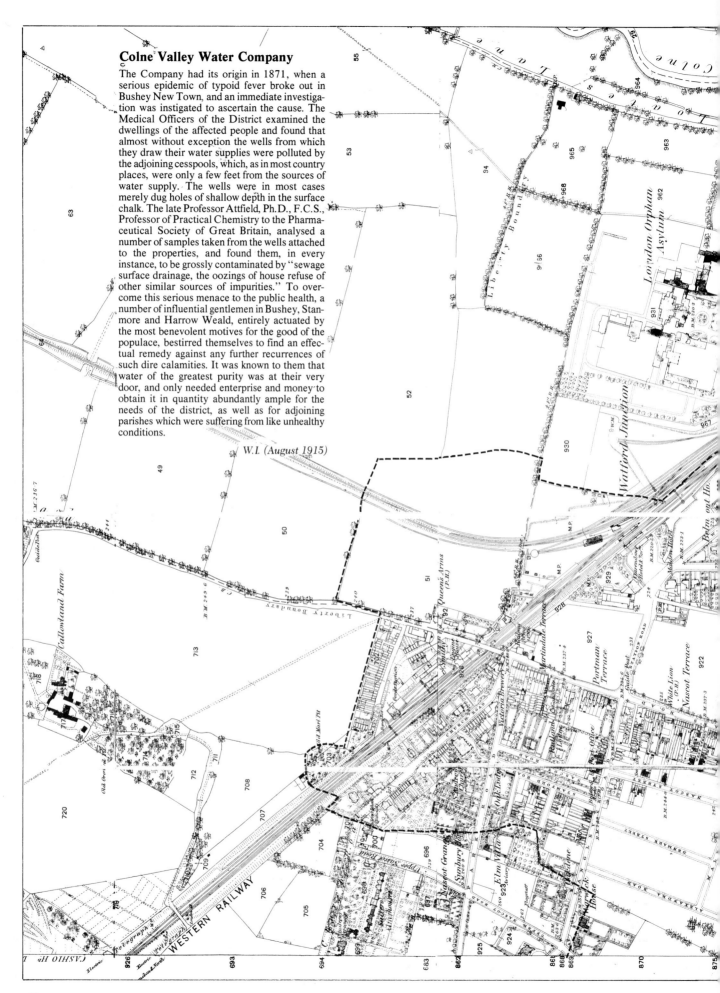

Colne Valley Water Company

The Company had its origin in 1871, when a serious epidemic of typoid fever broke out in Bushey New Town, and an immediate investigation was instigated to ascertain the cause. The Medical Officers of the District examined the dwellings of the affected people and found that almost without exception the wells from which they draw their water supplies were polluted by the adjoining cesspools, which, as in most country places, were only a few feet from the sources of water supply. The wells were in most cases merely dug holes of shallow depth in the surface chalk. The late Professor Attfield, Ph.D., F.C.S., Professor of Practical Chemistry to the Pharmaceutical Society of Great Britain, analysed a number of samples taken from the wells attached to the properties, and found them, in every instance, to be grossly contaminated by "sewage surface drainage, the oozings of house refuse of other similar sources of impurities." To overcome this serious menace to the public health, a number of influential gentlemen in Bushey, Stanmore and Harrow Weald, entirely actuated by the most benevolent motives for the good of the populace, bestirred themselves to find an effectual remedy against any further recurrences of such dire calamities. It was known to them that water of the greatest purity was at their very door, and only needed enterprise and money to obtain it in quantity abundantly ample for the needs of the district, as well as for adjoining parishes which were suffering from like unhealthy conditions.

W.I. (August 1915)

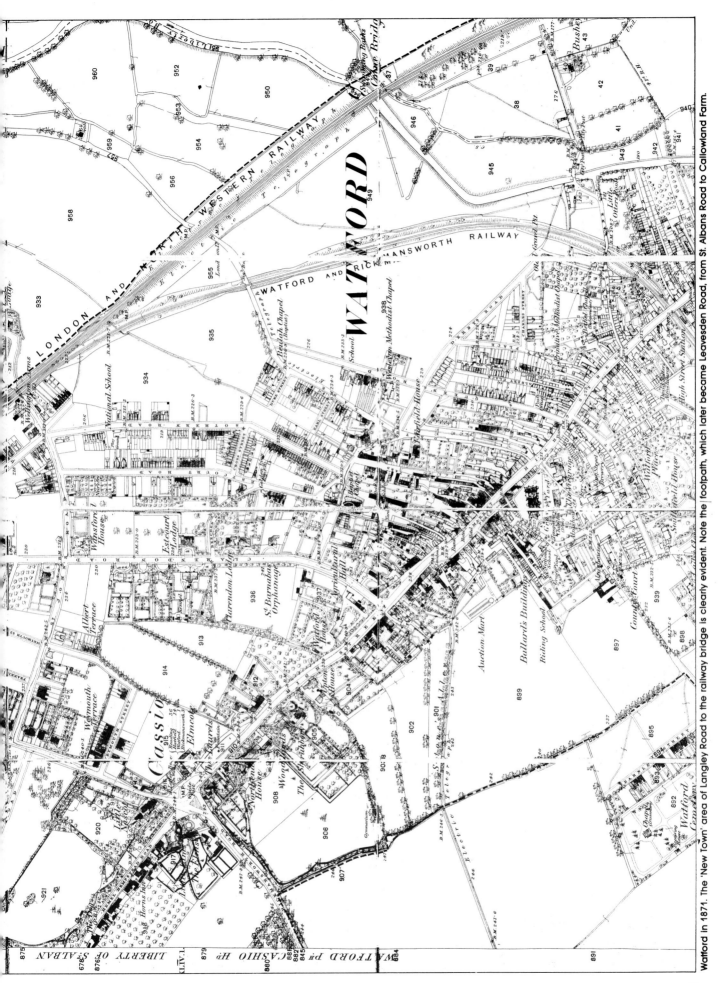

Watford in 1871. The 'New Town' area of Langley Road to the railway bridge is clearly evident. Note the footpath, which later became Leavesden Road, from St. Albans Road to Callowland Farm.

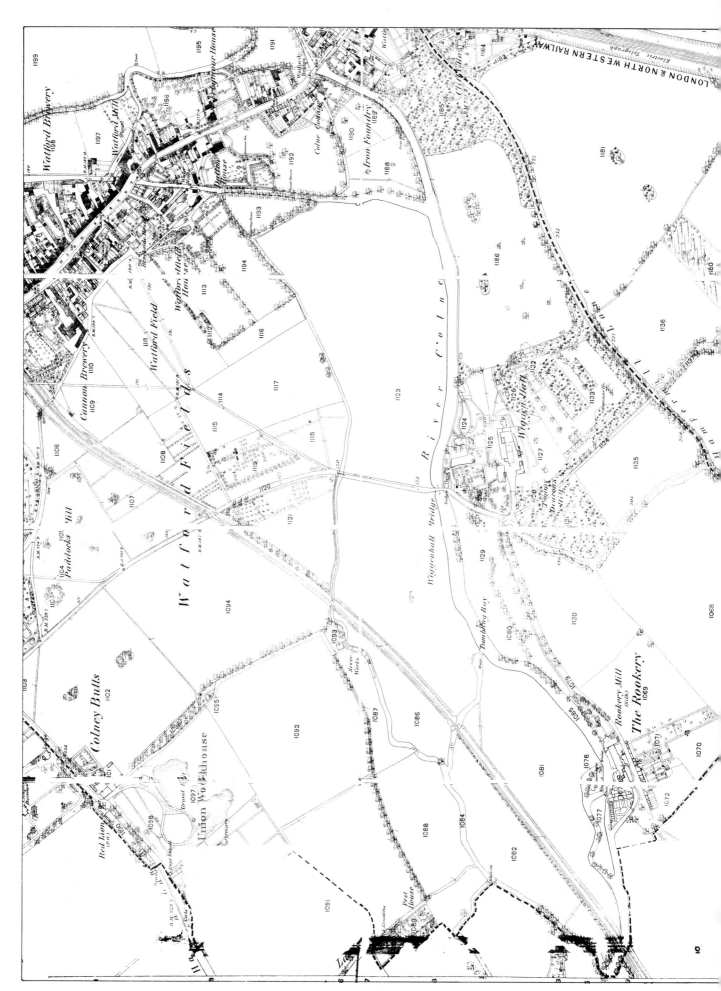

London & North Western Railway
Electric Telegraph

Watford Brewery
1198
1199
Watford Mill
1197
1196
1195
Tolpenmoor House
1194
1193
1192
1191
1190
1189
1188
1187
1186
1185
1184

Watford Field House
Watford Field
1113
1112
1116
1114
1115
1117
1118
1119
1120
1121
1123
1124
1125
1127
1128
1129
1130
1135
1136

Cannon Brewery
1110
1109
1108
1111
Watford Fields
1106
1107
1094

Wrights Hall

River Colne

Wiggenhall Bridge

Paddocks Hill
1101
1104

Colney Butts
1102
1103
1101

Union Workhouse

Red Lion
1100
1098
1097
1095
1096
1092
1093
1091

Sewer Works

1087
1086
1088
1084
1082
1089
1081

Wiggenhall Prospects
1126
1131
1132
1133
1134

Rookery Mill
The Rookery
1069
1070
1071
1072
1077
1078
1065
1079
1080
1068

Tumbling Bay

52

Watford Parish Church

Rebuilding the Parish Church . . .

A church has stood upon the site since the eleventh century.

The Rev. J. C. Clutterbuck said, in 1862, the walls of the nave are supported by six arches on each side, of the South which are Early English AD 1250, and the North, Perpendicular, AD 1430.

Throughout its history the Church has played a dominant role in the lives of its parishioners but by the

early 1800's it was in a quite dilapidated state. The pillars and arches, spurred out by weight, were repaired when the interior of the Church was restored in 1848.

The dilapidations of the outside were repaired in 1871 at a cost of some £6,839, during which time services were held in a 'temporary' iron church erected in the churchyard.

The Fig Tree

Countless burials had taken place around the church, many without benefit of coffins, with the result that earthwork grew so high around the church that the parishioners had to step down some three or four steps to enter the building. This, of course, caused both considerable dampness and inconvenience. During the lowering of the churchyard rows of skeletons were uncovered which appeared to have been buried side-by-side and were very probably remains of those who died in a period of plagues, (in 1540 some 47 burials between July and September, and in 1592, 1594 and 1625).

It was at this time that the 'Fig-tree' tomb, famous as an old legend that a fig tree had grown from the buried atheist lady's heart, accidentally

opened. It showed that the roots of the fig tree were not in the vault but in the crown of the arch, some four or five feet above where the lady's heart must have been.

The outer walls of the church were of rough-cast, which was removed, and replaced by a casing of flint. The entire roof was releaded and large stone 'pine-apples' removed and the top turreted to lighten the weight as the top of the tower was of solid stone.

Somewhat later, around 1880, alterations were being made to underground premises of Mr. Edmonds, ironmonger, when the workmen, in removing the earth, exhumed a number of human bones, which led to the supposition that at one time the churchyard extended to the High Street,

from the church gates, to Church Street, and that under the feet of the occupants rest the bones of many of the former inhabitants of Watford.

William's 'History of Watford'

●*No. 98 High Street, prior to rebuilding in 1959/60, was the shop of Spurriers, bakers, prior to which it had been that of Mr. Edmonds, ironmonger, who was established in 1798. The building carried an apothecary's sign in a recess in the upper storey, as may be seen in the illustration on page 276.*

53

Phillip Buck, Baker, in 1872 acquired No. 50 High Street and had a new shop front installed thus combining Nos. 48 and 50. The yard from which the horse and cart is emerging is Court No. 6, Edlin's Yard, which later led to Buck's Bakery. Buck's later acquired No. 52 and created a ballroom on the first floor. No. 52 had been the home of local architect Mr. C. P. Ayres. Among the buildings he designed during his career were the Work House Infirmary, Isolation Hospital and two extensions, the District Hospital, Derby Road Grammar School, the Girls' Grammar School, Victoria, Watford Fields, Leavesden Road and Parkgate schools, and several banks including Lloyds and Barclays, premises for Mr. F. Fisher and the Fire Station. *p.336 tl*

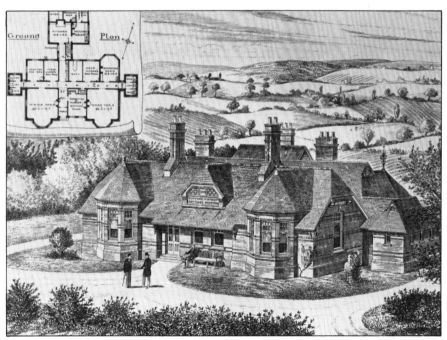

The Cottage Hospital in Vicarage Road was built in 1885, original accommodation being nine beds. In 1897, to mark the Diamond Jubilee of Queen Victoria a new six-bed ward and operating theatre was added. Five years later two additional six-bed wards plus dining rooms and staff accommodation were added, a total capacity of 27 patients. The original building cost £1700, and was opened by Lady Clarendon in 1886. The building still exists. *p.350 tr*

Plates. Inches.	With 1 Double Dark Slide and 2 Inner Frames.			Extra Double Slides, each.		
	£	s.	d.	£	s.	d.
4¼ × 3¼	3	4	0	0	13	0
6½ × 4¾	4	4	0	0	15	0
8½ × 6½	5	1	0	1	0	0
10 × 8	6	2	0	1	4	0
12 × 10	7	2	0	1	10	0

Typical high-class field camera c1880; note that no shutter is fitted—exposures are made by removing and replacing the lens cap.

Derby Road Endowed School for Boys and Girls, opened by the Earl of Clarendon on April 21, 1884 (boys) and April 22nd, (girls).

Endowed Schools

The new schools to be day-schools, and accommodation to be provided for 100 boys and 100 girls, or thereabout. Religious instruction to be in accordance with the doctrines of the Church of England; and any parent or guardian may claim, by notice in writing to the head master or head mistress, the exemption of any scholar from attending prayer or religious worship, or from any lesson or series of lessons on religious subjects, and such exemption will be granted. No teacher may teach systematically or persistently any particular religious doctrine, from the teaching of which exemption has been claimed. The head master's salary to be £100 per annum, with a payment from the capitation as may be fixed from time to time by the governors, at a rate of not less than £1 or more than £3 a year for each boy in the school. The salary of the head mistress to be £50 per annum, with proportion of capitation grant; each to have a residence, and to sign a declaration of their willingness to discharge their duties to the best of their abilities. The school to be open to all boys and girls of good character and sufficient health, residing with their parents and guardians or near relatives within an area to be fixed by the governors. Applicants for admission to the school to undergo an examination by the head master or head mistress, and none to be admitted who are not found fit for admission by the examination. Reading, writing from dictation, sums in two simple rules of arithmetic, with the multiplication table, to be the subjects for examination, to be graduated according to the age of the child. Beside religious instruction, the children are to be instructed in the following subjects: Reading, writing, arithmetic, geography, and history; English grammar, composition and literature; mathematics, Latin, French, natural science, drawing, drill, and vocal music. Other

modern European languages may be taught. An examination of the scholars to take place once a year by an examiner or examiners appointed or approved for that purpose by the governors, but otherwise unconnected with the school.

William's 'History of Watford'

Coffee Tavern Company . . .

at 87 High Street, is considerably enlarged, several bed and other rooms being added, and a hall at the rear capable of holding about 200 persons. It is also called the Temperance Hall.

William's 'History of Watford'

Printing Photographs

In 1882 an invention made possible the printing of copies of photographs by the letterpress printing methods. By having a finely-ruled special glass plate the tones of a normal photograph could be broken up into very fine 'dots', each dot varying in size according to the darkness or lightness of the original photograph.

Previously, illustrations had either to be hand-engraved in steel or copper, or of 'wood cuts', 'lithographed' from drawings upon stone.

● *The Free School was founded by Mrs. Fuller in 1704. Her endowments comprised rent charges from property and land she had owned. These were fixed charges and did not keep pace with the slow but gradual inflation between 1704 and 1880. In the meantime many other benefactors had helped to keep the school viable. Mr. Jonathan Cox Lovett, of Holywell, made a revisionary devise of certain of his estates, including Holywell Farm, to the Trustees of the school. The devise was not enrolled in Chancery and so became void. Had the devise become effective the income would have been fully sufficient to have supported the school. In the event, funds dried up and the school closed on August 10th, 1882.*

In the meanwhile, preparations were being made to provide new Endowed schools, and these were built in Derby Road, and opened in 1884, the residue of the previous endowments, and the Platts charity income being used subsequently.

Watford Field Road

Watford Field Road was formerly called Farthing Lane and therein stand the People's hall and Ragged Schools, supported by the Dissenters of the Town who are doing good work among the children of the lower classes.

William's 'History of Watford'

Market Place, Herts Yeomanry meeting outside the 'Rose & Crown' and 'Compasses'. Both this and the following picture show well the state of the road and market place about which Dr. Brett frequently complained. The yard entrance between Smith's and Longley's led to Chequer's Yard. When the new market was laid out in 1928 this entrance was then between the Midland Bank and Cawdells. Longley's, in this photograph, is now the open space entrance to Charter Place. The photograph is taken from the position of modern Ratner's.   p.334 b, 335 b   c1885

Court 18 off Farthing Lane (later Watford Fields Road); the girls are standing by the entrance to the Methodist Chapel (later the Town Mission and Ragged School).   p.274 tr

Names not altered and New Names	Old Names
Court 1	Butcher's Yard
Court 2	Well's Yard
Court 3 and 5	Two small Courts in Meeting Alley
Court 4	Wright's Yard
Court 6	Edlin's Yard
Court 7	Chequers Yard
Court 8	Ballard's Buildings
Court 9	A Court in Red Lion Yard, formerly Water-butt Square
Court 10	Hedge's Yard
Court 11	Holt's Yard
Court 13	Hudson's Yard, leading out of Chater's Yard
Court 14	Top of Crown Passage, formerly Clark's Buildings
Court 15	Boot Yard
Court 16	Between Nos. 184 and 186 (on map as 'Potton Yard')
Court 17	In Water Lane
Court 18	In Farthing Lane
Court 19	New Road
Court 20	Old Tan Yard
Court 21	Chapman's Yard
Court 22	Old Yard
Court 23	Malting Yard
Court 25	Neal's Yard
Court 30	Grove Place
Meeting Alley	Meeting Alley
Bell Alley	Bell Alley
Red Lion Yard	Red Lion Yard
Fenn's Yard	Fenn's Yard
Albert Street	Chater's Yard
Crown Passage	Three Crown Yard
Water Lane	Water Lane
Chapel Row	Chapel Row, in Water Lane
Pigg's Alley	Pigg's Alley
Swann Alley	Swann Alley
Watford Field Road	Farthing Lane

Henry Williams, Sanitary Inspector

Courtyards of Watford frequently changed ownership and name. In an effort to regularise the situation, Henry Williams numbered the Courts.

Herts Yeomanry meeting, outside the 'King's Head'. Saunders, late Kinder, is the butcher's shop reported destroyed by fire, together with the earlier 'King' Head' in 1828. (p.22)

p.277 tl, 334 c

Herts Yeomanry Cavalry

The annual training of the Yeomanry, which began on Wednesday in last week, was hampered considerably by the heavy thunder showers which prevailed for several days. On Friday morning the regiment paraded in the Market-place at 10.45, and marched to Cassiobury Park, but heavy rain came on and very little drill was got through. There was an improvement in the weather, however, on Saturday, and various evolutions with outpost duty, were undertaken in the Park until luncheon time, field movements, sword exercise, and a march past finishing the day's work.

WO (May, 1890)

Watford Town Band

The first summer promenade concert will take place on Wednesday, May 30th, by kind permission of J. E. Panton, Esq., at the Manor House, Church Road. A specially selected programme will be performed, and the grounds illuminated with numerous coloured fairy lights and lanterns. Commence at 7.45. Admission 6d. Thomas Mullett, Bandmaster. The last train to Kings Langley, Boxmoor &c, leaves Watford at 10.20. The Watford Town Band may be engaged for lawn parties, demonstrations, fetes, &c. Special consideration in regard to terms for engagements in connexion with charitable objects. Samuel Henry Baughan, Hon. Sec, Eva Villa, Gladstone-road, Watford.—(ADVERT)

WO (May, 1890)

Henry Williams, 1886

Watford Town Band at Dalton House, Lower High Street.

... planting of an Oak, junction of the Park Road with High Street ...

Her Majesty's Jubilee

THIS momentous event was celebrated in Watford, on Tuesday, with the greatest success.

The committee were Mr. S. H. Allen, Mr. R. Ashby, Mr. T. W. Bailey, Dr. A. T. Brett, Mr. P. Buck, Mr. F. Fisher, Mr. F. Gibbs, Mr. G. A. Heath, Mr. C. Healey, the Rev. R. L. James, Mr. G. E. Lake, the Rev. N. Price, Mr. H. Palmer, Dr. Stradling, Mr. G. Sturman, Mr. W. Taylor, the Rev. W. Y. Thomson, Mr. G. Urlwin, Mr. T. J. Villiers, and Mr. C. W. Edwards (hon. secretary).

At 9 o'clock there was a large assembly at the north end of the town to witness the planting of a tree by the Countess of Essex. The tree, a fine young oak from Cassiobury, was placed in position on the piece of green at the junction of the Park-road with High-street, and on the Park side of the drinking fountain. The Royal Standard was mounted near. Her Ladyship, accompanied by the Earl of Essex, arrived punctually on the ground, and was met by Mr. Humbert, the Chairman of the Committee, the Vicar of Watford, the Chairman of the Local Board, and the members of the Committee. The Band of the Watford Volunteers was in attendance and played before and after the ceremony.

The Vicar, in welcoming Lady Essex, said that she joined with them heart and soul in the proceedings of that day, and they had to thank her very much for her presence. He had merely to announce that Lady Essex would go through the formal ceremony of planting the tree which they saw before them, and to express the wish that great success might attend these efforts to perpetuate the memory of our noble and gracious Queen's reign. (Cheers.) It was with extreme pleasure that they saw such unanimity and cordiality throughout her extensive dominions. They did not wish to be behind others, and therefore Lady Essex had acceded to the united wish of the parish that she would plant that memorial of the day, and might God grant his best blessing on this and other ways in which they tried to celebrate the occasion. (Cheers.)

Mr. Humbert then handed to Her Ladyship a silver spade, with which she proceeded to place mould around the tree amid the cheering of the spectators, and the Band played "God save the Queen."

WO June 1887

Her Majesty's Jubilee

The arrangements were—and they were carried out as nearly as possible according to the programme—that the Union children, preceeded by their band, should march to New-street, and there fall in with the National School children; that the Union band should then proceed down High-street to meet the Bushey children; that the London Orphan Asylum Band should meet the boys from the St. Andrew's School in front of the Watford Railway Station, and proceed by way of Woodford-road to the Sotheron-road Schools, where the St. Andrew's School girls should join the procession, and the Beechen Grove school children fall in at the top of Sutton-road, and go by way of Queen-street to the Market-place. Having assembled there in good order, they marched with their teachers, who entered thoroughly into the arrangements of the day, and accompanied by the Town Band. the London Orphan Asylum Band, and the Union Band to the Agricultural Hall. The greater number were soon seated, and grace having been said by the Vicar, the children were quickly supplied with an abundance of good things by their teachers and

Most of the prominent members of the town, and Local Board, are at the tree-planting ceremony, Dr. Brett in uniform and the Earl of Essex at extreme right. The oak tree lasted until 1936. *sp.185*   18 June 1887

other willing helpers. It was a very gratifying scene upon which the subscribers in the galleries looked down, the appearance of the children being all that could be desired, and everything was carried out with the greatest order. After the tea the schools were again formed outside, and headed by the band proceeded to Cassiobury Park. Safely arrived in the park, the children dispersed to find amusement.

WO June 1887

● *To celebrate Queen Victoria's 50 years reign, the townspeople were involved in many suggestions as to suitable and befitting monuments. Architect C. P. Ayres suggested demolishing the houses and shops from the 'One Bell' to the Vicarage, thus exposing to view St. Mary's Church, and widening the road. The Earl of Essex suggested an extension to the library or building and endowing some almshouses. In the event insufficient interest and money was raised and celebrations were limited to planting a tree, giving the children a good feed and a fireworks celebration.*

Jubilee Committee

The following is the balance sheet:—Receipts: Total amount of subscriptions, £332 17s. Expenditure: Mr. Buck, for dinner, tea, &c., £200 2s. 8d; bands, £18 10s.; medals and favours, £14 11s.; sports committee, for prizes, £44 16s; fireworks, £15; expenses for planting the tree, £3 18s,; refreshments for the committee and the police, £5 11d.; Mr. Peacock, for printing, &c., £14 8s.; postage and stationery, £5 6s. 7d.; labour, £5 13s 9d.; Mr. Grant, for collecting, £5 6s.; total, £332 17s. Audited and found correct by Messrs. H. S. Allen and G. Heath.

(At the previous committee meeting a deficit of £20 14s. 0d. was noted. Further subscriptions reduced this sum to £1 14s. 11d.)

... it was ultimately agreed that the six members of the committee present should make the deficiency up themselves and the debt be paid accordingly.

WO November, 1887

The Bridge Over the River Colne

To the Editor of the Watford Observer.

Sir,—Let me endorse every word your correspondent "An old Inhabitant" writes on the subject of the bridge over the river Colne. If it really be the case that our Local Board intend to erect a foot-bridge by the side of the old one, I for one must raise my voice against any such "tinkering." Let our Board look the matter boldly in the face and set to work to provide a new bridge at once, such as your correspondent suggests. The cost would be nominal, with assistance from the County Authorities, which we might reasonably expect—a three-farthing rate would be ample. There are few in our town who would not give their cordial support to such an undertaking.

May I also ask when the sewer ventilators are to be removed? I understood the Board had arrived at a determination to this effect; if so, the delay is unpardonable. I would advise your readers particularly to avoid the gratings opposite Oxhey Church, the stench from these is abominable and undeniably dangerous to the number of people, particularly young children, who attend that church.

I am sir, your faithfully,
Another Inhabitant.
Watford, November 15th 1887.

Dinners for Poor Children

To the Editor of the Watford Observer.

Dear Sir,—During the winter of 1886-7 I was enabled through the benevolence of various donors to give dinners, at the school of cookery, for such children at the elementary schools as appeared most in want of nourishment, and whose parents were not in a position to provide them with sufficient food. The amount received was £20 19s. 6d. I have a balance of £1 0s. 8d. in hand. I propose to recommence what I look upon as a good charity as soon as I can make the necessary arrangements, and I shall be glad to receive subscriptions at the address below. I should like to add that preference is given to those children whose parents do not dissipate their earnings in drink, and that last winter we were enabled to provide nearly 2,000 dinners.

Faithfully yours,

Little Cassiobury, Watford,   Reg. Capell.
December 13th.

Allotment Gardens

Dear Sir,—I hope in the course of a week or so to mark out for allotment gardens a portion of the farm on the left of the St. Albans-road, now in the occupation of Mr. A .Johnstone, which that gentleman has most courteously allowed me to rent of him. The land is in good heart, and the rent will be to the tenants 6d. per pole, and the plots will be of about 10 poles each. Before finally settling with Mr. Johnstone, it is desirable I should know how many plots are likely to be taken up; and Mr. T. Turner (Cassiobury Saw Mills), has been so good as to say that applicants may register their names, etc., at his office. I hope this will be done at once. I subjoin the rules which have been in force in regard to the allotments on Harwoods Farm. They have worked well, and I propose to adopt the same for the Callow Land Allotment Gardens. Each tenant will have a copy, and will be required to sign a book, agreeing to abide by them before taking possession of his allotment.

Yours faithfully,

REG. CAPELL.

(1).   The rent of the allotments shall be at the rate of 6d. per pole per annum. All rents to be paid on the 25th March, 24th June, 29th September, 25th December in each year. Any tenant not paying his rent within seven days of the times stated shall be fined 3d.; if not within 14 days 6d., after which he shall be liable to be expelled,and to forfeit all crops on the ground.

WO January, 1888

● *In 1887 an Allotment Act empowered local Sanitary Authorities to provide allotments for the labouring classes—partly as a means of providing self-help for the unemployed. Sunday work on allotments was not to be allowed. Dr. Brett wrote "We the undersigned, being registered Parliamentary electors, residing in the Watford Urban Sanitary district, beg respectfully to submit to your Board that circumstances of the Urban District of Watford are such that it is the duty of the Authority to provide allotments for the inhabitants of the district and trust you will give the same your consideration" and appended signatures of 38 other gentlemen. The two questions to be answered were (a) was there a demand and (b) would allotments be found by voluntary arrangements.*

Vicar Reg. Capell was successful in obtaining land; and then there was later extensive discussions as to definition of 'labouring classes'. It was taken to include sedentary and shop workers so that these, too, could enjoy an 'open-air' activity.

Market Place c1887. Roger's on the left; Bucks & Oxon Bank (next to Roger's) has had a new imposing lower front installed since 1863. (p.45)   *p.115 tl*

Celebration arch across High Street from Clarendon Road Corner (Dudley's Corner) to Nos.40/42. *p.123 b*

Rickyard at Harwoods farm   1886

... anyone can go with a flock of sheep ... to sell them ...
... the market ... the stench they leave is not desirable ...

School of Music Examinations

Sir.—Has the idea ever occurred to the managing committee of the above excellent institution that the time allowed on an average for the study of vocal and instrumental pieces selected for competition at their annual examinations is scarcely sufficient for the thorough preparation of such works for instance as "Voi che capate" (Mozart), or Beethoven's "Sonata Pathetique." Works of such a high standard surely require more than three weeks' study to fit them for an examiner's ears. The committee are probably cognizant that the Royal Academy allows three or four months, and Trinity College likewise.

If you will kindly publish this plea for intending candidates at the next examination you will be sincerely thanked by

An Old Student.

WO March, 1887

Tenders for New Police Station

The following were the tenders for the New Police Station, now in course of erection in King-street:-

Haselgrove, W., Luton	£6475
Andrews and Sons, Watford	6275
White, John, Bedford	6185
Marriott Bros., High Barnet	6162
Grist, S., Aylesbury	6058
Ellwood and Son, Sandy	5990
Rhodes, W. A., London	5850
Willmott and Son, Hitchin	5846
Turner, Thos., Ltd., Watford	5839
Judge and Eames, Watford	5796
Miskin, Christr., St. Albans	5700
Bunting, Arthur, Fenstanton	5694
Dabbs, W. M., London	5580
Bonnett, S. T., Watford	5492
Waterman, G. and J., Watford	5396
Dupont, F., Colchester (accepted)	5185
Jarvis, Edwin, Banbury	5000

WO March, 1888

The Telephone Company & the Board

Dear Sir,—I have been somewhat surprised on several occasions to notice the opposition shown by the Local Board to all who wish to avail themselves of this most useful invention. It really seems their aim to suppress and retard by every means in their power any enterprise not immediately connected with their own body, whereas they should be the first to encourage anything which would advance the prosperity and trade of the town.

I trust it will not be very long before half our business houses in Watford will be connected with the London Exchange.

I am, dear sir, faithfully yours,
W. Pearkes.

THE South of England Telephone Company offer to connect their subscribers with a central office in Watford for £10 per annum. Mr. Henry Rogers, whose advertisement appears in the present issue, will supply telephones for short distances, including erection, at £3 17s. 6d., and for greater distance at £10, without any further payment whatever, this being at the same rate for the *entire purchase* as the Telephone Company charge *annually*. Mr. H. Rogers has recently fitted up telephonic communication between the central building at the St. Pancras schools and the Infirmary and other outlying offices, and is now engaged in telephonic work at Marlborough, Ballyclare, and other places.—[ADVT]

WO September, 1888

Watford Library—Newspapers

To the Editor of the Watford Observer.

Sir,—May I take up a few lines of your space to call the attention of the public to a mean act committed by some unknown person at the Public Library last Friday evening (February 3rd). The *Watford Observer* of February 4th had been on the table of the Public News Room but a short time when it was found that a letter had been cut therefrom. Probably the offender is not aware that upon conviction he would "be liable to be imprisoned for any term not exceeding six months, with or without hard labour." Such petty acts as these have not been unfrequent of late, and the Committee are thoroughly determined if possible to put a stop to them. A reward is offered to any person who shall give evidence leading to the conviction of offenders.

I am, sir, your obedient servant,
J. Woolman,
Watford Public Library,   Librarian.
February 8th, 1888.

J Woolman, Librarian

Moving the Market

The Chairman: In case we are compelled by the authorities to remove the market we may have certain compulsory powers; but you see that our idea as to what may be done is very vague.

Mr. S. Martin: I am in favour of removing the market, because it will remove the present nuisance. Outside the market place the beasts and sheep brought in are an abominable nuisance. Yesterday there was a flock of sheep along Dr. Brett's wall; there were more along the path for two hours outside Dr. Brett's house, and a flock outside my office, and the paths to-day are all left in the state they were when the cattle left. That I think shows the necessity for the removal of the market. I asked the question because I thought that if it were decided to buy this piece of land the remedy we wish to arrive at will be effected.

The Chairman: We cannot say the remedy will be effected until we get the power to remove the market; but if the Board had the premises and likewise the power to act as regards the market, we should of course issue rules for the regulation of it and prevent cattle and sheep, and what not, straying all over the place.

Mr. S. Martin: Then there is another question. What is the price asked for the land in question?

The Chairman: I do not think we need go into the price to-day, because when we come to the price we shall have to apply to a ratepayers' meeting of the whole Local Board district.

The Chairman: I can instance another place— the market at King's Lynn. They have there a very admirable cattle market, about 1½ acres, with iron pens and everything, and in an adjoining square dry goods and other things. I went through the cattle market a day or two after the market, and there was no smell whatever. The pitching is suited to the description of cattle which stand on it. The auctioneers go round to different pens, and the question of the lease-holder does not arise. It is absolutely an open market.

Mr. Austin: I do not think we require more room than we have already, if we find room for the cattle. I think we should spoil the trade of the town if we do not keep the rest of the market where it is now. Would Mr. Humbert move his cattle to his own land?

The Chairman: We cannot go into that. Mr. Humbert is not here. As leaseholder he could come here.

The Clerk: The difficulty would be this. If Mr. Humbert did move his sale, and the local Board had not acquired the rights, there would be nothing to prevent anyone else coming and selling in his place.

Mr. Austin: If the Local Board take it, cannot they be the master, as Mr. Humbert is?

The Clerk: Mr. Humbert is not the master. Mr. Humbert can take the toll of any person who comes into the market, but he has no exclusive right of selling. If an auctioneer claims a space he must find room for him. Anyone can go with a flock of sheep and claim a right to sell them in the market.

Dr. Brett: Has the Lord of the Manor a right to charge on Saturdays?

The Clerk: I am not prepared to answer that question.

The Chairman: Mr. Hoy asks the value of the tolls. According to the information given before the Commissioner they amount to £40 or £50 a year. He also asks what it will cost us for the market generally. It may surprise you to learn that it will cost about £5,000, taking it altogether. That is not saying anything about the site, but the general figure. If you have a general meeting of the ratepayers, which you can have as soon as you like, we shall be in a position to say exactly the price asked for the piece of ground and the quantity. Either we must make a friendly arrangement with Lord Essex or wait until we have compulsory powers. We have the lord to deal with and the lessee also.

Dr. Brett: I would rather hear other people speak their minds, but as I am called upon I will say something. I was asked what business I had here, because I do not live in the Market-place. I may say in justification that Colonel Ward's house is my property, and my children own a grocer's shop in the High-street, occupied by Mr. Bailey, and the baker's shop next it, so that I have a little interest in it.

I am old enough to recollect, and I daresay Mr. Hoy is, a place called Smithfield, where they used to have a cattle market, and it was found to be an intolerable nuisance to the London people; in our small way this is a second Smithfield. It is a nuisance from the cattle coming in, the smell, and the noise. I saw ladies rushing into Buck's shop yesterday, and although I am not much afraid of cattle, I had to stand by while the cattle passed me. As Mr. Martin has said, beasts and flocks of sheep stand in Clarendon-road, and the stench they leave is not desirable. I strongly object to the market being extended to our end of the town. If there were more room in the market-

Market Day. On the right No. 66 (the solicitors (Sedgwick, Turner and Walker), the Compasses, and then a small butcher's shop. Earlier this had belonged to Mr. Stone but Mr. Fisher had come to Watford in 1877 and bought the shop. He also owned the fields behind the shops. Auctioneer on his stand outside the Compasses has an almost entirely male audience. *p.164, 189, 324 t.* c1885

place trade would be increased; there really is not room for the beasts and cattle.

I think that the quadrupeds ought to be removed to some more convenient place where there is room for them. It is cruel to the poor animals, and I am sure that it is a nuisance to health. I need not repeat what I said at the enquiry, which was that the smell remains from week to week. Though the place is washed down, you can see pools of coloured liquid, apparently stinking urine. Mr. Williams and I do not quite agree as to the cause of the nuisance: he will tell you presently, if he is asked, that it is owing to horses. I am not skilful enough to tell the difference, but I know that the result of the accumulation of the droppings of swine and other animals is very bad. If you have cattle, you should have impervious material, which can be washed down like a slaughter house and leave no remains whatever. If you look at the Market-place you see pitching of various kinds—big stones which you could put your thumb between, and the urine and excreta get between them and cause a nuisance. In some places there are bricks and in others gravel. Mr. Humbert said that he had put 15 loads of gravel down lately. But if you make a farmyard with a gravel bottom, whenever you wash it you wash it further in. I do think that it would be for the advantage of the town and trade of Watford to take the quadrupeds from the Market-place. I think that the Board of Health ought to aim to make the town attractive—make it a residential place. There is no doubt that Watford might be made a place that people would think it an honour and privilege to live in. We have the soil, the country; every day in the week you can walk into a fresh park.

We all agree that to have a market in a town like this of very great value to us; it brings many people to the town, and it is of money value to us. No one wants to do away with the market, but the trade has increased so much that there is not space enough to do the business. If you have space for ten times as much the business of the market would be ten times as big, and bring ten times as many people to increase the trade of Watford. If you get rid of the quadrupeds in the street you will have more business done. It will improve the old market-place, and I think after first buying it you will make it pay, because when you get the tolls you can charge sufficient to compensate for the outlay. I think that it would be a good sound transaction.

The Clerk: I was asked as to the power of the Local Board with the view to acquiring the market. I think that it will be convenient to answer it to this extent at the present moment— that the Local Board can only acquire the market by consent, but I think we have every reason to believe that they will have compulsory powers within a very limited time. I think the question is this. If it is thought generally desirable to remove the cattle and sheep from the market place, is it not desirable before the opportunity passes to get a piece of the only land in the immediate neighbourhood of the market? If you can get it on fair terms, is it not desirable to get it? If then, going to Lord Essex and Mr. Humbert, they do not see their way to give you terms which are reasonable, you will only have to wait one or two sessions, when the Local Board, or the District Council it may be, their successors, will have power to take the market on fair terms. Perhaps I may state that Mr. Fisher—I am not divulging anything by saying this—has given us the refusal of the property until the 31st October. (Applause.) I think that we should move rapidly and make up our minds.

WO October, 1888

Watford Market

To the Editor of the Watford Observer.

Dear Sir,—Can you, through the medium of your paper, inform me who is responsible for the obstruction to trade and a nuisance to the people in upper High-street, on market days? Yesterday there was a large flock of sheep from 12 until 4 o'clock all over the road and on the pavement in front of my steps, close to the windows. It was impossible for vehicles to get near, and also most difficult for foot passengers to pass. I spoke to the owner of the cattle, and he, in a very abrupt manner said "I pay toll for them," and that I could have my remedy.

Is the Lord of the manor, the Local Board, or is Mr. Humbert responsible for this nuisance that is taking place every Tuesday. I maintain that those who receive the tolls should be compelled at once to find a proper place for the cattle; and not to be the means of sending customers away on market days.

I am sir, respectfully yours,
Watford,   Walter Allen.
Wednesday, October 31st, 1888.

Population 1888, c15,000

The new Police Station in King Street. Once or twice a year the Watford Observer would publish a woodcut or engraving of a notable building recently erected—the total extent of editorial illustration until the advent of reproduction direct from photographs in another year or two. Jan 1889. (Since 1962, the Robert Peel public house).

p.286 b

Conservative Club

The following are the tenders for the new building; architect, W. H. Syme, A.R.I.B.A.; clerk of works, H. S. Allen:—

Jones, F. C.	£3135
Sear, G.	£2300
Neal, W. B.	£2154
Waterman, T.	£2057
Sear, N. and E.	£2050
Turner, T. (accepted)	£1959

The new building will be ready for use in the early part of January.

WO September, 1888

Nets Needed

The 93rd Highlanders proved far too strong for the Watford Rovers, who went to pieces and were beaten by five to love.

The Scots played well together, especially in the back division. They were stronger than when the Rovers played such an even game with them before, but this severe defeat can only be accounted for from the fact that the "laddies" were "on the ball" and the Rovers were not.

The soldiers were unnecessarily rough, and one or two would doubtless have been ordered off the field by an Association referee. The 93rd are ordered to proceed to India shortly, so that the return match is hardly likely to come off.

The Rovers should secure official umpires and referee in their important matches, and thus avoid that abominable wrangling which has been too rife of late.

Surely some of the team must have known that the shot by the left wing at the outset scored a fair goal. It is a strong argument for goal nets.

WO (February, 1891)

The British Workman

To the Editor of the Watford Observer.

Dear Sir.—Will you kindly allow me a small space in your valuable columns to condemn a system practised by some of our prominent builders of Watford. We have seen of late many reports that have been made, showing how some of the largest business firms in the country grind down the workman to obtain the largest amount of labour at the least possible cost, thus depriving the working man of the privilege of having a fair day's pay for a fair day's work. As a working man, in speaking for myself I am speaking for my fellow workmen, that by a system of sub-contracting, or sweating, we are deprived of our just rights and privileges. Why are master builders distrustful of their men; why are we treated like a lot of slaves? For the purpose of lining the builder's pocket to the tune of 20 to 25 per cent. And what are our advantages? As soon as the builder can see the summer gone the men are discharged, possibly to lay out of work the greatest part of the winter; and what does that mean? Starvation. Then we are told if we ask for relief that we should look after a rainy day when in full work in the summer, and we ought not to want. Further, are we being fairly treated when we can hear of one of our employers trying to influence the other builders to cease building in winter, and also inducing them to let all their work, telling them he had done so, and it would be a saving of 20 per cent., and it mattered not to him what became of the men in winter? We all want to live, we want the confidence of the employers, we do not want charity, we want to earn what we get, but under the pressure of our friends'(?) influence with those we have to depend on mainly for our support we are having our bread taken from us, and it is time the working men in the building trade became alive to the tricks that are used to steal from them the privileges they should justly claim. Believe me to be

Yours obediently,
A Working Man.

WO October, 1888

The Coat-of-Arms For Watford

Dear Sir,—As we have now a coat-of-arms for Watford, I thought it might interest your readers to know the history of the movement. The idea of having a coat-of-arms for Watford originated with the Committee of the Library about seven years ago, so we cannot be accused of being rash and precipitate. When I was Chairman to the Library for the first three years, my years of office were rewarded by seeing the foundation stone of the Library building laid with Masonic honours, and the opening of it by the Lord Lieutenant, the Earl of Verulam. I am anxious that my second chairmanship shall be distinguished by clearing off two works that have been on the stocks many years—namely, the coat-of-arms for Watford, and the enlargement of the Library. We have obtained the first, and I trust we shall accomplish the second as soon as the turmoil of the County Council election is over. I should like to be permitted to explain why I have had to take a prominent part in this matter. I saw how desirable it would be to have some device for our work in the Library, in our certificates of merit, and for our books. The same is wanted much for the Endowed Schools. The Committee requested me, some years since, to obtain the opinion of those who were learned in heraldry or in mottoes, or who had artistic taste.

I need not trouble your readers with the details of the work we have had in Watford, at the British Museum, and elsewhere. I should like to mention that thanks are due for suggestions and for information to the following among many others:—The members of the Library Committee in general, and the Rev. Newton Price in particular, who is sponsor for the motto, "*Audentior*"; the Earl of Essex; the Earl of Clarendon; the Master of the Rolls (Lord Esher); the Hon. Arthur Capell; Mr. John Evans (the Treasurer of the Royal Society); Mr. Thomas Woods, of Durrants Farm; Mr. Henry Finch, J.P., Red Heath; Dr. Puckett, our Art Master, who took great trouble: the Vicar; Mr Charles Healey the First; Mr. Clement Heaton, and many others. The above are not responsible for the design at last adopted. I hope some day to send to your Notes and Queries columns an explanation of the coat-of-arms when time permits.

I remain, your obedient servant,
ALFRED THOMAS BRETT.

WO December, 1888

1888—A Car

In Germany Karl Benz's petrol-driven internal-combustion engined car went on sale. During the next five years 69 would be made and sold!

John Boyd Dunlop has produced a pneumatic bicycle tyre with separate air-filled inner tube.

. . . good gravel well laid, pleasant to walk upon . . .

The Roads and Footpaths

To the Editor of the Watford Observer.

Sir,—I beg you will afford me a small space in your paper for what I venture to term a public grievance in Watford, and from the remarks I hear on all sides I am confident that almost every one, whether resident or a visitor, is of the same opinion. I am referring to the state of the public roads and footpaths in the town, and am in hope that the members of our Local Board will themselves look into these matters and remedy the defects which so painfully force themselves upon our notice. When a road is relaid or repaired, the system, or want of system, in Watford, seems to be to spread over the surface a thick layer of stone, chiefly pebbles and flints—very good material for road making,—and then leave it to its own devices, or to be trodden and worn down by general traffic. The stones are never properly broken, numerous lumps are left as big or bigger than a large man's fist, which always remain as stumbling-blocks long after the rest has been worn down. It may be noted also that the centre of the road is hardly raised higher than the sides, and the ordinary traffic quickly pushes the loose stones from the centre to the side, so that by the time the road is worn a little smooth, its centre is on a level or even lower than the sides. It is said that the Local Board possess rollers and even use them, but one seldom has the good fortune to see them in this part of the town—St. Andrew's district. The stones are left loose on the roads for days and weeks to the great annoyance and detriment of the public, and if eventually the roller is employed it is too late, for the ballast has been displaced to the sides and the road is hollowed out in the centre and can never become either good or lasting. Everyone knows that the stones should be broken to a suitable size, and that directly they are laid, if there is no rain, they should be well watered and at once rolled, and it would pay well to use a steam roller.

Now for the footpaths, which are if possible worse than the roads. I would not myself wish to see pavement or asphalte, except in the main streets where there are shops, as gravel looks nicer, and good gravel well laid and properly rolled makes a good smooth path and pleasant to walk on, as one has in one's own garden, but the paths in Watford are infamous, and it is simply cruel to ask people to use them. They appear to be made of a sort of coarse shingly gravel, at least this is what always appears on the surface, and when laid they are neither watered nor rolled, and in consequence they are always either a surface of loose rough stone in dry weather, or of soft mud in wet. The badness of the roads and paths in Watford is a bye-word, and they are a disgrace to a civilised community. It would be absurd to say that they cannot be made properly. The Local Board can and ought to command the requisite technical knowledge and skill, but I have no hesitation in saying that any amateur would be ashamed to turn out such roads as we have to put up with. Again, as ratepayers we have a right to complain, as our money is being wasted, and not only have we to put up with disgracefully bad roads, but the roads only last half as long as they would if properly made, and are consequently far more expensive in the long run. In the interests then of the public, of their cattle, and of their poor feet, I call upon the Local Board and their agents to mend their ways.

Yours faithfully,
A Long-Sufferer.
Watford, October 10th, 1888.

Stephen Camp

At a distribution of prizes of the Literary Institute in 1871 Stephen Camp broached the subject of establishing a Public Library and Reading Room; the sequel was that a Building Committee was appointed by the Institute and this led to the building of the Public Library and School of Science and Art in 1874.

The Technical Instruction Act

A letter to the board:

Watford, 31st December, 1889.

Gentlemen,—In response to the invitation to the ratepayers, I for one would protest against the adoption at present of this Act.

Watford is not a manufacturing town, or noted for any special industry, and therefore the trade of the place would not be more prosperous if you could train up a few special local workmen, however distinguished they might become.

It would, I submit, be an act of injustice to tax all the ratepayers for the benefit of a few.

In a leader in the *Times* a few days ago it was said, "Polytechnics are excellent things, but it is not certain that they will succeed when they are directed exclusively by a class above the persons who use them. Mechanics' institutions of the latter kind are a declared failure because they were managed not by the mechanics, but for them, while on the other hand the self-governing institutes and clubs in Lancashire and Yorkshire, in which the men, women, and boys feel their personal honour to be involved are a conspicuous success."

Let those who want Technical Education in Watford pay for it. If they could get it for nothing they would regard it generally as worth what it cost.

Whether you get many communications or only a few on this subject, depend upon it there will be a great outcry, as there was against the adoption of the Libraries' Act, if the Board in the exercise of their powers make a penny rate or apply a sum equal thereto for the purposes of the Technical Education Act. Increased rents and increased rates are a burden which some of the tradesmen in Watford may find it difficult to cope with, and the Local Board will not contribute unnecessarily to the latter.

Yours obediently,
Stephen Camp.

Technical Instruction Act

Watford House

Gentlemen,—I wish to thank you for allowing me and other ratepayers to express an opinion upon the desirability of our adopting this Act in Watford.

I am strongly in favour of adopting the Act because I think it is capable of doing great good (if properly managed), and it may in the end decrease our rates.

It is not quite clear to me how best to carry out the Act.

It seems that the Science and Art Department is charged with it. I find that there are two institutions in Watford working in conjunction with South Kensington—the Watford Public Library and the Endowed Schools. I am informed that the grant obtained last year from South Kensington by the Endowed Schools (Boys) was £86 12s., I think by the Library £9, so that the boys schools do ten times the science work of the library, at least they got ten times the reward.

Under these circumstances, as I presume the governors of the Endowed Schools would be represented in the new Board of Management of the Technical Instruction Act, if the Governors could assist in carrying out the Technical Instruction Act for the benefit of the town, I think I may say they would willingly do so. Some plan might be devised that would obtain the help of both the educational institutions—the Watford Endowed Schools and the Watford Public Library. I enclose you a list of the subjects taught at the Endowed Schools.

I need not remind you that the Board of Health is represented on the Board of Managers of the Endowed Schools. Mr. J. J. Smith is your nominee.

I remain,
Your obedient servant,
Alfred T. Brett.

N.B.—The above remarks are made as a private ratepayer. I alone am responsible for the opinions.

WO January, 1890

To the Editor of the Watford Observer.

Sir,—I think the thanks of the ratepayers and the working men are due to our townsman, Mr. Camp, for his outspoken letter to the Watford Local Board. As to technical instruction, there is no doubt that it would be a great hardship to many. Supposing it could be carried out as it has been in Germany, what would it do? Cheapen the price of labour and so become a curse to the working man. If a trade is worth learning, it is worth paying for. Is it for the benefit of the working man? No, most certainly not; it is for the middle and upper classes. When the Public Library was first talked about, it was said what a good thing it would be for the working man. What do we hear now about the working man? Nothing. What we want is a public meeting in the Corn Exchange, not at the Liberal Club or at any other club. This is not a political question; it is a question of pounds, shillings and pence. It is also a question to me whether we should not be pauperising the upper classes in doing for them what they can do for themselves. If these penny rates go on they will soon be not penny, but shilling rates.

Yours, &c.,
A Ratepayer
(Who has paid to learn his Trade).
Watford.

WO January, 1890

At the corner of Derby Road/Queens Road a temporary Post Office was built in 1885. The horse-drawn Royal Mail Parcel Coach ran every night to London until 1908 when it was superseded by a motor van. Site of the photograph, Queens Road, across Derby Road. *p.352 t*

Watford Time

To the Editor of the Watford Observer.

Dear Sir,–Please allow me through the medium of your journal—only it is a weekly—to call attention to the somewhat serious discrepancies between the several prominent clocks in Watford. The other day I had the curiosity to compare my watch with the following clocks:–Morse's, Sims's, Judge's, and the outside and inside of the Post Office. Not one of them coincided. The time at which I did this was just after 10 o'clock, at which time I believe the clocks are supposed to be set. This is the result in a tabulated form:–

By Judge's I was	3	minutes slow
By Morse's I was	2½	minutes slow
By Sims's I was	2¼	minutes slow
By Inside Post Office I was	½	minute slow
By Outside Post Office I was	¼	minute slow.

That is to say that at 10 by my watch the mean time by these clocks was 1¾ minutes past. The difference is in some cases not very great, but as "an inch is a good deal on a nose," so is a quarter of a minute to train time. I have several times missed trains by a quarter of a minute, just because I was relying on one clock. Can anyone suggest a remedy for this? I should think that if the clock owners were to have a meeting every morning there might be some chance of, say two, coinciding, but that is hardly practicable. Thanking you in anticipation for inserting this,

I remain,
Yours in doubt as to what the time is,
Tempus

Watford, July 18th, 1889.

Keeping a Dog Without a Licence

John Whiteby pleaded guilty to keeping a dog without a licence, at Bushey, on June 20th.

Police-constable Reeves, S.604, said that a boy told him that he had been bitten by a dog chained up at the rear of the defendant's premises. He made inquiries and found that the dog had got loose and bitten the boy. The defendant said that he had not had the dog long, and he was about to take out a licence. He found that that statement was true. The defendant had since taken out a licence.

The Chairman said that it was clear the defendant had infringed the law, but looking at the short time he had had the dog they did not think that he intended to defraud the revenue. He would therefore only be fined 6d., with the costs 6s. 6d. The Chairman intimated to the police that in such cases they should see that the person without a licence took one out at once instead of being immediately summoned.

WO

The Post

At the beginning of the present century, c1800, the Post Office was kept in Butcher's Yard, opposite the 'Green Man'—and the cost of a letter to London was eleven pence. Next, it removed to a house nearly opposite Water Lane, and thence to Mr. Johnson at 87 High Street, later Coffee Tavern, then to a shop at the bottom of Carey Place. At this time the number of letters per day was around 30 or 40, the postman receiving 7 shillings a week for his labours.

From Carey Place the next move was to a shop in the High Street opposite King Street *(later Boots, later Ketts),* under the care of Mr. Morley. After an increase of business it was moved to a house built by Mr. Morley in Queen's Road but this also was outgrown. A site was purchased of Messrs. Watermans Brothers at the junction of Queen's Road and Derby Road and a new office built; there are, in addition, three other receiving houses and nine pillar and wall boxes. Ten persons are employed at the chief Post Office besides the Post Master.

William's 'History of Watford'

The WATFORD OBSERVATORY
QUEEN'S ROAD,
Facing the Public Library.

MORSE,
WATCH AND CLOCK MAKER,
JEWELLER, &c.

GREENWICH TIME BY TRANSIT OBSERVATION.

"The Patent Dust Proof Watch has been awarded the ONLY Medal for Perfect Cases, Inventions Exhibition, 1885."

Of B. S. MORSE *only* in WATFORD.

As part of the Bedfordshire Wesleyan circuit an early meeting place in 1813 in Watford was a room in Hedges Yard. Mr. Edmonds, tinman, was responsible for building a chapel in Water Lane in 1814/15 and in June 1889 this Wesleyan Church in Queens Road, corner of Derby Road, was opened.

Post Office staff c1890. Mr. J. Morley, Postmaster, and to his right Mr. J. H. Morley, chief clerk. The bicycles are fitted with the new invention, the pneumatic tyre, and direct-acting brakes work on the tyre.

In 1888 Francis Fisher had his two small cottage/shops (Nos. 74 & 76) demolished and the town's most impressive commercial premises built on the site. In the following year his former premises, between the Compasses and Rose and Crown, were demolished so creating an opening for a thoroughfare to connect the High Street with Merton Road, which at that time ran off from Vicarage Road into open fields. The new road was called Market Street. *p.335 tl* **1889**

Market Street

The land behind the 'Rose & Crown' was a sort of general-purpose hinterland, having upon it playing fields and being used as short cuts from the High Street to Merton and Vicarage Roads. Stone's Alley joined up with what is now Cassio Road and continued to Harwood's Farm and thence across fields to Cassio Bridge. The opening of Market Street was an event of considerable importance as it provided an eventual 'West Watford' link. In its early days the road took some degree of precedence in pavement make-up, much to the annoyance of residents in established parts of town not so well looked after.

Sales by Auction

Important Sale of unusually well-placed Freehold Building Land, being the first portion of the ROSE AND CROWN ESTATE, with immediate communication from the centre of the HIGH STREET, WATFORD, HERTS.

MESSRS. HUMBERT, SON & FLINT Are instructed by the owner to Sell by Auction, at the Rose and Crown Hotel, Watford, ON TUESDAY, THE 18th OF JUNE, 1889, at 5 o'clock precisely,
74 PLOTS of very valuable FREEHOLD BUILDING LAND, having frontages to the new roads now in course of completion, and suitable for the erection of good shops, and large residences. Many of the plots are within a few yards of the Market-place and High-street of Watford, seven minutes' walk from the railway station, and offering in every way exceptional and unusual advantages for the acquiring of freehold building land which will undoubtedly increase in value. The Estate stands on an elevated and dry site, with a valuable gravel subsoil. Gas and water mains will be laid in the roads, and the drainage connected with the main sewer, junctions being placed ready to connect with the various plots.

Particulars, plans, and conditions of sale may be obtained at the principal hotels and inns in the neighbourhood; of Messrs. Sedgwick, Turner and Walker, solicitors, 66, High-street, Watford; of Mr. C. P. Ayres, architect, 52 High-street, Watford; and of Messrs. Humbert, Son & Flint, land agents, auctioneers and surveyors, Watford, Herts, and 11, Serle-street, Lincoln's Inn, W.C.

Tenders.— The following tenders have been received for pulling down Nos. 74 and 76, High-street Watford, and erecting new house, shop, and slaughter-house for Mr. Francis Fisher. Mr. Charles P. Ayres, 52, High-street, Watford, architect:—

Brightman, C.	£2699
Judge and Eames	£2687
Andrews and Sons	£2678
Dove, H. M.	£2575
Turner, T. (Limited)	£2447
Neal, W. B.	£2397
Waterman, G. & J. (accepted)	£2337

WO May, 1888

The Rose and Crown still shows evidence of demolished butcher's shop; after this the Rose and Crown itself underwent a period of extensive rebuilding. The field behind, known as Rose and Crown field, was used by local schools and the town football team.

p.170 b, 324 c   **1889**

Result of Auction

MESSRS. HUMBERT, SON & FLINT

Mr. Humbert first put up the shop plots, pointing out their value, being in the centre of the town and close to the Market-place. The plots were small to suit purchasers, and it had been said that they were too small, but if they were two could be had. Four plots might be bought and three houses put upon them, or three plots and two houses built; but, he said in answer to a query, three plots would not be sold to put four houses on. There was no other building land for sale in Watford, and as was no doubt well known, the last sold, only a few weeks ago, fetched a very high price, £9 a foot frontage. Messrs. Andrews, who were always lucky, for whatever they touched seemed to turn to gold, were about the only holders of building land in the neighbourhood. No doubt they would want £5 or £6 a foot if they were asked. (Mr. John Andrews: We have none to sell.) He should not sell if he were them. Therefore the only land for sale was the Rose and Crown Estate.

The first bid for the shop lots was £70, then £80, the amount afterwards rising by biddings of £1 to £91, and lots 4 and 5 were taken at that price; the next two at £85; the next two at £88; lot 10 at £89; lot 11, £88; 12 and 13 at £87; 14 and 15 at £95; 16 at £92; 17 and 18 at £96; 19, 20, 21 and 22, at £85; 23 and 24 at £86. Lot 38 was then put up, and as biddings were slow, Mr. Humbert announced that though the price required was £88 a plot £80 would be taken for that day only up to lot 45. Proceeding then to the plots abutting upon Stone's-alley, the whole, from 93 to 103 were soon disposed of at about £90 each. Several of the plots between Marlborough-road

and Percy-road were then sold, the first price being £55, and the others being offered at £54, except the corner plots. The corner plot in Percy-road was sold, with the adjoining plot, for £132; that in Marlborough-road, with the next plot, for £160. The plots 199 to 210 were then offered at £70 a plot, 211 and 212 having been sold at that price. The number of plots sold was 47, the total sum realised being £3,096, the average being £83 per plot. The lots unsold are for sale by private treaty.

Rose and Crown Building Land

THE first offer by public auction of the freehold land on the Rose and Crown estate, belonging to Mr. Francis Fisher, took place on Tuesday, after the market. It is many years since land so near the centre of the town has been offered for building.

The principal street laid out, which has been named Market-street, opens directly from the Market-place, by the removal of the premises formerly occupied by Mr. Fisher (and in years gone by Mr. G. Stone) as a butcher's shop. The opening has on one side the Rose and Crown Hotel, which is being in great part rebuilt, and on the other the Compasses Inn.

In pulling down Mr. Fisher's premises the old wall of the house which is now the Compasses is exposed, and a quaint old window of the upstairs room has come to light just at the corner of the new street, showing that the gateway which adjoined had not always been built over.

Turning out of Market-street, which continues in a straight line until it opens into Merton-road on the far side of the estate, is, first, Marlborough-road, which, turning to the left, and running almost parallel with the old way known as Stone's-alley, runs into the old way across Monks Folly, or the continuation of Merton-road, leading to Park-road. Percy-road comes next, connecting Market-street, at somewhere about half its length, with Francis-road a street which leaves Market-street near the Merton-road end, and goes parallel with the old way to Marlborough-road. Mr. C. R. Humbert has purchased a good piece of the land between Stone's-alley and Marlborough-road for his sale yard, and a smaller piece adjoining is held for a similar purpose by Mr. H. B. Didsbury.

Between Marlborough-road and Percy-road a site, with a frontage also to Market-street, has been purchased for a Roman Catholic church. Then the rest of the estate is laid out in plots, with the exception of the frontage along the old way across Monks Folly (the Allotment Gardens). The whole has been laid out under the direction of Mr. C. P. Ayres, surveyor.

The sale took place in the Corn Exchange, in consequence of the building going on at the Rose and Crown Hotel.

WO June, 1889

Sequah was a travelling showman and in May 1890 he visited Watford where he held a meeting on the Rose and Crown ground which had been partly laid out for the building of Market Street and adjoining roads. The houses in the background are of Merton Road and the block to the right of the row became the site of the Empire cinema which opened in November 1913.

Although a number of plots were sold at the first auction in 1889, progress was slow and a second auction was held in 1890. The gravel-like line just above the heads of the crowd is the laid-out line of Percy Road, the photograph was taken near the site of the Holy Rood Church.

Sales by Auction

Sale of very Desirable Freehold Property, comprising 3 Shops and 7 Cottages, the whole producing £135 per annum.

HIGH STREET, WATFORD.

MESSRS. HUMBERT, SON & FLINT

Are instructed to Sell by Auction, at the Rose and Crown Hotel, Watford, on Tuesday, 9th July, 1889, at 5 O'clock precisely, in lots, the FREEHOLD BUSINESS PREMISES, having a frontage of about 41 feet to the High-street, Watford, and a depth of about 300 feet, well situated for business purposes and adjacent to the Market-place. The property comprises a butcher's shop and dwelling house, let to Mr. Watkins on lease, at the annual rent of £30, house and shop let to Mr. Eves on lease, at the annual rent of £23, and house and shop let to Mr. Ellis, as a yearly tenant, at the annual rent of £19 19s. 0d. There are also 7 cottages, with out-houses and laundry, let to weekly tenants at 3s. 6d per week. The property is situated in a most convenient position for business purposes, opposite the entrance to Queen's-road from the High-street, and with the increasing value of High-street property it offers a very secure and remunerative investment.

The New Catholic Church

The tender of Messrs. T. Turner, Limited, has been accepted for the erection of the new Catholic Church, which is to stand in Market-street, with return frontages in Marlborough-road and Percy-road; Mr. John F. Bentley, of John-street, Adelphi, being the architect.

The church will be in the late perpendicular style, and its outer walls will abut directly upon the three streets, without an intervening fence. The exterior facing will be of dressed flint, with stone quoins, windows, buttresses, &c. The main roofs will be tiled, and twin turrets springing from the chancel piers will surmount the whole. The plan shows a chancel 35 feet long, a nave 65 feet long by 25 wide, three chapels, two transepts, three aisles and a baptistry, of which rather more than half will be built now at a cost of just over £4,000. There will be a rood and rood loft, and its treatment, as well as that of the baptistery, the pulpit, and a double arcade and tritorium round the chancel, will be very picturesque. The tracing in the windows will also be noticeable. A clergy house will be erected next to the church, and behind this will stand the schools, while close by, the sisters, who undertake the education of the children, have secured a site for their house.

It is expected that Cardinal Manning will very shortly lay the foundation stone, and Messrs. Turner have undertaken to finish their contract by the end of February, so that the church may be consecrated upon Lady-day, 1890.

WO, July 1889.

● *Messrs T. Turner Ltd. were the owners of Cassiobury Saw Mills of St. Albans Road. The church was completed in 1897 at a cost of £20,000.*

WATFORD LOCAL BOARD.

NOTICE.

THE BOARD HEREBY GIVE NOTICE

That on and after the 1st day of AUGUST, 1890,

PROCEEDINGS will be taken against all Persons

Who, to the obstruction, annoyance, or danger of the residents or passengers,

Place or Leave any Furniture, Goods, Wares, or Merchandise, or any Cask, Tub, Basket, Pail, or Bucket, or who Place or Use any Standing Place, Stool, Bench, Stall, or Showboard on any Footway in the District of the Board, on any day of the week.

NO EXCEPTION IS MADE AS TO TUESDAY OR SATURDAY.

Dated this 17th day of July, 1890.

66, High-street, Watford.

By order,
H. M. TURNER,
Clerk.

Local Board Meeting, February 1890

●*Local Board meetings, in a room at the pumping station in Local Board Road, were almost invariably concerned with 'street' affairs; paving, cleanliness (or lack of), drainage, lighting, etc. This report is therefore little different to many others. The Medical Officer of Health's report is in its brief entirety and deals with the town's health very succinctly. It also is quite typical.*

Local Board

The usual meeting of the Board was held on Thursday. There were present Mr. E. J. Slinn (Chairman), Mr. C. P. Ayres, Mr. J. Weall, Mr. H. Thomas, Mr. E. Mead, Mr. J. C. Benskin, Mr. E. Clifford, and Mr. J. Andrews.

The Market Place

A letter from Messrs. Humbert, Son, and Flint, said that they had considered the request by the Local Board that they should pay 6s. a week for cleansing the Market-place instead of the sum they now pay. Inasmuch as paying for the cleansing at all was purely a voluntary act, they hardly thought that the Board should have requested them to pay a further sum. However, as the Board had done so, and they were anxious to fall in with their views, they would agree to pay the 6s. a week from the 26th March next. But they would like it to be understood that it was a voluntary matter on their part; they did not admit their liability to contribute towards the cleaning of the Market-place.

The Board received the following letter:–
"Elmleigh, Watford,
"January 28th, 1890.

"Dear Sir,–There is an old saying that "lookers see most of the game," and I trust you will allow me to bring to the notice of the Board a few matters that I think if properly attended to would conduce most materially to the comfort and convenience of the inhabitants of Watford. In the first place crossings are absolutely needed in very many of the streets and roads, particularly at the crossing of the St. Albans-road at the end of Langley-road, also from Mr. Dell's in the St. Albans-road to Mr. Cocks's premises, again in the neighbourhood of Queen's-road, Sotheron-road, &c., which is a much used thoroughfare into the town, three or four are required, and I have no doubt there are several other places where they are wanted. I hear that two or three 'carriage people' do not want them, as they say the springs of their conveyances suffer, but even if they did, surely the convenience of the few should not prevail against that of the many? But I have yet to learn that crossings, if properly laid down in the first instance and kept in good repair do occasion any appreciable damage or inconvenience even to the few, and if the Surveyor to the Board cannot keep them in order it is time that there should be someone who can. A great portion of the benefit derived from our new paths is done away with, when having to cross the road in wet weather you have to do it through a sea of mud. I am glad to see that one of the members of your Board, Mr. Thomas, has drawn attention to the way our roads are made. It is a source of amusement to me in my peregrinations to see the manner in which *green* stone is put on the roads, and then scraped up again in the shape of mud a few days after, and I often have a little chaff with an old friend of mine in this neighbourhood who is entrusted with the aforesaid scraping, as to

how long it takes him to get all the new material off again. Surely if we must have gravel roads there is some place where it can be exposed to the action of the sun and air before it is laid on. Strongly as I am opposed to adding to the rates for the new fad of technical education, I should be inclined to favour it if I thought that our Surveyor would become a pupil and learn the art of practical road and path making. Before closing this letter, I should like to ask when the residents in Church and Park-roads are likely to get their new paving? The first of these roads is very thickly populated, and the residents have, together with those of Park-road, paid rates and taxes for the last 25 or 30 years, yet I see mushroom streets that have only been called into existence the last two or three years have got their pavements, whilst these two are out in the cold. By all means let new streets be properly paved, but do not neglect the old ones because they have no one on the Board specially interested in them. I trust that we shall not be put off again on the ground that the money will be wanted in the shape of a technical education rate.
"Yours truly,
"Josceline F. Watkins."

Mr. Clifford: That's a scorcher!

Mr. Thomas: But there is a good deal of truth in it.

The Surveyor: And there is a good deal that is not true. We have not been putting "green" gravel on the roads.

The Chairman: Then we refer the Surveyor's report and Mr. Watkins's letter to the Highway Committee?

Mr. Mead: I propose that it should be dealt with to-day.

Mr. Benskin seconded.

Mr. Thomas said that it was a question for the future, not for this year, and he moved that it be referred to the Committee.

Mr. Ayres seconded.

The question having been put, Mr. Thomas's amendment was carried.

Numbering Houses

A letter from Dr. Brett was read asking the Board to have the houses in the different streets properly numbered, and pointing out the inconvenience of the present irregularity of numbering some streets.

It was resolved to instruct the Inspector to report.

The Lighting at Watford Junction

A letter from the London and North-Western Railway Company in reply to one from this Board was read, stating that enquiry had been made into this matter, and it was found that the Company had five gas lamps in front of the station, which were amply sufficient for all purposes in connection with the railway. Doubtless the open space in front of the station was inadequately lighted when the lights of the Malden and Clarendon Hotels were extinguished, but that was a question for the Local Board to deal with, and there were no grounds for calling upon the Company.

The Chairman said that the Company had five lamps there, but as a rule only two were lighted.

The Public Lighting

A letter from Mr. J. C. Binyon was read, asking whether we were really to go through the winter without light at night; if not, the sooner we got lanterns and hung them on the lamp-posts the better. Watford was supposed to be a flourishing

town, and yet was compelled by this Board to go back to the days of the curfew to save a few pounds.

The Chairman said that in putting out the lamps he thought they had begun at the wrong time of the year; it would do perfectly well in May, June, and July.

Mr. Clifford said that he could see that now, and he thought it desirable to make an alteration, that six weeks before and six weeks after the longest day they should not light the lamps at all.

The Chairman said that the saving from not having the lamps lighted would be very small indeed, but he thought that instead of at once proposing that they should not light them for six weeks before and six weeks after the longest day, they should use the time between now and next May in thinking out the best way of acting. He thought it was certainly the wish of the town that the lamps should be lighted now; the feeling was certainly in favour of continuing the old scale.

Mr. Clifford said that a lot of people were in favour of putting out the lamps early, and they asked him not to let the new arrangement be altered; but there were many people whose business began early in the morning who felt very great inconvenience, and so, having considered the matter further, he thought they ought to have the light.

Mr. Savil said that the memorial to the Board was signed by 157 inhabitants, most of the tradespeople.

Mr. Clifford said that people were asked to put down their names to that memorial whether they were ratepayers or not. What reply had been received in answer to their letter to the Gas Company?

The Clerk said that they had had no reply.

The Chairman said that looking at the number of personal applications he had, he thought that they ought to deal with the matter at once.

Mr. Benskin said that so far as he was concerned, he had a great many more come to him and express themselves in favour of his resolution, than he had people expostulating with him for it.

The Chairman thought they must be people who went to bed early and got up late.

Mr. Benskin said that he was told by a gentleman who goes up to London at 8 o'clock in the morning that all the clerks who go from Bushey agreed with his proposition.

Mr. Clifford said that he thought they had made a little error in beginning now.

Mr. Benskin said that from figures he had obtained from Mr. Rowell, the secretary to the Gas Company, he found that the total amount expended by the Board on gas in the six months of the summer of 1886 was £159, and the total amount in the two winter quarters was £447. Last year they carried out a proposition he made that the lamps should be extinguished at 1 o'clock, and this year, he not being present at the Board meeting, they went back to the old scale, and spent £113 6s. 9d. in three months. They could only save about £20 in the summer months if they put the lamps out for three months, on the figures of 1886, whereas in the winter months, if they put them out as they did at Rickmansworth and Hemel Hempstead, they could save upwards of £200.

Medical Officer of Health's Report for 1889

Paving

Mr. Andrews said that he believed loans for Hobman's paving had been made for ten years. Referring to the report, he asked whether if they passed it they would not be committed to paving Clarendon-road at the expense of the other roads. He thought that they ought to have a more lasting paving in the streets where the traffic was greatest.

After further conversation, the Chairman put the motion, when there appeared—For, 2; against, 8.

It was then decided to go into the matter *de novo*, and try to bring it to a settlement.

Mr. Andrews then said that seeing that a 6d. rate only produced £1,200 a year, and the paving in the roads that had been named, only about a fifth or a sixth part of the paths of the town, would amount to more than that sum—say £1,500, he considered that it was almost an absurdity to think of raising the money required by a rate. If the paving were undertaken in that way, it would take five or six years to do any satisfactory amount, and by that time the existing paving would require to be repaired or renewed, so that an annual rate of 6d. in the pound for paving would be established. He wished to avoid this by the adoption of permanent paving where the wear was hardest, so that no money would be required for constant repairing. Then besides the streets named in the report, Beechen Grove-road had been mentioned, and St. Albans-road, about which they had a petition. King-street also must be done on one side at least, also from Station-road to St. Andrew's Church, and from the Bushey viaduct to the Bushey Board school, and perhaps to Bushey Station. That would expend nearly a rate and a half. These and the others named, taking the cost at 2s. 3d. a yard, would come to £2,300, or even £2,500. So that it was totally impossible to do it under two rates. The 6d. rate would bring £1,200, so that they must agree with him that it would do only a fourth or sixth part of what it was desired to do. He might mention that Denner-hill stones could be taken up at certain places and permanent paving put down, and the Denner-hill stones more fittingly used for other purposes. At St. Albans the brick paving was done by a loan of £6000, and he could not hear that there had been a single dissentient voice. He was prepared to propose that this Board should proceed in a similar way. He thought at first that the amount should be £3000, which, borrowed for 15 years, would cost £290 yearly, or 4¾d. per head on a population of 15,000. But he would go further, and suggest that the loan should be £5,000 or £6,000, for as long a time as possible, say 20 years, for the best and most permanent paving, as to which they would have to decide. He should afterwards bring forward a motion, and show what could be done with local materials.

Mr. Clifford said that he would second Mr. Andrew's motion.

Mr. Savill having referred to the objections that had been urged to borrowing the money, even on the sewage farm,

Mr. Andrews, in reply, said that they would not require a second loan for the purpose of paving. In five years' time, after enjoying the benefit of the proposed outlay, no one would object to a 6d. rate if it were necessary.

Mr. Andrews submitted his resolution as follows:-
"That money be raised by loan for paving the town with some permanent paving."

Mr. Clifford seconded, and the resolution was carried, Mr. Benskin being the only dissentient.

Medical Officer's Annual Report

"Gentlemen,—I beg to submit to you my seventeenth annual report. It is for the year 1889.

"Vital Statistics.

"The population in 1881 was 12,162; the estimated population of your district in 1890 is 16,300. The number of houses is 3,335. The number of new houses in the year is 63. The number now empty is 73. In 1889 the new houses were 114, empty 79.

"Births.—The births were 457, giving a proportion of 28.03 in the thousand against 466 in 1888, and a proportion of 29.1 per thousand.

"Deaths.—The deaths were 237, that is 57 less than last year. In the Workhouse 24, that is 10 less than last year. Fifteen did not belong to the district. There were 80 under 5 years of age, 76 above 60; there were 17 above 80—5 males, 12 females; three were 90 or above; one in the Union House 95. Twenty-eight died of lung disease, 25 heart. The proportion of deaths per 1000 13.6. In 1888 it was 17.2. There were 10 inquests; in 1888 17.

"Marriages.—There were 44. Two males under 21, four females under 21. Ten were married at the Registry Office.

"Health of Paupers.

"In the Workhouse Infirmaries there was 246 cases, 114 acute, 132 chronic; 147 medical, 99 surgical. In 1888 there were 248 cases.

"Out-door Paupers.—New cases, 533. Surgical 99; medical, 434. Acute 151; chronic, 382. In 1888 there were 541 cases.

"Zymotic or Infectious Diseases.

"Deaths.—Measles 12, Scarlet fever 3, diphtheria 1, croup 4. This gives a percentage per thousand of 1.6.

"Smallpox and Vaccination.—No case of smallpox in 1889. In 1888 we had 10 cases and 2 died. The history of these cases showed the benefit of good vaccination.

"Re-Vaccination.

"All children should be re-vaccinated before they leave school, with as much regularity as in infancy.

"Remarks from my Journal.

"Register of Applications.—I have had 79 applications made to me on the following subjects:—Supposed smallpox, diphtheria, and supposed diphtheria, scarlet fever, typhoid fever, three cases (two in one house, the other imported), croup, nuisance from slaughter houses, w.c.'s out of order, want of water, houses not fit for human habitation, diseases of swine, rabies, overcrowding. I have sent you reports on typhoid fever, two on rabies, on diphtheria, and on the combined Isolation Hospitals. I have had consultations with you on the enlargement of your Public Library, and on the adoption of a coat-of-arms for Watford; you adopted both. Also consultations with your Hospital Committee and with Dr. Thomson. I have sent 30 notices to disinfect, and made 120 visits to houses and places.

Hospital Accommodation for Watford and District.

"The Cottage Hospital continues to do useful work. There were 73 cases, against 56 last year; 34 males, 39 females; 30 surgical, 43 medical. Nine patients at present.

"The Guardians' Isolation Hospital.—One typhoid fever, 4 scarlet fever, 4 measles, 12 mumps, 10 itch, 2 syphilis, in all 33, against 32 last year. No deaths. In 1888 there were 10 cases of smallpox and 2 deaths from it.

"The Joint Isolation Hospital for the Six Parishes of the Union for Private Patients.—We have had 54 cases, against 30 in 1888. Sixteen Urban from your district, 38 out of your district, Rural. Two diphtheria, 51 scarlet fever (two of these had whooping cough afterwards).

"Our Paths.

"During the year some of the paths have had asphalte laid down. The High-street, especially the defective and varied (six sorts) paving in the Market-place, demands attention.

"Gas.

"The gas has been above the legal standard in pressure, purity, and illuminating power. I often see it burning after 12 o'clock during light moonlight nights.

"General Remarks.

"The death-rate has never been so low, and the zymotic death-rate is very small. The general health was good. There are many buildings in a very dilapidated state, and although I cannot say they are injurious to health, yet they should be repaired for the credit of the town. At present they create an unfavourable impression. I allude among others to the crumbling Colne Bridge; houses just outside the Churchyard, and one inside the Churchyard walls. The approach to Watford from London might be improved, Aldenham-road East made wider; the corner by the Board School rounded. The Market-place requires Val de Traver cement, as in London. There is more smoke than there should be from manufactories.

"I remain, gentlemen,
"Your obedient servant,
"Alfred Thomas Brett,
"Medical Officer of Health for the
"Watford Urban District."

The Lighting of the Station Yard

To the Editor of the Watford Observer.

Sir,—In your account of the last meeting of the Local Board, I am reported to have stated that the Hon. Holland Hibbert had informed me that, in addition to paving a piece in the centre of the Station-yard, the London and North-Western Railway Directors would put up a good lamp column provided the Local Board would light the lamp. This is hardly correct, as what I said was that Mr. Hibbert was of opinion, or thought it possible, that the Directors would erect the lamp post, if the Local Board would provide the gas and light it.

I do hope the Boards, separately or conjointly, will arrange to light the yard in some way, as now, after dark, it is a disgrace to the town, and dangerous to the public.

Kindly insert this in your next issue and oblige

Your obedient servant,
52, High-street,   Chas. P. Ayres.
Watford, January 29th, 1890.

Population 1891, 16,819

'Vesuvius' on the slow down-line picking up water at the Bushey troughs. Mail trains would be equipped with automatic picking-up equipment to allow mail to be taken aboard for sorting whilst travelling. Similarly, sorted mail would be 'hung-out' and caught by station-side nets so saving necessity for the train to stop. This time-saving practice lasted about 100 years until ceasing c1970.

Watford to Rickmansworth line—level crossing at Loates Lane. Loates Lane, from the High Street, crossed first Derby Road and then Queens Road. Beyond the level crossing the lane continued its track as what we now know as Radlett Road. When the single-track line was doubled, to cater for the extension to Croxley Green and eventual electrification to London, this stretch of road was blocked and renamed Queens Place. The railway was carried over the new, and renamed, Radlett Road, by means of a bridge; this short stretch of new road under both railway bridges being referred to as the 'Death Trap'. In the 1930's improvements featured strongly in the Council's plans, but came to nothing.

To the Editor of the Watford Observer.

Sir,—As a regular passenger of the L. & N. W. Railway Company, I beg to call the attention of the authorities to the disgraceful way in which the passengers are kept waiting an unreasonable time at Bushey Station. We have to wait the convenience of the porters to allow us the privilege of passing out, which is not until the train has been despatched. At other stations between Euston and Watford arrangements are made by the respective officials to study the convenience of the passeners. Not so at Bushey. I have written to the District Superintendent respecting the same, and his reply was that we are not kept waiting more than half a minute, and that cannot be very serious, but he is wrong. Evidently no enquiries were made, or he would not contradict my statement. It has been my lot, with others, unfortunately, to wait four and five minutes. I have noted the time. I spoke to the only official on the platform (a porter) the other evening about it, and his reply was "Write to Euston, I cannot attend to everything." Quite true, it is not to be expected, but where is the stationmaster we rarely see on duty? I feel sure that the directors are not aware of the arrangements, or surely some measures would be taken to study the passengers.

I am, sir, yours truly,
J. Franklin Jacob.

Dear Sir,—I think Mr. Jacob, in his letter to you last week, is somewhat severe in his strictures on the Station-master at Bushey. No doubt he has grounds for complaint of the under-manned condition of the station. With the vast amount of traffic on the London and North-Western Railway, there must be some of the many stations where such an event happens as that of two, or even three trains arriving at the same time. Then comes the division of the small body of porters and some delay, probably, in releasing passengers from the station. But I am bound to say that the accusation brought against the Bushey Station-master is unjust, and I am supported in my opinion by numerous friends, who can state, with me, that they have never found him absent from his duty, except at proper times, and always most courteous and obliging. He compares most favourably with many Station-masters I could name.

I am, yours truly,
Carpenders House,   W. C. Wyles.
Watford.

WO April, 1890

KING & WEEDON'S TIME-TABLE
FOR JANUARY, 1891
LONDON AND NORTH-WESTERN RAILWAY.

DOWN TRAINS.

EUSTON	6 0	730	8 0	840	9 0	9 15	9 40	1015	1040	1140		1240	140	145	240	315	340	415	440
Chalk Farm	6 5		8 5	845			9 45		1045	1145		1245	145		245		345		445
Loudoun Rd.				848			9 48		1048	1148		1248	148		248		348		448
Kilburn ...	610		810	850			9 50		1050	1150		1250	150		250		350		450
Queen's Park				852			9 52		1052	1152		1252	152		252		352		452
Willesden ...	618	742	817	858	9 12	9 26	9 58	1026	1058	1159		1258	158	157	258	327	358	427	458
Sudbury ...	625		823	9 4			10 4		11 4	12 8		1	4 2	4	3 4		4 4		5 4
Harrow ...	633		830	911		9 38	1011	1035	1111	1215		1 11	211	2 6	311	337	411	438	511
Pinner ...	639		834	915			1015		1115	1219		1 15	215		315		415		
Bushey ...	645		840	921			1021		1121	1225		1 21	221		321		421		
WATFORD	650	759	844	925	9 30	9 50	1025	1047	1125	1229		1 25	225	218	325	349	425	451	520

DOWN TRAINS.   SUNDAYS.

EUSTON	520	540	545	6 0	640	710	740	840	9 5	9 40	10 5	1040	12 5	830	9 0	10 0	245	645	1015
Chalk Frm		545			645		745	845	9 45			1045		835			250	650	1020
Loudn Rd.		548			648		748	848				1048		840			254	654	1023
Kilburn ...		550			650		750	850	9 50			1050	1212	844			257	657	1025
Queen's P'k		552			652		752	852				1052		848			3 0	7 0	1027
Willesden	532	558	556	611	658	722	758	858	916	9 56	1016	1058	1218	853	912	1012	3 4	7 4	1033
Sudbury...	539	6 4			7 4	728	8 4	9 4		10 2		11 4	1224	859			311	711	1039
Harrow ...	546	611			711	736	811	911	926	10 9		1411	1231	9 8	924		319	719	1046
Pinner ...	550	615			715		815	915		1013		1115	1235	914			324	724	1050
Bushey ...	556	621			721		821	921		1019		1121	1241	922			330	730	1056
WATFORD	6 0	625	613	628	725	747	825	925	936	1023	1034	1125	1245	928	935	1032	335	735	11 0

DOWN TRAINS.

WATFORD ...	6 50	8 0	8 52	9 31	9 53	1047	1231	2 23	3 49	4 51	5 30	5 53	6 15	6 28	7 47	1034
King's Langly...	7 0	...	8 59		10 0	1056	1240	2 32	3 59	5 1	5 38	6 1	6 22	...	7 57	1042
Boxmoor ...	7 9	...	9 7		10 9	11 5	1250	2 42	4 8	5 8	5 47	6 9	6 29	6 40	8 6	1050
Berkhamsted ...	7 18	...	9 14		1018	1113	1 0	2 51	4 16	5 17	5 56	6 17	6 37	6 47	8 15	1058
Tring ...	7 26	...	9 23		1026	1122	1 12	3 1	4 24	5 25	6 7	6 25	6 44	...	8 28	11 6
Cheddington ...	7 36	...	9 33		1036	1132	1 22	3 12	4 32	5 34		6 34	6 51	6 59	8 38	...
Leighton ...	7 47	8 32	9 41	10 2	1047	1144	1 32	3 22	4 41	5 44			...	7 8	8 47	1120
BLETCHLEY ..	8 0	8 41	9 52	1011	11 0	1155	1 45	3 32	4 53	5 55			...	7 18	8 58	1130

(10 minutes earlier on Saturdays / Sats excepted)

Southern entrance to the Watford tunnel.

Watford and West Herts Sports Ground . . .

West Herts Sports Ground

Proposed Cricket and Football Ground

At the Public Meeting held in the Corn Exchange, Watford, on Wednesday, the 26th February, it was resolved that the generous terms offered by the Earl of Essex and Lord Capell for securing the 8 Acres of land on Harwood's Farm for this purpose should be accepted, as follows:–

"To lease the land for a term of 21 years at a rental of £100 a year, with the option of a further term of 21 years, at a rent to be fixed, and with the option of purchase at any time during the first of 21 years at the price of £6000.

It is estimated that the cost of laying out the ground, turfing, planting, fencing, building a pavilion, &c., will be about £1,200.

●*At a later public meeting it was made clear that an original proposal to form a Limited Company, to manage the new ground as a profit-making concern, would not be agreed to. The plans were changed to manage the grounds as a non-profit-making venture* . . .

"Chas. R. Humbert, Esq.

. . . In this letter I have only wished to express my hearty concurrence in and willingness to support this project, but have neither wished nor endeavoured to suggest any details as to how it should be carried out; those I leave to the judgment and decision of the trustees and committee when appointed, who will be much more competent to the task than I feel myself to be.

"Yours faithfully,

"Essex.

"P.S.— I cannot lose this opportunity of expressing our full appreciation of your disinterestedness, and of the zeal, energy, and intelligence you have shown in carrying out this scheme."

That goes plainly to show that Lord Essex never had the remotest intention or idea of letting the town of Watford have land considerably less than its worth to rent, undoubtedly less than its worth to purchase, with the view of a limited liability company being formed and profit being made out of it. Although I have not had an opportunity of seeing Lord Essex since the last meeting, I have seen his solicitors, and they emphatically endorse all that Lord Essex has said. So, if the company idea is persisted in, you will not have this land for the purpose of playing your cricket or football. Before going any further, perhaps you will expect to hear from me exactly what steps I took after the meeting on Thursday last. It appeared to me abundantly clear that it would be absolutely impossible that this scheme should take place if a company were formed, and in consultation with Mr. Turner and others I proceeded to send out circulars asking whether the subscriptions might be considered as donations, and if any profits accruing should be considered as belonging to the scheme itself, to be handled by the trustees, and dealt with for the further development of the land or its eventual purchase. The meeting being on Thursday, I sent them out on Saturday night, and by Monday morning I had received letters to the effect that out of £1347 promised before the meeting on Thursday £1305 were to be considered as donations. (Loud cheers.) That goes further, gentlemen, and shows that it was never the intention of the principal part of the subscribers to join in any company; in fact, many men who had been good enough to give their money for this purpose have taken the trouble to write me a little note on the form they have sent back, and nine-tenths of them have said, "If any company is formed, please consider my subscription as withdrawn."

Professor Attfield then said: My Lord and gentlemen, I have much pleasure in moving "That the resolution passed at the meeting of subscribers held at the Masonic Hall, on the 10th of April, 1890, in relation to the formation of a limited liability company, be rescinded." Now with regard to that meeting, although some good work, I think, was done, I suppose most of us will be of the opinion that a very large amount of time of a number of gentlemen was wasted (hear, hear), and when a great many men waste an hour or a couple of hours apiece it is apt to make them as angry as when one man finds he has wasted some 100 or 200 hours; they are all in the position of Matthew Mears. I do not know whether you are all acquainted with the history of that gentleman, which is summed up in the following rhyme:—

> "There was a man of Kirkcudbright,
> His name was Matthew Mears;
> He wound his clock up every night
> For six and forty years.
> But when that clock an eight-day clock
> Was clearly proved to be,
> A madder man than Matthew Mears
> You'd seldom wish to see."

(Laughter . . .)

Professor Attfield, referring to the question of adopting a name for the ground, expressed the hope that such a name would be chosen as would spread the interest in it over a wide area around Watford, so that more subscriptions might be available.

The Chairman, humourously remarking that "Elysium" and "Promised Land" had crossed his mind, asked whether "West Herts County Ground" would be acceptable.

The Hon. R. Capel suggested "Watford Cricket and Football Ground," which met with general favour.

Dr. Berry then proposed that Mr. E. J. Slim should be appointed hon. treasurer.

Mr. W. L. Smith seconded, and the resolution was carried unanimously.

Mr. Slim briefly returned thanks, and promised to do all he could.

Mr. G. Rooper, in eulogistic terms, proposed Mr. H. M. Turner as hon. solicitor.

Mr. R. Ashby seconded.

Mr. Turner, in his reply, expressed the hope that they would stick to the title of "Watford and Cricket and Football Ground," Watford being the capital of West Herts, and the centre of a large area from which they could provide the funds necessary for the support of the ground.

The Chairman, having made some remarks with reference to the last meeting, proposed Mr. Humbert as hon. secretary—a proposition that was received with continued cheering.

Mr. W. Pearkes seconded.

Mr. Humbert, in his reply, referred to the disheartening effect of the last meeting, and said that it had caused him to take off the twenty men and seven or eight horses and carts from their work of turfing and ground and to pull up the stakes. The work should now be pushed on as fast as possible, for if this were done and the grass not sown in April, they would not be able to play football upon it next season. Though he might not long be able to occupy the position of hon. secretary, he hoped that when he gave it up the affair would be a successful one.

A meeting of the committee was then appointed for Tuesday next, at 6 p.m.

Votes of thanks concluded the meeting.

WO April, 1890

To the Editor of the Watford Observer.

Sir,—In the large and earnest meeting in the Masonic Hall last night we heard many interesting speeches. I refrained from speaking, being afraid of prolonging the meeting. If I should not be considered impertinent, I should like to make a few remarks. (1). We did not sufficiently express the obligation we are under to Mr. C. R. Humbert for the part he has taken. I do not know any other man who could have got in £1400 in so short a time. Whether we are managed by trustees or by a company, I hope Mr. Humbert will continue to give us his valuable aid, so that the scheme so well conceived is fairly born and able to run alone. (2). I hope the directors will meet at once and approve of the works already begun by the Earl of Clarendon in buying turf—I mean in getting it for nothing—and the other works. (3). That they will continue them so as to save a year. (4). The company should raise enough capital to buy turf eventually, and only call up as much as is necessary. (5). We need not discuss how to spend the dividend till Christmas. It is prudent not to count the chickens before they are hatched.

Your obedient servant,

Watford, April 11th. A. T. Brett.

THE WATFORD OBSERVER
SATURDAY, JULY 5TH, 1890.

IT must be a gratification to the lovers of the manly sports to feel that though they may lose something through the stormy weather of the present season, it is a great factor in preparing for them the ground which is to be the future centre for Watford and the neighbourhood. When in the dry days of the spring the long desired land was secured and the levelling begun, there were fears no doubt that the turf and springing of the seed might not be such a success as was desired. Thanks, however, to the great determination and energy of Mr. Humbert, who had pledged himself to carry the matter through, we see the ground in such a state, by the aid of the copious showers, that cricket might by played on it at the present moment. The levelling has been admirably done, the splendid oak fencing is in a forward state, and this, we feel, is an earnest of the work being completed thoroughly. The land was in general estimation the best suited for cricket and football of any near the town, and its application to the purpose shows more and more how thoroughly well adapted it is. Time only is needed to make it one of the most delightful spots in the neighbourhood, and the belief that it is sure to be adequately supported will, we think, not turn out to have been unfounded.

First Photograph?

In the Watford Observer of 17th October 1891, was published, without comment a photograph with caption, "The new Board Room of the Local Board" and shows Dr. Brett and Mr. Slinn "from a photograph by F. Downer".

This is the first noted use of a photograph in Editorial context (some advertisements had previously used a half-tone block) and was to be followed by a series of head and shoulder portraits of local notables.

... Aylesbury builders, at least 20 or 25 per cent lower than Watford ...

Board Schools in Watford Fields

Sir,—Will you kindly insert the enclosed letter in your next issue of the *Watford Observer*, as I think it may interest some of your readers.

Yours obediently,
Queen's-road, Watford,   Chas. Brightman
September 4th, 1890.

"To the Chairman and Members of the Watford School Board.

"Gentlemen,—I am informed that the tender of Messrs. Webster and Cannon is likely to be accepted for building new schools in Watford-fields. As a ratepayer, I trust I shall not be out of order in protesting against an expenditure of over £4000 to accommodate 400 children, and, as I am certainly of opinion that your architects are fully capable of giving the accommodation for an outlay not exceeding £3,200, or £8 per head, I hope you will not allow the matter to proceed if the estimate is beyond that sum, for as other Board schools will shortly be wanted, the increase in our rates will cause a great outcry if you proceed on these lines. As a builder and ratepayer, I cannot help protesting against the schools being built by any outsider. Builders in Watford are numerous enough to ensure keen competition, and in matters of this kind it cannot be too much to ask that money raised by rates should, if possible, be spent amongst the ratepayers. I think I am within the mark when I say that the wages paid by Aylesbury builders are at least 20 or 25 per cent. lower than Watford, and, even if they pay at our rate on the job here, all the work being prepared at Aylesbury under the above lower rate, makes it unfair competition for us, who have to pay the increased rate of wages, and this fact I hope will have serious consideration from you, as I cannot but think you wish to be fair. I have not a word to say against Messrs. Webster & Cannon, for their work in Watford apparently does them credit, but I think it most unfortunate that they should be allowed to tender for such a job as this, which I argue belongs to Watford builders. There is no doubt that the bills of quantities will bear cutting up so as to make a considerable reduction in price, and, as such a radical alteration is necessary, I hope the Board will see its way clear to throw the job open again and confine it to the Watford builders who have already tendered, and in order to meet Messrs. Webster & Cannon I should like it to be possible to make them an allowance for the trouble they have had, and let them know that such a mistake is not likely to occur again. I am not thinking of the chance of getting the job myself, but of the principle which should be adopted. It is our money, and it will be true economy to spend it at home, and I am not at all alone in this opinion. I have no wish to harass or dictate to the Board, for like the majority of ratepayers, I feel grateful for the economical way in which their work has been carried out hitherto. Do not depart from that course; let your anxiety be still to keep the money where it is most wanted, namely, at home, and you will then merit as much support as you have already received.

"Apologising for troubling you,
"I remain, yours obediently,
"Chas. Brightman."
"Queen's-road, Watford,
"September 4th, 1890."

The New Board Schools

Sir,—In answer to Messrs. Webster and Cannon, I am still of opinion that it is the duty of our School Board, Local Board of Health, and Board of Guardians, as far as possible, to confine the contracts for various works required or goods supplied, to the tradesmen within the districts they represent, and in the matter of the School Board contract, I think the accepting of Messrs. Waterman's tender will prove of more benefit to the town than would have been the case had the tender of Messrs. Webster and Cannon been accepted at £190 less.

It was an unfortunate mistake that Messrs. Webster and Cannon were allowed to tender, and probably if I were in their place, I should make as strong remarks as they do; but being a Watford ratepayer I have done my best towards keeping work in the town, and Messrs. Webster's comparisons between Post Office, Railway Station, Bread Factory, and a Board School, do not to my mind at all agree. Private individuals and companies have a perfect right to go where they like, but when it comes to a building towards the cost of which I contribute my mite, I shall always kick against such jobs going away from home, and Messrs. Webster and Cannon have the same right at Aylesbury.

I am for free trade with fair competition, but I do not think it is fair to ask me to compete with any builder paying 6d. per hour where I am obliged to pay 7½d., and as to my being at Aylesbury six years ago, it is not my fault that I have not been there since, and Messrs. Webster and Cannon may rest assured I shall come again if I get the chance, and if I come and should run short of material, I shall not hesitate to ask Messrs. Webster and Cannon to accommodate me.

As to what rumour says about Mr. Ayres having shewn favour to Messrs. Webster and Cannon, that is perfectly ridiculous, for we all know very different, and I certainly believe that Mr. Ayres would rather see Watford work carried out by Watford builders.

Rumour also says that Messrs. Webster and Cannon have lost money over the Bank job; if so, they should feel obliged to me for trying to save them the possibility of further loss over the Schools. But it is of no use taking notice of rumour, for builders are always losing money.

Rumour says Brightman uses Swedish joinery. This is also wrong; I have certainly had some work prepared in London this year, in order to carry out agreements to complete works within time, but my workshops have been full of men as well, and the London men were paid 9d. per hour for my work.

I am glad Messrs. Webster and Cannon appreciate the sympathy of Mr. H. S. Allen, whose letter they say has fairly hit the mark; but I think it is strange that gentleman could not write about the School Board contract, without imputing dishonesty to working men who are industrious enough to earn a few shillings by a little labour after they have done their usual day's work.

Messrs. Webster and Cannon have my sympathy, which I can hardly expect them to appreciate, but I am glad the contract for building the new schools is likely to be kept in Watford.

Your obedient servant,
106 Queen's-road,   Charles Brightman
October 9th, 1890.

The Case of the Boy Sutton

Dear Sir,—The case of the boy Sutton, who was sentenced last week by the magistrates to a fortnight's imprisonment for stealing a pocket knife, is one which calls for more than passing notice, since it brings before us the fact that there is a class of boys in the town who are being allowed to grow up in vicious ways through no fault of their own, but simply because they are too poor for anyone to care at all about them. Clubs, institutes, classes, and amusements do not reach such as these. Ragged, untidy, rough, unrestrained in word and deed, their presence would soon end in driving all the other members away. Often, especially in winter, dependent for food upon what can be picked up in the streets, they frequently go the whole day with nothing to eat and (as I know was the case with Sutton last winter) sometimes have nowhere to sleep in at night. It is pitiful to see them struggling against their fate, trying hard to obtain work and being refused, owing to their untidy, suspicious appearance, or losing it through some trivial offence; no one caring whether they succeed or not. About twelve months ago I was induced to form a number of them into a class for instruction and amusement, but unfortunately my health completely broke down owing to this additional work, and I was compelled to give it up. I have, however, kept myself acquainted with many of them since, and they frequently ask me to resume the work. I write this, therefore, in the hope that someone may be induced to come forward and carry it on. The lads are extremely grateful for any simple act of kindness, and generous to any who are worse off than themselves. An instance that came under my notice was that of a little Italian boy whose means of livelihood, an accordion, had been stolen from him. The child was kept in food by a number of them (including Sutton) for nearly a week, and the money, fourpence a night, contributed between them for finding him a bed.

The Bench would have done an act of real kindness if they could have sent the boy Sutton to a reformatory instead of inflicting the penalty of 14 days' hard labour upon him for stealing a knife, thereby ruining his chances of obtaining honest employment on his release.

Yours faithfully,
C. H. Finmore.
8, Sutton-road, Watford.

WO July, 1890

RESULT OF AUCTION.

THE ROSE AND CROWN ESTATE, WATFORD.

MESSRS. HUMBERT, SON & FLINT

Beg to announce that at the second Sale by Auction of land on this estate, held last Tuesday, the 5th of May, 1891, at the Rose and Crown Hotel, Watford, the Freehold Plots of Land numbered in the particulars and on the sale plan as follows WERE SOLD:—With frontages to Market-street, Nos. 33 to 43, and 48 to 58 inclusive. Fronting Percy-road, Nos. 170 to 175 inclusive and No. 110 on Marlborough-road. The remaining plots were not sold, and may now be treated for by private contract

Auction and Estate Agency Offices,
Watford, Herts, and
11, Serle-street, Lincoln's Inn, W.C.

WO May, 1891

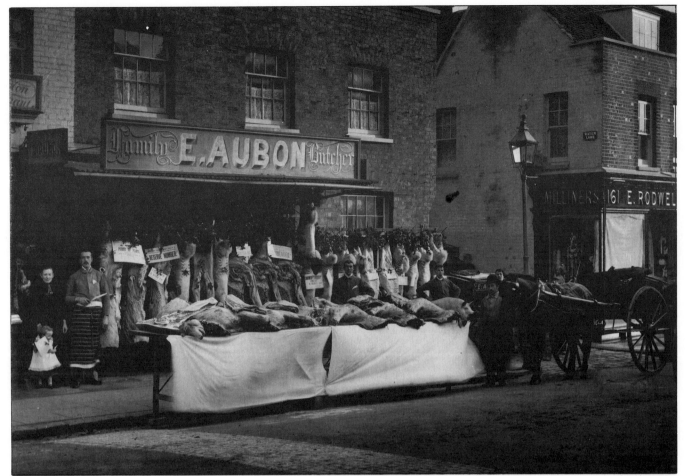

High Street, corner of Water Lane. Aubon's display of select carcases following the South West Herts Agricultural Show of 1892.   *p.256 t, 328 br*

Watford Local Board

This Board met on Thursday (yesterday), and had a secret conference with the Medical Officer of Health as to the condition of the town; in the meantime the reporters of the public press were denied admission. On the reporters obtaining entrance the Board proceeded to discuss certain alleged deficiencies of an incredible nature in the water supply to closets in the town. The members present were Messrs E. J. Slinn (chairman), E. Clifford, G. Capell, J. C. Benskin, Kead, Ayres, Coles, W. Wilson (Bushey) and Andrews. Mr. Weall was unable to be present at the commencement of the proceedings, but came in afterwards.

The Fearful State of St. Albans Road

Mr. Goss, jun., wrote to call attention to the state of the St. Albans main road, now in the district of the Watford Local Board. He supposed that nothing would be done until the Chairman or some other member of the Council were drowned. People had to go away and lodge in hotels.

Mr. Clifford asked why a state of things was allowed to exist here and would not have been allowed to exist 100 years ago? There was a lake 120 feet long, crossing the road.

The Clerk suggested that they should write to Mr. Judge.

The Chairman admitted that the road was in a shameful state.

Mr. Clifford: Are the public to put up with it month after month? The road, I repeat, is in our district. It is simply disgraceful.

Mr. Coles: It has been all right for 100 years—until the building commenced there.

No motion was come to.

The state of the Langley-road was also referred to, and the fault placed to the credit of the Highway Board.

The Surveyor recommended the purchase of granite or hand-picked flints for the roads.

The Lighting of the Town

A committee had had before them complaints as to the number of lamps in the town which were not burning at all, and they recommended that a man should be engaged to attend to them. They also fixed a day and hour to meet to look at the lamps, but it appeared that no one attended.

Mr. Benskin said he saw that Hertford was going in for electric lighting.

The Chairman: Ah, they have a river.

Mr. Benskin: So have we.

My. Ayres said it would be as easy at Watford as at Hertford.

The Chairman: They have the use of water power at Hertford.

Mr. Ayres: Could we not have the use of water power?

The Chairman: You would have to pay for it.

Mr. Mead said that a paper was read the other day to a meeting of engineers and others on the use of gas engines for generating electricity for lighting, and a deputation from Hertford had been over to his place to see his engines.

Mr. Clifford thought the Gas Company ought to take this question up seriously. Mr. Mead's mill would be a good station for electric lighting.

Mr. Ayres: Well, we pay now £1,000 a year for darkness; we might pay a third more and have light. Our public lighting is useless, and more than useless. A man going down the Clarendon-road has to strike a match when he leaves one lamp-post to find the next. (Laughter.)

The Chairman: That is a romance. (Laughter.)

Mr. Wilson said the lamps did not give any light when one was near them, and they certainly did not when they were far away.

The Chairman said the lamps were too high. They seemed to have been erected to light people to bed. They were three feet too high.

Mr. Clifford said it would be better to pay half as much again and have real light.

Mr. Wilson: We used to burn rushlights when I was a boy.—

Mr. Ayres: And they were better than our lamps. (Laughter.)

The Chairman: Mr. Ayres is not a shareholder in a gas company.

This discussion seemed to be much enjoyed by the members.

WHP January, 1893

The Roads

A report of the Highway Committee stated that on a report submitted to them by the Engineer, they recommend that 500 yards of broken hand-picked flints should be procured. A specification by the Engineer gave the amount of material required as 730 cubic yards.

Mr. Benskin asked the Engineer if he thought the flints would be more economical than granite.

The Engineer said said he thought so, on the present gravel roads.

It was then resolved to advertise for flints.

The Engineer said that he had put 400 tons of granite on the roads, and asked for 200 loads more, also granite chips.

The Committee recommended that 200 tons of granite and 50 tons of granite chips should be procured. The Board approved.

WO January, 1893

Church Street, cottages between Church and High Street, derelict and prior to demolition in 1893.

p.113, 132 tr

Old Cottages in Church-street

The Highway Committee recommended that tenders should be invited for pulling down the old cottages in Church-street.

The Engineer was instructed to prepare a specification.

WO January, 1893

Sale of Properties in Watford

Messrs. Humbert, Son and Flint offered by auction at the Rose and Crown Hotel, on Tuesday afternoon, two freehold residences, known as "Colne View" and "St. Ronan's," situate in Queen's-road, Watford, These were sold for the sum of £1220. A piece of land, described as suitable for the erection of villas, was next put up, and was not sold, although the bidding was very little below the sum that the auctioneer offered to accept for it.

The Sale room then rapidly began to fill, and some excitement was evident so soon as the first of the 51 plots of building land, situate on the Rose and Crown estate, were offered. This is the second sale of land on this estate, and lot 36, which comprised the first piece offered, has a frontage of 18 feet to Market-street, and a depth of 106 feet. This, together with the remaining similar lots, and two that were not included in the sale, were sold at the sum of £840. The next two lots formed a corner plot, with frontages to Market-street and Merton-road, for which the bidding was keen, and Mr. W. B. Neal bought these subsequently, together with the next lot, for £214. Seven sites adjoining were all sold, as also were the two following that were situate at the crossing between Francis-street and Market-street. The plots fronting on to Percy-road were now put up and mostly found purchasers. The sale altogether was a very successful one, and from the number of enquiries made of the auctioneer there can be but little doubt that a good deal more of the property was sold by him privately before he left the sale-room. The land being offered with the option of purchasers paying for the same on the easy system of payment naturally was a great inducement to residents and others to make small investments.

The amount realised for the land sold amounted to about £2,500.

Sale of Colney Butts Estate

Messrs. Humbert Son & Flint have received instructions from the proprietor to offer for sale by public Auction, at the Rose and Crown Hotel, Watford, early in February, 1893, upwards of **150** PLOTS of most eligible and advantageously placed FREEHOLD BUILDING LAND, situate as above, with suitable and important frontages to the Vicarage, St. James's, and Cardiff-roads, and to other roads in course of construction, and with depths of from 100 to 150ft.

The Colney Butts Building estate is within easy distance of the centre of the town and Market Place, within 500 yards of the High Street Station, and adapted to the erection of private houses, shops, and business premises, for which there is an unlimited demand in Watford.

The new roads, sewers, gas, and water supply will be forthwith constructed and laid on.

WO January, 1893

School of Music

The Rev. Newton Price said that a concert had been arranged to take place at the Agricultural Hall on the 20th April. They were obliged to take this building because they had 100 performers, but unless they were well supported the concert would result in financial loss.

Mr. Benskin suggested that the people should be admitted to the galleries at 3d.

The Rev. Newton Price said they would not go below 6d. unless Mr. Benskin wanted them to pay the people to go in.

Dr. Brett said that he was at the County Council on the previous day, and he was told on the highest authority that music had been recognized as a technical subject. Schools of music in other parts of the county were going to apply to the County Council for money, and it had been suggested that Watford should communicate with the other schools of music with the object of making this a sort of joint question. Watford School of Music was much more developed than other schools of music in the county, and he suggested that it should apply for £50.

The committee was of opinion that the Watford School of Music should act independently in the matter of application for grants.

WO March, 1893

Watford National Schools

Dear Sir,—For the information of the subscribers to the above schools will you please insert the following Government reports, and oblige

Yours faithfully,
REG. CAPEL

BOYS' SCHOOL.—"This is a well disciplined school, and the boys are taught with intelligence and considerable success. The reading and recitation of the upper standards are admirable, the handwriting is uniform and neat, the problems in the III. and IV. Standards are praiseworthy. History has made an excellent start. Geography is good except in the lower standards, and some very creditable maps were drawn. The points requiring attention are the composition of the VI. Standard, the arithmetic of the V. and VI. Standards (especially the latter),and the work generally of the I. Standard, which no doubt suffered from the weakness of the staff in the autumn."

GIRLS' SCHOOL.—"The discipline and general tone are excellent and Swedish drill and singing by note (both now taken for the first time) are admirable in every way. The elementary work is taught with thoroughness and intelligence, problems (especially in the VI. Standard) being worked with unusual success. Recitation is said with marked expression, and despite some weakness in the composition of the VI. Standard, and the arithmetic of the V. Standard, and in the intelligence of the reading, the highest grant is well deserved. Needlework and English show further improvement, and deserve special praise."

WO March, 1893

Watford Bathing Place

The hot weather has caused a large number to use the Bathing Place this year. The largest number in one day was 560—last Saturday.

WO June, 1893

Smallpox

The INSPECTOR reported that all the cases of smallpox had been discharged, and he was cleansing the Pest House under the direction of Dr. Berry.

The Board awarded the nurse, in addition to a testimonial, £5 5s. for extra services.

WO July, 1893

Scarlet Fever

The Chairman said that scarlet fever had been put an end to at Croxley Green and the schools reopened, but a child was sent home from the Isolation Hospital and in three or four days the fever broke out again in the same house. There seemed to be something radically wrong, and it was destroying the advantages of isolation.

WO July, 1893

●*Arthur Algernon, 6th Earl of Essex since 1839, had seen the complete tranformation of the town. Actively associated with town affairs, he did not enjoy robust health during his later years, although he achieved the good age of 89 years. Upon his death in 1892 he was succeeded by George Devereux de Vere Capell—who was to carry out further changes affecting Watford.*

Dumbeltons, Lower High Street, opposite Farthing Lane (Watford Fields Road).   p.93 t, 275 tr

Fire in Langley Road

A fire, which at one period threatened to involve a great part of Langley-road, occurred on Wednesday evening. At half-past four information was received at the Volunteer Fire Station of a fire at Mr. Suttle's oil shop in Langley-road, and not many minutes afterwards both the Volunteer and the Local Board Fire Brigades were on their way to the scene of the conflagration. The Watford Brewery Fire Brigade, which did not receive the call until after the others, lost little time in proceeding to the spot with their steamer. At a quarter to five little was to be seen but smoke, and it was not thought necessary to use the steam engine. A few minutes afterwards all was changed. The stock which was almost entirely composed of combustible materials, took fire. The flames shot across the road and made it impossible to get near the premises, a plate glass shop window on the opposite side of the road soon cracked, and the flames began to lick the wooden door of the side entrance to the private house opposite.

The explosion when the barrels of oil caught fire was tremendous, and the firemen soon found themselves unable to cope with the flames. The stock in the shop, consisting of oils, firewood, glues, paints, etc., blazed furiously, and the services of the steamer were soon afterwards called into use.

Under Superintendent Taylor a good pressure was got up, and the steamer supplying the three hydrants, a diminution was at once apparent. There seemed, however, a strong probability that the whole block of four shops with dwellings above would soon be ablaze. However, after a time, the fire in the lower part of the house having consumed all the combustible material, eventually succumbed to the strong jets of water, and attention was next directed to the upper rooms and roof.

Several long ladders were sent for, and two having been planted in the front the flames were partly reached from that direction. This was soon found to be insufficient, and at length a ladder was successfully placed at the rear of the premises. Several firemen got from the ladders on to the roof, and with the aid of hatchets attempted to arrest the progress of the flames by breaking the slates. Cheer after cheer from the large crowd assembled below greeted these attempts. It was soon evident that the united efforts of the three brigades, greatly assisted by the Watford Brewery steamer, had obtained some mastery over the flames, although they had not been quite able to prevent them spreading on to the next roof.

After an hour's hard work it was evident that the further progress of the flames had been arrested and at a quarter to eight Captain Ashby and his men left with their steamer, leaving Supt. Geo. Urlwin and the Volunteer Fire Brigade in charge.

There was an excellent water supply throughout and the police under the immediate charge of Inspector Duke rendered all possible assistance in keeping the crowd at a proper distance and clearing the road so that the firemen might not be hampered in their work. The Deputy Chief Constable, Mr. C. M. L. Pearson, was also present, while Inspector Duke gave great personal assistance to the firemen. The three brigades worked well together, and throughout the evening all co-operated harmoniously.

The premises where the fire originated are insured and are the property of Mr. F. Fisher. The tenant, Mr. Suttle, has only been there a short time, and came to Watford from Limehouse. It is not known how the fire originated.

WO 1893

Bricklayers' Strike

There is no change to chronicle with regard to the bricklayers' strike, nor can there well be any if one side or the other does not give way, and it only remains to be seen which will hold out the longest. The T. Turner Company having signed the bricklayers' rules, the latter are of course bound to them, while the other masters in Watford hold to the amended rules they submitted to the Bricklayers' Society. What work there is in progress is being done quietly with a little outside help.

WO June, 1893

Death of Mr. Henry Williams

Mr. Henry Williams died on 28th October, 1893, aged 65 years. He began his business career as a photographer—a very primitive process in those days—but his liking and aptitude for newspaper work led him to change his vocation and he became a reporter, as representative in Watford and the surrounding district, on behalf of the "Buckingham Advertiser." Later, he became Sanitary Inspector at Watford, and, presumably, followed his bent for writing in his spare time. Sometimes he wrote absolutely for the amusement of his friends; then, the humorous element came very much to the top. He wrote a very amusing "Soliloquy on Public House Signs."

His "History of Watford"—the first history of its particular kind—gave him a double dose of work. When he had passed the proofs and they and the original "copy" were at the printers, the printing works was destroyed by fire and he had to re-write the manuscript.   *J.W.G.*

WHP (August, 1928)

Earl of Essex, 1893

Watford Junction Station and staff; the station decorated for the Earl of Essex's arrival after his wedding. The station front was extended and rebuilt in 1909.   *p.238, 311, 342*

Marriage at Westminster

ON Thursday afternoon, at the handsome church of St. Margaret's, Westminster, situated under the shades of the historic Abbey, and well known as the "Speaker's church," and a fashionable resort of American families when in London, and in the presence of a very large and aristocratic assembly, the marriage was duly solemnized of the Right Honourable the Earl of Essex (George Devereux de Vere Capell) and Miss Adèle Grant.

The Bridegroom traces his descent from Mr. Arthur Capell, who was Member of Parliament for the county of Hertford, in the Long Parliament, and was created "Baron Capell of Hadham," and for his loyalty to the "Royal Cause" was beheaded in 1649. He was succeeded by his son (second baron), who was created "Viscount Malden" and "Earl of the county of Essex" (peerage of England, 1661). He was appointed Viceroy of Ireland, 1672-1677, and for sometime First Commissioner of the Treasury, but being accused with Lord Russell of connection with the "Fanatic Plot" was committed to the Tower, where he was found dead in 1683. His son, the second earl, was a lieutenant-general in the army, and Constable of the Tower of London, and died in 1709, and was succeeded by his son William, as third earl, who died in 1743. His son, William Aune, the fourth earl, died in 1799. The fifth earl, George, "D.C.L." who assumed the name of "Coningsby," died in 1839, and was succeeded by his nephew, Arthur Algernon (son of the Hon. John Thomas Capell, second son of fourth earl), who was sixth earl (and grandfather of the present peer), who on his death last year in September, was succeeded in the family estates and titles by the present peer, who sits in the House of Lords as "7th Earl of Essex."

The Bride, the charming and accomplished Miss Adèle Grant, is a famous American beauty, and eldest daughter of the late Mr. Beach Grant, of New York, and Mrs. Beach Grant, of 35, Great Cumberland-place, Hyde Park, London, W., and granddaughter of the late well-known General Stewart, of America, and niece of the late Mr. Thomas A. Scott, a former President of the Pennsylvania Railway Company.

WO December, 1893

Reception of the Earl of Essex

LORD and Lady Essex would travel by special train, consisting of an engine and three coaches, from Euston, arriving at Watford Junction at a quarter to 6. Number 1 platform, at which the train stopped, had been specially and appropriately decorated under the superintendence of Mr. Braide, of the Permanent Way Department.

Over the steps had been placed an elaborate shield of red trimmed with variegated holly, the Essex crest having been ingeniously worked with cotton wool in the centre with the words "Welcome Home" underneath. One side of the shield bore the stars and stripes, the other the Union Jack. The windows on the left were all aglow with the light of red fires outside. The steps were carpeted in red, and the roof of the subway was lined with white material, the decorations being continued to the station entrance, where, on the station buildings, a great pole had been erected, on which was flying a flag bearing the arms of the London and North-Western Railway Company.

One company of Volunteers formed at the Station-yard under Major Lake, and had proceeded to keep the Park gates, while another company formed at High-street, under Major Humbert, and proceeded to the Station-yard, and marched after the carriage behind the torch-bearers. The Malden and Clarendon hotels were illuminated, and the scene was made more brilliant by the coloured fire. The procession went by way of Woodford-road and Queen's-road to High-street, all the way being brilliantly illuminated.

As soon as the procession turned the corner of Queen-street coloured fires were lighted on the front of some of the houses in High-street, and in the market-place, the beacon fire upon the triumphal arch having been previously set ablaze. Upon a decorated platform erected in front of the Corn Exchange were assembled Lady Edith Villiers, Lord Hyde, the Vicar of Watford, Mr. E. J. Slinn (Chairman of the Local Board), Mr. H. Morten Turner, Dr. Brett, Professor Attfield, Major Humbert, Mr. C. Healey, Dr. Berry, Mr. W. T. Boydell, Mr. W. T. Coles, Mr. Hubert Thomas, Mr. E. M. Chater, Mr. C. W. Edwards, Mr. A. Spicer, Mr. G. P. Darby, Mr. W. J. Flint, Dr. Christmas, Mr. J. Weall, Mr. G. Stone, the Rev. J. Stuart, Mr. J. C. Benskin, Mr. D. D Downer, Mr. F. Downer, &c., and many ladies. When the carriages stopped amid enthusiastic

cheering Mr. Slinn, who stood in front of the platform, addressing Lord and Lady Essex, said: It is with very great pleasure that the inhabitants of Watford meet you here this evening to welcome you on your wedding. I hope that in your progress here from the station they have received you with acclamation the whole of the distance, and also your bride. With your permission I will ask Mr. Turner to read the address to you from the Local Board of Watford as the governing body of the town."

After the address, the carriage passed on its way up the High-street towards Cassiobury. There were the same signs of welcome all along the route, indeed the inhabitants seemed to vie with each other in the demonstration of their goodwill. From the almshouses to the Cassiobury entrance there was a chain of fairy lights on the side next the West Herts Ground, also fairy lights on the almshouses and along the space to the entrance. At the gateway itself the windows of the lodges were outlined with fairy lights of different colours, and on either side of the arch were the letters "G" and "A." Here the carriage stopped while the horses were put in. His Lordship bowed to the crowd, and under the escort of the Yeomanry the carriage proceeded through the park to the mansion.

WO December, 1893

Marriage of the Earl of Essex

Sir,—I should like through the medium of your columns to tender, on behalf of Lady Essex and myself, our most sincere and heartfelt thanks to the people of Watford and the neighbourhood for the most cordial and unanimous reception which they accorded us on our arrival here last week. It was one, the remembrance of which, will, I know, never fade; and will be a continual reminder to us of the good feeling which exists, and which I hope will not only ever exist but will grow stronger as time goes on between the House of Cassiobury and the people of Watford.

Yours faithfully,

ESSEX.

WO December, 1893

... Watford, with technical instruction, took the lead as the most scientific town in Herts ...

Local Government

The initiatory steps towards the new order of local government was taken by the County Council who at their meeting had before them the report of the special committee appointed to bring into operation the Local Government Act, and under their directions a local enquiry was held by Mr. J. C. Earle, barrister-at-law, on the 27th June, respecting the division of the parishes of Watford Union. The effect of the Act on Watford was that the parish was divided into two parishes, that part which was within the district of the Local Board being the "Urban Parish," and the residue the "Rural Parish." A similar division took place in the parish of Bushey.

During September several important matters were brought under public notice. The School Board made provision for the erection of new schools at Leavesden-road for 480 boys, and the first annual meeting of the Committee appointed under the Technical Instruction Act showed a distinct advance in organised education work. At this meeting Dr. Brett bore testimony to the great success of Watford with regard to technical instruction, which, he said, took the lead as the most scientific town in Herts. The great advance made in respect of the Public Library was shown by the Committee at their annual meeting. Twenty years ago the income was only £80 a year; now the rate money is more than four times that, namely, £320 a year.

In November the Society for Improving the Condition of the Poor, at its annual meeting, was able to show an excellent year's work, the good resulting from which cannot be too highly commended. The ninth exhibition of Chrysanthemums was larger and more imposing than any previously held, thus testifying to the great progress made by the Society. It is not necessary to dwell on the important events of the past month they are so fresh in the public memory.

The Local Board, Rural Sanitary Authority, and ex-officio Guardians ceased to exist, the latter authority being succeeded by the Rural District Council, comprised solely of representatives of the rural parishes in the Union. The Urban District Council takes the place of the old Local Board, the election for which was marked by great interest. The newly constituted Boards in town and district enter on their work for the year with great possibilities, and judging by preliminary meetings held already give promise of realizing many of the hopes entertained of them.

January, 1895

Care of Market Place

THE Clerk stated that he had had an opportunity of considering the matter, as to who was liable for keeping the Market Place in order, and the opinion he had arrived at was this—the whole of the Market Place, from house to house, was clearly dedicated to the public, subject to the rights of the lord of the manor to hold his market there on Tuesdays, and possibly, to a limited extent, on Saturdays. Therefore, as the place was to be treated for the purpose of a highway, he thought it was the duty of the Board to prevent its being dangerous, and to make it passable for her Majesty's subjects. If through the use of the place as a market, it was necessary that a portion should be treated differently from a highway, he thought the duty rested with the lord of the manor, and where it was so treated, it was clearly his duty to keep it in repair.—Mr. Andrews believed the lord of the manor paid for the cleansing of the place, and he presumed he was also responsible for the repairing.—The Chairman said he thought the path the public were complaining of now was where the old fountain stood.—The Clerk said they might call upon him for that. After some discussion, it was decided to give notice accordingly.

WO December, 1894

Building

	1891	1892	1893	1894
Houses	96	418	264	328
Other erections	67	55	96	77

New Streets—The Board have during the past year approved plans for making and sewering 7 new streets:—Garfield-street, 173 yards long; Shakespear-street, 190; Parker-street, 158; Milton-street, 208; Cecil-street, 208; Judge-street, 193; Ridge-street, 188. Total, 1318 yards. The whole of the above streets are in the Callow Land district, and some are now in course of construction.

Private Streets—Great progress has been made during the year in completing the works required to be done to private streets before being made public, under Private Street Works Act, 1892. Works of sewering, metalling, channelling, kerbing, paving with 2in. indurated stone slabs, and lighting have been carried out in the following thirteen streets, and the whole, except Victoria-road, have been declared public:—

	Yards long	Cost. £	s.	d.
Percy-road	158	276	3	6
Ebury-road	111	320	13	6
Shaftesbury-road	157	422	16	4
Stanmore-street	130	206	17	0
Copeswood-street	286	439	6	1
Leavesden-road	275	466	13	8
Lowestoft-road	130	258	6	6
Grover-road	316	778	14	7
Oxhey-street	132	280	16	9
Westland-road	200	349	6	4
Wellington-road	137	245	11	5
Canterbury-road	123	222	18	6
Victoria-road estimate	225	500	4	11
Total yards	2,380	£4,768	9	0

Street Improvements

Upton-road—This street has been completed by paving the footpath with indurated stone slabs 2in. thick, and declared a public highway. St. Albans-road—One side of this street has been completed by kerbing and channelling from Bedford-street to Leavesden-road, and paving the whole from the railway to Regent-street with 2in. indurated stone slabs. By arrangements with the owners of the property the water troughs in front of the Stag and Leviathan public houses have been moved to the edge of the footway. The corner of Leavesden-road has been widened, the land required for this improvement having been given by Messrs. Benskin and Co., and the L. and N.W. Railway Company. Vicarage-road—In consequence of building operations near the Union House, it was found necessary to ask the builder, Mr. T. Clark, to set back his frontage line to get the road 36 feet wide. The piece of land was purchased by the Board. To further improve this road also the Board purchased a strip of land from Messrs. Benskin and the Trustees of the Wesleyan Mission Room, and the improvement will be carried out when the conveyances are completed.

Numbering of Streets—Progress has been made in numbering the new streets in the Callow Land district, and the other new streets are now receiving attention. The following rule is being adhered to, in all new streets—Odd numbers on the left, even numbers on the right. Begin at the end nearest the Central Post Office, or nearest the main road. One number to be left for each vacant plot of ground.

WO January, 1895

OLD HOUSES IN THE HIGH ST

One of a series of drawings of Watford, made by Colonel Healey. (Printed in WO 7th February, 1891)

Frederick Downer, photographer extraordinary; Watford's first block-maker? . . .

Mr. Frederick Downer

THE County of Hertford should feel complimented in being selected as a home for Art, and especially that portion of it situated within a few miles of the Metropolis on the London and North-Western Railway. Bushey, as everyone knows, is the centre of a great Art education system founded some years ago by Professor Herkomer, R. A., who has here built himself a magnificent mansion, while many of his pupils, past and present, have taken up their residence in close contiguity to the famous Bushey Studios where so much artistic work is successfully carried on. Prominent engraving firms in London, also, have formed branch establishments in Hertfordshire, because they find that not only are rents more moderate, but that daylight is superior and more reliable all the year round than is found to be the case during those months in town when fogs are rampant.

One of the most recent instances of business enterprise in this direction is that of Mr. Frederick Downer, the well-known artist and photographer of Watford, who has there started, in conjunction with his sons, an engraving establishment of his own. Like many others who have made their mark in the world, Mr. Downer began in a small way, encouraged by his own enthusiasm for Art to persevere, until we find him what he undoubtedly is,—the most successful photographer in the County. He is distinctly a Hertfordshire man, for he was born in Watford, where he has lived ever since, his father, Mr. David Downer, being a hairdresser and stationer there. Leaving school at an early age, the son had some experience for a year ot two in a lawyer's office, and, after spending a short time at a stained-glass factory, he acted as his father's assistant, the boy's duties necessitating his presence behind the counter for about twelve hours daily. But his heart yearned for higher things than such as the stationer's shop afforded, and he aspired to become an artist.

There was no School of Art in Watford at that time, but—and this proves the inborn determination of the youth—there was a train leaving Watford for London at ten minutes to five o'clock in the morning, by which he decided to travel to the Metropolis for the purpose of becoming a student in the early morning life-class at Leigh's (now Heatherley's) Drawing School in Newman Street, Oxford Street. He accordingly arranged with the policeman on night duty to arouse him every morning at four o'clock, when he jumped out of bed and soused his head in a basin of cold water to avoid running the risk of falling asleep again. During the whole of the summer of 1860, while he was a student, he only missed the train once by neglecting this precaution, and he has not yet forgiven himself for it. The Art class of which young Downer was a member was held from 6 a.m. to 8 a.m., and when it was concluded he would usually have some business to transact for his father before returning to Watford by about 10 o'clock.

The year after, Mr. Downer decided to give up his connection with the stationery business, and to take up photography as a profession. With the aid of books and the valuable advice and assistance of some amateurs, he quickly acquired a knowledge of the subject, and began his career by rigging up in his father's garden a simply-contrived tent, being merely a framework of wood covered with canvas, for which, however, he soon substituted a small glass studio. Almost from the first he received much encouragement from his patrons, earning a fairly substantial sum by these initial efforts in the production of "glass positives"—the predecessors of the sensitized-paper prints which are now so familiar. He then

resolved to give still greater scope to his operations by renting a stable adjoining his father's residence, converting the same into the necessary offices and dressing-rooms, and building out over the yard a commodious studio.

Here he remained for some time, reaping golden opinions from his *clientele*, and practically holding the monopoly in the locality for this class of work, his only competitor being a daguerreotypist, who eventually retired. A few more years elapsed, and the business so continued to prosper, that Mr. Downer was induced to purchase a plot of land in Loates Lane, on which he erected his present large and well-lighted studio, specially constructed to suit all requirements of the profession. The principal front is a handsome one, built from a design by Mr. W. H. Syme, M.R.I.B.A.

Entering the studio, the eye is first attracted by the numerous photographic pictures adorning the walls, including portraits of celebrities and other familiar faces. Mr. Downer has had the honour of sittings from many of the nobility and gentry both in and beyond the County, and from others who have distinguished themselves in Literature, Science, Art, and the Drama. To mention but a few, here are lifelike presentments of the Earl of Clarendon (Lord-Lieutenant of the County) and the late Countess of Clarendon, the Lady Edith Villiers (in the pose and dress of Millais' well-known picture, "Cherry Ripe"), the late Earl of Essex, the present Earl and the Countess of Essex, Lord Maldon, Mr. T. F. Halsey (M.P. for the Watford division), Professor Herkomer, R. A., Professor Rudolf Lanciani (the noted Italian antiquary who recently visited England to receive the degree of D. C. L.), Mr. W. S. Gilbert (of comic-opera fame), Dr. Stradling F.Z.S., with his boa-constrictor, &c., &c. Mr. Downer is always particularly successful in photographing family groups, children, and animals; in fact, nothing comes amiss to him, and his portraiture of dogs are as artistic in treatment as are his pictures of human subjects.

Both ends of the studio are utilised as backgrounds, one for ordinary plain effects and interiors, the other for outdoor scenes; while attached to the studio are large grounds for taking equestrian groups or figures, these grounds also affording a pleasant promenade for visitors whose requirements cannot be immediately attended to. Mr. Downer executes on the premises all silver and platinotype printing,—a branch of the work which many photographers relegate to others. Photos. are also taken by him in badly-lighted rooms or in dull weather by the aid of the magnesium flash-light, highly successful results being thus achieved.

His lenses are by those noted makers, Dalmeyer and Ross, the largest of which cost 60 guineas, the camera itself being worth another 20 guineas, the studio is furnished with about a dozen cameras, capable of dealing with negatives of varying dimensions, from stereoscopic to 15in. x 12in., larger sizes being produced by enlargements. Here, in a corner, and as much out of sight as possible, is an "instrument of torture" familiar to those accustomed to sitting for their portraits,—I allude to the head-rest, with its adjusting screws, &c.; but it is only fair to say that Mr. Downer avoids its use as much as possible, and only avails himself of it when, owing to a bad light, the sitting is likely to be prolonged; in these days of rapid exposure, however, the head-rest is seldom resorted to.

As enough has been said to prove Mr. Downer's high standing in the County as an expert and artistic photographer, a special reference must

be made to that new enterprise to which a brief allusion was made in the beginning of this article. Mr. Downer is now justified in styling himself a Photo-Engraver and Photo-Etcher. He cannot only furnish a photographic print, but also a reproduction of it in metal, suitable for book illustration, and examples of his work will be found in the present article as well as in previous numbers of the *Hertfordshire Illustrated Review*. The engraving department is under the management of his eldest son, Mr. Fredk. Downer, who is assisted by his two brothers, Edward and Arthur. His second son, Harold, an electrician by profession, is partly responsible for the installation of the electric light in the studios and show-rooms, and for the fitting-up of necessary appliances. All Mr. Downer's sons have artistic tastes, Fred. and Harold being clever designers.

The art of reproducing paintings, drawings, and photographs is known as "Process" engraving, and a brief account of the method by which nearly all the illustrations in the *Hertfordshire Illustrated* are produced will probably prove interesting to my readers.

"Process" is a comparatively recent development, for it was only a few years ago that the means were discovered of applying the principles of printing through the agency of light. The original picture is first photographed, the camera being mounted on a sliding platform, by means of which the difficulty of focussing is minimised. The electric light is generally used even during the day at Watford, as it is always ready to be switched on, and supplements the strength of the natural light. The plate glass for the negative is prepared in the usual manner, and after the necessary exposure in the camera it is conveyed to the "dark-room" to be developed and intensified. The negative is next taken to the printing-room, and placed in a wooden frame (similar to those used by photographers, but much heavier) in front of a highly-polished zinc plate which has been sensitized by means of a specially-prepared solution. The glazed front of the frame is now exposed to the light, which, for several minutes, is directed through the negative and upon the sensitized surface of the zinc. The metal plate, after sufficient exposure, is removed from the frame, but nothing is visible upon it until it has been rolled up with transfer ink and developed in a bath of water, when, by rubbing with cotton wool, those portions of the sensitized film are removed which have not been fixed by action of the actinic rays of light, the parts so fixed being a

78

Mr. Downer has been established 33 years, during which time he has photographed almost everyone of note; every newsworthy occasion, and almost every new building.

From the time when his photographic equipment verged on the primitive, and of coating his plates before he could make his exposure, he now has at his command better lenses and better plates.

Photography, so far, has been the province of the professional or perhaps, at best, a very small number of dedicated amateurs. Although block-making of photographs has been possible for a number of years editors of newspapers have not yet realised that their readers would appreciate more photographs to support the text.

So far without serious competition, he now faces the threat of Mr. Coles, recently established in Queens Road, who quickly builds up a business of quality to prove a serious rival. A newish American firm called Kodak has made a film which anyone can load into a suitable camera; and furthermore, has designed a device by which the film may be processed in daylight. The new cameras can be used in the hand without the erstwhile cumbersome tripods.

If the situation looks bleak, Mr. Downer's experiments with 'process engraving' have to spring some surprises, surprises which have preserved Watford in images available from no other source. In a short while he would have finely-printed postcards on sale.

Double-ended studio with as many as 12 cameras available.

Five-and-a-half horse power four-stroke gas engine driving a dynamo.

replica of the original picture—in fact, a photograph of it. The plate, after being again rolled up with ink in order to give the lines a firm acid resist, is transferred to the etching-room, and the large surfaces which will appear white when printed are painted out with a preparation consisting of shellac in solution. When this is dry, the plate is placed in a bath containing diluted nitric acid, which eats* away those parts not protected by the acid resist. When the plate is sufficiently etched, a proof is taken, and, if satisfactory, it is mounted on oak to make it "type high"—that is to say, after the plate has first been punctured for rivets and the superflous margins cut away. At this stage the engraving is called a "block," which must be trimmed and touched up with the graver before it is ready for the printing-press. It is a remarkable fact that such a block will yield about 50,000 impressions before exhibiting an appreciable amount of wear and tear.

The above description similarly applies to the reproduction of "line" work (that is, all drawings executed in lines) and to "half-tone" work (drawings in wash, or photographs), the latter, however, being the more delicate operation, requiring greater skill.

There is one feature of "half-tone" engraving that should be mentioned. Those who examine with a powerful glass any such reproduction of a wash drawing or photograph will observe that the various degrees of light and shade are made up of minute square dots. This peculiar texture is obtained by means of a screen formed by two sheets of glass attached to each other, each having upon its inner surface a series of minutely-engraves parallel lines; on one p late these lines are vertical and on the other horizontal, or they may be engraved diagonally, to the right and left respectively. † It will be easily understood that when such a screen is inserted in the camera between the lens and the negative, the engraved lines (sometimes numbering 200 to the inch) cut up into minute squares the image of the picture as it appears on the negative, except in those parts which are solid black. After the negative is printed on the zinc plate (as already described), the latter goes through several acid baths, between each of which it is dusted with an acid-resisting powder. On closely inspecting the plate when it leaves the etchers, one can detect the effect of the glass screen in the minute squares of metal which form the picture *in relief.*

From the above it will be seen that the art of "Process" engraving is not so simple as it might at first sight appear. It obviously means great pecuniary expense, as well as steady perseverance in overcoming difficulties and disappointments, before success is assured, and Mr. Downer is to be congratulated in having achieved such results as those he has already attained in so short a time. Here, in Loates Lane, he has made the most of the accommodation at his command, this being necessarily somewhat limited. A 5½ nominal horse-power Otto high-speed gas-engine and a brush dynamo machine generate the electricity and motive power required for the various operations. In the photographic studio connected with the engraving department are two arc lamps (Brockie-Pell), each affording light equal to 2,000 candles, and, in addition, there are a number of glow lamps for purposes of general illumination. One of the rooms (that now used for enlarging and the production of lantern slides) contains thousands of negatives!

† These screens, being very difficult to produce without a flaw, are very expensive, even those of moderate size costing as much as £60.

*The word "etch" is from the Dutch word *etzen,* to eat.

Hertfordshire Illustrated Review, 1894

Market Place, Market Street to Green Man; No. 68, the Compasses, No. 66, offices of Sedgwick, Turner and Walker, solicitors, of which partnership Henry Morten Turner held prominent office in the Local Board and then Urban District Council; also Registrar's Office of Births, Marriages and Deaths.

Beyond No. 66 is an ironmonger dealing in garden and farm agricultural implements, and in the corner with placarded wall, the 'Green Man' inn. *p.296*

Electricity

Unlike the industrial north and midlands, Watford was essentially agricultural and would stay so for a number of years more. However, with gradual sale by the Earl of Essex of parcels of land the time was approaching when industry would become dominant. Larger factories, such as the paper mills, made full use of steam power both for heating and driving engines to provide power for machinery by means of shafting, pulleys and belting.

Smaller factories, rather than install steam engines, relied on the alternative power plant offered by the single cylinder slow running stationary gas engine with its distinctive 'pop, pop, pop' which could be heard emenating from many sheds and yards. Gas engines powered plant at Waterlow's, Acme Tone Engraving Company and at the Paget Plate Company (as remarked in a fire report on page 95).

But Mr. Downer, as did the Paget Prize Plate Company, used the gas engine to generate electricity.

In the meantime the Urban District Council, which had grudgingly accepted the telephone, belatedly acknowledged that a municipal electricity generating undertaking would prove remunerative to the operation.

Some public functions had been electrically lighted many years earlier by lamps strung across a hall and powered by batteries loaned by Henry Rogers.

The generating plant was conceived principally to provide light in substitution for gas. When the Cardiff Road plant was operational, (and to save costs shared the same chimney as the refuse destructor), street lamps were soon changed, though not without criticism. The first carbon filament lamps were the equal of a modern 30 watt bulb; the arc-lamps in the market place gave more light but needed regular replacement of the carbon rods after about 100 hours use.

The 'Green Man' inn, old established commercial house, proprietor D. Podmore, offers first-class accommodation for bicyclists and tricyclists. Next door is the Swan Iron works whose ownership had just changed from Mr. Childs, farrier, to that of Mr. Horton, who had previously owned the 'George Inn', (at 91 High Street where Marks and Spencers store now is) before taking up this new business in 1887. *p.262 tl*

Railway Bridle Path

Sir,—I am glad to see by your report of the proceedings of the Urban Council that Mr. Ayres is not going to let the action, initiated by himself and Mr. Pridmore some little time ago, with reference to the state of the bridle path from the St. Albans-road to the Station, drop.

I took some little trouble four or five years ago, and I am glad to say successfully, to get the Railway Company to open up a continuation of that path direct to the Station, thus saving a longer and less pleasant route round the "Clarendon," and I have incessantly since then pointed out to the late and present Chairman of the Council the state of their path as described so truthfully by Mr. Ayres, but wholly without effect. Binding gravel or granite chips properly rolled and kept rolled with the steam roller is all that is required, if a proper drain is placed at the head of the path in the St. Albans-road to keep the water from washing the mud down from the road on to the path. We have suffered for years from unjustifiable neglect on the part of the authorities in this respect, and I hope Messrs. Ayres and Pridmore will not rest until the path is put into proper order. I believe the traffic over this path is as large as that over any street in Watford.

Yours obediently,
JOSCELINE F. WATKINS
Stratford Lodge, Watford, August 31st, 1896.

Christ Church, Callow Land

SATURDAY was a day of rejoicing in the parish of St. Andrew's, the occasion being the dedication and opening for divine service of the new temporary church at Callow Land, by the Bishop of St. Albans. The new church has been erected on the land given some years ago by the late and present Earl of Essex for the purpose, adjoining the St. Andrew's Parish Room, on the St. Alban's-road.

The church is lofty, and consists of nave with side aisles, the nave having clerestory windows. The ventilation is on modern principles, and the lighting by incandescent gaslight. Tenders were obtained from various iron church builders, and that of Messrs. Harbrow, of Bermondsey, for an iron church to accommodate 400 persons, at a cost of £508 was accepted, exclusive of furniture and fittings. Towards the cost of the new building £616 has already been subscribed, and £220 for endowment. The furniture and fittings are at present incomplete, but kneelers will be provided for all the seats. The interest taken in the new church may be seen from the fact that much of the furniture has been given, and some of it made, by members of the church. The pulpit, which is not yet finished, is the gift of Mr. J. S. Daw, one of the churchwardens of St. Andrew's, and the choir stalls, which are not yet in their places, are the gift of St. Andrew's congregation.

WHP 1896

Dr. Brett . . .

*For much of his working life in Watford Dr. Brett
worked closely with colleagues Dr. Wilson Iles and
the Reverend Newton Price; they were a formidable
trio, constantly crusading on behalf of the working
class, the poor and the town in particular. Dr. Iles
held almost as many posts as did Dr. Brett and
between them they forwarded plans for building
Watford's first hospital. Dr. Iles did not see the plans
come to fruition; he died in 1883, aged 49. He had
performed a tracheometry operation during which he
suffered a small cut to a finger. This became infected
and he died of the resultant blood-poisoning.*

*During Dr. Brett's time a Foundation, Platts,
provided for a Free Grammar School at Aldenham,
with places for a certain number of children from
adjoining parishes, including Watford. As, however,
the distance from Watford to Aldenham prevented
children attending, the object of the founder, as far as
it concerned this parish, was not achieved. Upon
making changes to the school endowments in 1876,
the Charity Commissioners set aside £13,333 for the
purpose of an endowed school at Watford. This
endowment was neglected for a number of years, and
would have been lost forever had not the efforts of
Dr. Brett restored it.*

Death of Dr. Brett

The community of Watford mourns this week
one of the most prominent of its oldest inhabitants, Alfred Thomas Brett, M.D., of Watford
House, who died on Saturday morning last. Dr.
Brett's health had been failing for some time; he
suffered from chronic Bright's disease, of which
there was no amelioration; about eighteen months
ago he had an attack of influenza and bronchitis,
and in December last, pleurisy. Though he
cannot be said to have departed "full of years,"
being only 68, he lived to the physicians' age, and
bears all the honours of the aged, for his years
were full of work; he had done much for the
inhabitants of the town to which his footsteps
were led early in life.

Dr. Brett, the youngest son of the late Mr. J. T.
Brett, of Fishmoor, Walton-on-Thames, was
born in Hinde-street, Manchester-square, London, in 1828. His professional education was
received at Guy's Hospital, where he was successful in obtaining all the appointments open to
students. He obtained distinctions in chemistry
and anatomy. He was dresser with the late Dr.
Bransby Cooper (nephew to the first Sir Astley
P. Cooper), through whose influence it was that
he came to Watford in 1850, and afterwards
became partner with the late Dr. T. A. Ward. He
became M.D. of St. Andrew's, 1850, and after-
M.R.C.S. Eng. and L.S.A., 1850 (Guy's); Fellow
of the Royal Medico-Chirurgical Society; Member of the British Medical Association; Vice-
President of the Medical Officers of Schools'
Association. He was the representative of Herts
in the Metropolitan Branch of the British Medical Association; active in forming the Medical
Officers of Schools' Association, and became a
Vice-President (the head of the Association
being the President of the Royal College of
Surgeons). Dr. Brett was on the Council of the
Society of Medical Officers of Health, and a
member of the Volunteers' Medical Staff Association. He was Hon. Secretary for more than
thirty years, most of the time Treasurer, and
since President of the West Herts Medical
Association. That society was formed in 1849,

and he attended nearly every meeting since its
formation. The public offices Dr. Brett held in
connection with his profession were—Medical
Officer of Health for the Watford Urban District,
Medical Officer for the Union and Parish of
Watford, Public Vaccinator, Certified Factory
Surgeon, Hon. Surgeon to the Watford District
Cottage Hospital, Medical Officer of the London
Orphan Asylum, Watford, and Surgeon London
and North-Western Railway.

Dr. Brett married the daughter of Mr. Reeves,
of Chalk-hill, Watford, and had four daughters,
also a son who died in infancy. Mrs. Brett died in
1865. Their daughters living are Miss Brett,
Miss Edith Brett, and Mrs. St. Leger; Mrs.
Lacon, the wife of the Rev. Edmund Lacon,
having died soon after her marriage.

Dr. Brett will be remembered as one of the
most earnest promoters of the growth of Watford
institutions. When building became general, when
new streets were laid out, and Watford began to
assume the character of a suburban rather than a
country town, the necessity for institutions such
as the locality had not before possessed became
apparent, at times assuming such an urgent
aspect that except to the most sanguine the
provision of funds by voluntary means seemed
almost impossible. But this did not deter Dr.
Brett.

It was a characteristic of Dr. Brett that his love
for the various works that he undertook did not
cool, but his interest carried him on from year to
year with a devotion that was remarkable. Before
the establishment of the Public Library, he was a
supporter and Chairman of the Science and Art
Classes in connection with South Kensington:
for he was always enthusiastic in regard to the
acquisition of knowledge in science, art, and
indeed in literature. He joined in the proposal to
substitute the Public Library for the more private
Mechanics' Institute with all his heart. The
Public Libraries' Act was adopted in 1871, and
the foundation of the present building was laid in
1873, in Masonic form, by the M.W.P.G.M., the
late Bro. William Stuart, of Aldenham Abbey, and

opened by the late Earl of Verulam, Lord Lieutenant of the County. For the first three years Dr.
Brett was chairman of the institution, and again
occupied that position in 1888, when enlargement was in progress. It was at that time, by his
influence, that the coat of arms for Watford was
adopted for the Library.

In the same way he pushed forward the
schemes for Technical Education, leading the
way with those gentlemen who had made it more
particularly their study. It is a matter of gratification that he lived long enough to count up in some
measure his successes. The establishment of the
Public Library as a library and reading room,
with science and art classes, grew into the
Watford College of Science, Art, Music, and
Literature, and he rejoiced over each success,
marking the standing of the Technical branch in
1894 by congratulating the Committee that Watford was still taking the lead. But the connection
of Dr. Brett with the Public Library is the history
of that institution.

When the possible loss to Watford of a sum of
£13,333 6s. 8d. for education seemed imminent,
Dr. Brett, who had previously been one of the
Governors of Mrs. Fuller's Free School in the
Parish Church-yard, threw all his energies, with
other gentlemen, into the endeavour to secure the
money, and to add to it the endowment of Mrs.
Fuller's School, to provide a school for Watford
above the elementary class. That he succeeded is
evidenced by the present Watford Endowed
School.

He rejoiced to say at a meeting of the Old Boys
Association, that from a school beginning with
67 boys there were 320 ex-boys at the time. But
the Endowed School was at its foundation only
the secondary school on somewhat modernised
lines, and in the addition of those branches of
technical instruction which are now taught, Dr.
Brett took a leading part. Cookery at the girls'
school, and principally, chemistry at the boys',
were undertaken, and a laboratory was built, for
which the County Council Technical Grant is,
through his energy, forthcoming.

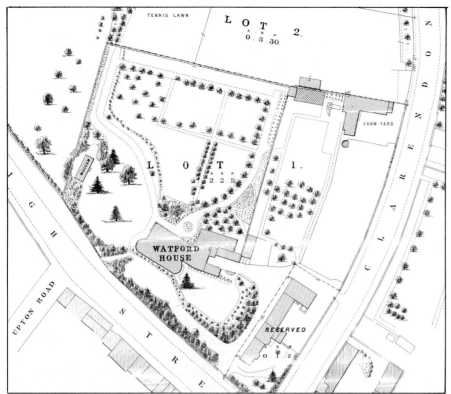

Watford House, built c1775 by Thomas Clutterbuck Jnr. was the home of Robert Clutterbuck, a historian of Hertfordshire. The house and grounds were sold after Dr. Brett's death in 1896; Clement's store now occupies part of the site. Dr. Brett's museum housed his natural history collection—he was president of the Herts Natural History Society. Upton Road is now the Exchange Road flyover.

Sale of Dr. Brett's House and Land

THE first part of this was described in the particulars as highly valuable freehold residential property, adjoining the High-street of Watford, and the main road from London, 800 yards from the station, and close to the centre of the town and Cassiobury Park, possessing an extremely valuable building element. The property includes the commodious old fashioned family residence known as Watford House, which is approached by a carriage drive and well removed from the road, from which it is sheltered by a line of well grown and grand timber trees and shrubs, standing in the midst of a beautiful and lovely old-fashioned garden, which has had great care bestowed upon it, and is well stocked with the best fruit trees and flowering shrubs. There is a large room on the lawn used as a museum, overshadowed by a grand cedar-tree, and on the opposite side of the garden a model farmery. The land has an area of 3a. 2r. 22p. The corner piece of the property, on which stands the surgery, was reserved.

The next property that I have to bring before you, said Mr. Humbert, is Watford House, where our old friend Dr. Brett lived a vast many years of his life, and I do not hesitate to say that in course of my career in Watford I have never had such a saleable thing through my hands—I have never had to deal with an estate which can be bought and developed without the expense of a single shilling. The roads exist—the High-street and Clarendon-road—and are made up; there is nothing to pay for road-making. You can sacrifice the house if you are so disposed, and sell the whole of the frontage on the High-street in about half-an-hour; in fact, I will undertake to do it. Apart from that you have the old-fashioned house—a charming old place which has taken many years, all Dr. Brett's life and his predecessor's, to make it what it is. I am not going to wade through all the particulars, because you have all been to look at the property and know its capabilities, and whatever I say you will take no notice of.

Bidding began for Lot 1 at £3,000, and went on rapidly up to £4,250, but then began to drop off. It stopped at £4,320, and the lot was knocked down to Mr. W. Judge. "Will you take the field?" asked Mr. Humbert. "The whole," replied Mr. Judge; so that he takes the whole of the property for £7,320.

The next property offered was Nos. 5, 6, and 8, Derby-road. No. 5, which was of the rental of £30 per annum, the auctioneer said he could have let at £36 over and over again, the drains having been renewed and put in perfect order. The bidding began at £300, and only reached £390, at which price Mr. Humbert said he could not sell it. No. 6, let for £38, went up to £395, and he passed that also. No. 8, rent £30, went to £390. Mr. Humbert said that he could not sell at that price; anyone could have either of the houses at £400 that night; to-morrow they would be £450.

"The Kennels," Chalk-hill, was next put up, let at £50 a year, on a lease expiring in 1900. It was sold to Mr. E. Clarke, the tenant, for £620.

"Copthall," Chipperfield, an old-fashioned house with 3½ acres of land, let at £31 a year, came next. After reaching £500, the bidding went up £1 at a time, causing some amusement, until it reached £556, when it was knocked down to Mr. Eales, the tenant.

WO October, 1896

Twenty-three years ago Dr. Brett became the first Medical Officer of Health for the Urban District of Watford, upon the passing of the amendment of the Public Health Act establishing that office. In order to take that position he resigned the seat on the Local Board, or as he always preferred to call it, the Board of Health, which he had filled for many years. The commencement of his work could not have been pleasant; there was a great deal to be done in improving the sanitary condition of the town, and the prejudices to be contended with were not few. It will be safe to say that even what were regarded as his whims and fancies have to a great extent been carried out. Year after year in his reports he was persistent in recommending different improvements, one being the alteration of the bridge at the lower part of High-street, not only on account of its narrowness, but the annually recurring nuisance of rotting weeds that the arches detained in their course down the Colne. He saw the day when he was able to support in the County Council the proposal to build a new bridge, and afterwards used the present substantial structure in his daily drives. With regard to this office it will be remembered that he bore the burden of the beginning. He resigned only a few weeks ago, and his son-in-law, Dr. St. Leger, has been chosen his successor.

The circumstances of his election may be remembered; how, when he had been instrumental in calling public meetings at which the candidates were brought forward, he at the last moment offered himself, and was elected by a good majority. His platform, said the *Lancet* on the occasion, was "Sanitation; public health; all means to improve the physical, and moral condition of the people." The ideas that he had formed as to the sanitary needs of the town and district he carried with him to the County Council, and we find him, while supporting general matters, bringing forward a proposal for the supervision of the rivers and water-ways of the County.

One of the movements which he took up with great earnestness was that for the provision of

allotments, and he did not rest until the Local Board were proceeding in the matter. Summing up the result of this movement, he remarked that (including the previous provision of allotment gardens) there are now five fields set apart for the purpose, with 600 cultivators.

Dr. Brett joined the Watford Company of Hertfordshire Volunteers when the movement began, in 1859, as, he used to say, "a full private." He became surgeon to the Company, and was assiduous in his attendance, being studiously present on all great occasions. Time brought him the rank of Surgeon-Major, the Queen's medal for 32 years' service, and the addition of Lieutenant-Colonel to his title.

It would be difficult to sum up such a life as that of Dr. Brett if it had not been lived before the people; not indeed for applause, but because the work that was done could not be hidden. He found his pleasure and reward in what he did for the good of the community. He gained esteem, respect, reverence, for he had a faith in the ultimate success of his endeavours that sustained him against opposition, and with it, unbounded geniality. We have said nothing as to religion, but he was a Churchman of the moderate school. Possibly, knowing his habit of thought and study of nature, we should not be wrong in saying that his whole life was worship; but if we speak more particularly, it would be to say that, usually he worshipped with the children.

WO July, 1896

Missing Doctor Brett

IN how many ways the kindly presence and influence of the late Dr. Brett will be missed has yet to be experienced. On Tuesday last a meeting of the Directors of the Corn Exchange Company was to have taken place, but nothing could be done for lack of members of the Board. In such cases Dr. Brett was most attentive; except it were absolutely impossible for him to attend, he might be expected to be present in any business that he undertook.

WHP July, 1896

High Street looking towards the Market Place. Loates Lane is beside Longley's and the Churchyard entrance is on the left of the picture. Nos. 91-95 would later become Marks and Spencer's. No. 114, on the left, has had the 'flower basket annexe' added whilst the rest of the shops on the left stand comparison with the 1832 drawing on page 28. Occasion is Queen Victoria's Diamond Jubilee, 1897.   *p.333*

This wagonette bus service operated between Callowland (water trough, Gammons Lane,) and Bushey Arches. With driver Mr. G. J. Bence and a conductor, four passengers were carried at a fare of threepence each for the single journey. Popularity led to frequent overloading and consequent breakdowns and the service was withdrawn. The vehicle became the possession of the Standard Range and Foundry Company. Story page 188.

◀ This 1897 Diamond Jubilee celebration bonfire built at Harwoods Farm may have been similar to that which was built a few years later for the Coronation of King Edward VII, the postponement of which caused riots.

Members of the Urban District Council, and others, include, l-r: Messrs. Boff, Waterhouse, Camp, Fisher, Brightman, Slinn, Ayres, Darvill, George Capell, Clifford, Brightman, Andrews, Jackson and Tearle. This list includes the UDC Engineer, an Architect, and no less than four builders!

... 30 kw capacity for day use ...

Watford Electric Lighting

Although the question of electric lighting has been before the Urban District Council on several occasions, it was not till June of 1896 that any serious move was made, and it was then decided to advertise for a consulting engineer to advise the Council generally on the matter. As a result, the Council placed the drawing up of a report in the hands of Mr. W. C. C. Hawtayne, who presented a long report in October of the same year, in which he advised the Council that the establishment of municipal electricity supply works should prove remunerative.

The Council desired that the scheme presented should be one to embrace the complete public lighting of the town. Mr. Hawtayne's scheme dealt with this, and of course the laying of mains in a considerable portion of the town for supplying private customers as well as public lamps.

The system recommended was the high tension alternating current transformer system with distribution at low pressure, and the scheme was estimated to cost, approximately, £19,000, if the buildings could be combined with new sewerage works that the Council were about to construct at the old sewerage sites, which are distant about a mile and a quarter from the centre of the town, or about £21,000 if the two undertakings were not combined.

As an indication of the rapid growth of Watford, it may be mentioned that whereas the number of public lamps set out on the plan was 414, the actual number now being connected to the mains is exactly 800. The contract for the cables for both public and private lighting was placed with Messrs. Henley's, who have carried out the work in a very thorough manner. It was originally intended that a number of arc lamps should be placed in High-street and Queen's-road, but the Council afterwards decided that they would rather go in for incandescent lighting throughout, except in the Market-place, where three arc lamps are to be installed, and in the railway station approach, where there will be one. Separate mains are laid throughout for the public lighting, which is controlled from six switching-on points. The high tension mains are connected to transformers at a ratio of 2000 volts to 400 volts, from which the low tension mains run to the groups of street lamps, each lamp-post being fitted with two 200 volt 8 c.p. or two 16 c.p. lamps in series across the 400 volts in all the streets with the exception of a few in the centre of the town, where two 20 c.p. lamps are to be placed in each lamp-post. Existing posts are being adapted in the majority of cases, but in the centre of the town new lamp-posts are being erected.

The installation has several features of interest. In the first place, taking the last census as the guide, there are but two Municipal installations in England with a smaller population to serve, namely Taunton and Whitehaven, and but one in Scotland, Ayr. We are not therefore surprised that Mr. Hawtayne, the consulting engineer, originally advised the adoption of small units, namely, three of 75 K.W. each and one of 25 K.W. for day load.

Before the contract was definitely placed, however, Mr. Hawtayne recommended an alternative of the Brush Company, which was in due course accepted, comprising two 150 K.W. sets and one 30 K.W. set for day load.

The station has been designed to take a third 150 K.W. set before the temporary cable requires to be removed, and we are glad to learn that this space is not likely to remain long unoccupied, owing to the rapidity with which premises of all kinds are being wired for connection to the mains.

It is a most business-like combination, and the way in which it performed its 6 hours' full load test leaves nothing to be desired. Not only were the bearings "stone cold" at the end, but almost the same could be claimed for the armature and field coils of generators and exciters. In no case did the temperature exceed 40 degrees F.

The engine has but a single crank, the vertical compound cylinders being arranged tandem. Each cylinder is in itself single acting, but the H.P. piston is active upwards, and the L.P. downwards, so that the crank receives two impulses per revolution.

The two large engines develop 250 I.H.P. at 300 revolutions per minute. The valves are of the Corliss type, and our readers may remember that notwithstanding the use of only two valves, automatic expansion is accomplished without any of the usual throttling effects.

WO May, 1899

● *Frequent references in the local newspapers drew invidious comparisons with other large towns and cities which had adopted electricity and and which were mainly in the industrial midlands and north.*

However, no private enterprise had made an attempt to establish an independent generating station in Watford and so the Urban District Council filled the gap, building the station in Cardiff Road.

As the third smallest municipal generating undertaking in the country, the capacity of the plant was planned on an appropriately small scale with 225 kw main (night) load plus 25 kw day load. But before installation this was increased to 300 kw main load and 30 kw unit for day load.

The early electricity pioneers apparently visualised electricity as being a power for lighting only—consequently they could see little day demand: 30 kw being an insignificant amount.

Highway Offences

David Edmonds, of Chiswell Green, was charged with riding asleep on the cart of which he was in charge, at Watford, on August 7th.

Police-constable Hadder found the defendant asleep in the bottom of another man's cart in company with the other man. The second cart ran into a barrier placed in the street where a new crossing was being put down. The man in charge of the barrier said that he led the first horse past the barrier, but the second horse being tied to the first cart, the second cart came in contact with the barrier.

The Chairman said that the Bench would adjourn the case for the attendance of the man who was in charge of the barrier.

Edmonds pleaded guilty, and he was fined 2s. 6d.; costs 6s. Allowed a week to pay.

Charles Gibbs, the man in charge of the second cart, pleaded guilty.

Fined 2s. 6d.; costs 6s. Allowed a week to pay.

Water Supply

Messrs. Wells and Co.'s application.—A letter dated 20th inst. from Messrs. Wells and Co., was read, stating that they desired to extend the water laid on to the stables at their premises, to a portion of the brewery. The Committee recommended that the application be acceded to on the following terms:–(a) the costs of the necessary pipes and meter to be paid by the Company. (b) An agreement relieving the Council from all liability in the event of the supply being at any time deficient, and empowering either party to determine the arrangement on one month's notice to be entered into. (c) That the charge for water supplied be at the rate of 1s. per 1,000 gallons, with an annual minimum payment of £10.

"Water Supply. Application from Dr. Tibbles' Vi-Cocoa (1898), Ltd.—A letter dated 26th inst. from Mr. R. W. Price, was read, stating that this Company, having purchased 50 acres of land bounded by St. Albans-road, Bushey Mill-lane, and the branch line from Watford to St., Albans, were about to construct two roads on the lower portion of the land and to build a factory, and enquiring whether the Council would be prepared to lay water mains before the roads were made, and on what terms they would supply the factory with water. The matter was referred to the Engineer for consideration and a report.

WO July, 1899

Fire Brigade

In 1867 an advertisement in the 'Watford Observer' led to the formation of a 'volunteer' fire brigade on November 23rd.

A new engine was purchased from funds, amounting to £148, raised by public subscription.

This engine, names 'Vesta', was horse-drawn, and the pumps were worked by hand. With 200 feet of delivery hose it was capable of pumping 140 gallons of water per minute to a height of 130 feet. Delivery of the engine was taken in March, 1868.

The Volunteer Fire Brigade remained an independent unit until 1898 when it was taken over by the W.U.D.C., but members were still unpaid volunteers.

Cassiobury Park Gates, Rickmansworth Road

p.293 t, 338 bl

Shepherd's Lodge, Rickmansworth Road.

p.338 br

Rickmansworth Road, looking towards Watford; ground in front of Cassiobridge Lodge was Cassiobridge Common where gypsy encampments gave much trouble; the lane to the left was Rousebarn Lane where after taking the ford of the Gade one could proceed to Chandlers Cross. *p.339 b*

Rickmansworth Road, looking towards Cross Roads, building on left is stables of the 'Elms'—note the huge elm tree *(s.184)*—later site of Town Hall. Straight ahead for Nat. West. Bank! *p.339 t*

The Fire Brigade

Mr C. H. Peacock, writing in answer to a letter from the Council asking if he would drill the firemen at Callow Land, said he was quite willing to drill the men when there were any. (Laughter.) If the Council would provide outfits for about six men, they could soon be picked out. He added that he should be glad to see the application for tenders for the new fire station at Upton House.

Mr. Thorpe said that he had received a fire engine at Callow Land that day. It was a very ancient one, somewhere over 50 years old. He should like to know whether they were to have a more powerful engine.

The Chairman: This one used by the Volunteer Brigade will find its way there when a small repair has been carried out.

Mr. Thomas enquired when the plans would be ready for the fire station. If the obsolete engine mentioned was a sample of their fire protection it was quite time they took the matter thoroughly in hand.

Mr. Ayres: I shall be able to have the plans ready, and, if they are approved, the estimates in, in about a month. The engine spoken of is not the engine we use in the town. There is a better engine always ready.

Mr. Pitkin asked if there was really a fire brigade of any description existing, and if so, whether the men ever practised? He pointed out that they must consider not only the needs of Callow Land, but the requirements of the whole district.

The Chairman: That question can be raised on the reference to the Committee of Mr. Peacock's letter, and the Committee can bear in mind there is a strong feeling in the town that the present provision is inadequate.

Mr. Thomas: There is a great amount of dilatoriness and drifting at present.

Mr. Ayres said that he was advised it would take 12 months at least to get an engine, and he proposed it should be an instruction to the Committee to consider the advisability of at once ordering an engine.

Mr. Pitkin pressed his question as to whether there really was a fire brigade. He had been told by men who should know something about it that they had a new fire escape, but that it was perfectly useless, as they had not a man who knew anything about it.

Mr. Thomas said that the town was totally unprotected against fire. The arrangements were quite inadequate for a place half the size of Watford.

Mr. Trew said he had a very short time of the committee, and he thought Mr. Peacock was the man who was more thoroughly up in the matter than anybody on the Council. However, as most of them were aware, Mr. Waterhouse had made every preparation—and he believed at the last meeting they approved of his suggestions—for extending the water mains, or rather increasing their size and doing away with a number of deadends, so that they would have a certainty of a good supply for any emergency. They had the same advantages and same fire engines as they always had, and Mr. Peacock was, he believed, still interested in the work. Whether the men had been practising as much as some might think he could not say, but he would get the information Mr. Pitkin asked for and report at the next meeting.

Mr. Thorpe asked whether Mr. Peacock was really acting as captain or not, because some time ago he resigned from the Volunteer Fire Brigade, and now was rather uncertain whether he was acting under the Council or not.

Mr. Trew said they understood Mr. Peacock was still acting as captain, but he would see him and get something definite from him.

The whole matter was then sent to the Committee, who, it was understood, would consider the purchase of a new engine.

WO June, 1899

Firemen's Suits

Tenders were opened for the supply of eight fireman's suits, consisting of trousers, tunic, and cap. They were as follows:–Messrs. Shand, Mason and Co., £19; Mr. Austin, Watford, £16 16s.; Mr. J. P. Taylor, £2 17s. 6d., £2 14s. 6d., and £2 7s. 6d. per suit.

On the motion of Mr. Cossham, Mr. Austin's tender was accepted.

Fire Station at New Bushey

Mr. Pitkin brought forward a motion of which he had given notice with regard to the provision of a fire brigade station at New Bushey. He had understood that the question was to be dealt with all over the district and a thorough scheme of protection against fire adopted. At Callow Land a station had already been provided, and what he asked for was a similar one at New Bushey. The expense would not be great, or he should have considered seriously before bringing this forward. They had two manual engines, one of which had gone to Callow Land, and he suggested that the other should be sent to New Bushey.

WO July, 1899

New Fire Engine

It was reported by the Water Supply and Fire Brigade Committee:–

"The following tenders for the supply of a fire engine capable of throwing 350 gallons per minute, with accessories, were received and opened—Messrs. Shand, Mason and Co., £362 10s.; Messrs. Rose and Co., £375; Messrs. Merryweather and Co., £435. The Committee recommend that the tender of Messrs. Shand. Mason & Co. be accepted subject to the Engineer being satisfied with the specification."

In reference to Mr. Pitkin's motion, the report stated:–

"The Committee considered Mr. Pitkin's motion for the establishment of a fire station at New Bushey, and resolved to recommend that a hose reel be obtained for New Bushey."

WO August, 1899

The Fire Station

Tenders for the erection of the Fire Station at Upton House were opened as follows:–

	£
H. Martin, Northampton	2020
Clifford and Gough, Watford	2037
George Wiggs. Watford	2011
H. V. Watkins. Watford	2085
Henry Brown, Watford	2298
Clark Bros., Watford	1928
R. L. Tonge, Watford	2099
F. Dupont and Co., Watford	2228
H. M. Dove, Euston-road	2237
G. and J. Waterman, Watford	2267

The approximate estimate was £2,250.

Mr. Cossham moved that the tender of Messrs. Clarke Bros. be accepted.

Mr. Longley seconded.

WO October, 1899

Highway Offences

Frederick Gurney, of Hemel Hempstead, was charged with riding asleep, at Watford, on October 30th.

Sergeant Hassell stated that the horse and cart in this case was standing behind the other. When the first horse stopped this one stopped.

Fined 10s.; costs, 6s. In default, seven days' hard labour.

Population 1901, 26,327

An early manual fire pump, originally in the use of Hamper Mill.

Watford's early fire pump of c1800-1820, photographed in Albert Street, in the 1920's.

Watford's Fire Brigade wearing their new Watford uniform. Behind is 'Vesta', the double-horse-drawn manual fire engine of March 1868, i.e. 31 years old at this date.   (1899)

Summer 1900, the new fire station, next to the U.D.C. offices in the High Street, completed and open for business.

p.289 t, p.322 b

The Fire Brigade

The time fixed for the trial was half-past six, and a few minutes after that time the new engine, which is very smart in appearance, was driven up. Unfortunately the weather was bitterly cold.

Mr. Trew lit the fire, and in 6 mins. 45 secs. steam of 100 lbs. pressure was registered. Those present were able to check the time for pressure at 5, 10, 20, 30, 60, and 100lbs., on cards which were handed round for that purpose. The engine was started by Mr. Trew when the 100 lbs. was reached. Interesting tests followed. First with 60 feet of hose a 1⅛ in. jet was thrown to a height that would command any building in Watford; then two deliveries, with ¾in. nozzle, were put on 160 feet of hose; after that two breechings of one into two, giving four ⅝in. jets were worked, 360 gallons per minute being thrown; and last the biggest spray possible was shown with two lines on, breeching of two into one, with 1½ in. jet. The result of the trials was regarded by those competent to judge as most satisfactory. The absence of oscillation in the engine was remarkable considering the work done. When she was working at top pressure the body and wheels were perfectly steady, and there was not the slightest signs of rocking. The weight of the engine, it may be mentioned, is 32 cwts., the hose bringing it up to two tons. In each of the four ⅝in. jets referred to was obtained the same power as could be got from the old manual at full pressure with 22 men at the levers, and this with, of course, only two men working, the stoker and driver.

With the adoption of a new call-bell system, which is under favourable consideration by the Council, there will be, what has not been the case for many years, adequate fire protection for the town. That is a fact which it is most satisfactory to record.

In order to celebrate in an informal way the opening of the new Fire Station adjoining Upton House, the Brigades taking part in the Whit-Monday procession, were entertained to dinner on the new premises, by permission of the Urban District Council, by Mr. C. H. Peacock, captain of the Town Brigade. About forty sat down, the company including the members of the Town Brigade, Sedgwick's Brigade under Deputy-Captain Harold Sedgwick, and Croxley Mills Brigade.

WO June, 1900

Police Christmas Boxes

By Colonel Daniell's time (1880-1911) public relations had improved somewhat, but this improvement itself created problems. From around 1888 onwards the citizens of Watford began at Christmas to offer gratuities out of appreciation for the work of the police. However, by Christmas 1897 the police had fallen into the practice of calling round to the houses of various residents in the borough and, while not specifically asking for a Christmas box, making it quite clear what they had called for. A certain Mr. Moore wrote to the Chief Constable and complained of this practice. Colonel Daniell, naturally, was furious. Captain Wymer, the commander of Watford Division and Deputy Chief Constable of the county, was forced to resign, but only after Daniell had threatened to dismiss him summarily from the force. Wymer was turned out of his house at Watford police station in spite of appeals for a stay of execution on account of his family's health. The inspector of the division retained his job only after a pathetic letter begging for clemency on account of his wife's nervous ill-health. The £26 that had been collected was offered back to the donors. It is perhaps indicative of the state of the relations with the public that out of the £26 only £5/11/6 was received back by the donors. Daniell followed up this action with the following general order on February 7, 1898:

"All the officers and constables stationed at Watford are aware that from the point of view of the Secretary of State in the Home Department, with whose opinion every chief officer of police must be in absolute accord, a very grave breach of the regulations concerning the police has been committed by local police at Watford going round private residents and places of business collecting Christmas boxes. Nothing can be more destructive to the morale and discipline of the force. How would it be if a constable in the witness box were asked in cross-examination "Did you go into the plaintiff's (or defendant's) house for a Christmas box?" "Yes." "Did he give you one?" "No." Would not counsel immediately make a point that the police were against his client on having been refused a Christmas box? If anyone sends money to the police station as a Christmas box for the men the sum so received will be divided, but there must be no collecting."

In 1892 the first full-time plain-clothes officer had appeared at Watford. He was supplemented by a second officer in 1894.

This move was designed to cope with the growing liaison between Watford and London and the consequent increase in crime.

'The Story of Hertfordshire Police'

Cycles—Hertfordshire Police

Daniell was very concerned with the new forms of personal transport being developed. Bicycles came into general use after one had been bought as an experiment in 1893 in Watford. In 1895 Daniell ordered that "names and numbers of officers of all ranks competent to ride bicycles

Watford Steamer returning from a trial call out.   c1910

are to be sent into this office, and names of officers are to be sent in as they learn to ride a machine." By 1896 there were eleven county-owned cycles in use by the Hertfordshire Police. In June of that year Daniell announced that officers could use their own cycles for police work with an allowance of 3d. per hour (this high allowance was given because Daniell regarded cycling as a very dangerous occupation). Early introduction of cycles on a fairly large scale was one of the reasons why the mounted section of the force was never very strong. Characteristically, Daniell surrounded police operations on two wheels with a mass of paper work. Each cycle trip had to be fully documented.

In 1899 the magazine "Cycle" reported the proposed setting up of a cycle corps in the

Hertfordshire Police, which the magazine feared would be extremely hard on speeding cyclists or "scorchers." The fears were not entirely unfounded, for many speeding cyclists were caught by the corps. These officers, who operated largely on the Great North Road, were distinguished by the wearing of a forage cap instead of a helmet.

'The Story of Hertfordshire Police'

Test Call

The year, about 1910, the occasion, a test call to Hunton Bridge, and Molly and Tommy did the run in 11 minutes flat, and the older members never let you forget it either, as numbers 2-4-6-8 were still serving when I joined the Watford Volunteer F. Brigade in 1923.

The actual Photo shows the crew and appliance returning from this test call and was taken about 200 yds North of the "Dog" public house in Hempstead Road, Watford.

The crew comprised:- 2nd Officer Graham Neill, Fm Dick Wise, Bill Hilliard, Charlie Crawford, Chief Officer Thorpe, Fm Dan Fountain, Dick Hatton, and Freddie Heath. All the men here except the C/O and Fm Wise were Council employees.

W. Chana (Sub O ret'd) H.C.C. Fire Brigade (1963)

● *The photograph above had been in the fire station, forgotten, for many years, and was only rediscovered when the station was demolished in 1962.*

Early morning by the Lime Tree Temperance Hotel in the High Street (near modern W. H. Smiths, No. 39). On the corner opposite is the house which once was the surgery of Dr. Iles (now Nat. West. Bank).

High Street, left to right, Nos. 30-16. Courtyard entrance is to Wells Yard (modern day Wellstones); shop and cottage on right is now Jackson's, Jewellers. *p.173 tl, 336 b*

War Fund

... Now, at the end of nine months, the company are still in the field. The have done hard campaigning work, to which reference has been made from time to time in our columns. They have lost a few of their number in battle, and more through disease. When they return they are assured of a great welcome from Watford townspeople, a committee of whom have all the arrangements for the home-coming in hand. While on this subject, it may be mentioned that a War Fund, started by the "Watford Observer," was responded to most liberally, and reached a total of £282. Also, it should be added, that Major the Earl of Essex was invalided home, and was on a bed of sickness for weeks after his return from South Africa, his recovery being regarded with the greatest pleasure by everyone in the town. Lieut.-Colonel Healey, too, who went out in command of the South Wales Borderers, came home, broken in health, to receive a cordial welcome from the people amongst whom he lives.

WO February, 1900

The Royal Visit

An escort of Yeomanry attended the Prince from the railway station to the Market-place, where from a covered stand, on which stood most of the public men of the town, an address of welcome to his Royal Highness was read. In his reply, the Prince referred to the growth of the town, which, he said, he had visited in 1874 with the 7th Hussars. He also expressed his gratification at the loyalty of the inhabitants. As he drove away the crowds broke into lusty and prolonged cheers. The route to the new schools was lined with people. The ceremony connected with the new

institution was notable in many respects. With such of the ritual of Freemasonry as could be gone through before the eyes of the uninitiated, the Prince laid the stone well and truly, to the honour of the Craft and the glory of God. The building, which is to cost nearly £100,000, is now proceeding apace, the site being on the Bushey Grove estate.

WO May, 1900

The Relief of Mafeking

Like the rest of the country Watford celebrated the relief of Mafeking with great enthusiasm, the scenes in the streets both on Friday and Saturday evenings being unparalleled in the history of the town. The decorations which had been used the previous week to welcome H.R.H. the Duke of Connaught came in most handy. High-street, Queen-street, and the Broadway were in gala day garb. The festoons of Chinese lanterns which were so effective on the 12th along the Broadway were again lighted and were again admired. But it was not only in the main thoroughfares that flags were displayed. Away in side streets tiny banners peeped from the windows or were waved by youngsters in the garden—the same youngsters who had on Thursday night been drawn up in the school playground and had cheered for Baden-Powell, and been given a day's holiday because Mafeking had been relieved.

It was about half-past ten on Friday evening when the news arrived, and in less than half-an-hour from that time a dense crowd blocked the thoroughfare. The good news so eagerly awaited had come. Men did not stop to ask whence it had come, or whether it were official. Someone was certain of its authenticity, and that was enough.

The loyal and patriotic residents of Watford rushed from their homes on hearing the first shouts and the first cheers. They swarmed into the High-street, where, with unrestrained enthusiasm, they woke up echoes in the little back streets. All the town, or very nearly all, knew the great news before midnight. Everywhere it was received with joy. The people who had given the Herts Yeomanry such a magnificent send-off two months ago were just the people from whom one could expect a great outburst over the end of the sufferings of heroic Mafeking. As time passed the uproar grew. The heaviest sleepers in the neighbourhood were awakened, and as it dawned upon them that the noise meant the arrival of the news for which they had waited with such feverish impatience for days that seemed weeks, they rushed, half dressed and cheering lustily, into the street. How they sang "God Save the Queen"; and with what expanse of lungs they hurrahed for Baden-Powell!

The Artizan Staff Band turned out, and the singing of "Rule Britannia" and the National Anthem, now led by the band, rose louder and louder. Women, looking on from the windows above, waved flags and now and again joined in with treble notes that could be distinctly heard above the bass roar of the crowd. A number of people carried torches, and that old-time expression of jubilation—the bonfire, was not lacking. At several points in High-street the flames threw a glare on the faces of the hundreds that tramped by. The police did not interfere; they only kept a watchful eye on the bonfires.

WO May, 1900

High Street, timber-framed houses dating from 1714, Nos. 186 & 188. The Railway Tavern, next to the railway station, is No. 184. Just beyond the Tavern can be seen the narrow entrance which led to the station platform. On the left of the photograph is an Urban District Council street-watering cart used to spray the streets to settle the dust; comment p.145.   *p. 330 tr*

The War—A Soldier's Letter

Private S. Dolamore, writing from Kroonstad, on June 28th, to his mother at Watford, says:–

"I dare say you have been worrying about me not writing for so long, but I could not write before as we have had such a lot to do since we left Bloemfontein to go to Pretoria. I must tell you that it was very hard marching, and plenty of fighting, but not so much as we expected there would be; and I am very glad to tell you that my regiment, the 5th Mounted Infantry, was one of the first regiments to enter Pretoria. We had a fight outside of Pretoria on the 4th of June, and marched past Lord Roberts and on through Pretoria on the 5th, and camped the other side. We stopped there two days, and then came back through to this side. Then my regiment went on to try to knock Botha out. I was left behind because my horse died. I was there for three days, but I did not write because I was waiting to hear if there were any orders about coming home. I have not heard anything about it yet. Then I was sent down to Johannesburg to get some horses, but we could not get any there, so we had to come down here to Kroonstad to get some. We came by train, and were nearly blown up by De Wet, and delayed for three days because the line was torn up. It was at the same place that De Wet captured our mails and burnt them, but we found several letters all intact. We had Mr. Winston Churchill and the Duke of Westminster on the train.

WO July, 1900

Monmouth House, The Parade, High Street. Mrs. Bishops house, later to be converted into shops.

Entrance to Red Lion Yard, High Street, later to be entrance to new market site in 1928.

Lower High Street. The 'Angel' in the distance (behind the girl). The top of the Mill may be seen and Dumbeltons, butchers, with the shop blind. By the wagon are the 'Brewer's Arms' and 'Leathersellers Arms'. *p.75, 162 t, 331 tl*

Single line, uncovered platform of High Street Station on the Watford to Rickmansworth line. c1900. *p.330 tl*

The 'Angel', now site of George Ausden's Yard. *p.330 b*

Lower High Street. On the right-hand side, between trees and near house, is Farthing Lane, and between trees and far block of houses, Local Board Road.

The 'Anchor' and the 'Hit or Miss' *p.332 tr*

Lower High Street, Nos. 262-266, now site of High Street Service Station. White-fronted building on the left is the 'Angel' and beyond is 'Grove Place', Court

No. 30, demolished and now George Ausden's.

p.330 b

WATFORD ENGINEERING WORKS.

SOLE AGENTS for

STEAM AND OIL MOTOR CARS.

Petrol.   Motor Spirit.

These Cars may be inspected and tested by appointment, and can be supplied on the

EASY PAYMENT SYSTEM.

MOTOR CARS REPAIRED.

Motor Cycles, 2-h.p., guaranteed, £35.

George Tidcombe's engineering and iron works was started in 1827 and purchased by Henry J. Rogers in 1885, when the name was changed to 'Watford Engineering Works'. Henry and his brother, Roger, continued a business first started in the town in 1777. *p.124 c*

Grove Place, Court No. 30, Lower High Street, centre left-hand houses in the photo above.

A Charter For Watford?

The important subject of Incorporation was again put on the agenda, and once more did the Council decide in favour of seeking a charter. The necessary steps, however, towards obtaining it remain to be taken, and though this journal has persistently advocated incorporation and laid stress on its advantages, there seems to be lacking a public man sufficiently interested in the matter to see it carried through. The paving of the town has been taken in hand, and about £15,000 is being spent on it. Towards half of this sum the County Council contributes two-thirds. During the year the Council added another to their officials by appointing a building inspector, whose duty it is to see that the byelaws are adhered to, and that no "jerry building" goes on.

WO December, 1900

Paget Company's Premises Gutted

Soon after 2 o'clock on Thursday morning a fire broke out on the premises of the Paget Prize Plate Company, Limited, Callow Land, with the result that one block, that in which the photographic plate business is carried on, was practically destroyed. The Company have been established in Watford some twelve years, and employ a considerable number of hands mostly girls, some 50 or 60 of whom found on arriving at their work on Thursday morning that, owing to the fire, they had to return to their homes. The outbreak turned out to be one of the most serious that the Brigades have had to contend with in the town for years.

The fire started in the engine room. An employee named Samuel Brooks was on duty, and it appears that while he was in the boiler-house his attention was called to a bright light in the engine room near by. He soon discovered that this particular room was in flames, and at once gave the alarm. The Callow Land District Brigade, under Lieutenant R. A. Thorpe, turned out with promptitude, and, after connecting their hose with the hydrant, they ran out a length of over 300 yards and tackled the flames by breaking entrances through the windows. The town Brigade, led by Captain C. H. Peacock, and Messrs. Sedgwick's Brigade, under Captain Harold Sedgwick, followed in quick time. It should be added that the London and North Western Railway engineers also assisted with a couple of lines of hose from the railway supply. The police, under Superintendent Wood, also rendered considerable assistance. At half-past 2 the reflection from the flames could be seen in the sky for a long distance. Immediately the nature of the fire was known, instructions were sent out to the pumping station for the best possible force to be put on, and by this means sufficient water was obtained to keep the steamer well supplied.

The block in question was the original one in which the Watford business was commenced, the other premises being extensions. The fire burnt with great fierceness. In the engine room ventilating fans were at work, and these accelerated the progress of the fire, which had a clear run along the roof of the block, owing to a false ceiling. The two six-horse power engines for driving the electric dynamo were much damaged. The other rooms in the department were given to photographic plate work, and the stock and machinery burnt is of considerable value.

The cause of the fire is probably connected with the electric wiring. The firemen deserve great praise for their efforts. Every man was wet through to the skin, and considerable risk was run through the falling roof, iron shafting, and cisterns of water.

WO April, 1902

U.D.C. offices, 14 High Street. Proclamation of King Edward VII. 30th January, 1902.   *p.289*

Electric Street Lighting

Dear Sir,—I should like to recommend any of your readers, who desire an object lesson, to walk down High-street to the new showrooms of the Watford Gas Company, and compare the town electric lamp and the gas lamp of the Company. Being an electrical engineer myself I can hardly be accused of holding a brief for the Gas Company, but I am very anxious that the matter should be carefully gone into, and the Council urged to make their electric street lamps a better advertisement for their undertaking than it is at present. As a ratepayer I am also anxious that we should get the best system of lighting at the least expense.

The following figures may interest those who consider that the matter at all affects their pockets as ratepayers.

The gas lamp outside the Gas Company's showrooms, I am informed, gives 700 candle power, and consumes 20 cubic feet of gas per hour; this, at 3s. per 1000 feet (the price the Company are charging their customers) costs about three farthings per hour.

The ordinary incandescent electric lamp absorbs about 3½ watts per candle power, and at the price of 5d. per unit, about one farthing (the price charged by the Council), 700 candle power absorbs about 2,450 watts, at a cost of about one shilling per hour.

Again, the two eight candle power electric lights in the street lamps absorb about 56 watts per hour, costing 5d. per unit, about one farthing per hour, against a 50 candle power incandescent gas burner consuming about three cubic feet per hour, at 3s. per thousand, burning over two hours for one farthing.

With these figures it certainly behoves us to either turn over the street lighting to the Gas Company, or cast about for some method of improving matters.

I do not know why electric arc lamps are not used more than they are in Watford, for instead of absorbing about 3½ watts per candle power, the arc lamp gives about three candle power per watt, or ten times the light for the energy absorbed.

As an electrical engineer I am certainly very anxious that the bad advertisement electric lighting is now receiving in Watford should be improved, and as you state in your issue of last Saturday, "every ratepayer is a shareholder in the undertaking," we should all see that the electric lighting of the streets is energetically and efficiently carried forward with as much business acumen as an ordinary private firm would have to show.

I beg to remain, dear sir,
Yours faithfully,
H. Cecil Hodges.

WO November, 1902

What date?

Many photographs have been added to the Central Library collection long after they were taken. In consequence the accurate dating and identification of events is not always possible.

The two photographs on the following page have been variously described as 'King George V's visit' and 'King Edward VII's Coronation'. King George came to the throne in 1910 and in the top picture Boot's premises were not yet built—this gives a 'probable' span of 3 years, during which no visit is reported. The guard provided indicates the degree of importance but similarly no such visit is reported of King Edward VII— especially unlikely during his coronation year. Both monarchs visited Watford, but by car, and these events are well commemorated by Downer's postcards.

In 1900 the Duke of Connaught visited Watford to lay the foundation stone of the Royal Masonic School at Bushey and large crowds were gathered. But at that time the electricity supply was not far enough advanced to permit decorations upon buildings. The fourth alternative—the visit of H.R.H. Princess Henry of Battenburg—seems the correct answer and it suitably explains why the crowds are proceeding DOWN the High Street when there would appear no other tangible reason for so doing.

H.R.H. Princess Henry of Battenburg (daughter of Queen Victoria), accompanied by Lord Hyde, passes through the High Street on her way to lay the foundation stone of the Royal Caledonian School, Aldenham Road, Bushey.

The Watford Observer reported in May 1902 "An escort of the Herts Imperial Yeomanry, under Captain Gilliat, "with their scarlet tunics and burnished helmets gave a welcome splash of colour". 17th May, 1902.   *p.329 b*

Whilst the carriage passes Chater's (between Queens Road and Water Lane) the crowd throng behind. (Between what are now Woolworth's and Littlewood's.)

Coronation Postponed

So advanced were the arrangements for the carrying out of the festivities in Watford that some reference to the indefinitely postponed programme may be made.

The celebrations promised to be on a scale in every way worthy of the reputation of the town. Our readers hardly need reminding that the permanent local memorial of the great occasion will take the shape of a new district hospital, towards which already over £3,000 has been subscribed, and for June 26 itself an excellent programme of festivities had been arranged, the cost being estimated at £800, and the money now in hand being approximately £700.

WO June, 1902

Riots in Watford

ON Thursday evening scenes which were an absolute disgrace to Watford occurred in its main street.

It appears that among a certain rowdy element the postponement of the festivities for the Coronation was regarded as a grievance. The Town Committee, over which presided Mr. F. Fisher, as chairman of the Council, met on Tuesday evening, immediately after the official news of the King's dangerous illness was received. The committee unanimously decided to postpone all the festivities—a course which commended itself to all reasonable people.

On Wednesday, however, a number of roughs were heard to express their determination to cause trouble on the following night.

On Thursday morning Mr. Fisher, who seems to have been especially singled out by the rowdies, was hissed as he went about the town.

As the day wore on, the rumour that riotous conduct was expected drew large crowds into the streets. A feeling of subdued excitement prevailed, but at 8 o'clock the police had matters well in hand.

At 11 o'clock there was a huge crowd in the High-street, including about 50 or 60 of the lowest characters in the town, who were determined to create disorder. Stones began to fly, a number of windows were broken, and an attempt was made to fire the shop of Mr. F. Fisher. The police became powerless to deal with the mob. Two shops belonging to Mr. G. Longley were sacked, and considerable damage was done to the shop and residence of Mr. Fisher.

A few mounted police proved unequal to quelling the disturbance, and it was not till a large number of special constables were sworn in that a semblance of order was restored. Special police were drafted into the town next day, a recurrence was feared, but fortunately there was no breach of the peace the following day. Police Court proceedings followed, no fewer than 62 persons having been apprehended on charges of riotous conduct and larceny. Of these 56 were summarily convicted, three were committed to the Quarter Sessions, one was dismissed, and two cases were withdrawn. The prisoners sent to the Quarter Sessions each received terms of imprisonment. The claims which had afterwards to be paid by the County Council to tradesmen whose property had been wrecked amounted to over £1,000.

WO 1902

● *The Watford Observer was caught with a type-set story which did not happen. Running to several columns all references to 'had happened' and sports prizewinners 'had been presented with prizes of . . . and value' were hastily changed to 'were to have happened' and 'would have been presented', etc.*

Following the rioting those arrested were remanded in custody at St. Albans gaol where they stayed until brought back for trial at Watford Court on the following Tuesday. This is the scene as the procession passed through the High Street site of the greatest damage. Longley's shop appears to be still undergoing repairs. *p.277 tr, 300 t*

The Coronation

EARLY on Friday the town began to assume a gay appearance, and by the evening most of the decorations were completed. Crowds paraded the main streets, and between 7 and 10 o'clock the High-street and Queen-street were in parts almost impassable, owing to the density of the people. It is not too much to say that the decorations were on as elaborate a scale as they would have been had the Coronation taken place on the date originally fixed. Across the narrower portions of High-street hung lines of flags and bunting, and in some instances the designs worked out with lights were very striking after darkness had set in. One saw such patriotic sentiments as "God save the King" and "God bless our Queen" on every hand, the words being either in red, white or blue.

Though the Coronation Festivities programme for Watford was necessarily on a smaller scale than it would have been on June 26, thousands of people found enjoyment on Saturday in Cassiobury Park, so kindly lent for the occasion by the Earl of Essex and the Hon. Mrs. W. Peel. The weather, that all-important element when outdoor demonstrations are held, was fortunately beautifully fine.

There had been in the morning a special service at the Parish Church, and the streets from 12 till 2 o'clock were full of people, rejoicing right loyally. At half-past 2, throngs passed through the Park gates. Inside on the left of the main path were roundabouts, and all the side shows, which are of such entrancing interest to the juvenile mind. Further across the greensward were stands around which a Pierrot banjo team and a company of comedians drew small crowds.

WO August, 1902

Chequers Yard. Just off the Market Place (location p.56) later to become part of the new market site in 1928.

At the time of the Coronation postponement riots, Longley had two shops which were extensively damaged and had to be boarded up pending repairs—photograph on previous page shows ladders, whilst procession of rioters return in wagons after trial at St. Albans. 1902 Longley's main shop passed into the ownership of Mr. Cawdell and the smaller into ownership of J. P. Taylor.

s.209, p.300 t

Watford Town Mill, Lower High Street.

p.162 t, 330 b

Grove Mill, Grove Mill Lane.

● *Lt. R. A. Thorpe became Captain of the Watford Fire Brigade upon the resignation of C. H. Peacock later in 1902.*

Livestock Sale

The 49th Great Annual Sale of Store Stock in connection with
WATFORD MARKET.
HERTS,
Adjoining the High-street, close to the Market Place and Rose and Crown Hotel, and ten minutes walk from the Junction Station.

MESSRS HUMBERT & FLINT
Beg to announce that they will hold this sale on their land adjoining Marlborough-road, on Tuesday, 25th August, 1902, at one o'clock punctually.

5,000 SHEEP and LAMBS, including a choice selection of full-grown Cheviot and Scotch and Masham ewes, wethers and lambs specially selected and consigned direct from Scotland for this sale, and suitable for grazing, &c.; also half-bred Scotch sheep for turnip feeding and grazing, and well-bred Hampshire Downs, South Down and half-bred ewes, wethers and lambs; also a number of store SHORTHORN and HALF-BRED CATTLE, comprising steers, heifers and cows.

Watford Camera Club

Another successful meeting of this club was held at headquarters on Thursday evening, the 5th inst., when representatives of Kodak, Ltd., gave an interesting exposition of their specialities. Mr. W. Coles, who presided, referred to the revolution hand cameras and their specialities had created, some of which they would have the opportunity of examining. He was pleased to see so many members present, and as he understood that a portion of the evening would be devoted to the consideration of members' work and other difficulties experienced he was certain that a club formed on such exquisite lines must prove successful. The lecturer then proceeded to demonstrate the advantages derived by the use of the new pelloid films and the daylight developing machine, and some excellent prints were also made by gaslight on Deko paper. A number of interesting slides, all made from negatives taken by Kodak hand cameras, were next shown, the lantern having been kindly lent by Mr. Mennisieur.

WO February, 1903

Local architect Whitford Anderson, ARIBA, extensively photographed Hertfordshire for posterity, of which this is Mill End, Rickmansworth. A number of his views of Watford taken between the years 1893 and 1903 are used in this book.

Bushey Village, looking towards Watford.

The morning after the Vi-Cocoa fire, story below.

p.280 t

Vi-Cocoa Factory Gutted

THE largest fire that has ever occurred in Watford broke out between 7 and 7.30 o'clock on Saturday evening in the factory erected in the Callow Land district by Dr. Tibble's Vi-Cocoa Company. The extensive block of buildings, which was put up some three years ago, stands on an eminence on the confines of Callow Land, and runs alongside the St. Albans branch of the London and North-Western Railway Company. At the factory are employed nearly 600 hands, two-thirds of whom are young girls, the rest being men and boys. Although the premises are known as the Vi-Cocoa factory it is understood that the business is confined to the preparation of chocolate in various forms. The resident manager is Mr. Boisselier, and almost without exception all the employees live in the town.

The alarm of fire seems to have been given in the first instance by one of the workmen named Eames, who lives in the Balmoral-road near by. No one was on the premises at the time, the factory having closed at one o'clock on account of Saturday, but a night watchman was on duty, and to him the alarm was given by Eames. The hooter was promptly blown, and this was followed very quickly by the pulling of the fire-bell outside the residence of Captain R. A. Thorpe. The time was now about half-past seven, and Captain Thorpe, who was then at dinner, rushed out, and, with the nearest men available, hurried to the scene with the escape, the steamer and men, under Superintendent Butler, following from High-street. Soon, Messrs. Sedgwick's Brigade, under Superintendent Taylor, were on the spot, and then the Bushey, Rickmansworth and Croxley Brigades.

The fire had evidently broken out in the basement of the south corner and fanned by a fairly-stiff south-west breeze was carried with marvellous rapidity over the greater part of the several wings which complete the factory and which cover more than half-an-acre of land. The roofs of the several departments were well alight before the fire brigade could get to work, not that the latter lost a single moment either. Quickly a connection was made with four-inch main and Capt. Thorpe directed the Brigade to try and

save the engine rooms and also the boiler sheds, a step which met with the approval of Mr. Boissilier, who had arrived upon the scene. This the Brigade did, Supt. Butler and others taking to the roof of the building for that purpose. They had a difficult duty to undertake, and to the ordinary spectator the work of the steamer and the brigade seemed a waste of time. But it proved otherwise.

At the time the fire broke out a steady trade was being done in the town in the many places of business, but the way in which the town was illuminated by the fire some two miles away was the means of completely clearing all the shops and denuding the main streets of people, who hurried off to witness the spectacle on the Vi-Cocoa Estate. As time went on the crowd increased in density and it was estimated that no less than 20,000 or more persons were congregated in the locality. They came from all parts of Watford, Bushey, Hendon, Uxbridge, St. Albans, Rickmansworth, Hemel Hempstead, Kings Langley, Boxmoor, Chesham, and many other places, and from localities even further afield than Uxbridge.

The close proximity of the St. Albans branch of the London and North-Western Railway Company, which really runs alongside the factory, made many doubtful whether it would be possible for trains to safely pass the burning buildings. This doubt was entertained by some of the railway officials as well as by others, with regard to the train which leaves at 7.55 for St. Albans. To settle the point, a pilot engine was sent to try the experiment, and the trial being satisfactory the passenger train was allowed to depart.

The work of the Brigade in saving the large engines and boilers has been spoken of, but there remains more to be said as to the saving effected. Outside the boiler houses were huge heaps of coals, representing scores of tons and had the boiler-houses gone, there is but little doubt the coal heaps would have vanished also. Not only that but a little way beyond the same spot were some huge stacks of timber, cut and shaped ready for use in the room set apart for carpentry and which is of the value of £4,000. All this was saved. Then too, at the rear of the boiler-houses

and engine room, or rather on the other side of them running parallel with the line was what we may describe as the carpenters' shop. This is some 40 to 50 yards in length and contains a large number of steam saws, a large quantity of timber and boxes already manufactured and ready for use. It seems a marvel how this was saved, especially when it is pointed out that the fire extended right up to the partition wall of this part of the factory. All this was saved in connection with the factory proper, and it must not be omitted that the cottage which was occupied by the caretaker and which stood close to the storeroom was likewise saved. The fire brigade therefore accomplished some most valuable work and their efforts are the more creditable when the low pressure of water available is considered. The men generally and likewise Capt. Thorpe and Supt. Butler, the responsible officers, worked with the greatest enthusiasm and time after time ran no small degree of personal risk, but happily each time escaped unhurt.

The workers in all number about 550. The great majority were girls, but there were also a number of men and boys and the number of unemployed in the town is already unpleasantly large. In many cases we know girls employed there were the sole support of their homes, and it is feared there will be much distress as an outcome of the conflagration of last Saturday. On the Monday morning the following notice was pasted up:–"We regret that owing to the extensive damage done by the fire, the works will be compulsorily closed, and in consequence all will receive a week's wages and notice to leave our employment. It is proposed to start rebuilding immediately, and Mr. Boisselier would like to speak to the hands in their mess-room on Monday morning between nine and twelve. A registry will be made of names and addresses, any change to be notified to the office.—(Signed) Vi-Coca Ltd."

WHP February 1903

Vi-Cocoa Poor Relief Fund

Dear Sir,—Mr. Gorle, in his letter to the "Leader" of the 17th inst. entirely ignores the fact that the Society for Improving the Condition of the Watford Poor has 33 visitors in Watford, all of whom have been distributing relief to the unemployed since the middle of November. They had, up to the end of January, given away to applicants for relief 1,051 tickets, varying in value from 1s. to 2s., besides naving given upwards of 5,000 to 6,000 dinners to poor children.

It is quite unecessary to have a multiplicity of funds, as the persistent cadger will by this means obtain relief from many sources, which is the form of relief most to be deprecated.

The Committee of the Vi-Cocoa Relief Fund has, very properly, placed itself in communication with the heads of the factory, with the object of avoiding this over-lapping of relief.

I invite Mr. Gorle to let our society and Vi-Cocoa Fire Relief Committee know the names of those whom he is assisting, and to what extent.

It would also be interesting to know the names of the unemployed "who have helped to make Watford what it is," and in what way they have achieved the result.

Donations may be sent to any of the banks at Watford, or to any of the Committee.

Any further particulars may be obtained from

Yours truly,
HENRY J. ROGERS.
Hon. Secretary.

WO February 1903

Victoria Boys' School

On Saturday afternoon last the new Victoria Boys' School, Watford, which has recently been erected to meet the growing scholastic requirements of that part of the town in which the present block of buildings named after the late Queen are situate and more especially that part known as Harwood's Estate, were formally opened by Mr. E. M. Chater, the chairman of the School Board.

Mr. R. A. Thorpe, as chairman of the Works Committee, first gave an official description of the new building, the points enumerated being as follows:—The school is arranged on the central hall system to satisfy the requirements of the Board of Education for 600 children. The central hall is 73ft long by 33ft wide having a gallery 53ft wide across the south end. The class rooms are ten in number each arranged on the Board of Education scale to accommodate 60 pupils, being 24ft x 24ft 8in and are entered from the central hall. They have six ranges of deal desks. The four back rows are on stepped platforms and a space is provided behind the last row to allow the teacher to pass.

Isolation Hospital

Sir,—I feel the time has come when the ratepayers of Watford should insist upon there being a resident medical officer at the Watford Isolation Hospital. I understand there are seventy-two cases of one description or another in the Hospital at the present time, and if a patient should be suddenly taken worse, the shortest time a doctor could get there in is half-an-hour. In the case of my own child, who was taken with convulsions, while they were telephoning for a doctor he had a fit and died. Now, I contend that had there been a doctor on the spot his life could most probably have been saved. Another thing I have to complain about is that the staff of trained nurses is inadequate. When I was called to see my child's body at the Hospital last Saturday there were two young probationer nurses, girls about seventeen years old, in charge of two big wards, and the poor little fellow was lying in a little boat shaped cot, with barely enough room for him to turn round. Trusting you will spare me a little room for this in your valuable space,

I am, respectfully yours,
HENRY LAKE.

Year End Summary

. . . As to improvements in Watford, we are pleased to record that the re-erection of the bridge over the Colne is half done. To Dr. Brett, no doubt, who for many years, year after year, pointed out the necessity of this alteration, the first thanks must be given, then also to the gentlemen who have pursued the matter to its present stage. Another improvement which ought not to go unrecorded, is the widening of Church-street. This is an instance of not letting a favourable opportunity slip, and the result should have due applause for the Chairman and members of the Local Board. The year has also seen the completion of the church of St. John, which was consecrated in July, adding largely to the church accommodation of the town.

A step has been taken by the proprietors of what has up to a few months ago been known as the Agricultural Hall to make that building of greater general utility and consequently a better investment. The name has been changed, and as "Clarendon" Hall it is hoped that it will become the general meeting place for large gatherings. The best, possibly, has been done with that object. A cherished institution, the Watford District Cottage Hospital, is always to be remembered, and in saying anything at this time, the Society for Improving the Condition of the Poor must not be left out of sight.

WO 1903

WO February, 1903 ◀ ● *The schools had been in use since 1897.*

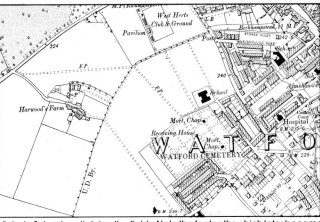

Victoria Schools, adjoining the fields. Note the footpaths which later became Addiscombe and Durban Roads.

Vi-Cocoa works, rebuilt after the fire.   *p.346 tr*

St. Albans Road, looking north to Langley Road. 'White Lion' public house is behind the wagon; Canterbury Road to the right. The shops (latterly Darley Motors for many years) were demolished in 1985 and built in their place was an exhaust fitting centre. Despite the area being zoned as 'residential' there is currently no plan for much-needed small shops. Upon West Street site (opposite Dean Park Hotel), (cottages demolished) at time of writing is advertised a 'prestigious office block'. *1903p.290 cl, 346 cr*

Self-contained Watford New Town . . .

At the beginning of the century the open market and the many shops lining the High Street served to attract the indigenous population and visitors of every social level. If the services of Longley and J. P. Taylor, gentlemens' outfitters, were enjoyed by those in a high income bracket the Penny Bazaar catered for the needs of the working class. For food and provisions the choice of vendors was more than adequate but Henry Kingham's enjoyed the reputation of being the oldest established grocers in the High Street.

Ironmongery for the farm was expressly the province of Horton's (Agricultural Engineers) for Watford was very much a market town. The needs of householders were well served by Rogers and Gowlett, whose range of products extended into the specialised and luxury classes.

The majority of shoppers' requirements were then more mundane but their shopping expeditions were more frequent since homes were not equipped to keep perishable food for more than two or three days as the only 'cold place' was a marble slab in a ventilated larder. For clothing and other domestic needs Saturday afternoon/evening was the traditional time for shopping.

The central area was still heavily populated and for many residents the facilities of a shopping centre little more than a walk away. Queens Road was rapidly establishing itself as a competitive shopping area. With the Library at the High Street end, the General Post Office in the middle and interposed by a large number of shops specialising in a variety of goods, it could best be described as an artisans' shopping centre. The accent was on value for money and Queens Road traders offered serviceable rather than ostentatious clothing, also footwear, bicycles and accessories, tools of all descriptions, household wares and drapery—the basic requirements of families whose breadwinners would most likely be employed in building, labouring, brewing, or printing.

Watford New Town, as the name suggests, was a self-contained, if not self-sufficient, town which grew up in the area centred around the section of St. Albans Road from Langley Road/Station Road to the railway bridge. Here a community of independent shopkeepers formed to cater for the needs of the workers of the railway, the brewery, Cassiobury Sawmills and the newly developed printing and blockmaking factories in the Milton Street and Copsewood Road area.

Within this short stretch of road bakers, butchers, fishmongers, grocers, sweet shops, household hardware, bicycle shops and a dairy supplied the daily needs of this relatively small township. With even more shops in Langley Road just beyond New Town Post Office, the area was virtually self-contained.

When Leavesden Road was constructed and the area developed with more shops established between the railway bridge and Balmoral Road, the shops between Station Road and the bridge still retained their importance and popularity. It was not until the post-war years, when the public changed its shoppings habits, that the years of prosperity ended.

St. Albans Road, from Weymouth Street, looking north. On the left would be built the Oddfellows Hall and the Nascot Motor. Now the underpass after road widening in 1971. *p.290 b*

St. Albans Road, Langley Road. Fisher's butchers on the corner. The stretch between Station Road to just over the railway bridge was made into dual carriageway at the time of widening the railway bridge, c1961-3. *p.346 b*

Cameras and Clubs

After preliminary meetings in October 1902, at the Library in Queens Road, the inauguration of the Watford Camera Club was not without incident. Disagreements about the premises and the degree of involvement in the educational aspect of the Library caused a split and the formation of two organisations, the Camera Club and the Watford Photographic Union.

At the first meeting of the Watford Photographic Union, Whitford Anderson, ARIBA, spoke on the need to make and preserve a complete record of the changing face of Hertfordshire.

The two clubs continued in rivalry until 1910 when a merger was successfully negotiated and the original name, Watford Camera Club, adopted. With the outbreak of World War 1 the Club was closed to be restarted in Autumn 1919 with Mr. L. H. Haines as President. The Club was again forced to close in 1939 when war was declared. It was reactivated in 1944 by W. Mitchell Bond, ARPS.

The cameras illustrated are some of those popular about 1905. No. 1 being a typical Press camera; No. 2, the serious worker's reflex model; No. 3, the rather new-style roll-film Kodak; No. 4 the completely universal studio, field and copying camera.

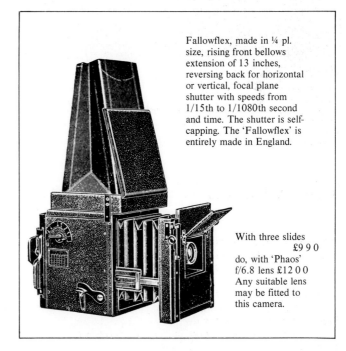

Fallowflex, made in ¼ pl. size, rising front bellows extension of 13 inches, reversing back for horizontal or vertical, focal plane shutter with speeds from 1/15th to 1/1080th second and time. The shutter is self-capping. The 'Fallowflex' is entirely made in England.

With three slides £9 9 0
do, with 'Phaos' f/6.8 lens £12 0 0
Any suitable lens may be fitted to this camera.

Minimum Palmos, by Carl Zeiss, ebonised black wood, focal plane shutter, cross and rising front. For 3½ x 2½ in, with 3 double dark slides
f/4.5 Tessar £13 18 0
ditto for 5 x 4 in
f/4.5 Tessar £16 11 0

Kodak folding cameras from 21/- (3¼ x 2¼) to £7 7 0 for a half-plate (6½ x 4¼) model.

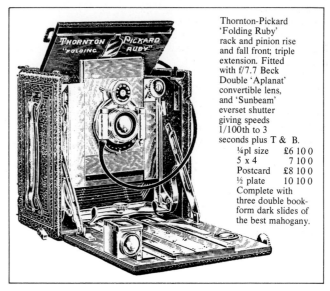

Thornton-Pickard 'Folding Ruby' rack and pinion rise and fall front; triple extension. Fitted with f/7.7 Beck Double 'Aplanat' convertible lens, and 'Sunbeam' everset shutter giving speeds 1/100th to 3 seconds plus T & B.
¼pl size £6 10 0
5 x 4 7 10 0
Postcard £8 10 0
½ plate 10 10 0
Complete with three double book-form dark slides of the best mahogany.

Watford Heath, showing original school at which Rev. Newton Price set a precedent by having girls taught to cook. *s.112*

Bushey Station goods yard, from which coal was taken by horse and cart to the High Street gas works.

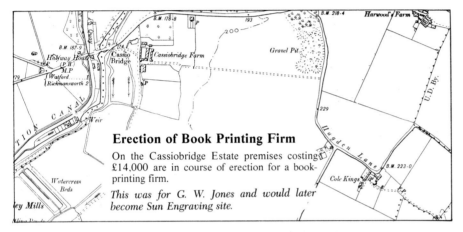

Erection of Book Printing Firm

On the Cassiobridge Estate premises costing £14,000 are in course of erection for a book-printing firm.

This was for G. W. Jones and would later become Sun Engraving site.

Watford in 1904

During the year which has just drawn to a close the town of Watford has not stood still. There has been a steady increase in the population, and although building operations have not been so extensive as was the case five or six years ago, houses are still being erected on the outskirts of the Urban District, and the town is steadily pushing its way into the surrounding country, especially to the west and north.

The rates now stand at 8s 11d. in the £, made up of 4s 3d. general district rate, 3s 8d. poor rate, and 1s. for the water. A prospect has recently been held out by the Finance Committee of the Urban Council that their rate may be reduced next year to 4s.; on the other hand, the poor rate, which is made to cover school expenditure, shows a tendency to increase rather than go down.

Quietness and solitude on the canal approaching Capel Wharf from the north, wide barge loaded with coal and horse-drawn. Canal continued to be in constant use, particularly with coal, until second world war, although horse-drawn had largely given way to powered barges.

The flood at Watford, June 16, 1903. Bushey Hall Road. Urban Council free ferry.

Flood, June 1903, Lower High Street. A frequent occurrence after the building of railway embankments on the north side of Bushey Arches. Newsagent's premises, entrance to Bridge Place (Old Yard). *p.258 tr*

New Railway Schemes

The two largest schemes which have been brought forward this year concern the electric light and the water supply, and the expenditure on the former work will be about £26,000 and on the latter £27,000.

A proposal to alter the name of the Callow Land district has not met with much success. Many of the residents in that locality hold an objection to the name, but historical research has shown that it has existed for centuries.

Last winter there was considerable distress in the town, and a number of unemployed were found relief work in levelling the Vicarage-road recreation ground. This winter a Joint Conference on the Unemployed has been sitting, and the Urban District Council have provided work at the gravel pits. Fortunately there has not been, so far, any long stretch of severe weather.

WO December, 1904

THE projects remind us that a petition has been signed extensively in Watford during the past few days asking the Metropolitan Railway Co. to obtain powers to construct a line into Watford, with a station in the vicinity of the Harwoods Estate. This they can do very easily, as we have pointed out on previous occasions, as they already have a line which runs nearly to Croxley Green. The Metropolitan Railway Co. have before now had an eye upon Watford, and about a dozen years ago a deputation visited the town to go into the very scheme now proposed. The Company will certainly be received with open arms by Watford, as another railway in the town is absolutely necessary. A connection with the Metropolitan could be effected in about two miles, and with a station near the West Herts Enclosure, and a thickly populated district. The Junction on the L. and N.W. is on the opposite side of the town, and as a matter of fact there is plenty of room for the successful working of a loop line as above described, by which passengers could run straight into Baker-street Station.

WHP December, 1904

See. p.126, the 'Met' line was opened in Watford in 1925.

Trial 'Bus Service

The trial trip of a motor 'bus service between Edgware, Stanmore, Watford, Rickmansworth, St. Albans, Dunstable, Luton, and Harpenden was run at the end of November. A company is being formed in connection with the undertaking.

WO 1904

Taken from the railway embankment, this photograph, looking towards Watford, shows the site of the George Stephenson College (the middle). Line of hedge and tree on the water's horizon is Water Lane and Watford is in the far distance. To the left is Sedgwick's Brewery. *p.258 b*

Faded, scratched and battered at the corners as are so many old photographs—but treasured keepsakes for all that. This photograph by Jesse Landon of Queens Road is of the Thorne family and was taken in 1904. It shows Mrs. Wilkins as a babe-in-arms; her story is alongside.

The White Feathers

An early adventure out in 1904, although at just a few weeks old I didn't know anything about it, was to Landon's studios in Queens Road where my parents had a group portrait made. We were living in Queens Road and a few years later I started at St. Andrews Girls School opposite the Church. There were four classes for boys and four for girls and boys and girls had their own entrances. Girls were upstairs, boys down.

I well remember the bustle of weekday market, but my mother had told me to hurry home and not dilly dally round the market. Just past the umbrella maker (near where the Green Man was) was a clairvoyant who always seemed to frighten me—anyway I always hurried past, and across to Meeting Alley.

I left school at 13 because we moved out of Watford for a short while; but when we came back I got a job at the Penny Bazaar and soon rose to be first-hand on ironmongery. I stayed for about three years but on a day when some men were not in, I and a friend were asked to unpack some cases in the yard. Being first-hands we refused at first, thinking others should do the job, but eventually we gave in and did the job.

We received our cards at the end of the week!

Soon after we came back to Watford the Great War was on; we had a soldier and sergeant billeted on us and they shared a room: we children had to share rooms together.

My brother was a lampman on the railway; a responsible job, but the taunts of the soldiers on the trains and them constantly showing him white feathers made him volunteer. He was killed just before his first leave. My other two brothers were called up and returned safely.

I did not find it easy to get work after I was sacked and I cycled all over the place trying to find a job—I got one eventually at Delectaland, foil wrapping chocolates. I was there only nine weeks when my mother died and I had to leave to look after the family. At 17, the youngest, and perhaps rather spoiled, I had a lot to learn, quickly!

During the war my sister worked at Waterlows as checker; my other sister at the Munitions Factory as examiner and my mother also worked there for a while as powder filler, but when my brother was killed, she left. She'd have no more to do with it.

Shortly after my mother's death my father came into a largish legacy, around a hundred pounds or so; which, in those days, was a lot of money. Discussions were held and it was felt that mother would have liked something sensible done, and so father decided to use the money as deposit on a house. He soon found one he liked, in what is now described as 'Nascot Village', and it cost £275 and of course the balance was on a mortgage which, at times, was a bit of a struggle to pay. But it was worth it; it is now my home in my old age.

Mrs. Wilkins
Recollections 1987

●*At the time of writing a house in the same terrace was advertised for sale at over £60,000. For comparison purposes an average North Watford 1900 terraced house is currently marketed at c£60,000, and still rising!*

PUBLIC MONEY, PUBLIC CONTROL.

A PUBLIC MEETING

WILL BE HELD IN THE

CLARENDON HALL, WATFORD,

On THURSDAY, APRIL 27th, 1905, at 8 p.m.,

TO PROTEST

AGAINST

THE COUNTY COUNCIL SCHEME

TO EXTEND THE

WATFORD GRAMMAR SCHOOL.

1.—WHAT IS THE SCHEME? It is proposed to obtain "A Loan of £15,250 for the purpose of Building a Secondary School for Girls at Watford, such sum to be repaid within a period not exceeding 30 years from the date of the borrowing thereof. That half of the principal and interest on the Loan to be raised be charged upon the Urban District of Watford, the remaining one half to be charged on the County as a whole." It is further proposed to adopt the principle of "differential rating," which will enable the County Council to charge upon this district such proportion of the cost of maintenance as they think well.

2.—WHY THE SCHEME SHOULD BE OPPOSED :—

(a) Because the Watford Grammar School is a Private School. Under the Scheme half its Governors will continue to be privately appointed.

(b) Because its income from Endowments is less than half what it derives from Public Funds, and under the New Scheme the additional expenses will make much greater demands on Public Funds.

(c) Because it is not proposed to modify the Scale of Fees and Charges, which for children over 10 years are a minimum of from £7 10s. to £8 12s. 6d. per year. Thus the School is absolutely out of the reach of the great majority of families, however much they may desire the advantages of a Secondary Education.

(d) Because as the Scheme only provides for 250 Students it is inadequate. There are upwards of 7,000 Children in the Elementary Schools of the district.

(e) Because the School is Sectarian.

3.—WHAT WE REQUIRE :—

There should be a County Council Secondary School entirely under Public Control, accessible to all classes, and free from all religious tests.

The following Gentlemen will take part in the Meeting :—Messrs. A. Aronson, J. Davies, F. H. Gorle, J. Gowers, A. J. Harman, F. S. Judd, G. W. Judge, E. B. Staples, W. Stimpson, Rev. J. Stuart, Rev. D. Tatton, E. W. Thomas, A. J. Waldegrave, and H. J. Wallington.

PEACOCK, PRINTER, WATFORD.

The New Girls' Grammar School

A scheme to build a new Grammar School for Girls on a site of seven acres at the Crescent, Watford, towards which the County Council decided to make a grant of £10,000 to the Governors of the foundation, aroused considerable opposition from the Watford Urban District Council and the Watford and District Free Church Council.

At the meeting of the Urban District Council on February 1st the Free Church Council wrote stating that the scheme contained objectionable features, and asking that it should be given the very fullest consideration, in order that no provisions unfair to the ratepayers of the district should be imposed. The Clerk informed the Council then that as soon as the amended scheme reached him copies should be placed in the members' hands.

On February 15th, on the motion of Mr. S. J. Ellis, seconded by Mr. E. B. Staples, a resolution was passed—Mr. J. C. Benskin alone opposing—setting out in detail the Council's objections.

On April 19th it was agreed to ask for a local enquiry by the Board of Education. The subject was next heard of at a meeting of the County Education Committee in June, when Sir John Evans moved that a sum of £10,000 should be borrowed, half of the instalments of principal and loan to be charged on the parishes of Oxhey and Watford Urban. This motion was adopted.

On July 24th Mr. W. C. Fletcher, senior inspector under the Board of Education, conducted an enquiry in the Council offices. The Urban District Council and the Free Church Council were legally represented; but many of the former's objections were cut away by the Inspector ruling at the outset that the financial aspect of the matter was outside the scope of the enquiry.

A conference during the luncheon interval resulted in the Urban District Council withdrawing their opposition on the understanding that they should appoint eight Governors instead of six, and that the County Council would not charge exclusively upon Watford for any part of the annual grant it was suggested should be given to the school to make up for loss of income consequent upon selling stock to purchase the land for the erection of the school buildings.

The Free Church Council submitted that a denominational basis for a public school was unfitted to present-day requirements, and that it would be better to have a County Council secondary school on Cowper-Temple lines and with lower fees.

The scheme was ultimately passed.

WO 1906

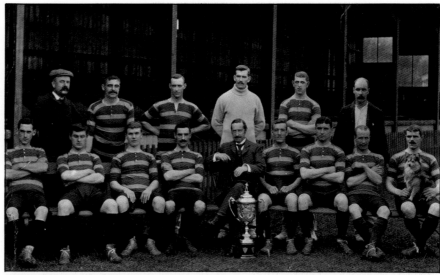

Watford Football Club 1906-7; Upton (trainer,) Richardson, Aston, Biggar, Brooks, Goodall, *seated* Soar, Fyfe, Law, Turner, R. A. Thorpe, Esq. (Chairman), Foster, Niblo, Hitch, Main. The Trophy was presented by George Broadbridge in September 1905 to the United Football League, and was won by Watford in the first season. The final league placings were: Watford, Crystal Palace, Leyton, Luton, Clapton Orient, Swindon, New Brompton, Brighton and Hove, Grays United and Southern United. In April 1906 Watford were 15th in the Southern League, Division 1.

London Orphan Asylum

LONDON ORPHAN ASYLUM.—In order to relieve to the utmost the very large number of candidates seeking admission to the institution, the managers have resolved to receive fifty orphans at the approaching January election. Contributions in aid of this enlarged and costly effort are very urgently needed. An earnest appeal is therefore made for generous contributions at this season, the need being especially felt of an increased number of regular annual subscribers. Five hundred orphans are now in the institution, and upwards of 9,300 have already received the benefits of the charity. Subscriptions and donations will be very gratefully received by the secretary, Mr. James Rogers, 21 Great St. Helens, E.C.

● *The postcard, below left, carried the carried the following message:*
"Being such a very fine day I will meet you outside this building at 5 p.m." and was addressed to Miss Bracey, Eleanor Villa, St. Johns Road, Watford.

Trams?

The Light Railway Commissioners sat at Watford on July 2nd, to consider an application from the County Council for an order to authorise the County of Hertford (Watford) Light Railway, and to extend the time for the Bushey Light Railway Order. Opposition to the scheme was forthcoming on the ground that Queen's-road, which formed part of the route, was too narrow for a tramline, and until the gap at Stanmore was filled, linking-up with the Middlesex lines was impossible. The order and the extension were granted.

WO July, 1906

King Edward VII

His Majesty the King passed through Watford, on his way to Mentmore, in his motor, on Saturday, July 7th, and was loyally received. His Majesty also passed through on his return to London on the following Monday.

WO July, 1906

The London Orphan Asylum, latterly known as Reed's School.

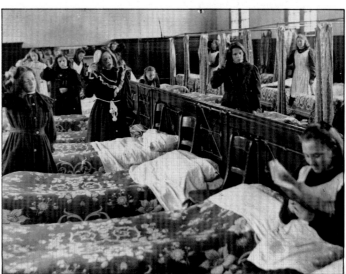

Part of a girls' dormitory at the London Orphan Asylum.

In 1908 Fred Oatley had three shops; that at No. 177 dealt in boys' and youths' suits and juvenile outfits; that at No. 19 sold mechanics' clothing, hats, caps and hosiery and No. 181 undertook High Class Tailoring. Shoppers from Rickmansworth leaving the station opposite would be reluctant to cross the muddy or dusty road and would turn left towards the town and past the competing business of M. W. Steabben at Nos. 176-178, was also a men's outfitter, and dealt in mechanic's clothing.

The old gas lamps (the two large hanging lanterns) had given way to modern electric light, of which Mr. Oatley had two installed rather higher up and in addition, a globe in the porch and many lamps in the windows. In a few year's time, 1911/12, the railway was widened for the Croxley line and electrification to London, and the building was demolished. The alley at the right-hand side is New Road, opposite High Street Station.

Fred Oatley

In 1892 Mr. Oatley assisted John Ellis and his brother to inaugurate the Lantern Mission in the Corn Exchange. These entertainments were later transferred to the Clarendon Hall where as many as 1,500 people would attend each Sunday evening. Collections at these meetings resulted in several hundreds of pounds being given to charity.

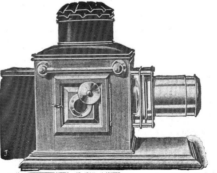

THE "IMPERIAL" PATENT AUTOMATIC ACETYLENE GAS GENERATOR.

PATTERN "C."

COLD GENERATION OF GAS.

Bean and Ringwood's Patents.

Size.		£	s.	d.
No. 1, for 2 lights, 5 hours	.. .. ..	1	5	0
No. 1½, for 3 lights, 5 hours	.. .. ..	1	15	0
No. 2, for 4 lights, 5 hours	.. .. ..	2	0	0

Price includes 1 Patent Carbide Holder to each machine.

PATENT CARBIDE HOLDERS FOR "C" PATTERN GENERATORS.

Size.							£	s.	d.
No. 1	..	..	..	..	..	each	0	8	6
No. 1½	..	..	..	..	..	"	0	9	3
No. 2	..	..	..	..	..	"	0	10	0

Typical lantern for 3½ x 3½ slides, price £7 7s. 0d., and one of many makes of acetylene lamp equipment.

Between the Railway Tavern, No. 184 and No. 186 is Court No. 16, erstwhile Potton Yard; shops to the left later to be absorbed into Benskin's premises.

p.313 t, 330 tr

Sedgwick's Brewery.

Hemel Hempstead road, from the Cross Roads. The pub in the distance is the 'Horns', and around the bend a little further on is the 'Dog'. Past both pubs runs a road which winds its way through fields and woods. The wall and gate belong to the 'Elms' and later they and the cottages would be demolished to make way for the Town Hall. Opposite the Horns the Library would be built and a little further along on the right, Hyde Road. *p.305 b*

Hempstead Road looking towards Cross Roads. Both carts are in what is now the precinct of the Central Library. *p.322 tl*

High Street, outside future Woolworth's. Placard proclaims 'Watford v. West Ham United'. Note hand cart with lady passenger. At this date the first Vicarage still existed in the yard behind Mullett's shop; the second Vicarage in its own grounds behind the trees further along the road. Both Vicarages were demolished before the end of 1916. Between Tipple and Mullett is the entrance to Gregory's Yard. *p.333 tl*

Same stretch of the High as above but looking in opposite direction. Vicarage ground, trees on the right, would later become shops of which we now have Dolcis as the best-known. The occasion is the passing through Watford of His Majesty King Edward VII, on his way to Mentmore in Buckinghamshire, on Saturday July 7th, 1906. 'Most loyally received', he returned through Watford to London on the following Monday. *p.325 t.*

Dorrofield's, later Duke's, 38 Queens Road, noted shop for all art requisites. Demolished, later part of Trewin's site. *p.341 t* 1904

Library and School of Science and Art in Queens Road. After building of new library in 1928, used as 'Technical School'. *p.340 t* 1874

Death of Rev. Newton Price

With great regret we have to record the death of the Rev. Newton Price, vicar of Oxhey, who passed away on Saturday afternoon. The rev. gentleman was 73 years of age.

The Rev. Newton Price was a B.A. of the University of London and also of Trinity College, Dublin, and was ordained deacon in 1866 and priest in 1867. For ten years, from 1858 to 1868 he was headmaster of Dundalk Grammar School, and afterwards held various clerical appointments. Before he was appointed Minister of Oxhey Chapel in 1872, by the Right Hon. W. H. Smith, he had rendered assistance in the parishes of Watford, Bushey, and Chorleywood. It was mainly through his efforts that Oxhey Parish Church was built. He rallied many friends round him in raising the necessary funds, and the church may be regarded as a monument to his energy. He became the first vicar upon the consecration of the church in 1880, and his ministry has been continuous for the last 27 years.

Deeply interested as he was in the welfare of Oxhey, the rev. gentleman's activity was not confined to his parish. For years he took a prominent part in local education affairs. He had the distinction of being the first man in England who adopted the teaching of cookery in elementary schools, though he only achieved this end after a protracted conflict with the Education Department of the day. This was in the seventies. The late Mr. William T. Eley built a kitchen at the old church school at Watford Heath, but the Government stopped the grant when the matter came to their knowledge. In the end Mr. Price won Mr. Mundella over to his side, and the teaching of cookery became recognised as a legitimate adjunct to the curriculum of elementary schools.

But it will be for his work in connection with the Watford Public Library that the Rev. Newton Price will be chiefly held in grateful remembrance in Watford. Enthusiastic as he was in promoting a love of literature and science, being secretary of the Science and Art Classes in

Watford, the rev. gentlemen saw in the Public Libraries Act, when it was brought within the scope of Local Board districts by Act of Parliament, an opportunity for the education advancement of the people which was not to be missed. With the late Dr. Brett and others he secured, in 1871, the calling of a Town's Meeting—the recognised methods of procedure—and a resolution was passed adopting the Acts, Watford being the first Local Board in the country to take this course. From this time, up to 1895, he devoted all his great abilities to laying the foundation of the institution as it exists to-day. His work on behalf of the Library was incessant,

no detail was too small to secure his attention; he was the moving spirit week in and week out for 24 years. Either as chairman or hon. secretary he had charge of the educational department, and by rotation presided over the meetings of the Library Committee. By writing and speaking on its behalf he obtained a considerable sum of money for the institution. The School of Music was founded by him, and the University Extension Lectures were started at his instigation.

In a wider field Mr. Price was associated with the late Sir Henry Cole at South Kensington, and was also a contributor to the "Times" on educational subjects. In the history of his own parish he was naturally deeply interested, and to his friends he was fond of showing a copy of a charter of 1007, of Oxangehaeg, the original form of "Oxhey." This charter was discovered among waste paper by accident in Ireland, and now lies in the Bodleian Library. The chapel itself dates even farther back than the charter, for it is believed to have been founded by monastic settlers in 790. The present building dates from 1612.

During his career it is estimated that Mr. Price was successful in raising for Church purposes and public institutions no less a sum than £70,000.

WO 1907

Watford Public Library

School of Music

Instruction is given in Pianoforte, Singing, Violin, Violoncello, Viola, Clarinet, Theory and Harmony. In addition there is a Ladies' Choir, Orchestra, and Choral Union under the conduct of the Principal.

On the Staff, besides the Principal, are two Professors of the Royal Academy of Music, one of the Royal College of Music and other exceptionally qualified Instructors.

The Fees for separate instruction range from 15/- to 105/- a term, and for the Classes 3/- to 21/-.

Goodrich "Guide to Watford"

Road Crossings

A letter, dated 18th ult., from the Superintendent of the Line (London and North-Western Railway), was read, asking whether the Council can see their way to dispense with the crossings, one opposite the Green Man Inn, in Market-square, the other opposite Three Crowns Inn, High-street. The committee recommend that these crossings be removed when the road is repaired, and also that all other road crossings in the town be taken up as the different roads in which they are now situate are repaired with granite.

Mr. Andrews said he had no objection to the two crossings complained about by the London and North-Western Railway Company being taken up, but he objected to the recommendation "that all other road crossings be taken up." Did this mean that the continuations of the footpaths were to be taken up?

Mr. King: It means take them all up.

Mr. Andrews: That would be the greatest mistake you could possibly make. I cannot imagine the Council will do such a thing. I have never been into a town where the footpaths are not continued with these crossings.

Mr. King said they had received so many complaints about the crossings that the committee thought it best for them all to come up. Now that the roads were made of granite and well rolled these crossings were not required.

Mr. Andrews moved an amendment to the effect that the crossings be taken up except those which were a continuation of the footpath at the end of a street.

Mr. Staples seconded.

Mr. Brydges said it was agreed some time ago that they should all come up, but it had never been done. These crossings were quite dangerous for horse and other traffic, and for foot passengers they were quite as dirty as the roads.

Mr. Tucker said he agreed with Mr. Brydges that the crossings were quite as dirty as the roads, and they might as well be taken up.

Mr. Thorn said he drove about the town a good deal, and he found these infernal crossings a great nuisance, especially to people who had weak backs, like Mr. Andrews. Now that they had plenty of sweepers their roads were kept nice and clean, and he thought it would be safer, cleaner, and better if the crossings were taken up.

WO November, 1907

● *Pedestrian road crossings from pavement to pavement were cobbled and generally placed at main street junctions or other busy crossings. Roads surfaced with coarse gravel were gradually improved until by this time (1907) they were given a hard compacted granite surface. Many photographs show such roads with smooth surfaces thus conveying a deceptively modern appearance. The unbound granite surface became the norm for many years. The Hertfordshire County Council contributed, in the form of a small grant, towards the cost of tarmacadaming the St. Albans Road and Rickmansworth Road in 1919.*

The Old and the New

The Watford to London Parcel Coach, which has been running every week-night during the last 23 years, has now been superseded by the modern Motor Van. A good crowd saw the Coach leave for the last time at 9.15 last Thursday evening, and a still larger assembly watched the new service start at 10.10 the following night. The horse coach was remarkable for its punctuality, and may be said to have been

Church Street, c1902; twin archway entrance to the National School on the left and in the distance the road meets the High Street. The public conveniences behind the 'Bell'/'Kings Head' have yet to be built.

p.334 tr

A Free 'Paper'

The "Newsletter," now in its third month of publication, came out with no great flourish of trumpets. We left the "flourishing" to the Watford public, the members of which have most kindly and efficiently performed that part of the business. At the same time, we now find it necessary to explain away certain misapprehensions which have arisen concerning the methods adopted by us to guarantee that 4,500 Watford homes—and, therefore, practically the whole population of Watford—receive a copy of the paper weekly. The method is by *free* distribution, and we hope no more people will visit this office asking what they owe for the papers left at their houses. To ensure the paper being kept after reading, we have had the popular competitions for children, and the results to the far-seeing advertisers who have used our columns prove the success of their adoption. The distribution scheme is of the completest character, streets necessarily omitted one week being covered the next, the actual number of houses in each street being supplied on lists to the distributors who have a corresponding number of copies. These facts, together with a certificate of the circulation, can be respectively proved and obtained by all interested, if they will favour us with a visit at The Printing House, 8, King-street, Watford.

Watford Newsletter
March, 1908

slow but sure. On Tuesday evening the new Motor failed, and stood in the Lower High-street all night. The parcel mails had to be conveyed by train.

WN May, 1908

Cassiobury Park, lock gates and keeper's cottage.   *p.263 b*

Cassiobury Mill, originally used as a corn mill and later used for pumping water to the mansion. Became derelict mid-1900's and as a dangerous structure was demolished in 1956.

The Watford Poll Committee.

POLL OF THE TOWN.

re Cassiobury Park.

This Committee has been formed for the purpose of taking a Poll of the Town in order to decide whether the town, as a whole, is in favour of purchasing a portion of Cassiobury Park for a People's Park and pleasure ground, or not, at a cost of £16,500 The Committee have resolved to take the poll on the method previously decided upon by the Urban District Council's Poll Committee, which is as follows :—

To every elector resident in the district upon the 1907 Register of Voters, being the Register now in force, will be addressed an envelope containing a voting paper and an addressed envelope, in which to cover the return of the voting paper.

The voting papers are being delivered to-morrow, Friday, September 11th, and will be collected on Monday, September 14th. Any person on the Register of Voters referred to above, who by reason of removal or otherwise does not receive a voting paper by noon to-morrow, Saturday, September 12th, is invited to call at the Committee Room, Lime Tree Hotel, High Street, Watford, either on Saturday, September 12th, before 6 p.m., or on Monday, September 14th, not later than 10 p.m., and then and there to record their votes.

No voting paper will be received under any circumstances after Monday, the 14th September, at 10 p.m.

By order of the Committee.

J. B. RYDER,
Chairman of the Committee and Returning Officer.

Watford Poll Committee Room,
Lime Tree Hotel, High Street, Watford.

THE WORRIES OF CITIZENSHIP.
What's the matter wid yer, Bill? Yer looks worried.
Yus, it's this ere park. Blowed if I knows whether to buy it or not.

WN, 1908

Cassiobury Park

Arthur, 6th Earl of Essex, died in 1892 and George de Vere Devereux succeeded to his title; within a short period parts of Cassiobury Estate were being sold piecemeal. In 1900 Cassiobury House was available on a letting basis; George and Adele were living in London. In 1908 Ashby and Brightman purchased 184 acres for housing development. They offered a large area to the Watford U.D.C. for use as a park but this move aroused considerable controversy in the town with the 'Watford Newsletter' taking a strong 'anti' stance. A ballot resulted in a majority vote against the purchase but despite public feeling the U.D.C. eventually purchased 65 acres in 1909. A further 25½ acres was acquired in 1912 by the Watford District Council and in the autumn of 1932 the purchase by Watford Borough Council of the West Herts Golf Course, for £24,500, was completed.

Green Lane, Oxhey, private road to Oxhey Place, belonging to Blackwell's.

In front of the Corn Exchange, High Street. Declaration of poll in 1906 when Nathaniel Micklem (Lib) defeated T. F. Halsey (Con). 24th January, 1906. The Corn Exchange, next to the Essex Arms was built following the destruction of the Market Hall (1858). The Essex Arms building was demolished to make way for a new Timothy White's and Taylor's store which opened in May 1931. The Corn Exchange site is now part of the Charter Place entrance mall.

The Bucks and Oxon Bank opposite Market Street was rebuilt (1889), the year after Mr. Fisher's butchers shop almost opposite. Unlike Mr. Fisher's shop, the character of which changed upon alterations in late-1950's. the by-now Lloyds Bank building was rebuilt in 1983 with the front unaltered. After rebuilding, the premises were used as a retail shop, with Lloyds Bank moving next door into completely rebuilt premises. (No. 67). For the greater part of this century No. 67 had been firstly J. P. Taylor, men's outfitters, and then Cawdells, drapers, some little distance from Cawdell's main store.   *p.59 t, 323 b*

The Essex Chapel in the Parish Church; built for Sir Charles Morrison on a licence granted by the Archdeacon of St. Albans in 1596. Bridget, Sir Charles's mother, Dowager Countess of Bedford, was buried here in 1601 but the monument and other Russell connections were removed to Chenies in 1907.   *p.349 bl*

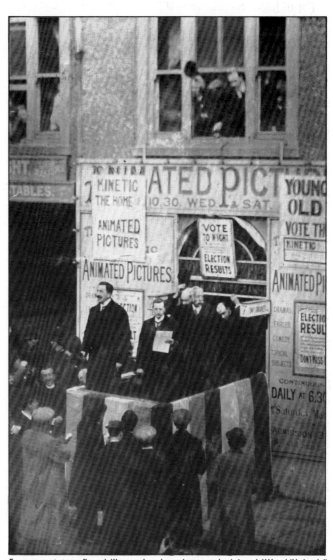

Four years later, after a bitter and acrimonious contest, Arnold Ward (Unionist) defeated Nathaniel Micklem, 28th January, 1910. Arnold Ward was the son of Mrs. Humphrey Ward, popular novelist early this century, who lived at Aldbury, Herts.

In the intervening four years, 'animated pictures'—the cinema—had taken the public's interest and the Corn Exchange had become a popular venue for film-goers.   *p.335 cl*

Rickmansworth Road at Cassiobridge. The road just visible at the left is Whippendell Road along which, at a little distance, is a new printing factory built for Mr. Jones. We know it today as the 'Sun'. Note the Watford to Croxley bus at the 'Halfway House'.

p.321 b   c1909

Callow Land To Go?

A letter from the Callow Land Ward Association appealed to the Council to use its best endeavours to remove the name of the Callow Land district, and re-name it North Watford. The matter was referred to the Town's Improvements Committee.

The Council decided to send to the Postmaster-General a copy of another letter from the Callow Land Ward Association which complained of the altogether inadequate Postal facilities in that district.

WO 1909

● *The name Callow Land gradually went out of use after the title 'North Watford' was adopted in 1916.*

The omnibus . . .

The earlier 'wagonette' service (p.84) did not last long; the early Daimler was not up to the demands placed upon it and reliance was again placed upon horse-drawn vehicles plying between Station and Town.

Railway companies had been experimenting with motor buses for a few years and locally the LNWR took the plunge in April 1906 when they started a service between the Station and Croxley Green. An hourly service was provided at a fare of fourpence.

Later in the year another service was started from the Station to Harrow and Wealdstone Station, via Bushey Arches.

In 1907 the Croxley Green service was extended, beyond the Station, to Callowland and on 12th May 1913, further extended to the 'Three Horseshoes' at Garston. On 1st September 1913, a new route was established to Hemel Hempstead calling at Hunton Bridge, Kings Langley, Apsley (for Apsley Mills) and Boxmoor.

The garage was in Leavesden Road, next to St. Albans Road and this later became the base for the LNWR Road Motor Engineers Department.

In 1914 the London General Omnibus Company ran a service from South Harrow Station to Watford as route 173 but this lasted only a few months.

In April 1915 all services except workmen's services between Watford and Boxmoor were withdrawn, the reasons variously given as 'vehicles being requisitioned for war use' and (by Downer in Watford Illustrated) that 'the services would cease owing to shortage of drivers and conductors so many having joined the colours'.

The Watford to Boxmoor service ceased in 1917 and no further services were provided until 1919, one year after war's end.

MOTOR OMNIBUS SERVICES.

WATFORD TO HARROW.

Watf'd Station	Queen's Rd P.O.	Q'ns Rd Bank	Bushey Station	Old Bushey	Bushey Heath	H'rrow Weald	H'rrow Station
6 45	6 48	6 50	6 55	7 0	7 15	...	...
...	...	...	7 45	7 50	8 0	8 11	8 24
7 43	7 46	7 48	7 53	7 58	8 10	...	...
...	...	...	8 25	8 30	8 39	8 49	9 2
8 25	8 28	8 30	8 35	8 40	A	...	...
...	...	...	9 28	9 33	9 42	9 52	10 5
10 45	10 48	10 50	10 55	11 0	11 9	11 20	11 35
†11 40	...	11 45	11 50	11 55	12 5	...	...
S12 20	12 23	12 25	12 30	12 35	12 44	12 55	1 10
12 45	12 48	12 50	12 55	1 0	1 10	1 25	1 39
1 45	1 48	1 50	1 55	2 0	2 9	2 20	2 35
2 25	2 28	2 30	2 35	2 40	2 50	...	...
†3 20	...	3 25	3 30	3 35	3 44	3 55	4 10
3 50	3 53	3 55	4 0	4 5	4 15	...	...
†4 20	...	4 25	4 30	4 35	4 45	...	...
4 55	4 58	5 0	5 7	5 12	5 19	5 30	5 44
Sx5 17	5 20	5 22	5 29	5 35	5 45	6 0	6 14
S 5 26	5 28	5 30	5 35	5 40	5 50	...	...
5 50	5 53	5 55	6 0	6 5	6 14	6 25	6 39
6 50	6 53	6 55	7 0	7 5	7 14	7 25	7 40
7 50	7 53	7 55	8 0	8 5	8 14	8 25	8 40
8 50	8 53	8 55	9 0	9 5	9 14	9 25	9 45
S 9 30	9 33	9 35	9 40	9 45	9 55	...	...
9 50	9 53	9 55	10 0	10 5	10 15	...	...

WATFORD TO CROXLEY.

Watf'd Station	Market Place	Golf Links	Cassio Bridge	Croxley Green
7 5	7 8	7 16	...	...
7 37	7 40	7 48	7 52	8 0
9 7	9 10	9 18	9 22	9 30
10 0	10 3	10 11	10 15	10 25
11 0	11 3	11 11	11 15	11 25
12 20	12 23	12 31	12 35	12 45
1 32	1 35	1 43	1 47	1 55
2 32	2 35	2 43	2 47	2 55
3 37	3 40	3 48	3 52	4 0
4 32	4 35	4 43	4 47	4 55
5 27	5 30	5 38	5 42	5 50
6 17	6 20	C		
6 42	6 45	6 53	6 57	7 5
S7 30	7 33	7 42	7 45	7 55
7 45	7 48	7 56	8 0	8 10
S8 30	8 33	8 41	8 45	8 55
8 50	8 53	9 1	9 5	9 15
9 50	9 53	10 1	10 5	10 15

S Saturday only.
Sx Saturdays excepted.
A Runs to foot of Clay Hill.
C Runs to Whippendell Road.
† Runs *via* Market Place.

The Fare for a "Small Want" in the "Watford Newsletter" is 6d. It is more than worth it.

HARROW TO WATFORD.

H'rrow Station	H'rrow Weald	Bushey Heath	Old Bushey	Bushey Station	Q'ns Rd Bank	Queen's Rd P.O.	Watf'd Station
...	...	7 28	7 37	7 40	...	...	...
...	...	8 12	8 20	8 25	...	...	...
...	...	B	8 47	8 52	8 56	8 58	9 2
8 50	9 5	9 14	9 22	9 27	...	...	...
9 45	10 0	10 10	10 22	10 28	10 33	10 35	10 40
10 40	10 55	11 4	11 12	11 18	11 23	11 25	11 30
...	...	12 15	12 22	12 28	12 33	12 35	12 40
12 30	12 45	1 0	1 22	1 28	1 33†	...	1 40
S 1 25	1 40	1 49	1 57	2 3	2 8	2 10	2 15
2 20	2 35	2 44	2 52	2 58	3 3	3 5	3 10
...	...	3 15	3 22	3 28	3 33†	...	3 40
3 30	3 45	3 54	4 2	4 8	4 13	4 15	4 20
...	...	4 15	4 22	4 28	4 33†	...	4 40
...	...	4 50	4 57	5 3	5 8	5 10	5 15
S 4 45	5 0	5 9	5 17	5 23	5 28†	...	5 35
Sx4 55	5 10	5 19	5 27	5 33	5 38	5 40	5 45
...	S	5 50	5 57	6 3	6 8	6 10	6 15
Sx5 55	6 10	6 19	6 27	6 33	6 38	6 40	6 45
S 6 15	6 30	6 39	6 47	6 53	6 58	7 0	7 5
6 45	7 0	7 9	7 17	7 23	7 28	7 30	7 35
Sx7 18	7 34	7 44	7 52	7 58	8 3	8 5	8 10
7 45	8 0	8 9	8 17	8 23	8 28	8 30	8 35
8 45	9 0	9 9	9 17	9 23	9 28	9 30	9 35
...	S	9 55	10 2	10 8	10 13	10 15	10 20
...	...	10 15	10 22	10 28	10 33	10 35	10 40
10 10	10 25	10 34	10 42	10 48	10 53	10 55	11 0

CROXLEY TO WATFORD.

Croxley Green	Cassio Bridge	Golf Links	Market Place	Watf'd Station
...	...	7 22	7 30	7 34
8 0	8 7	8 11	8 19	8 23
9 30	9 37	9 41	9 50	9 55
10 30	10 37	10 41	10 50	10 55
11 45	11 52	11 56	12 5	12 10
12 45	12 52	12 56	1 5	1 10
1 55	2 2	2 6	2 15	2 20
2 55	3 2	3 6	3 15	3 20
4 0	4 7	4 11	4 20	4 25
4 55	5 2	5 6	5 15	5 20
5 50	5 57	6 1	6 10	6 15
...	D	...	6 30	6 35
7 15	7 22	7 26	7 35	7 40
S8 0	8 7	8 11	8 20	8 25
8 15	8 22	8 26	8 35	8 40
S9 0	9 7	9 11	9 20	9 25
9 15	9 22	9 26	9 35	9 40
10 15	10 22	10 26	10 35	10 38

S Saturday only.
Sx Saturdays excepted.
B Starts from foot of Clay Hill at 8.45 a.m.
D Starts from Whippendell Road at 6.25 p.m.
† Runs *via* Market Place.

Every care has been taken, but we do not hold ourselves responsible for errors.

Market Place, opposite Market Street corner. Bus service Watford Junction to Harwoods Farm and Croxley Green. The bus is a solid-tyred 24hp Milnes Daimler taken into service 15th March, 1906. To the left of F. H. Willis is the entrance to Chester Yard (plan p.37). *p.335 tr*

Purchase of Cassiobury Park

SIR,—I am directed by the Local Government Board to state that they have had under consideration the Report made by their inspector, Mr. Willis, after the inquiry held by him with reference to the application of the Urban District Council of Watford for sanction to borrow £16,500 for the purchase of a portion of Cassiobury Park for purposes of public walks and pleasure grounds and £1,200 for the widening of Rickmansworth-road.

The Board learn from the Inspector's Report that by the price proposed to be paid by the Urban District Council for this land the vendors would obtain £60 more per acre than was recently paid for it by them. It would further appear that, if the land is acquired by the Council for purposes of public walks and pleasure grounds, the vendors will be relieved from an obligation to contribute half the cost of constructing a road 50 feet in width and a mile in length, with lamp-posts, sewers, drains, &c., while adjacent land belonging to them will certainly be increased in value.

In these circumstances the Board are of opinion that the Council are being charged too high a price for the land.

I am, Sir,
Your obedient servant,
H. C. MONRO.

Population 1911, 40,939

The Ashby & Brightman Syndicate

To the Editor of the "Watford Newsletter"

DEAR SIR,—Excuse the liberty I am a taking of in writin' to you, but I thought if other chaps could write to the papers, a working man could do the same. Well, my mate Bill and me was havin' half a pint, and I 'ad bin a readin' about the new park what some chaps wants to sell us. Bill carn't read, so I told him all about it. I told him that they calls chaps what sells parks sinderkits, and he says, "What's that?" Well, I told him it was a lot of chaps had bought some ground, more nor they could pay for, and they wanted us working men, who pays all the rates, to buy it off them, and get 'em out of a hole. "But," says Bill, "you told me there was only two chaps in the sinderkit." "Yus," I says, "there is only two a sellin' of it, and all the others lays low—in a way of speakin'—they does the talkin' outside, a recommendin' of us to buy it." "Well," says Bill, "that is artful, if you like." "Yus," I says, "I agree with you, Bill, specially when them other chaps is on the local board, or whatever they calls it, and gits paid for servin' the likes of us." Well, just then the landlord—I won't tell you 'is name—he chimes in, and says, "Yus, my brewer is one of the sinderkit, or some of the company is, and o' course 'e reckermends the public to buy it; but don't you say nothing about what I told yer, or else he might tern me out of this house." Yer see, the public are not surposed to know how the sinderkit 'as been worked. "Well," says Bill—yer know, if Bill carn't read, he 'as 'is 'ed screwed on all right, as they say—"if we buys it, how are we to pay for it?" After we 'ad called for another two 'arf pints, I says, "Why, the local board is goin' to borrer the money, and then we 'as to pay it back agin on what they calls the *Times* system,

so much a week, and they collect the money from you and me, and all the others." "Yuss, that is all very fine," says Bill, "but I don't want no park; that is only for the toffs, who lives just outside. Give me a good allotment for a little money, that is park enuf for me." Now, I thought that very senserbul, and Bill and me ain't goin' to have our rent put up to pay no *Times* system, to get a sinderkit out of a hole.

Yours respectly,
A Working Man

[Notice.—We cannot spare space for any other of the communications which have reached us on this subject.]

Visiting Watford's Largest Factory

Visitors to Victoria Works—Watford's largest factory—cannot possibly see everything in a single afternoon, and it requires more intelligence and power of observation than I possess to understand thoroughly all that can be seen, while to remember everything interesting is well-nigh impossible in this vast acreage of productive plant.

Hundreds of people have been taken round the works recently, and to-day about 150 people, from all parts of the country—one gentleman coming from Leeds—will be shown the making of Vi-Cocoa, the cleanly methods employed to produce Boisselier's Chocolates, and the making and packing of the delightfully odorous Freeman's Glass Lemon.

Watford Newsletter

III

"Selling" the Town . . .

By rail Watford was less than thirty minutes travelling time from the Metropolis. By road the journey was beyond contemplation, except to the privileged few who would enjoy the convenience, if not reliability, of the motor car, which was then coming into vogue.

The prospect of escaping from the smoke, smells, grime and sulphur-laden fogs during the long winter months and the unremitting heat in the summer attracted the Londoners many of whom lived in terraced houses or flats. Not surprisingly the green fields, orchards and wooded countryside of Watford tempted the city dwellers. Without question Watford was a desirable place in which to live.

With the ever-increasing availability and efficiency of electric power Watford was also viewed as a desirable place in which to set up business.

As early as 1908/9 the Watford Urban District Council was confident that utilities and other essential services could meet any demand made upon them. With the major obstacles overcome the Council was convinced, with some justification, that by attracting new, non-traditional, industries, the town's rateable income could be increased without burdening the existing ratepayers.

In a contemporary brochure these bountiful attributes were short-listed as progressive steps towards that end.

The Urban District Council operated the Municipal Electricity Undertaking which at that time had no less than 670 consumers taking a supply of current. From a service, designed for the provision of lighting, emerged the first power station generating sufficient power to drive electric motors to the extent of 'several hundred horsepower'.

Statistically the town was exceptionally healthy with a death rate of 10.3 per 1000 population; lower than many acclaimed 'health spas'. The Municipal Water Works supplied particularly good and pure water. Additionally the same authority attracted engineers and observers from all parts of the world to view and inspect the efficient and well-run sewerage disposal works. The town's drainage system had been designed to take storm-water to natural water courses while sewerage was treated at Holywell Farm and Cassiobridge Farm.

The fields on which the effluent was discharged produced excellent crops of mangolds, oats, rye grass and clover. The fields which were 'resting' produced maize and vegetables.

The farms operated at a profit. As an adjunct collected refuse was burned by a refuse destructor; at an average of 27 tons a day the heat generated was used to provide power to pump the liquid sewage. The unburnable residue — clinker — was sold, again at a profit, at prices from 1s. (5p) per ton, ex-works. The refuse destructor was stated to be one of the Council's most profitable investments.

With the town's affairs so well organised the Council wisely decided to publicise the benefits of moving to Watford by publishing a 68-page brochure. It was profusely illustrated with photographs taken by Frederick Downer and Sons and printed from blocks made by them. The blocks were 150 and 170 screen and the printing by Bemrose Dalziel.

The list of new industries, though relatively short, represented a promising mix. Included were such undertakings as Paget Prize Plates (photographic materials); Vi-Cocoa (food products); Blyth and Platt (Cobra/Wren polishes); Nicole Nielsen (watches); White's (Bushey laundry); G. W. Jones (printing); as well as the 'newly arrived' International Health Association (Granose Foods).

Urban District Council Water Works in Local Board Road.

Urban District Council generating plant in Cardiff Road.

The municipal utilities, roads, market, housing, factories, schools, churches and excellent rail facilities in a clean-air environment made Watford an exciting and appealing town in which to live and work. This potential for production and expansion would be unexpectedly and fully utilised five or so years later in 1914.

In 1908/9, the majority of houses in Watford were new, or nearly new, with the exception of the High Street with its timber-framed houses and shops, and numerous medieval courtyards. Overall the quality of housing was of an acceptable standard although some sub-standard properties existed. Residents generally lived in conditions that would have been the envy of many Londoners.

The design of many central buildings conveyed the age in which they were built, and the same may be said of the terraced houses built by Clifford and Gough in the late 1860's in the Sutton, Sotheron, Estcourt, Stanley, Derby Road area. It could also be said of the terraced houses built by the same company in the 1880's in Oxford, Souldern and Aynho Streets.

To satisfy demand while using the area of land available, and to allow a low letting price, the units were compact and relatively inexpensive.

Messrs. Ashby and Brightman entered the building industry when Watford's development was at its peak, their first major works being the laying out of the Bradshaw Estate. Ashby and Brightman houses were of slightly larger proportions than those of Clifford and Gough, they were built in close terraces to existing designs, and again, the same frugality was exercised in the use of land.

Towards the end of the century Ashby and Brightman purchased 35 acres of the former Callowland Farm from the Earl of Essex on which to develop many working class residential areas including Parker Street, Copsewood Road, Milton Road, etc. Here too, the properties built were in small, close terraces, the building costs of some houses being as low as £80.

In 1898 Dr. Tibbles purchased an area of North Watford bounded by St. Albans Road, Balmoral Road, Southwold Road and Bushey Mill Lane. The Vi-Cocoa factory was built for Dr. Tibble in this area and he became a respected employer of an extensive labour force.

Estate plans and specifications were prepared for the development of roads in this North Watford area, including Windsor, Sandringham and Parkgate Road, and among the building guidelines was a directive that no house should cost less than: detached, £175; pairs of semi-detached, £275; terraced houses, £135 each to build — a sum considerably in excess of the prices for houses of the early Ashby and Brightman estates. The plots sold slowly at first but before 1914 the estate was virtually complete.

The 'minimum price' procedure was later adopted by Ashby and Brightman when they planned the Cassiobridge Estate (p.126) where the gardens were large and the building cost was specified as 'over £300'. The days of the terraced houses were numbered.

In 1919/20, with a huge demand for houses to be satisfied, the Council, influenced perhaps by the Garden Cities, and faced with the large acreage of 'Hossacks' for development, went even further in the direction of luxury and expense. The Harebreaks Estate was conceived with wide roads, gardens and greens and, for that era, luxury houses. The estate soon became a show piece for visitors from home and abroad. The houses, together with land, cost over £1,000 each, with Messrs. Brightmans Ltd. making an agreed profit of £23 per house. This massive step from the £80 house of little more than 25 years earlier is hard to justify, taking into account that inflation was not of the levels achieved in the 1960's and 1970's.

The aerial photographs on pages 150 and 151 show clearly the differences in styles between 1880 and 1920. On page 151 the West Watford terraces may be identified while on page 150 the Cromer Road/Bruce Grove/Bradshaw Road area, the Parkgate Road estate and the Harebreaks are plainly visible.

The estates yet to be developed off Bushey Mill Lane and Balmoral Road are still cultivated fields.

The lands used for the development of Callowland belonged to Fellows of the Merton College, Oxford, from about 1380 and was acquired by the Earl of Essex in 1881 who in turn sold off parcels of land of varying size to speculative builders.

Watford UDC Refuse destructor, Cardiff Road.

New Girls' Grammar School, in course of erection in the Crescent, 1908.

119

Bushey Hall Road. The factory of Andre & Sleigh, printers, built in 1899.

Nicole Nielsen's watch factory, Whippendell Road.

Bemrose & Dalziel—Bemrose and Sons plus Dalziel Foundry, 1903. Became Waterlow Bros. & Layton c1910.

Christ Church is an eccesiastical parish, formed in 1909 from the parish of St. Andrew. The church was consecrated in 1905 and this group of workmen are those of Messrs. Darvill who built the church, with nave, aisle and transept, seating 800 persons, and which replaced the temporary iron church built in 1896.

Paget Prize Plates, St. Albans Road.

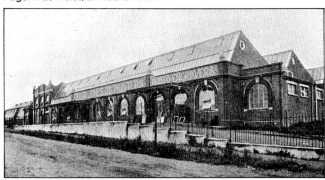
G. W. Jones factory in Whippendell Road.

Large Public Institutions

The fact that so many large Public Institutions have been erected in and around Watford, furnish eloquent testimony to the general healthiness of the district. Space will only permit a brief reference to these fine Institutions which are as follows:—

The London Orphan Asylum

This famous Institution was opened in 1872 with accommodation for 600 orphans, it is beautifully situated on the east of Watford Junction Station, adjoining the railway, and stands in very extensive and picturesque grounds.

The Royal Masonic School for Boys

This was opened in 1903, with splendid accommodation for some 400 boys, ten years of age and upwards. There are twenty resident masters. The grounds, which are beautifully situated, cover some 66 acres, while the buildings are a triumph of architecture.

The Royal Caledonian Asylum

This well known Institution was founded in 1815, the first building for the reception of orphans being erected in 1819 in Cross street, Hatton Garden, London, E.C. Ten years later it was found necessary to provide greater accommodation, and land for the purpose was acquired in Islington, the Orphanage erected there serving a most useful purpose until 1903, when the present fine buildings were erected at Bushey. The object of the Orphanage is to maintain and educate the Children of Soldiers, Sailors and Marines, natives of Scotland, who have died or become disabled in the service of their country, as also the children of necessitous Scotch parents resident in London.

It is of interest to add that at the present time about 170 children are accommodated.

Clergy Orphan Girls' School

St. Margaret's School, Bushey, the Girls' School of the Clergy Orphan Corporation, educates and clothes one hundred girls, the orphan daughters of the Clergy of the Church of England. This Society was founded in 1749, and incorporated in 1809.

The girls receive a first-rate education and, being the daughters of educated men, they make a good return for all that is expended on them.

Homes for Aged Women

Among the Public Institutions of the Town Mr. Gosling's Homes for Aged Women are worthy of note; situated in Cassio Road these Homes provide furnished rooms for a number of respectable women upwards of 60 years of age, at a very low charge. This excellent work of Mr. Gosling's is much appreciated.

Goodrich 'Guide to Watford'

A Lavatory?

Mr. Ryder said that having in view the poor property of old buildings which stood on one portion of the Market Place he thought that the time had arrived when it would prove a good investment to the Council were this property purchased by them, some handsome premises erected on the site and the land at the rear used for the public conveniences, a double set of the latter, of course, the main street to be reached by an ordinary subway. There could be a Central Hall and the first and second floors would find ready tenants to use them for office purposes. Further, the Council would have a chance of erecting buildings which would be at once an ornament and credit to the town, thus setting an example to the builders of Watford. (Hear, hear and laughter.)

Mr. Trewin said that objections would be raised, as before, to the use of the Market-place for this institution, and, speaking for himself, he knew that if he possessed premises there he should most strenuously oppose the scheme tooth and nail.

Mr. Gorle asked Mr. Trewin or anyone else to suggest a better alternative site. There would be objection wherever the conveniences were placed, and seeing that the matter had hung about for so long, he urged that it be dealt with straight away, in spite of the likes or dislikes of those property owners and others of whom Mr. Brightman and Mr. Trewin had spoken so much.

Mr. Thorpe endorsed the remarks of Mr. Gorle. The best site was the Market-place. The matter must be dealt with quickly.

Mr. Oxley said that all questions of usage or prejudice must be set aside in this case. The necessities of a growing and important town could not be ignored, and therefore proposed that the Council at once proceed to acquire powers to purchase a Market-place site and proceed with the work.

Mr. George said he had been very quiet, but desired to say a word on that question. (Laughter). He was strongly opposed to the spending of any more of other people's money by that Council. They were always spending something. (Loud laughter).

The matter was eventually referred to Committee.

In moving the adoption of the Relief Works Committee, Mr. Staples said the total amount which had been spent amounted to £628 17s. 6d. 290 tickets had been issued, employing an average of 100 men per day. It was pleasing to record that the work had been performed by the men satisfactorily, and that many homes had been saved in Watford by the Relief work provided. They were doing as much as possible.

WO November, 1909

High Street looking towards Queens Road. 'Eight Bells' on the left. *p.325 t*

Sorting room, Post Office, Queens Road.

Rickmansworth Road c1900

Watford Bathing Place, Five Arches, Water Fields. *p.354 t*

Clarendon Road, the 'Skating Rink' closed for rebuilding; behind the Palace Theatre, built 1908, (out of sight) is the Agricultural Hall, later the Clarendon Hall, later the Drill Hall. *p.247 c*

High Street, Clarendon Road Corner. Across the road, the 'Coachmakers Arms' (No. 32), a tailor and then Well's Yard. Just past Well's Yard is what is now Jackson's, jewellers. Around the corner, out of sight, Clements, but the corner, to be most memorable for Garner's 7x Bakery, is not yet developed. Extreme left, just at edge of picture is entrance to Wright's Yard. *p.173 tl, 269 b, 316 t*

Watford Camera Club

Candidly, we were surprised and delighted at the quality of the exhibits in the Show, opened by the President of the Watford Camera Club (Lord Hyde) last evening, at Buck's Restaurant.

Mr. S. J. Ellis presided at this inaugural function, there being also on the platform, in addition to Lord Hyde, Mr. Arnold Ward, Mr. Eric S. Hervey, and others.

Lord Hyde congratulated the Club on the exhibition, and the congratulatory remarks in the Judge's report. His Lordship said many felicitous things, as did also Mr. Ward, and the company forthwith proceeded to make a tour of the charming room, in which Messrs. Couper Matthews' (of the Parade, Watford) magnificent photograph of the noble President, was conspicuous.

The requirements of getting to press early, and the crowded state of the room last evening, prevented our reviewing the show, but we hope to have the pleasure of publishing a notice next week. The exhibition remains open until ten o'clock to-night (Thursday).

November, 1908

Simple Advice About Lenses

Both the Amateur and Professional Photographer is uncertain on which Lens to make his final decision. A popular notion with many amateurs is that the better or more valuable the lens the easier and more certain will be the results. This is, however, quite a mistake, and a common landscape lens will often give finer results than a high-class anastigmat to the beginner. The value of the superior lenses is to be found in their treatment, and the thoroughly practical worker who understands his anastigmat can make it a universal lens suitable for Portraiture, Landscape, Copying, Snap Shot, Architectural and Interior Work. Of course, it is impossible to lay down hard and fast rules about exposure, stops and distance. But the universal rule for amateurs is:- use the smallest stop and the longest exposure possible.

After reading this many will say, "That is what I do now." When next those people take a snapshot of Group or Landscape they will in all probability use F8 and 1/50th instead of F11 and 1/25th, which would have given ample exposure right through the emulsion, and by using F11 the corners and nearer objects would have more sharpness. Again, these same people when taking a church interior will give, say half-an-hour at F16, when two hours at F32 would result in a far finer negative.

Then, again, distant landscapes can be brought into the plate by using one combination, and it is sometimes forgotten that this arrangement needs 4 times normal exposure, because with F8 and an R.R. Lens one combination becomes F16.

Use the longest focus lens suitable to your camera.

Remember that a high-class Lens must be carefully focussed, and that more care must be given to the rising front and swing back of the stand camera and the focussing of the hand camera when such lenses are in use. A single non-achromatic lens gives less distortion and often a greater depth of focus, but cannot be compared to the present day Anastigmatic or superior Rapid Rectilinear—if used by a practical photographer. The question of selecting a Lens depends so much on the worker that I can only advise when I have full particulars of Camera and class of work it is wanted for.

Fallowfields's Photographic Annual, 1909-10

Council offices, 14 High Street. Proclamation of King George V.

p.289 t

High Street, Clarendon Road corner; companion view to bottom of preceding page. The Conservative Club premises have been rebuilt and renamed Halsey House (1889). In 1920 Halsey House was sold for conversion into shops and the site renamed Dudley's Corner. The building has since changed hands and trades several times but the exterior is still substantially as built. Across the road may be seen Buck's shop with an imposing bow window to the upstairs ballroom. The road repairers are rolling and compacting granite chips which are not tar-bound.

Construction crew at Watford believed to be working on Croxley or Euston extensions.

Bushey Arches, construction of viaduct for electric line to Broad Street, Euston and Baker Street/Waterloo, (the Bakerloo line) over Oxhey Park, 1912. In the right foreground can be seen the Wheatsheaf—recognisable in the bottom 'tollgate photograph' on page 48. In front of the newly-constructed viaduct is the early Watford Engineering Works, built near the river at or near the site of the wide marshy ford which gave Watford its name.

The reason for this photograph has not been discovered, but the basic form of loco and platform was later used by the National Union of Railwaymen in the design for their new Banner which first went on show in 1915 at the Mayday Rally. *p.343 cr*

Croxley Branch Line

Of the works of building the Watford–Euston electric line, the section between Harrow and Willesden, and Watford to Croxley is complete.

The Watford–Croxley branch will open on June 15th. For the first few months North London carriages will be used, the handsome electrically propelled trains being put into service when the line is electrified. The public will, of course, appreciate the policy which decided that, rather than keep the public from the convenience provided by the new line, old coaching stock has been got out and well prepared for temporary use pending electrification.

Watford Newsletter, June 6, 1912

1912 Retrospect

The opening of the Harrow-Watford section of the new line from Euston in February.

The waiting-rooms, offices, and platform of Croxley Green Station were burnt down by Suffragettes in March, and in April a similar outrage destroyed Roughdown House, Chorley-wood.

. . . During the year a lot more has been heard of the tramway scheme of the County Council. A difference of opinion arose between the Urban District Council and the County Council as to the widenings which were necessary in High-street.

The Light Railway Commissioners sanctioned the proposals of the County Council, and at the same time made the suggestion that a larger scheme of widening was necessary to carry out a town improvement. They indicated that if the Urban District Council would favourably consider this suggestion, they would be prepared to direct that the County Council should hand over £2,000 towards the cost. The idea did not commend itself to the Urban District Council. There the matter rests at present, though the Urban District Council have not withdrawn their opposition, and have submitted their case to the Board of Trade.

In connection with this matter, the "Observer" pointed out that the opportunity should not be lost to so improve Church-street as to obviate the great danger arising from such a narrow turning into the chief thoroughfare.

The bad condition of the Watford roads led to severe criticism of the Council's methods in this department of their work, one of the chief points to which attention was attracted being the making up with gravel instead of granite such roads as are used by heavy traffic. The Council were eventually moved to action. A fresh Chairman of the Highways Committee was chosen at the annual meeting, the Surveyor's department underwent re-organisation, and a new highways surveyor was appointed. The result has certainly been an improvement, but a good deal still remains to be done.

The Council have acquired powers over Watford Heath, and—after a very long delay—over Cassiobridge Common. Water Field Recreation Ground, which, owing to its proximity to the railway and its generally neglected appearance, was well described as "one of the worst advertisements the town could have," is to be taken in hand, a suggestion that a landscape gardener's advice should be sought having been adopted.

After prolonged discussion, a housing scheme has been adopted by the Council. On allotment land near Pest House-lane, off Vicarage-road, 16 cottages at 4s. and six houses at 4s 6d. a week rent are to be erected.

In November the Council came to a decision to exercise their option to purchase an additional 25 acres of Cassiobury Park at a cost of £7,000. The vendors, Messrs. Ashby and Brightman, reduced their price £500.

WO 1912/13

Are The Trams Dead?

Rumours have been current in the town lately that the proposal to bring the trams to Watford from London—and which has been the subject of the debates in the Urban District Council for a space of 13 years—has definitely been abandoned. Incidentally to this suggestion, another has been existence for some time, viz., that the London General Omnibus Company were contemplating running a service from Charing Cross to Watford, on similar lines to the one they inaugurated from London to St. Albans some time ago. Among these statements is one that the fare to Watford was to be 8d. We enquired this morning of the London General Omnibus Company, as to what the position of affairs is, and they inform us that the matter is certainly under consideration, but the time is not ripe for the publication of any details. The Company has been running trial buses lately, and this explains why people have seen so many busses of a different kind to those usually seen in Watford.

WN December, 1912

Bad roads stop trams?

Electromotive power saw the upspring of trams in many towns and cities. For nearly 80 years rail travel had been swift; the trams promised an equal advance. In Watford the roads, as remarked by the Watford Observer, were little better than 20 or 30 years previously and a shake-up in the surveyor's department took place. The tram routes suggested were from Stanmore into the town and from the Junction, along Queens Road, the High Street, Market Street and out to Whippendell Road. The problems of very narrow roads proved stumbling blocks and before they could be overcome the Great War halted such proposals. At war's end motor cars and lorries started their ascendency and the tram proposition was dead.

First Cinema

'Films' had been shown at various places, including the Agricultural Hall, Corn Exchange and the Palace. By 1909-1910 the length of show had increased to around two hours and in May 1911 the Cinema Palace was opened in the High Street. The site was recently that of Ponderosa, (closed 1987).

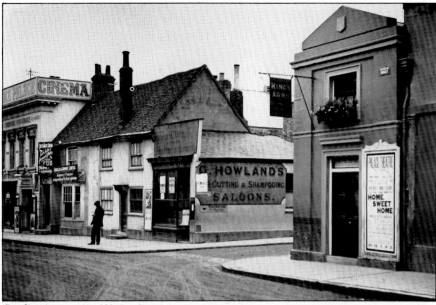

King Street corner. No. 132 High Street, Howland's Hairdressers, and house next door were replaced by Barclay's Bank. Both before and after the rebuilding, the play 'Home Sweet Home' is advertised on the placard. *p.325 b* c1912

No. 122 High Street, Ellis cycle makers, have moved with the times and have turned their site, and skills, to the servicing of the new invention—the motor car. There are others; Christmas, lower down on the other side; and another just below High Street Station. Yard alongside Tipple, butchers—Gregory's Yard/Tipples Yard; next to A. E. Smith—Hedges Yard/Ellis's Yard. *p.325 b*

Waring & Gillow have had a shop in Watford for some time; this photograph though, has nothing to do with that, but is, nevertheless a fine example of a typical road train of the time. Tractor is a Wallis and Steeven 4½ ton compound motor tractor.

125

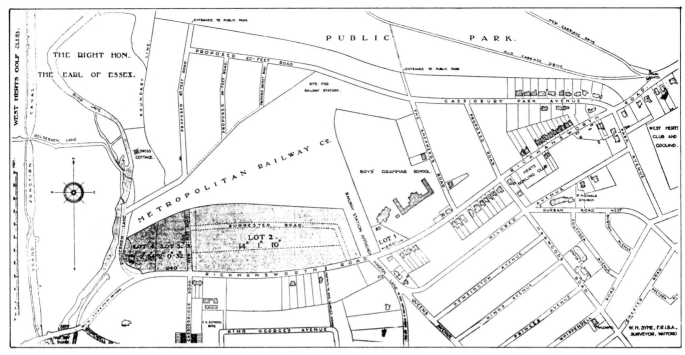

Harwoods estate had been developed for some time though few houses were yet built along Rickmansworth Road. There were a number of houses in Cassiobury Park Avenue—these feature in subsequent Peace Celebration photographs of 1919 on page 144.

THE DEVELOPMENT OF WATFORD.

MESSRS. ASHBY & BRIGHTMAN'S PLANS.

THE CASSIOBURY PARK AND CASSIOBRIDGE BUILDING ESTATES.

In August last the Metropolitan and Great Central Railway Company completed the purchase of 5½ acres of the Park estate for their terminal for passengers and goods traffic, and this fact, combined with the already existing extension of the LNWR at Watford West and Cassiobridge, had facilitated the development for building purposes of part of the Cassiobury Park Estate, which for rural charm is not to be surpassed in the whole county of Hertfordshire. The plan on this page shows where the new station will be erected, and where the new roads and approaches from Cassiobury Park Avenue and Rickmansworth-road are to be constructed.

Messrs. Ashby and Brightman incurred a considerable outlay in the formation of roads, and in passing, the face may be noted that certain stipulations as to building values have been made, with a view to not only protecting those who have already built, but adapting the remaining the remaining plots and frontages to suit residential and business purposes without prejudice to either. The land will doubtless become more valuable as soon as the railway is started.

No one can doubt for a moment that the Grammar Schools have already attracted residents to the district. A few years hence those who hesitated to acquire land in this improving district will regret their mistake.

Plans have been passed by the Watford Urban District Council for the main roads and sewers, and the work of laying the sewers will proceed as quickly as possible. The new road from Shepherds-road through the estate to Rousebarn-lane has already been marked out.

It is hoped that Swiss Cottage and grounds will be kept as a pleasure resort. As the town extends it would be desirable to keep such a charming

little bit of rural Watford intact so that we may retain a local beauty spot and a quiet retreat.

Seventy-five acres of the estate have been

DETACHED RESIDENCE, RICKMANSWORTH ROAD.

acquired for a Public Park, and to-day no one regrets that the purchase was made. In the development of the remaining portion of this most desirable estate, no effort will be spared to make it worthy of the town as one of the most attractive and desirable places to live in near London.

Whippendell Road, which is 45ft. in width, will eventually become a very busy thoroughfare owing to the proximity which it will enjoy to three railway stations as soon as the Great Central and Metropolitan is constructed in the Cassiobury Park Estate.

We already have the Speedometer Works at the corner of this road—a most successful enterprise with such a largely increasing business that the owners have secured more land for further extensions. The Menpes Printing Factory at the lower end of the road, is another growing concern

employing a large number of hands, and there is also Messrs. Kasner's Engineering Works, which provides work for a number of mechanics.

It will, therefore, be noticed that only desirable factories have been introduced, providing work for high-class workmen. The greatest care has been taken to keep out any business that is objectionable.

Builders and others who have done business in Harwoods and other estates opened up by Messrs. Ashby and Brightman have no cause to regret their dealings with the firm and the present time is most opportune for further dealings as there is a considerable demand for houses of almost every class. Messrs. Ashby and Brightman have spent large sums in the development of these estates and have full confidence in the future, as they had nearly 14 years ago when they started at Cassio-road.

Every information, together with Plans and Particulars, may be obtained of the Vendors, or of Messrs. Humbert & Flint, Surveyors, Watford.

Many of the plots in this new road are from 140 to 190ft deep—quite an old fashioned depth for a garden—and they are suitable for detached and semi-detached cottage residences from £300 upwards, with no danger of being built in and at a price within the reach of a thrifty working man, every facility being given by easy terms for him to become a freeholder. Builders can secure the option on a number of plots by payment of a small deposit, reasonable terms, free of interest, being given by arrangement for development.

Extracts from prospectus published in
WO March, 1914

The Pond and High Street looking towards the Cross Roads. Access on the left-hand side of the pond allows horses easy entrance for watering. The washing of carts was frowned upon! A few years later, during the war, railings were added.

p.337 t

the outbreak of war . . . and Mr. Downer's last surprise . . .

Munition factories and similar works transformed Watford in many ways; considerable areas of the Station Estate (Balmoral Road) being used for H.M. No. 1 Munitions Works, part of which later became Penfolds, and part the Co-op (demolished in 1985). A further large munitions works, H.M. No. 2 Filling Works, in Bushey Mill Lane, alongside the St. Albans branch line, later known as Greycaines. H.M. No. 1 Factory was described as a Powder Factory, making 20 and 50lb bombs.

In West Watford Mr. North's enlarged works were producing speedometers and later became better-known for making magnetos essential for motor and aeroplane engines.

Troops, billeted in large numbers among local families, used the local parks and grounds for training. Later they suffered considerable inconvenience from the grave shortage of hospital accommodation.

Hardship followed as men were called to the colours—the greater the number of men from a family, the greater its 'patriotism'.

Instances of overcharging and of selling adulterated milk became commonplace soon after war's outbreak. Food shortages occurred in 1917/18 for which the local population was quite unprepared.

Conscription took all able-bodied men in ruthless 'comb-outs', with 'exemptions tribunals' sitting weekly. In some respects social conditions for the remaining men and womenfolk improved with, for example, shorter hours for shop staff.

After the war, promises of 'houses for heroes' were hard to fulfil, but the Council embarked upon far-reaching housing programmes which produced houses of good quality and design.

The war saw Mr. Downer's last, and biggest, venture—that of producing a weekly illustrated newspaper. Troop movements in the town were considerable, and without censorship they were photographed and printed with full unit details. Printed on better quality paper, the newspaper gave a graphic account of one aspect of the time. However, unlike the Observer and Post—both of which carried masses of advertising and reported meetings, etc., at voluminous length, the "Watford Illustrated" carried extremely little news and, beyond perhaps three or four adverts, no advertising.

For 52 issues this continued then censorship put a stop to giving troop details. From then on one platoon looked the same as dozens before; Downer's reason for sale had been taken away. At issue No. 80 the reason for closing was given as cost and shortage of materials but, as the other papers appeared unchanged, it must have been that, without advertising revenue, failure was inevitable and so "Watford Illustrated" closed. With his sons' aid Downer's photographic business continued but his truly extraordinary venture into high-quality letterpress printing died.

For nearly 60 years his camera had recorded Watford's transition from hamlet to a bustling, thriving industrial town in an incredible show of photographs.

127

Watford Territorial Infantry

The Watford Territorial Infantry were the first of the three arms to mobilize for active service.

The men paraded at the Clarendon Hall early on Wednesday morning, August 5th, and proceeded to the Headquarters at Hertford.

They had just undergone a week's training under canvas at Ashridge Park, Berkhampstead, and certainly looked very fit with their tanned faces.

It was not until 5 o'clock on Monday morning that the Battalion had the order to strike camp, which order was very quickly executed, and the Watford men were home by mid-day, with instructions to hold themselves in readiness and await further orders.

The Company was under the command of Lieut. V. H. Palmer, with Lieut. Lemare and Capt. H. A. Rudyard (R.A.M.C., attached), and numbered one hundred non-commissioned officers and men.

Capt. Scott Gatty took over the command of the Company, on arrival at Hertford.

In the ranks of the Company we noticed Private Webb, who served in the Volunteer Company sent out from the Battalion to the South African War.

On Saturday, August 8th, they left Hertford for Romford.

The Watford Artillery and Yoemanry were occupied on Wednesday and Thursday in selecting and buying suitable horses. They left the town on Saturday. Major G. R. Holland was in command, and under him were Capt. E. A. Horsman Bailey, Lieut. A. G. Agnew, and 2nd-Lieut. R. C. Foot, with one hundred and seventy-four non-commissioned officers and men. They, like the Infantry, had only just returned from a camp suddenly broken up, for it was only on Saturday, August 1st, that they went into training at Bellingham, Northumberland, and they were back in Watford on Monday night.

To see the excellent way in which they marched through the town, one could scarcely believe that the horses had had practically no training in running in teams of six.

The Yeomanry, at full strength, under the command of Major H. J. Wyld, with Lieut. Arnold Ward, M.P., Lieut. L. A. J. G. Ram, Lieut. R. F. Barnett, and 2nd-Lieuts. Holland-Hibbert and W. Holland-Hibbert, followed closely on the Artillery in the march to active service, and with them also one noticed the excellence of their horsemanship.

They have gone at their King and Country's call, willingly and uncomplainingly, a unit in a mighty army standing and fighting for justice; and whatever duty they are called on to perform, Watford is confident that they will acquit themselves as soldiers and men, and from her heart wishes them "God's Speed."

The Watford Post Office have lost twenty-six of their staff of Postmen, who have either been called up to the Regular Forces or have gone with the Territorials.

Large numbers of people have taken advantage of the public spirit of the management of the Conservative Club in exhibiting outside the latest news obtained from the Central News Agency.

About one hundred Special Constables were sworn in at the County Court on Saturday afternoon last by Mr. J. F. Watkins, Mr. W. F. Goodrich (Chairman of the Council).

The Watford Voluntary Aid Detachment are holding working meetings in St. John's Hall for the purpose of making uniforms. On the afternoon of our visit we found about fifty ladies hard at work. The Countess of Essex has offered Cassiobury House to the Detachment for a hospital.

Four private wireless installations have been sealed at Watford by a Government official.

It is with regret that we have to mention that

Sheep being driven to Market; High Street, outside Clements.   *p.336 b*

Later, the same stretch of road.   *p.336 b,*

the Earl of Clarendon, the Lord-Lieutenant of the County, is ill and has been forbidden to transact any business. The Earl of Essex is acting temporarily as his Deputy-Lieutenant and will attend to official and county duties.

A disturbance took place in the Market on Sunday evening about 9 o'clock. The Socialists were holding their usual meeting when one of the speakers made disrespectful remarks with regard to the King and Lord Kitchener, at which the large crowd took offence and finally upset the platform. The speaker was escorted to the Police Station and detained till it was safe for him to leave, which he did by a back way.

The Watford and District Master Builders' Association held a meeting on Friday and decided not to work more than three-quarter time on general work in order to provide labour for the greatest number.

WI August, 1914

Killed in action

The first Watford man to lose his life for his country in the present war, so far as is known is Sergeant Horgan. He was in the 2nd Batt. Royal Inniskilling Fusiliers. The only intimation which the father, Mr. Michael Horgan, of 20, Westbury Road, has had from the War Office is to say that his son had been killed in action in France. Mr. Horgan and his family have Watford's sincerest sympathy in their loss.

WI September, 1914

First bus operators were, paradoxically, railway operators. They saw the need for 'feeder' services to get people to and from the stations to be able to use the trains; from this grew the network of bus services. In this group the destinations are: Croxley Green, Harwoods Road, Boxmoor, Garston and Bushey Arches.

Shown clearly is one of the town's few arc lamps. "When I was a youngster we'd watch the lampman wind down the lamps to replace the carbons; the ends were thrown out and we'd scramble for them! The arc lamp was turned off at about 11 o'clock and the two smaller lamps used, but they were quite dim".

Left to right the buses are: 1911 Leyland, 1914 Daimler, 1912 and 1911 30hp Leylands.
p. 238, 311 b, 342/3

Close proximity to an excellent rail-head plus ample areas for training and houses for billeting meant that Watford was a busy military depot. This view of the High Street was taken not long after the start of war, September 1914.
p.333

The London Scottish regiment marching along St. Albans Road en route for France, 19th September, 1914.

Recruits

During the past week, nearly 150 recruits have been enrolled at the Clarendon Hall, making a total of about 400. This is a great improvement, but others are wanted, and next week we hope to be able to state that more than double this number have offered themselves. It is true that Watford has so far supplied as many men as all the rest of the County, but this is not sufficient: let Watford be far and away at the top, and it will be an incentive for other towns in the County to follow and strive to do better.

WI September, 1914

Some regiments noted in the 'Watford Illustrated' during the first year of the war and before the imposition of censorship:

The London Scottish
King Edward's Horse
15th Bttn. City of London Regiment
7th Bttn do
6th Bttn City of London Rifles
15th Bttn do
16th Bttn County of London Rgt (Queen's Westminster Rifles)
15th Bttn County of London Rgt (Civil Service Rifles)
13th Bttn do (The Kensingtons)
14th Bttn do (London Scottish)
2nd Bttn London Scottish
The Hampshire Regiment
The Suffolk Regiment
The Norfolk Regiment
The Sherwood Foresters
and Herts Volunteer Regiments.

The Late Earl of Clarendon

The Earl of Clarendon, P.C., G.C.B., G.C.V.O., M.A., whose death, which we very much regret to record, took place at The Grove, Watford, on Friday, October 2nd. His lordship was the fifth Earl, and was born in London, February 11th, 1846. He was A.D.C. to the King, Lord Lieutenant of Hertfordshire since 1892, formerly Lieut.-Col. Commanding and afterwards Hon. Col. of the Herts Yeomanry; Lord-in-Waiting to Queen Victoria, 1895-1901; Lord Chamberlain of the Household, 1900-05; President and Chairman of the Herts Territorial Association, a County Councillor for Watford (Rural) Division of Herts, a Magistrate for Warwickshire and Hertfordshire, Deputy-Lieutenant for Warwickshire and Chairman of the Board of Governors of the Watford Grammar School.

He had the 1st class Order of the Red Eagle of Germany and of the Ernestine Order of Saxe-Coburg, the Grand Cross of Charles III. of Spain and the Danish Order of the Dannebrog; and was sworn of the Privy Council, November, 1900. He was educated at Harrow and Trinity College, Cambridge, unsuccessfully contested South Warwickshire in 1868, and sat as M.P. for Brecon (L.), 1869-70. He succeeded his father, the fourth Earl in 1870, his elder brother having died in infancy. The estate consists of about 5,000 acres (The Grove, Hertfordshire, and Kenilworth, Warwickshire).

The late Earl married in 1876, Lady Caroline Elizabeth Agar, who died in 1894; eldest daughter of the third Earl of Normanton, and in 1908, Emma Mary Augusta, daughter of the late Lieut.-Gen. George Cliffe Hatch, C.S.I., and widow of the Hon. Edward Roden Bourke. He had two children by his first marriage, Lord Hyde who now becomes the new Earl, was born in 1877; and married in 1905 Adeline Verena Isabel, sister of the sixth Baron Somers. There are two children, George Herbert Arthur Edward Hyde (who now becomes Lord Hyde), and Nina Joan Edith Virginia. Lady Edith, born in 1878, married in 1911 Viscount Valletort, only son of the fourth Earl of Mount Edgcumbe.

His lordship had been ill since the beginning of August, but after two weeks in bed he was able to go away for a change, on his return he was still far from well.

He was present and was sworn in as Hon. Chief Commandant of the Special Constables, at the Clarendon Hall, on Tuesday, September 22nd, although he was too ill to address the parade. This was his last public appearance in Watford, but on the following Tuesday he motored to St. Albans and witnessed the review of troops by Lord Kitchener. On Wednesday evening he took to his bed, and gradually became worse, passing peacefully away at 3.30 on Friday afternoon.

He took a great interest in the welfare of Watford, and was closely associated with its public work. His death came as a very sudden shock to the town and the loss of his genial personality will be greatly felt.

The funeral took place on Thursday, at 12 o'clock, in the Grove Park, in a private vault which has been specially built and consecrated. The spot is in a beautiful part of the park, in what is called Heath Wood, and just behind the gardens. The service was quite private.

A memorial service was held at the Parish Church, Watford, at the same time as the funeral, and was most impressive, and attended by a very large congregation.

A service was also held at St. Margaret's, Westminster, at the same time.

WI October, 1914

● *Lord Hyde, Earl of Clarendon, later assisted in obtaining the Borough Charter in 1922; he became the Borough's first mayor. His son, George Herbert, Lord Hyde, died in 1935 of accidental shooting.* s.191, 265

The old and the new. Watford's 'latest modern motor fire engines, and for comparison an old manual of about 100 years ago!'   *p.87 c*

No. 1 and No. 2 engines

Watford's Fire Protection

We are indebted for the following account of the Watford Fire Brigade to the courtesy of Mr. R. A. Thorpe (Hon. Captain) and Superintendent H. M. Pratchett, and from what we have seen and heard, Watford may well be proud of her organization for dealing with outbreaks of fire.

In the first place, we will deal with a "call." Now, very few people are aware of what takes place when one of those emergency fire alarms, which we have all seen and become so familiar with in the various streets, are made use of. Immediately the handle is pulled, an indicator drops down on the switch board at the fire station, showing the name of the street from which the alarm came, and a bell continues to ring for some minutes. If the call is given at night, the whole of the ground floor of the building is illuminated automatically and a second bell rings in the Superintendent's bedroom. He at once jumps out of bed and, by moving one switch, rings up all the men of the Brigade at their houses. He can if he wishes communicate with each one separately, so that should he only require two or three, he can call them up without disturbing the others. Each man's name is written on a tablet above the bell push which rings in his house. Should the alarm be given by telepone, the same thing happens with regard to the lighting of the building, but of course information as to the whereabouts of the fire will have to be received over the wire, and while this is being ascertained the men will have already been warned.

The Brigade consists of 24 men, three of whom, including the Superintendent are paid firemen, the remainder are Council employees. They all live within easy reach of the station, and can turn out in a very few minutes after a call has been received; in fact, they have done so in as short a space of time as half a minute. At the fire at Mr. Luckett's shop, in Queen's Road, just recently, they were actually playing on the fire in four and a half minutes from the time they received the call. Those men who are not present when engine starts, follow on bicycles, for instructions are always left behind as to the destination.

Now for the engines.—These consist of two 60-h.p. motors with turbine pumps, propelled and pumped by the same power, so that all that it is necessary to do on arrival at a fire is to switch over from the driving gear and use the motor for pumping.

No. 1 Engine, which is for town use, carries 1,000 feet of hose; and No. 2, for use outside the Watford area, 2,000 feet. They will both throw 350-400 gallons of water per minute, to a height of about 150-160 ft. with one inch jets. No. 1 has a 55 feet escape mounted on it, which can be immediately run off, for directly the wheels touch the ground it clears itself. No. 2 Engine, instead of the escape, carries a 35-foot extending ladder, and can attain a running speed of 39-miles per hour, the speed of No. 1 being rather less, 37 miles per hour. The brigade is supplied with what are known as "hand controlled branches," which are the nozzles of the hose and which are held to direct the jets of water. With these branches, the damage by water is reduced to a minimum, for the fireman directing the hose has complete control of the water supply, and can turn it off and on at will, and does not have to wait while it is manipulated from the engine or standpipe. Further than this, by a simple arrangement, a spray of water can be formed in front of the fireman, which protects him to a great extent from heat and also tends to drive the smoke from him, so that with this appliance he can approach nearer to the flames than he would otherwise be able to do.

No. 1 machine is fitted with what is known as a "first aid tank" of 35 gallons capacity, and supplied with 180ft. of one inch tubing. This is for use in extinguishing fires in early stages, when a small jet of water is only required, and being fitted with the hand controlled branch it can be at once shut off, and saves needless damage by water.

Superintendent Pratchett was Station Officer in charge of the Central Station of Tottenham Fire Brigade before he came to Watford, and served 12 years with that Brigade. He was during that time recommended three times for life-saving, and was awarded a certificate from the Society for the protection of life from fire.

Previous to taking up fire brigade work Mr. Pratchett served six years at sea, in the merchant service and is an expert at knot tying which he finds very useful in his work. He showed us how to make the chair knot for saving people by a rope and we saw several men let down by it from the tower. After the knot is tied, one loop is placed under the arms, and the other behind the knees, and although the person be unconscious, it would be impossible for them to slip out. After seeing the Brigade at drill, and the way he instructed the men, with the able assistance of second Officer Dent, we were more than ever impressed with his abilities.

Tottenham were the first Brigade in the United Kingdom to adopt motor machines, and Supt. Pratchett was a driver for six years, and it was then that he saw the great advantage they were over the horsed machines, and it is in some measure due to him, that Watford is at the present time in proud possession of two of the finest machines it is possible to obtain, and to his initiative that it has such an excellent staff to man them.

WI October 10th, 1914

Capt. R. A. Thorpe.

St. Mary's new Parish Hall in George Street, Watford, 'to be opened on Wednesday, December 16th, 1914'.

The Workmen's Dwellings erected by the Urban District Council in the re-named Willow Lane (previously Pest House Lane).

Church Street, narrow entrance into the High Street; Messrs. Kingham's on the other side of the High Street. Empty space by the side of the horse and cart was the site of the cottages of p.74.

"I realised a great ambition and spent 24 hours in the trenches."

Extracts from letters received from Lance-Corporal A. Dodwell, of the Herts Territorials, to his parents at 294, St. Albans Road, Watford:—
Received Nov. 21st.

Last Wednesday morning we went out trench digging, we were in France then, and at about 11.30 a.m. the order was suddenly given to pack up. We had a five to six-mile march home again, and on arriving found about forty motor buses waiting to take us to the front. Of course we were all rather excited, but when we had spent almost eight hours on the top in the pouring rain and bitter cold, I can tell you our excitement soon died away.

It was past 9 o'clock before our journey ended at a town some six miles from the firing line, and then we had to march there. It was a march too. We could hear the big guns blazing away and several times we saw small houses on fire, but that was nothing to what was to come. As we marched through a large town, the whole place was in ruins and houses were burning, while the Germans were still shelling the place. We had a near shave, one of two of their shells bursting over our heads; but we reached our destination in safety. Our quarters were some distance away from the actual fighting and consisted of small "dug-outs" covered with straw and leaves. We stayed there until yesterday, when we had more orders to advance to relieve another regiment in the trenches. Yesterday, a German aeroplane gave the enemy the range of our homes and we had to clear out in quick time. The shrapnel simply rained down, but only one or two were hit and they were not badly injured.

Received Nov. 23rd.
. . . As you want to know where we are at this time, I will tell you straight out. It is the Front. Yesterday I realized my great ambition and spent 24 hours in the trenches.

The Germans attacked twice in the night. Our trench was protected on both flanks by Regulars. Excitement!—we couldn't see any Germans, we could hear the attack and several bullets struck our shelter. In the morning we had the first real sight of a battlefield, and it was not very nice to see the dead lying about, but we soon got used to it.

At the present time we are under shell fire, and one of our chaps has just been hit by shrapnel.

Letter from Sergt. Kempster, of the 1st Herts Regt. to his sister at 17 Langley Road, Watford.

428 Sgt. G. H. Kempster "D" Company,
1st Battalion Territorials
British Expeditionary Force

Sunday, Nov. 2nd 1914.
Just after I sent you the last letter we were ordered up to the trenches, and marched two or three miles through inches of mud and slush and miserable rain. Half the Battalion went into the trenches Saturday night till Sunday night, and our Half Battalion Sunday night till Monday night, when we were relieved by the _____ Troops. When we went in, we relieved the _____ Infantry. It was a wearisome time: we had nothing to do, only watch and wait, but no Germans came. In front of our wire entanglements laid dead Germans all over the place, not a very pleasant view. We left there Monday night, and went back to our dug-outs: they are holes dug in the ground for anything from two to twelve men to get in, and covered with sticks and straw and then earth on top, to be shrapnel-proof. We were shelled for a week by "Jack Johnsons," tremendous shells, but not one hit us, but one landed in a farm yard, where our headquarters and stores were, and killed one man and wounded several others and smashed our grub, worse luck. Needless to say, they soon shifted the headquarters into our wood. You see, we have to keep out of the sight of aeroplanes.

Last Wednesday or Thursday, E Company were in the trenches and had several killed and wounded. We get rum served out every night and plenty of smokes and food. Friday night, we left the dug-outs at 10 p.m. and marched away to where we are now, right away from the fighting. We were on the road from 10 p.m. till 5 a.m. Saturday morning, then stopped about an hour and had some hot tea and rum, and then continued our journey. We passed Billy How's sons and several we knew from round Watford.

The Battalion arrived here at 11 a.m., after thirteen hours on the road. Some came a good distance out of _____ into _____. It was a glorious sight, for there is snow all over here, and it is bitterly cold. We are in billets here. I am with five others in a nice little house, a bootmaker. I made him understand Dad was a bootmaker.

Troops at rest and on the march in St. Albans Road.

Christmas Eve, 1914, The Parade, Sainsbury's.

Christmas Eve, 1914, Queens Road, Boot's corner (present day Ketts).

They look after us splendidly. Last night the daughter was making pillow lace, just like mother does. She was quite excited when I let her know Ma made it. It was a treat to sleep under a roof after being out in the woods, for the cold is rotten and we had wet feet, and plastered with mud for over a week. You ought to have seen me when I got here yesterday, no shave for ten days and no wash for a week, so you can guess I looked very pretty. I was very pleased to get your letter during the week; they are worth their weight in gold. Keep bright: it is much better for all of you. It is bad enough for us out here; but for those at home it is worse, wondering all the while where we are.

You ought to see where the fighting has been, it is awful. Poor Belgium. Their country is absolutely ruined. We have been to where all the severest fighting has been. The fields are all cut up with trenches and shells, the woods chopped up and smashed, their towns burnt down and shelled down, simply awful: it will cost millions and millions of pounds to put right again if ever they can. We went through one town you have read about a lot lately, and it was terribly smashed up, simply heaps of ruins and single walls standing. Near where we were was a big farm, and a "Jack Johnson" caught it fair and set it on fire; next day, just a heap of ruins was left. Every night we can see fires all round caused by shells. We have seen as many fires as a fireman sees in a lifetime. It is terribly hard out here: what with the war and the weather, a day's hard work in England is child's work compared with this. It is awful, and I shall be more than glad to get home, and so will every one. I would prefer to be a practical plumber than a fighting soldier.

No one can realize the hardships of a soldier's life, only those who go through it. But I am very glad to think you are all safe at home. I would rather be out here fighting for you than be at home with war in England and be a civilian and everything smashed up. Now we are here, we are going to do our bit, but I am looking to the finish of it, for I have had quite sufficient of it. How is the old cat? Give him a stroke for me and keep him all right till I get back.

WI December, 1914

Christmas Eve, 1914, Upper High Street (towards present day W. H. Smith)

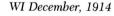

Girl delivering milk.

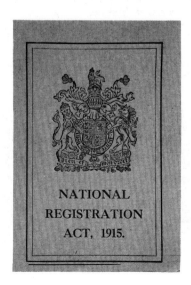

The latest "Domesday."

We cannot remember anything in English history exactly like the national registration which is now taking place. Of course the census comes along periodically but that differs in many respects, for example, in its whole object and purpose, from the present Register. Most people will by this time have supplied the information the Government requires. The young man of military age, who has not yet done his bit for his country, will have had to acknowledge that fact. Possibly his form may also suggest some reason and justification for his holding back. But at any rate, among other advantages of the Register, the Government will get to know exactly the number of men of military age who are not yet drawn into the fighting forces, and also the numbers in the still more select circle of those who are not serving, though of military age and unmarried—neither martial nor marital, if we may so speak. A good many ladies, again, who shrink from specifying the exact number of summers they have seen, will have had to set it down with precise and painful accuracy. But these and other susceptible folk may trust to the loyalty of the local authorities and their helpers not to make this public, or state information a matter of private gossip. The Register is a big and important business and should help considerably towards a better national organisation directed to the one great end of victory in the present war.

W.I. August, 1915

● *In the issue of Watford Illustrated dated 24th April, 1915, is was reported that "The London and North Western Railway Company have been obliged to stop their motor bus services in the town, owing to so many of their drivers and conductors joining the Colours."*

15th Bttn. County of London Rgt. entraining in the goods yard.

Hampshire Regiment at muster in Lowestoft Road.   1915

Recruiting drive in the Market Place, June 1915. The posters in this (dated) photograph help date many other Market Place pictures hitherto undated.

Callow Land Halt

We have had several requests from readers, who either reside or work in Callow Land, to try and induce the L. & N.W.R. Co. to stop more trains which now pass through Callow Land Halt. It has been pointed out to us that very little time would be lost to the trains between Watford and St. Albans, and that now the 'buses have stopped running, the people of Callow Land would greatly appreciate a more frequent service. We feel sure that the Railway Company will note the requirements of this growing district, and that the increasing number of workers near Callow Land Halt will receive every consideration. Trains suggested to us that might be stopped with advantage are the 6.55a.m. and 1.34p.m. from the Junction, and the 8.40a.m., 1.58p.m., and 5p.m. from St. Albans.

WN August, 1916

Appeals

G. A. P. Warren (36), Gladstone-road, painter and decorator, appealed on the ground of domestic hardship. Passed for "C2."—Conditional on remaining on work of national importance.

F. Marland (33), Sandringham-road, munition worker, sole support of invalid father. Other domestic reasons. This case was adjourned for medical examination. Applicant had passed for active service.—Dismissed.

E. Lavender (18), Brightwell-road, butcher's assistant, was appealed for by his mother, who said that he was the only son left at home. She had three sons in the Army, and a fourth had been killed. The employer of E. Lavender also put in an appeal.—The mother (crying): It seems hard to lose them all. I lost one in South Africa. I have been left a widow twice.—The Chairman: We don't want to be hard upon you. You can retain your boy until June 1st.—The mother: I hope, please God, the war will be over before then.

R. H. Roberts (18), Brightwell-road, brush trimmer, was appealed for by his mother, who said that she had four sons in France, one of whom had won the Military Medal. This young boy was the only one left.—Adjourned for medical examination.

WO February, 1917

The Eastbury Road pumping station, opened in August 1915. The Woolf condensing rotative beam engine is capable of raising and pumping 2,000,000 gallons of water per 24 hours into the Bushey Softening Reservoirs.

Line of cars parked in Clarendon Road, from the High Street to past Beechen Grove Baptist Church. The owners were attending a meeting, at Halsey House on the corner, to organise a 'Volunteer Driver' brigade to help aid war works.
p. 122 t

The Rev. R. Lee James had been Vicar of Watford for 60 years; he resigned on October 1st, 1915 and was succeeded by the Rev. C. F. Ayerst who was instituted on the 6th November, 1915.

The Vicar

The Watford Parish Magazine of January, 1912, said of the Rev. Richard Lee James, LL.B., B.C.L., Vicar of Watford 1855-1915:

"It would be impossible, even if we were able, to give any adequate outline of the work done by the Vicar during his Vicariate; but it may be safely said that he was the first to place the Services of the Church upon a proper footing, and to awaken Church life in Watford.

"He, too, has seen the restoration of the Parish Church (a work which has only recently been completed), in every part of which may be seen some evidence of his loving care for the building, or his generosity as to its furniture: for example, the beautiful oak in the Vestry, which, alike with other things, in the church, bears testimony to his love for the classics.

"Then there is the beautiful church of St. John, in the building of which he took so lively an interest, and which is a splendid example of careful building.

"But perhaps the greatest debt of gratitude which churchmen in Watford owe to their Vicar is the way in which he saved the Church Schools at the time of the passing of the Education Act. Happily they are still efficient and vigorous, and had his people the same courage as their Vicar, they might be enlarged and filled to overflowing. We believe nothing would give the Vicar greater pleasure than to see this done. When the free school, erected and endowed by Mrs. Fuller, was incorporated with the Grammar Schools, the purchase of the beautiful old school was effected by the Vicar, by subscription, and placed under trust as the Church House of the parish, and is valuable, as the Guilds and Societies in it find a home. An effort is now being made by a representative committee to erect a large Parish Hall, the site for which was secured by the Vicar (on lease), the present hall not being large enough for present requirements.

"It would be interesting to know how many couples he has married, and how many children he has baptized during his long term of office; for they, too, must almost be a record.

"The Parish Hall mentioned above has now been erected and was opened only last month.

"The venerable Vicar attended the service at the Parish Church on Sunday morning and pronounced the Blessing; and, considering his age, he is still quite active."

WI February, 1915

Of three vicarages this was the earliest, on the site of the present Woolworth's. In the distance, through the courtyard entrance, can be seen hoardings around the site at the corner of Queens Road/High Street marking the building of Boot's new shop (now Ketts). The vicarage was demolished c1914 to allow Woolworth's to be built.

The familiar dome of Boot's, built in 1913 on the corner of Queens Road, identifies the site of this ancient tithe barn behind the Vicarage as the spot where Woolworth's now is. When the first vicarage ceased as such it was altered and continued in use as cottages. This was Gregory's Yard.

Second vicarage site; the second vicarage was demolished in August 1915 and the site cleared—the last tree being cut down on Christmas Eve—"to be replaced shortly by a row of modern shops." *325 tr   1915*

Training and muster on what it now Harebreaks, Russell Lodge, at the top right, was at the corner of Longspring/St. Albans Road until demolished c1960. *p.270 tl*

Lord Derby's Volunteers, waiting outside recruiting centre at No. 62 Queens Road. They volunteered some months before their call-up date became due, and so gained the benefit of extra training. Note Watford Motor Company at No. 60. June 1916.

Peark's grocery stores at the corner of Red Lion Yard, reputedly the oldest building in the town, was virtually destroyed by fire. Peark's moved across the Market Place. *p.277 tr* 1916

Female ticket collectors at Watford Junction.

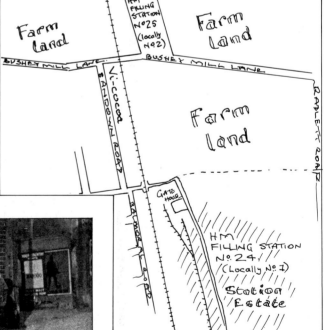

Girls delivering the post.

● *The 'munitions' story is reported at some length because, unlike other industries which continued production and existance, the munitions works closed extremely quickly and almost all account is lost without trace.*

The Munitions Factory Disasters . . .

Two local areas were selected as suitable to accommodate munition factories, Bushey Mill Lane and Station Estate better known as Imperial Way, Balmoral Road.

In accordance with national practice, local industrialists were asked to manage such factories. The Watford Manufacturing Company Limited, previously known as Dr. Tibbles Vi-Cocoa, was approached to this end.

H.M. No. 1 Factory (Imperial Way) was described as "making 20lb and 50lb bombs" and the plant in Bushey Mill Lane (Greycaine) as H.M. No. 2 Filling Factory. Both establishments were engaged in all engineering aspects of the manufacture of mortar bombs, grenades, smoke cannisters, small arms magazines and other ancillary equipment.

On 6th February, 1917, an Examiner in the Department of Munitions did not panic when he saw a mortar bomb which had ignited. With great presence of mind he grabbed the bomb from a pile and threw it out of the building. For this act of bravery he was awarded the Edward Medal of the Second Class.

A week later, Tuesday 13th February 1917, a fire occurred which could have been disastrous for the Town, and about which the strict censorship has prevented the full details being generally known except as excerpts in isolation.

A young lad, helping with grocery deliveries recounts:

"At that time Balmoral Road was only a lane and really finished at the little bridge. I was only a young boy and had been helping with some grocery deliveries to the factory, to earn some pennies. The alarms went and we were chased off the premises; our horse and cart had just got to the bridge when we had to quickly pull aside to let the galloping horses and fire engine pass through."

A. R. Green recounting his recollection of the 1917 Munitions fire, (Oct. 1986).

The West Herts Post reported:

Great Fire Prevented

Soon after eleven o'clock on Tuesday morning, the Watford Fire Brigade and other Brigades were called to a serious outbreak of fire at some works just beyond Watford Station, which threatened to involve many adjacent buildings.

The factory, which employs hundreds of girls, caught fire, and the flames spread so rapidly that, but for the exceedingly prompt action of the firemen on the spot, the Brigade from the Victoria Works, the Council Brigade, and Messrs. Sedgwick's disastrous results might have had to be recorded.

The girls were marshalled off the premises, and people living in the vicinity were warned that the fire might assume alarming dimensions.

A large body of constables and "specials" were soon on the spot controlling the traffic and assisting in various ways.

Unfortunately, two succumbed in the District Hospital, to burns, and several persons were injured, but the management is to be congratulated on the fact that an outbreak of such inflammable material was so ably coped with.

February 1917

And later in the year, a rider:

Great Fire Prevented

On February 13th a big fire broke out at a large local factory, and only the promptitude of the various brigades and their remarkable skill in dealing with the blaze prevented the most disastrous conflagration. Two workers were unfortunately burned to death, but the loss of life would undoubtedly have been great had it not been for the magnificent work of our firemen. So splendid did they act that Lord Clarendon and other public men called them together in the Council Chamber and publicly thanked them for the splendid bravery displayed by one and all.

S144   *December, 1917*

Apart from the public thanks the Watford Fire Brigade men received no other acknowledgement until after the war's end.

Meanwhile, the Works' Brigade fared rather better:

The *London Gazette of 22 June 1917* announced the award of the Edward Medal of the Second Class to Thomas Luther Burt, Chief of Police at H.M. Factory, Watford with the following brief citation:

'On 13th February last an outbreak of fire occurred at the Watford factory at which explosives are manufactured. Burt, who was on his round of inspection at the time, at once rushed into the building, which was burning fiercely and full of suffocating smoke. He carried out Mixer Price and immediately returned to rescue Mixer Morecroft, the smoke by then being so dense and the heat so great that he was compelled to crawl along on his hands and knees before he could reach Morecroft. Afterwards he worked hard in assisting in the removal of explosives from the burning building.'

And in February 1920 the 'Watford Observer' reported:

Mr. Burt, who was formerly a sergeant in the Herts Constabulary, received the Edward Medal at the King's hands in October, 1917. He also received the Carnegie certificate, and £20, as did also the following:—Messrs. S. Poultney, P. O'Keefe, W. R. Knight, N. Hill, R. Swift, and R. Blane (son of the general manager).

The 'Watford Observer' also reported:

We understand that the Home Office have intimated that they are prepared to award three O.B.E.'s to the Watford Fire Brigade in connection with gallantry shown at a fire at the local Munition Works in February, 1917.

but as a mix-up occurred regarding names submitted for these honours the awards were increased to four . . .

. . . At the time the fire occurred, so strict were the regulations of D.O.R.A., that no details of the circumstances under which two men lost their lives was allowed to appear in the Press. The official announcement simply stated that "a small fire took place on Wednesday at a factory in Hertfordshire. Although little damage was done, two

Both factories were 'Filling Factories', neither employed women under the age of 21. Officially Nos. 24 & 25, they were known locally as No. 1 (Station Estate) and No. 2 (Bushey Mill Lane). No. 1 filled smaller weapons and for the for year of 1917 production included 113,342 rifle grenades at 3/-, 390,035 2"

trench mortar bombs at 17/10d each, and 458,007 Red and White Phosphorous, and other 4" bombs at an average price of 39/-. The year's production totalled £815,040.

... the greater part of Watford would have been destroyed ...

workmen unfortunately lost their lives." These men were Charles Moorcroft, a licensed victualler, of Harpenden, and William Pride, a shopkeeper in Percy-road, Watford. On Tuesday, February 13th, 1917, they were in No. 2 mixing house at the factory, mixing an explosive powder in a mixing machine. Suddenly there was a flash, but no loud explosion. The foreman of the department stated at the inquest that he was near the deceased, and was blown into one of the doorways. He was dazed, and knew nothing of what happened to the other two.

Thomas Luther Burt, Chief of the Factory Police and Fire Superintendant, gave interesting evidence. About 11.20 a.m. he was on a round of inspection when he heard a slight booming noise, and saw smoke rise from No. 2 mixing house. He immediately ran out two lines of hose. He saw the foreman stagger out of the packing house, which adjoined the mixing house. Through the door witness saw Pride, who was practically in a nude condition. Witness got him to his feet, and he walked to the door of the packing-room. Returning, witness saw Moorcroft on his knees, trying to get to the door. The smoke was so dense that witness also had to get on his knees to assist Moorcroft outside. The mixing house during the whole of the time was one dense mass of smoke, and was very hot. Evidence was also given as to the machinery being lubricated, and the bearings not over-heated. Both men were terribly burned, and died in the District Hospital from shock. The verdict returned was "Accidental death."

The Works Fire Brigade did fine work until the arrival of the local Brigades. In the packing room adjoining the mixing house were stocked tons of high explosives, and had the flames reached these the effect would have been terrible. In all probability the greater part of Watford would have been destroyed. How narrow an escape the town had on this occasion was only fully realised by a few. It is therefore, fitting that those who played an heroic part should be rewarded, though in the case of the Watford firemen the recognition is somewhat belated.

S138   *WO February 1920*

After the Armistice local authorities and others responsible for fire brigades were invited to submit recommendations for the Medal of the Order of the British Empire (approximately equivalent to the present day Queen's Gallantry Medal). The recommendation covered only the fire on 13 February 1917 and was on the following terms:

'On arrival the brigade found a building used as a powder mixing room on fire. Superintendent Pratchett was informed that he must stop the fire from spreading to adjoining buildings at all costs. Superintendent Pratchett and his men, with Mr. Brace, acted with the utmost coolness and promptitude. They soon had the fire completely under control and extinguished, although the roof required a considerable amount of cutting away. If the fire had extended it could have been disastrous to the whole town. Superintendent Pratchett himself carried out the first case of T.N.T. from the burning building and all the men got to work removing it, assisted by the works brigade. There is no doubt that all present faced an appalling disaster which was only averted by their own courage and devotion and the skill of Superintendent Pratchett.' (P.R.O. H.O. 45/11016/377171)

Examination of this recommendation by the Home Office showed that Superintendent Pratchett, Firemen Fountain and Wise and Driver Robinson were first on the scene, followed shortly afterwards by the other men; and that they had carried the branch into the burning mixing room and succeeded in damping down the material inside sufficiently to prevent an explosion.

Superintendent Pratchett and his three colleagues received their medals from the Lord Lieutenant of Hertfordshire, Brigadier-General Viscount Hampden, at a ceremony in Clarendon Hall Yard, Watford, on 10 November 1920.

At the same ceremony W. J. Foxen received the Medal of the Order of the British Empire. His name appears in the same 'Gazette' as the four firemen with the citation:

'for great courage and devotion to duty at a filling factory, particularly on the occasion of an explosion which caused a great deal of damage. His control at the time was considered to have prevented a most serious loss of life.'

The 'Watford Observer' of 14th February 1920 carried the following story:

In October of the same year another explosion, in which three lives were lost, occurred at the Factory, and, in this instance, too, no publicity could be given to the facts. There were three victims—Clara Frost, Henry Frederick Turner, and Charles F. Tolfrey, all of Watford.

At the inquest the Coroner told the jury that in the afternoon of October 4th the deceased woman was engaged in soldering a box containing propellant charges, and the two deceased men were standing by to move the box when finished. A report was heard, and a witness saw the place in flames. Assistance was at once obtained, and the three were got from the building. Unfortunately the injuries they had received were so severe that they afterwards succumbed.

The evidence showed that the accident occurred in the Trench Warfare Department. The fire was extinguished very quickly, the hydrant being at work in less than a minute. There was no direct evidence as to what caused the explosion. The deceased woman had been on the same work for some months.

The jury returned a verdict of "accidental death," and expressed their appreciation of the efficient way in which the fire was extinguished.

A sixth medal was due to be presented but the recipient, R. A. Boyle, was absent abroad. His medal was also gazetted on 7 July 1920 *'for great courage in continuing to work in a poisonous atmosphere although repeatedly burned and gassed'*. Again, it is not clear whether Boyle worked at the Watford factory.

Medal award details: WO and Major J. D. Sainsbury T.D., courtesy of 'Medals and Awards' issue November 1980.

Banknotes

To replace the withdrawn one and half-sovereign coins, £1 banknotes are to be introduced. These are to be printed by Messrs. Waterlow Ltd. in Milton-street, Callow Land.

At No. 25 Filling Station production centred around filling bombs and in the nine months ended in March 1917, considerable expense was incurred in laying roads, railway and in providing new building and equipment. Nine

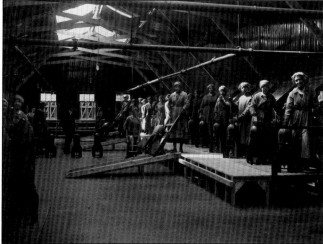

months production included filling 222,041 M/M bombs at £8 10s. 0d. each; 2,930 20lb bombs at £4 each; 9,692 bombs at £8 each and 3,031 3cwt bombs at £33 8s. 2d. each. Nine months production totalled £2,017,910.

This photograph carried the caption 'Munitions Factory, Station Estate, 1914-18'. Subsequent enquiries pieced together the stories of the fires and dangers. It would appear that this photograph, showing about 380 people, is of the staff of H.M. No. 1 Factory. This occupied a very large extent of the land between the new Imperial Way and Radlett Road. The photograph includes Thomas Luther Burt wearing his Edward Medal, presented to him by the King in October 1917.

The building behind the group had connections with the munitions works but it is known that the height of the top floor exceeded the level of the water reservoir which supplied the area and so there was no water on the top floor either for manufacturing or firefighting. At one time, after 1920, used for furniture manufacturing, it later became the works of T. H. Lewis for repairing and overhaul of Express Dairy vehicles. It was then used from c1964 for about 20 years as a 'temporary' sorting office for the Post Office before they vacated it for larger premises at Ascot Road. Empty for two or three years, it was demolished in 1986 and site redeveloped as small industrial units. *p.280 t*

L & N W Electrification

"The chief reason for deferring the running to Watford of the electric trains has been the want of suitable rolling-stock. Instead of constructing the necessary vehicles at their Wolverton Works, the London and North-Western Railway ordered the trailer and motor coaches of a private firm, and for some reason or another the vehicles are not yet available, nor does there appear any immediate likelihood of the vehicles being ready in the near future. The coaches for working the through service need to be of a special design, because of the difference in the height of the platforms on the new Watford line and those on the Baker-street and Waterloo Railway. Everything else being ready for electric working, the Baker-street and Waterloo Railway made experiments with trains composed of trailer cars of the Great Northern, Piccadilly, and Brompton Railway, and motor coaches of the Central London Railway, and by an ingenious arrangement these coaches have been made suitable. Passengers alighting at the stations on the Watford new line will merely have to step up from the carriage on to the platform, and when entraining they will step down."

Shortage of labour and materials, due to the war, have delayed construction between Willesden and Euston. The service starts during mid-April.

WO April, 1917

A Letter

2.7.17
Watford Herts

Mr Levey/ Sir you have a yellow powder you are now useing at your No 2 filling Station Watford which staines the hands and face very much and i am medicaly informed tenders to shorten the lives of the girls working in it   I understand that it is your wish that one and all shall take thire turn in working in it so that one shall not do more of it than another   now this system unbeknown to you is not being carried out there being girls in it at present working for weeks and weeks and likely to remain there   others who appear to be bits of favourits with the matron who up to the present have not soiled their hands with it and this is causing great discontent   if this is not at once seen into and rectified I shall place myself in communication with the government Inspector and the minister of munitions to see if something can not be done in the matter (let one and all take her share)

I am Yours Truly
An Interested Party

Horse Chestnuts for Munitions

Sir,—We have always looked upon horse chestnuts as of no commercial value, and they have been the perquisite of the boys for the noble game of "Konkers."

This war has taught us many things, and amongst them that it is possible to extract a spirit from these chestnuts, which is of use in the production of high explosives. A ton of chestnuts saves 10 cwt. of barley, so that it is easy to see how valuable they are to the country.

Every chestnut is wanted, and it is hoped to secure 250,000 tons this year. I have been entrusted by the Herts County War Agricultural Committee with the duty of organizing their collection, and I want to enlist the help of the schoolboys in the County schools; but I now appeal to all landowners, householders, and farmers who have chestnut trees to be good enough to have the chestnuts all picked up as they fall and reserve them. If they will kindly send me a postcard, saying about what weight they have on hand, I will send them word what to do with them. I hope to have a local receiving agent in every village and district, who will take in small quantities; but in the case of those who can collect a ton or more, I should then notify the Ministry of Munitions, who will send a motor lorry for them as soon as possible.

I hope that Herts will do all it can to help provide "surprise packets" for Fritz.

Yours, etc.,
COLIN TAYLOR, C.C., J.P.

August, 1917

Superintendent Pratchett, firemen Robinson, Hatton and Fountain shown with the medals won in February 1917 and presented in November 1920.

H.M. King George V worked to an extremely busy schedule; many investitures were held at factories, hospitals, etc, countrywide. That he visited Watford is not in doubt but at time of writing (August '87) the date has not been ascertained with accuracy from the Royal Archives.

Death of Mr. F. Fisher

It is with great regret that we have to record the death, which occurred early on Saturday morning, of Mr. F. Fisher, of Roseberry, Hempstead-road, Watford, in his 68th year. He had been in poor health since he had a slight seizure three years ago, but he was not taken seriously ill until a fortnight ago. The end came very peacefully.

FHOTO, W. COLES, WATFORD.

Born in 1849, at Aylesbury, the son of Mr. William Fisher, farmer, dealer, and wholesale meat salesman, the deceased, one of a family of 11, was educated at Howard House Academy, Thame. He married the eldest daughter of Mr. Edmund Keen, of Hemel Hempstead. He commenced business at Kings Langley, and came to Watford in 1877, purchasing the business of Mr. George Stone, at 70, High-street. A few years afterwards he bought the Rose and Crown estate and developed it, building himself, at 74 and 76, High-street, new premises and abattoirs, with every modern improvement, including one of the finest private cold storages in England. He also built up a large connection at Deptford. As time went on his keen business instinct led him to buy and develop land on the Bushey Hall Estate and other large estates in Essex. In 1903 he retired, and went to reside at Roseberry. He left the Watford business in the hands of his son, Mr. F. E. Fisher. A second son, Mr. Arthur E. Fisher, is a wholesale meat salesman at Luton; a third, Mr. William Fisher, is farming in Buckinghamshire; and a fourth, Mr. Percy Fisher, is an officer in the Northumberland Fusiliers. There are also two married daughters.

The deceased was held in great public esteem in Watford. He was a member of the Urban District Council for eight years, and Chairman in two very eventful years—1901-2 and 1902-3. He gave a memorable banquet at the Clarendon Hall to the Herts Yeomanry on their return from the South African War. His official position necessitated his taking a leading part in the local arrangements for commemorating the Coronation of King Edward. It was in connection with the postponement of the festivities, on account of the sudden and serious illness of King Edward, in June, 1902, that the town was brought into unenviable notoriety by rioting. The Council had no option but to postpone the dinner to the aged and deserving poor and the distribution of money to school children, but a disorderly element obtained the upper hand on the night of July 26th, and created disturbances. Damage was done in the town which cost the county over £1,000 in compensation. Of 62 persons who

were apprehended on charges of riotous conduct and larceny, 56 were summarily convicted. No one felt the stigma which had been cast on the town more deeply than Mr. Fisher, and it was very unfortunate that his term of office was marred by such a lamentable occurrence, especially as he had thrown himself into his public duties with remarkable zeal and devotion. When he retired from the chair of the Council high praise was bestowed upon his work by his colleagues, but Mr. Fisher never had the same taste for public work afterwards. He continued, however, to be a member of the school authority. He was made a Justice of the Peace in 1906, and attended the sittings of the Bench fairly regularly.

WO August, 1917

No Football This Season

Owing to the fact that they have been excluded from the London Combination, and also that the West Herts Club and Ground have declined to continue to rent them the ground, the directors of the Watford Football Club have decided not to make any fixtures this season, and to give football a rest until more propitious times.

The Executive Committee of the West Herts Club and Ground sent the following surprising letter to Mr. W. Swain, secretary of the Watford F.C.:-

"That in view of the fact that there has been some loss of subscriptions and opposition to professional football, the Committee regretfully decided that they could not entertain an application to re-let the ground for that purpose.

WO August, 1917

Shorter Shopping Hours

Darkened streets, and fear of possible air-raids, combined with the withdrawal of nearly all the male assistants from the shops have brought about considerably shorter hours in retail businesses, and this is all to the good.

Before the war the average number of hours for a shop to be open in the week was about 72, and war-time conditions have conclusively proved that these were much longer than necessary.

The Early Closing Association, which has done wonderful work in the past to improve the lot of those employed in shops, is now pressing for a 48-hour week (exclusive of meal times) and there is very little doubt that when the "boys" return from the front they will expect and deserve working hours of this description, as they remember only too well the few opportunities they had in the past for open air exercise and enjoyment.

WO November, 1917

Big Blaze at Victoria Works

Soon after 9 o'clock on Thursday evening the Watford Fire Brigade was called to an outbreak of fire which occurred at Victoria Works. A store-room containing dried milk, nuts, advertising literature, and a consignment of Vi-Cocoa about to be dispatched to the troops, was ablaze, and the nature of the contents of the building soon made possible, and even probable, the prospect of the disastrous consequences of Feb., 1903, when the greater part of the works was destroyed. The night was pitch dark with occasional flashes of lightning illuminating the heavens, while a gusty wind favoured the conflagration. The reflection of the flames on the low banks of cloud made the fire seem more serious than it actually was, and hundreds of people

rushed over to Callow Land to witness the blaze, although really little could be seen, for the Works Brigade, under Captain Brace, with the Watford Council Brigade, under Captain Thorpe and Supt. Pratchett, were assisted by the Croxley Mills Brigade, Messrs. Sedgwick's, and Bushey Brigades, and the whole of these firemen worked like Britons, getting the fire well under control within an hour, and by superhuman efforts saving the Freeman Factory and the main building adjoining from destruction. Two or three firemen were slightly injured by falling debris, and Captain Thorpe fell from a landing-stage, bruising his face and straining his wrist. But apart from having a black-eye, Mr. Thorpe looked little the worse for his accident the next morning.

The Works Brigade continued on duty for 15 hours without a rest, and so well did all the Brigades work that on Friday morning every employee was able to go on as usual, and there was not the slightest disorganisation.

WO September, 1917

The British Tradition

HE sat in a pool of water, with his hands before his face. He was almost the colour of the mud; hands, face, clothes, all stained and caked with it. His shrapnel helmet has a large dent in the side and under the rim of it a bandage tinged with red. Now and then, at some concussion greater than usual, he shuddered. The air was alive with death all round him, and from time to time a fresh deposit of mud and sandbags would hurtle into the trench.

By all the rules of the game he was a "casualty," but you could not have made him realise that. He was badly shaken, and had been almost unconscious when his "pals" delved him from a collapsed dug-out. But he was glad no officer had been present to order him to the aid-post. He knew that the Germans would counter-attack presently, and he waited. That is the British tradition.

He was right in his surmise. The bombardment died down and the counter-attack began.

He rose unsteadily to his feet to take his place with his comrades on the fire-step. His lips were dry and swollen, and he moistened them with his tongue, while he pressed home a clip of cartridges in his rifle. For half-an-hour those obstinate men in grey tried to force their way into the trench, but the British stood firm, and the man who was the colour of mud stayed at his post, firing steadily into the grey mass.

When the German attack was finally broken up, and an exhausted remnant of field-greys surrendered, the little band of British lit their cigarettes and sat down again in the water, nursing their rifles.

It was unpleasant sitting in water, but they were too tired—far too tired—to stand. Many of them were casualties, but they still waited. That is the British tradition.

The man who was the colour of mud dug his teeth into his lips for fear the others should see his pain.

The Platoon Commander did not see many casualties when he came down the trench. They turned wounded arms and legs away from him, they pulled their helmets further down on their heads to hide bandages; men who were too hurt to sit up lay against the wall of the trench and sang and made a show of cleaning their rifles, trying to control the trembling of their hands. They thought another effort might be wanted from them, and they knew how much their officer cared for their wounds, and how he would have

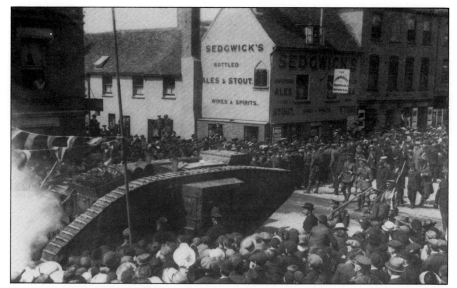

Arrival of 'Julian' in the Market Place.   *p.166, 174t, 189*

STOUT PARTY: These ration cards are a dashed nuisance.
THIN PARTY: Are they? We didn't have any where I've just come from.
STOUT PARTY: Please name that happy place, sir!
THIN PARTY: *Ruhleben*—a prison camp in Germany.

sent them back instantly as casualties. So they hid their pain and waited, according to the British tradition.

When they were relieved, the man who was the colour of mud laughed. It was a dry, rather shaky laugh, but there was a smile with it.

"Rest," he said. ". . . bit done up . . . good fight, though . . . bloomin' good fight . . . Thank Gawd they dug me out in time for it."

They passed down the communication trench laughing and every man who could speak sang; the others smiled, and left cigarettes for those who had to be taken on stretchers; and the man who was the colour of mud carried his exhausted chum's rifle. . . . That, again, is according to the British tradition.

WN March, 1918

Food Rationing

For a foil to his comfortable, well-fed grumbler our artist pictures the wasted frame of a man who has been immured in the German camp for civilian prisoners of war at Ruhleben. Many hundreds of Englishmen have been detained there for three and a-half years, and those who have lately returned to England all tell the same story—that they had very spare living indeed and had to depend for food to keep body and soul together almost entirely on parcels sent to them from England. Did they grumble about their lot? Not a bit of it. On the contrary, they accepted the fortune of war cheerfully and "kept their tails up" all the time. The sailors who guard us on the seas, the soldiers who are fighting our battles in France, have times of difficulty about rations. Do they grumble? Not a bit of it. They growse, but growsing is different from ill-conditioned grumbling, and their letters home always declare they are "in the pink." We at home, thanks to the sailors and soldiers, have food enough for all if it is evenly shared, and *rationing is the only means by which even distribution can be assured.* Here and there the machinery of rationing may work irregularly at first, and where there is such mischance let everyone approach the difficulties in the spirit of making the best of it and setting the irregularity right without a fuss. A little patience, plenty of goodwill—these are ways in which we may all manifest a real patriotism.

The story of the Ruhleben internment camp shows the value of a rationing system well organised and well administered. The camp leaders there saw to it that the parcels from England were shared out so that all had food even if the quantities were spare. The Germans provided only a daily ration of potatoes for their prisoners, and the parcels from England alone saved the situation. There was not a man there who called the system of sharing the parcels "a dashed nuisance." All were in the same boat, and all shared alike. One result was that many Germans in Berlin envied the English prisoners, and Mr. E. L. Pyke, who was lately released, says that the Prussian authorities more than once had fears that the mob would attack Ruhleben in order to get at the English parcels!

WN April, 1918

Watford's Rally Round the Tank

Watford lived up to its fine reputation for responding to every appeal made in the interests of the nation, and last week the Tank Bank had such a busy time that when the final figures were announced on Saturday evening, they were a source of pride and gratification to every townsman. In the four days that "Julian" stayed in the Market-place, £162,020 was invested in War Bonds and Certificates, and the crowds that collected each evening, especially on Saturday, were almost unprecedented.

On Thursday evening, Mr. W. Pearkes again presided on the Tank and appealed for the money to help to win the war.

Mr. Dennis Herbert said the appeal from the Tank was an appeal to one and all, no matter to which class they belonged. The best they could do for the men at the Front was to deny themselves. He felt certain that without the big money already subscribed it would be easy to raise Watford's total to £150,000 before Saturday by means of small amounts.

WN May, 1918

How Watford Celebrated Peace

The great news of the signing of the armistice between the Allies and Germany was received on Monday forenoon with jubilation. Every hooter in the district sounded, and the majority of factories closed for the day. Flags and bunting were immediately displayed, and the streets soon thronged with joyful crowds of citizens. In the evening the arc lamps in the Market-place once more brightened up the town. The Market-place was simply packed throughout the evening, and young people gave vent to their feelings. There was some singing but no rowdyism, and the Deputy-Chief Constable, Mr. W. Wood, reported to the Magistrates the next morning that there was not a single case of drunkenness or disorderly conduct.

At the Churches thanksgiving services were held, and there was a general spirit of deep relief sobered by the thoughts of those who will not return to enjoy the blessings of peace.

WN November, 1918

No. 25 National Filling Factory,
Bushey Mill Lane,
Watford.
14th November, 1918
Brigadier General Milman, C.M.G., R.A.,
28 Northumberland Avenue,
W.C.

Dear Sir,

The Armistice being signed, the work for which I originally came forward, namely Production, is at an end. Under these circumstances I should be grateful if I could be released to go back to my own business.

During my tenure of office of nearly three years, I have been supported by a truly loyal staff, and in particular have I been fortunate in the services of my two Superintendents, Mr. H.C. Spratling at No. 24 Factory, and Mr. F. Stanley at No. 25., and I should esteem it a great personal favour if you would appoint them respectively, to take charge of the winding up of these two factories. They are naturally conversant with all details, and are, I know, fully competent to carry the responsibilities attaching to this work. You can also rely on my placing my assistance at their disposal, should they feel they need it.

May I take this opportunity of tendering my most earnest thanks for the great courtesy and consideration which I have received at your hands, and from every member of your staff with whom I have come in contact.

Believe me,
Yours sincerely,

● *The copy of the letter was unsigned, but the General Manager was Louis Levi.*

141

... a cheap hospital for a peace memorial? ...

The Coal Position

The Coal Controller most emphatically warns the public that in consequence of the cessation of hostilities there must not be any relaxation of the effort to save coal and light, and to win coal from the mines. The demands of our Allies, France and Italy, must for some time continue to be of a very exacting character.

The fuel situation in this country is still precarious, and the demand for coal is far from being met. It will be impossible to materially alleviate the coal situation in the immediate future. The public are requested, in the national interest, to continue exercising the utmost economy in the burning of fuel and light at the present time as they so loyally did under a condition of war.

WN December, 1918

Wages of Council Employees

The Urban District Council held a special meeting on Monday,Dec. 16th, to receive an application from the Council's workers for an increase of wages. Mr. R. A. Thorpe presided, supported by Mr. G. Longley (vice-chairman), Messrs. Andrews, Staples, Trewin, Clark, Pearkes, Long, Oxley, Southam, Poultney, Moffat, Tucker, Julian, Gorle, with Mr. W. Hudson (Clerk) and Mr. D. Waterhouse (Surveyor).

Mr. Palmer, who represented the Workers' Union, spoke very earnestly on the men's behalf, pointing out that the abnormal increase in the cost of living justified the demands which had already been laid before the Council, and unfortunately turned down. He urged upon the Council to reconsider the matter, as feeling was very strong among the workers, and failing compliance a strike was imminent. He asked for an increase of 4s. a week for all employees, and 12½ per cent. on earnings of all men of 21 and upwards. Even this would leave them below the amount which the Committee of Production adjudged as providing a living wage, this amounting to 28s. 6d. additional per week.

Mr. Longley read a table showing the present increases to date as follows:-

Employees	July, 1914			Dec. 1918		
	£	s.	d.	£	s.	d.
Carpenters	2	4	9	3	15	0
Blacksmiths	1	12	0	2	14	0
Strikers	1	7	0	2	3	0
Lamp-cleaners	1	2	0	1	18	0
Masons	1	15	0	2	11	0
Labourers	1	5	0	2	5	0
Other Labourers	1	5	0	2	1	0
Park-keepers	1	5	0	2	1	0
	1	4	0	2	0	0
Labourers	1	4	0	2	0	0
	1	6	0	2	1	0
Sweepers under 60	1	4	0	2	0	0
Sweepers over 60	1	4	0	1	14	0
Destructor Stokers	1	12	0	2	8	0
Dust Van Assistants	1	12	0	2	8	0
Dust Van Assistants	1	6	0	2	2	0
Dust Van Drivers	1	8	0	2	4	0
Engineers Drivers	1	18	0	2	17	0
Engineer Stokers	1	10	0	2	11	0
Farm Carters	1	5	0	2	1	0
Sewage Destructor Men	1	4	0	2	1	0
	1	5	0	2	2	0

Some general idea of the increase could be gained by realising that two or three rises had been given during the war, and it amounted to an average 16s. for unskilled and 20s. for skilled labour.

December, 1918

Death of Mr. F. Downer

We regret to record the death, which occurred early on Monday morning, of Mr. Frederick Downer, the well-known Watford photographer, aged 78 years. He had been in failing health for some little time, and passed away in his sleep after a paralytic stroke.

Deceased was born in Watford, where he lived all his life. He commenced his career as a clerk in a lawyer's office, but being very fond of drawing, he used to get up early in the morning and attend classes in London, at Lee's Artistic Studio, returning to take up office work at 10 a.m. When photography became popular he bought a camera. He erected a studio at the back of his father's offices at 97, High-street, and later had a shop at 110, High-street; eventually he built up the premises in Loates-lane, where he had of late years carried on business. He had an extensive connection. Twice he photographed the late King Edward—once when, as Prince of Wales he attended the Royal Agricultural Show at St. Albans, and again in a group at the Grove. Deceased also went to Carlton House to take pictures of the Jubilee procession. It is hardly too much to say that Mr. Downer's camera had been seen at every important local function for the past 50 years. Deceased took no active part in public affairs. He was keenly interested in the Volunteer Fire Brigade, which was formed in 1867, being on the committee and a pioneer. Later he became a member of the Brigade for a few years.

WO January, 1919

Lack of Hospital Accommodation

During the past four and a half years the situation at Watford with regard to accommodating wounded soldiers has been almost pathetic and would have been serious but for the heroic efforts of such kind-hearted people as Mrs. Morten Turner, Mr. Pierpont Morgan, Mr. Barton-Smith, and other devoted ladies and gentlemen.

When the first big return of our wounded boys necessitated the help of practically every town in the kingdom, and the Watford Hospital was viewed as to its capacity for assisting the military authorities, we had to confess that our hospital was scarcely large enough to deal with all the private cases that came along, and it was not greatly to our credit that we were unable to meet a demand such as conditions at that time particularly required.

But think for moment what might have been if the town had possessed a fine spacious hospital such as is suggested by the Peace Memorial. If we had been foresighted enough to offer our pennies, our shillings, and our pounds towards a building that would have done the community credit, we might have welcomed many hundreds more suffering lads and given them comfort whilst healing their wounds.

The troops who passed through the town in the very early days, and also those who have been billeted round about, are almost unanimous in their praise of the treatment accorded them; and, indeed some of the Norfolks and Suffolks became very much attached to their Watford friends, and many a landlady spent days of anguish when the Norfolks were reported missing in Gallipoli, and no trace could be found of most of the men who left Watford to join in this unsuccessful fight for Constantinople. How much more then have the wounded who have been attended to at Lady's Close, Wall Hall, or the Croxley V.A.D. felt when they had gone back to their regiment or to their homes, that the kind-ness extended to them at Watford would never be forgotten, and that the town would be a remembrance to them of happiness.

It is our great opportunity at this moment to say whether we desire a cheap hospital for a Peace Memorial, or whether we would wish Watford to erect a building with the most up-to-date appliances. Even shillings make a difference, and a bigger difference than many of us imagine, because a multitude of shillings given by those who can only spare so small an amount soon mount up to the price of erecting an extra ward, and also show the breadth of appeal and the interest taken in our hospital.

If you cannot send pounds will you please send shillings, and you cannot start the new year better than by resolving to help forward by every means in your power this great Peace Memorial which we have set our hearts upon erecting.

WO January, 1919

National Factory For Sale

It is announced that the Government have decided to dispose of munition factories at Watford, Trafford Park (Manchester), and Dudley (Worcestershire). The first two have been used for the manufacture of explosives, and the third has been a projectile factory. The Watford factory stands on a site of 33 acres, and the buildings cover 124,100 square feet.

It is understood, says the "Daily News," though the Ministry of Munitions on Tuesday declared that no official announcement can be made on the point at the moment—that the decision to dispose of these three factories will probably be followed as rapidly as possible by the sale of many other of the Government factories which have been erected during the war.

The sale of the three factories named above will have to be by tender. A large number of enquiries have been made about them.

WO January, 1919

● *This refers to No. 2 Factory in Bushey Mill Lane.*

German War Trophies

A letter was read stating that it had been decided to offer to the town as war trophies a damaged German machine gun, an ammunition box, and ammunition belt, carriage forward.

The Clerk: Just about what I expected.

Mr. Mills: Are they worth troubling about? I will propose that we ask them to hold them over until we have formed a museum to put them in. (Laughter.)

On the motion of Mr. Batchelor, seconded by the Chairman, it was agreed to accept the trophies.

Mr. Mills: I will move that the proposer and seconder be appointed trustees to take care of them. (Laughter.)

The Chairman: We could have an auction sale and make more of them than the carriage will cost.

WHP February, 1919

● *Two German field guns were sited just inside Cassiobury Park Gates on the greensward facing the toilets. They were elevated to aim above the toilets but elevation and traverse wheels on both guns had rusted solid and the wooden handles were splitting. This was in the early 1920's.*

Anonymous boyhood memory, 1987

Land For New Houses

THE Watford Urban District Council have decided to purchase, subject to the sanction of the Local Government Board, 130 acres of the Callow Land estate, for housing purposes. The price is £27,500.

The Council were of the opinion that they have made a good bargain, and there was no opposition to the purchase. The scheme, if it should go through—and it is probable that the Local Government Board will bestow upon it a speedy benediction—will mark an important step in the development of Watford. The growth of the town was to be expected to the north and west, particularly to the north.

The Watford Manufacturing Company recently bought 210 acres of the Garston House estate. The Government intend, so it is stated, to adapt part of the munition works as a clothing factory.

It is apparent, therefore, that, apart from the existing demand for houses, building operations on a large scale will be necessary in the near future in Callow Land. The Council are pledged to the erection of 280 houses, a number which the local Labour Party ask should be increased to 500.

The Watford Council have all along shown that they are aware of the urgency of the problem, and anxious to do what they can to relieve a situation which becomes more serious every month. In the meantime they are not disposed to be dragged into the Greater London scheme of the London County Council. We entirely agree with the advice tendered to them by the Herts County Council on this point. If the Watford Council allowed themselves to be swallowed by Greater London, they would be abrogating power of local government and practically admitting inability to settle their own affairs; it is almost certain, too, that the expense to the ratepayers would be very much greater.

WO February 1919

Snow Clearing

A letter was read from the Secretary of the United Builders and Labourers' Union stating that members of the society had been offered 6d. per hour for clearing the snow away from the streets, and the Union considered that that was not enough, considering the present cost of living. The men did not want help, only work. Mr. Julian: Was anyone taken on at 6d. an hour? Mr. Trewin: No.

WO February, 1919

WATFORD & DISTRICT PEACE MEMORIAL HOSPITAL

	£	s.	d.
Amount previously acknowledged (Feb. 18th, 1919) 13800		3	4
Mr. J. F. Clark	1	0	0
Mr. P. Buck	5	5	0
"A Friend"	10	0	0
Mr. C. Morland Agnew	250	0	0
Mr. Albert Dunn	1	1	0
Mr. S. H. Hunt	10	0	0
Loyal Phœnix Lodge of Oddfellows (per Mr. Frank Roberts)	15	15	0
Mr. J. Harris Mayes	5	0	0
Mr. C. Knight	3	0	0
Mr. Arthur H. Inns	5	5	0
Messrs. W. E. Pearkes and Son	100	0	0
Watford Postal Staff Fines and Gowns Fund (per Mr. V. Corry)	5	0	0
Mrs. Sherry	10	0	0
"Observer" Shilling Fund (Ninth List)	500	5	0

Donations sent to the Hon. Treasurer, Mr. Henry Brown, Lyndale, Upton-road, Watford, will be gratefully acknowledged.

St. Albans Road, Cromer Road, Balmoral Road, Hossack estate on left-hand side, later to be called 'Harebreaks'.

Housing Hustle

The way the Housing Sub-Committee of the Watford Council is moving is calculated to take away the breath of some of the older Councillors, who have never been accustomed to anything in the nature of hustle. The official intimation that the Local Government Board are paying the cost of housing schemes above a penny rate has warranted the adoption of a policy to meet local requirements to the fullest extent. There is now no excuse for doing things by halves. Enquiries have shown that there are two or more families in eight per cent. of the houses in Watford. Over three hundred applications, mostly from men who have served or are serving in the Forces, have been received by the Council for new dwellings. Last week an advertisement in the "Observer" of a 10s. 6d. house to let at Oxhey, was answered in a few hours by over 150 people. In view of such facts as these, the Council cannot be accused of overstepping the mark in approving a scheme for 750 houses. By their purchase of the Callow Land and Wiggenhall Estate for £27,500 and £14,000 respectively, they are already in possession of the necessary land.

WO March, 1919

Property Derequisitioned

The Clerk reported that he had received an intimation from the officer commanding the troops in this district, that the military proposed to retain North End House, Clarendon Hall, the Skating Rink, Beechen Grove School House, and Halsey Hall.

It was stated that Little Nascot and Chater Schools would be vacated.

WO May, 1919

County Council's Road Programme

The Highways Committee reported:–

Road Reconstruction.—Road and Bridge programme, 1919-20.– The Surveyor submitted correspondence with the County Surveyor upon the above subject, and reported that the net result of the negotiations with the County Council was that they were prepared to make a grant of £9,752 towards the cost of re-surfacing with tar macadam St. Albans and Rickmansworth-road, the estimated cost of the work being £25,678, and that no grant was proposed to be made in respect of any of the other roads, the subject of the Council's applications.

WHP WO June, 1919

Retrospect of 1919

For the first time in the history of the town, Labour has had a majority on the Urban District Council, the Party, thanks to good organisation and to the apathy of their opponents, winning eight seats at the March election.

In January it was announced that the Watford Munition Works, standing on a site of 33 acres, with buildings covering 124,100 square feet, was for sale. Later the works were adapted as a clothing factory by the Government.

In March the Watford Rural City Society Ltd., purchased, as a Public Utility Society, 17½ acres of land adjoining Gisburne House, their scheme being to erect four houses to the acre. In April it was reported that 556 applications for houses had been received, over 300 of the applicants having served in the Forces.

In May instructions were given for the "lay out" of the Hossack Estate, with sites for a public hall, public baths, and a branch library. By this time 739 applications for houses had been sent in.

In May, Mr. George R. Bolton, Sub-Librarian of Stoke Newington, was appointed Librarian at a salary of £250 a year. In July it was announced that a site in King-street for a new Library had been presented to the town by Mr. S. H. Timms.

In August it was announced that to recognise the services of the Hertfordshire Regiment during the war, and the attachment formed between that Regiment and the Bedfordshire Regiment, owing to the enlistment into its ranks of many Hertfordshire men, the name Hertfordshire Regiment was to be altered to Bedfordshire and Hertfordshire Regiment.

In September it was suggested that open markets should be established in Watford. Mr. W. Hurst Flint, the owner of the market rights, stated that he had no objection if open markets would be for the good of the town, but asked where it proposed to put them, and what about the collection of the tolls. It transpired in the course of correspondence with Mr. Flint that he would not oppose the acquisition of the Market rights providing it was in the interest of the town to acquire them. The subject is still under consideration.

WO January, 1920

DEMOBILISATION.—Percy Landon, photographer, 125, St. Alban's-road, Watford, having been demobilised, wishes to thank his numerous patrons for their support during his absence.–ADVT.

Arrival in Cassiobury Park for the Peace Celebrations.

. . . fun fair just inside the Park Gates.

Atlantic Flown

Alcock and Brown left Newfoundland in an open cockpit converted Vickers Vimy twin-engined bomber which had a cruising speed of 90 mph. The attempt was to cross the Atlantic to win a Daily Mail prize of £10,000. After sixteen hours and twenty seven minutes flying—during which Brown had to climb on the wings to chip ice from the carburettors—they crash-landed in an Irish bog.

The Magnetos, made at North's Factory in Whippendell Road, had performed faultlessly.

WN June 1919

Peace—And After

So far as can be gathered, there was not a single untoward incident to mar the success of the Peace Celebrations in West Herts on Saturday. It is true that a drizzling rain fell in the evening, but this perversity of the weather had hardly any appreciable effect on the spirits of the holiday-makers. Every town, village, and hamlet gave vent to its feelings in a carnival of rejoicing.

There has never been seen such a wealth of decoration. From church tower and public buildings floated the Union Jack; business premises were almost hidden in flags and bunting; streamers and fairy lights hung in countless gardens, and from the windows of humble cottages small flags added to the wonderful glow of colour.

The Peace Celebrations in Watford July 19th were upon a large scale, and proved very successful. On the Sunday prior to the 19th a united service of thanksgiving was held on the West Herts Ground. On the 19th there was an impos-

ing procession through the town, a fete was held in the Park, and tea was given to the wives and children, to the number of 3,900, of ex-Service men. A series of dinners was afterwards arranged for ex-Service men in the Clarendon Hall, and the number who attended these dinners, which were held on five separate evenings, was 2,150. The money for the celebrations, £1,378, was all subscribed, so that no call was made upon the rates.

WO July, 1919

Peace Memorial Hospital Site

Mr. S. J. Attenborough read the report of the Sites Committee (Messrs. R. A. Thorpe, George Longley, Henry Brown, C. H. Peacock, and S. J. Attenborough, and Mrs. Schreiber), which stated that, in considering the question of a site, they had had the following principles in their minds, viz.:–That the site selected should be in a prominent position in the town and worthy of the memorial to be erected upon it; that it should be free from building or other restrictions; that it should have no buildings upon it; that a sufficient area of land should be acquired so as to render the Hospital capable of enlargement in the future if rendered necessary by reason of the growth of the town and district. The committee had found a site, viz., the "Elms" paddock in the Rickmansworth-road, of about three acres, having a frontage of 390ft in the Rickmansworth-road and a depth of 820ft., which they thought complied in all respects with the principles enunciated above.

Apart from the question of price, the only difficulty which arose was that the "Elms"

paddock could not be acquired unless a purchaser could be found for the house and gardens, to which it is appurtenant. A purchaser, however, should not be difficult to find, having regard to the price for which the committee had secured the option to purchase the property. By the contract the committee had by payment of £200 secured the option to purchase the "Elms" estate at any time on or before the 31st December, 1919, for the sum of £12,250. This £200 has been found by Messrs. Arthur Kingham and Stanley J. Attenborough in equal shares, and these gentlemen will bear the loss of it in the event of the option to purchase the estate not being exercised, while the £200 is to be treated by the vendors as paid on account of the purchase-money in the event of the option to purchase being exercised, in which event the £200 would, of course, be repaid to the two gentlemen who had found it.

The "Elms" estate is of a total area of 10a. 1r. 9p., and consists of a house, outbuildings, gardens, and orchard, and six cottages, together with the paddock, which paddock the Sites Committee recommended the Executive Committee to acquire as a site for the erection of Watford's Peace Memorial. With the exception of four of the six cottages, the estate is freehold, the four cottages being copy-hold of the Manor of Watford. The house, with the stabling and other outbuildings, gardens, and orchard, are subject to a tenancy agreement for three years from August 9th, 1918, at a rent of £300 per annum, the cottages bringing in in addition about £50 per annum. The paddock has been requisitioned by the Watford

Peace Celebrations, Cassiobury Park; houses visible are at the town end of Cassiobury Park Avenue.

Urban District Council as garden allotments, for which they paid 6s. a week. The Committee hoped it would be possible under the scheme to obtain the Elms Paddock for £5,000.

Mr. R. A. Thorpe said that the Committee thought five acres were necessary. He knew it had been suggested that three acres would be sufficient, but they were looking forward to the time when the town would be double the size it is, and the Sites committee and Executive Committee were of opinion that the five acres should be acquired.

The Chairman: That will give plenty of room for expansion.

Mr. Thorpe thought the General Committee would be well advised to take the five acres. It was generally agreed this was the most suitable site.

Mr. W. Hudson pointed out that they had that liability wherever they bought land in the town. After all it was only a matter of an additional acre and a half between Mr. Hofland-Hibbert's estimate and the Executive Committee. They were putting this hospital up for all time.

Everyone who signed the report earnestly hoped that they would use every endeavour to secure the Elms Estate for the benefit of Watford, and the paddock for the Peace Memorial for Watford and district. It was thought five acres was ample for hospital accommodation. This was the cheapest site that had been offered in Watford. Across the road £5,000 was being paid for 2¼ acres, and the Committee had 10¼ acres, and if they did a bit of multiplication, he thought they would agree with the Sites Committee that this was one of the most reasonable prices that had been put before them.

WO November, 1919

A Good Bargain

The estate known as "The Elms," standing at the corner of Rickmansworth and Hempstead-roads, Watford, is to be acquired by the town. When the Peace Memorial Hospital Fund was started the paddock of "The Elms" was regarded as an ideal site for a new Hospital, and the Sites Sub-Committee were enterprising enough to secure an option to purchase the whole property for £12,250. They decided to offer the Urban District Council the benefit of the contract, on the understanding that the Hospital site should be retained at a price of £5,000. The Council thus had an opportunity of securing the house, cottages, orchard, gardens, and grounds, an area of about five acres, for £7,250, and at their meeting on Tuesday evening, they unanimously decided to close with the offer.

Some two or three months ago we pointed out that the Council ought not to allow the opportunity of acquiring this property to slip. The Council's administration has suffered in the past from a lack of foresight and failure to grasp the possibilities of the growth of the town. Otherwise there would have been years ago municipal offices worthy of Watford; the patchwork additions to Upton House would have been avoided, and proper accommodation would have been available for recent developments in the Public Health Department, and such new departments as those devoted to Infant Welfare Work and War Pensions.

The purchase of "The Elms" on such advantageous terms will materially assist in solving a problem that might have given the Council great trouble in a few years' time. When all the details are settled and the sanction of the Local Government Board obtained, the Council will no doubt consider whether it would not be a good financial move to sell the property on which the existing offices stand, and remove to "The Elms" site. An alternative scheme might provide for the removal of the Public Health and one or two other departments.

WO January, 1920

One of the ex-Servicemen's dinners at the Clarendon Hall; menu—steak and kidney pie.

Hertfordshire and Road Transport

The Herts County Council are applying for a Parliamentary Bill enabling them to own and run motor omnibuses. We take it that they are adopting this course for two reasons—first, because they desire to protect Hertfordshire from the encroachment of other counties. Both the London and Middlesex County Councils are promoting Bills which give them power to run motor 'buses over a wide area, including the Metropolitan Police District. When these schemes were put forward, the Herts County Council sent representatives to conferences with various Councils round London.

At the same time they submit a solution—which neither the London nor the Middlesex Bill contains—of the transport question for Greater London. They ask for the setting up of a Joint Committee of the Councils interested in the provision of motor omnibuses. Broadly speaking, what it is hoped to effect by this arrangement is that each county, while absolutely preserving its own rights, shall have running powers, where desirable, in adjoining counties. Thus the services would be planned according to the needs of localities, and there would be no stopping and changing at geographical boundaries. The Hertfordshire County Council, in the proposals they put forward, show that they are alive to the future. Some such action was inevitable if they were not to stand supinely by while the first step was taken in the encroachment on Hertfordshire by Greater London. The danger of this encroachment has greatly increased in recent years. Places like Bushey and Watford have the strongest objection to being swallowed up in the vast agglomeration of the County of London. A moment's reflection will show how desirable it is for all the Hertfordshire local authorities to join together in thwarting the new Metropolitan policy.

WO January, 1920

Street Watering

Mr. Woodstock inquired why the streets were not being watered.

The Chairman replied that it was a question of horses.

The Surveyor said that if the streets were watered they could not tar them, and it was also a question of traction.

Mr. Woodstock said they wanted the streets watered, so let them get horses.

Housing—£1,000,000

Before the war the mere mention of such a sum for any local scheme affecting a population of 50,000 would have been regarded as a symptom of municipal lunacy; now it passes without a word of comment from any Councillor, being looked upon as, perhaps, rather a heavy item, but really quite unavoidable, and, therefore, not worth worrying about. It will be found, we imagine, much easier to talk of a million than to raise it. The Ministry of Health want local authorities to finance their own schemes, and local authorities are protesting, and calling for a national housing loan.

There are suggestions of mortgages, bonds, and the issue of County Stock. Nobody seems quite clear what will eventually be done, although housing has been the most important problem in domestic politics for well over a year.

No decision has been reached on the question of rent, which must enter into any discussion on the financial soundness of housing undertakings, the fact being that everyone knows that a £1,000 house ought to fetch twice or three times as much rent as the local authorities will dare ask. It is all a muddle.

The Ministry blame other people, and other people blame the Ministry. There are fine promises—1,000 houses for Watford this year, for instance—but little performance.

Much of the difficulty has arisen from the initial mistake in practically shutting out the private builder, who met all past needs, instead of giving him every encouragement. In the meantime the Watford Council are sending deputations to the Ministry, appointing officials, discussing types of houses, arranging loans where possible, and generally immersing themselves in detail. They have started on a few houses, and have arranged with a local firm to erect 813 houses on Harebreaks Estate "subject to the money being available."

There are now over 1,200 applicants in Watford for new houses, and those who were earliest on the register must have almost abandoned hope. They do not want excuses for delay; they want houses. Possibly the Council can give a more or less reasonable explanation why the housing eggs have not been hatched after a year's sitting. It is not an unfair conclusion to draw, that if the Council majority had been constituted differently from what it is to-day, we should have had some wild denunciation at the forthcoming municipal elections.

WO March, 1920

IV

The False Dawn

The veterans who had avoided death in the trenches returned home with the promise of a land 'fit for heroes to live in'. Their expectations could not be fulfilled overnight. The reality of the dream was indecision and delay. The shattered economy could not be switched to the demands of peace easily, although Watford had embarked on an expansive and costly housing programme the size and quality of which exceeded all earlier projects.

The nation mourned the loss of its sons and did not disguise its abhorrence of the cost in human terms as the wounded, disturbed and permanently disabled exservicemen and women returned home. Social conditions had irrevocably changed and men found their places taken by the new civilian army of women workers particularly in shops and stores. Before the war the suffragettes had campaigned, with little effect, for greater freedom. Ironically the war gave them the opportunity of proving the point that they had been making as they successfully undertook all manner of employment previously thought to be the prerogative of the breadwinner of the family.

The right to vote was given to men on reaching the age of maturity (21) and to wives of householders as well as women over 30 (reduced to 21 in 1928). The opening hours of shops were drastically reduced. The men who had faced death on land, sea and in the air were required to adjust to these new and liberated conditions.

The long term prospects of trade and commerce were bright, making good the deficiencies of a society deprived of all luxuries and many necessities. Motor transport was beginning to take over from the 'horse-age' which had largely determined the speed of progress. The job opportunities for returned drivers and mechanics exceeded the supply as new garages were opened and light trucks and vans replaced the erstwhile horse and cart.

In much the same tradition as the 1865 Red Flag Act which discouraged the early development of steampowered road transport, the post-war era applied severe weight and speed restrictions on motor cars, buses and lorries. Mechanical transport had made excellent progress prior to 1914, progress which accelerated with the demands of war.

Road construction and maintenance did not follow suit. Little changed and for the most part roads had deteriorated. Few were tarmacadamed; between towns and villages the majority were still rutted dirt and gravel. In towns they were generally of rolled and compacted granite. No surface could successfully resist heavy vehicles with solid tyres carrying excessive loads at excessive speeds.

An enterprising ex-serviceman named Scammell conceived a means of overcoming part of the 'weight' problem by designing an innovative articulated vehicle. In later years the same firm developed the famous and ubiquitous Mechanical Horse which successfully replaced the horse in the movement of goods in town and city. A generation of men and women had matured and aged before their time. Work was available if not plentiful. Inflation had forced up prices and wages were not far behind. The future augured better living conditions, even prosperity.

It was not to be.

Watford Athletic Ground

Lovers of sport in Watford have always been haunted by the fear that sooner or later the West Herts ground would fall into the hands of the builder. Hence, there will be great gratification at the announcement that through the generosity of Mr. Dodwell the ground is to be purchased and conveyed to a central committee for the benefit, in perpetuity, of sport in the town.

To all intents and purposes Mr. Dodwell makes a gift, of the value of over £8,000, to Watford. Apart from any question of sport this is one of the most considerable benefactions the town has ever received.

The West Herts ground has been a great asset to Watford for nearly 30 years. It has been the local centre for the two national pastimes of cricket and football, and there, also, lawn tennis and hockey have been regularly played. With the rapid growth of the population its facilities have been more and more appreciated. On one occasion this year ten thousand people gathered to watch a football match.

To replace the ground would mean an expenditure of many thousands of pounds, and moreover no site equally central is available.

In our report of the special meeting of the West Herts Club will be found full details of the scheme, which, there does not appear to be any doubt, will be in operation in a very short time.

Messrs. Benskin, who bought the ground some time ago, and were coming into possession on the expiry of the Club lease, have acted very handsomely. They made the purchase in order to ensure the continuance of first-class football, and, with a commendable spirit, readily fell in with the scheme of Mr. Dodwell, doing at the same time what they could to assist future developments.

Mr. R. A. Thorpe, who financed the Football Club in the past, has generously waived a claim for an old debt standing, it is said, at something like £2,000. The Watford Athletic ground, as it is now to be called, starts with excellent prospects.

A central committee, on which all sections have representatives, with the Trustees as *ex-officio* members, will govern its affairs. The difficulties which often arose through the conflicting claims of cricket and foorball ought now to disappear.

WO May, 1920

The Pond is no longer a watering place for the military horses and for a few years more, before the top end of the town is developed, reverts to peaceful rusticality.

New Motor-Bus Service

The restoration on Wednesday by the London General Omnibus Company of the motor bus service formerly worked by the North-Western Railway between Garston and Croxley, via Watford Junction station, has been appreciated by the people of Watford and by those dwelling in the Garston and Croxley districts in particular. Running at 15-minute intervals during the busier hours of the morning and evening and at 30-minute intervals during the other periods of the day, the new service connects at Watford Junction with the electric trains working between that station and the Metropolis. The journey time between the Garston terminus, the Three Horse-shoes, and Watford Junction occupies 14 minutes and the fare is fourpence; between the Croxley Green terminus, the Sportsman, and the Junction the journey time is 27 minutes and the fare sixpence. The through fare between Garston and Croxley Green is tenpence.

The new daily service between Bushey station and Boxmoor runs at hourly intervals by way of the High-street, Hunton Bridge, Kings Langley and Apsley End, the fare for the through journey being 1s. 1d. This service, No. 145, is a welcome augmentation of the weekend service, No. 146, recently inaugurated by the General Company between Golder's Green and Boxmoor traversing Watford en route.

The fare between Watford High-street Station and Hunton Bridge Church is sixpence, between the former point and King's Langley, Saracen's Head, eightpence, and between Watford High-street and Apsley Mills, tenpence.

The intention of the L.G.O.C. to develop its motor bus services in the Watford district is shown by the Company's recent opening of a garage at Leavesden-road, from which a large number of the motor buses working on local routes will be operated and which, incidentally, should provide employment for Watford workers. With the materialisation of new housing schemes in Watford and the neighbourhood and the need for additional facilities for travel, the Company hopes to be able to install motor bus services to

such places as Rickmansworth, Berkhamsted, Hemel Hempstead and St. Albans.

Full particulars as to the routes and times of the new services are given in Peacock's Railway Timetable.

WO August, 1920

Watford in 1920

The chief feature of the year has been the alarming upward tendency of public expenditure. The rates have reached an unprecedented level. In Watford they now stand at 18s. 4d. in the £, and a further increase is probable when the new budget is made. Several reasons have been adduced for the additional burdens thrown on the ratepayers. The County Council claim that their hands are forced by new schemes which the Government call upon them to undertake. The Urban Council have been faced with increases of salaries and wages and the dearness of materials. The cumulative effect has been a demand for economy—a demand so strong that it cannot be resisted, so that in the near future it may be expected that local authorities will exercise the most rigid economy.

The most important subject which has engaged the attention of the Urban District Council during 1920 has been that of housing. The estimated number of new dwellings required is roughly 2,000, including 500 to replace houses in insanitary areas. Four separate schemes are in hand—at Harebreaks, Callow Land, Willow-lane, Sydney-road, and Wiggenhall. The first-named scheme provides for 1,000 houses; the land alone cost £27,500, and the making of roads and sewers involves the outlay of over £100,000. The houses will cost, roughly speaking, £1,000 each. The total expenditure on housing in Watford will, it is anticipated, eventually reach the huge total of two millions.

It may be interesting to take the events connected with the schemes in something like chronological order.

In January it was reported that the sanction of the Ministry of Health to the Harebreaks Estate loan had been received. The same month, at a meeting held in the Clarendon Hall, it was stated that the Council had given an undertaking to build 1,000 houses this year. A resolution was passed protesting against any reduction in the standard of houses.

In February this question was discussed by the Council, and a protest entered against the abandonment of plans drawn up by architects engaged by the Council, and the substitution of plans provided by the Ministry of Health. In March it was decided to inform the County Council, who were proposing to issue county stock for housing that the amount required for Watford was £1,000,000.

A contract was accepted with Messrs. Brightman and Sons to erect 813 houses at a cost of £980 per house on the Harebreaks Estate. Further contracts were entered into with the same firm to put up 40 houses in Gammons-lane, at £850 each. In March it was stated that the amount allocated by the County Council from the issue of County Stock was £615,000.

In April the Clerk of the Council reported that the Ministry had sanctioned the borrowing of £32,400 for the 40 houses in Gammons-lane, and a loan of £100,500 for street and sewerage works on the Harebreaks Estate.

In June the rents of the houses in Willow-lane and Sydney-road were fixed at 12s. 6d. each, with 4s. 10d. rates, making a total of 17s. 4d. The Ministry of Health paid for the abandoned plans made by the Council's architects, the cost being £6,239 16s.

At the same meeting the Council made an application to the County Council for a loan of £100,000 from the County Stock.

The same month a flying visit was paid to Watford by the Inter-Allied Housing Congress. In July, at a special meeting of the Council, the rent of the new houses was discussed, and a resolution was proposed asking the Ministry of Health to reconsider the amount fixed for the

147

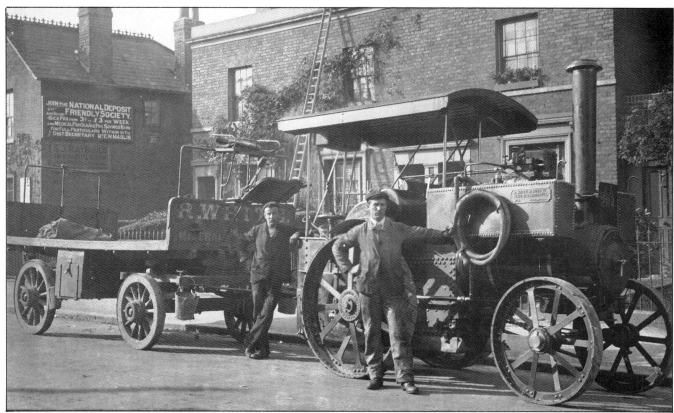

R. White, mineral water manufacturer of King Street. Water filling stop in Queens Road.

p.346 cr

Willow-lane cottages, as "it is considered that no tenants should be called upon to pay more than one-sixth of his wages." This resolution was lost by the casting vote of the Chairman.

In July it was suggested that the men engaged on the scheme should be asked to work an extra hour a day, so as to expedite building. The men, on a ballot, refused; it was stated that they would probably work an extra hour in the morning, but objected to working an hour longer in the evening.

In August the Ministry sanctioned a loan of £12,400 for the erection of 10 houses in Rickmansworth Road.

At the September meeting it was reported that the men were dead against overtime, and would not consent to it. In November Messrs. W. King and Sons offered to put up 68 houses at a cost of £1,185 per house, and the Council wrote to the local Master Builders' Association with a view to

other builders following suit. The rents originally fixed were decreased as the result of a deputation to the Ministry of Health, the figures being 16s. 3d., 19s. 4d., and 22s. 4½d., these sums including rates. At the Council meeting in December, it was stated that some 50 houses were occupied and more were nearly ready for occupation.

ably increased. In October it was reported that five acres had been secured in King's Ward, which would provide 70 or 80 permanent new allotments, while in Harebreaks Estate 200 new allotments had been staked out.

In November, the sale of Church property in Watford by the Church Lands Charity, realised £7,000, the High-street Infant School fetching £3,100, and the Vicarage-road recreation ground £2,300.

In December, Mr. R. A. Thorpe resigned his

position as Captain of the Fire Brigade, after 20 years' service, and the Council passed a vote of thanks to him for his services. Certain alterations were made by the Council in the pay and duties of the firemen.

In January it was announced that the Watford Conservative Club premises, High-street, had been sold to Messrs. Dudley, for conversion into shops, and that North End House had been purchased for the Club. The new premises, which were redecorated and renovated, and to which was added, at a cost of £3,000, a new billiard room, were opened in July, and re-named Halsey House.

WO December, 1920

Photographed in Market Street near the Rose & Crown stables. In 1987 the name is the same but the telephone number, 530, has a few more digits in front.

Pond Cross Roads looking towards the town. Triangle with signpost, fountain and Queen Victoria's Jubilee oak tree is on the right.   *p.185 b*

WANTED, SMART LAD to solicit and de-liver orders, by cycle; salary 25s.—Apply, J. Sainsbury, The Parade, Watford.

WO March, 1920

● *David Downer recollections in WHP June 1, 1920. David at age 83 (born 1837, Frederick's brother). Until 1900 he ran the stationer's business started by his father.*

● *The W.C.C. restarted in Autumn 1919, President F. H. Haines.*
● *Gibbs & Bamforth moved from 42 High Street to Carey Place in March 1920.*

Elizabeth Kingham opened a small shop in the High Street c1790 dealing in provisions and groceries. In 1835 her eldest son, Henry, inherited the business and henceforth traded as 'Henry Kingham' (pic. p.97). He purchased the freehold of the shop in 1851. His five sons took an active part in the by now widespread business and in 1911 a private company was formed to manage the firm's affairs after their father died, with son, Arthur, as Chairman and Managing Director. Arthur maintained an active interest until his death at the age of 80 in 1941.

Prior to 1913 the firm relied upon horse transport (and were noted for the excellence of their stabling), but in that year they hired a Foden steam wagon. During the early days of war their valuable horses were requisitioned and more Fodens were brought to replace them. This photograph shows their fleet of Foden wagons c1922.

Henry Kingham & Sons Ltd. were noted retail and wholesale grocers, specialities being tea and coffee blending and bacon curing. They packaged many products under their 'Larkspur' label. By 1951 they had 455 employees engaged in supplying retail outlets throughout Hertfordshire, Bedfordshire, Buckinghamshire, Cambridgeshire, Essex and parts of North London and Middlesex.   *p.277 t, 291 b*

1925/6, the new By-Pass (top of picture), built and opened; Harebreaks built and Watford Manufacturing Co.'s new factory, the large squat square building just above centre, empty, later to become British Moulded Hose, the site of former H.M. No. 2 Munitions Factory off Bushey Mill Lane, a clothing depot for some while, would shortly become Greycaines.

p.288

Vicarage Road, the Union House, later Shrodells but before that known colloquially as No. 60 (Vicarage Road). The disused gravel pit became the ground of Watford Football Club.

s.153, 155, p.350 tl, 351

The Library staff 1921, new Librarian, Mr. George Bolton, with the book.

High Street reconstruction 1923, corner of Queens Road.

New Librarian

When librarian George Bolton was appointed, the Watford library occupied purpose-built premises in Queens Road. The facilities offered by the library were renowned but although the building had already been enlarged, space was again at a premium.

In an age, some 50 years or so before modern photocopiers made their mark, the only means of copying a rare document was photographically. In fact, many earlier plate cameras were well-designed, with long bellows extensions, to get near and focus accurately.

George Bolton was keenly interested in photography and used his equipment to very good purpose in making copies of such items as church register pages and rare, fading photographs. From this work, and probably inspired by men such as Whitford Anderson—who was prolific in photographing places and antiquities of Hertfordshire 'for posterity'—he saw the wisdom of starting a local collection.

This has survived and has been added to from that date. Much of George Bolton's work is among the collection, but difficulty exists in definite identification. Whilst the local professionals used plate cameras—and would do so for many years to come—George Bolton was a relatively early exponent of the use of both cut-film and roll-film, which meant lighter and more portable cameras.

He recorded progress of road changes, for example, the Cross Roads; bridge building at Wiggenhall Road; reconstruction of the High Street, and rebuilding of Cassio Bridge. Some of his photographs of the years 1921 to 1939 are used in this book, of which that left shows Queens Road corner. The High Street was in course of reconstruction in 1923 when new foundations were laid and the road given a tarmac surface.

Rebuilding Hunton Bridge

Messrs. K. Holst and Co., London, are now engaged in rebuilding Hunton Bridge, which was not considered strong enough to carry modern traffic. The structure will be of reinforced concrete and consist of a centre arch having a span of 31ft. 6in., leaving a roadway 26ft. wide and a footpath 5ft. in width. The amount of the tender was £4,050 and the Ministry of Transport have agreed to make a grant of 50 per cent. towards the cost.

WO September, 1922

● *Reconstruction of the High Street and London Road; the tender of Mr. Chas. Ball of Letchworth amounting to £25,630 was accepted.*

Population 1921, 45,910

Football in Watford

A party of journalists were invited by the directors of the Watford F. C. to inspect the new Vicarage-road football ground on Friday evening.

The area of the ground is 6½ acres, and the total estimated accommodation is 33,000, for 5,000 of whom cover is provided. The grand stand will hold about 1,400, and there are two other stands. Commodious dressing-rooms are provided, together with bath-houses (including shower baths); there are also a directors' room, cashier's room, referee's room and bath, a bar, and store rooms, and—as autioneers say—the usual offices.

WO August, 1922

Concerning Water

The Water Supply, Fire Brigade, and Baths Committee submitted the following report:—

"Proposed Sale of Bushey Sub-Fire Station Site.—The Committee again considered the desirability of disposal of this land, in accordance with the suggestions made from time to time by the Captain of the Fire Brigade, and recommend:— (a) That the existing Fire Station be closed as a Fire Brigade Station. (b) Moved by Mr. Oxley, seconded by Mr. Goodrich, that the land be not sold. Amendment, moved by Mr. Andrews, that, having regard to the unsuitability of the site, the same be sold. Messrs. Andrews, Thorpe, Mobbs, and Ellis (four), voted for the amendment; and Messrs. Brightman, Oxley, and Goodrich (three), voted against, and the amendment was declared to be carried as a recommendation to the Council.

WO November, 1922

Engine off the Rails

Shortly after midnight on Thursday a railway accident of an extraordinary nature occurred on what is known as the Kings Langley loop—a siding used for goods trains so that fast traffic may go through.

An engine, with a tender, was being driven from Crewe to London, and, for some reason, ran into the loop, crashing into the buffers near the bridge. The engine went over the embankment, falling into the road, and taking part of the woodwork of the buffers with it. As shown in the photograph, the engine blocked the road to Abbots Langley.

The driver and the fireman had marvellous escapes, neither being injured.

WO September, 1922

PAINT NOW AND GIVE EMPLOYMENT

Travellers to and from Hunton Bridge from Hillside and Abbots Langley will recognise the railway bridge, unchanged since being built except for the addition of pedestrian tunnel to the right (under where the engine is in this photograph). Beyond the bridge, to the left (not in view), the 'King's Lodge'.

High Street; one of many photographs made for sale as postcards, in this instance by Frith Bros. Frith's work was always serially numbered and so can be dated, this being 1921.

p.245 b, 323 t

J.M.W.Turner Esq.r R.A. del.t — View from N. West. — Hill, aquatinta.

. . . Cassiobury is now only a name in local history. Watford, which has absorbed it, has history yet to make . . .

Sale of Cassiobury

CASSIOBURY, a Royal domain from the days of the Cassii tribe, with which the whole history of Watford is bound up, is one of the last of the stately Homes of England marked down for sale by auction, on June 8th, unless previously disposed of. It touches a sad chord and marks the sign of the times to see these historic mansions come under the hammer. Messrs. Humbert and Flint, the estate agents who for years have had the Essex properties in their care, are offering (in conjunction with Messrs. Knight, Frank, and Rutley) the freehold estate in seven lots, if not sold as a whole. Lot 1 and 2 will be offered together; they consist of the noble residence and 100 acres, the home farm, &c., and a valuable building estate, making together over 433 acres; Lot 2 is LITTLE CASSIOBURY, over 2 acres; Lots 4 and 5 are pasture land; Lot 6 is the West Herts Golf Course; and Lot 7 Whippendell Wood.

We believe some members of the Royal Family came from Windsor last week for a private view. Would that the whole property, with its valuable and historic contents, its paintings, staircase, Grinling Gibbons' carvings, could again become the home of royalty.

The sale of the contents of the Mansion will start on the 12th June for ten days. There are some 3,000 lots to dispose of.

WO April, 1922

Cassiobury Sold

We understand that the greater part of Cassiobury Estate, together with the mansion, has been sold to a local syndicate. Though the names of those comprising the syndicate have not been made public, it is rumoured that it consists of no fewer than nine members, of whom two are members of the Watford Urban District Council. No information is available as to the price, but in business circles the figure is put down somewhere in the neighbourhood of £55,000.

Cassiobury was put up for auction by Messrs. Humbert and Flint, in conjunction with Messrs. Knight, Frank and Rutley, in London, in June. It was then stated that 11¼ acres of pasture had been sold privately. Mr. W. Hurst-Flint suggested an opening bid of £90,000, and came down to £50,000, but no offer was made.

For Little Cassiobury £1,000 was offered, but on a final bid of £3,600, the property was bought in at £4,000. Since that time, however, it has been privately sold to Mr. G. Blake. Mr. Flint suggested at the sale that the estate could be adapted as a hydro, country club, or public institution, but expressed the hope that some wealthy man would preserve it in its present character. Referring to the noted Grinling Gibbons carvings in the mansion, he stated that he had had them valued, and it was estimated that they were worth anything from £14,000 to £20,000. The West Herts Golf Club's Course embracing about 261½ acres, and having over 5,000 feet of existing road frontage, leased until

1932, at £600 per annum, was taken in at £10,500.

Since the auction, it has been known that attempts have been made to form a syndicate, and at first three or four names were mentioned as being interested. Others apparently joined them, and the deal was arranged at the end of last week. The land purchased is bounded on the west side by the river Gade and Grand Junction Canal, and on the east side by Hemel Hempstead-road. The intention of the syndicate is to develop the estate for building. What will be done with the mansion remains to be seen.

A report appeared in a London paper to the effect that the Watford Urban District Council had acquired 50 acres "of the lower picturesque portion of the ground, through which the river Gade flows and which adjoins the present Park allotments, representing a portion of Watford Park proper."

At the June meeting of the Council Mr. G. Blake suggested that the question of securing an extension of the Park should be considered, and a sub-committee, consisting of Messrs. T. R. Clark, G. Blake, R. A. Thorpe, and H. B. Watkins was appointed to deal with the matter. It is probable that negotiations have taken place between the sub-committee and the vendors, but we presume that no bargain would be completed before discussion in open Council.

Swiss Cottage by the Gade, celebrated local beauty spot. Pathway on the left is Rousebarn Lane leading to Chandlers Cross. Location of Swiss Cottage in relation to Rousebarn Lane and Rickmansworth Road can be seen from the Ashby and Brightman development plan on page 126.   1921

The End of Cassiobury

The announcement made this week that the greater part of the existing Cassiobury Estate has been sold privately to a local syndicate means that the final step has been taken in the disintegration of the historic home at Watford of the Earls of Essex. The intention of the purchasers is to develop the land as a new building estate. The mansion, now that all the furniture has been sold, stands as an empty shell.

From a sentimental point of view, this is a matter of no inconsiderable regret. The town would have been a very different place from what it is to-day had the Cassiobury Estate remained intact.

It is just a quarter of a century since the late Earl made the first of a series of sales to Messrs. R. Ashby and C. Brightman—two men to whose enterprise and foresight the development of Watford in recent years has been largely due. They started with purchases in Callow Land, and followed these by the acquisition of the Harwoods Farm Estate, Cassiobridge Farm Estate, and extensive tracks of Cassiobury Park. From them the Council were wise enough to buy 75 acres to make the public Park.

On land which formed, a little over two decades ago part of the ancient estate, are now miles of streets. Judge-street, Victoria and Chater Elementary Schools, the Boys' Grammar School, St. Michael's Church, and other places of worship were erected as the new areas filled up with private dwellings. The growth of Watford during this period put the town far ahead of any other place in Hertfordshire, and strengthened its claim, now happily conceded, to larger municipal powers. If the late Earl had been able and disposed to say that the rural character of his inheritance should remain unchanged, Watford would have remained confined to comparatively small boundaries, and its development would have been stifled. As it is, the break-up of the estate coincided with the creation of new urban needs, and the final disposal of the mansion and adjoining land has been inevitable for some time.

There remain the West Herts golf course, Whippendell Wood, and a portion near the river Gade, which is being offered to the Urban Council as an extension of the public Park. That prospective purchase, by the way, is a matter which ought to be thoroughly discussed in open Council meeting. The price mentioned in this connection, £4,100 for 59 acres, would, of course be very low if the land were, like the other portion, suitable for building. It is a matter of some satisfaction that the syndicate referred to are all Watford men, and therefore are more likely than outsiders to have due regard to residential and other amenities. Cassiobury is now only a name in local history. Watford, which has absorbed it, has history yet to make.

WO August, 1922

● *At the same time as Cassiobury was being sold, the recession and down-turn in trade was hitting local industry; the Watford Manufacturing Company—in process of having a large new factory built at Delectaland—was in trouble.*

Watford Manufacturing Co. Ltd.

An extraordinary general meeting of the Watford Manufacturing Company, Ltd., was held at the Cannon-street Hotel, Cannon-street, London, on Monday, for the purpose of considering, and, if thought fit, passing a resolution to wind up the Company voluntarily.

The Chairman said he regretted that they were meeting that day in accordance with a resolution of the directors conveyed to them in the Company's circular dated August 24th, 1922. The proposal that the Company should be wound up voluntarily was no doubt a great disappointment to every individual shareholder, particularly to those who had been for so many years associated with the Company. Naturally they desired to know the reasons why the directors were asking them to take the course proposed.

In one word, it was the direct result of falling market prices. For the past twenty-four months manufacturing companies throughout the world had been experiencing conditions of which they had no previous experience or even precedent. The cessation of hostilities created an unprecedented demand for goods, and there was no doubt that almost every individual manufacturer expected that demand for replenishing war depleted stocks to be still greater during 1920 and 1921; instead of which the years 1920 and 1921 were possibly the worst years for demand experienced, owing to the inability of the world, especially Central Europe, to finance the replenishment of their depleted stocks.

The huge readjustments which had been necessitated in many of the largest manufacturing and trading companies had unfortunately resulted in the fact that business under those altered conditions could only be carried on at a serious loss. It would not be right, nor would it help them, to refer by name to the number of other companies who had suffered enormous and unprecedented losses during that period. Fortunately for them, most of them had been able to weather the storm by drawing on their reserves to liquidate their losses. Unfortunately their Company had no reserves to fall back upon with the exception of its capital. The ordinary shareholders of the Company came forward last year, and agreed to the sum of £225,000 being written off their ordinary shares, but they would see from the accounts that further heavy losses had been made.

That naturally had resulted in a weakening of confidence of the bankers of the Company, and they had become increasing insistent in their demand for repayment of their overdrafts. At the present moment they owed their bankers about £450,000 in round figures, and other creditors about £83,000, a total indebtedness of £533,000. The simple fact, therefore, was that their creditors were insisting, not unreasonably, upon the complete liquidation of their overdraft, and it was that position which had given their directors no option but to ask the shareholders to attend that meeting, and, with their consent, to carry the resolution on that agenda paper.

Mr. Banks said that the Chairman had stated that the loss was mainly bought about by falling markets. Could he state the amount due to the bank on account of the new and unfinished factory?

The Chairman said that it was rather hard to reply specifically to that question because the bank overdraft did not necessarily mean money expended on building. The new building and plant purchased for it approximately amounted to £350,000 and the building was not yet completed.

WHP August, 1922

New Football Ground Opened

The Watford Association Football Club's new ground in Vicarage-road was opened on Wednesday evening by Colonel Charles Healey prior to the match with Millwall Athletic. There was an attendance of over eight thousand when Mr. F. W. Jeffs asked Colonel Healey to perform the ceremony.

The Company of which Colonel Healey is a director, was of some little assistance in developing and equipping the ground. Those present who knew the ground five months ago could hardly realise the transformation that had taken place. It was a waste wilderness then, but now it was a beautiful area covered with lovely and very fine turf. He trusted that it might be enjoyed by future generations of Watford for many, many years.

Mr. F. W. Jeffs presented Colonel Healey with a silver key, and also the silver lock and chain from the gate.

The padlock bore the following inscription:—
"Presented to Colonel Charles Healey, C.M.G., on the occasion of the opening of the football ground, Vicarage-road, Watford, 30th August, 1922."

WO September, 1922

The Borough Charter . . .

The Incorporation Campaign

IT is well over 30 years since Incorporation was first discussed at Watford, and it is probable that but for the war a Charter would have been obtained six or seven years ago. Leaving out of account the persistent advocacy of Incorporation by the *Observer*, the body which has played a greater part than any other in the movement was undoubtedly the Watford Tradesmen's Association. In 1910 they appointed a special committee to visit a number of boroughs of similar size to Watford, and were hoping to complete their campaign by arranging for a "petition of inhabitant householders," when the outbreak of war put an abrupt end to their activities. Prior to that, however, it had been made clear that Incorporation was regarded as desirable by practically all parties and classes in the town. Here and there were to be found opponents, but their number was always negligible.

Leading car of the procession is that of Watford's M.P. Mr. Dennis Herbert who has handed to Watford's Mayor, the Earl of Clarendon, the Charter of incorporation at the Borough Boundary at Haydon Road/London Road. Photographer on the steps in the background is Mr. W. Coles.

Drawings on the right illustrate the ingenious and practical 'tripod ladder' in use at this time.

The New Borough

Watford has every reason to be proud of the wonderful success of the Charter celebrations. It was the day of days in the town's history, and the scenes in the streets will long be remembered. To those responsible for the arrangements a great deal of credit is due; but if there had not been, on the part of the residents generally, feelings of gratification and pride that Watford had become a Borough, the proceedings would, inevitably, have fallen flat. The presence of the Lord Lieutenant of the county, the High Sheriff, the Mayors of Hertford, St. Albans, and Hemel Hempstead, and the Bishop, assured the pomp and dignity of the ceremonial of the reception of the Charter. The procession was worthy of the occasion. It was not only representative of the public and social life of the town, but it included many men prominent in the local government both of the county as a whole, and of West Herts in particular. In this respect the gathering was unique as far as Watford is concerned. Hitherto, the town has been merely an urban district, with no municipal status above places with a thousand or two of population, and claiming only the passing interest of its neighbours; now the Borough of Watford, with a Hertfordshire nobleman as Mayor, and with possibilities of the highest standard of civic life, comes into its own, rising at once to a new status.

WO October, 1922

Charter Day Arrangements

THE programme of Watford's Charter Day celebrations on Wednesday next is now practically complete. The order of the procession was given in our last issue. The official timetable is as follows:-

12 noon.—Reception of the Charter at the Borough boundary at the corner of Haydon-road and Chalk-hill. Mounted and walking detachments are requested to be ready to take up their positions at 11.15 a.m., and conveyances at 11.30 a.m.
12.10 p.m.—Start of procession.
1.30 p.m.—Procession forms up in the Marketplace for Proclamation of the Charater.
1.45 p.m.—Luncheon to invited guests at Buck's Rooms.

3 p.m.—Public meeting in the Palace Theatre.
1.30 p.m. to 5 p.m.—Free cinema performances for school children at the Super-Cinema, Central hall Picture House, Electric Coliseum, and Empire Cinema.
7.30 p.m.—Grand firework display in Cassiobury Park.

WO October, 1922

Town Council Elections

IT is satisfactory to know that a great deal of public interest is being taken in the election of members of the Watford Town Council. There will be contests in all the eight wards, and 43 candidates have come forward for the 24 seats. Fifteen of the candidates are being run by the Labour Party, who are carrying the fight into all the wards except St. Andrew's and Oxhey. The election of Aldermen, which takes place at the first meeting of the Council, may necessitate several bye-elections. It is extremely improbable that the Aldermanic bench will be filled from outside the Council, but in our opinion it would be unwise for the members not to consider the claims of a few prominent men who have given the best years of their lives to local public service. This Aldermanic election is on an entirely different footing from those where Councils have been long established, and where a recognised system of promotion prevails. The contests next Wednesday are almost certain to result in new faces being seen in the Council Chamber. The two ladies who have the support of the National Council of Women may do well if they have the consistent backing of voters of their own sex. In 1919, when Labour secured a majority on the Council, one of their successful candidates was a lady, whose term of office was, however, short.

It would appear that the chance of Labour regaining the power which was easily wrested from them a year last April is extremely remote.

Watford has had one experience of Labour government, and is hardly likely to want another.

In municipal life the Labour member is the most expensive luxury imaginable.

The fact is, as Mr. Harry Gosling, a Labour leader, said in 1919, "If you are going to have a real live Labour movement rates are bound to go up."

It was only apathy and indifference on the part of the general body of the Watford electors that enabled Labour three years ago to dominate the Council. The importance of the forthcoming election is made the more apparent by that fact. Watford, entering upon a new municipal status, has good reason to fear reckless and extravagant expenditure, and to object to any foolish experiments in Socialism on the part of representatives of a political party who are avowedly out to upset the economic and social order upon which the prosperity of the country depends.

WO October, 1922

Radio

May, 1922, radio station '2LO' started in London and for several months it was not allowed to broadcast music! In November 1922 the British Broadcasting Corporation, an association of manufacturers of wireless apparatus, received its licence to broadcast and regular London programmes began. First receivers were of headphone and crystal detectors, gradually giving way to receivers with valve amplifiers.

Horton's new garage in Loates Lane near Derby Road. Demolished for relief road widening c1965 and the business moved to corner of St. John's Road/ St. Albans Road.

St. Albans Road 1922, looking towards Cross Roads; one of a series of photographs made by Mr. O. Brookman in 1922 when he came to Watford to find a garage site, below.   p.103tl, 347 b

Euston and Watford Electric Line

The new electric line between Watford and Euston was opened for passenger traffic on Monday.

The section between Willesden and Harrow was opened for steam driven trains in June, 1912, on which date the Watford to Croxley Green branch was also opened for steam traffic. In February, 1913, the extension from Harrow to Watford was opened, steam still being the motive power. During the intervening years to 1915, the Bakerloo tube was extended from Paddington to Queen's Park, and opened early in that year. In May, 1915, electric trains from Elephant and Castle ran through to Willesden, and in April, 1917, onward to Watford. At the same time the electric service between Watford and Broad Street was inaugurated.

WO July, 1922

Scammell

In an era of post-war weight- and speed-restriction on commercial vehicles, Alfred Scammell, with his brother James, designed and built a revolutionary articulated vehicle which could be registered as a single vehicle. This was shown in 1920, was permitted to travel at 12mph rather than be restricted to 8mph and carried a legal payload of 7 tons. The reaction to the prototype led to further machines being built and exhibited at the 1921 Olympia Motor Show, where firm orders for 50 vehicles were taken.

The modest premises in London would not support production on the scale needed, and ground in Tolpits Lane, West Watford, was used to build a factory where, in 1922, a workforce of some 60 men was employed to start production.

In 1922 the right-hand unit was built, to be quickly followed by the second. Named the Nascot Motor Works, Brookman & Co. the business later became that of Tucker Bros. after moving from their High Street premises (next to Ponderosa site) and thus continued until demolished for 1970/71 road widening. The Oddfellows Hall was built alongside. Otto Brookman started with the 'Singer' car agency, was a keen photographer and at one time President of the Watford Camera Club, c1935.   p.290 bl, br

St. Albans Road, looking towards Garston, Lowestoft Road corner just visible by the lamp-post.   1922.

1921: Riverside Road/Rookery area before development. The silk mill factory building at the extreme right was, in the late 1880's, the Watford Steam Laundry, and later a piano factory. The farm and woodland on the right-hand site became Blackwell Drive, Deacons Hill and Oxhey. The carriage sheds, centre, were demolished June 1987.

Lord Leverhulme's Offer

A meeting of the creditors of the Watford Manufacturing Co., Ltd., was held on Friday at the Cannon-street Hotel. The chair was occupied by Mr. F. D. Arcy Cooper, the liquidator, in the voluntary liquidation of the Company, who submitted a statement of affairs, which disclosed liabilities of £538,653.

The assets were estimated to realise £427,709, or a deficiency of £110,944. The principal asset consists of the properties, which stood in the Company's books at £622,506, but which had recently been valued at £307,000.

The Chairman stated that he had received an offer from Lord Leverhulme to purchase the assets of the Company, as a going concern, for a sum of £543,000, payable in cash. Lord Leverhulme desired that in the event of his offer being accepted, the liquidator would obtain the approval of the Court to the sale of the assets. The liquidator pointed out that he did not anticipate that any better offer could be obtained for the business, and if Lord Leverhulme had not been so deeply interested in the Company the creditors would not have obtained payment in full, which could now take place.

A resolution was unanimously passed in favour of the liquidator applying to the Court for leave to accept Lord Leverhulme's offer.

WHP October, 1922

Duke of York Visits Watford

On Tuesday the Duke of York paid a visit to Watford, and spent over an hour and a half inspecting the various departments of Messrs. Waterlow Bros. and Layton's printing works in Milton-street.

The party were first conducted through the Treasury Notes departments and those in which the unemployment and insurance stamps are printed, and the Royal visitor was shown the printing, perforating, and reeling machines. In the photogravure department a portrait of the Duke, in the uniform of the Royal Air Force, was being printed, and the processes were explained to him. The tour concluded in the artists' department, where many fine posters were in course of reproduction. The various stages of the preparation of posters deeply interested his Royal Highness, and he saw several posters being printed off.

WHP November, 1922

Bridge over the River Colne, Wiggenhall Road, prior to rebuilding; Blackwell Drive can be seen as can the first new houses of Riverside Road.

... the Bridge looking towards Watford; railway carriage shed on the left built 1914/15 (and demolished June 1987), and in the background, behind the tree, Benskin's brewery.

Local Traffic Returns

As stated in last week's "Observer," a complete census of all the vehicles passing stationery points on eight of the main roads around Watford was taken between the hours of 6 a.m. and 10 p.m. during last week, concluding on Saturday evening. The official figures for the first three days were given last week; those for the rest of the week (Wednesday, Thursday, Friday, and Saturday) were as follows:—

Colney Street: 635; 580; 670; 1,138
Leverstock Green: 595; 449; 522; 868
Garston: 1,097; 1,006; 1,125; 1,660
Kings Langley: 1,669; 2,066; 1,593; 2,699
Bushey: 2,626; 1,945; 2,768; 3,896
Elstree Road: 669; 913; 618; 1,110
Croxley Green: 1,394; 1,286; 1,491; 1,931
Rickmansworth: 1,126; 942; 1,224; 1,756

The census is being taken only on the Ministry of Transport's classified roads throughout the country, with a view to the allocation of money for their upkeep. This district has been supervised by the County Council Surveyor's Office, in Mildred-avenue.

WHP August, 1922

Sub-Letting on Harebreaks

The complex problem of sub-letting in Council houses was the subject of a debate introduced by Councillor Mansfield, who drew attention to a paragraph in the report of the Tenancy Sub-Committee of the Housing Committee, instructing the Housing Official to commence proceedings for the possession of three houses at Harebreaks, where overcrowding was alleged. Councillor Mansfield said that in these cases there were in the respective houses 10, 12 and 10 people. His point was that if the Council took action to turn the sub-tenant families out of those municipal houses, they would simply force those families to overcrowd other houses, where the conditions were less tolerable than at Harebreaks.

If overcrowding in present conditions had to exist, it was better it should exist at Harebreaks where there were, at least, baths and air space, than in the conditions prevailing in some of Watford's dreary side streets.

In reply to a question, the Town Clerk said that the Housing Committee had power to act. He mentioned that action in one of the three cases had been deferred for a month.

WO February, 1924

Wiggenhall Houses

In reply to an enquiry, the Housing Committee had informed the Ministry of Health that of the houses erected or being erected at Wiggenhall, 50 are for general applicants, and 74 for people removed from property scheduled for closing.

The Public Health Committee reported as follows:-

"Ballards Buildings, etc.—Demolition Orders. —The Medical Officer and the Sanitary Inspector reported that all the new houses at the Rookery had been allocated, and that all the tenants selected by the Tenancy Sub-Committee had removed from Ballards Buildings, New-street, and Lamb Yard. The Sanitary Inspector reported that every house in Lamb-yard was empty, but in Ballards Buildings a few houses were still occupied.

The Medical Officer reported that the next areas to be dealt with were the following:— Meeting-alley, 30; Butchers'-yard, 11; Watford Fields and Fox-alley, 6; Lower High-street, 6; Woodman's-yard, 3; Water-lane, 2; Carey-yard, 2; Wheatsheaf Cottages, 2; Tibbles'-yard, 1; Cassio Hamlet, 2; total 74.

WHP February, 1924

Most photographs (as below) show Ballard's buildings as a 'peep' through the courtyard entrance; but this photograph is rare in that the photographer has ventured in to show a different view, not long before the buildings were vacated for demolition under a slum clearance order.

Ballard's buildings to go . . .

The buildings had gained a reputation perhaps more unsavoury than deserved. Very old properties, they were at one time in the ownership of Mr. Dyson who had a small brewery at the end of the yard. In the 1830's they housed a considerable number of railway workers from which spread the story that Ballard's buildings had been built for that purpose.

Most courtyards consisted of a few dwellings, such as Meeting Alley which was just one row of cottages, but Ballard's buildings contained rather more buildings. Other more odious and delapidated properties were demolished as slums much earlier but Ballard's buildings survived. Because they were near to the Church and Market Place, and in the public gaze, they perhaps disturbed better-off residents' consciences not a little.

Watford, as a town, had a better reputation than most for dealing promptly with property which did not meet sanitary and health requirements. Many tenants had lived long in some houses, were satisfied, and maintained them in spick and span order, and resisted the orders to demolish and move. Above all, they resented the implication that THEY were the cause of the 'slum' in which they lived.

New Street, entrance to Ballards Buildings on the right.

p.349 br   c1914

Watford Town Mill, morning after the disastrous fire . . .   p.93 t, 99 tl, 330 b   Dec. 1924

and later up for sale but without buyers. The mill and water rights were bought by the Council for £2,250 and mill was demolished in 1938.

Roger's timber yard, blaze of 1921. The site became, in the 1950's, Beechen Grove car park and then part of Charter Place.

Flour Mill Fire

A disastrous fire occurred in the town, on Wednesday night, which resulted in damages, estimated roughly at £20,000, to the Watford Flour Mills, High-street, the property of Messrs. T. Bailey, Ltd., in which the interests are held by the well-known milling family of Messrs. Putnam, who have been associated with the industry in this part of the country for a period extending over half a century. The mills constitute one of the oldest structures in the town, and have been in existence many generations. They consist of a pile of buildings imposing by their plainness, solidity, and commanding height, as, with their elevators, they tower right above any of the adjacent property.

John Welbys, of Watford, seems to have laid a claim to the Mill Pond at Watford in 1431, but the result of the suit, which arose between himself and the Abbot, is not given. In the time of Abbot John of Wheathampstead a sum of £41 3s. 6d. was spent on repairs to the mill. About the same time certain inhabitants of Watford began to erect a horse mill, but were successfully opposed by the Abbot. "The Fishery and all the shops recently erected upon the waste at Watford were granted in 1579-80 to John Farnham, and the mill in 1609 to Edward Ferrers and Francis Phillips, the fee farm rent of £13 from the Mill paid by them being granted at the same time to Sir Christopher Hatton and others." "Ferrers and Phillips sold the Mill in the same year to Sir Thomas Lord Ellesmere, who died seised of it in 1616-17, and it subsequently passed with the Manor to the Earls of Essex. The present Watford Mill is the representative of this old Abbotial Mill." (Victoria History of the Counties of England, Vol. 2, p.452.)

The building up of the banks of the Mill stream above the Mill, which extends for more than a mile, is attributed to the monks. The present structure was built by John Guest in 1826 upon the site of the old Mill, but being larger, one corner of it encroached upon a piece of the Turnpike road, and amongst deeds is an interesting document conveying that small portion of the land from the Trustees of the Sparrows Herne Turnpike road to John Guest for the sum of 10s. The Mill was installed with two breast water wheels and seven pairs of stones, together with the necessary dressing tackles. This machinery was the best that engineering skill could produce, and made Watford Mill one of the best in its generation, and was in its time the "talk of the county." The engineers who dismantled this machinery bore testimony to its substantial and perfect design. The introduction of the Roller system made it necessary to destroy obsolete though magnificent machinery in order to make room for a modern system.

The Mill was remodelled in 1921, and brought up to date by the present proprietors, Messrs. Thomas Bailey (Watford), Ltd., under the managing directorship of Mr. Gilbert Putnam.

WO December, 1924

● *The Metropolitan line extension to Watford, which was planned before 1914, was completed during 1925. The Watford Station was formally opened on Saturday 31st October, and full services provided from Monday 2nd November, 1925.*

The Peace Memorial Hospital . . .

The nature of a practical memorial expressing thanks for peace after the horrors of the Great War was readily apparent. The Cottage Hospital in Vicarage Road was totally inadequate to cope with the normal requirements of an expanding community and it was common knowledge that lack of hospital facilities had forced the authorities to find alternative accommodation for the war wounded.

The land was purchased soon after the war's end, the Council was determined not to let the opportunity pass, and as Chairman of the Appeal Fund, the Earl of Clarendon, backed by C. H. Peacock of the Watford Observer, as Treasurer, set about raising £90,000 by voluntary public subscription and money raising events.

The success of the campaign was apparent when in July 1923 the foundation stone was laid and in June 1925 the Princess Royal, Princess Mary, opened the Peace Memorial Hospital in Rickmansworth Road next door to the 'Elms'. Its 87 beds soon proved inadequate. Further extensions costing £70,000 were added in 1937, providing a total of 154 beds.

Leica

A camera, using 35mm perforated cine film, had for some years been the subject of perfunctory development by the firm of Leitz, who, needing a business boost, decided to put the camera into production. It was shown at the 1925 Leipzig Fair and had some degree of success. It had a focal-plane shutter with speeds 1/20th to 1/500th sec and a non-interchangeable f/3.5 lens. 869 of this model were to be made in the first year.

● At first this small camera was more of a novelty, and not sophisticated enough to compete with competently handled press cameras. In time it was improved and became a living legend . . .

Peace Memorial Hospital nearing completion.   p.338 t   1925

Princess Mary en route through the Market Place to open the Hospital.

Dedication of Sculptured Group; the work of local artist Mrs. Mary Bromet, the figures represent 'The Spirit of War'; the left-hand figure representing the agony of the bereaved and those never to return. The right-hand figure is dedicated to the maimed and is depicted as blind and groping; the centre is Victory 'We have won! It is over!'
                                                         p.249 br, 322 tr   1928

163

The By-Pass . . .

The quiet-looking Cross Roads (p.149 b) belied the congestion which the town could suffer, particularly on market days.

In an attempt to cut unemployment a plan was made to build a road from Mill Hill past Stanmore and around Watford, joining the Hempstead Road near Hunton Bridge.

Started in 1924, the By-Pass was completed in about two years and when finished afforded considerable relief to Watford.

The photograph below shows the High Street during its last years as a venue for the ancient street market. (The 'Compasses' was rebuilt in 1928 at the time the street market was transferred to its new site.

The cars are parked on the old 'Market Place'. When the market closed considerable disquiet was expressed at the use of this space as a car-park. After much discussion it was taken into use as a carriageway as shown on page 189.

The North Orbital Road—the By-Pass—on the sweep from Hunton Bridge (at the bottom). Photographed in 1928, the road was constructed between 1924 to 1926. In the foreground, leading right, Russell Lane. Leading to, on the left side, High Road, Leavesden. Land on the left later King George V Playing Fields, later Leavesden Aerodrome.

Market Place on non-market days is used as a convenient car park; the viewpoint for this photograph is the same as that of 60 years previous (p.45) but the use of a slightly wide-angle lens has made the far buildings appear more distant.

p.61, 189   c1924/6

Watford High Street c1926, street market in progress.

165

Crowds gathered at Market Street at the end of the strike, May 12th. The first bus of that day had just passed, signifying that, for better or for worse, the strike was over, but not without incident at the Lower High Street bus garage (story below).
p.174

General Strike . . .

In 1919 and 1920, when the full impact of the war casualty figures was beginning to be appreciated, the economy appeared to be in a healthy state. The public demand for consumer goods was insatiable and confidence was growing. Suddenly the bubble of prosperity burst and legislation was not then regarded as a tool by which the economy could be manipulated. As the money ran out so demand and prices tumbled.

Locally, the Watford Manufacturing Company, which at its Annual General Meeting of 1920 expressed optimism in all aspects of its manufacturing and trading outlets, reported also that its employees, through the Company's social welfare arrangements, received dental and eye inspections. This same company were to find themselves greatly overstocked with raw materials purchased at top prices and, worse, a new £300,000 factory partly completed. With bank overdrafts of £500,000, it went into voluntary liquidation in 1922.

Compulsory wage cuts throughout industry were common-place. Exported coal fetched only one-fifth of the price it had commanded a few years earlier. The payment of subsidies to miners was stopped. The key industries of power, transport, printing, etc, went on strike in support of the General Strike called on 4th May, 1926.

With a year's prior warning of this possibility, the Government had made emergency arrangements to maintain essential supplies. With comparatively few homes enjoying the luxury of wireless receivers, news was hard to come by. Some newspapers published a single-sided sheet little bigger than this page. The news sheets were eagerly purchased and read before being passed on.

The T.U.C. called off the strike on May 12th as nothing appeared to have been achieved. The miners were forced to continue their struggle alone for another six months. John Dickinson & Co. banned unions and set up an in-house Union with a £50,000 grant.

World economic conditions, beyond the control and understanding of the man-in-the-street, generated long-lasting bitterness and strife. In 1929 America exacerbated the international problems with its own brand of economic depression.

Bus Windows Smashed

On Wednesday when the first National buses came out of the High-street garage, windows of three of the vehicles were broken by stone-throwing. News that the service would resume soon spread, and in addition to the strike pickets and a large body of members of the Transport and General Workers' Union, with which the National 'busmen are associated, there was a considerable crowd round the garage.

The previous day there had been activity in the yard of the garage, and on Wednesday about half-past eleven, the first 'buses, labelled for Garston, drew up to the entrance gates. The first one, driven by a National 'bus driver who had gone back, came out. He was greeted with both cheers and jeers, and although the strikers were predominant vocally, many in the crowd shouted words of encouragement. This 'bus was manned by a volunteer conductor and a special constable. It got about seventy yards when a stone was hurled through a window. This was the only damage done to it.

The second and third 'buses then came out and were subject to attacks. Finding that the police were busily engaged in cleaving a passage round the garage, a crowd of men and youths armed themselves with stones, and lined the road as far as the end of the hoardings, which stretch from the garage gates to the line of old houses, and the second and third 'buses had to pass through a rain of missiles. The drivers shielded themselves as best they could with their left arms, and the conductors and special constables covered their heads with their arms and turned their backs to the shower. The police immediately cleared the road and the path, and were reinforced by two more car-loads of officers.

Mr. E. G. Yates, of the Typographical Association, a member of the Watford Strike Committee, came up in a two-seater car, and standing

Small group in Queens Road reading a news bulletin displayed in Trewin's window.   *p.211*

up he appealed to the strikers not to throw stones, but to disperse. The 'Bus Company had a perfect right, he said, to run their 'buses. The strikers should persuade the public to boycott them, but not stop them running. This was a free country.

Several voices disputed this fact, and queried it. One man shouted something about the police and soldiers.

WHP May, 1926

General Strike and Observer

The "Observer" of May 15 was produced under very considerable difficulties. Though the general strike was called off on Wednesday, the printers were not given permission by the Typographical Association to return at once to work. Consequently, on Thursday morning they were very unsettled. They were torn between loyalty to their employers and to their Union. It became known that in Watford the printers and the bricklayers were expected to remain out until the National Omnibus Company had reinstated all their drivers and conductors. What connection there was between print and bricks and buses was not clear, nor was it plain why any trouble should be raised after the signal to cease hostilities had been given.

The typographical staff of this journal had responded to the call to strike with the greatest reluctance. Many of them had been with the firm for long periods, and their relations with the proprietor had been of the most pleasant character. They had no grievance, and left the office, at the call of their Unions, in dejected mood. Last Thursday morning they returned in a body to find all their places open for them.

But the tension was by no means over. The local Union officials were not prepared to see their authority upset. In the evening a note was

delivered to the father of the "Observer" chapel, and the men were ordered to report at headquarters the following morning. If this order was obeyed it clearly meant that their unanimous promise to produce the "Observer," made on Thursday morning, would be broken. Consultations followed, and the men, who were working the usual extra hours on Thursday evening, announced their intention of continuing straight on. They felt that, the great strike being over, they could not be accused of anything in the nature of "black-legging," and they wanted no persuasion to see the paper out.

The men who went out on the rounds all returned with stories of the delight of the newsagents in receiving the paper. One shopkeeper, thinking that a further supply of the London sheets had arrived, said she did not want any more papers, but when told that the parcel contained the week's "Observer," she snatched at it eagerly.

For our failure to publish an issue on May 8—the first time this journal has not appeared since its establishment in 1863— we do not think we need apologise, because the circumstances are so well-known.

WO May, 1926

The "Post" and the General Strike

The Editor has received the following interesting letter from Mr. Ernest Spence, past President of the Watford Typographical Association dealing with an article which appeared last week.

We feel sure that many readers will read the letter with interest, and we give it in its entirety.

Sir,–As a regular reader of the "Post" I naturally looked forward to its Jubilee publication, and must congratulate you and the staff on the splendid achievement attained.

I was very interested in "T.L.B.'s" article on page 15 dealing with the "Post's" career during the General Strike of May 1926. That paragraph interested me very much because I was the representative of the strikers detailed to interview Mr. J. W. Gibbs on that occasion.

Therefore, it might interest your readers if I told the story of how the "Post" was published then although not one copy was sold. The Strike Committee obtained information that the edition was printed, and we sat in solemn conclave as to the ways and means of stopping publication.

Mr. H. Julian and myself were detailed to interview Mr. Gibbs, and on arriving at the door at the rear of the old office, were duly admitted to explain our errand.

Mr. Gibbs was very courteous but pointed out that his instructions were to publish, and that order he intended to carry out. We explained that if that were so, trouble would ensue with the large crowd who had by this time surrounded the office, and we asked that he should phone the Directors at St. Albans before publishing. Mr. Gibbs promised us that and would let us know the result later.

After waiting outside about an hour a car drove up and I recognised Mr. H. S. Gibbs and two other gentlemen enter the office.

Asking admittance again we were met by Mr. H. S. Gibbs who refused to discuss the matter, but ultimately relenting said "I will see one of you" and indicating myself invited me in.

On entering the office I was confronted by half-a-dozen stalwart policemen and the two gentlemen who had come with Mr. H. S. Gibbs and was asked to state our case.

To the best of my ability I did this, even asking permission to purchase the entire edition sooner than allow publication. At the conclusion of my appeal one of the gentlemen (a huge smiling man) walked over to Mr. Gibbs and said "What Mr. Spence has promised he will carry out, and I will answer for his integrity." I was dumfounded, who the gentleman was, I then had not the slightest idea.

Mr. Gibbs then dismissed the police, much to my relief, and we further discussed the matter, finally deciding that I was to distribute about 80 per cent of the edition to the strikers, and Mr. Gibbs the remainder among his friends, free of cost.

The interview over, the tall gentleman turned out to be Mr. John Baum who was at one time my apprentice at Smith's Printing Agency at St. Albans.

Needless to say I was delighted to meet my old colleague again although at the time I failed to recognise him, but it was through his influence that the interview was terminated so peacefully.

If this should catch the eye of Mr. Baum, for his good comradeship I tender him my sincere thanks.

ERNEST SPENCE.

Past President,
Watford Typographical Association.

WHP (1937)

Ermanox

A Press-type camera, available in sizes taking 3½ x 2½in. in film packs or plates, or VP.

The larger size has folded strutted body, the smaller is rigid. Focal plane shutter gives speeds 1/10th to 1/1000th sec.

The Ermanox is fitted with an Ernostar lens having the exceedingly fast aperture of f/1.8.

. . . the Freedom of Watford

After giving up farming in Lincolnshire Alderman Thorpe came to Watford where he started the Wells (Red Lion) Brewery, in St. Albans Road. He did not marry, but worked hard to build the successful brewery. He took an active part in sport and, as Captain of the Fire Brigade, assisted at many fires. With his unique perception of what was 'right' for the town he took advantage of the sale of the Essex's estates. He made sure that much of the land was not developed but became public parks and lands in the ownership of the people of Watford. In conversation with the Editor of the West Herts Posts he remembers:

"I looked round for a site or premises. At first I considered some premises near the railway bridge in St. Albans-road, but they were not large enough.

"Then I bought some land next to the St. Albans-road Police Station. The 'Paget Prize Plate' proprietors had an adjoining site; they said their site was more level than mine, and eventually we agreed to exchange sites.

"Having decided on the site, of course, I started building, but only in a small way. The building was completed in 1890. As the trade grew, I extended until the premises reached their present size.

"I had to do a bit of everything. I brewed in the early morning; then I went up to London getting and seeing after business; and at night I saw the draymen in.

"I knew, from certain information that came to me, that the late Earl of Essex was placing some part of Cassiobury Park on the market, and I wanted the Council to buy it. What happened eventually was that certain people acquired a large portion of the estate, and it was from them that the Council bought 50 acres of the land they had acquired.

"Before we got this purchase through, I had to meet tremendous opposition, but since then everybody has recognised how important it was that we should get some of the park. What would have been our position now if we had not taken our chance at that time? There would have been nowhere for children to play. Watford without a park! It is unthinkable now!"

By the unaminous vote of a special meeting of the Watford Borough Council, held at the Oddfellow's Hall, on Wednesday night, confirmed with enthusiastic unanimity by a large and representative town's meeting held subsequently, Alderman Ralph Alfred Thorpe, J.P., was made a Freeman of the Borough of Watford—the second honour of the kind which has been bestowed since the Incorporation of Watford as a Borough in 1922.

The occasion was unique in that for the first time a meeting of the Borough Council was held in a public place, and in the presence of an audience many times larger than is usually to be found in the Council Chamber. The venue of this gathering was chosen as a matter of convenience, and some 200 or 300 representative Burgesses of Watford had the unusual experience of seeing the Mayor and Aldermen of the Borough ushered into the Oddfellows' Hall, preceded by the Mace-bearer (Sergt.-Major Maxted) and formal Council business transacted, under the Chairmanship of the Mayor (Alderman T. R. Clark).

The formal part of the meeting was brief in character. At the request of the Mayor, the Town Clerk read the notice convening the meeting, and he subsequently read letters of apology for inability to attend, received from Councillor H. W. Higgins, Councillor H. J. Bridger, and Councillor W. Bickerton. The Mayor then formally moved the following resolution:—

(a) That this Council in pursuance of the Honorary Freedom of Boroughs Act 1885, do hereby confer upon Mr. Alderman Ralph Alfred Thorpe, J.P., second Mayor of Watford, the Honorary Freedom of the Borough as an expression of the high esteem in which he is held by the inhabitants of the Borough (b) That the Common Seal be affixed to an engrossment of the foregoing resolution.

The Deputy-Mayor formally seconded, and the Council carried the resolution unanimously.

Alderman Thorpe signed the Roll of Honorary Freemen of the Borough, the Mayor and Town Clerk attaching their signatures thereto as witnesses.

This concluded the business of the Council meeting, and the public part of the proceedings then commenced.

The Mayor said he considered himself extremely fortunate that evening, because, in his opinion, with which they would, he was sure, agree, no more pleasing duty could fall to the lot of the Mayor of the Borough of Watford than that of putting his hand to the resolution conferring the Honorary Freedom upon Alderman Thorpe. To attempt to enumerate the many virtues of Alderman Thorpe before an audience of Watford people in a general way was an exercise which was as unnecessary as it was pleasant. They all knew him, and their presence there that night was a sufficient testimonial to his conspicuous and well-deserved popularity. (Applause.) It might not be out of place if he briefly enumerated some of the matters which had specially received Alderman Thorpe's attention. He said some advisedly, because it would be hopeless to attempt to give anything like an adequate account of Alderman Thorpe's beneficent and many-sided public activities. Six times was Alderman Thorpe elected Chairman of the old Urban District Council. He was named in the Watford Charter as substitue Mayor to the Earl of Clarendon; was the first Deputy-Mayor of Watford, and was the second Mayor of the Borough, serving in that office for two years. As Mayor, he had the honour of receiving Princess Mary on the occasion of her visit to Watford to perform the opening ceremony of the Peace Memorial Hospital. Alderman Thorpe was at present, and had for many years, been Chairman of the Watford Joint Hospital Board, and was also a member of the County Council and a County Alderman. In connection with the Hospital, he was, at the inception of that great undertaking, chairman of the town's meeting and a member of the original Committee. He was Captain of the Watford Volunteer Fire Brigade for a great number of years, and he held the long service medal of the National Fire Brigades' Association. He had also been for many years a Governor of the Watford Grammar Schools, and had been President of many sports associations, and either president or vice-president of numerous societies and organisations. His donations made for public purposes, and his private benefactions must total a very considerable sum indeed. Many of such as the Hospital, the Football Club, and

others, had necessarily been known to the public; but he ventured to say that Alderman Thorpe's private generosity, which on many occasions had been known only to himself, and only guessed at by others, probably reached, if it did not exceed, the very considerable sum which, during all those years, had been subscribed openly by him to any cause which had for its object the good of the inhabitants of Watford. (Applause.)

Some of them remembered the great struggle which took place over the acquisition, in 1909, of Cassiobury Park, and the strong fight put up by Alderman Thorpe at that time, in favour of securing to the public a park which, he ventured to say, was the town's proudest possession. To those who remembered the fierce antagonisms that arose, the attitude of Alderman Thorpe on that occasion would ever remind them of some of those qualities for which he was eminent in a marked degree—the qualities of fearlessness, foresight, and sound judgment. When such qualities as those were possessed together in a high degree by one individual, together with a most striking generosity of character, it was only to be expected that the result should be remarkable. In that sense Alderman Thorpe was undoubtedly a most remarkable man. He had been very fortunate in having the help of Mrs. Godson, especially in the performance of his many duties socially as Mayor, during his years of office. (Applause.) The Mayor thanked Alderman Thorpe personally for the great assistance he had rendered to himself, both on the Council and in other directions. He (the Mayor), with the exception of Alderman Tucker, could claim to have had the longest public association with Alderman Thorpe of anyone else now on the Council. He had been struck with the diligence Alderman Thorpe had shown in his work on the Council. During 1916-17, when he was elected Chairman of the Urban District Council, Alderman Thorp was his vice-chairman. The Mayor also referred to their work together on the Tribunal during the war, and to Alderman Thorpe's wisdom in grasping details and of his keen anxiety to see that nothing but justice was extended to all who came before him.

The Deputy-Mayor (Alderman H. B. Watkins) said that the Mayor had dealt so very fully with the many good qualities and the great services rendered to Watford by Alderman Thorpe that he had left very little new for him to say. Alderman Thorpe came to Watford about forty years ago, and throughout the whole of that time he had identified himself with every philanthropic institution in the town. He would like to refer to Alderman Thorpe's work for sport in the town. It was not generally known that he played cricket when he first came to Watford. He had been identified with the West Herts Club and ground and the football section of it from the beginning. At one time Alderman Thorpe carried the Watford Football Club on his back. (Laughter and applause.) Had it not been for Mr. Thorpe, there certainly would not have been any first-class football in Watford to-day. It had very nearly petered out. The money he advanced for football at that time amounted to practically £2,000, and when the ground was bought by the late Mr. G . B. Dodwell and handed over to the town as a gift, Alderman Thorpe generously agreed to forego that debt which was due to him. (Applause.) Alderman Thorpe had never had full credit for the gift he made then. (Applause.)

Councillor H. Horwood said that was the most unanimous meeting he had attended for some time. He felt he could support that resolution both as a member of the Council and as Chairman of the Watford Trades and Labour Council. (Applause.) He did not know of any member of that Council or any member of the general public who would not agree that the honour they had just awarded had been well and truly earned. (Applause.) They know of his sterling work in connection with the Fire Brigade, and in the development of Watford's electricity undertaking, and the town's water supply. What had amazed him was how it was that Alderman Thorpe had managed in his spare time to put in so much public work when he was engaged successfully in another enterprise also connected with water—although treated in a different manner. (Laughter.)

The Alderman's Thanks

Alderman Thorpe, whose rising was signalled by loud and prolonged applause and the singing of "For he's a jolly good fellow" and cheers for Mrs. Godson, said it took him some time to collect his thoughts and think of what he could say on the numerous points made by the Mayor in his speech. Many of them seemed to come back like old times. Those had been rather hard times, but they were, he believed, for the good of the town. (Hear, hear.) He had tried to do his best. Many times it had been hard work, but the people of Watford had always been kind to him, and he thanked them. One of the times in which he had gone rather wrong in Watford was over the question of Cassiobury Park. Everybody had seemed against him, but he had stuck to it, and they got 50 acres, and the Corporation took another 25 acres before the option expired. (Applause.) The Town Council was not satisfied with 75 acres. He did not know how many acres they had got altogether, but it was one of the best investments Watford had ever made. (Applause.) He thanked the Mayor and Corporation for the honour they conferred upon him, the illuminated address, and for the portrait of himself. He felt that after all those years it was a great honour to be made the second Freeman of the Borough. (Applause.)

WO June, 1927

44 High Street, the "Empress Tea Lounge and Gardens" (more recently known as "Next"), the subject of an oft-told story about being built as the Watford Met Station. The account below explains that there was a possibility of this happening but no more. This photograph shows the "Empress" before it became "Cedars". No. 42, Stratton's, had previously been the offices and works of the Watford Newsletter and West Herts Post before transference to Carey Place. In 1937, whilst rebuilding was being carried out, the entire shop front collapsed, killing one man. To the left of 'Wren's' may be seen the small courtyard entrance.

Water-Cress Losses

Nowhere is the aftermath of the floods being felt more keenly than among local growers of water-cress. The season never looked liked being a good one, but the recent floods have left more than one grower on the verge of ruin. The loss, locally, runs into thousands of pounds.

There are few greater cress-producing counties than Hertfordshire, and in the valley which runs between Watford and Berkhamsted, no fewer than nine growers have been affected by floods. One of the biggest of these is Mr. H. G. Sansom, of Cassio Bridge, from whose sixteen acres of "beds" goes out more water-cress than any other grower in the county produces.

His "beds," extending over sixteen acres, stretch from here to Uxbridge, a very big deposit being at West Hyde. The floods came, sweeping the tender cress from its "beds," and scattered it here, there and everywhere.

In the presence of the "Post" man, Mr. Sansom turned up his last year's records.

In the corresponding week then his output was four tons. This week there is nothing, and there will not be anything for a month.

The enormous demand which Mr. Sansom has to meet each year is illustrated by the fact that in a single week in a normal year, his output has reached twelve tons, which means 600 baskets.

What Watford eats is practically negligible compared with Mr. Sansom's total output. The most he has ever had to supply in Watford is less than a ton, 40 baskets to be exact.

Whatever the price of water-cress during the next few months, the demand will probably be as strong as ever, for thousands of people look upon it as nature's own medicine. It holds a high reputation in the treatment of many kinds of diseases, such as consumption, gout, rheumatism, anæmia and constipation.

Dr. Harold Scurfield, among other eminent medical men, has advocated the more extensive use of water-cress, which, he said, is believed to contain all three vitamins.

WHP January, 1928

The Metropolitan Line

Watford had a double-sided 615ft platform, 30ft wide, capable of handling a full length main line steam train and sheltered by a 280ft wood and glass canopy supported on steel girders. Locomotive escape roads were positioned each side of the platform roads. The platforms were lit from the traction current, the rest of the station from the local supply. A well-equipped seven-road goods yard contained a large shed, five-ton crane, horse and carriage dock and cattle pens, all reached by a new 40ft wide approach from the main road. Watford Council has insisted on this, not wanting vehicular traffic along Cassiobury Park Avenue, which the passenger station fronted, as this was designated a residential road.

Management of the new branch was in the hands of the Watford Joint Railway Committee, reconstituted by the Metropolitan and the LNER in November 1925. Both companies provided a train service when the line opened to the public on Monday 2 November 1925.

Some consideration was given to moving the terminus closer to the heart of the town. Early in May 1927, J. M. Clark, who had been resident engineer for the branch construction and was now in the Metropolitan Railway Engineer's office at Edgware Road, noticed that premises at 44, High Street, with 2¼ acres of backland extending to Cassio Road, were on the market. He sent a memorandum to Selbie in which he suggested that this property would provide adequate space for a small passenger terminus and outlined two possible approach routes, one in tunnel for part of the way to avoid property demolition. Selbie took his usual positive attitude, getting the board to agree to purchase of the property 'in view of possible future eventualities'. The transaction was made through a third party in October 1927, the LNER not being told until after the event. Although parliamentary sanction for the acquisition to pass openly to the Metropolitan Railway was given in the Metropolitan Railway Act, 1929, there had been new developments by that time. In 1928 the property was sold at a profit to the Metropolitan puppet company, N. W. Land & Transport Co Ltd, who leased it to a furniture retailer, ensuring it could be re-possessed without difficulty should it ever be needed. But that it would be a railway station had now become much more unlikely.

London's Metropolitan Railway,
Alan A. Jackson

◄ Cassiobury House, contents sold and buildings demolished.   1927

22nd September, 1928, was the last day of the old street market. At that time the Compasses on the corner was being rebuilt. Here, a little earlier, the shops adjacent to the old 'Compasses' are being built. In the middle ages the right to hold a market was one of the most valuable privileges that a king or lord could grant to a body of his subjects. It was in King Henry I's reign that Watford's first charter was granted.

p.334 c

Jimmy Marsh presents a basket of fruit to the Mayor after the formal opening of the new Market Place.

Watford's £20,000 Library

On Saturday morning, Mr. F. J. B. Hemming, Chairman of the Watford Public Library Committee, laid the foundation stone of the new building, to cost, including the ground, about £20,000. The location is excellent—a site in Hempstead-road, on the Little Nascot estate, not far from the Junction and the town's four main roads.

In August, 1911, the late Dr. Andrew Carnegie offered a grant of £4,750. In 1920, Mr. S. H. Timms gave a site, "Garfield House," in King Street, but this proved unsuitable and the present site was decided upon in 1927. Subsequently, Mr. Timms generously agreed to the sale of the site in King-street, and the allocation of the proceeds towards the cost of the new site. Since the approval of the plans by the Carnegie United Kingdom Trust, which continues the munificent work instituted by the late Dr. Carnegie, the Trust have added ten per cent. to the original offer. The Library Committee have also received the sums of £500 and £250 respectively as the result of a diversion of footpaths on the Munden

and Bradshaw estates in 1919. In this respect, thanks are due to the Hon. A. H. Holland-Hibbert, J.P., D.L., and the Bradshaw Trustees, also to Mr. T. Moffet, a former Chairman of the Library Committee, who secured these gifts for the town, when acting on behalf of the Watford Fieldpath Association.

WHP March, 1928

New Industry

Chain-link fencing was started by the Germans; and works started in Belgium. The business of three factories is to be transferred to Watford where a new factory by the name of Penfold Ltd. is being prepared upon the Balmoral Road site. The machinery is being sent by rail direct to the site and as many as 100 local men will be found employment and training given; the new chain link fencing is expected to be in much demand.

WHP March, 1928

Historic Change at Watford

ALL WATFORD seemed to meet in the Market Place on Saturday, with the result that the crush on the narrow roadway and pavement was greater than ever.

Even those who, as a rule, try to wriggle out of the merry-go-round of cars, 'buses, prams and packs of people as quickly as they can, lingered on to have a last look at the busy scene.

The stream of vehicles through the High-street was like a tidal wave which threatened to sweep everything in its wake. How it is that more accidents have not occurred, goodness only knows!

A "Post" reporter who looked round the market found Mr. Henry W. Butler, popularly known as "Curly," selling fish just as he did nearly 30 years ago. Mr. Butler's rent for his stall used to be fourpence. On Saturday it was 5s. Some, he said, paid as much as 30s.

The price of his fish now is three times as much as it was 27 years ago. As a comparison of costs, he said that he pays as much for empties now as he used to pay for his fish.

WHP September, 1928

Market Street corner; the bus in Market Street has halted outside the coach and bus waiting room. Post-1947 on, it was the London Passenger Transport Board information room and depot.

p.66, 324 c

The 'Woodman', Red Lion Yard, behind the market and convenient for market traders. Demolished to make way for Charter Place site.

The 'Swan' 216 High Street.

The 'Fox', 206 High Street. *p.274 tl*

Opening the New Market

The Mayor, declaring the Market open, said that the opening coincided with the closing down of the old market across the road which had been in existence for 800 years. Watford at that time must have been a very small town, for if they only went back as far as eighty years they were told that the population at that time was only five thousand. There was then practically only one street. Watford had developed and developed very rapidly since that time, especially so during the last decade when its development was such that the High-street was a great menace to pedestrians on market days. Negotiations were opened with a view to the purchase of the market rights. A successful deal was accomplished about three years ago, thanks to the energy of Councillor F. Williams, then Chairman of the Market Sub-Committee of the Corporation. The result was that although they spent something like £20,000 for the purchase of the market rights, they were satisfied and able to go forward with a scheme for the removal of the market from High-street. The new market site and its equipment had cost £9,500, and all would agree that the eyesore of the slums of Red Lion-yard and Chequers-yard was a disgrace and was better removed. The new market occupied an area of 1,955 square yards. There were 187 covered stalls, including five for meat, eight for fish, and 174 general stalls. That meant an increase of 57 stalls and 400 feet frontage over the old market. The rents, including lighting, would be reasonable, compared with those of other towns.

At the conclusion of his speech, the Mayor was presented with a handsome basket of fruit, including a pineapple, grapes, oranges, and apples, by Mr. "Jimmy" Marsh, one of the largest stall-holders.

WO September, 1928

● *The dissatisfaction about the market site and facilities continued for many years until the Watford Borough Council in 1925 made an offer of £19,500 to Mr. W. H. Flint for the franchise of the Watford Market.*

Later in 1925 the Town Improvement Committee authorised the Town Clerk to make application for the compulsory purchase of a site in Red Lion Yard.

Slum clearance of Ballard's Buildings and Ashwell's Yard, enabled the market plans to proceed.

Loss of Banknotes

Announced that the Bank of England will in future undertake the printing of treasury notes, with the consequence that Messrs. Waterlows, of Milton Street, who have printed them since their introduction will lose a considerable amount of business. It is stated that several hundred men, women and boys will be affected. Questions were asked in Parliament but to no avail.

WHP March, 1928

The Wesleyan (Methodist) Church at the corner of Harebreaks and St. Albans Road, being officially opened by Mrs. Hunt, 22nd October, 1928.

The new church and school cost £12,500; at the start of the opening ceremony it was announced that £2,000 was still owing; a collection raised £550 and later in the evening it was announced that the remainder was promised and the church free from debt.

Municipal Buildings

The Royal Institute of British Architects nominated Mr. E. Vincent Harris as assessor in the Competition for Best Designs.

New Library Opened

WATFORD'S new Public Library in Hempstead-road, the culmination of 17 years of effort, and erected at a cost of about £20,000, was formally opened yesterday by Sir Fredrick G. Kenyon, G.B.E., K.C.B., Director and Principal Librarian British Museum, Chairman of the Departmental Committee on Public Libraries, and Past-President of the Libraries' Association, etc.

In every way the town has secured a splendid home for its Library. Lieut.-Col. J. M. Mitchell, O.B.E., MC., M.A., Secretary of the Carnegie United Kingdom Trust (which contributed a grant of over £5,000 towards the cost), paid this high compliment: "You have, on the whole, the best Library of its size in Britain."

WHP December, 1928

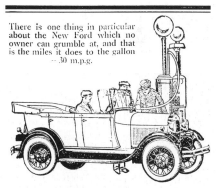
There is one thing in particular about the New Ford which no owner can grumble at, and that is the miles it does to the gallon -- 30 m.p.g.

The NEW FORD TOURER

Strong as steel, because made of steel. Three speeds, four-wheel brakes, 14.9 engine, complete equipment (including bumpers). £170 at works, (

By-Pass Ice Rink

With sudden ice, as frost followed rain upon the By-Pass approach to Hunton Bridge, any driver brave enough to take the risk had more sport than expected. A number of nasty accidents occurred, fortunately without serious injury; cars, buses and lorries all came to grief.

The Watford branch of the British Legion was presented with its standard by Lord Clarendon; after receiving the banner the procession marched to the Parish Church for a Service of Dedication; *(above)* the Mayor and Town Clerk have passed and representatives of other local Legion branches, with their banners, are following. WO March 1929 *p.246b, 265 tr*

Memorial to War Heroes

At a ceremony noteworthy for its simplicity and the reverence of the large audience, the Memorial Cross, erected in Watford Cemetery under the instructions of the Imperial War Graves Commission, was unveiled and dedicated on Sunday afternoon. This Cross, which is 12 feet high, has attached a sword in bronze. On the base of the cross is an inscription, which reads:

"This Cross of Sacrifice is one in design and intention with those which have been set up in France and Belgium, and other places throughout the world, where our dead of the Great War are laid to rest. Their names liveth for evermore.

"Erected by the Imperial War Graves Commission in Watford Cemetery, to the memory of members of His Majesty's Forces who gave their lives for the country in the Great War, 1914-18, and who lie buried in the Borough of Watford."

When the shroud had fallen from the memorial, the Mayor said he regarded it as an honour, as well as a privileged civic duty, to unveil that memorial. It must be very gratifying to them all to know that Watford had been selected as one of the parishes in which the Imperial War Graves Commission had decided to erect a stone in memory, not only of those who had fallen in battle, but also to the memory of those who during or since the period of Great War had lost their lives through illness, due to injuries or wounds.

With marked significance to all assembled, but especially to men present who had gone "through the dust of conflict and through battle flame," there burst forth the martial notes of "The Last Post," sounded on the bugle by ex-Trumpeter S. J. Simmons who, after the completion of two minutes of silence, given up to the remembrance of those who made the great sacrifice, and solemn thoughts devoted to personal examination and the plea for peace, played "The Reveille."

The concluding prayer was said by the Vicar of Watford, who also pronounced the Benediction. At the close of the service all present joined in the singing of a verse of the "National Anthem."

WHP February, 1929

'Wetford' Market

The Rev. Reginald James, Vicar of St. John's, Watford, has sent to the "West Herts Post" a spirited appeal for something to be done that will improve conditions for both traders and the public at the New Market.

The state of affairs on wet days, he depicts as deplorable, and urges that, failing anything better, the whole of the market should should be covered. His letter is set out below.

Sir,—Anything more pitiful than the conditions for marketing on an ordinary wet day would be difficult to behold. On Saturday last it was literally a "wash-out."

The stalls are so arranged that the water pours from the coverings all over the customers, who are confined in such narrow alleys that they get soaked by the overflow from both sets of stalls.

Five minutes of this with no umbrellas—for there is no room for such things—is bad enough for the public, but what must it be to the stallholders all day? The conditions are very bad underfoot; pools and running water abound.

The stallholders are arranging a petition asking to be moved back to the proper Market Place, and for this present miserable spot to be used as a car parking site.

What can be done to help the general public and these hard-working and up-to-date plucky traders to do business in comfort? The town ought to have a first-class market. If no other site can be found, at least this one should be completely roofed-in, and protected against the weather.

The stalls should be given far more space to do business in. I believe 40 stalls, on an average, are now unoccupied, and could be removed.

The resident traders should be given preference over the itinerant merchants, who in some cases even bring their own food in order not to spend more than is necessary in the town.

Again, what a vision of beauty, with encouragement to enter, did the designers of this new market exhibit when they arranged the obscure, narrow and mean entrances. "Abandon hope all ye who enter here" would be an appropriate warning overhead.

I think it has been a very poor effort by our Council. In place of a bright and busy market in our street twice a week, we have now, every day on view, the smelly, dirty tail ends of a number of cars and vans. It is just as dangerous for traffic, for these cars back out suddenly into the road without warning. The shops on the parking side of the street are obscured every day instead of twice a week, and lose business.

Yours, etc.,
REGINALD JAMES

WHP February, 1929

The 'Coachmakers Arms', High Street, opposite Clements. *p.91, 122, 355 tl*

The 'Queen's Arms' St. Albans Road, now the site of New Hertford House.
p.345

'Verulam Arms Hotel' Station Road, now site of Nat. West. drive-in bank.
p.292

Watford Market

Sir,—The Israelites of old were glad to be led out of Egypt, but as soon as something failed to please them they turned round on their leaders and said: "Why were we brought out of Egypt; let us get back there at once;" and recent letters to your paper show once more how difficult it is to please everybody, and how easy it is to criticise adversely.

The old market was a constant source of complaint, but two correspondents have recently held up the new market to scorn, and have loudly cried: "Let us return to our old market!"

As far as I am concerned—and many Watford people agree with me—I am sure that the new market is a great deal better than the old one, though I do not say that there is not still room for improvement. A market must be central, and where else was there a site in the centre of the town? The entrances may be narrow, but would the objector to them undertake to prevail on Messrs. Cawdell, Messrs. Kingham, or the Bank to remove part of their premises to permit of the enlargement of the market entrances? The rain does drip down your neck, but so it did in the old market, and when a biting wind whistles down the high-street, the new somewhat sheltered market is infinitely preferable to the old, entirely unsheltered one. Moreover, a scheme is on hand for covering in the market entirely.

Unless you have a habit of walking in the road, the danger to pedestrians from cars backing out of the old market place is very slight, and the people who park their cars there have enough thought, if only for their own property, to see that there is no danger of collision with other vehicles. As for so-called "road hogs," short would be their shrift if they tried any of their little games in Watford High-street.

The stalls in the new market are carefully arranged, and the actual tables are much cleaner and more hygienic than those in the old market.

As for saying that the old market was an attractive feature of Watford, anyone who remembers the untidy array of stalls of all shapes and sizes, many of them in a very dilapidated condition, will be very doubtful as to the truth of this statement.

The new market is not perfect, but it is a great improvement on the old one, which was dirty, dangerous, and a disgrace to Watford.

Yours etc.
E.M. BRIDGER.

WHP February, 1929

Watford Motor Traffic

After many months of cogitation, the Watford Town Council have decided to put down white lines at dangerous corners in the Borough. The first spot to be treated is the junction of Harwoods-road and Rickmansworth-road, where many accidents, some of a serious nature, have occured.

The annual licensing meeting may also do something to clear the air. A great deal of comment has been caused by the fact that no sooner was the market cleared away from High-street than the available space was utilised as a parking-place. Whatever objections may be taken to this practice, either by the shopkeepers whose entrances are affected or by the public who are inconvenienced, it appears that at present neither the police nor the Council can take action, unless obstruction, in a legal sense, can be proved; nor is it possible to collect any tolls.

WO March, 1929

De-rating

Under Mr. Winston Churchill's famous De-rating scheme, companies and firms carrying on "productive industries" in Watford will be relieved of paying 75 per cent. of their rates on about £25,000 of rateable value.

This is an absolute gift, except that in the case of brewers, certain additional taxation is imposed under this year's Budget, as an offset to the rate relief.

In Watford, in respect of "agricultural" claims on £1,100 rateability, the whole has been allowed. The properties concerned will be exempt from ALL rates as from April 1st last. In respect of "industrial" hereditaments, claims on £35,000 of rateability were submitted. The amount allowed is £25,000.

The list below sets out how claims by some of the largest manufacturers in Watford have fared:-

Firm	Original Valuation £	Amt. Alwd. to rank for 75% Reduction £
Watford Engineering Co.	420	420
Gazelda Ltd.	450	450
Benskin's	3350	3272
Herts Ice Co.	700	512
Scammell's	1200	1200
Watford Steam Laundry	600	572
Sun Engraving Co.	1800	1800
North & Sons	1600	1600
Cassio Photographic Paper Coy.	550	550
McCaskey & Co.	465	461
Waxed Papers, Ltd.	480	480
Wells Brewery	400	370
Waterlow's	1850	1850
Co-op Bakery	300	248
Delectaland	4200	4073

WHP May, 1929

173

The rebuilt "Compasses". The ancient window, discovered when Market Street was opened up in 1889, has been moved and preserved at the left-hand side of the building. It still exists. Of interest is the size of the Post Office before the present building was constructed in 1932.   *p.335 tr*

American Firm Coming to Watford

The £350,000 factory which was built at Delectaland six years ago, and has never been used, was sold last week.

An American firm has bought it—the Electric Hose and Rubber Company. British interests are concerned as well.

There will be work for hundreds. Where possible, preference will be given to local people. The factory may open in September.

This is, undoubtedly, the biggest industrial development Watford has experienced for years.

Messrs. W. S. Weller and Son, the well-known local firm of auctioneers and estate agents, had the distinction of conducting the deal on behalf of Delecta, Ltd.

The story of the deal affecting the Watford factory has a strong flavour of American hustle about it.

Only two hours before, Mr. Green had been talking on the 'phone to Mr. C. D. Garretson, of Delaware, U.S.A., who authorised him to make the purchase.

They were hoping, he said, to open in September, but the process of converting the factory and installing machinery was being put in hand almost at once.

"As far as possible," he said, "the purchasers are going to use English machinery and fittings, but certain things will have to come from America."

This great North Watford factory, which was erected in 1922-23, has been a source of mystery to local people. For six years the massive pile of brick, steel and concrete has remained silent.

It is the biggest structure for miles around. Steel-framed throughout, it is a six-storey affair with a floor space of 158,000 square feet.

Mr. C. D. Garretson is the President of the Electric Hose and Rubber Company and was over here in March.

He was impressed not only by the actual building and by its splendid position in regard to transport facilities, but by the progressive atmosphere of the town of Watford.

The class of workers appealed to him, and so did the type of houses which were being erected in North Watford. Moreover, he quickly discovered that obstacles were not placed in the way of new industries, whose advent could not fail to help mould the development of the town.

The Electric Hose and Rubber Company specialise in the production of braided hose, which they originated 30 years ago, and nothing else but this will be made at Watford.

There is a big market for this hose, which is rapidly becoming the understood thing in shipping and coal-mining, where it is used for the conveyance of air, steam and water.

The Colonies are big buyers, and they will be supplied from the Watford factory. That will mean a big saving to the company, for there is a heavier duty on American goods taken into British Colonies than there is on goods sent from this country.

WHP May, 1929

Big Holiday Attraction

At 3 p.m. at Vicarage-road Football Ground, on Whit-Monday, May 20th, the Watford Football Supporters' Club, in conjunction with the Watford and District Auto Club, are holding another of their popular Motor Gymkhanas. A splendid programme has been arranged, commencing with a Motor Cycle Football Match between Watford and the Famous West Bromwich M.C.F.C. Other events include an Obstacle Race, Long Kick, Slow Riding, Trick Riding, Cow-Punching, Relay Race, and a Polo Match. Gates open at 2.30. Admission, 1s. (including tax); school children, 3d. All stands 6d. extra. Refreshments may be obtained on ground.—(Advt.).

WHP May, 1929

The Market

THE MANY complaints that have been made about Watford's new Market are apparently producing results.

Among recommendations adopted at Tuesday's meeting of the Council was a proposal to borrow £4,200 for roofing the Market.

The figures for the new Market make very good reading. From April 1st to June 25th this year, the receipts were £858 14s. 3d., compared with £481 1s. 3d. in the same period last year.

WHP May, 1929

Watford as Training Centre

The Ministry of Labour have acquired the large single storey building opposite Parkgate-road School, which Delecta Ltd. have used for offices, printing and box factory, etc.

This will be converted into a training centre for 400 unemployed men, who will be drawn mostly from the distressed mining areas.

Among the trades which will be taught at Watford are building in its various phases; furniture making, upholstering, and cabinet making; motor manufacture work, body painting, etc.

WHP May, 1929

The line of the suggested Colne Valley road, mentioned in the Hertfordshire Regional Planning Report. It is stated that by improving the southern end of the High Street near Watford bridge, particularly at the corner near the railway arches, and the construction of a new road leaving the High Street slightly north of this point, leading under the Five Arches alongside the Colne, a valuable connection will be provided with the Watford By-Pass south of Aldenham." WO 1928.

Nearly sixty years later—1987—this projected road is under discussion as the 'M1 Link Road'.

Central Hall Cinema, King Street, c1928. In 1929 sound projection equipment was installed and upon re-opening the cinema was renamed the 'Regal'. Before eventual closure to become the present Bingo Hall, it was re-named the 'Essoldo'.

Footpath from the High Street to Albert Road and Weymouth Street. The Plaza cinema was built before the parade of shops which later adjoined the site.   *p.285 br*

Watford's New Cinema

Watford's magnificent new cinema, The Plaza, was opened on Monday by the Mayor of Watford (Alderman F. J. B. Hemming). He was accompanied by the Acting Deputy Mayoress, Mrs. M. Peakman, the Vicar of Watford (the Rev. Henry Edwards) and members and officials of the Corporation.

WHP May, 1929

Death of Mr. W. T. Coles

We regret to record the death, which occurred this (Friday) morning, at his residence, the Shrubbery, High-street, Watford, of Mr. W. T. Coles, who had reached the great age of 92 years.

For over fifty years Mr. Coles had taken a prominent part in the public life of Watford. In 1874 he was elected a member of the Board of Guardians, and was Chairman from 1895 to 1900. He was made a Justice of the Peace in 1894. He was a member of the old Local Board, and in 1896 was appointed Chairman of the Urban District Council, succeeding Mr. E. J. Slinn, the first Chairman. He was a director of the Watford Gas Company.

Mrs. A. F. Broad, a member of the Watford Corporation, is a daughter of Mr. Coles.

WO June, 1929

Death of Alderman R. A. Thorpe

WE regret to record that Alderman Ralph Alfred Thorpe died on Sunday at his home, "Lindum," Park-road, Watford. He leaves as an example to those who follow him in public service, a record remarkable alike for its quantity and quality. He was an Alderman of both the Hertfordshire County Council and Watford Town Council; a Freeman of Watford; a Justice of the Peace for Hertfordshire; on six occasions he was elected Chairman of the Watford Town Council; he was Deputy Charter Mayor and twice Mayor of Watford.

WHP June, 1929

Fifty years hence there will have grown up generations to whom Watford's rulers in the earlier part of the twentieth century will be scarcely known, even by name. Just occasionally, there will be people who, inspecting the handsome municipal buildings of those days, will, on reaching the Council Chamber, pause to read the names, inscribed in gold on oak boards, of the ladies and gentlemen who, through the long succession of years, have presided over the authorities responsible for administering the town's municipal affairs. They will see the name of Ralph Alfred Thorpe occurring six times as Mayor of Watford.

The frequent recurrence of that name will cause this comment to flash to mind: "He was a big man!" The people in those far-on days will be using that expression to describe his high importance in the affairs of the town, but actually, though unconsciously, they will also be crystallising into a sentence the life and character of Alderman Thorpe.

He was a *big* man.

That can most truly be said of Alderman Thorpe. Could any man wish for a finer epitaph?

WHP June, 1929

An aching head—

at the end of a busy day is not inevitable, but is due to eyesight defect, which proper glasses will correct. Have your eyes tested. Consult C. R. Turner, F.B.O.A. (Hons.), 11 St. Albans-road, Watford. Telephone 639—(Advt.).

Baths at Watford?

Sir,—One can hardly expect your columns this week to be overcrowded with congratulations to the sub-committee which has been dealing with the question of supplying baths for the convenience of Watford's bathless, on their speed. That the sub-committee have awakened and presented a report must have really caused the main committee to have a severe shock. (How many of them have advocated 'baths' in their Election Addresses for many years?)

Does the sub-committee think that 24 baths, twelve for each sex, is enough? Their estimate of the number of people who would patronise public baths is amazing, considering the number of houses without that convenience has not appreciably diminished. It is to be hoped that the total number of slipper baths will be nearer 70 than 24; besides, if only 24 is to be the number, how can the Mayor, if he, as first citizen of Borough, publicly opens the building, ask the Corporation to have "one" with him if there are not enough to go round?

Yours etc.,

W.J.DAVIES

WHP July, 1929

● *On most important issues the local papers usually were in accord; on the question of 'Baths' the West Herts Post was definitely anti. Open air baths were OK; covered baths a waste of money which they labelled 'Squandermania'. This stance must have delayed for years the building of the Public Baths.*

The New Register

Yesterday, the new list of Parliamentary Voters came into operation. For the Watford Division the figures are:-

MEN 25,719
WOMEN 30,303

Total 56,022

Thus, women have a majority of 4,584.

WHP May, 1929

St. Albans Road, at the Cross Roads. House on the right is 'Little Nascot', once belonging to Messrs. Humbert and Flint, and on the left, wall of the grounds of 'Elmcote', later to be the parade of shops by the pond.
p.185 b

Cross Roads looking towards the Town. The Plaza cinema is built and the parade of shops partly built. In the above two photographs, and top, p.185, can be seen the AA Patrolman on traffic control point duty. The Automobile Association was founded in 1905; one of its main tasks being to help motorists in difficulties whilst on the road, and to present the motorists' point of view to obstructive Parliament, particularly as regards unduly restrictive speed limits.
p.185, 305b

The 'Dog', Hempstead Road, demolished 1969.

Council Houses in Eastbury Road

Sir,—I read, with some alarm, in your report of the Watford Borough Council meeting, held on the 7th inst., that certain residents in the Eastbury-road locality have signed a petition, requesting the Council to reconsider their decision to erect 130 houses on a site abutting on Eastbury-road, and that other house owners in the district object to the Council's plans.

I cannot help feeling how very selfish these people are, to come forward at this juncture and try to delay, and if possible prevent, the erection of only 130 new houses, especially in view of the urgent need for houses in the town. The present official waiting list is, I am told, over 900 families.

In your issue of 12th December, I read a heartbreaking case of a man, wife and four children living in one room in Gladstone-road, and I feel sure that no father or mother living in Woodways, etc., would like to live under those conditions. Judge Crawford gave this family instructions to quit on 18th January, last Saturday, but where are they to go? Where is there a house to let within their means? Who wants a lodger with a wife and four children?

These are the sort of cases the Council are trying to help. As the few houses they are building will only accommodate one tenth of the need in the town, they will, therefore, only be able to help the most necessitous cases.

If the petitioners only knew of the terrible overcrowding that exists in Watford, I feel sure they would never have signed such a petition. I hope the Council will proceed with the scheme as soon as possible, and bring a little happiness to 130 families, who at present have no home of their own to live in, and are anxiously waiting for one.

Yours etc.,
ARTHUR BENNETT.
WHP January, 1930

Gladstone Road

. . . the houses in Gladstone Road were originally quite grand; three storeys and basement. The basement leads to the garden backing onto the railway line. Many houses held three or four families; often a family of four or five in the basement, and goodness knows how many in the rest of the house.

The main recollection is of the flickering gas lamps—the mantles didn't seem to last long, or perhaps there weren't enough pennies to feed the meter, and in the winter, the problem of keeping warm. Thin, threadbare blankets with layers of brown paper in between to aid warmth, which rustled and crackled; perhaps the noise made one feel warmer.

The tin kettles never lasted long; just something like the crying of the baby to distract attention long enough for the kettle to boil dry. Until a pot mender could be bought from Woolworth or Roger and Gowletts the hole would have to stay and a saucepan used in its stead.

Nowadays, many of the houses are split into self-contained flats with all modern services.

Recollection 1987

Rowdy Street Scenes in Watford

A feud, which has already resulted in a certain amount of conflict between parties of Watford youths and Welshmen who are at the Ministry of Labour's Training Centre at Callowland, has caused a great deal of excitement in the town during the last few days, and the police have had to interfere.

Last night, there was a wild scene in the High-street. Razors and lengths of lead piping were flourished, and there were several free fights.

The police, who had been keeping close watch on the Watford party during the evening, acted promptly. They arrested two Watford youths and took them to King-street Police Station.

Although there have been exaggerated reports of casualties and the drafting in of extra police, actually only one injury has been reported, and the Watford police were able to quell the disturbance without assistance.

One of the leaders of the Watford youths told a "Post" reporter last night that the trouble started on Saturday evening, when the Welshmen set upon a Watford youth and hurt him. Since then, the Watford youths had formed themselves together and hunted the Welshmen down.

On Sunday evening, he continued, two of the Welshmen were ducked in the pond in High-street.

A remark of another youth suggested that employment questions were connected with the trouble, for he said: "When the Welshmen go we shall get work."

WHP January, 1930

"The Parade," High-street

BUILDING development at the Pond end of High-street has led to much confusion over numbers

The outcome is that the Town Council have instructed the Borough Surveyor to re-number the section of High-street from the Pond crossroads to Clarendon Corner with odd numbers.

The Council have also decided to call that section "The Parade."

WHP February, 1930

A Word With Mr. F. C. Jarvis

IN my judgment, one witness for the opposition did not help their case. He was Mr. F. C. Jarvis of Oxhey-road, who, when the Inspector pointed out to him that his front door is a quarter of a mile away from the Council's estate, said: "Yes. But a housing estate means children, and they have a capacity for not liking their own roads."

The mentality behind such an observation in this twentieth century is amazing. I am not going to try to follow the gymnastics of Mr. Jarvis's mind; it will suffice if I say he has set me wondering whether, in the great hereafter, he hopes to dwell in a little heaven all on his own, with a notice outside: "Children must not pass this way."

It was not surprising that women at the back of the room applauded when the Town Clerk commented: "You don't object to sewage farms, but you object to housing estates and you object to children."

WHP March, 1930

●*A tireless and energetic worker in seeing the Harebreaks scheme to fruition, F. H. Gorle also took responsibility for naming the estate and many of its roads.*

The estate name 'Harebreaks' was taken from an old ordnance survey map; in 1871 the woods alongside St. Albans Road, opposite Lea Farm, were named Harebreaks (the wood area is now the site of Spring Gardens and Holland Gardens).

F. H. Gorle in a talk given in Watford after his retirement.

Meeting Alley, between Salmons and Roger's Coal Office, which led to Beechen Grove and Estcourt Road.   *p.40, 251 t*   Feb. 1928

The Geordies and the Taffies . . .

In the wake of the false boom years after the 1914-1918 war followed an economic depression on a scale the world had not previously experienced. As financial systems collapsed and America's Wall Street crashed, fortunes were lost as banks and businesses failed. Britain did not escape the depression although the light industry of Watford suffered far less than the heavy industries of the North East and South Wales.

After the General Strike of 1926 the unemployment level rose until, in 1931, it reached a figure of two million, at which level it stayed for a number of years.

(When comparing unemployment figures it must be remembered that today's insured workers include a great many wives and mothers, the workers of 1931 were principally male. Husbands and sons were then looked on as the breadwinners of the family—"a woman's place was in the home."

The two million unemployed of 1931 represented approx. 20% of the country's workforce, the three million of 1986 represented about 8%.)

In 1931 unemployment benefit was cut by 10% and a 'means test' introduced for the long-term unemployed. Literally any casual earnings, even a few shillings, were required to be declared and were deducted from the benefit received.

Local relieving offices at Shrodells (Union Workhouse), Vicarage Road, and at No. 1 Glencoe Road, Bushey, dispensed (after the hated 'means test') weekly meal tickets which were redeemable at local grocers and butchers such as Melia's on the corner of Cary Place, Lipton's and the Home and Colonial.

The high rate of unemployment meant that where a job became available it would often be filled by cheap labour, ('if you don't want the job there's others who do'). Consequently, a man's wage for a 48 or 50 hour week's labouring could be no more than 35 or 40 shillings.

In the early and mid 1930's many men would travel from the north of England, or walk from South Wales to seek work, or attend the North Watford Government Training Centre in Southwold Road. That some of these men found jobs locally would cause annoyance among some Watford men who had been unsuccessful, and the taunt of 'Taffy go home' may have caused more than one local Welshman to cultivate a change of accent!

Market Street, Camfield's next to cattle market entrance. Postered wall is the Post Office site. The bus queue rails were introduced in June 1926 and removed one month later. At the 'Palace', Will Hay.

177

High Street prior to the 'Wheatsheaf' being demolished and rebuilt on a site set back from the road. Horse and cart is one of a regular procession which delivered coal from the Bushey Station coal wharf to the gas works in the Lower High Street. *p.331 b*

The Ministry and the 'Buses

The Ministry of Transport have forwarded to the Watford Town Council their decision on the recent 'bus appeal. Three local proprietors of 'buses were, it will be remembered, refused a renewal of licences by the Council on the ground that certain conditions had not been observed. The proprietors, feeling that they had a grievance, took their case to the Ministry, who appointed an Inspector to hold an Inquiry. The proceedings extended over five days, and the upshot is that the licences are granted on condition that the services in question do not cover more of High-street than the section between the cross roads and Clarendon-road.

The terminus is at Watford Junction. In their endeavour to restrict High-street traffic the Council may therefore be said to have gained their end. It was unreasonable, in the first place, to insist that services on the Hempstead-road route should carry their passengers no farther than the cross roads, and the decision of the Ministry seems a sensible compromise.

The extra-ordinary part of the whole business is that this common-sense solution was not reached in the discussions between the Council and the proprietors.

It would be interesting to learn how much money the protracted Inquiry has cost the rate-payers. We do not know whether the appellants regard their costs as money well spent, but the Watford public will not appreciate the municipal purse being opened to pay lawyers for nearly a week's work in arguing to what extent a few 'buses should use High-street.

We recognise fully that the Council has to assert their authority as far as 'bus traffic is concerned, and we appreciate the difficulties arising from uncertainty as to the extent of their powers. But to put the matter quite bluntly, they have only themselves to blame for the muddle which arose over licences.

At one time they had the proprietors working to agreed time-tables, and on a system of inter-changing return tickets, but they permitted trouble which led to this agreement being torn up. They have complained, probably with good cause, that they could get no guidance from the Ministry, but they have never attempted to take a strong line on their own initiative or manifested any real determination to get their own way. Whether the position will be improved as the result of the recent Inquiry remains to be seen.

If the Council will only lay down certain lines on which they intend to act in future and adhere to them instead of losing themselves, as they have done in the past, in a maze of petty details, the situation may eventually be eased. The Council may feel some satisfaction over the Ministry's decision on the appeals, but regarding the subject as a whole there is certainly nothing upon which they can plume themselves.

WO April, 1930

The Wheatsheaf Widening

The decision of Watford Town Council on Wednesday to carry out a widening scheme in Lower High-street, opposite the Wheatsheaf Inn, will effect a much needed highway improvement. The opportunity arose through the Cannon Brewery Company, owners of this ancient hostelry, resolving to demolish the present building, and erect a new public-house on land at the rear, set well back from the new road.

At this point the road has only a width of 32ft., and through this narrow thoroughfare an ever-increasing volume of traffic is poured from the roads which converge at Bushey Arches. The Corporation Highways Committee, on learning of the contemplated re-building, approached the Brewery Company, and the negotiations have resulted in an agreement, under which the Company will make a gift of the land necessary for the road improvement conditional on the Corporation constructing a loop draw-up to the new inn.

Negotiations have been entered into with the adjoining owners and land acquired so that the street will be widened for a distance of 300 yards from the river bridge to Eastbury-road. At the point opposite the new Wheatsheaf the road will have a width of 60ft. Here the present road dips, as the inn itself is low-lying, and it is proposed to raise the surface at this position.

The old Wheatsheaf has stood for well over 200 years, and is a link with the earlier Watford in the more leisurely age of the toll-gate and the pack-horse, before the coming of the trains and motor cars. The new building will be in modern style, and the work of construction is just commencing, but the road improvement cannot be effected until the business is removed and the old inn demolished.

WO April, 1930

The Plight Of Eight Old Ladies

The eight old ladies who occupy the Essex almshouses behind Watford Parish Church are wondering what is going to happen to them.

Their little houses are on the market, and they are in danger of being cast adrift on the world, with a contribution from the proceeds of the sale, to fend for themselves.

The fate of the almshouses has become the topic of the town, consequent upon the keen debate which raged in the Council Chamber last week. At that meeting, the proposition was made that the Corporation should consider the possibility of the purchase of the site for its use as a car park.

WHP June, 1930

By The Way . . .

To the memory of Alderman R. A. Thorpe, Deputy Charter Mayor and for two years Mayor of Watford, and his services for many years as Churchwarden of Christ Church, the parish propose to erect a Thorpe Memorial Hall in St. Albans-road.

WO July, 1930

The Right Type Of Houses

A housing scheme in the Eastbury-road locality is reaching a definite state. There will be 80 houses for letting, and all are to be non-parlour, which means that the workers in the lesser-paid trades will stand a better chance of meeting the rent of a Council house without sub-letting.

WHP July, 1930

● *The Eastbury Road housing scheme (p.176 and this page), was named 'Thorpe Crescent'.*

No exit

. . . Another point was the proper planning of roads. Was any place so difficult to get out of as High-street, Watford? From the "Wheatsheaf" to King-street there was only one outlet—Farthing-lane. He was not throwing stones—he was a Watford man and loved the town. The poverty of concept in estate development was one of the most fruitful causes of depression.

A member said that when he came to Watford 7½ years ago he wondered whether there was any town planning. He saw a row of shops pushed up in front of the Parish Church, and learned that years ago the Council had an opportunity to buy them at a mere song.

WO August, 1930

Co-op Expansion

The Watford Co-op started in 1895 at No. 58 Leavesden Road, moving within a short while to St. Albans Road; Market Street branch opened in 1902, Oxhey in 1906, Model Electric Bakery in Brixton Road in 1912, dairy depot in 1926 and the latest new store at 187/9 St. Albans Road in 1928.

The Society employs 520 people, all of whom are members of a Trade Union, receive Trade Union wages and work under Trade Union conditions. The Society has 17,000 members in an area covering Wealdstone, Harrow, Oxhey, Watford, Bushey and Kings Langley.

Programme of the official visit of the Prime Minister (Ramsey Macdonald) to open the Trade Union Hall, Watford, 30 January, 1931.

... lavatory and bathroom should be separate ...

Women's Idea of Ideal Homes

The 13 suggestions of the Ladies' Committee were as follows, the Housing Committee's decision being given in brackets:—

A deep sink with a plug in every house. (The Committee directed that deep sinks be provided.)

The copper placed near the sink to avoid the carrying of heavy baths and pails. (This is always arranged where possible.)

The windows over the sink should all be made to open, thus allowing steam and cooking odours to escape more readily. (The Committee recommended this window have push-out vent).

That gas cookers be placed away from draughts. (This is done).

That larders, wherever possible, be built away from the sun, and one of the shelves to be of slate, for keeping food cool in the summer time. (The Committee consider concrete shelves should continue to be provided).

As much cupboard room as possible, and a corner one in small bedrooms where space will not allow a square one. (The Committee directed that provision be made for a corner hanging curtain and footboard).

That doors be placed so that they open several inches away from the corners of the room, to avoid brushing the wall in passing. (This is usual practice wherever space and planning permit).

A more liberal allowance of window at present in Council houses, three or four casements at least, with two-thirds opening. (The Committee agreed to a more liberal allowance of window, where desirable).

In the non-parlour houses, the kitchener should be convertible and economical and, if practicable, should heat the water for baths and so keep the house warm. The cost of gas for heating water by the gas copper method, as at present installed, works out at 6d. for a bath, and 9d. to a 1s. to do the weekly wash, which is altogether too heavy for small incomes. (The Borough Surveyor will consider and report).

That the question of planting privet hedging in the back gardens be seriously considered. Lack of privacy is a source of much trouble in Council Housing Schemes. (The Committee directed that Penfold or similar fencing be provided on the next scheme).

That a piece of wood fencing 6ft. high and at least 6ft. long be placed by the side of every house near the back door to prevent immediate overlooking. (The Committee directed that where back doors face each other a fence be provided).

Wherever possible, lavatory and bathroom should be separate. (The Committee state that this is done wherever practicable).

WHP November, 1930

Dining room of a 16th century Cassio Hamlet cottage

High Street Improvements

An Order for the compulsory purchase of certain premises in connection with the Corporation street improvement schemes in Lower High-street and near the old Market-place, was the subject of a public inquiry held at the Municipal Offices on Monday morning, by Mr. C. G. Mitchell, of the Ministry of Transport.

The problem of Watford High-street was very acute. Over 100 years ago, looking at a plan of Watford, one could see that the town simply consisted of one long street—the High-street. Watford was a town or village on one of the main coaching routes to the North. About 100 years ago the London and Birmingham Railway was made, and the result was that traffic was shifted off the High-street to a considerable extent on to the railway, and the town spread out in a number of other directions. That being the case the problem of Watford High-street, which would no doubt have early become serious, slumbered for 100 years or so. But after the war, owing to the advent—beneficent or otherwise—of motor traffic, the problem suddenly awoke, and awoke to some purpose. And the problem to-day was an exceedingly serious one. The Corporation from time to time as they were able had taken steps and had, so far as they could, taken time by the forelock, with the object of dealing with the very serious situation which had arisen.

The first step was after the war when the Corporation, with the help of the County Council, totally reconstructed the whole of High-street. The High-street up to that time had been what was called a water-bound road, and it was reconstructed with a foundation of nine inches of concrete, reinforced where necessary with steel mesh, and with a surface of asphalt. Then as various properties became vacant the Corporation took steps to acquire them. In 1923 the Corporation acquired No. 283, High-street. Then in 1925 they bought Nos. 275 to 281, and also No. 289. All these properties were necessary in order to make an improvement which had been carried out so far as it had been possible, and for which the purchase of the properties Nos. 293a, 293b, and 293c, were necessary in order to complete that improvement to make it properly effective.

In 1926 the Corporation acquired a further property with a frontage of 20ft. wide, extending to a considerable distance on the opposite side and immediately north of the proposed improvement, and a strip in front of Dalton House.

In 1929 the Corporation, at considerable cost acquired Nos. 96 and 98, High-street, and subsequently No. 100. These three properties with Nos. 92 and 94, which they were now seeking to acquire, formed the island site. In addition to the acquisition of these properties the Corporation in 1928 removed from High-street the old market, which had been held in the Market-place for many hundreds of years. One of their main objects in acquiring the market rights and the new site was to relieve the High-street and make it more available for traffic. In the spring of 1930 the Corporation faced a long and difficult inquiry before an Inspector of the Ministry of Transport, the result of which was that the Minister of Transport upheld the Corporation's view and imposed on the omnibus proprietors certain conditions which in effect prohibited them from running down High-street further than Clarendon-road corner.

Mr. W. W. Newman, Borough Engineer, confirmed the Town Clerk's statement, and said the traffic problem in High-street was getting worse. For the proposed improvement on the east side of the Lower High-street, just above the bridge, he considered that the acquisition of the proper-ties mentioned was necessary. In regard to 293a, 293b and 293c, only the forecourts were required. The improvement would be the continuation of an improvement already acquired up to the old Mill, giving the road a width of 57ft. The present width of the road opposite No. 291 was 38ft. 9in., and the improved width would be 52ft. Opposite No. 293 the present width was 41ft. 10in., and the improved width would be 52ft. Opposite No. 293 the present width was 41ft. 10in., and the approved width would be 48ft. 4in.; and at the end of the improvement the width was 44ft., and the improvement would give a width of 50ft. The improvement was necessary because on one side of the road was the National omnibus garage and on the other side the entrance to the Gas Works. The road opposite Mr. Frost's premises was only 26ft. in width, and would not accommodate four moving vehicles.

Regarding Nos. 92, 94, 94a and 94b, High-street, the acquisition of the properties was necessary in order to open up Church-street and to complete the Market-place improvement. This was the narrowest part of the High-street, and the worst spot for traffic.

Mr. Weaver: I take it that one of your objects is to enable traffic to come from Church-street into High-street?—

Mr. Newman: It will allow that, but it is more advantage to High-street itself.

It would increase traffic into an already narrow street?—It would increase the number.

Where would that traffic go to?—

Vicarage Road, I should think.

Is there not enough service at present down Whippendell-road and Market-street?—Market-street is pretty congested.

And then you have King-street, an artery for traffic to come into High-street from the same direction?—Yes.

And the width of the High-street where King-street joins is no wider that the width at the island site?—I cannot say from memory. It is certainly more than 34ft. 5in.

The Town Clerk went on to say that Mr. Wilson seemed to be of the opinion that it was not worth while obtaining the Order unless the whole of the improvement ultimately projected could be carried out. That was not the view of the Highways Committee of the Town Council. They were content with the Order as it at present stood, and were of opinion that it would give them what they wanted for the moment, and they were content to wait if necessary for the falling in of the lease of No. 98 before absolutely completing the ultimate improvement that the town was entitled to.

Mr. Wilson: Then if the Highways Committee are satisfied I am quite content.

The Town Clerk said that as to Mr. Weaver's point that the Order was premature, the Highways Committee did not consider it premature in any way.

The Inspector then declared the Inquiry closed.

WO March, 1931

Leica 1930/31

The Leica I is now available with an interchangeable lens.

Population 1931, 56,799

Queens Road, looking across Derby Road to the High Street.　　*p.340 bc*

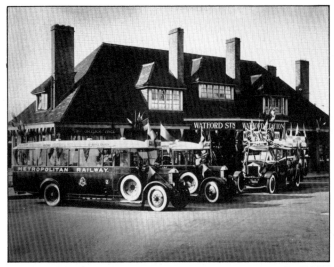

Planned in 1914, (p.127) the Watford 'Met' station was not opened until 1925; the Metropolitan buses celebrating a Watford 'Shopping Week', October 1928. The 'Met' was granted four licences for a circular service between the Station and St. Mary's Church from November 1927, but, at a time when transport licensing arrangements were somewhat chaotic, the service did not last more than a year until it was handed over to the Lewis Omnibus Company Ltd., thus gaining access to Watford Junction, an access previously denied.

Watford Printers Limited

PRINT and progress, two prime essentials of modern industry and civilisation, are outstanding features of the business of Watford Printers Limited. This Society of working printers, keen craftsmen with ideas of their own as to what could be accomplished by the application of new business methods to problems of management and control as applied to their own trade, commenced business on a Co-partnership basis in October, 1921, at the rear of premises in Watford High Street. The development of a printery was found to be an expensive process, and the Society has had many difficult problems to solve in keeping pace with pressing demands for new plant and machinery which are a natural corollary of an expanding business.

This Society was the first to publish an illustrated booklet of a Political Party, they being responsible for the production of "Labour Personalities in the House of Commons," which publication enjoyed a very large circulation and contained portraits and a short history of each Labour Member returned to the House of Commons in the 1921 General Election.

With the help of our friends the future of this Society is bright, and it is confidently anticipated that with steady progress the number of Co-partners employed will be ever increasing.

Sun Engraving

The photographic studios here remind one forcibly of a film-set erecting-room at Hollywood. They are immense. There are none like unto them anywhere. The customer's goods, for natural object photography, come into special storage rooms. And it does not seem to matter whether it is an iced birthday cake or an Axminster carpet, a dozen foulard ties or a tulip, when they have passed through these coldly staring, north-lit studios, wherein illusion cannot exist, their reproduction from an origin in fact to a facsimile in paper is not a matter of conjecture, but of cast-iron certainty. The incontestable veracity of the camera is the basic element here.

And the trained skill of the etcher paints the lily of the job thereafter. No man with a remnant of a conscience can say, when the colour printing of his object has come through in its finished state: "My original is better than this reproduction." Because the real and the printed copy placed side by side are as one.

The colour engraving of the "Sun" has always had a high reputation, but these new studios at Watford enable them to give their friends a better service in the future than, good as it has been, they have given in the past.

Colour-photogravure is one of their specialities, upon which they have spent many thousands of pounds on experimental and research work. It is the photogravure process before which the spirit of the average printer very naturally quails. Members of textile firms, requiring a high grade of smoothness on their cylinders for calico printing, have often expressed astonishment and envy, when visiting the works at Watford, at a photogravure cylinder surface of a perfection that they themselves can never attain.

It interests this writer immensely to be shown an industrial gadget that nobody else possesses. The attitude of the makers and owners of it is always so amusing. In the presence of their "baby" they become quite inarticulate, or else volubly technical, which to a layman is much the same thing. We stood in the shadow of a monstrous machine at Watford which is unique in all the world. An eight-colour photogravure machine, about sixty feet long, which does eight printings at once, and turns out seven to eight thousand complete coloured interiors of a magazine or a catalogue in an hour from the blank sheet which feeds into it at the centre.

"Where does it come from—Germany?" you shout in the uproar. "Certainly not!" they shout back. You feel you have indeed said the wrong thing. It appears to have been home-made—that is as to it specification: it was the result of the collective brains of the Watford men. And its fame having spread abroad, dozens of people try to see it.

Yet it is not all firms that give one this sense of stability in production, this rigorous cleaving to quality even when great quantity has to be handled. One supposes it is that equilibrium in effort that only comes with continual self-testing through the years, and that a really great reputation can only be gained and kept by using the best methods and ignoring every other kind. This, anyhow, seems The Way of the "Sun"—which has brought them to their present eminence.

Programme of the official visit of the Prime Minister (Ramsey Macdonald) to open the Trade Union Hall, Watford, 30 January, 1931.

Changing Watford

One half of the Watford Market Place improvement scheme is now nearing completion and it is anticipated that the whole scheme will be finished in about a month from now. As soon as the portion which was used as the old Market Place has been completed the traffic will be diverted to the new roadway for the old portion to be taken up, refaced, and relevelled.

The old Market Place used to slope down from the kerb to the roadway for drainage purposes, but as this will now be utilised for north-bound traffic only, it has been necessary to give the whole of the new roadway a new camber. This has necessitated a double kerb on part of the Market-street side of the Market Place.

When the new scheme is in operation all north bound traffic will use what used to be the Market Place, and south bound traffic will travel on that part which is now used for the traffic both ways. Already new lamp standards of the latest type, and two traffic signs indicating "one-way traffic," have been erected.

"The worst part of the work has already been done," stated the Borough Surveyor (Mr. W. W. Newman) to the "Observer" this week, "and there were difficulties in connection with the sewers and drains which had to be met."

The centre of Watford High-street has now completely changed its appearance. The historic old hotel, "The Essex Arms," has entirely disappeared, and on its site Messrs. Timothy White, the cash chemists and household stores, have erected their big new branch which opens on Thursday next. Alongside is the reconstructed and greatly enlarged drapery establishment of Messrs. J. Cawdell and Co.

WO May, 1931

The Baths Spring Another Leak

For years now, Watford Town Council have been criticised for not providing a suitable swimming bath. When, at last, they really did decide to have one, there was another outcry against the amazing expense to which they proposed going; and lately they have been subjected to further criticism for not making haste with the scheme now that they have decided on something definite.

WHP August, 1931

180

Essex Almshouses Surprise

AFTER a discussion lasting three hours, Watford Town Council, at a special meeting on Monday evening, decided to inform the agents for the Essex Almshouses that they (the Council) were not interested in the purchase of the site.

The Deputy-Mayor (Alderman F. J. B. Hemming) proposed the adoption of a recommendation of a sub-committee that the site should be acquired for highway purposes, and that the Almshouses should be demolished. An amendment moved by Councillor W. Bickerton, in what was perhaps the most eloquent speech ever heard in the Council Chamber, that the Almshouses should be purchased and preserved, was lost by two votes.

A further amendment, proposed by Alderman T. R. Clark (Chairman of the Highways Committee and a member of the sub-committee mentioned), that the Council "inform the agents that we are not interested in the purchase and we leave them absolutely alone," was carried by 15 votes to 7, and subsequently adopted as a substantive motion.

Reference was made to the starting of a voluntary fund to save the Almshouses, and the possibility of the Council becoming subscribers. It was also understood that the question of town planning the site as an open space will be considered.

WO August, 1931

Essex Almshouses

THE response to the Mayor of Watford's (Alderman W. Bickerton's) appeal for funds for the repair and preservation of the Essex Almshouses has been quite generous, but if the desire to do the work during the coming summer is to be fulfilled, further support will have to be quickly forthcoming.

It is hoped to start the repairs and renovations early in the spring, and it is estimated that £800 will be required to do the work, £100 per house.

Three local gentlemen have offered to be responsible for a house each, and a fourth is covered by the £100 donation of Watford Corporation. The Mayor's appeal for the other £400 has so far realised £222, so that nearly £200 is still required.

WHP January, 1932

Housing Density

In connection with the new housing scheme of the Watford Town Council on the Leavesden Green estate, a discussion took place at Tuesday's meeting on the question of how many dwellings should be erected to the acre. The Ministry of Health have fixed the density at 12. Councillor T. H. Simmons suggested 18-20, with a view to reducing cost and making possible a rent which is not an undue strain on the average working man. He proposed a resolution embodying his views, but was beaten on a division by two votes.

The Ministry will not depart from their density regulation except under very special circumstances, and in their opinion, in Watford there is no case for exception. We think the Ministry are absolutely right. No doubt the comparatively high rents charged for Council houses are a hardship to many tenants, but the remedy is not to crowd small houses together; that would simply mean the creation of future slums. The houses they erect must be a credit to the town and provide the amenities to which the tenants are entitled. The density rule is the outcome of experience, and lays down a standard that has been readily and generally accepted. The Council would only have been wasting time if, as was suggested, they had sent a deputation to the Ministry to press for a lowering of this standard.

WO May, 1932

LMS Line—Water troughs at Bushey. Water was supplied by railway company reservoir and softening plant in Oxhey Road. Loco 6019, 'Llewellyn', down 'Royal Scot' 19th May, 1929.

A. Christmas & Co. Ltd., garage at rear of Clock House, 54 High Street; were previously at mid-Lower Higher Street at 141/143, and were established in 1822 as coachmakers.

Sun Engraving Co.—process department, half-tone colour etching studio. c1930

... Watford in 125 years—a huge car park of six storeys? ...

A Vision of Watford in 2057

... Before strolling down the High-street, I looked at the cross-roads. No A.A. scout was on duty, as the St. Albans–Rickmansworth-road dipped under the Hempstead-road, and on the opposite corner a strange notice caught my eye: "Offices of the Hertfordshire County Local Municipal Committee."

Before enquiring the meaning of this notice from a man sitting beside me, I saw that he was reading a "Watford Daily Post."

I eventually gleaned from him in conversation that all Boroughs and Urban and Rural District Councils were done away with about 1970, and their powers taken over by the County Councils and administered by local committees. My informant seemed to remember being taught in school that in about 1930 the first move was made to that end by the County Councils absorbing the bodies called "Guardians," who controlled the places then called "Workhouses" (but he wasn't quite clear about it, saying that of course those places didn't exist in his time!)

Strolling down the road, I noticed that at regular intervals there were subways for pedestrians to cross, and I afterwards learnt that none were allowed to cross main motor roads except by subway—offenders being heavily fined—if not killed, of course.

A huge car park of six storeys and covering about two acres stood at the corner of Upton-road, on the site of the old Council Offices, and I stood for some time, fascinated, watching the silent cars creeping up and down the elevated sloping roadways to the various floors.

On the opposite side was Rigby House—altered, certainly, but recognisable, being apparently the oldest building within my view; all the buildings I had known south of this, as far as where Buck's Restaurant used to stand, had been swept away, and a large 'bus station existed.

I have often imagined, when struggling on to a 'bus in Market-street, what a super 'bus station might be like, but the sight of this one almost took my breath away. It was called the "Central Road Station" and comprised magnificent waiting rooms, reading rooms, restaurant, covered platforms, and four storeys of shopping arcades above.

Crossing the road by the inevitable subway, I entered the booking hall, wondering if my 1930 pennies would be accepted by the automatic booking office machines. Luckily, all was well, and I took a 2d return ticket to North Watford, just to see that part of the town.

I had stood on the platform 15 for about 30 seconds when a "North Watford Circular" bus swept silently in, discharged its passengers, picked up more, including my bewildered self, and accelerated swiftly and silently up the town.

When I looked out of the window, we were passing over a wide bridge and pulled up again just past Leavesden-road. We were off again in a few seconds and silently floating at about 55 miles an hour along the widened St. Albans-road, with its low walls guarding the paths and regular subways.

In this stretch I had the greatest surprise of all. All the small shops had disappeared altogether, and that part of St. Albans-road, and all the roads I could see that converge on to it were built up with ultra-modern sun residences and flats—each with its roof garden and 'plane landing place, verandahs and garage underneath. Before I had got over my surprise, we had stopped and started again.

I asked my companion where the Council houses were. He smiled and said he had certainly heard about them from his father, and understood they were demolished about the time he

was born, as they were an endless expense and not wanted in those days. The ground was sold, and the rates benefited thereby.

We shot over the much-widened by-pass by a bridge, and I looked in vain for the gasometer, but on enquiry my companion looked puzzled and said gas was last used about 2000 A.D.

The whole countryside seemed dotted with the modern flat-topped houses with their sun verandahs, tennis courts and lawns, and only here and there an old house still stood. It was evident to me that town-planning had come at last, even if late!

... My head was still in a whirl when we returned to Station-road and stopped at the Junction Station. Two of the old hotels I used to know still stood, though slightly altered, and the station had a new front built out and looked, not sooty and drab, but really attractive.

WHP March, 1932

Covering Watford Market

The work of covering Watford's market is now making progress, and a large part of the girder work is now in position. The whole of the work will not be completed, however, till the end of January. Operations started with levelling on September 19th.

Twenty-one men are employed on the job at the present time, nineteen of whom are local, and it is expected that that number will be increased to thirty shortly.

WHP November, 1932

"To One Car Park—£15,000"

Sir,—With regard to the report of the last Watford Town Council meeting, and the comments of Mr. John T. Clarke, I feel that it would be well to enlighten him on modern methods. A municipal car park should be on the main road for entrance, and most certainly as central as possible. The proposed site I consider excellent. Who wants to drive a car up to the Elms Estate.

Our friend would do well to visit Rosslyn-road, Upton-road, or the Parish Church, on a Saturday evening. 3,000 cars per week, at 6d. per car approximately £75 per week cash. Not a very heavy burden for the ratepayers, and then there is the sale of good frontage for shops, &c.

Watford grows daily, cars increase daily, and a central municipal car park is most urgently required. I have watched the development of this growing town for the past ten years. Can our friends find a better Council? I think they all take a real stand for economy.

A visit to Windsor would give our friend a good idea of a municipal car park; perhaps our friend is not a motorist, and therefore disinterested.

Yours faithfully,
PROGRESS, MOTORIST and RATEPAYER

WO December, 1932

Watford's New Fire Engine

The Watford Fire Brigade's new engine, which is now complete and ready for service, underwent exacting tests this week at the headquarters of the London Fire Brigade; and on Tuesday, after an extensive demonstration which included speed tests, it was formally christened by the Mayor of Watford (Councillor J. Evans), who broke a bottle of champagne over its front spring.

The fire engine is the first made by Messrs. Scammell, Ltd., the well-known firm of lorry manufacturers, of Watford West, and was designed with the close co-operation of the Watford

Fire Brigade. It is the first fire appliance to be fitted with the Stone turbine pump which has hitherto been only used in liners and docks. This pump can deal with 400 gallons of water a minute, and with a ¾in. nozzle the jet can reach a height of 139 feet. Two ⅝in. nozzles used together can send jets to a height of 115 feet.

The engine was taken to the Watford Waterworks on Tuesday afternoon, and in the presence of a large number of fire chiefs from the home counties and the Midlands, water tests were made. The hoses were run out and with the ¾in. nozzle the jet of water reached the top of the waterworks chimney stack, which is 120 feet high. Tests were also made with two and four nozzles working at once, and the first aid extinguisher was also demonstrated.

At Messrs. Scammell's works the engine developed a speed of 50 miles an hour on the road.

The design of the machine is of the most up-to-date character. It is fitted with one of Messrs. Scammell's famous four cylinder 40 horse power engines, but can develop 85 h.p. A new escape and scaling ladder extending to 55 feet, foam generators, and gas cylinders are included in the equipment.

WO January, 1933

Watford's All-Electric Baths Open

Watford's new public bath, erected at a cost of £37,000, and believed to be the first all-electric baths in the world, were in use by the public for the first time to-day.

The swimming bath presented an animated scene last night, for following on the official opening by the Mayor in the afternoon, a gala was held, and expert swimmers provided a display of grace and thrills combined.

Occupying a site just off the Hempstead-road, almost opposite the Public Library, the baths have an imposing appearance, and first impressions, coloured by a graceful approach and a dignified flight of steps, are not misleading.

The building, with its wonderful system of heating and modern equipment, will certainly be one of Watford's show places. Local pride is enhanced by the fact that the Borough Engineer (Mr. W. W. Newman, A.M.I.C.E., F.S.I., L.R.I.B.A.) has been responsible for the design and carrying-out of the scheme, with the assistance of the Chief Electrical Engineer to the Corporation (Mr. A. W. Barham) in connection with the electrical heating and lighting equipment.

WHP May, 1933

● *A petition was filed in the High Court of Justice by the Westminster Bank against Messrs. North, of Whippendell Road and London. March 1933*

Interior of Watford Baths, shortly after opening.

Near the top, corner of Upton Road, the new office/shop block (inc Elliott's) — the style of the future. In Market Street, next to the 'Compasses', the Post Office is being built. At the bottom of the picture, the market stalls, prior to 'permanent roofing'. Just above centre, at the right, the white roofed building is the Drill Hall, just below it the cottages of Meeting Alley and below those the chimneyed building of Roger's sawmills. Behind

Clement's store may be seen the rows of greenhouses of earlier farm days. The distinctive 'dome' of the Midland Bank can be seen at the bottom of the picture and next to it the new building of Cawdell's. From Cawdell's to Drill Hall is now Charter Place.

Plaza cinema and the Pond.   *p.247 tr*   Cassiobury's Lime Avenue in days of splendour; Cassiobury House in the distance.

Watford Slum Clearance

WATFORD CORPORATION'S slum clearance proposals were the subject of an Inquiry held by Mr. W. H. Collin, on behalf of the Ministry of Health, in the Council Chamber on Tuesday and Wednesday. The Corporation asked for confirmation of Clearance Orders in respect of eleven areas, and Compulsory Purchase Orders in respect of three areas.

On the opening day the portion of the room reserved for the public was filled with tenants of the houses concerned, and on several occasions they made themselves audible with interruptions. The feeling of the tenants who attended was, judging by the applause, against the suggested demolition.

. . . Mr. Salter Davies in a general concluding statement, said that the slums in Watford were not of the appalling magnitude found in other towns, but he submitted that these areas were thoroughly slum in character. The only remedy was their demolition. It was proposed to re-house the people on a very pleasant estate on the by-pass road in houses at 7s. a week, which were in the very strongest possible contrast with the houses mentioned in these Orders. They would have amenities which would give them a decent standard of life and a chance of living such as they had never really had before.

The Inquiry then closed.

WO May, 1933

The Man Who Made Watford Grow

Mr. Ashby was born in Bushey in November, 1842, and came to Watford at an early age, so that he lived in Watford for nearly the whole of his life.

For 50 years he was employed at Sedgwick's Brewery, and for a long period was manager there. It was during his managership that the Brewery became a concern of the first rank amongst Watford industries.

Watford, at the beginning of the century, had a population of just under 30,000, and Mr. Ashby could recall when it was little more than the single street of the old coaching days.

About thirty years ago a number of large estates were thrown into the market. Mr. Ashby, in partnership with the late Mr. Charles Brightman, purchased Harwoods Farm, Cassiobridge Farm, both of which belonged to the Earl of Essex, and also an estate in Callowland. These the partners developed as building land, and later, in 1908, they also purchased 180 acres in Cassiobury Park and developed this in the same manner.

WHP June, 1933

Cassiobury's Lime Avenue

THOUGH not a vestige of the noble mansion of Cassiobury exists, the magnificent avenue of limes in what is known as the second park remains, and it is gratifying to know that its preservation has become the special concern of Watford Town Council. Fear was recently expressed that some of the trees, from their great age, might be in a state of decay and prove dangerous to those seeking their shade. The advice of an expert, Mr. W. J. Bean, late curator at Kew Gardens, was therefore obtained, and his report, presented to the Council this week, is very reassuring. He does not know "a lime avenue of an age and size equal to this where the trees are in better condition." Lopping need not be considered at present; it would be wrong to spoil the beauty and dignity of the avenue in this way. What could be done was to clear away from the base of the trunks the huge clusters of "adventitous" branches that in summer completely hide them, thereby robbing the spectator of the sight of a stately succession of tree trunks suggesting the columns in the nave of a cathedral. Without loss of time the Council have commenced this work.

WO April, 1934

Leica

In the few years since its introduction, the Leica has proved a formidable tool, and since 1932 has been available with a coupled rangefinder for automatic setting of the lens to correct subject distance. The shutter speed range is extended from 1 second to 1/1000th.

The original f/3.5 Elmar was joined by the faster f/2.5 Hektor in 1931 to which is now added the 50mm f/2 Summar. The first wide-angle (35mm f/3.5 Elmar) was available in 1932, and the first long-focus lenses (73mm f/1.9 Hektor; 90mm f/4 Elmar) in 1931. Thus the Leica is now a system camera.

Felix H. Mann, having started an illustrious career using an Ermanox plate camera has, like many other gifted German photographers, started to use and exploit the unique advantages of the small Leica camera—which would have a quite astonishing effect for Watford in a few years' time.

North Watford Library

The question of providing a public library for North Watford was again before Watford Town Council on Tuesday, when a scheme to cost approximately £10,000 for the buildings alone was dealt with.

The Finance Committee stated that they had deferred consideration of the question of the plan and cost, but approved of the purchase of the site.

An Aerodrome for Watford?

A definite proposal came before Watford Town Council on Tuesday, that they should purchase 118½ acres of land (the asking price being £25,000) for the purpose of a municipal aerodrome, subject to contract and the Ministry of Health's sanction.

WHP July, 1934

Traffic Lights

Watford's first traffic lights were installed at the junction of Langley Road, St. Albans Road and Station Road. The signals were worked by traffic-actuated road pads. The second set of lights were at Queens Road/High Street and Kings Street. The installations cost £700.   June 1933

Pond Cross Roads looking along St. Albans Road (counterpart to p.176 t); part of 'Little Nascot', is being removed for road improvements. *p.279 tl, 339 t*

Watford Roundabout

IT is understood that work will be commenced shortly on a traffic roundabout at Watford High-street cross-roads. The estimated cost is in the neighbourhood of £12,000; 60 per cent. of this will be covered by a grant from the Ministry of Transport, and the balance will be provided in equal parts by the County Council and the Corporation. There has been considerable delay over the scheme. It was put back because of the national financial crises, and revived twelve months ago when the County Council gave conditional approval; they expressed the surprising opinion that it was not absolutely necessary from a traffic point of view, but had been promoted by the Corporation for obtaining a layout on town planning lines. As we said at the time, a little appreciation of the volume of traffic at this spot and the absolute necessity for regulation at all hours of the day dispelled any idea of that sort. However efficient the A.A. patrols may be, the time has clearly come for the breaking up, by means of a roundabout, of the converging streams of traffic. Fortunately the structure will not materially affect the most attractive part of High-street. It will be a new and useful feature of what is planned to be Watford's civic centre.

WO May, 1935

Watford's Municipal Offices

THE decision of the Assessor appointed by the Watford Corporation in the architectural competition for designs for the new Municipal Offices and Town Hall was announced at the meeting of the Town Council on Tuesday.

Mr. Vincent Harris stated that he had awarded the first place to Mr. C. Cowles-Voysey, of 14, Gray's Inn-square, W.C.1.

At the meeting of the Town Council in April it was stated by Alderman Hemming, who is Chairman of the Municipal Offices Sub-committee, that the assembly hall would accommodate 2,000 and the banqueting room 200. The competition was to be limited to six architects chosen by the Assessor, and Mr. Vincent Harris was nominated as Assessor by the President of the Royal Institute of Architects. Each competitor complying with the conditions is to receive a premium of 150 guineas.

WO June, 1935

Jubilee Tree Gets The Chop

The construction of the traffic roundabout at the junction of St. Albans-road, High-street, Rickmansworth-road, and Hempstead-road has caused the removal of some of Watford's oldest and most historical trees.

In the former category are two huge elms—or at least the remains of them—probably the last of the original elms after which the house was named.

They are believed to have been at least 250 years old. One of them was hollow practically the whole way through.

Of historical interest was the oak at the Rickmansworth-road end of the island at the junction of this road and High-street.

This was planted in June, 1887, by the Countess of Essex in commemoration of the jubilee of Queen Victoria.

Every effort was made to preserve this tree, but it could be neither moved and replanted nor included in the roundabout, so there was no alternative but to cut it down.

The second pond at the Cross-roads—it was a pond before it either dried up or was drained—on the Hempstead-road side of Little Nascot, is being filled in.

WO January, 1936

Pond Cross Roads prior to roundabout construction. The oak tree on the left, in the triangle, is that planted to commemorate Queen Victoria's Jubilee in 1887. Westminster Bank marks the futhest extent of the Parade but the ground adjoining is up for sale for building. 1935 *p.149 t, 268 t, 339 t.*

Death of King George V

TUESDAY bought to a close a week of unforgettable memories—the passing of a beloved king, the proclamation of his successor and, then, the funeral, with its mile-long procession through a crowded but silent London.

Only in the middle of the night has Watford High-street ever been so quiet and deserted as it was during Tuesday dinner-hour and the early part of the afternoon.

Life seemed to have come to a stand-still in what is normally the busiest throughfare in the county.

At 1.30 three maroons boomed out—one in Cassiobury Park, one in Oxhey, and one in North Watford.

It was the signal which had been awaited for days.

For two minutes Watford stopped altogether. Silence prevailed; even the wind seemed to stop bending the boughs of the trees.

It was the climax to events which had followed the death of the King.

Many Watford people had already attended some service of remembrance, though the official service was not until an hour and a half later.

Councils had arranged, and some had held, meetings to pass resolutions of condolence with the Royal Family and loyalty to the new King, and declarations of the accession of the new King had been made.

Watford had joined in the world-wide tributes to the passing of a great and noble king.

Few shops stopped at the Chamber of Trade's lead to close from noon to five o'clock; the majority closed all day.

Banks shut from 11 till 2; most offices closed from 12 till 5 or did not open at all, and cinemas were not opened till six o'clock.

Many people went to London early—mostly by train—to pay their last respects as the funeral cortege passed through the streets; many, too, went to Windsor, mostly by car, to join the silent throng that waited in the shadow of the royal castle.

WHP January, 1936

Crematorium?

Watford Town Council decided on Tuesday to ask Watford Joint Burial Board to consider the installation of a crematorium on a site adjacent to the North Watford Cemetery.

Councillor E. J. Baxter had given notice to move the resolution. In doing so he said that cremation was the most sanitary and convenient way of disposal now in use. It had many advantages over other methods of disposal, and those which would appeal to the Council were that there was no paupers' corner, that the garden of remembrance could be used in perpetuity and became increasingly beautiful the longer it was used, whereas in burial grounds the ground became swiftly filled and became the scene of desertion and decay, an eyesore to surroundings and to the coming generation.

WHP March, 1936

Open Air Bath to be Closed

Watford's open-air bathing place at the Five Arches is to be closed, but the Baths Committee is to consider the possibility of providing other suitable facilities for open-air bathing.

It was revealed at the Town Council meeting on Tuesday that a report of the analysis of the water showed evidence of sewage and manurial matters.

The Baths Management Sub-Committee recommended the closure following the analysis.

WHP May, 1936

The 'Elms', cross-roads roundabout under construction, 1935. *p.337 b*

Town Council and Unions

Watford Town Council at their meeting on Tuesday officially approved of the principle of collective bargaining for public employees through their Trade Unions.

The Council passed the following resolution:

"The Council, recognising that collective bargaining is in the interests of employers and workers, places on record its willingness to receive the duly accredited officials of the Unions at the appropriate Committee in connection with negotiations on wages and conditions of employment."

There was a time in the bad old days when employers imposed conditions on their workers. Now it was recognised that the worker was entitled to receive fair consideration, and that full and satisfactory relationships were obtained between employer and employee through collective bargaining.

Most industries, and many local authorities, including the Herts. County Council, recognised that.

Watford Parking Problems

WHAT is to be the solution to Watford's car parking troubles?

It is by now quite evident that the provision of the large Municipal Car Park at a cost to the town of something like £15,000 has not touched the roots of the problem. Daily, Watford tradesmen are worried by their customers protests that they are being "harrassed" by the police when they bring their cars on shopping expeditions, daily the car park stands almost empty.

WHP July, 1936

Hertfordshire's first nursery school opened at Wiggenhall House, Oxhey. The school, which used the Montessori method of education, was paid for by private subscriptions, but the organisers hoped that Hertfordshire County Council would soon take it over.

Death of Famous Sculptor

The artist who executed the famous group of statuary fronting the Watford Peace Memorial Hospital, Mrs. Mary Pownall Bromet, died at her home at Lime Lodge, Oxhey, on Thursday, after a long illness. She was 74 years of age.

In her autobiography, published in 1935, Mrs. Bromet says that it was at a memorial service at Croxley Green to Nigel Newell, killed in the war, that she saw "as in a vision" the three figures that now stand in bronze in front of the Hospital. She modelled the first two figures during the war, but the third was not commenced until some time afterwards. The group was unveiled in 1928. When the work was seen by Sir William Gascombe John, R.A., he turned to Mrs. Bromet with the words, "I congratulate you; they are beautiful. I admire their reticence and the work you have put into them."

WHP March, 1937

Derelict Mill Purchased

Twelve years ago last December the Watford Flour Mill in Lower High-street was destroyed by fire. Ever since the burnt-out roofless shell of the building has stood as the firemen left it. Even to-day, charred beams hang precariously from the upper storeys, while the wooden floor below is rotting away. Grass and weeds grow on the walls. The Watford Borough Council have approved a scheme to acquire the premises for £2,250. They will then be able to control the sluices. The Mill was one of the four mentioned in the Domesday Book. The "Observer" understands that the remains of the building are to be cleared.

WO March, 1937

'Kodachrome'

16mm Kodachrome was introduced, in USA, in April 1935, and Double-8 in Spring of 1936, followed by 35mm cartridges. In Germany Agfacolor Diafilm was introduced in November 1936.

. . . road line for future M1 and M10?

Another Plea for Lower High Street

Sir,—At the meeting of the Watford Town Council on Tuesday, February 2, Councillor Lock noted that it was proposed to spend £230 on the Pond fountain for Coronation celebrations, because the Watford people were proud of their Pond and also because it was a part of old Watford.

So far, so good.

But what about Lower Watford?

Have we not the Old Mill, and is not that a part of old Watford?

If our Council can afford to spend £230 on the Pond, I am sure they can spare a pound or two on our local eyesore, especially as residents and shopkeepers below High-street Station are not included in the Borough scheme of illuminations.

RATEPAYER (No. 2).

WHP February, 1937

Opening of Gaumont

Watford's newest cinema, the Gaumont, was opened on Monday evening by the Mayor, Alderman Henry Coates, J.P. He was supported by the Mayoress, Mrs. Coates; Cllr. C. E. Last, (deputy mayor), and Mrs. Last; Major A. J. Gale, I.B.E., (directors); Mick Hyams (theatre controller); F. A. Boyd (general manager); E. Pearson (house manager), and Mr. Johnson (publicity director.)

The guest of honour was Mr. Will Hay, the popular stage, screen and radio star.

The building is a fine structure in High-street, and is one of the finest buildings of its kind in the country.

The facade is on dignified lines and modern in its conception. The entrance hall is spacious and beautifully laid out as also is the lounge on the first floor. On the first floor, too, is also a modern cafe which will soon be opened. Here will be a popular rendezvous for Watford people.

The theatre itself is beautifully decorated and every seat in the building provides an excellent view of the screen and every sound can be heard without distortion. The proscenium is draped in a colour scheme of gold and brown and the curtain is of rich golden coloured velvet.

Every seat is comfortably upholstered and ample knee room is provided. The carpets were specially made for the Gaumont.

The Mayor welcomed Mr. Will Hay, and said the British public appreciated good clean humour.

Mr. Will Hay was received with prolonged applause. In his speech, he said that London might well be proud of such a fine cinema. Referring to the Mayor's remarks on British films, Mr. Hay said that a great deal of work and skill was being put into them and it was no longer true that America led the film industry. There was a time when a British cinema would be qualifying to have its doors closed if it stated that it would show British films, but all that had now gone.

He was doing his bit to help in keeping British films to a high standard.

WHP May, 1937

Sunday Games

THE Town Council have decided that they will not sanction games in the public parks on Sundays. This does not apply to games by organised clubs but simply to the throwing open of the parks for games for the general public.

The discussion on Tuesday evening was conducted on a high plane, and both sides stated their case with dignity, sincerity and restraint.

The question of Sunday games, like that of the cinemas, is one that seriously exercises the minds of a large number of men and women who want to do the right thing. Where are we to draw the line? If it is right to open the baths for a portion of Sunday, can it be wrong to grant similar facilities to non-swimmers who want to play tennis or other games?

Again, if there is a moral or religious objection to public games, then there must also be the same objection to allowing games by clubs.

If Sunday games are allowed, then it will not be long before Sunday cinemas are permitted.

We have suggested on a previous occasion that this is a matter for a plebiscite. Both sides could state their case if this were done, and many councillors who are now in doubt as to what the public really wants would have a definite ruling one way or the other.

Eventually, this will be found to be the only satisfactory way out.

WHP May, 1937

Mr. P. Fisher's Home On Fire

Fire broke out in a reception room at "Duddenhill," Clarendon-road, the home of Mr. and Mrs. Percy Fisher, on Friday, and damaged a quantity of valuable furniture.

It is believed that an electric heater was accidentally left on close to heavy curtains which ignited. The whole room was quickly alight, and before a maid discovered the outbreak, it had achieved considerable proportions.

A collection of carved ivories in the room escaped damage.

Mr. Percy Fisher was going abroad when he was called back on account of the fire. He left immediately after ascertaining the extent of the damage.

"Duddenhill" was recently bought by the Herts County Council for the future erection of Watford's new Police Station.

WO June, 1937

"Bigger Than Anyone Realises"

"Bigger than people yet realise" was the comment of the Mayor (Alderman H. E. Coates) on the proposed lay-out of the King George V. Recreation Ground, put before Watford Town Council at Tuesday's meeting.

The estimated cost of the lay-out is over £30,000, including:

Sixteen grass and four hard tennis courts.

Three bowling greens.

Three cricket pitches.

A running track.

Football, hockey and netball pitches.

A children's playground, and

A £15,000 pavilion or a number of smaller pavilions, and conveniences.

The original estimate in 1935 was just under £20,000. Now the total cost, including the cost of the land, has reached £54,500, but the Herts. County Council has made a grant of £4,700, and a further grant will come from the King George V. Memorial Fund, and there is a grant of £1,000 from the Playing Fields Association.

WHP July, 1937

Oh to Live in Hempstead Road!

Sir,—A lady enquired last week through the medium of the "West Herts Post," why the class distinction between higher and lower High-street, Watford.

If she reads the report of the Mayor's Banquet she will find her answer, when a certain gentleman said in his speech, "all the Mayors come from Hempstead-road."

All the public offices and amenities are in Hempstead-road or very near.—Baths, Public Library, prospective Town Hall, Electricity Showrooms, public convenience, and the Illuminated Pond.

Now they have all that is necessary we of Lower High-street, Watford Fields and Oxhey can hope for improvements.

Perhaps I can suggest a couple which are essential.

A Belisha crossing at Farthing-lane and a public convenience.

Ratepayer No. 1.

WHP November, 1937

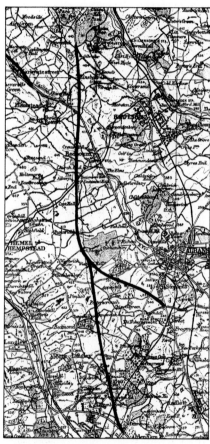

Through the courtesy of the County Surveyor (Lieut.-Col. A. E. Prescott), we are able to publish this map showing the line of the proposed new by-pass road for St. Albans. The line proposed by the Ministry of Transport, as shown in the map, joins up with the Watford by-pass at Garston and, travelling due North and skirting Gorhambury on the West, intersects the Watling Street at Flamstead and links up with the Harpenden-road slightly South of Luton. Travelling South, the new by-pass forks to the South-East at Gorhambury, and links up with the North Orbital-road at the point where it joins the old Watling-street.

Herts Advertiser, August, 1937

... 826 necessitous families benefitted ...

New Town Hall

WATFORD Borough Council, at their meeting on Tuesday night accepted the tender of £146,471 by Messrs. Richard Costain Ltd., of London, for the new Municipal Offices.

The actual cost to the ratepayers may be either 4.21d. in the £, or 5.01d. in the £, according to whether the Council decide on a 60-year or a 30-year loan period.

WHP September, 1937

Sunday Cinemas

THE discussion at the Town Council on Tuesday on the question of Sunday Cinemas brought to a head a matter that has caused a sharp division of opinion for some time.

It is not a question whether the Town Council approve of Sunday cinemas, but whether the electors should be allowed to decide this matter for themselves.

The responsibility is now off the shoulders of the Council, and during the next few weeks we shall see a campaign by the "pro and anti-cinema" people in the town.

It would be well if an effort was made to decide this question calmly and without bitterness. In fact, we believe most people have a pronounced opinion one way or the other on the matter, and it only remains for them to express it.

There is one difficulty, however, the single young people who are vitally concerned, will not have votes.

For both sides there is much to be said. Those in favour of Sunday opening point to the fact that Harrow and other neighbouring towns have Sunday cinemas, and that the opening of the cinemas prevents a considerable amount of horseplay—and worse, in the streets and parks. In a town where so many young people are in lodgings, it is well that something should be provided for them.

Those against Sunday opening express concern at the desecration of the Sabbath and say that ample opportunity is provided for cinema-going in the week.

They also fear that it is the "thin end of the wedge," and that Sunday labour will become more general if we give way on these matters. Further, they point out that young people have the religious services from which their parents derived spiritual strength in the past, and that it would not harm them to go to church more frequently than they do.

Well, those are the main points. It is up to the electors to take their choice. We live in a democratic country, and there is no reason why the issue cannot be disposed of in the best of spirit.

WHP January 1938

Many Families Benefit

No fewer than 826 necessitous Watford families benefitted as a result of the Mayor's Christmas Appeal this year. A total of £342 was raised out of which subscribers to the "Post" Shilling Fund contributed £65.

At Tuesday's meeting of the Watford Town Council the Mayor (Cllr. T. Rigby Taylor) expressed his thanks to all those who had contributed to and worked for the fund.

He directed especial thanks to Mr. S. Jump who distributed the gifts.

The Mayor added that, as in previous years, there was a small balance left over which would be spent on coal for the most needy cases.

WHP January, 1938

Watford's Historic Mill

A TENDER for the demolition of the old flour mill in Watford High-street was accepted by the Town Council on Tuesday. For just over 13 years the building has stood derelict, after being practically gutted by a fire which did damage estimated at £20,000. The Council bought the mill and the water rights for £2,250. They will now be able to control the flow and level of the water, thereby preventing, or at least reducing, flooding. In this matter they will work in conjunction with the Thames Conservators. The present mill was erected in 1826, and a short time before its destruction had been entirely remodelled. The structure was depressingly plain in character, and its final disappearance will be regretted by none. There are, however, centuries of history behind it.

In monastic times Watford mill belonged to the Abbot of St. Albans by virtue of his jurisdiction over the Manor of Cashio. The fact that no corn could be ground but at Abbey mills was one of the causes of the Peasants' Rebellion of 1381, in which men from this district took part, joining with others in rushing the Abbey, forcing a charter of liberties from the Abbot, burning records and breaking up millstones, pieces of which were carried away in triumph. In their charter they claimed the right to use hand mills in their houses "with freedom from suit at the Abbey mill." How John Ball, Gryndecobbe (surely a good name for a miller) and 15 others were hanged at St. Albans after the rising, is read by every schoolboy. Later, certain inhabitants of Watford began to erect a horse mill, but Abbot John of Wheathampstead was not to be thus defied, and soon put them out of business. The building up of the banks of the mill stream above the mill, which extended more than a mile, is attributed to the monks.

The mill was, in later days, so modernised that we find it described as "one of the best in its generation and the talk of the county." Soon, only the site will remain, but its associations will appeal not only to historians, but to all those who find delight in conjuring up visions of the past.

WO January, 1938

Watford's First Bus Driver Dies

Watford's first busman, Mr. George James Bence, of 46, Grover-road, Oxhey, Watford, died on Monday.

He was 67 years of age.

The first bus was run in 1898 and the service was between Bushey Arches and the water-trough at Callowland, with Mr. Bence as driver. The fare was 3d.

Its very popularity led to disaster. Built to carry four passengers and a driver and conductor, people clambered on to the bus in such numbers that the bus often broke down.

This happened so often that the service fizzled out and the bus was bought by the Standard Range and Foundry Company and was transformed into a lorry.

The vehicle was an 8 h.p. Daimler.

Mr. Bence was one of the earliest motor drivers in the country. After his experience as a bus driver, he became inside driver for the Daimler Company.

He then went into private service, and one of his duties was to make a journey a week to Margate.

In later years, and until his death, Mr. Bence ran his own private hire service.

WHP January, 1938

A Dangerous Corner

Sir,—A serious accident at Garston on Sunday causes me to write this letter, as this occurrence is the latest of a great many which have occurred at the same spot. I feel that the Borough Council's attention should be drawn once again to this very dangerous corner—the junction of the Watford-St. Albans main road with the North Orbital. Surely the ratepayers' money would be better spent in the construction of a roundabout at this place, which is very dangerous and a disgrace to any town in its present state, than in widening a road which is already amply wide enough, and where accidents are almost unknown. I refer to the proposed widening of Horseshoe-lane. I can write with experience, as I have lived in Garston for a great many years.

Yours truly,
S. GRAHAM WEALL

WO March, 1938

SUNDAY CINEMAS WON
RECORD POLL

"WE BOW"—Opposition
"HARDEST FIGHT"—Proposers

FOR	9,565
AGAINST	6,908

A 50% poll was recorded.

WHP March, 1938

Irresponsible

ON the other hand there is the problem of the irresponsible cyclist. There are far too many of them on the road, and the worst are not the careless children, but the factory workers who flood the roads at certain times without the slightest consideration for anybody else. Not all of them behave badly, but a large proportion do. I have myself been ditched in a narrow road by a wild stampede of works cyclists, several of whom would certainly have been massacred had there been a car on the road.

The only possible remedy is some system of registration for all cyclists, so that prosecution and punishment are possible in cases of dangerous and careless behaviour. This would necessitate some nominal tax, and unpopular though this would be, it seems to be the only fair way of dealing with the problem.

WHP May, 1938

No road sense?

The years 1930-1937 are the worst-ever for road deaths. Motor transport is in its infancy and all road users still naively believe they have an absolute priority on the highway; pedestrians cross willy-nilly at any road point and fail to estimate oncoming vehicle speeds. Roads are still not marked at junctions and first across wins! Night driving is hazardous as long as headlights are inadequate; oil lamps gave way to acetylene (mid-late 20's) and to electric lighting. Car headlamp systems for open-road driving are as inefficient as street lighting, where it exists. On meeting oncoming vehicles the main headlamps are 'dipped' by extinguishing the nearside lamp and dipping the off-side. A pedestrian crossing the road is virtually invisible.

Local newspapers regularly report such accidents.

Market place, early Spring 1938 ▶

A camping-ground in Lees Wood, for the Countess of Clarendon's Own Groups of Scouts, in memory of Lord Hyde, was opened. The Bishop of St. Albans conducts the dedication service.

The Earl of Clarendon performs the opening ceremony (above). The camping ground is today an essential and most popular part of the South West Herts Scout movement.

Memorial to Lord Hyde

Lord Hyde, the son of Lord Clarendon, died aged 30, in South Africa during 1935, from an injury sustained when his gun was accidentally discharged as he put it down.

A corner of Lees Wood, on the Grove Estate, was formally opened in memory of the late Lord Hyde by his father the Earl of Clarendon, as a camping ground for the 1st and 2/1st South West Herts (Countess of Clarendon's Own) Groups of Boy Scouts. A Sarsen stone carries a tablet, cast by members of the 2/1st Group, to commemorate George Lord Hyde who had been a Scout and Rover of the Group.

Watford's Cheap Electricity

TWO lectures on subjects of momentous importance to the town were given at a meeting arranged by the North Watford Ratepayers' Association held at the North Watford Methodist hall on Wednesday.

"The Watford Electricity undertaking" was the subject chosen by Ald. Henry Coates (Chairman of the Electricity Committee of Watford Town Council), while Capt. H. W. Carter addressed the meeting on air raids precautions.

Ald. Coates pointed out that the electricity undertaking was the largest industrial enterprise in the town. It was run by the Council for the burgesses and primarily for those wishing to consume electricity.

The fact that Watford was such a smokeless town considering the large number of industries carried on in it was due to the fact that most factories used electricity as their motive.

From an infant the Watford Electricity undertaking had grown in 39 years to a lusty adolescent.

Watford was the first town to have its streets entirely lighted by electricity.

The plant now supplied no less than 100 square miles with electricity. Towns such as Hemel Hempstead and Bovingdon benefitted from Watford's enterprise.

The people in Aldenham were causing some trouble and holding up the progress of the system in their area because they could not see that an extra charge for their current was justifiable. It was so because additional cables had to be laid, houses were further apart than in the town, and losses by transformers had to be taken into consideration.

In 1922 the plant outgrew the old building and the enterprise had to be extended. Three phase current was generated instead of the old single phase, and the voltage was raised.

In 1910 the undertaking had plant capable of generating 1,880 kilowatts; in 1922 there was 4,000 which supplied 4 million units a year; and in 1938 the plant could generate 36,000, which supplied 63 million units a year.

Ald. Coates explained how the 1926 Electricity Act controlled the business of generating electricity.

When the Act was passed Watford was told that their station would be shut down.

After a period Watford applied for a new plant and were told that they could not have it and they would have to take a supply from the grid.

The Grid prices were higher than the charges made for Watford produced current and the town

could not be forced to take its supply from the grid.

Watford was then asked to become a selected station to supply the grid, to which the committee agreed.

Ald. Coates estimated that the town saved £10,000 a year by virtue of the fact they were using their own electricity and not that of the grid.

WHP May, 1938

Historian of Watford

IT is with deep regret that we have to announce the death, which occurred on Thursday last, of Mr. William Raymond Saunders, of "Uppershott," Toms-lane, Kings Langley, at the age of 67.

The son of a straw hat manufacturer in Luton, Mr. Saunders began his teaching career there, and in 1896 joined the staff of Watford Field School. He was for a time at Victoria School and was transferred to Callowland in 1922, retiring in December, 1930. He was a past president of the Watford Branch of the National Union of Teachers, and was particularly interested in schoolboy football.

He is perhaps most widely known as the historian of Watford. When he saw old parts of Watford beginning to disappear and its old courts and alleys demolished, he decided to write a history of the town. He spent a number of years on this work, and his searches led him to documents in the British Museum, Somerset House, the Public Record Office, Watford Public Library and the registers of the Parish Church. The result was a fascinating story of Watford's growth from Saxon times. His history was published first in serial form in the "Observer," and in 1931 as a separate book by Messrs. C. H. Peacock, Ltd.

Shortly after the war Mr. Saunders went to live at Toms-lane, Bedmond, and took a prominent part in the erection of the Village Hall, in which he retained his interest until the end. Only two days before his death he was wheeled up to the hall and saw it for the last time.

WO April, 1938

May 1938, Town Hall foundation stone laying ceremony.

Members of the Mickey Mouse Club at the Odeon Cinema, Watford.   *p. 285 br*

Vickers 'Vildebeest' with Bristol 'Pegasus' engine—a machine of this type had been presented by the makers to the Watford Squadron of the Air Defence Corps, for ground instruction.

Town Hall Foundation Stone Laid

Yesterday was a momentous day in the history of the town of Watford, probably the most important day yet.

The foundation stone of the new £150,000 municipal offices and town hall was laid, but to Watford people who are proud of their town there was much more in the ceremony than that.

They hope it will be the first step in a new sense of civic dignity and interest, that it will be the means of breaking down that oft-expressed feeling that Watford is merely a dormitory town for London's workers.

WHP May, 1938

Watford High Street

BECOMING impatient over delay in the scheme for widening High-street, Watford, the planning Committee of the Corporation recently instructed the Town Clerk to press the Ministry of Transport and the County Council for details of their requirements. The Ministry replied, as was to be expected, that the Council were responsible for the future width of the highway, but they considered that the suggested 80 feet seemed appropriate. The Committee have now directed officials to prepare a report showing the approximate cost of adopting widths of 64 feet, 74 feet and 80 feet. No reason is given for these curious alternatives. The County Council are to be approached to see what grant they are prepared to make towards the scheme. That authority will no doubt want to know just what is in the minds of the Corporation. Apparently the idea is to acquire any property that becomes vacant and set back the frontage. To purchase whole blocks of shops and demolish them for widening purposes would entail colossal expenditure which, in the state of the town's finances, it is impossible to contemplate. The fact is that any wholesale widening is out of the question, and the appearance of High-street, at least as far as the roadway is concerned, is not likely to be materially changed for many years to come.

WHP June, 1938

Cadet Flying Corps For Watford

With the object of creating a body of 20,000 youths familiar with aircraft and with flying, a new organisation is being started in the country.

It is to be called the Air Defence Cadet Corps, and squadrons are being formed in all big centres.

The "Post" has the privilege of giving first details of the scheme to be started in Watford.

Watford has a great opportunity to make national history by being the first Corps organised.

It is hoped in Watford to raise two squadrons of 100 cadets each. Only 200 cadets will be enrolled, and this number will not be exceeded.

Cadets will be selected, approved and enrolled by a local Committee, consisting of the Deputy Mayor, Alderman H. Coates, Squadron Leader Burge, Alderman J. Evans and Mr. E. McGregor, and must be between the ages of 14 and 18.

They will be taught the elementary principles of aircraft engineering and maintenance, the handling of simple work shop tools and instruments, the general theory of flight, the identification of aeroplanes, the morse code, message carrying, meteorology, fire action, and model aeroplane making and flying. They will be fully trained in air raid precautions, and be given an insight into the working of the Observer Corps, the Balloon Barrage Companies, anti-aircraft gunnery, searchlight and sound locator operation, and all other forms of passive defence.

WHP June, 1938

With no parking restrictions busy days become a free-for-all. This is the High Street between Bucks' and W. H. Smith.

p.336 tl

Wanted—a Car Park

A MUCH-NEEDED improvement for the lower end of the town is being ridiculed in certain quarters. This is typical of the mentality which has been responsible for the neglect of Lower High-street and that has made this thoroughfare a cause of shame to every citizen who takes a pride in the town as a whole.

In Lower High-street, Queen's-road and King-street are traders who have been ratepayers for many years. They have helped to lay the foundations of Watford's prosperity, and they should not now be penalised because the trend of commercial development is northwards. It may be interesting to recall that of eleven firms who advertised in our Jubilee issue last year that they had been in business for more than fifty years, eight of them are in the lower end of the town.

Contempt has been poured on the scheme for a car park in Albert-street. All sorts of difficulties have been raised, and it has been suggested that no car park is needed at this spot.

The true position is this. The piece of waste ground it is proposed to convert into a car park is already being used by about 30 motorists a day. We have checked this, and found that it excludes a battered perambulator that others appear to have discovered.

We have consistently urged that there is no need for an expensive scheme. It is not even necessary to concrete the yard. So far as an attendant is concerned, he could be paid a moderate wage and take what he could in tips from motorists. This is done in other towns and cities not far from Watford, and would not make the Council responsible for the cars in any way.

Three banks, two newspaper offices and sever-al business offices, the police station, and the only railway station in High-street are nearer Albert-street than they are to the Municipal Car Park.

One-way traffic could easily be introduced, even through Carey-place.

The High-street car park, useful though it is, is too far from the business centre of Queen's-road and Lower High-street to be adequately served by it. A modest expenditure on levelling and improvement of the entrances is all that is required at Albert-street, and the business interests of the lower end of the town demand it.

WHP February, 1938

● *Albert Street was eventually cleared and demolished c1960 and the open space bounded by Derby Road, Queens Road and the rear of the High Street premises became better known as 'Sainsbury's car park' when Sainsbury's occupied the old library site in Queens Road from 1970-1986.*

More About Sunday Washing

Sir,—I am glad to see the subject of Sunday washing raised in your paper. At one time in this part of the town people used to put their washing out on Monday and Tuesday, and then no more was put out until the next Monday and Tuesday. But now it is put out every day in the week, including Sunday. Surely housewives can do all their washing on six days of the week and leave us free from this disfigurement on Sundays. Sunday is so much more enjoyable if we make it different from other days.   R.L.K.

WHP May, 1938

Local Charities To Benefit?

Notification that the Home Office have made an order extending Sunday cinemas to Watford was received at the meeting of Watford Town Council on Tuesday.

The Town Clerk (Mr. W. Hudson) said that under the Cinematograph Act 5 per cent of the profits went to the Cinematograph Fund. The County Council were the licensing authority for Watford so that if any other conditions were to be laid down on the grant of the licences it would be for the County Council to formulate them.

The Council could make suggestions to the County Council, for instance as to funds for charities to benefit in addition to the Cinematograph Fund.

In reply to a question the Town Clerk said that the amount to go to charities could be had up to the whole of the profits.

It was agreed that the Council ask the County Council to bear in mind the claims of the Watford and District Peace Memorial Hospital and the Watford and District Nursing Association.

WHP June, 1938

"Suitable and Wholesome Films"

The Council suggested that performances should start after the ordinary hours of church services and that the type of film shown should be suitable, wholesome and fit for people of all ages.

It also asked that the existing conditions that music be of a sacred or classical nature should be rigidly enforced.

WHP July, 1938

193

Watford's new Town Hall taking definite shape. This shows the administrative centre and, to the left, the assembly halls.   *p.337 b*

Watford One-Side Waiting

THE unreasonable objections to unilateral waiting in Watford High-street have at last been overcome. The Town Council, after acquiescing in police suggestions that the scheme was impracticable because of the narrowness of the road and the existence of bus stopping places, recently made representations to the County Council, who have now granted an order for an experimental period of three months. The old market-place section, where there are two traffic lines, is excluded. If the Corporation had shown a firm attitude in the first place this means of relieving traffic congestion, adopted in so many other towns, would have been in operation long ago. The "Observer" has been advocating unilateral waiting since April, 1936.

WO June, 1939

Garston House to be Demolished

Reputed to be one of the most ancient buildings in the county, Garston House is to be demolished to make way for a modern building estate.

The estate, comprising 55 acres of land adjoining Garston Park on the St. Albans-road has been purchased by Messrs. W. J. Rice and Sons and the lay-out of an estate to contain 500 houses has been provisionally prepared.

This 55 acres is the remnant of a huge property so old that its origin is lost in history. It is, however, certain that a house of some kind existed in the twelfth century while parts of the present house date back to the fifteenth and sixteenth centuries.

The estate, which had for 20 years been the property of Mr. A. D. Bradford, is not well-known by the general public. Its great antiquity has hitherto escaped wide notice, and many of those who attend the big Conservative Fete in the

grounds on Saturday will view the house with fresh interest.

With the sale there passed into the lands of Messrs. Rice a large number of interesting legal parchments of the reigns of Henry VIII, Queen Elizabeth, Charles II, right through to George III.

These deal with such widely divergent subjects as the various sales of the estate through the centuries, tenancies, court proceedings conducted by the Earls of Essex and even marriage agreements. The seals of Elizabeth are exceptionally interesting and almost complete.

Penned in Gothic script, the parchments could only be deciphered clearly by an expert, and obsolete, intricate legal phrasing make the task even more difficult. Those of the time of Elizabeth are in Latin.

All have been presented to the Public Library, where expert assistance is being obtained for translations.

The earliest document is of the year 1542, recording a sale from Ruth Cartor to John Randall. From histories of Hertfordshire in the Watford Public Library and the documents the following facts come to light.

Nicolas, son of John de Garston, gave the tenancy of certain land at Garston in the 12th century and the manor was conveyed in 1368 from Bartholomew Blaket to John Curteys of Wymington.

In 1455 William Halle, of Schildyngtone, in the county of Bedford (Shillington) granted the manor to John of Wheathampstead, 33rd Abbot of St. Albans. The Abbot and his successors continued to hold the manor till the dissolution of the monasteries by Henry VIII. On July 12, 1544 the Tudor King granted the manor to Richard Carter and Thomas Palmer.

Half the land was then sold to John Randall and his wife from whom that portion went to

Michael Sayer of Marsworth, Bucks. Meanwhile William, son of Richard Carter had died and his son, Richard, inherited half of the land and subsequently bought the other half again. In 1636 another William Carter sold the estate to John Marsh, in whose family it remained till conveyed in marriage to Thomas Beech. Thomas Beech sold up in 1729 to Richard Capper of Bushey, a family name still surviving. One of his descendants married Mary, the daughter of Robert Ord, then Lord Chief Baron of Scotland.

In 1816 the estate passed by sale to Stephen Moore, and thence in 1854 to Henry Cobb, and then to his widow in 1873. At that time the estate comprised 400 acres but in 1904 when Mr. Thomas Farries lived there the estate dwindled to 184 acres.

The sale of the estate by Robert Capper makes strange reading in the old document—

"I, Robert Capper, for the sum of 10s and for other considerations do sell, release and confirm unto the said Stephen Moore, the manors, lordships and reputed manors and lordships of Bushey, Bournhall and Garston together with the capital or mansion houses, buildings, gardens, farms, lands, tithes, etc." One wonders what the "other considerations" were. In another document, however, is mention made of a sum of £2,000 which Moore paid to Capper.

Messrs. Rice are conveying a portion of the land to the Corporation to be added to Garston Park. This includes a lake in the grounds.

With regard to the lay-out, Garston-lane is to be widened to a 50ft. road and will go through in the direction of Munden.

WHP July, 1938

The Town Hall assembly rooms, entrance in Rickmansworth Road, taking recognisable shape.   WO August 1938

Wing Commander Hodsell, Inspector-General of ARP, inspects Watford's Auxiliary Firemen during black-out and defence exercise, November 1938.

Watford's Entrances

NOW that Watford Town Council have completed the work started by the fire many years ago, and pulled down the old mill in Lower High-street, this entrance to the town, once so dingy and dirty, is greatly improved.

The erection of new buildings on two sites there will also add to the freshness of the outlook, but it cannot yet be said that every aspect pleases.

The chief offenders to the view now are a number of bill posting sites. If these could be altered or removed, this entrance to the town would give visitors a much better introduction.

There can be little complaint of the other main roads into Watford from the aesthetic point of view.

Hempstead-road will present a dignified appearance when the road works now in progress are completed, and with the imposing town hall dominating the town end of the road.

The entrance by St. Albans-road has also been improved recently by the laying-out of the round-about on the same lines as the Pond roundabout.

WHP May, 1938

Assembling The Respirators

A magnificent piece of work was put through in Watford in assembling the 60,000 to 70,000 respirators necessary.

Authorities were not allowed to assemble the respirators until instructed.

Instructions were given first in Watford early on Monday morning. These were countermanded and then at 11 a.m. the order was again given.

The Mayor (Councillor T. Rigby Taylor) got into touch with the Sun Engraving Works, the Model Laundry, the Watford Steam Laundry, Millars Laundry, and Silverdale Laundry, and asked them to supply the staffs to assemble them. They agreed.

Then it was found there were no jigs for assembling.

The Mayor and Councillor E. J. Baxter went to two regional stores and obtained jigs.

At 2 p.m. on Monday assembly started, and by midnight three hundred employees at the Sun and three hundred at the laundries had assembled 50,000 masks.

The others have been assembled since.

The Mayor wishes to make it quite clear that Watford was not behind in the distribution of masks, as some people have alleged.

WHP September, 1938

Fitting of Respirators

WE appeal to our readers to heed carefully the letter which we publish in this issue from the Mayor (Councillor T. Rigby Taylor) regarding the necessity for expediting all measures to be taken in the Air Raid Precautions Services within the Borough of Watford.

One of the most important of these is the fitting of respirators to all residents, and we ask that everyone concerned will do their best to make the gigantic task of fitting the population with gas masks as easy as possible by reporting to their respective polling stations when required to do so.

There is no need for alarm. The fitting of respirators is inevitable, and as a house-to-house visit would take many months, it is hoped by asking residents to attend for fitting, to complete this important work within three weeks.

The Authorities have done and are doing their part, and it is up to the public to assist.

WHP September, 1938

A Message from the Mayor

The Mayor of Watford (Councillor T. Rigby Taylor) addresses the following message to the burgesses of Watford—

"Though all necessary precautions are being taken in case of dire emergency it does not follow that war is inevitable.

I would ask the population of Watford to be calm and to avoid panic.

I can assure them that everything has been and is being done for their protection.

I wish to thank all workers for their efforts."

WHP September, 1938

The Ill Wind, Food Hoarding

ONCE more the proverb of "the ill wind" comes to mind. The windy bravado of the Dictators during the past two weeks may indeed blow the English community a great deal of good—especially around London.

The past ten years has seen a growth of new and old towns around London proceed at an amazing pace. That growth has been so quick that outer London could be called little more than an agglomeration of dormitory building estates. Division between one district and another became purely arbitrary, for pride of town had not time to grow. There was no community spirit because, firstly, business interests were usually centred elsewhere and leisure pursuits were purely self-centred.

A.R.P. has probably done more than anything else since the war to change all that. By force of circumstances the new districts have of a sudden been welded into a unit of common effort to a common cause, and whatever wind may have blown the seed there, once implanted, must by the nature of things continue to grow.

FOOD hoarding was as prevalent in Watford during the crises as elsewhere, and the wireless warning that shopkeepers were not bound to take back inordinately large purchases found plenty of interested hearers.

In one instance a housewife had ordered 100 tins of condensed milk, accepted delivery and then wanted to send them back when the crisis had passed. Grocers in many cases were unable to make deliveries of orders within twenty-four hours owing to the tremendous demands made upon them.

It was mentioned at an A.R.P. meeting by Councillor Mrs. Armitage that a shopkeeper had said to her, "The women of Watford are thinking of nothing else except stocking their larders."

WHP October, 1938

Home Secretary to Inspect A.R.P.

The Home Secretary (Sir Samuel Hoare) and the Inspector-General (Wing Commander Hodsell) will be among those who will witness the Air-Raid Precautions exercises in Watford and Rickmansworth in the County black-out on Saturday.

The Black-out will be the biggest A.R.P. exercise held in the country. It will cover approximately 640 square miles and about 12,000 volunteers who have enrolled for the different services will be called upon to take part in the exercises.

All sections of the general public, including motorists, are asked to co-operate by extinguishing all lights between 11.45 and 2.30, and by remaining at home.

All of the regular services, the police, the St. John Ambulance Brigade, the British Red Cross Society, the railway companies, and the Post Office are collaborating.

WHP November, 1938

The Picture Post story starts . . .

Felix H. Man (Felix Sigismund Baumann) was born in Freiburg im Breisgau in 1893. As a contributor to the *Munchner Illustrierte Presse* and the *Berliner Illustrirte* from 1929-1934, his photo essays covered all spheres of life. In 1934 in England he was the leading photographer with *Weekly Illustrated* when it first came into existence and, when *Picture Post* started in 1938, he was appointed Chief Photographer by the Editor. He remained with *Picture Post* until 1945 and returned as their colour specialist in 1948-1951.

His one-man shows have been exhibited in public museums and art galleries all over the world.

His books on lithography and *European Artists* were published in the 1950s and the 1970s.

❝ In spite of the 'Ermanox' camera, with a lens with an aperture of f/1.8, if indoor photographs had to be taken by available light, or people such as conductors were to be photographed, it has to be remembered that negative sensitivities then were only a fraction of what they are today. The present-day photographer knows nothing of these difficulties, as all these problems have been solved mechanically—usually to the disadvantage of the eventual result. In the early days, with the limited means at our disposal, it was nearly always the rule that the negative was under-exposed, and had to be reinforced after development, in spite of the fact that exposure times varied between one-half and one-eighth of a second. For this reason, all indoor photographs had to be taken with a tripod, as it was impossible to hold the camera steady. No light or distance meters were available. Distances had to be estimated, and only on rare occasions was it possible to look through the viewfinder, and never possible to control the picture on the matt-screen.

The number of photographs we could take was limited, as we had to work with glass plates in metal cassettes; as a rule, not more than 15 to 20 of these could be carried on an assignment. We hardly ever exposed more than one negative of the same subject. We did not then conform to Bernard Shaw's idea that 'the photographer is like a cod-fish who lays a million eggs in the hope that one may hatch'—an idea which makes more sense today, when photographers may take 300-500 pictures for one story, of which perhaps 20 or so will be selected later by the editor who has encouraged these methods. The technical limitations of the early days demanded great concentration and creative capacity. Each exposure had to be a hit.

I left Germany for good in May 1934. I had to leave everything behind me and travelled with only a small suitcase, to avoid suspicion. I had been told that the best way into England was by Calais and Dover. Passport control took place on the boat, during the crossing. 'How long are you going to stay in England' asked the Immigration Officer. When I replied that this depended on my work for various continental papers, my passport was stamped with an oval stamp, with the words 'Leave to land at Dover this day, 31 May, 1934, on condition that the holder does not enter any employment paid or unpaid while in the United Kingdom'.

As a journalist I could do free-lance work, even working for an English paper, provided I was not employed and paid a fixed salary or retainer, but paid separately for each job.

A few days after my arrival I met, by sheer accident, my old friend Stefan Lorant, the Hungarian former editor of the *Müncher Illustrierte*;

he had been imprisoned soon after Hitler's take-over, but released through pressure from the Hungarian Parliament. 'You are exactly the man I would most have liked to meet at this moment' he exclaimed 'I need you, as I am planning a new weekly illustrated paper with Odhams Press.' Neither of us had known of the other's presence in London before we met. For years we had worked together in Germany, he as editor, I as his principal contributor. We were a team, complementing each other. Was it coincidence, or fate?

At that time, photo-journalism did not exist in England. The continental method of writing essays with a camera was unknown, and there were no illustrated weeklies of the continental type. The world's first illustrated paper, *The Illustrated London News*, published news photographs, pictures taken by scientists or explorers, or photographs of prominent society people.

Soon after his arrival in England in May 1934, Stefan Lorant had learnt that Odhams Press were planning a reorganisation of some of their magazines. He made contact with the management, and suggested that they should publish a new illustrated weekly of the continental type. Odhams agreed, and their dying magazine *Clarion* was incorporated— in small type—with the new magazine, *Weekly Illustrated*.

The preparatory dummy was put together by Lorant in June 1934, in the continental manner, using a number of my old picture-stories. As time was short, I started, that month, to produce photo-essays for the new paper. When the first number of *Weekly Illustrated* came out on July 1934, the bulk of the picture stories were mine; Lorant had laid out, on the usual two pages each, four photo-essays of mine. I had worked on my own, as usual, with a personal assistant, also providing the facts for the captions and the brief texts. I was paid according to the number of pages of my work which were published; for several months the paper was largely dependent on my work, and I was earning it between £40 and £50 a week. This naturally caused some jealousy from others on the paper. Maurice Cowan, thinking after a few months that he knew how to run such a paper, plotted how to get rid of Lorant and myself.

I was overworked, and my permit to stay in England was due to expire at the end of August. I decided to take a continental holiday, leaving about eight stories behind, to be used in my absence. Lorant only hesitantly accepted my suggestion that a German friend Hübschmann should take over in my absence; the latter and I agreed that he would fade away on my return. Later on Kurt Hübschmann changed his name to Hutton.

When I returned to Dover in October, the Immigration Officer again used the oval stamp, giving me another three months in England. In the meantime the squabbles at *Weekly Illustrated* were mounting. Lorant, fighting to retain his own position, was not able to give me sufficient support. A month after my return, I left the paper, predicting to Lorant that he too would be leaving within a couple of months, a correct forecast as it turned out. *Weekly Illustrated* stumbled on without its founding fathers, until killed off by the overwhelming success of *Picture Post* in 1938; it was then reborn as *Illustrated*.

Until today, the importance of *Weekly Illustrated* as a picture magazine has yet to be assessed. It was through this paper that photo-journalism was introduced into England. When Henry Luce was preparing the publication of *Life*, he came to England to study the back issues of *Weekly Illustrated*.

I kept in close contact with my old friend and

colleague, Stefan Lorant. When in the mid-thirties, he started to publish a magazine of his own, the pocket magazine *Lilliput*, it was only natural that I become a contributor at once. In about June 1938, Lorant sold *Lilliput*, for what was then a substantial sum, to Hulton Press, and then entered into negotiations with this young but financially very sound publishing house, about starting a weekly illustrated paper on the continental model. The new enterprise, to be called *Picture Post*, was due to start in October 1938, so there was little time for preparations.

When the first number of *Picture Post* went to press, trenches were being dug in Hyde Park to protect the civil population against air raids. In contrast to this fatuous improvised protection, the first issue of the paper, which was intended to conquer England in a quick assault, was well prepared. This issue, of 750,000 copies, was sold out and had to be reprinted. By the spring, the circulation was nearly 1.4 million. Meanwhile Chamberlain had been and gone to Munich, the clouds of war had receded, the race for re-arming was on, and the economy was prospering.

Many experts had forecast that a new picture paper could not succeed. Was not the fate of *Weekly Illustrated* proof enough? Conditions in England were said to be completely different from the continent, and everything was against such a venture. The large editions of the Sunday papers would, it was said, leave no room for an illustrated weekly. Their large organisations and printing facilities enabled them to change words and pictures up to the very last moment; this was something that *Picture Post* would never be able to do, as this would involve changing a whole photogravure cylinder, covering sixteen pages, a long and costly business.

The phenomenal success of *Picture Post* made nonsense of all these predictions. Why, then, was the weekly such a smashing success? There were a number of causes, but the most important of these lay in the conception and direction of the paper. Stefan Lorant, the editor, and the two principal contributors, Hutton and myself, were all experienced in our fields. We had mastered our jobs and worked together as a team. Tom Hopkinson, the assistant editor, had learnt a lot in four years with *Weekly Illustrated*. His main job was to oversee the 'words' part of the weekly, while Lorant as editor and picture-expert held his protective hand over the whole project. The British public was, for the first time, introduced to abundant well-composed large-scale picture essays about ordinary, everyday things, which people were familiar with, but had never consciously observed.

In issue number one, published on October 1 1938, there were 80 pages for what was even then a ridiculously low price of three pence. There were 39 pages of pictures, 22 of reading matter, and a four-page colour supplement on great British painters. The buyer needed several hours to go through the magazine thoroughly.

Unlike the German weekly illustrated papers, where essays or interviews were limited to two or three pages, *Picture Post* spread important pieces over six, even eight, pages. The accompanying text had to be much more detailed, so a number of journalists were taken onto the staff. Coming from a different branch of journalism, they tried to dominate the photographers. As I resisted these attempts, I was not very popular with the journalists; I insisted that, when on a job, photographers came first, as we were, after all, an illustrated paper.

The leading political figure before, and at the beginning, of World War II was the Prime Minister, Neville Chamberlain. When he returned from his meeting with Hitler at Munich in

1938, did he really believe that 'Peace in our time' was secured by the famous piece of paper he waved at Croydon Airport? Or was it his intention to gain time for Britain, then largely unprepared, to re-arm?

A couple of weeks before the war started, I found a cottage in the Chilterns with vacant possession; anticipating what was going to happen, I installed myself there at once. 'The Old Forge,' my eighteenth-century cottage, was at Flaunden, a small hamlet of about 20 houses, with a church, a pub and the Flaunden General Stores, a tiny shop where cigarettes and postage stamps could be bought.

The fear of the enemy within, the fifth column, caused me problems. As my time in Canada counted towards residence in Britain, I had been in a position to apply for naturalisation six months before the war broke out. My case was under investigation, but the outbreak of war stopped all naturalisation. I had become friendly with Sir Stafford Cripps, who tried to get me into the Ministry of Information. But no alien could be employed at the Ministry; as the Home Office ruled that naturalisation could only be granted to aliens already working for a ministry, it was a vicious circle. 'Enemy Aliens' such as myself had to go before a tribunal. Before this took place, I could not travel more than six miles from my home. I could cycle the four miles into Watford, where the *Picture Post* offices had moved to, but my contributions stopped.

In June 1940, I was planting flowers in my garden at Flaunden, when the peaceful silence was broken by five men coming through my garden gate, four of them in uniform. The other said 'I must arrest you' and posted the uniformed men around the cottage to prevent any attempt to escape. This man, the Police Superintendent from Hemel Hempstead, gave me half-an-hour to get some things together, and then took me off to a single cell in Bedford Prison. He managed to collect a fair number of aliens in this way, and after a few days, we were taken by train to Euston, and then marched across London under military escort to Victoria Staion, heartily abused by those we passed on the way, who supposed that we were dangerous spies. Hampton Court Race Course was the assembly-point for thousands of internees, and we were all cross-examined there. The MI5 Colonel who interviewed me at once realised that a mistake had been made. He told me 'I cannot help you at present, but I can give you some advice. Be persistent in your efforts to get out. Try everything, and you will eventually succeed.'

He was right. Three months later I was free, back at Flaunden and working again for *Picture Post*. But the Police Superintendent evidently regarded me as a dangerous person still. One day I looked out of an upstairs window of the cottage and noticed somebody hidden in the bushes opposite. I went down and found the village policeman lying in the ditch. He was very embarrassed at being discovered. I said 'I am not going out today so you are waiting in vain—you had better go home.'

Stefan Lorant, though not interned, had suffered from a number of restrictions, one of the reasons why he had given up his position and emigrated to the United States in July, while I was interned. Tom Hopkinson **99** had taken over as editor.

Back to the Middle Ages

Later that day began the worst pogrom since the Middle Ages. Looting went on all over Germany and Austria. The houses of Jews were broken into, children were dragged from their beds, women were beaten, men arrested and taken to concentration camps. Foreign journalists were prevented, as far as possible, from gathering details, but it is known that in Berlin several Jews were stoned to death. In the provinces, the number must have been higher.

The police did not interfere. The fire brigades turned their hoses only on non-Jewish buildings. All Jews in the streets or in wrecked shops, who were not manhandled, were arrested. In Munich, 10,000 Jews were rounded up and ordered to leave within 48 hours. This order was later rescinded, but not before hundreds of terrified Jews had run into the forests to hide from the mobs. In Vienna and the Sudetenland, Jews were made to crawl in the streets.

On November 11, arrests were continued all over Germany. Many Jews, despairing, committed suicide. German shops refused to sell food to Jews.

Goebbels told foreign correspondents that he sympathised with the people in their desire to protest, denied that there had been looting or that he had organised the pogrom. "Had I done so," he said, "it would have been done more thoroughly." Not a single synagogue, hardly one Jewish shop, remained unwrecked.

PP November, 1938

The amalgamation of unrivalled production facilities, plus the original gifted editorial team, produced a magazine which had profound effects upon the whole country. Fearless in reporting war time inefficiency, and in reporting troops' derogatory comments about the quality and standard of their equipment, Picture Post's revelations about degrading social conditions in many towns and cities paved the way for almost universal demand for quick social reform. Picture Post's crusading stance on the subject played no small part in the country's returning a Labour government to power in the first post-war general election.

Preparations . . .

ARRIVING 20 minutes behind schedule the Inspector General of A.R.P. (Wing Commander Hodsell) who was accompanied by Flight Lieut. Eardley-Wilmot (Regional Inspector of the London Area), Major General Tindal-Lucas (Chairman of the Hertfordshire A.R.P. Committee), Mr. Elton Longmore (Clerk to the Hertfordshire County Council), Captain J. E. Slattery (County A.R.P. director), and A.R.P. representatives from Buckinghamshire, Middlesex, and Surrey, reached Watford Fields House at 11.40 p.m. Here he was received by the Mayor (Councillor T. Rigby Taylor), and the Deputy Mayor (Alderman H. Coates), and was introduced to Councillor E. J. Baxter, Borough A.R.P. Chairman and other officials. He inspected the decontamination centre and the lecture rooms, and was also shown the demonstration gas chamber.

As he was leaving Watford Fields House, the sirens in the town could be heard giving the signal for the "blackout." The darkened streets, with red Hurricane lamps substituted for street lighting

and even the traffic signals masked so that only small crosses of light could be seen, and all neon signs extinguished, gave the town an eerie appearance. The first call by the Inspector General was to the air raid post at 14, Derby-road. *(pic. p.207)*. Normally a gas meter testing depot it was sandbagged effectively and all the A.R.P. workers had tin hats—a surprise feature which caused one of the officials to ask how Watford had managed to get them! The post consisted of an operating room, which had a map of the two or three streets under the control of the post, and a rest room whose furniture included a bed for anyone off duty.

From there Wing Commander Hodsell went to Watford's "nerve-centre"—the control room behind the fire station, with eight telephones and elaborate maps dotted with small flags. He next visited the Car Park Attendant's office *(pic. p.203)* which was the centre of operations of the demolition squads. Operated by ex-Royal Engineers it presented a very business-like appearance, and the Inspector-General was particularly struck with a multi-coloured notice-board which showed at a glance where each section was.

In the car park were the ghostly figures of 100 auxiliary firemen with their four pumps, motorcycle dispatch riders, and a Scammell 'mechanical-horse' fitted for demolition work.

The Inspector was introduced to Superintendent S. Manning, the Chief of Watford's fire service and with him and the Mayor inspected the Auxiliary firemen, expressing his congratulations on their smartness and efficiency.

On his way to the Car Park the Inspector-General had looked into the duty room of Watford Fire Station and had seen the switch which simultaneously sounds all Watford's air raid sirens; these sirens are all electrically connected to the fire alarm system of the town.

At Watford Fields he saw repair squads working at a bomb crater, and at Whippendell-road he paid a brief visit to the depot where squads of workers of the Watford and St.Albans Gas Company and Watford Electricity Works were in readiness for emergency work. He then went on to Watford Baths, where a hut was set on fire and the Fire Brigade called. The fire was quickly extinguished and the ambulance took away three or four casualties. Lastly he visited the first-aid post at Little Nascot, and expressed the opinion that a permanent building was needed for training and use should the occasion arise.

Speaking to an "Observer" representative before leaving Watford, the Inspector General said "Watford put up a very good show. I was particularly impressed with the arrangements for decontamination and rescue work, and the notice-board I saw in the latter centre was the first I have seen in England. I was very impressed with the keenness of everybody. Watford is building up an excellent organisation."

The Watford Borough Control Room was in the Recreation Room of the Fire Station and was in charge of Mr. G. G. Crook (Deputy Borough Treasurer) and was fully staffed. The Postmaster was an interested spectator. This room was fitted with four telephones for incoming calls and four for outgoing calls and wireless. Messengers were in readiness to carry the reports of the "casualties," etc., to the waiting ambulances and fire tenders. Members of the auxiliary fire service drawn up in the car park were inspected.

At No. 1 Whippendell-road an inspection was made of a Rescue and Demolition Party and a Gas Party Squad. In this particular case there were three "casualties," who were quickly removed in an ambulance converted from a Watford Steam Laundry van, to the first-aid post at "The Hut," at Little Nascot. *WO November, 1938*

Opening of the North Watford Odeon, November 27th, 1938.

p.261 b

WATFORD 5912 | WATFORD 5912

ODEON REGD.
NORTH WATFORD

SATURDAY, NOV. 27   DOORS OPEN 7.15
GRAND OPENING CEREMONY
BY
HIS WORSHIP THE MAYOR
(COUNCILLOR T. RIGBY TAYLOR, J.P.)

SUPPORTED BY E. HENRY LOYD, ESQ., D.L., J.P.

SPECIAL ENGAGEMENT OF THE BAND OF

1ST BN. ROYAL SCOTS
THE ROYAL REGIMENT
BANDMASTER : MR. H. C. MACPHERSON
By kind permission of Lt. Col. G. H. HAY, D.S.O., and Officers of the Regt.

ON THE SCREEN—ALL COLOUR PROGRAMME
HENRY FONDA   ANNABELLA
WINGS OF THE MORNING
HOLLYWOOD PARTY   ORPHANS PICNIC
FOX NEWS   (Walt Disney)

BOX OFFICE
for
**OPENING
PERFORMANCE**
OPENS
WED., NOV. 24th
at 2.30 p.m.

**BOOK
EARLY**

A New Incendiary Bomb

Since my last article it has been announced that a new incendiary bomb has been invented. It is called the "kilo-electron" and makes use of the light and extremely inflammable metal, magnesium. It has been stated that the bomb burns at 1,300 degrees centigrade.

They will probably be released some ten or twenty at a time and owing to wind resistance will spread out as they fall. It has been calculated that a bomber flying at 200 miles an hour at 5,000 feet or more and releasing 20 bombs per second, might be able to start a fire over 60 or 70 yards, providing the area was covered by 15 per cent buildings.

Experimental work has been carried out on methods of extinguishing this bomb, but so far the results have not been of any great importance. The use of the water spray is at present being developed. One can stop the bomb penetrating a building by a quarter-inch mild steel plate, one layer of closely packed sandbags, or four inches of reinforced concrete. From these facts it will be seen that the incendiary bomb of the future will be an exceedingly formidable weapon, against which we have at the moment very little defence.

The effects of the high explosive bomb, better known in the services as "H.E.," are the most terrible of all the weapons which can be used from the air. They have been known to weigh as little as 60 lbs., but only few over a ton have been dropped in the world's war zones so far. These bombs have a tremendous power of penetration downwards, and it is difficult to provide a measure of protection against this.

WHP December, 1938

New Town Hall

Sir,—I was a little concerned to see scaffolding erected round the tower of our new Town Hall, and to find that demolition has already started! Certainly it is not a "Thing of beauty," but would have been useful as a factory (if permitted by Town Planning regulations), a block of flats (if not "too many to the acre"), or even a lodging house for Jewish refugee children! It seems a pity not to use it for some purpose, but if demolition is intended to be complete, the site could be laid out as a pleasant public garden. It looked quite nice before they put the building on it.

Yours faithfully,
J. A. WELLER.
WO January, 1939

The New Town Hall Critics

IT is time someone said a good word for Watford's new municipal buildings, and we are going to say it, though, to be candid, the clock turret cannot be described as a thing of beauty; somehow or other it does not seem to fit in with the general design. But to ridicule the structure as a whole, as some of our correspondents have done, and to describe it as "something to shudder at and pass by," or as being suitable for housing Jewish refugee children, is to carry criticism to absurdity. The design was selected as the best in a keen competition, the adjudicator being a well-known architect of great experience. It is not fair to judge the building in its present incomplete state. Tastes differ in architecture, as they do in most things, but it is something to be spared one of the ultra-modern monstrosities which some people admire and rave about. These new municipal buildings will eventually bear comparison with the best erected in recent years in towns of the size of Watford, say the amateur architects what they will. But we should like to see that clock turret reconstructed.

WHP January, 1939

Demonstration of Scammell firefighting equipment mounted on a 3-wheel Mechanical Horse.

Bradshaw Post Office, Bushey Mill Lane, air raid siren not long installed. November, 1938

Cattle Market and Car Park

THOUGH the site of the proposed municipal cattle market for Watford (the old Ballards Building area near Church-street) is not everything to be desired, the advocates of the scheme can certainly make out a strong case. The original idea of the Council was to take a 999 years' lease from Messrs. Fisher at £300 per annum, but this has been altered to a 15 years' lease at the same figure, with an option to purchase for £7,500 at the end of that period. The market would be let to an auctioneer on one day a week for something like £200 per annum, to which has to be added a similar amount for tolls. The loan charges on the cost of the lay-out are estimated at £600 per annum, and at the end of 15 years, when that loan drops out, another for purchase would replace it, and, being for 60 years, the charges would not exceed what had previously been paid. It may be mentioned that the cattle market at St. Albans practically pays for itself, the balance on the wrong side last year being only a few pounds. The probability, therefore, is that the new cattle market will not be an appreciable burden on the rates. Tradesmen in the centre of the town will benefit from the country people visiting the Market, which it is presumed will be held on Tuesday. The only criticism of the scheme offered at Tuesday's Council meeting was that a nuisance would be caused by cattle and sheep being driven through the streets, but nowadays practically all the stock sold in the existing private cattle market held off Stone's-alley is brought in and taken out by carts and lorries.

This cattle market project would probably not have been put forward but for the possibility of combining with a car park available for six days a week. To provide proper access to Church-street the suggestion is to remove the existing mortuary building and to secure an option on the lease of the old National School, at present used for offices, with a view to demolition. In time the whole row of buildings facing the Church may come down. This work, however, may not be undertaken for years to come. Another car park, right in the heart of the town, would serve a useful purpose and leave motorists no excuse for parking in adjacent streets.

WHP January, 1939

7 p.m. Curfew for Market and Shops

FAR-REACHING effects of a bylaw that Watford Town Council propose to adopt, in an endeavour to secure a uniform closing time for large numbers of shops, were discussed at Watford Chamber of Trade's quarterly meeting on Monday. With the exception of certain classes of exempted shops, the bylaw is aimed to secure a general closing time of 7 p.m., and in this category the Council will attempt to include the Borough Market, newsagents, and street vendors of newspapers, &c.

Strenuous opposition from the newsagents was forthcoming at the Chamber of trade's meeting, which was presided over by Alderman H. W. Beall.

The Secretary (Mr. B. J. Andrews) said that a deputation comprising Mr. S. J. Weaver, Mr. H. Buskingham, Mr. L. Ive and Mr. H. Swann would, it was hoped, be received by the Borough Finance Committee on Tuesday. The four points they proposed to raise were: The effect on the market; street vendors; receiving offices; and exhibitions.

Alderman Beall said they would try to see that the order was carried out strictly in every way. At present the hairdressers had kept out, but now they wanted to come in. He had had it more or less brought to him that the hairdressers would like to come in if possible.

He thought the earlier closing would help those who needed more time for A.R.P. duties in Watford.

If the scheme came into force, added Alderman Beall, they wanted it to be universal.

A member referred to confectioners who kept groceries "under the counter," and said this scheme would give those people a good footing.

WO March, 1939

Proposed New By-pass Road

DETAILS of a huge road scheme for by-passing St. Albans, at an estimated cost of 1¾ millions, were given at a Ministry of Transport Inquiry, conducted by Mr. H. Martyn Hooke, at the Town Hall, St. Albans, on Wednesday.

Mr. Rowland Hill (divisional road engineer), who presented the case for the Ministry of Transport, first dealt with the necessity of diverting traffic from St. Albans, through which the London-Holyhead trunk road (A5) and the London-Carlisle trunk road (A6) passes. Consideration was given to the location of a bypass which would take through traffic from both A5 and A6.

The scheme commenced on the A6, just south of Luton. The Watford Spur left the route at its junction with the Leverstock Green-St. Albans road and took a southerly direction by Potters Crouch and passed over the North Orbital-road at Waterdale. It then passed west of Bucknalls, crossed the St. Albans branch of the L.M.S. Railway from Watford, near Mutchetts Wood, and proceeded through the Munden estate to the Watford bypass, which was utilised until it met the A5, south of Elstree. Consideration was being given to the construction of flyovers at several points. The length of new roads to be constructed was 16½ miles, while the North Orbital and Watford bypass roads were to be widened so as to provide duplicate carriageways and cycle tracks for a distance of 5½ miles. The length of trunk roads to be superseded was 26½ miles. The cost of the scheme was estimated at 1¾ million pounds.

WO March, 1939

The Town Hall Critics

SOME months ago we published a number of letters criticising Watford's new Town Hall. The building was likened to a workhouse, a cocoa factory, a block of flats, "something to shudder at and pass by," and suitable only for housing Jewish refugee children. One correspondent, with heavy sarcasm, wrote that it was at all events "a very suitable building to house our worthy Council"! This condemnation was unfair because it was directed against an incomplete building hidden to a great extent by scaffolding. The Town Hall is now practically finished apart from furnishing, and it would be interesting to know if the critics are still of the same opinion. For our part we regard the design of the building and its general appearance as admirable. We make an exception of the clock turret, for which nobody has a good word; surely some improvement could be made here. The surroundings of the Town Hall have been planned with good taste, and altogether Watford has good reason to be proud of the new centre of its municipal life. Possibly the staff will move in before Christmas, but nothing has so far been settled about a formal opening ceremony; the matter is not likely to be discussed until it is possible to gain a clear idea of what the future holds. We are waiting, too, to hear about the proposed sale of the site of the old offices and other Council property which is in the market; the proceeds should be a considerable set-off against the large expenditure on the Town Hall.

WO August, 1939

On November 1st, 1938, the 343rd (Watford) Field Battery of the Herts Territorials was converted into an Anti-Aircraft unit. This is a training session in the use of height finder/predictor.

Watford's Town Hall

IT is understood that Watford's new Town Hall will be formally opened, probably by royalty, early next year. The municipal staff may move in before that date. In the meantime it is announced that the Corporation, through a firm of London agents, are prepared to consider offers for a building lease of the site of the old offices, including the fire station, in High-street. The first idea was to sell the freehold, but, later, it was decided that leasing on 99 years' terms would be more profitable, taking the long view. Little Nascot, the building on the St. Albans-road corner of High-street, now used as public health offices, with a hut serving as a Welfare Centre, will also come onto the market, as a new Centre is to be erected on a site near the Public Library.

The Town Hall is costing Watford £150,000, so that a substantial set-off is very welcome. Some idea of the value of High-street property may be gathered from the fact that recently Messrs. Rogers and Gowlett's shop fetched at auction £546 per foot frontage; even higher figures were realised a few years ago for other property.

WO May, 1939

... further training ...

West Herts Ready For Evacuation

FOLLOWING an announcement by the Ministry of Health yesterday preparations for receiving children and other "priority cases" evacuated from London were set in motion throughout West Herts.

The "Observer" understands that Hertfordshire is to receive 84,000 evacuees. Watford and Bushey are the only towns in this area where there will be no billeting; they are officially termed "neutral zones." In every other town, village and hamlet London school-children with their teachers, and expectant mothers, are to be billeted.

Although not receiving any evacuated children permanently, Watford will be a "distributing" centre. Children will be brought to Watford Junction station and entrained from there to country districts. It is understood that they will come to Watford by bus, coach and tube, and in this connection a considerable portion of the bypass road from Finchley-road to the Elstree roundabout, will be a one-way traffic road for vehicles leaving London. There will be no interference of early morning traffic from Watford stations, but during the day services will be curtailed.

WO August, 1939

and the 79th HAA Regt., TA, ready to move off to camp for a month's training.   June 1939

London evacuees; for these Watford was a reception and distribution centre; a short rest and meal break at the Labour Club premises before making for new 'homes' in the area.

Others changed trains for Kings Langley and Boxmoor.

Delivery of Anderson Shelter components.

The A.R.P. Problem

IT was reported at the meeting of Watford Town Council on Tuesday evening that £1,279 is being paid out in wages each week to workers in A.R.P. services in the Borough. This works out at over £66,000 per annum, or nearly £200,000 if the war should last three years. Though this sum may not be so large as in some places, it is sufficiently alarming, and when it is remembered that expenditure on this scale is being incurred all over the country it will be seen what a vast drain on the national resources is involved. For the time being the Government will repay the whole cost on personnel to the local authorities, but that is little consolation to the taxpayers. The wage bill at Watford includes £463 for the auxiliary fire service; and, as Councillor Baxter (Chairman of the A.R.P. Committee) pointed out, another six men are wanted before the Home Office requirements are reached. He said that the Committee were out to save money wherever possible, and no doubt in some cases voluntary service will be substituted for paid service.

WHP October, 1939

The British-made Ensign cameras were popular but even at these seemingly low prices needed a week's work to obtain one, hence the '12 months at 5/9d'! The Leica had been joined by the Zeiss Contax in the 'system' class; and by the Kodak 'Retina' and Agfa 'Karat' in a simplified pocket-camera style. For the serious workers, the Rolleiflex and Rolleicord, introduced in 1928, began to help establish reputations.

V

The Missing Years, 1   1939-1945

The possibility of the introduction of the Sunday Cinema occupied the thoughts of many residents during 1938. Sunday opening had been discussed at Council level over a number of years. The Council voted 'no', the majority of Watfordians voted 'yes'.

The clouds of war were gathering in Europe as the concept of air raid precautions was implemented in this country. Prime Minister Neville Chamberlain met with Adolf Hitler to try to avert the impending disaster as the Fuehrer's well-rehearsed military machine became more agressive. Chamberlain thought he had concluded a pact which would ensure a long-lasting peace. Many of Britain's leaders thought otherwise and the belated re-armament programme was accelerated especially in regard to the production of a new genre of aircraft. The League of Nations with its many branches throughout the land still worked for a peaceful solution throughout the turbulent 30's right up to 1939 but Hitler's racial hatred and territorial ambitions were not to be deterred. In spite of his promises he attacked Poland at the beginning of September 1939. Great Britain honoured its commitments not knowing that Hitler had released demoniac forces which, before they were expurgated, were destined to kill more than 53 million people world-wide in just a few years.

When war was declared both old and young were involved. Veterans were re-called to the Colours, and conscripted young men to the local call-up centres. Rationing was slow to be applied but gas masks were quickly distributed, for who could believe Hitler would wage a conventional war. The rate of conscription was speeded up and some women were directed to the armed forces or the Land Army. Those beyond their fighting years became the backbone of the Royal Observer Corps, the Fire Services, and Home Guard, and many women joined the Women's Voluntary Service.

Conscripts and volunteers, trained in unfamiliar and often remote parts of the country, were posted overseas to places they would otherwise never have seen. Unemployment fell below the 2-million figure of 1931 to less than 1.5 million and for the first time poverty as an ordained way of life was confounded by a rationing system that ensured an adequate amount of food and clothing could be bought with money earned by regular work.

As early as 1942 women realised they were receiving women's wages for doing mens' work and it was not forgotten. The exciting prospect of the newly conceived Beveridge Plan (November 1942) became the widespread hope for the future. The report was the greatest single influence on the making of the Welfare State, it tackled the problems of health, education, housing and unemployment. The days of the Friendly Societies were numbered. The hope was even expressed that economic planning would be made to help the country out of the inevitable years of post-war depression.

Many local men were called up at the beginning of hostilities and served a full six years in the services seeing little or nothing of their home town. Those who served their full overseas tour not only saw little of Watford but also little of the country for which they were fighting.

The photographs between pages 194 and 221 inclusive were taken by Greville's, which local studio had contracted to provide 'news' photographs for the Watford Observer as the newspaper employed no photographic staff at that time.

Fortunately these photographs have survived. Apart from the odd 'snapshot', little in the way of pictorial evidence of the period is available for reasons which deserve explanation. The armed services received most of the film stock and allied photographic products, and only a little was released for amateur use. Professionals were allocated a proportion of their pre-war consumption and, with an increasing demand for portraits to give to loved ones, very little film and printing paper was used to record local views and events.

Throughout the days of 'hard slog' on the home front, aggravated by rationing, blackout, and fuel shortages; and for serving men and women boredom, danger and hardship; there was a common bond of friendship and the will to help others in every bodys' hour of need. There also existed the will to win.

The news of victory by the Allies in Europe was received with intense relief tinged with horror and disbelief at the exposure of the atrocities perpetrated by the Nazis. In August 1945, Japan surrendered under the additional presure of the atomic bomb, and after nearly six years the war was over.

Council to Erect Shelters

OF the 12,000 "Anderson" shelters to be provided free to householders in Watford, the Borough Council estimate that 4,000 cannot be erected by the recipients owing to physical incapacity or other reasons, and at a special meeting of the Council on Tuesday it was agreed to exercise the necessary powers to enable the Council to erect these shelters at a cost that may run into nearly £30,000. Of this some nine or ten thousand pounds will fall on local ratepayers. The Civil Defence Committee and the Town Clerk were given exceptional powers in order to avoid delay.

WHP July, 1939

Now Do You Want a Shelter?

Only a few weeks ago the "Post" told the story of the delivery of the first Anderson steel air raid shelters.

More than a few people due to receive them refused for some reason or another—some did not want to spoil their gardens; others did not want the trouble of erecting them, and perhaps a few did not like to advertise the fact that their income was less than the prescribed amount.

Most of those who refused are now regretting it and applying for delivery again. Some are even complaining of delay, but these will have to wait their turn again. Everyone wants a shelter now, and there is possibility that Watford Council may take away any shelters that have been lying about, not in position, for more than a week and deliver them to persons who require them.

Not until deliveries for the free list have been completed—and some 2,500,000 come into this category—will those who intend to pay be accommodated.

It might be added that the Council have power to make an advance to any householder who wishes to buy a shelter but cannot afford the full outlay immediately. *WHP September, 1939*

Profoundly Touched

Sir.—As head teacher of one of the evacuated London schools, may I express on behalf of my colleagues and myself, our most grateful thanks to all the people of Kings Langley for the way in which they have received our children and their teachers.

We could never have believed that we should meet with so much kindness. From the voluntary workers who took charge of our weary children so sympathetically on arrival—to the new "uncles" and "aunts" who opened their homes to them so willingly and spared no thought or effort to make them at once part of their own families—everyone seemed possessed with the same spirit of kindliness and the desire to help. We shall never forget our reception here—we have, indeed, been profoundly touched.

A LONDON HEAD TEACHER.

WHP September, 1939

When the Sirens Sounded

SUCH a complete surprise was the air raid warning on Sunday morning that in many parts of Watford the house-holders, instead of making for shelter as they had been instructed, congregated in the streets to converse with neighbours. Some took little notice, fancying that the signal was just a rehearsal, but many in central Watford who took the warning more seriously were considerably alarmed when a warden in one area mistakenly rang a handbell for the "raiders passed" signal. Realising that the ringing of a handbell had some connection with gas, but forgetting that it was the "gas all cleared" signal a number of persons rushed for their gas masks and took shelter.

WHP September, 1939

Sand bag filling for protection of the ARP post in the Shrubberies car park. Showing at the Gaumont was Will Hay in 'Ask a Policeman' and Basil Rathbone in 'Hound of the Baskervilles'. *p.247 b, 336 t.*
2nd September, 1939

HMS Courageous was built in 1917 and converted to an aircraft carrier to handle a complement of 40 aircraft. It was not at strength at the time of sinking on 17th September but its loss was an early shock. This scene at Dudley's Corner (Clarendon Road/High Street). So soon after the start of war greengrocers (here, Walton's) had an ample stock of fruits, including later-to-a-vague-memory—bananas. Bateman's, opticians, had windows covered criss-cross with tape to prevent flying glass in event of bomb blast.

The Approach of Rationing

NOW that the National Register is virtually complete and the 40,000,000 rationing cards are being made out for distribution, we may expect rationing to be in force in the latter part of this month. In view of all the difficulties, especially in regard to transport, that war has caused, there has been remarkably little delay. Nor has there been any serious shortage of any foodstuffs, except perhaps bacon in some districts. If we remember the strain thrown upon rail and road traffic by the transport of an army of 158,000 men to France with all its modern equipment, to say nothing of the supplies required by the Navy and the Air Force, we may wonder that civilian life has been so little disturbed. When rationing comes into force, we may count upon each household and each district getting a fair share of the foodstuffs, few in number, that will at first be controlled. There is no need to suppose that the national stocks are inadequate—the contrary is the truth—but at the outset of what may be a long war the Government is right in taking full precautions against even a temporary shortage anywhere.

WHP November, 1939

203

Watford Fire Brigade's second Scammell fire engine; there is a proposition to build a new fire station, costing £25,000, in Nascot Road.

Air-raid precaution exercises, Shrubberies car park..

Women manning watch-room at the fire station.

AIR RAID PRECAUTIONS

BOROUGH OF WATFORD
FIRE BRIGADE

The Chief Officer of the Fire Brigade requests Householders to PLACE BUCKETS OF WATER OUTSIDE THEIR FRONT DOORS AT NIGHT. This would ensure a sufficient supply of water to enable Wardens or Stirrup Pump Parties to get to work immediately and in many cases enable a fire to be quickly extinguished before much damage is done.

S. B. MANNING,
Chief Officer Fire Brigade.

● *The 'Nascot Road' suggestion was an alternative to a Radlett Road site. War intervened before these plans could be furthered. Just prior to outbreak of war the Government formed the 'Auxiliary Fire Service' and, locally, volunteers were trained by the W.F.B.'s full-time professional firemen. In 1941 the A.F.S. was disbanded and replaced by the National Fire Service which lasted until 1948.*

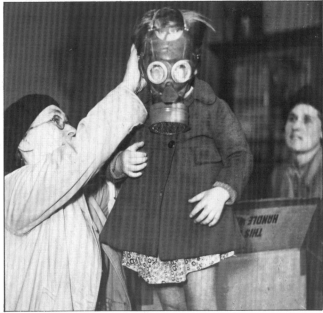

Fitting child's respirator.

At Chater School, preparation for issuing ration books.

The new Town Hall had been substantially completed for some time at the outbreak of war. Many buildings not fully utilised were requisitioned for war use. It is stated that to avoid this happening to the Town Hall the Mace Bearer's flat was 'occupied'. Some departments had moved in and the first Council meeting, at which Alderman L. H. Andrews was elected mayor, took place on 9th November 1939. The 'official' opening took place on 5th January 1940; here, the Countess of Clarendon speaking.

Town Hall opening

WITH befitting ceremonial, Watford's new Town Hall was officially opened on Friday afternoon, the ceremony taking place in the large assembly room. The Municipal Buildings, standing at the corner of Rickmansworth and Hempstead-roads, and costing about £186,000, have taken two years to erect, the foundation stone being laid in May, 1938. Based on a modernised version of Georgian tradition, the buildings are from a design by Mr. C. Cowles-Voysey, the contractors being Messrs. Richard Costain, Ltd. The assembly hall has seating accommodation on the floor for about 1,300 people, and a further 300 in the gallery, while there is a capacious stage with seats in tiers.

It was a great disappointment that the Earl of Clarendon (Charter Mayor of Watford) was unable, owing to indisposition, to fulfil his promise to perform the ceremony, this duty being graciously undertaken in his absence by the Countess of Clarendon, who was accompanied by her daughter, Lady Joan Newman. Representatives of neighbouring boroughs and other local authorities attended, and in the hall were representatives of all departments of the town's activities, with burgesses and many others from adjoining districts. The Member of Parliament for the Watford Division (Sir Dennis Herbert) and the Chairman of the Herts County Council (Sir David Rutherford) were on the platform.

WO 12th January, 1940

205

... Dunkirk. The wounded arrive ...

In a few short months Europe is over-run; Denmark, Holland, Belgium and France conquered and occupied.

40,000 British and French troops are trapped in Belgium but by an unexplained act the German advantage is not immediately exploited and in ten days, with sunny weather and calm seas, a rearguard action halts the Germans long enough for 330,000 troops to be evacuated by 'little ships' off the beaches of Dunkirk.

Britain stands alone whilst the horrors of Nazi-dominated life start for the newly-conquered and vanquished.

The Battle of Britain commences; every Spitfire and Hurricane is desparately needed and used sparingly. Against overwhelming odds the 'few' repulse attack after attack against airfields, in Hitler's effort to cripple the Air Force. When the Germans are almost to the point of success they change tactics and start to bomb London and other cities. The airfields are saved to be patched up to continue the fight.

Britain's solitary 'finest hours' had passed and Hitler had had his first defeat.

Dunkirk—May 1940
Battle of Britain—June to Sept. 1940

Urgency

There is a freshening spirit in the Government and the people of Britain. The first German bombs have fallen on English soil—the first drops of the shower of steel that Hitler has threatened. German troops are only 25 miles from the coast of Kent. German parachutists must be expected at any moment from now on. Britain faces the most formidable trial in her history without despondency or alarm.

Picture Post, May 1940

B.E.F. Wounded Are Here

WE make an urgent appeal to everyone, not only in Watford, but in the whole of the district served by this newspaper, to come to the immediate aid of wounded men of the B.E.F., who have been arriving in Watford in their hundreds since the gallant evacuation of Boulogne and Dunkirk.

Many hospital trains laden with their maimed and broken human freight have been arriving almost daily at the station. Here their field dressings, many of which are, of necessity, rough and improvised, are supplemented before the men are placed in the waiting ambulances which convey them to the various base hospitals distributed throughout the county. Owing to the very nature of their wounds, the importance of these heroes receiving immediate attention on their arrival cannot be emphasised too greatly, but such attention requires suitable materials for bandages, pads, etc.

Here, then, is where we call upon your sympathy and gratitude which can be shown in a practical manner by supplying these men with a few comforts.

WHP June, 1940

Watford's Century of Printing

AT a meeting of the Guild of Young Printers, in connection with the Watford Branch of the Typographical Association, held in the Oddfellows (Small) Hall on Friday evening, Mr. David Greenhill, of the Sun Engraving Company, gave a very interesting lecture on "Printing and its Development in Watford." Going back to its earliest days Mr. Greenhill recalled that John Peacock was the first Watford printer. He started as a printer, bookbinder and cardmaker somewhere about 1800 or just after at premises where High-street Station now stands. In the Public Library there is a poor-rate book, dated 1834, with the imprint "Peacock, Printer, Watford," and in the "Observer" office there is still an American hand-press dated 1820. The firm possess many specimens of work done in these early days. John Peacock was followed by his son Samuel, who in 1863 established the "Observer," the offices then being in Queen's-road near the old Library. Samuel died in 1880, and his elder son, Thomas J. Peacock carried on on behalf of his mother. At the mother's death in 1893 Thomas sold his interest to his younger brother, Charles Herbert Peacock, who then became proprietor, and ran the business very successfully till his death in 1930, since when his son, Kim Peacock has been director and manager. Mr. Kim Peacock, who has taken a great interest in modernising the plant and in improving the "Observer," had been assisted by at least two, and possibly some other very able men. The two referred to were Mr. F. H. Barnes, the editor, to whom he was indebted for the forgoing information, and Mr. W. J. Tamplin, who largely ran the works side of the business.

When he came to Watford, some 35 years ago, Mr. Greenhill said, the "Observer" office was prominent among the small number of printers.

So far as he could remember there were:
Bemrose and Sons, who had the works at Milton-street, North Watford, now used by Messrs. Novobax Ltd. *(Waterlows.)*
Acme Engraving Co., process engravers and printers, who were in Acme-road, near Bemroses.
Mr. Edward Voss, in Loates-lane.
Mr. T. C. Warren, of the "Record" Printing Works.
Mr. Michael (who was father to Percy D. Michael, the Home Counties Alliance Secretary), in Queen's-road, and who later joined Mr. Voss.
Castle and Parker, of 151, High-street.
Mr. J. E. King, of 42, High-street.
Messrs. Curtis Bros., of King-street.
Messrs. Stone and Cox, who started about 1904/5.

André and Sleigh, of Bushey, who made a great reputation for fine engraving and later for fine colour printing, started about 1890.

There was also a Mr. Ashworth, who started in partnership with Mr. Meredith in 1901. He began at Bushey, and then moved to Clarendon-road in 1906. In 1902 Mr. Ashworth made the first colour process engraving for the cover of "The Motor," and he believed he had continued to do them ever since. Mr. Ashworth still kept his flag flying in Fleet-street, London, and must be nearing the three score years and ten!

With regard to the more recent development of printing in Watford, Mr. Greenhill gave the following short summary of dates:
1914.—Sun Engraving Company Ltd. developed from Anglo-Engraving Co. and André and Sleigh, of Bushey, in 1914, and in 1918 took over the works in Whippendell-road, formerly owned by the Menpes Press. As you will probably know, the Menpes Press was a rather beautifully built and very well designed printing factory, planned by Mr. Geo. W. Jones, the eminent printer.

1918-1919.—Hudson and Stracey. Mr. Hudson was at the Menpes Press when the "Sun" took over.
1919.—Bournehall Press.—Mr. Lewis Blower now had a very nicely equipped plant doing very good work.
1919.—Gibbs and Bamforth Ltd. started in Watford by purchasing the "West Herts Post" and the "Watford Newsletter," and combining them into one paper.
1924-25.—Davey and Winterson started a small business in North Watford.
1926.—Messrs. Greycaines started in Watford.
1929.—Messrs. F. E. Blower and Co. took over Mr. Warren's business—the old "Record" office.
1935.—Messrs. Edsons (Printers) Ltd. came from Stoke Newington and built a very nice modern factory, very well equipped, and now doing a very good standard of work.
1936.—The great firm of **Odhams Ltd.,** came to Watford and started Odhams (Watford) Ltd.
1936.—The Chiltern Printing Works started in Clarendon-road.

WO July, 1940

Hertfordshire Police

After World War I the trickle of road accidents became a flood. In 1927 fifty-seven people were killed on Hertfordshire roads, in 1936 this figure rose to seventy-five and in 1939 the total was 101. The figure has remained around 100 ever since.

New Printing Machine

Watford Town Council on Tuesday decided to buy a multilith printer and accessories from the Addressograph Multigraph Co., Ltd., at a cost of £564 3. 8d., on which to print all the Council minutes and printing work.

In discussing the question of economy, Councillor' E. J. Baxter mentioned the proposed spending of £560 on the machine, and suggested that it might be wise to ascertain how the operators might be affected by rules of the Typographical Association or any other printing union.

Council E. T. Warren replied that movable type was not used. This was simply a duplicating machine.

Councillor F. Williams stated that at first he thought here was the Council trying to economise and then they were going to spend £565, but looking further one realised that sometimes it was necessary to spend money to economise.

Councillor Williams asked for an assurance that all the printing of each department would be done on the one machine.

Alderman J. Evans (Chairman of the Finance Committee) said that the Town Clerk suggested the purchase of the duplicating machine from his experience at his previous appointment. The Commitee had seen the machine working and it seemed to turn out very fine work. They would make a considerable saving. At the present time the printing of the minutes cost £490 a year. They could duplicate them for half that amount.

The whole of the printing would be under the Town Clerk's department.

The machine would pay for itself in a year or two.

WHP September, 1940

Corporation as Pig-keepers

WATFORD TOWN COUNCIL are about to start a scheme for the collection of pig food. Householders are to be asked to keep in a receptacle separate from the dust-bin all sorts of food scraps, which will be collected by the dustmen. The Council are buying two 60-gallon boiling pans, and intend to increase the number of pigs on the Corporation farm. Surplus food will be sold. The dustmen are to be paid 1s. per cwt. on the quantity they bring in, and it would seem that the experiment will have to be a big success if this outlay is to be covered. At Tottenham the salvage is run on different lines. The dustmen have themselves formed a Pig Club. They have erected piggeries in their spare time on vacant land at the refuse disposal works, and have acquired a herd of 42 pigs. For these they already have ample food and are selling tons of surplus. The vehicles are equipped with pig-food containers, and it is anticipated that the weekly surplus will soon be 20 to 30 tons. Watford Corporation have had a pig farm for many years. The Farm Bailiff has specialised in show specimens, and has been a very successful exhibitor at leading shows. He knows his business and there is no reason why, in a short time, he should not have a large utility herd under his control, besides preserving the strain he has made famous.

WO January, 1940

Getting Fit For Service

On Wednesday evening 230 Watford men responded to the "Fitness for Service" campaign organised on Watford Football ground by the Central Council of Recreative Physical Training and the Football Association. Our picture shows Mr. S. F. Rous (secretary of the F.A.) discussing plans with local officials. Left to right: Alderman J. Evans and Mr. W. Findlay (Watford F.C.), Mr. Rous, Mr. H. Richardson (County Physical Training Organiser), and Councillor T. Rigby Taylor (Chairman of Watford F.C.).

WO July, 1940

How Watford Hospital Has Grown

The last annual meeting of the Watford Peace Memorial Hospital as an unincorporated body was held yesterday. Although the actual incorporation took place in February, a resolution was required at the annual meeting to regularise certain matters arising from the incorporation and this was duly passed.

Sir John Caulcutt, the Chairman, commenting on the annual report, which has already appeared in the "West Herts Post," said that one or two useful comments could be made. The Peace Memorial Hospital was opened in 1925, and a report published in March, 1927, showed that at that time there were 87 beds in the hospital. In that year 1,126 in-patients were treated at a cost of £10,600.

Since that time, further accommodation was found necessary, and in 1937 the hospital possessed 154 beds, while the annual cost was by then £25,000. When the work now in hand was completed the number would be 308.

Up till 1937 the Committee had made both ends meet in regard to maintenance. But for the last three years there had been respective deficits of £1,908, £1,492 and £1,480. This was partly due to the increased cost of medical stores, which in many cases had gone up almost 50 per cent.

A total of £145,000 had been provided by people in Watford in order that the hospital might be built, furnished and carried on.

Since the outbreak of war, the Board of Management had been very much alive to its responsibilities towards the town. They had been doing all they could to increase the accommodation with the result that two shell wards would soon be available.

WHP July, 1940

Pig food collection, Holywell Farm. At this time the weekly collection amounted to some 10 tons of waste food.   1940

Stanley Rous inaugurates a 'Fitness for Service' campaign at Watford football ground.   *p.350 tl*   1940

Wardens' Corps Efficiency Presentation, ARP post at corner of Loates Lane/Derby Road. Kingham's warehouse in the background.   1940

207

Slow Fund Support Criticised

Strong criticism of Watford's support of the Spitfire Fund was made at the meeting of Watford Town Council on Tuesday, and summing up his speech, Alderman H. Coates said: "If we don't get the amount required in the next three weeks or month Watford should be ashamed of itself."

Councillor S. W. Smith raised the matter. He said that the last amount published was £1,500. That figure, compared with collections in Watford in the past, would be considered stimulating, but when they compared it with the figure required it was a long distance off.

To raise the sum of £6,000 would mean a widespread, well-organised and highly concentrated effort with all possible initiative put into it. He had received letters disparaging the organisation of the scheme.

The Mayor stated that the total was now £1,650. The money was coming in slower than he anticipated, but it was coming in steadily.

There were several things they hoped would bring in reasonable sums. An auction at the Town Hall for which they required gifts, a dance, a boxing tournament, etc.

He did want, he said, more subscriptions direct from the public, and if possible some substantial ones.

Alerman Coates said that it was a very unsatisfactory response that only £1,650 should be raised in five weeks. It was unfortunate that Watford could not be aroused to the enthusiasm of many towns. It was a shame that this effort had not been considered worthy of the people.

Why are not the people of Watford ready to go out and say to their friends, 'Let us do something for the fund.' It should be sufficient that the Mayor is at the head of the Fund. Everyone should feel it his duty to get on with it."

Alderman Coates recalled that during his Mayoralty he made a special appeal for the Hospital. He expected £5,000 at least. It was depressing to find that only £750 was given.

No matter what it was, there had been a lack of enthusiasm among the people of Watford. Watford looked upon itself as a dormitory town, and that the residents came here to sleep.

"I would like people to come here and wake up," he continued.

He hoped, he went on, that a very big effort would be made.

WHP November, 1940

The New Police Court

ERECTED at a cost of £70,000, Watford's new Police Court was formally opened this week. For some 80 years the local Magistrates have shared the building in King-street with the County Court, the police headquarters being a short distance away. Now, the administration, including that of the Magistrates' Clerk, is centralised in Clarendon-road. In quite a central position, the new building is a worthy addition to the public institutions of the Borough. It is admirably designed to meet a need that had become more pressing as the population grew. Fortunately the scheme was too far advanced to be affected by the outbreak of war.

There are doubtless older inhabitants of Watford who remember the primitive police station situated in one of the yards off Lower High-street. The next move was to premises in Estcourt-road, later occupied as the Weights and Measures office. The King-street station was erected about half-a century ago, and had become just about as inconvenient and incommodious as the old Municipal building in High-street.

WHP October, 1940

BUY FURNITURE NOW! DELAY IS UNWISE

OAK BEDROOM SUITE, finished medium Jacobean colour, consisting of 4ft. Wardrobe, with shelf inside, 3ft. Dressing Chest, containing 3 drawers and triple mirrors, and 3-drawer Chest.

£7'10'0

Owing to Government requirements, timber for new Furniture is almost impossible to obtain. Stocks will be difficult to replace. Prices are steadily rising. BUY YOUR FURNITURE NOW!

BARGAINS IN WHITEWOOD

The whole extensive stock of useful and inexpensive Furniture for all purposes is offered at low prices.

THREE-PIECE SUITE, consisting of Settee and two Easy Chairs. Constructed on strong, well-seasoned frames. Upholstered in various coloured, hard-wearing Tapestries.

£9'18'6

JAMES CAWDELL & CO.   **Phone 4404**

The Canal Towpath

FOR a considerable time negotiations have been proceeding between Berkhamsted Urban Council and the Grand Union Canal Company with regard to the public right-of-way along the canal towpath, and it is satisfactory to note that a compromise has now been reached. The Council agree to take no further action to remove the Company's notice boards prohibiting the use by the public of the tow path, and the Company, on their part, will grant an irrevocable permission of use. Watford Town Council and other local authorities through whose districts the canal passes are parties to the agreement, but the credit must go to Berkamsted. In the first instance Mr. E. V. Thompson, when chairman of the Citizens Association, took the matter up and has since been a delegate, with others, to the Company, who, for their part, showed quite an amicable spirit in receiving representations.

The canal, the name of which was changed from the Grand Junction to the Grand Union, passes through some of the most lovely scenery in West Herts. It enters the county at Marsworth, and the summit level there is the highest water level in England. Passing Berkhamsted, it runs through Kings Langley, the Grove and Cassiobury Park and on to Rickmansworth, and so through to Middlesex, entering the Thames near Brentford. Construction was begun in 1792, and the canal was opened in 1805.

WO February, 1940

£85 Expenses on Spitfire Fund

THE Deputy Mayor (Alderman L. H. Andrews), during whose Mayoralty the Watford Spitfire Fund was launched, is deeply concerned regarding the fact that the Fund having reached £5,001 has the not inconsiderable sum of £85 to pay in respect of expenses incurred. These include printing, postages and many other items which always accrue.

Alderman Andrews has appealed to us to give the necessary publicity to this fact, hoping that when once it is appreciated that Watford's own Spitfire is almost within grasp, the public will respond and see to it that Lord Beaverbrook has Watford's cheque for the full amount in his possession in the shortest possible time, particularly in view of the fact that it is now five months since the Fund was inaugurated.

The Deputy Mayor might like to know that we have good reason for believing that if, say, £50 or £60 is subscribed by the public, a certain well-known local gentleman will provide the balance of the amount outstanding. This is an extremely generous gesture, for we know that this person has already made a liberal gift to the Fund.

We have it on good authority that if the public make a good response to this final appeal, the Fairy Godfather will do the rest.

All subscriptions should be addressed: Mayor's Spitfire Fund, Town Hall, Watford.

WHP December, 1940

Simple-Minded People

Sir,—A few days ago a man remarked: "Oh, well, if the Germans win, at any rate I have my pension and they can't touch that."

There is reason to believe that there are other simple-minded people in Watford who are similarly deceived. Can nothing be done to convince these that if so appalling a catastrophe as a German victory should overtake us, pensions and every other source of income would cease to be available. We should simply be slaves, entirely under the control, in every department of our lives, of the Germans. Everyone would be compelled to work for whatever wages and during whatever hours the Nazi rulers might dictate.

C. CARR.

WHP December, 1940

Two Games on Christmas Day

It was decided on Tuesday afternoon that Watford and Luton will meet twice on Christmas Day.

The match at Watford will take place in the morning at Vicarage-road, kick-off 11 a.m., and at Luton in the afternoon.

Watford and Luton are the first clubs to decide to play both fixtures on the same day. Many other clubs are likely to follow their lead.

The decision of Luton to agree to the double fixture is welcomed by Mr. William Findlay, Watford F.C. manager, who is responsible for the idea.

On Monday, when a decision had not yet been reached by the Luton directors, Mr. Findlay pointed out to me that the cancellation of Boxing Day football means that Luton would play Watford at Vicarage-road on Christmas Day, a large crowd would be certain to congregate—in all events the largest of the season—and Luton would derive half the gate-money. On the other hand, had this return fixture in the afternoon not been arranged, Watford would not have had the opportunity of reaping in 50 per cent. of the takings at Luton

WHP December, 1940

Death of Mr. James Cawdell

WE regret to announce the death, at the age of 73, of Mr. James Cawdell, of 17, Rickmansworth-road, Watford, who 37 years ago established the draper's business in High-street, which is still carried on in his name.

In 1904 he bought the business of the late Mr. George Longley in Watford, and, with the encouragement of his late wife, developed it from the days when Mr. and Mrs. Cawdell lived over the shop and had only 14 assistants, until 1924, when the turnover was six times greater and they had 50 assistants.

In the days when Mr. Cawdell was in business the cattle market was still held in the Market-place, and occasionally sheep and cattle rushed through the entrance of his shop.

In 1929, in view of his rapidly increasing business, Mr. Cawdell bought from Trust Houses Ltd., the Essex Arms Hotel, one of the largest hotels in Watford, whose premises included the old Corn Exchange, which had been converted into a dance hall. With the buildings he had to acquire the publican's licence of the premises, and for four months, until he allowed it to lapse at the next Brewster Sessions, he was actually a licensed victualler as well as a draper. In that year he converted the firm into a private limited company, and went into partnership with Mr. David Greenhill, under the name of James Cawdell and Co., Ltd. The new firm demolished the existing shop and hotel, and on its site built the present large store in the Market-place. Mr. Cawdell remained in active association with the firm as managing director until 1935, when he retired from business life.

WO February, 1941

Bomb-damaged All Saints Church, Croxley Green

. . . St. Johns Road

. . . Rosary Priory, Caldecote Towers, Bushey.

209

53rd South West Herts (St. Peters) Scouts group, Bushey Mill Lane, scrap metal collection . . .

. . . and waste paper salvage collection.   1940

The Air Raids

During the period of the blitz upon London, a considerable number of enemy planes crossed and dropped bombs upon Watford and the surrounding district. All incidents were recorded; many were of unexploded bombs which, nevertheless, had to be dealt with. Falling anti-aircraft shells added to the incident roll.

The main incidents during 1940 and 1941 were: 27th September 1940, fires started at Greycaine's and an unexploded bomb in Sandringham Road; October, damage in Souldern Street; 31st October 1940, house wrecked in Cassiobury Park Avenue; 16th November 1940, house wrecked in Tudor Avenue; 5th December 1940, damage in St. Johns Road, five dead; 9th December 1940, damage in Eastlea Avenue, 4 killed and 2 injured; 2nd January 1941, incendiary damage to Trewin's store; 17th January 1941, damage in Norfolk Avenue, four injured; 30th January 1941, three injured in Park Avenue; 15th March 1941, damage in Crossmead, 7 casualties.

After this period of activity attacks a parachute bomb was dropped near the top of Scots Hill on 17th February 1944; on 16th June 1944 a flying bomb caused damage near Rosecroft Drive and on 26th June 1944 in Oxhey Lane. The last incident was in the early hours of Sunday morning, 30th July 1944, when a flying bomb damaged 50 houses beyond repair in Sandringham Road, 100 severely and 500 to a lesser degree. 40 people were killed and many more injured.

More bombs fell in wooded and open areas, causing little or no damage. There is no evidence of 'planned' attacks upon the area or upon particular targets.

Cassiobury Park Avenue, and (above) Tudor Avenue.

Park Avenue.   January 1941

Queens Road; incendiary bomb hit on Trewins. Nearly two years into the war paper shortages were not yet serious; newspapers were still of fair size and unlike a few years later, published a number of photographs.

Via neutral countries, the enemy could still get British newspapers which were then methodically scanned to glean information about effectiveness of air attacks. To counter this, no photographs could be published which included town or store name. In this photograph, the legend 'Trewins' was obliterated by the censor and only careful recent work on the original plate reveals it—for the first time!

In addition, stories were delayed and place names identified as 'a town in the Home Counties . . .'

p.167, 305t, 310c

War Weapons Weeks

THIS district of Hertfordshire is at length coming into line with other parts of the country in organising War Weapons Weeks. A start was made at Bushey on Monday evening by the decision to make an effort from March 22 to 29, and a figure of £100,000 has been mentioned as the goal. Rickmansworth, on Wednesday, fixed as the period April 12 to 19, aiming at a similar amount. In each case the local authority is giving active support. Committees representative of local industries, banks, schools, British Legion, W.V.S., and Savings Groups have been formed and organisers appointed.

In Watford, which we should have liked to see taking the lead in such a vital movement, the date we have heard suggested is April 19 to 26, which appropriately enough, will include St. George's Day, with a quarter of a million sterling as the minimum. To ensure success a much more vigorous organisation will be required than that behind the long-drawn-out and only partially successful Spitfire Fund. Given a bold lead, with enterprising and effective management, no doubt need be entertained as to the ultimate result of such a popular contribution to the national war effort.

WO February, 1941

The Toll of the Road

ACCORDING to a police report presented to the County Council this week, 824 road accidents occurred in Hertfordshire last quarter. Of these, 23 proved fatal, as against 14 in the corresponding period of last year. Eleven people were killed by careless or dangerous driving, and seven pedestrians met their death through carelessness on their own part. This toll of the road is very disquieting, and raises the question whether Magistrates are sufficiently severe on motorists whose guilt is clearly proved.

How far the returns are affected by the blackout in the winter months is not shown, but undoubtedly night driving in pitch darkness with war-time lights is a contributory cause. Another factor is the recklessness to which some drivers of Army lorries are addicted. On the other hand, the complaint of motorists about "jay" walkers is proved by the statistics to be well founded. Pedestrian crossings are often ignored, and it is common for people to step straight on to the road without troubling to look for on-coming traffic, or, if they do look, to do so one way only. The rules of "safety first" are thus forgotten, often with lamentable results. The authorities will sooner or later be forced to take more drastic steps than any they have hitherto taken to deal with this question of road accidents.

WO May, 1941

PUBLIC NOTICES

PRELIMINARY ANNOUNCEMENT

WATFORD WAR WEAPONS WEEK

APRIL 26 to MAY 3

OUR AIM is —

HALF A MILLION for a DESTROYER H.M.S. WATFORD

211

Eastlea Avenue.   9th December 1940

Thanks A Million

Watford and District War Weapons Week ended on Saturday and with the termination of this greatest of savings campaigns disappear any doubts—if there were any—that the public would rise to the occasion.

At the inaugural war weapons meeting held five weeks ago, a target of £500,000 was the aim. Most people were of the opinion that it was a modest sum, but despite optimism there were few who conscientiously believed that Watford's effort would reach the final enormous figure of £1,275,629, a sum equal to £12 7s. 8d. per head of the population.

The result is a tribute to local patriotism, proof of public confidence in the Government, and what is even more outstanding, it reveals the unity of purpose existing in the country—for in unity lies strength, and in a strong and well armed Britain lies the assurance of a Victory which will bring with it the dawn of an era of Peace in our time, and, we hope, in our children's lifetime.

WHP May, 1941

Watford Grammar Schools

MRS. WHEELWRIGHT, a Watford member of Herts County Council, speaking at a meeting of the local Rotary Club, revived the Watford Grammar Schools controversy, which has been more or less dormant since 1935. It will be recalled that when the Governors applied for a capital grant of some £18,000 for a pavilion they were told that such a grant could only be made on condition that the Schools were transferred to the County Council. The Governors would not forego their trust, and in this decision were practically unanimously supported by the townspeople, a public meeting showing how strongly local opinion had been aroused by the suggestion. At that time Mrs. Wheelwright ran counter to the general feeling in the Borough, and now talks about the Schools being left out of the post-war educational programme. They have, however, gone along very well since the County ultimatum was presented and, in any event, the war has put any new building out of the question.

The County Council do not allege that the Watford Grammar Schools have been badly managed, or that the standard of education is not as high as that at any similar school in the country. They object to the Governors not being completely under their control: in other words, they want to be sole masters. Local pride in the foundation they dismiss as mere sentiment. To their standardised minds it is nothing that the Schools date back well over two centuries, that the founder, Dame Fuller, is a revered figure in Watford's story, and that generations have been brought up in the old Fullerian tradition. For no good reason at all they want to destroy Watford's pride in the individuality and historic associations of its Grammar Schools. It may be that they want to be in control when Watford, with 75,000 in population, seeks county borough powers, so that their hands are strengthened if they decide to oppose. So far, fortunately, there is no sign that the Governors are in the least inclined to surrender their independence. They realise that if they tamely handed over the heritage of the Schools they would bring on their heads a great storm of protest.

WO May, 1941

Watford Electricity Profits

WATFORD electricity undertaking made a net profit last year of £30,225, which was slightly less than for the preceding twelve months. The sum allocated in relief of the rate was £6,500. It may reasonably be asked why this amount has not been larger, especially as the legal maximum is in the neighbourhood of £10,500, and Luton's transfer is £14,000.

For some years now Watford Corporation have been only making transfers from the income derived from the Borough itself, leaving out of account that from outside districts, whose objection to helping to "subsidise" Watford rates from profits to which they contributed became very vocal some time ago. There were several good answers to these protests—one was that outlying places had made no contribution to the capital outlay on the scheme—but to placate opposition the Council decided to adopt the principle mentioned. Whether the matter will be reconsidered in the future remains to be seen.

Despite the war, the undertaking continues to flourish. On the sales for public lighting there has been a drop of nearly a million units, but so small is the margin of profit in this branch of the business that the effect on the balance sheet has been insignificant. The annual accounts (just published) of the Chief Engineer and General manager show what a vast volume of business is being done. An addition of 1,696 consumers during the year brought the total up to 31,832, and the tariff is among the lowest in the whole of England.

It is some 44 years since an Order was obtained to supply electricity to what was then the urban district of Watford. From time to time the area of supply has been extended, until it now covers 61 square miles. The rapid development at Hemel Hempstead, Bushey and the villages round has increased the mileage of cables to 541. Showrooms and offices have been erected, and trading powers have been exercised.

In its early days the undertaking did not show much promise of becoming a valuable asset to Watford. As a matter of fact, its sale to a company was seriously suggested, and it was only the determined stand made on the Council by the late Mr. J. C. Benskin, who was then chairman of the Electricity Committee, that saved the scheme. Though enjoying the advantage of a monopoly, the undertaking undoubtedly owes a great deal to highly efficient and enterprising administration.

WO May, 1941

War Weapons Week; procession along Gammons Lane into St. Albans Road.   1941

Weapon demonstration outside Town Hall.   1941

Change at West Herts Post

The copyright and goodwill of the "West Herts Post" have been purchased by Home Counties Newspapers Ltd., who have been in part associated with the management of the paper for the last twenty years.

With the exception of a few minor changes on the technical side, the paper will continue as usual under the editorship of Mr. W. Fleet Huson, supported by the present editorial staff.

Commencing with next week's issue, the "West Herts Post" will be published on Thursday afternoon instead of Thursday morning, and will appear in a much more convenient and handy form, a change that we are certain will be warmly welcomed by our readers.

WHP October, 1941

●*The West Herts Post from 1887, when it was founded, followed until 1919 the style of the Watford Observer in having the front page consisting of advertisements, mostly classified. Then, for a year, the West Herts Post cleared advertisements from the front page and ran news stories in their stead. This did not last and in 1920 they reverted to the 'Observer' style.*

In the 1941 change the front page was cleared and given over to news stories, the page is halved to tabloid size and the number of pages increased. Layout is stylish, presentation snappy and stories are given good length and display.

Pleased—And Displeased

Sir,—Congratulations to the new "West Herts Post!" Both for its make-up and content. On its present form it should be the medium for all progressive thought in Watford and district.

It is fitting also that it should seize on the question of production as the most vital one of the moment, and I venture to forward a few suggestions on this all important question.

First, we must have production committees in every factory, on which properly elected workers' representatives must sit, in conjunction with the owners.

All the cards must be laid on the table at conferences of these committees. Safeguards of living standards must be given, and guaranteed by mutual agreement. On the question of "hold ups" the workers must have equal access to all information relating to any given circumstance.

After supplies, comes manpower, and many of the Government's difficulties are due to their stupid handling of this question.

At the moment we have enforced labour, with no proper sense of distribution. Some firms have too many workers, others not enough. Under the present "cost, plus ten per cent" system, it is profitable to engage workers to do nothing. No wonder workers are cynical, and fed up.

The Production Committees could alter this. Amicable arrangements by voluntary agreement could soon be made to remedy these anomalies.

Wages, too, lag behind the cost of living, and but for constant overtime would be insufficient to maintain proper living standards in these times of high prices. This is a source of great discontent.

Firms also should be forced to recognise trade unionism. Many still refuse to do so. Workers will not exert themselves for such masters, nor the people fight with a good heart to preserve them.

In advocating these "war-time" measures, we have an eye also on the "New Order" of the future, when the workers will, and must have, a voice in the control of a peace-time economy. Self-preservation and progress demand it. To refuse it at this critical stage of world history may well mean our extinction as a race.

John Bruce.

WHP November, 1941

Home Guard, on an Anti-Tank training course at Russells. 1941

Over 18's women registering for first call-up.

Knight's
Castile

FOR *face appeal*

STANDARD TABLET *(1 coupon)* 4ᴰ

IMPORTANT

Government Announcement to Women

Ministry of Labour and National Service

There must no longer be any doubt in anybody's mind that every available woman in Britain will have to serve to win this war.

The Registration of age groups will proceed steadily. But this process, which necessarily involves interviewing, takes up precious time, and thousands of volunteers are needed at this moment in the A.T.S. for work that cannot wait. In the hour of their country's need, the Women of Britain have always responded, unselfishly and most courageously, to the call for service. The hour of need is upon us now.

You are being asked to volunteer to-day ahead of your age group. If you have already registered do not wait for your interview. Come forward, and say you want to help now.

There are many different ways in which you can serve, but the need of the AUXILIARY TERRITORIAL SERVICE is very great indeed. This service demands personal integrity, good intelligence and willingness to maintain a high standard of efficiency.

Members of the A.T.S. are working side by side with men in the Army and are also taking over vital work which releases men for the front line. Come forward now and help to build the mighty army that will lead a great country to Victory.

Post this to-day

Address it to The Auxiliary Territorial Service, AG18 99A, Hobart House, Grosvenor Gardens, London, S.W.1.
Please send me full story of life in the A.T.S. and details of the opportunities it offers. This does not commit me in any way.

Mrs/Miss _____ Age _____ *(In confidence)*

Address _____

Age limits, 17½ to 43. (Parents' consent needed under 18) Ex-Service women may volunteer up to 50.

(Unsealed envelope, penny stamp)

★ *Please call and have a talk at any Employment Exchange or A.T.S. or Army Recruiting Centre. They are there to help you.*

200,000 ATS urgently needed

Women Demand Equal Rights

If an employed man is injured through the war he will receive compensation of 35s. a week. If a woman is similarly injured she will receive only 28s. a week. Pension rates are much less, too.

That is how the law stands at the present, but it will not remain so if the women can help it.

Women are very upset about this discrimination, and a campaign is in progress to secure equality.

Watford women (men are invited, too) will have an opportunity to register their protest at a meeting to be held at Watford Town Hall on Friday, December 5. Watford Branch of the National Council of Women is calling the meeting, and Mrs. Tate, M.P., will speak.

Angry Women M.P.s

Miss E. E. R. Bradford, chairman of the Branch, told a "Post" reporter that all the women M.P.s are angry about the differentiation, and were organising a campaign to try and get the matter reconsidered. The National Council of Women were arranging for a petition to be signed.

"The position," continued Miss Bradford, "is very unfair. Women are exposed to the same dangers as men, and are doing jobs which hitherto were men's prerogative."

"The old argument that men should have more because they usually have a family to keep does not apply because dependants are provided for separately."

WHP November, 1941

M.B.E. For Mr. George R. Bolton

Mr. George R. Bolton, Borough Librarian, of Watford, who was awarded the M.B.E. for his work as controller of 17 Group of the Royal Observer Corps, attended at Buckingham Palace on Tuesday when the King invested him with the honour.

Mr. Bolton was announced by Lord Clarendon, who has so many associations with Watford.

WHP July, 1941

Coal Must Be Saved

IT is as necessary in the home as in the factory that coal should be saved this winter. An appeal has been made by the Minister of Mines to all local authorities, urging the greatest economy in the use of fuel. All departments of Watford Corporation have been circularised to this effect by the Mayor, and doubtless industries not engaged upon war work will be recipients of a similar urgent appeal.

The bright autumnal weather of the past few days will have relieved many a housewife or maid of the task of lighting fires, and the equally disagreeable task of cleaning up the grates in the morning. But with the vital requirement that the national war effort should reach its peak at the earliest possible moment, it is imperative that the domestic user should practise the greatest economy, not only in coal fires, but in the use of gas and electricity, and every other fuel.

The employer and worker in business and the woman in the home must be linked in this great fuel economy campaign.

WO October, 1941

This Spitfire goes into action carrying Watford's coat of arms. The machine was paid for by subscriptions and it is one of our fastest and hardest hitting aircraft, carrying two 20mm cannons and four machine guns, with a speed approaching 400mph. WHP October, 1941

Casting name-plate 'HMS Watford', at Tividale Foundry, Local Board Road.

Mayor, Councillor Price, leads waste-paper collection drive. Outside Town Hall.
1942

5,000 Meals Daily

Plans for the opening of five or six British Restaurants throughout Watford will be under way shortly.

This encouraging statement was made by the Mayor on Tuesday at the official opening of the British Restaurant in the Baptist Hall, Leavesden-road.

When these restaurants are completed the Borough of Watford will be able to provide 5,000 meals per day.

The Mayor pointed out that this scheme should to some extent remedy the "queue" epidemic that is now rampant in the town.

Mr. W. Blackwood, Assistant Division Food Controller, who was representing Major C. R. Dudgeon, proposed a vote of thanks to the Mayor and in doing so praised the Mayor's power of oratory, a well-deserved tribute. He added that Watford's first British Restaurant was the most ideal he had inspected throughout the Division. (The Division includes all Hertfordshire and Essex.)

WHP November, 1941

Training 8,000 Fireguards

ARRANGEMENTS are complete for the training of Watford's 8,000 fire guards, and organisation is well forward.

Eight thousand fire guard armlets and steel helmets have been ordered.

All fire guards will attend a course of about eight lectures of about an hour each, spread over eight weeks.

The lectures will be given by the head wardens and the deputy wardens of the A.R.P. service, and will consist of two parts: (1) essential training, and (2) supplementary training.

The essential training is compulsory, but the supplementary training is voluntary, although fire guards are being urged to take the additional lectures.

The essential training will consist of lectures on incendiary bomb control.

WHP November, 1941

Well Done, Chater Infants

An outstanding achievement in National Savings is reported from Chater Infants' School, who aimed at a target of £300 to buy an ambulance, and have raised just over £317.

WHP December, 1941

Watford Challenge to Luton

Watford is out to beat Luton once more—this time in the towns' Warships Week next March.

Watford's challenge to beat Luton's total each day, to reach one million pounds before Luton, and to exceed Luton's total both in amount and per capita was accepted last night (Wednesday) with the comment, "Your audacity can only be surpassed by our achievement."

The challenge was sent by the Mayor of Watford, Coun. W. H. Price, after a meeting of Watford Joint Savings Committee at the Town Hall on Friday, in the following telegram:

Watford Joint Savings Committee issues the following challenge, which please convey to all workers in Luton Warships Week effort. We have chosen the weapons—each a light cruiser—for Warships Week next March. Watford challenges in these terms:

"The citizens of Watford will beat Luton's total each day, will reach the million pounds mark before you, and, finally, Watford's grand total will be greater than Luton's both in amount and per capita.

WHP November, 1941

Women's War Work Inquiries

The two Government Training Centres in Southwold-road and Hempstead-road are anxious to fill every training vacancy available, and so enable them to send out qualified engineers to the many war munition factories in the Home Counties.

One question which many women have been asking is: "Why, if I have got to register for essential war work, is an appeal made to me to offer my services?"

The answer is that registration necessarily takes some time to come into effect. If a woman who volunteers now is worth a score when registration day arrives, how much more valuable is a volunteer who has already undergone a course of engineering training!

"That women have an aptitude for engineering," an official stated, "has been proved strikingly in many factories in Hertfordshire. While many employers are still a little reluctant to employ women on engineering work, this county has not been behindhand in trying out experiments.

"For example, two factories have gone so far as not only to employ women on men's work, but also to try out an idea of doing part-time shifts."

WHP December, 1941

History of the Last War Helps This

A HISTORY of the last war, extending to several large volumes, was proudly brought to the Mayor of Watford (Councillor W. H. Price) by a small boy, when he visited Watford Fields during his "paper-chase" tour of the Borough, on Saturday afternoon, in connection with Watford's paper salvage drive. The boy came struggling out of a house with them, and handed them to the Mayor, who put them in a civil defence league vehicle, which followed the loudspeaker car, and which was used as a touring collection depôt.

"Wait a minute, I've got some more," said the boy, after the Mayor had thanked him, and handed him one of the lucky tickets which may bring him a prize. And into the house he went again and brought out the rest of the volumes.

The Mayor started from the Town Hall, and made a three-hour tour of the borough. With the aid of the loudspeaker he urged the people of Watford to make every effort to salvage paper. His tour took him down the High-street, round Oxhey Ward, Watford Fields, Harwoods Ward, the St. Albans-road, Bushey Mill-lane, the Harebreaks, and Kingswood.

Quite a number of housewives were on the look-out for him, and came out with bundles of newspapers and books. One lady on the Kingswood Estate cleared the shelves of her bookcase of all the cheap sixpenny volumes she had.

WHP January, 1942

Trader's War Problems

WATFORD Chamber of Commerce has soon got down to the problems with which the second interim report of the Retail Trade Committee of the Board of Trade has confronted them, as reported in last week's "Post."

Though they have not yet decided what action they will recommend locally in regard to the main issues—the closing or merging of shops—the Executive Committee on Monday went into the difficulties arising from such action.

The Committee decided to send a resolution to the National Chamber of Trade, the Drapers' Chamber, and Sir Dennis Herbert, M.P. for Watford, pointing out that to safeguard businesses there should be some form of registration and licensing of premises so that those closed can be re-opened after the war; some reasonable compensation for any losses sustained through closing; and some form of moratorium to protect the assets of a business, so that the owner can benefit now and not have to wait until the assets have disappeared.

WHP February, 1942

'Ceremonial queue' for the opening of Watford's second British Restaurant (corner of St. Albans Road/Balmoral Road). Premises used for a time postwar as training centre for Hoover Ltd.'s salesmen.

Soap Rationing

FROM Monday, February 9th, soap may be bought only against a coupon or buying permit. The oils and fats used in soap manufacture occupy much shipping space, and some of this must be saved for food.

You will have 4 coupons in each 4-weekly period, and will be able to use these how and when you like within the period. There will be no registration, and you may buy from any shop stocking the kind you require.

Rationing will not apply to shaving soaps or dental soaps, shampoo powders, liquid soap, or scourers.

WHP February, 1942

H.M.S. Capetown Is Ours

THOUGH Watford failed to beat Luton in the Warship Week challenge their accomplishment in exceeding their aim of a round million pounds by over £200,000 was very commendable.

The cruiser, H.M.S. Capetown, can now be looked upon as another of Watford's tangible contributions towards the war effort, to be ranged alongside the destroyers paid for in War Weapons Week and the Spitfire donated by the Town.

The final total for Watford Warship Week, made known only yesterday, is £1,225,809.

Luton's final, as announced on Monday, was £1,421,714.

Watford therefore ensured being able to adopt H.M.S. Capetown, with nearly a quarter of a million to spare, but the effort, splendid as it was, failed to uphold the three-fold challenge to beat Luton on the aggregate, the day to day total, and the amount per head of population.

WHP March, 1942

Railings Will Go Soon

Quite a number of people in the last few weeks have put the question, "When are Watford's railings to be taken for scrap?"

Some have gone on to criticise Watford Town Council for not getting on with the job.

The railings are to be collected any day now, and let us take the opportunity right away of saying that the delay is nothing to do with Watford Town Council, and neither are they responsible for the collection, so don't blame them after the event for any damage that may be done. The removal and collection of these railings is undertaken directly by the Ministry of Works. The reason for the delay is that the Ministry are dealing with the job town by town.

WO June, 1942

2nd British Restaurant

The idea of communal feeding was carried a step further in Watford on Monday, when the new British Restaurant, at Alpha House, on the corner of St. Albans-rd. and Balmoral-rd. was opened by the Mayor, Councillor W. H. Price.

The dinners served at Leavesden-road have been such a success that it is now proposed to start on teas at Alpha House, which is trying the experiment of staying open from 12 to 6.30, in order to serve an early evening meal to factory workers leaving about that time.

High teas of baked beans and welsh rarebit, or even an occasional egg can be obtained for 8d. while a more refined afternoon tea is only 4d.

Otherwise the scale of prices remains the same with the main dish 7d., sweet 3d., tea or soup 1½d.

The new restaurant which provides seating for 80 people at small tables, is to be served from the kitchen at Leavesden-rd., which is very well equipped and quite capable of the additional work.

The food supplies, travelling in special insulated containers which keep it hot for four hours, will be delivered by the two new Ford emergency food vans in time for lunch.

WHP April, 1942

None Were Idle

Saturday's registration in Watford of the 1900-class women yielded many fewer with young and dependent families, and should thus mean an increase in volunteers for factories and shops.

There is plenty of opportunity for women workers, full or part-time, in Watford, and the "Post" is assured that all volunteers from this or other registrations could be absorbed locally at once.

Eighty per cent. of the women who registered were married, and of these 60 per cent. were engaged in household duties. The rest were fairly evenly divided between full-time and part-time work.

Of the single women, 85 per cent. were working full time, and the remainder either doing part-time work or occupied with household duties. None were unemployed.

WHP July, 1942

War work

War work was obviously the thing and after a short course on basic engineering at the Government Training Centre in Southwold Road, the job to which I was directed was at Norman Reeves next to the High Street station.

Ford dealers? War work? As with most garages they had a couple of lathes, and any firm with machine tools was pressed into use. The work was for Scammell's, turning cast brass air filter covers for tank transporter tractor units. But, in mid-winter, with no garage heating except for a coke stove, it was no fun to operate a lathe clad for warmth in gloves and overcoat . . .

Cox's was a vast change from the lathes at the back of Norman Reeve's repair shed; a complete hive of industry by day, and to a large extent, night.

Car, lorry and tank seats, aircraft seating, tank periscope assemblies all among the perpetual crackle, smoke and sparks of the welders, and adjacent to the odours of the paint spray shop. Working in the machine shop were men and women producing a wide variety of small machined components. The women tended to stay longer as the men faced call-up and disappeared.

In the black-out all roads were dark but Aldenham Road, with hedges and trees alongside was something else again—after all, a carefully-shaded and hooded cycle lamp didn't lose much light downwards, but what little light the dynamo gave wasn't much. Once at work the bright spots were the overhead gas heaters—welcome particularly on night shifts—and the 'lunch' break which would see a trek across the road to the Busy Bee Cafe—open all hours!

Recollections 1987

"Mr. Percy Grillo, one of Watford's best-known tradesmen, is, as our picture shows, doing his bit as an ARP Warden, thus carrying on a tradition of which the firm of M. Grillo and Son are justly proud. Four of the principals of the firm are British ex-service men. " *WHP*

First Carnival Queen to be crowned in the new Town Hall, Joan Glenister being given given bouquet by Miss Ellen Pollock. (4th May, 1940)

Dieppe Raid

SOME Watford men who took part in last week's large-scale raid on Dieppe will have thrilling stories to tell when they are free to relate their experiences during that exciting day.

Two who will have particularly exciting stories to tell are:

Trooper Fred Craft, of 26, Home-way Mill End, and Trooper Sid (Nobby) Clarke, of 240 Whippendell-road.

Both are aged 22, and both were members of the small party which, not strong enough to capture a six-inch gun battery, worked round behind it, sniped the gunners to such good effect, that in desperation the Germans turned the guns on the snipers, and so could not shell the beaches, where the Canadians were landing.

The Watford district was also represented on the naval side of the operations by Ldg./Seaman Patrick Edgar, of 37, Lower Paddock-road, Oxhey, who was serving in one of the destroyers that took the Commandos over.

WHP August, 1942

More Women Needed

ALTHOUGH women in Watford and district have responded well to the call for workers in factories in the district, there is an urgent need for many more, both for full and part-time employment.

That need is growing daily and when the comb-out of young men, which Mr. Bevin promises, comes about the need will be pressing.

Every women who can offer her services can be placed locally.

The shortage of women is holding up production of vital war requirements.

This is a call to you to come forward to help on the war effort in the best possible way. Watford wants to know why women are not coming forward.

WHP July, 1942

Tanks—£40,000 Short

Unless the small savings of Watford and district reach £40,090 this week there will be no tank-naming for the town. The position is,that if Watford is to name ten tanks they must reach £253,000 by Saturday night. If they fail, then not even a small tank will go into battle carrying Watford and district's name.

Since the "Tanks For Attack" campaign started ten weeks ago the total had reached £213,756 by last Saturday. The total for the week ending September 19 was £24,658, which must be nearly doubled this week.

Street group secretaries have toiled unceasingly, and the schools, social organisations and industrial groups have been no less enthusiastic, and they will do their utmost during these last few days to see that Watford does not suffer widespread disappointment.

WHP September, 1942

Offensive Inspires Workers

The great victories in Egypt and Libya have inspired Watford factory workers.

Now there is the feeling abroad that at long last the great Allied offensive is under way, the workers are roused to a new enthusiasm and a new solidarity.

The first important task of the new Mayor of Watford will be to receive a deputation from Watford factory workers and Trade Union organisations, to hear about a suggestion that there should be a Libya Production Week in Watford.

The idea is to draw all Watford workers and citizens into the greatest effort ever to increase production, and economy.

When the lead for such an idea comes from those who will themselves have to make the effort, we know that the right spirit exists.

WHP November, 1942

Church Bells on Sunday

Church bells all over the country will ring out on Sunday in celebration of our Egyptian victory.

WHP November, 1942

Restaurants to go?

The deficit for the period from the opening, October 29, 1941, to March 31, 1942, on British Restaurants and the cooking depot at Watford was £612, plus £95, being proportion of central administrative expenses, and also 2 per cent. in lieu of bank interest lost.

In respect of the months April, May, June and July, the deficit was £10.

The Emergency Committee reported at the meeting of Watford Town Council on Monday that it was reasonable to suppose that some loss would be incurred in the future.

It appeared from correspondence that the Ministry of Food were not, at present, inclined to refund the deficit, notwithstanding the fact the the Corporation had acted under their directions as their agents in the matter, stated the committee.

WHP November, 1942

Naming Ten Tanks

The Watford Savings Committee are now seeking to name the ten Churchill Tanks which is Watford's prize for collecting the magnificent total during the ten-week Tanks For Attack Campaign.

Each tank will bear three names, meaning that thirty local names in all will appear on the tanks as they go into action. The following have been asked to submit names for the tanks: Ten street groups, six groups in the rural district, six schools, six industrial groups and two social groups.

In the rural district, Sarratt, Abbots Langley, Radlett, and Aldenham have been asked to submit names, and a further two will be named by groups in the Watford district.

The Social Group and the Voluntary Services are also naming two, while the production, transport and commerce side of industry will also submit names.

The group in Kelmscott-close have given "Kelmscott," Kingsfield-road "Kingsfield," and Parker-street "Parker Group."

It is hoped that next week the "Post" will be able to give all thirty local names and also the numerous groups who narrowly missed naming a tank, but in the words of the Savings Committee were "highly commended."

WHP November, 1942

Sea Cadets head 'Wings for Victory' procession, St. Albans Road (between railway bridge and Station Road traffic lights).
p.290 tr

Savings campaign, theme—beat the 'Squanderbug'.
1943

Another Million?

WITHIN the next few days Watford will announce its target for the "Wings for Victory" Week, which is to be held from Saturday, May 8, to Saturday, May 15. It is expected that the target will be at least one million pounds, the same as in Warship Week, but this may be affected if the Rural District does not join in Watford's effort.

At a meeting of Watford and District Joint Savings Committee on Monday, Mr. R. Mugford, Chairman, said, "I think this should be Watford's greatest effort of the war, even if we fail valiantly to reach our target."

All targets are to be named in terms of aircraft. If Watford decide on a million, they will put it in the words of 50 Mosquito fighter-bombers.

These aircraft, stated to be the fastest fighter-bombers in the world, have distinguished themselves in recent actions against the Axis.

WHP January, 1943

Gas Buses

A new type of 'bus is to be introduced by the London Passenger Transport Board on routes No. 301 and 302, and as a consequence the position of the "Request Stop" signs are to be rearranged.

These 'buses will be driven by their own producer gas plants, instead of by petrol. They are much slower in acceleration, and the L.P.T.B., notifying Watford Town Council of the introduction of this type of vehicle, stated that experience had proved the necessity of limiting the number of "request stops."

At the Council meeting, on Tuesday, the Highways Committee reported that the Borough Engineer had inspected the points affected, and the police had been notified of the proposed change.

It was agreed that the matter be left in the hands of Ald. T. R. Clark, Chairman of the Committee.

In response to a request by Coun. Mrs. A Primett, Ald. Clark said he would bring before the Committee the question of approaching the L.P.T.B. to get them to install stops at the end of St. Albans-road.

WHP March, 1943

New Cox's Production Drive

THE great example of Cox and Co's production drive has led Watford's Drive for Victory Campaign Committee to hope for a united town effort, which will stimulate the whole of Hertfordshire, if not the whole of Britain.

Mr. J. H. Price, Secretary of the Watford Drive for Victory Campaign Committee, has asked Cox and Co's Joint Production Committee to join with them in a scheme which will embrace all the local manufacturers, and the "Post" understands that this scheme is now under consideration.

Cox and Co's campaign was introduced in December last as an inter-departmental production competition, arranged to cover the four weeks in the month, with prizes of National Savings certificates given to the winning department. Interest was stimulated by means of speakers from the fighting services, and film shows.

The competition was voted a definite success and resulted in an increase in output in nearly all departments.

This led to another campaign being introduced for March, and this time, in addition to the interdepartmental competition, prizes are also offered for individual effort among workers who excel.

Full details of the scheme were reported in the "Post," and are now being circularised by the Watford Production Committee to upwards of 35 firms in the area, who, it is hoped, will inaugurate their own competitions in an all-out effort to increase production at this vital time.

WHP March, 1943

New Freemen Honoured

IN a ceremony which was simple, yet strikingly impressive, Watford on Monday honoured three of its most deserving public servants by conferring the Freedom of the Borough on Lord Hemingford, Alderman T. R. Clark and Mr. William Hudson, the former Town Clerk.

The historic significance of the occasion was marked by the wide interest displayed and the number of county dignitaries present.

There was scarcely a vacant seat in the hall, and the pageantry of the proceedings was followed intently especially from the balcony where there were a large number of schoolchildren, and American and Canadian guests.

The simplicity of the celebration was, perhaps, its greatest worth. There were no fanfares, no grandiloquent flights of oratory, but just straightforward, plain expressions of goodwill, carrying the convincing ring of spontaneity and sincerity as their hall-mark.

"The boast of heraldry" was supplanted by a fervent good-fellowship, and a spirit of appreciation of sterling service fully rendered to the town, whose people were now saying a simple, yet unanimous, "Thank you!"

All who witnessed the ceremony were deeply moved, and the new Freemen more than any, and it was obvious that, like all of us, they recognised the event as the crowning joy of their careers, for what greater encouragement or reward can be expected by a public servant than a whole community's "Well done!"?

WHP March, 1943

"Coasting" Trains

BY planned "coasting," 8¾ tons of coal are being saved every day on the L.M.S. Euston-Broad Street-Watford electric services.

In the operation of electric trains it is usual, in order to give economy in energy consumption, to accelerate rapidly, and then shut off power and coast to the point at which it is necessary to apply the brake for the next station stop.

By calculation and experiment, the L.M.S. has determined the most economical points, and fixed a "coasting board" at these points for the guidance of drivers.

WHP April, 1943

Self-generating gas-unit powering an LMS delivery lorry.

Overcharging

Maurice Houtman, St. Albans-road, Watford, who pleaded not guilty, was fined £25 with £7 costs at Watford Police Court on Tuesday for selling a second-hand table at an excessive price at Watford on September 30.

Mr. L. Jones, prosecuting for the Board of Trade, said the price of the table should not have exceeded the first-hand price plus purchase tax, which would have totalled about £7.

Robert Kettle said that he bought the table as a solid oak one at £18 18s. He found that it was made of white-wood.

Cecil Walker, a trade expert said that in 1942 the table would have cost about £7, including purchase tax.

Houtman said he bought the table for £12 15s. at Hendon in 1943. He was of the opinion that the bottom of the table was oak. Plywood would not crack and was preferable to oak. Before selling the table for £18 18s., he compared prices elsewhere for similar articles, and found they were selling at 25 to 27 guineas.

WHP March, 1943

50 Mosquitoes

WITH "Wings for Victory" Week opening on Saturday, the whole of Watford is on its toes for what promises to be the greatest small savings effort in the history of the town—the raising of £1,000,000 to build 50 Mosquitoes.

Everywhere there are signs that small savers are alive to the need for special exertion on their part, and the keen interest already being shown in the many R.A.F. novelty attractions in the course of erection shows the "Wings" Campaign Committee to have done its job in stimulating faculty.

WHP May, 1943

Giant Bomber on Show

Most interest so far is being shown in the giant Lancaster bomber, in the course of erection outside the Town Hall. The bomber, which is the same as was shown in Trafalgar Square during "Wings" Week, has been on 27 operation flights, including 13 over Germany and one over Berlin itself. It has also raided Italy, and has taken part in many daylight sweeps over Occupied France.

WHP May, 1943

Save The Blade

There are more ways to keep safety razor blades on the job a little longer.

"Shave with a slanting or sawing movement—don't just pull the blade down your face," is the advice. "Shave down your face only. If you shave upwards it may give you a close shave, but it is helping to make the hair tougher.

"Lather your face for at least two minutes before shaving.

"Drying is the most important part of the care of a blade. This is the correct way. Put the corner of a smooth towel on a flat surface, lay the blade on it and draw the blade towards you without touching the edges with your fingers.

"Turn over end to end and dry the other side the same way. And remember, a damp atmosphere is just as deadly to a blade as water left on it."

WHP May, 1943

'Wings for Victory' week, American contingent in march-past which included personnel from all branches of forces including ATS, WAAF, etc. May 1943

Refreshment van presented by American Red Cross to W.V.S.

Lancaster in course of assembly outside Town Hall, May 1943.

3rd Birthday of the Home Guard; march-past of the 10th Bttn, and part of the 7th, Wings for Victory Week, dais outside Town Hall.   *p.263 tr*   1943

Crikey!—Mosquitoes

More than two years ago a silvery streak flashed through the skies, and from the lips of all who saw it there sprang the involuntary cry, "Crikey!"

That was the name by which the now famous high-speed reconnaissance fighter-bomber De Havilland DH.98 Mosquito, became known to R.A.F. and Observer Corps personnel during its experimental days. The only things known about it in those days were its amazing speed and almost incredible manoeuvrability, which, of course, gave rise to the exclamation, "Crikey!"

Since then the remarkable exploits of this plane over enemy-occupied territory and the heart of Germany itself, Berlin, have inspired many more exultant cries of "Crikey!"

The Mosquito was reported in action for the first time in an attack on Oslo in September 25 when it broke up a Quisling rally. It had been in service many months before that.

The Mosquito is unique in that it is one of the first all-wood aeroplanes to go into service with the R.A.F for many years, and its method of construction results in one of the strongest airframes yet designed, combining the qualities of lightness with perfection of streamlined form.

Following its amazing exploits over the Continent, the makers issued this description in the trade journals:—

"Anopheles De Havillandus-offensicus. Characteristics: Furious and aggressive. Prolific. Flies great distances at high velocity to deposit eggs which are both distasteful and harmful. When molested shoots unpleasant streams from multiple probosci. Possesses penetrative and recording eyes. Habitat: Met in increasing numbers in Axia, where inhabitants are apprehensive of the imminence of a plague which promises to cause considerable inconvenience."

This also caused cries of "Crikey!" in trade circles.

When it became known that during its "Wings" Week, which opens on Saturday, Watford aimed to raise £1,000,000 to buy 50 of these super planes, there were many more cries of "Crikey!" in the town, but we are confident that when the final result of Watford's "Wings" Week is declared there will be an explosive cry of "CRIKEY!"

More seriously, our "Wings for Victory" Week, more than any other previous savings effort, calls for a major effort. Its success depends on the small savings of the people. The astounding totals reached by Watford in previous efforts were a tribute to the willingness with which the wage-earner lent his savings to the State, but they also owed a great deal to the investments contributed by large firms and institutions like banks and insurance companies. This year presents a different picture.

Those firms who had sold their stocks, and had been unable to replace them were persuaded in War Weapons Week and Warship Week to lend their excess capital to the Government until peace returned and factories could once more produce for the civilian public, and not the armed forces.

These firms responded so magnificently that many of them have already invested all they can, and have no reserve left to assist the "Wings for Victory" total. Other companies are so rigidly taxed that they need all the capital they have to finance their war production. In this third effort, therefore, though we know they will do all they can to help, we cannot expect it to be on the same large scale as before.

So it is that we come back to the small saver. Fortunately there is plenty of evidence that the small savings will be forthcoming in quantities that will fully make up for the loss of large investments.

There is no question that the R.A.F. is dear to the heart of everyone. Their sacrifice in our defence, their gallant attacks on the enemy have brought home to every man woman and child the true nature of the debt we owe to the men of the R.A.F. Without exaggeration we owe to them our very existence as a nation, and even as individuals. The call to lend on their behalf will not fall on deaf ears.

The wage-earners of Watford are in many ways fortunate in their circumstances. High wages are being earned, higher than ever in history. There is little on which money can sensibly be spent, and no one can deny the urgent need of the State.

The great thing to remember is that Watford must have an average of £5 from every man, woman and child if it is to equal the achievements of previous campaigns. Sixpence is not too little, not £1,000 too much, to invest. The R.A.F. deserve more than the best we can do.

WHP May, 1943

"Wings" Well Earned

Watford's "Wings for Victory" Week total has now risen to £1,150,326, and may soar even higher when final returns are received.

With a target of one million pounds the organisers of the effort, and Watford residents generally, can take pride in this splendid result.

WHP May, 1943

220

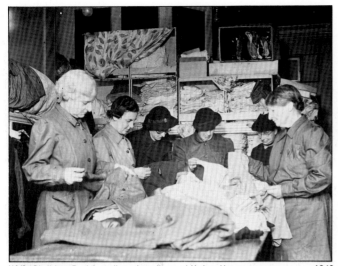

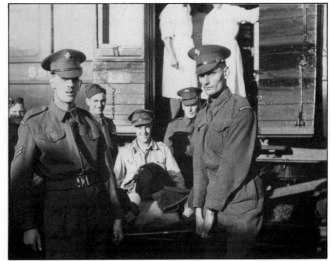

WVS 'Clothing Party', sorting donations at Upton House.　　1943　　War-wounded at Watford Junction.　　1943

Still Stepping Up Output

Representatives of the Ministry of Production attended a meeting arranged by Watford Drive for Victory Campaign Committee and held at Watford Town Hall on Friday.

In a frank discussion many points affecting workers and the managements were raised, and a deputation to meet the Eastern Regional Board was appointed. Plans for a still more stimulating drive in Watford are under consideration, and it is hoped to invite the full support of the Eastern Regional Board.

The meeting decided to send a congratulatory cablegram to General Alexander on the wonderful victory in North Africa.

WHP May, 1943

HMS Capetown Plaque

H.M.S. Capetown, Watford's adopted ship, will now have a bronze plaque, designed in Watford, and made in Watford of gifts of old bronze by Watford people, to perpetuate the town's link with the ship.

In exchange, Watford borough and Watford rural, associated in Warship Week effort, have each received a plaque bearing the badge of H.M.S. Capetown.

Following the adoption of H.M.S. Capetown in Warship Week, residents were asked to give old bronze articles to be melted down and converted into a plaque for the ship.

One donor gave his 1914 Mons Star.

The plaque, which weighs 40 lbs, was cast by Watford Iron Foundry, the design being sculptured by Montague W. Jackson, Watford School of Arts, and the finishing touches being applied by the Novobax Engineering Co.

Rectangular in shape, it bears the borough arms in enamel, and is inscribed: "To commemorate the adoption of H.M.S. Capetown by the Borough and Rural District of Watford, Warship Week, March, 1942."

The presentation of the plaque took place at a special meeting of the Town Council on Tuesday night and it was received on behalf of the Captain, officers, and ship's complement by Vice-Admiral A. L. Snagge, representing the Admiralty and National Savings Committee.

WHP July, 1943

German Prison Ship

LIFE aboard a German commerce raider . . . men packed into the tanks of a tanker turned prison ship . . . running the British blockade . . . forty prisoners jumping from a train taking them to Germany . . . others tunneling by night out of a hut, under the barbed wire and out beyond their prison camp to freedom . . .

These are some of the incidents in the thrilling story, which can now be told, of Seaman Jack King, whose return to Watford in July was described by the "Post."

Jack, aged 18, believed to be the youngest prisoner of war, was a deck boy aboard the s.s. African Star, sunk in the Atlantic, but let him tell his own story.

Here it is:

"We were homeward bound from Buenos Aires when one morning we sighted a big steamer flying the Russian flag. She approached and fired a shot across our bows and signalled us to stop.

"We at once sent out an S.O.S. and continued steaming, but the raider then began to shell us. The first shot tore half our bridge away and more shells crashed into the ship, stopping our engines.

"We took to the boats, and the raider signalled us to come on board.

"Seventy four of us, including the captain and two women passengers, climbed on board the raider, which we found was a German.

WHP August, 1943

Italy Surrenders

Within a few hours of the news of Italy's surrender, Watford National Savings Committee had posters circulated all over the district urging people to celebrate by making a thanksgiving investment in War Savings.

First response to the appeal was made by a local Councillor, who invested £75. This was followed by a street group member who brought in £39.

Mr. R. Mugford, of Cawdells, who is Chairman of the Watford Savings Committee, went along to his Observer Corps savings group and invested £500 in 3 per cent. bonds.

WHP September, 1943

Oranges—New Quota

WATFORD has received its quota of oranges for the under-fives, and on Tuesday and again yesterday, pavements had little bits and pieces of orange peel as traps for the unwary.

Watford Town Hall steps were not immune, and one of our elderly councillors nearly came to grief through slipping. He righted himself with a rather comical effort, and turning to the "Post" reporter who witnessed the incident, he wagged an admonishing finger and said, "No names, now! No names!"

WHP October, 1943

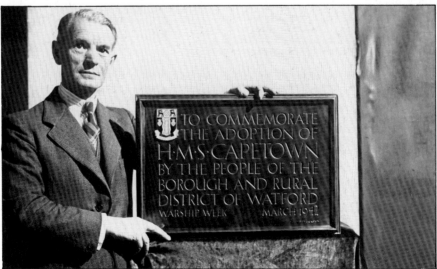

Mr. M. W. Jackson shows the HMS Capetown Plaque.　　1943
HMS Capetown was a 4200 ton cruiser launched in 1919, and completed 1922; in the 1944/5 issue of 'Jane's' it was stated to be 'due for retirement soon'.

221

The bargees survey the scene after firemen toil all night fighting a blaze at Croxley Mills.

Fire watching

Whilst the drone of enemy bombers overhead kept many families for night after night in their cold and damp Anderson shelters, to emerge into an equally cold and dark dawn, volunteers were organised into fire-watching and fire-fighting groups. On a rota system, those on duty during an alert would be called upon to patrol a given area and to deal with outbreaks of fire should such occur. Promptitude with buckets of sand to quench the initial effect of an incendiary bomb; and follow-up with water from stirrup-pumps to attempt some form of control until greater help could arrive.

Women fire watchers on Cawdell's roof—the Parish Church is bold behind the smaller premises of the 'King's Head'.   *p.348 t*

Berlin Raid—D.F.C.

HELPED to shoot down a German fighter while rear gunner in a Lancaster during a raid on Berlin . . . while in great pain from wounds to both feet and in the leg subdued a fire in the turret with an extinguisher and finished it off with contents of coffee flask . . . remained at his post and helped to drive off two other fighters . . . unconscious . . . now the Distinguished Flying Cross.

This briefly sums up the experiences of Flying Officer Cyril Govier Pascoe, of 8, Vale-road, Bushey, on the night of August 31.

For "displaying a high order of courage and fortitude" is the official reason for the award of the D.F.C., just announced.

The official citation states:

"When nearing the Dutch coast the aircraft was attacked by a fighter, but the assailant was destroyed by the determined and skilful fire directed by F/O Pascoe and the mid-upper gunner.

"Shortly afterwards the bomber was hit by fire from another fighter. The intercommunication system and the rear turret were rendered un-serviceable. A fire broke out in the turret, but F/O Pascoe, although in great pain from wounds sustained to both feet and in the leg, obtained an extinguisher and subdued the flames, finally extinguishing them with the contents of a coffee flask.

"Displaying great fortitude he remained at his post and, later on, when the bomber was subject to interference from two enemy fighters, he assisted in driving them off before losing consciousness.

WHP September, 1943

●*Cyril Pascoe, to whose memory this book is dedicated, suffered the loss of a leg. He found employment in Cornwall, and passed away there only recently, in December 1985.*

Jitterbugging at Dances

SHOULD jitterbugging be banned at Watford dances?

Coun. Mrs. Beall thinks it should, and said so at a meeting of the "H.M.S. Capetown" Comforts Fund Committee on Wednesday.

"In certain other places jitterbug dancing is being stopped and I think we should stop it here. Old-time dances are becoming very popular," she said.

The matter arose following a suggestion to organise a dance in aid of "Capetown" Fund and it was decided to book a provisional date to be confirmed later.

Looking ahead, the committee has arranged a whist drive for May 1, 1944, at the Town Hall.

It was announced that £450 had been sent for distribution among the ship's crew. This left a balance of £48.

WHP October, 1943

Oxhey 'Plan'—Opposition

QUESTIONS may be asked in Parliament on the London County Council's proposal to settle 15,000 bombed-out Londoners on Oxhey Place Estate, which includes Oxhey Golf Course and Oxhey Woods, some of the most famous beauty spots in Hertfordshire.

A petition signed by more than 50 Bushey residents has been sent to Air Commodore W. Helmore, M.P. for Watford, protesting against the idea.

Bushey residents, who have for many years taken their Sunday walks on the Oxhey Estate, hope that the House of Commons will see their point of view and will veto the L.C.C.'s scheme.

WHP November, 1943

Satellite Town Protests

Sir,—Like charity, love of the beautiful can be a screen for other sins. The protests about the proposed satellite town seem to show a greater regard for personal pleasure and convenience than for the preservation of rural beauty.

The increasing encroachment of town on country, regarded from one angle, is indeed grievous, but nevertheless inevitable. The resultant losses, however, as Mr. Odell has indicated, need by no means be total if the new towns and settlements are intelligently planned. This is the point that most of the protestants appear to overlook.

Councillor E. J. Baxter has described the L.C.C. plan "as a good one, and better than any speculative builder could envisage."

A study of the County of London Plan, recently published by the L.C.C., also gives good ground for supposing that the authors of such a well-conceived scheme are hardly likely to botch a small cottage estate of 15,000 inhabitants.

The estate, presumably, is intended to accommodate a few of those who will need to be transferred from the slums if London is to become a city for our pride and not our shame, as much of it is at present.

And is there nothing to be said of the benefits accruing to the 15,000 fortunates who will be our neighbours? Is it to be pleasant Sunday walks for the relatively few, or health and happiness for the many?

And do Carpenders Park residents really think that the St. Meryl Estate is a thing of beauty and a joy for ever?

E. H. LARGE.

WHP November, 1943

. . . new estate at Oxhey for LCC . . .

Watford Pigs for Farms of Europe

ALTHOUGH they may not be aware of their role, the housewives of Watford are playing an important part in laying the foundations of Europe's future livestock herds. The scraps and kitchen waste which they assiduously put out for collection each week are being converted into flesh, blood and bone—in fact, the finest pedigree pigs—at Watford's own municipal farm.

Homesteads will have to be rebuilt, farms re-established, and broad acres of grassland stocked with livestock to replace the herds stolen by the hun.

And this, says Mr. Farquharson, the Borough farm bailiff, is where Watford comes into the picture. The breeding qualities of the Watford herd are known all over the world—so much so, says Mr. Farquharson, that many of the pigs that will become the nuclei of the Continental herds will be Watford pedigree stock. There will be Large Whites, Middle Whites, and Wessex Saddlebacks of best quality, all bred at the Borough's own farm—Holywell Farm—which lies just off Tolpits-lane, in the south-west corner of the town.

As a result of the steady stream of auxiliary pig food supplied by patriotic local housewives, the size of the herd at Holywell Farm has not only been maintained at its pre-war level, but it is now 250 strong—bigger than ever before.

Sales of pigs, mainly from pedigree stock, at Holywell Farm during the nine months from April to December, 1943, brought in £2,500. The best animals fetched anything up to 80 guineas. In December alone sales totalled nearly £700. Some of the porkers became somebody's tasty Christmas dinners; others are being used for breeding.

The Corporation did not exhibit their pigs in any of the national shows until 1934. Then in that year they audaciously launched out and entered their best Middle Whites in the Royal Show of England—the "Cruft's" of the pig world.

The Watford pigs swept the board in the class in which they entered. They took the cup for the Middle Whites female champion, and the prize for the supreme Middle White champion of the show.

From that day boars and sows from Holywell Farm have taken big prizes at all the principal shows up and down the land. Such a degree of excellence, indeed, has been attained by Watford's pigs that they have been exported for breeding purposes to over twenty countries. Watford Corporation supplied the first Middle Whites ever sent to South Africa.

WO January, 1944

New Camera Club

TO-MORROW evening, at Watford Central Library, a number of Watford camera enthusiasts will meet to discuss the possibilities of forming an active photographic society in Watford.

It is felt that "leafy Hertfordshire," with its many beauty spots, provides wide scope for such a society, and Mr. W. Mitchell Bond, of 76, Harford-drive, Watford, the convener of the meeting, is anxious to hear from all who are interested in photography.

WHP February, 1944

L.C.C. Wants Oxhey Estate

The fate of the Oxhey Place Estate is now in the balance, the battle having reached its climax at Watford Town Hall on Monday and Tuesday, when Mr. W. H. Collin, ex-Chief Inspector of the Ministry of Health, came out of retirement to hear the London County Council's case for confirmation of a Compulsory Purchase Order and the arguments put forward by the opposition, including Watford Town Council, Herts County Council, Rickmansworth Urban Council, and the trustees of the Blackwell Estate.

Defining the attitude of Watford Town Council, the Town Clerk, Mr. G. Salter Davies, said that although they sympathised with the L.C.C. in its problem of having to provide housing for 100,000 families after the war, they considered that there should not be one standard of accommodation for the wealthy and another for those referred to under the Act as "persons of the working class."

They did not want Watford drawn into the London maelstrom, but if the Order materialised Watford Town Council would do its best to make the people feel at home.

WHP April, 1944

Post-War Plans

Watford Town Council decided on Tuesday that as post-war expenditure will be restricted for the first three years, the town's five-year programme should be spread over eight years.

Schemes which have been prepared by the various committees are estimated to cost £728,000 and the suggestion is that by delaying some of them the town will get better value for money, and it may be possible to finance them without increasing the rate burden in respect of loan charges.

Councillor Smith said he considered the committee had paid too much attention to the rate aspect. He added: "I do feel that the urgency of important schemes must over-rule the rate question."

Referring to housing, Councillor Smith said they were hearing quite a lot on this subject, and he felt the people would press them on this matter to a far greater degree than they had suggested.

The citizens will want houses, and a very considerable number of them," he said.

WHP May, 1944

Gone for a Pub Crawl

The High Street had long been reputed as a street with many pubs. By 1944 many had gone but there were enough left to make a pub crawl a test of stamina . . .

Towards the Arches:
Eight Bells
Three Tuns
Leather Seller's Arms
King William

from the Arches to the town:

Wheatsheaf	*One Crown*
Jolly Anglers	*Kings' Arms*
Hit or Miss	*One Bell*
Anchor	*King's Head*
Swan Inn	*Spread Eagle*
Fox	*Rose & Crown*
Railway Tavern	*Compasses*
White Hart	*Green Man*
Three Crowns	*Coachmaker's Arms*

Embarkation leave

Sheila carries daddy's gas-mask,
Peter carries daddy's gun.
Mother's chattering on and laughing
As if parting were just fun.

She's put apples in his pocket,
He's got photos in his book,
When he isn't busy fighting,
He'll have time to have a look.

Dad is going to fight for England,
For a world where men are free,
Better times for all but — mostly
He'll be fighting for these three.

SALUTE THE SOLDIER

The soldier is giving up all he holds most dear. What can we do to show our gratitude? We can salute the soldier by saving. SALUTE THE SOLDIER

Fourth Million

WITH £100,655 still needed on Saturday morning to enable Watford to reach its "Salute the Soldier" million pounds target, the Campaign Committee felt a bit anxious and issued special bulletins.

They need not have worried. The town and district made a great last-minute effort, put in £232,605 that day, and so carried the total to £1,131,950.

Even this was not the finish. The final balancing of accounts showed the total to be £1,142,058, or not far short of the £1,150,236 raised in Wings Week.

A particularly bright feature was the great part played by small savers. They beat last year's figure of £12 7s. 2d. per head of population by 2s. 7d., much to the satisfaction of those responsible for this side of the effort.

WHP May, 1944

223

Members of the British and Allied Services, who took part in Bushey's 'Salute the Soldier' parade, recline 'at ease' on the lawn behind Bushey House waiting for the address by General Sir Frederick Pile. (The target £125,000 to beat a challenge of £200,000 by Berkhamsted.)

"D" Day

THE news that the Great Day had dawned was hardly credited in Watford during the earlier part of Tuesday.

Scepticism at first followed the German broadcast. Then there was speculation that it might be just a feint landing.

When the B.B.C. announced a landing in force the mood of the people took on a noticeable change.

There was visible excitement wherever groups of people gathered, and as bulletin followed bulletin, early excitement and enthusiasm gave place to a somewhat more sober mood, with a fuller realisation of what the great assault betokened.

The roar of the great armada overhead before dawn was the first indication that something unusual was astir, and throughout the day, as the planes streamed to and fro, eyes were lifted towards the sky—eyes that held a new light of hope and faith.

WHP June, 1944

Invasion View

FLYING in a Lancaster bomber on "D-Day," Flight-Sergt. Hutton, of Watford, had a bird's-eye view of the start of the invasion of Normandy.

Describing the scenes Flight Sergeant Hutton said, "It was an unforgettable sight, to be followed later on our return journey by an even more imposing spectacle.

"Suddenly, stretched away as far as the eye could see, were two massive convoys, one on our port bow and the other to the starboard.

"These were no small fry, but big ships in line astern, with their escorts of destroyers and corvettes which fussed around them like chicks round an old hen.

"Some were flying balloons and the sight sent the pilot bouncing up and down in his seat and clapping his hands with joy. One of the crew counted 55.

"That was our big moment, for these two great convoys steamed steadily on course as if such a thing as war and opposition were out of the question."

WHP June, 1944

Made Homeless by Flying Bomb

EARLY on Sunday morning a flying bomb crashed on to an area in Southern England. Deaths and injuries were caused and property was damaged. The most amazing thing was that Anderson shelters stood undamaged.

An A.R.P. worker on duty shortly before the bomb crashed told our representative that the missile dived. A fire followed. The N.F.S. and rescue squads were quickly on the scene. There was no shortage of willing helpers, prominent among these being Service men of all ranks and a number of American officers and men.

The work of rescue was considerably handicapped by scores of morbid sightseers, who in some cases even broke through the cordons.

The spot where the bomb fell is near where a bomb fell in the early days of the war.

WO August, 1944

District Mourns Flying Bomb Victims

A district's last tribute to victims of the flying bomb which fell on a housing estate was paid last week when a sympathetic crowd gathered as the funeral went to the cemetery.

Flags were at half mast, blinds were drawn and people gathered at street corners to watch the cortege pass.

A reporter writes: On our way to the cemetery we climbed a steep hill, and came upon a small group of people standing outside a gate.

We entered, and just beyond saw the robed figure of a clergyman waiting to receive the mourners. He walked to and fro in deep meditation.

"Silence, please," in a peremptory but sympathetic voice, caused all heads to bow, and the chief mourners in deep black walked slowly past and filed round the grave.

The coffins, draped with the Union Jack, were lowered, and a reverent hush fell as the clergyman moved to one side of the grave. He commenced to speak.

His voice, though sombre, was full of solace and reassurance. He said, 'I want you all to feel that you are supporting and sympathising with the bereaved."

He spoke of the victims, and muffled sobs were heared as he referred to an eight-years-old child. The sobbing stopped as he quoted a Psalm.

"I want all of you to feel that you are the mourners, that these people are our brothers and sisters," said the clergyman. He paused to pay tribute to the local Council for the manner in which they had arranged the burials.

"They have arranged it," he said, "that everyone of these people, though sharing a common grave, shall have their own funeral.

"They are not unknown," he said. "They are our brothers and sisters. They were sleeping in the same district as us. Some of them were very near to us.

"They lived their lives as we do, and their lives—in their own ways—were much like yours and mine."

The speaker was inaudible for a time as a fleet of aircraft roared overhead on their way to the battle fronts. Retribution was the keynote of those engines, and as the silver specks disappeared in the clouds the speaker continued:

"Let us pray for these people," he said, "that they may gain their eternal reward."

WO August, 1944

● *'D' Day was June 6th, 1944. The flying bomb disaster occurred early on Sunday a.m., July 30th, 1944.*

V1 and V2 rockets totally destroyed 24,000 houses in the Greater London area and damaged another 760,000 as to make them uninhabitable. Sandringham Road flying-bomb disaster.

The invasion had been launched over two months ago and penetration into France is not yet deep. Hitler launches a 'last-fling' weapon—the flying bomb. Miniature pilotless aircraft powered by a rocket-type motor, which cuts out when fuel is exhausted; after a few seconds of deathly hush there follows an explosion; in July 1944 one fell on Sandringham Road, causing a death toll of 40. Rescue workers face the harrowing task of searching for survivors and digging out bodies . . . .

...'Sun' to merge with Hazell Watson & Viney...

L.C.C. to Build at Oxhey

BY his decision to confirm the Compulsory Purchase Order of the L.C.C. The Minister of Health allows practically the whole of the application—with some minor exceptions.

A little over 921 acres will therefore be acquired for development as a cottage estate to meet post-war housing needs. All the land is situate in Herts, and comprises the Oxhey Place Estate of Mrs. T. A. W. Blackwell. The Order apparently does not apply to 50 acres of land owned by the Artisans' and General Dwellings Company, which is within the Middlesex boundary.

It will be remembered that at the Inquiry it was stated that the L.C.C. would be prepared to exclude the ancient Oxhey Chapel and to preserve a part of Oxhey Woods. It is by no means certain that the mansion of Oxhey Place will be demolished.

Also of timely interest is the fact that the whole of the land which will be acquired by the L.C.C. is an area for which Watford Town Council are applying to be brought within the Borough boundary.

WHP October, 1944

A Forgotten Generation

Sir,—There is much talk of better education for children and I think most people will agree that it is desirable. One point, however, causes me a little concern.

When the children have had the advantage of this new education, is it not likely that the relationships between parent and child will provide us with a ticklish problem?

The present parents of school children, and those young people who have left school and will be the parents of the future, must inevitably find themselves at a disadvantage with their children unless some opportunity is given them to at least equal the knowledge to be absorbed by their offspring.

How, I wonder, can this problem be solved, as the Education Act does not provide for the teaching of present or prospective parents.

Bushey   T.F.

Demand for 8,400 Homes in 10 Years

DEMANDS for the erection of 8,400 houses in Watford in the first ten years after the war, to relieve the housing shortage, are made in a 23-page memorandum to be presented to Watford Town Council.

The memorandum has been prepared by a joint committee of the local Labour Party and Trades Council. It is based on a survey which revealed that 4,271 Watford people are without adequate accommodation.

One proposal likely to cause much heart-burning is that a site of 112 acres in Watford's most "select" residential quarter—the Cassiobury Park estate—at present reserved for large houses, built four or six to the acre, should be used for the erection of 10-to-the-acre working-class dwellings.

The survey sums up its findings as follows:

Dwellings required, 1,499; houses required (included in the above), 1,438; flats required (included in the above), 61; number of people expressing preference for a Council dwelling, 1,117; expressing preference for non-Council dwelling, 367.

Wishing to buy accommodation, 136; wishing to rent accommodation, 1,279; serving men and women requiring accommodation, 400; bombed-out families requiring accommodation, 69.

WHP February, 1945

Firm's Merger Not Ominous

The "Post" learns that the amalgamation announced yesterday, of the printing firms of Messrs. Hazell, Watson and Viney, and the photogravure and letterpress printing business of the Sun Engraving Co., Ltd., will not result in any displacement of workers at Whippendell-road, Watford.

The transaction includes Rembrandt Photogravure Ltd., but does not include the process engraving section in London and Watford of the Sun, or the London typesetting section or any of the foundry departments.

WHP March, 1945

"London Pride"

WATCHED by hundreds of proud eyes, a Halifax bomber, streaming flags of the United Nations, zoomed gull-like over Leavesden Aerodrome on Monday afternoon.

It was a very special bomber, the 710th made by those who watched—employees of London Aircraft Production. It was also the last they would make before, with victory assured, returning to their peace-time jobs; and last, but not least, it bore the gallant name "London Pride" with the appropriate flower painted on it.

That was the end of the story, but perhaps it will be as well to leave the cheering, happy crowds for a moment and retrospect to a different scene—on December 15, 1941.

That was the date when Halifax No. 1 became airborne from the same field that saw the first flight of "London Pride."

Following an urgent appeal by the Minister of Aircraft Production, Sir Frederick Handley-Page—who witnessed Monday's ceremony—set about gathering his forces to produce "at the earliest possible time the largest number of bombers his resources would allow."

Reviewing this period on Monday, Lord Ashfield, chairman of L.A.P., said: "It is unnecessary for me to remind you that at that time no employee of the Group (L.A.P.) had any knowledge of aircraft production."

The Group consists of five concerns, among which is a section of L.P.T.B.

Their deficiency of aircraft knowledge was soon a thing of the past for those who witnessed the culminating triumph on Monday.

The ceremony took place in No. 3 hangar. As soon as the workers saw "the last of the many" bombers, they spontaneously broke into a loud cheer.

Lord Ashfield read a telegram which he had received from Sir Stafford Cripps, Minister of Aircraft Production, in which the Minister offered his congratulations on the memorable occasion.

Lord Ashfield told the crowd: "To build 710 bombers has been a wonderful achievement and an experience none of us will ever forget."

After a tribute to Sir Frederick Handley-Page, Lord Ashfield said he would christen the aircraft in the knowledge that a gallant crew would make it play its part in helping to rid the world of a bestial and ruthless tyranny.

He then named the bomber "London Pride" while the band of Duple Bodies and Motors, Ltd., played the "Knightsbridge March" by Eric Coates.

In the hands of the Chief Test Pilot, "London Pride" thrilled the watchers with an exhibition that proved it will be able to more than hold its own in the final routing of the enemy.

Said an employee afterwards: "It gives one the impression of having completed a job well worth doing."

WHP April, 1945

Drawing To The Close

WHEN the Allied armies were chasing a beaten and disorganised enemy back into Germany, and the Allied air forces were raining destruction on the Fatherland at a rate never before contemplated, even in this war, it was freely predicted that when the end came it could come suddenly.

There was a general feeling that under this intensive attack from without and within, the battered Nazi edifice would crash, topple and fall almost overnight.

Events have shown how wrong we were. The cracks appeared—the most ominous of the earlier ones was the attempt on Hitler's life last year—but still the Third Reich, against all the laws of nature, held together.

There have been other and wider cracks since then. The biggest ones, both within the last few days, have been Himmler's offer of unconditional surrender to Great Britain and the United States and the death of Hitler, the fanatic whose evil genius created and maintained the Nazi hegemony.

The second event, which must in the end add to the consequences of the first has, however, been made the occasion of an attempt to stave them off.

The appointment of Admiral Doenitz as Hitler's successor suggests a temporary suspension of the peace negotiations being carried on by Himmler, for how long cannot as yet be judged.

So we must, for the time being, remain on the tenterhooks which have kept us in suspense all this week.

In Watford, as elsewhere, the last few days have been memorable, if rather tantalising, ones. Everybody has been keyed up to expect the great announcement almost hourly.

WHP May, 1945

Thousands In Streets For VE-Day

HEAVEN'S artillery sounded its salvos as though to herald the dawn of VE-Day. For three hours a tropical storm, more violent than any since that which was the prelude to the day when we declared war on Germany, rent the darkness with vivid flashes, and torrential rain put out the pre-VE-Day bonfires. But the great day dawned calm and clear, the birds sang blithely, and Watford awoke to a glorious day—glorious in every minute of it!

Grey, soaked streets warmed quickly to brilliant sunshine; the bedraggled flags and bunting, in such profusion everywhere, flapped out the moisture, and soon Watford was gay again.

Then the streets filled—streets that were soon sun-drenched—and the hearts of the people warmed to the "King's weather." Lads of the Forces, especially those in hospital blue, received handshakes, even kisses, from perfect strangers. Everyone was happy and glad to go to the Town Hall in the morning for an act of thanksgiving—but not all could be crowded into the great hall.

Then followed gaiety in its many forms—singing, laughter, street tea parties, illuminations, dancing, bonfires. Watford was determined to enjoy every minute of this great occasion.

WHP May, 1945

● VE Day, Victory in Europe, 8th May, 1945.
VJ Day, Victory in Japan, 14th August, 1945.

. . . Watford street lights will go on again . . .

Lights Go On Again

With the exception of a few lamps which have been broken, Watford street lights will go up again on Sunday evening, following the putting back of clocks one hour to British Summer Time.

The Borough Engineer told the "Post" yesterday: "Everything is ready except for some lamps which are out of order but which we are to replace as quickly as possible.

WHP July, 1945

Victory-Joy Sweeps Watford

ALL Watfordians were tucked snugly in bed at midnight on Wednesday when Mr. Attlee made his momentous announcement that the world was once more at peace.

When they woke and learned the news yesterday morning it was with quiet thankfulness and subdued satisfaction.

Not until the afternoon, when the sun burst through the clouds, did it seem that full realisation that the war is over, the boys will be back, and life will return to its normal courses, burst upon the consciousness of Watford.

Then the shops closed, streets filled with gay, happy crowds, victory parties sprang up, bonfires were lighted, and the town gave itself over to a celebration appropriate to the historic occasion.

Watford did not really swing into celebrating mood until the evening, when old and young let their feelings go in victory parties which sprang up all over the district.

WHP August, 1945

The Hell of Belsen

A MEMBER of a Field Transfusion Unit with the B.L.A., whose wife lives in Gammons-lane, Watford, has been with the mercy mission at Belsen. What he has seen has so shocked him that he has written a "lest we forget" description of the horrors.

"This is the most tragic thing in my life, worse than any action I have been in." he says. "Since I have been away from home I have at times wondered what we were fighting for. I had heard yarns of seemingly exaggerated German atrocities, and had taken them all with a pinch of salt. But not now! Never has anyone on earth, other than the people responsible, seen anything like this."

Here is his description of a long, narrow building known as "The Human Laundry."

"Outside a long line of ambulances waited with their loads of living death. This building is appropriately known as the 'human laundry'. All along one side are benches, and to each one is an S.S. woman—a huge Amazon, callous and depraved. The patients are off-loaded by the few remaining German prisoners. There are men and women. They seem dead, but still breathing—a horrible sight. It's quite impossible to say how thin they are, only a covering of skin over the bones. To give you an idea: sometimes they bring two women in on one stretcher.

"Well, these S.S. women proceed to scrub them from head to foot thoroughly and powder the hair with anti-louse powder. They are then passed down to where they are put into clean blankets and sent to the Army hospital. I suppose this is their first wash in five years or whatever length of time they have been in the camp.

"We went into the concentration camp, which is full of typhus, TB., scabies, dysentery, and everything under the sun. The awful stench is too over-powering for some.

"There are delapidated old huts, rags, sacks, straw and everything conceivable which these people had tried to make out of nothing in order to provide some sort of shelter. The majority we saw were women. It was awful and hopelessly impossible to ascertain the ages. Girls of 18, 19, 20, looked like old wizened grandmothers.

"These women crawl out from under their roofing of sacking and attend to all needs of nature. Self-respect, decency, is all gone. They are lower than animals. Those who can walk shuffle along in faltering steps of six inches or so a time.

"We left the hut area and visited one particular place which had just been vacated. I do not know whether it was curiosity or a determination to see for myself, which compelled me and others to go inside. On the floor was a squelching mess about nine inches thick, and on top of that was such a collection of filth I can never hope to describe. Horribly stinking rags which just dropped off these people were strewn everywhere; tins, bottles, God knows what else, there was so much.

"At the end of this place three girls were still living! But the little room they had was more presentable. They looked reasonably well, having not been there long, and they had taken advantage of this room when the rest cleared out to go to hospital. I don't think they had been there more than a matter of months, hence their comparative good appearance, but their decency had gone even then.

"We went to the grave area. Huge pits of bodies alongside a heap of human bones 10 feet high. The most amazing thing was that there was a heap of boots and shoes stacked 15ft high, 30ft long, and 15ft thick. Thousands upon thousands. They had been taken off the dead and placed there as a reminder to the living of the fate which awaited them.

"We met these wrecks, wandering aimlessly around with an insane smile on their faces, looking with envy at the graves, hoping that they soon would find peace. On every building one saw the notice marked out in chalk: "Dead here. Will lorry please call." A few medical students were there, trying to straighten things out, but they had a hopeless task.

"That is very briefly what I saw. Fortunately, instead of going into a concentration camp to work, I am working with these patients after they have been de-loused and washed. We have 1,500 here; they are all T.B., typhus, etc. They are dying off rapidly. I suppose they cannot yet get used to receiving humane treatment, being fed at regular intervals, and a proper bed to lie in.

"At Belsen a squad of German Medical Corps personnel was sent there to help. When they met one of the S.S. Guards they set about him and practically murdered him. Yes, I am convinced that the blame is only on a clique, which so foolishly the German people have followed so blindly.

"These ordinary people are trying hard to make friends with us. They respect us, there is no doubt, in spite of the fact that they are compelled to do all the dirty work here. They are aware of the orders issued to us about no fraternisation, and I feel that they are trying to prove by their efforts to impress us, that they had nothing to do with this state of affairs.

"They did, I suppose, because they allowed the Nazis to rule them. I am certain, however, that they will not tolerate the Nazis again, and I believe they will become a democratic people, for they have been humiliated beyond description.

"Every word in this letter I have written is true, nothing exaggerated—rather understated. It is impossible to find the suitable words."

WHP June, 1945

VI

The Missing Years, 2   1945-55

War-weary Watfordians celebrated VE Day (Victory in Europe) in May 1945. For many families with loved ones still in the Far East the celebrations had other meanings as the seemingly invincible Japanese experienced their first major military reverses.

By VJ Day (Victory in Japan) in August 1945 when the atomic bomb bought the war to a premature and dramatic end, some of the first servicemen to be called up were being 'demobbed'. The process was both ponderous and frustrating as the analogous compulsory recruitment for National Service continued. A positive and material commitment was essential in Europe and the Far East to police the occupied and defeated countries and restore their governments and economies until they were once more self sufficient.

For the housewife little had changed except she no longer had to fear the dreaded telegram and the blackout. Consumer products were scarce and the shortages persisted. Newspapers carried a minimum number of pages, and food (as well as milk), was still rationed.

Plans for providing residential accommodation had been made as factories switched to the manufacture of the pre-fab, specially in London. Large housees were converted into flats but the insatiable demand for more housing continued. Couples who had married during the war years now needed more space for their children. The newly-elected Socialist Government discouraged free-enterprise as it legislated, controlled and allocated. Restrictions dictated the course of events but the population, used to a war-time environment, patiently accepted the privations.

To replenish the national coffers, depleted to pay for the war, factories which had quickly turned to peacetime production became exporters of the goods intended for home consumption. Battered, deprived, war-weary Britain now faced even more years of toil to recover from six years of all-out war effort. The country's pre-war foreign assets had been sold or bartered to pay for essential war needs. There was no prize for winning the war. 'Physician heal thyself' was a truism that all had to accept. Consumer and luxury goods, cars, radios, cameras, foods, confectionery, toiletries, any manufactured products for which there was a market, were sold abroad. The population went without.

The new Town Hall proved a successful venue for the exhibition of goods manufactured locally and Industrial Exhibitions geared to business-generating promotions became a regular feature in the town's calendar.

The 1951 'Festival of Britain' marked a turning point not in austerity but in outlook, as a new hope was injected into an otherwise mundane existence. Some had complained of its unwarranted cost but in retrospect and in psychological terms it was a good investment. (Television sets (black and white) many with 10 inch screens, were becoming available and demand accelerated as the Coronation of June 1953 approached.)

Gradually the housing shortage eased as many new estates were built. When the tenants had faced and paid some of the costs of setting up home, those who had served away looked around for means of regaining some of the freedom they had enjoyed during the war.

Travel. They wanted a car.

Except upon strict priority allocation there weren't many, and second-hand pre-war cars were quickly sold. During the early 1950's small numbers of new cars began to trickle through, and even with 66⅔% Purchase Tax, soon sold.

Many semi-detached properties built in the middle thirties offered 'garage space' but terraced properties gave the car owner problems as parking lights were compulsory. The paraffin hurricane lamp was found to be an effective substitute except it failed to meet the requirements of 'white to front, red to rear' and the driving window parking light connected by crocodile clips direct to the battery became a universal practice. There was one major disadvantage; the dread of every motorist on a damp cold Monday morning as to whether he would face a flat battery.

In 1953 an extensive 'land-use' survey was carried out in what was later to become the 'Central Area', an area bounded by the St. Albans Road Railway Bridge, the Town Hall and High Street Station. During 1954 a traffic census was arranged, the results of which were published in 1956. The report prepared by the Borough Engineer Mr. Sage, and the County Planning Officer Mr. Doubleday, was out of date before being printed.

Austerity was still the norm; restrictions were still severe with £15 the basic holiday travel allowance.

By 1955 the postwar 'missing years' were beginning to recede into the past. Cars were coming onto the market and could be found by dextrous searching. The pent-up demand for consumer goods was due to explode. Watford, with its traditionally long, narrow High Street, and few ineffective roads to relieve traffic pressures, which had survived relatively unchanged for a millennium, was now going to come under threat.

After sixteen long, uneasy years the time was ripe for positive action.

... squatters at the derelict U.S. camp ...

"Squatters" in Langley Way Camp

THE "squatters" are here. Following the example of those in other parts of the country, local families, tired of living in pent-up conditions and tired of the futile trek and inquiries for a home of their own, have invaded the derelict American Army camp in Langley-way.

They came in force. Within a short while 50 families had staked their claims, and others had chalked their names on the few remaining huts. Dozens were turned away, but were not dismayed, and indicated they intended occupying some empty huts at Leavesden.

Some disquiet is being shown by those in the comfortable residential area of Cassiobury Park Estate, and by the Corporation, who have been approached to make water and electricity available.

WO August, 1945

Swift Switch to Peace Programme

WATFORD factories—managements and work-people alike—are straining at the leash to switch over to peace-time production, following the nation-wide cancellation of war contracts announced by the Government yesterday.

Several big local concerns have already begun the transition, and many others have their plans ready to put into operation.

Typical of this class is Scammell Lorries, Ltd., of Tolpits-lane, peace-time commercial vehicle makers, whose contribution to the transport needed by the Army, Navy and R.A.F. and essential home services during the war was colossal.

They produced for the Government 1,449 heavy breakdown and recovery tractors, 786 heavy artillery tractors, 6,074 four-wheel tractor conversions, 676 "mechanical horses," 4,268 trailer under-carriages and hundreds of other vehicles.

Government requirements for those types of vehicles and equipment will continue for some months, and as these taper off, production will be gradually switched over to supply the needs of the commercial work.

Example of a firm which did make a wide departure from its usual work is that of Dickinson's Paper Mills, who cut down on their manufacture of beautifully finished notepaper to produce anti-radar "black strips" and jettisoning petrol tanks for aircraft.

WHP August, 1945

Labour Gain Watford

Claimed to be the heaviest poll on record, 69,825 people representing 72.6 of the electorate, cast their votes. The final figures were:-

Major J. Freeman (Labour) 32,138
Air Commodore W. Helmore (Con) ... 29,944
Major E. Harben (Lib) 7,743

Major Harben failed to poll an eighth of the total and thus loses his £150 deposit.

WHP August, 1945

"Nachrichten" in its Millions

When in the late afternoons of last autumn Watfordians looked skywards and saw, high up a long procession of four-engined British and American bombers streaming towards the Continent they looked at each other with knowing glances and said, "Jerry's going to get another pasting to-day—a few more block-busters will teach him his lesson."

Sometimes an employee of the Sun Engraving Co., Watford, was within earshot. He could have told them that those planes weren't carrying bombs but newspapers—thousands of them.

He had helped print them at the Whippendell-road works, but he could not enlighten his acquaintances, for he was bound by the strictest measures of security silence.

From July 14, 1944, to May 14, 1945, the Sun took part in a deadly type of psychological warfare which had as important a part in bringing about the German capitulation as bombs, shells and bayonets.

Every day during this important closing phase of the war the Company produced anything from a million copies of a propaganda newspaper in German—"Nachrichten Fur Die Truppe" (News for the Troops).

They were packed on the spot in special containers and dropped by plane the same day in the vicinity of German troop concentrations.

There came a time when the effect of "Nachrichten" was more devastating than bombs. Reading of the good food and honourable treatment they would receive as prisoners, thousands of Germans, sick of war, rushed to give themselves up. Opposing armies that might have taken weeks to beat in the field disintegrated overnight. Those newspapers, printed in Watford, helped to make the final, swift drive on Berlin possible.

WHP September, 1945

Sun's Atom Bomb Research

HAD it not been for extensive laboratory research work carried out at Watford during the past two years, the atomic bomb, conqueror of Japan, might not have been possible.

The work, carried out at the Sun Engraving Company's Whippendell-road works, was shrouded in such secrecy that even the "Sun's" workers engaged on it did not know until recently that they were participating in the construction of the atomic bomb.

After British and American scientists had carried out a tremendous amount of theoretical and experimental work into the possibilities of concentrating the energy of the split uranium atom to the point of a devastatingly explosive force, Imperial Chemical Industries were entrusted with the contract for the development of the "diffusion" plant essential to the construction of the bomb, it is recorded in a White Paper, "Statements Relating to the Atom Bomb."

In this work they were assisted by two sub-contractors, one of whom was the Sun Engraving Company as the leading experts on the deposition and electrolytic processes affecting metals.

A small laboratory was set up at the Sun's Whippendell-road premises, and here research workers worked seven days a week.

Their particular problem was to discover a method of treating metal so as to make possible the building of plant necessary to the gaseous diffusion of the uranium isotope known as "U.235."

A technical expert who had a considerable amount to do with the research at Watford told the "Post":

"The work was very exhausting and at times taxed our ingenuity to the utmost. But we had the satisfaction in the end of being able to inform I.C.I. that we had found what they wanted."

WHP September, 1945

De Havilland's to Stay at Leavesden

SECRECY surrounding De Havilland's intentions regarding the future of their factory sited on the King George V Playing Field at Leavesden was lifted by Ald. T. H. Simmons at Watford Town Council on Tuesday when he revealed that the company wish to continue their occupation for the production of aero engines.

He emphasised that De Havilland's were tenants of the Air Ministry, by whom the playing field was requisitioned in 1939, and that in any event De Havilland's would have to work to Air Ministry instructions.

Alderman Simmons was defending the action he took prior to the last Council meeting, when, replying to an enquiry from De Havilland's as to the Council's future intentions with regard to the site, he had informed them, through the Town Clerk, that the Council "favoured the retention of the aerodrome."

"I have had an opportunity of consulting with the managing director of De Havillands and his deputy," continued Ald. Simmons—"especially in view of the possibility of the firm going.

"There was the risk of the loss of employment for several thousands of workers there. If we had said, towards the end of 1944, "The Council wants the playing field back" what kind of a row would that have caused? I think I have a shrewd idea."

WHP September, 1945

Nr. 327, Freitag, 9. März 1945

NACHRICHTEN FÜR DIE TRUPPE

Eisenhower geht über den Rhein

Starke USA-Kräfte fassen auf dem rechten Ufer Fuss

DER schwerste Schlag gegen die Verteidigung des Reiches im Westen seit der Landung der Alliierten in der Normandie ist jetzt am Rhein

"News for the Troops" reporting U.S. Rhine crossing.

... penicillin made at British Moulded Hose ...

Fairfield's Part in Air Warfare

WHEN a large, white-painted Wellington bomber, repaired and equipped with the latest Radar devices, took off from Aldenham airfield at midday yesterday, the Fairfield Aviation Company's last war job was done and the factory, employing 1,100 Watford workpeople, officially closed down. A grand "saved from the scrap-heap" task had been completed.

Jobs have already been found by the Ministry of Labour for practically all the displaced workers. They have been smoothly absorbed into other local industries.

Since August, 1940, when they came to Aldenham as a war-time subsidiary of Redwing Aircraft Ltd., Croydon and Wolverhampton, Fairfield's have repaired and refitted 1,809 fighter and bomber aircraft for the R.A.F. A portion of Odham's factory was placed at their disposal.

Their task was to rescue smashed-up aircraft from the scrap-heap and put them back into the air. This they achieved at the rate of practically a plane a day.

Working day and night, often at nerve-wracking pressure, they took badly shot-up Blenheims, Wellingtons, Hawker fighters and other types and made them airworthy again in a matter of hours.

"Our employees worked wonderfully," Mr. Frank Collins, Fairfield's welfare officer, told a "Post" reporter. "The majority, among whom were many girls and women, came to us untrained and entirely without technical knowledge. They proved tremendously adaptable and within a few weeks became amazingly skilled and efficient."

Fairfield's speciality was the Lysander Intruder. To them, in conjunction with Wing-Commander "Freddie" Pickard, of "Target for Tonight" fame, goes the credit for the development of this specialised aircraft.

Developed from the old Lysander Army co-operation 'plane, the Intruder became a deadly thorn in the side of the foe.

Painted dull black, it flew across the Channel night after night, transporting patriots and supplies to aid underground movements in enemy-occupied territory.

High spot of Fairfield's activity was during the Battle of Britain. As the struggle reached its climax so many 'planes were being shot down or seriously damaged that mobile squads were sent out from Fairfield's to repair them on the spot. These squads, who repaired a total of 593 aircraft and worked wonders at improvisations, became famous up and down the country for the motto stencilled on the back of their jerseys, "Ubend'um, Wemend'um."

WHP October, 1945

Kingswood is Exception

Watford Education Committee decided on Monday that although approval should no longer be given for the use of schools for social events such as children's parties and dances, an exception should be made in the case of Kingswood School.

Couns. C. W. Tyrwhite and S. W. Smith pointed out that Kingswood is a remote district with no other facilities for social events.

WHP December, 1945

Getting the Houses Built

THIS is the problem confronting alike Parliament and the Local Authorities, and even more intimately many of their constituents. Demobilisation from the Forces and the resettlement of industry is enhancing the urgency. The bulk purchasing of housing materials and components, including complete factory-made houses, described by the Minister of Works in the House of Commons on Monday, when speaking on the Building Materials and Housing Bill, should, if operated with vigour and foresight, considerably assist in providing houses. For that is the vital need.

Briefly stated, a short-term policy this report propounded was for 350 dwellings in the first and 550 in the second. A long-term policy involved 7,500 houses in ten years, including replacement of temporary houses. If the new Housing Committee bring forward schemes for the speedy erection of dwellings we feel sure that support will be forthcoming from other Groups on the Council—for let it be remembered that the Borough has no mean record in respect of housing.

Meanwhile, the Mayor and Housing Chairman are appealing to residents for "spare-room" accommodation for urgent cases. A register is being prepared on the response to the appeal, which it is hoped will help to relieve the situation of some of the 2,500 applicants on the Corporation's waiting list.

While many smaller households have done their bit during the war years in billeting troops and workers in essential industries, there may be a good deal of accommodation available in larger houses.

WHP November, 1945

Watford's Penicillin

ON the fifth floor of a large Watford factory is an elaborately equipped laboratory in which a small army of workers—60 per cent. of them local women— are working seven days a week to produce penicillin.

They make the new "wonder drug" at the rate of 1,000,000 doses a month.

During the latter stages of the war this laboratory was producing a very high proportion of all the penicillin made in Britain. At that time its activities were on the "highly secret" list, and although it is now possible to tell the story of its work, none of the 120 employees knows the formula to which he or she is working.

That is still a secret of the British Medical Research Council and the U.S. Office of Scientific Research.

Branch of a Greenford firm of manufacturing chemists, the laboratory was established under the auspices of the Ministry of Supply in the top storey of the British Moulded Hose Company's premises at Sandown-road, Watford, early in 1944. Delicate and costly apparatus was installed and stainless steel had to be specially diverted from armament production to provide some of the essential equipment.

A "Post" reporter who visited the laboratory this week saw girls deftly handling hundreds of flasks containing penicillin mould which passed slowly along on a conveyor belt.

He was told by the manager: "Here you have intricate laboratory work carried out on factory production scale. Something like 90,000 flasks are growing penicillin mould here at any one time, and as a fluctuation of only one degree in temperature can seriously affect the growth, the care that must be taken can be readily understood."

WHP December,

KILLED IN THE WAR, Europe

	Armed Forces	Civilians
American	170,000	—
British	333,000	60,000
French	250,000	270,000
German	3,250,000	3,640,000
Russian	13,600,000	6,000,000
Yugoslavian	300,000	1,300,000
Dutch	10,000	100,000
Total all nations		
(inc. others not listed)	19,070,000	14,730,000
Murdered Jews		5,978,000
Asia and Pacific		
American	50,000	—
New Zealand	10,000	—
Australian	30,000	—
British	40,000	—
Chinese	3,500,000	10,000,000
Japanese	1,700,000	360,000
	5,330,000	10,360,000
Total worldwide losses	53,300,000	

Putzger, Historische Weltatlas

No Later Shopping

From now until March, 1946, Watford shops will have to close not later than 5.30 p.m.

Watford Town Council has made this decision under Defence Regulation 60AB, which continues to remain in force. Tobacconists, confectioners and newsagents are exempted from the Order, while barbers and hairdressers are allowed to remain open until 6.30 p.m.

WHP December, 1945

Spotlight on Cinemas

Watford Town Council is to ask Herts County Council for information regarding Sunday opening of cinemas in Watford.

Ald. Last, stressing that his question was not a criticism of the operation of Sunday cinemas in Watford, and that he had no grounds for believing that there were any irregularities, asked on Tuesday for details of the amounts paid to local charities, and also whether the cinemas were observing the conditions laid down regarding Sunday staffing.

Very stringent conditions were fixed regarding payments to hospitals and conditions of labour when the licences were granted, Ald. Last reminded the Council, and he had been asked to raise the matter. If he could be given an assurance that these conditions had been observed he would have nothing further to say.

Coun. Mrs. Bridger wanted to know whether Ald. Last had any specific knowledge of infringements, and whether he had been approached by an individual or by an organisation.

Ald. Last replied that he was not prepared to divulge who had approached him. He had no specific knowledge of any irregularity, and he was not criticising the cinemas. There was "a feeling" in the town and he had been asked to raise the matter.

WHP December, 1945

● *North Watford residents of the 1930's, before the advent of Odhams and the new estates, viewed the North Watford gasometer as an 'imposition' and 'hideous eyesore'. It was frequently complained of in the local newspapers.*

The Pond, frozen. 1946

Woodside, Leavesden.

The car without registration letter or number can belong to only one person—the King. Passing North Watford roundabout on a visit to the Canadian 'Khaki University' at Leavesden are HM King George V I and HM Queen Elizabeth.

Upon their return to London they passed through Watford, where it was remarked that the 'King looked pale, drawn and tired' whilst the Queen, in a red coat, looked bright. Feb. 1946

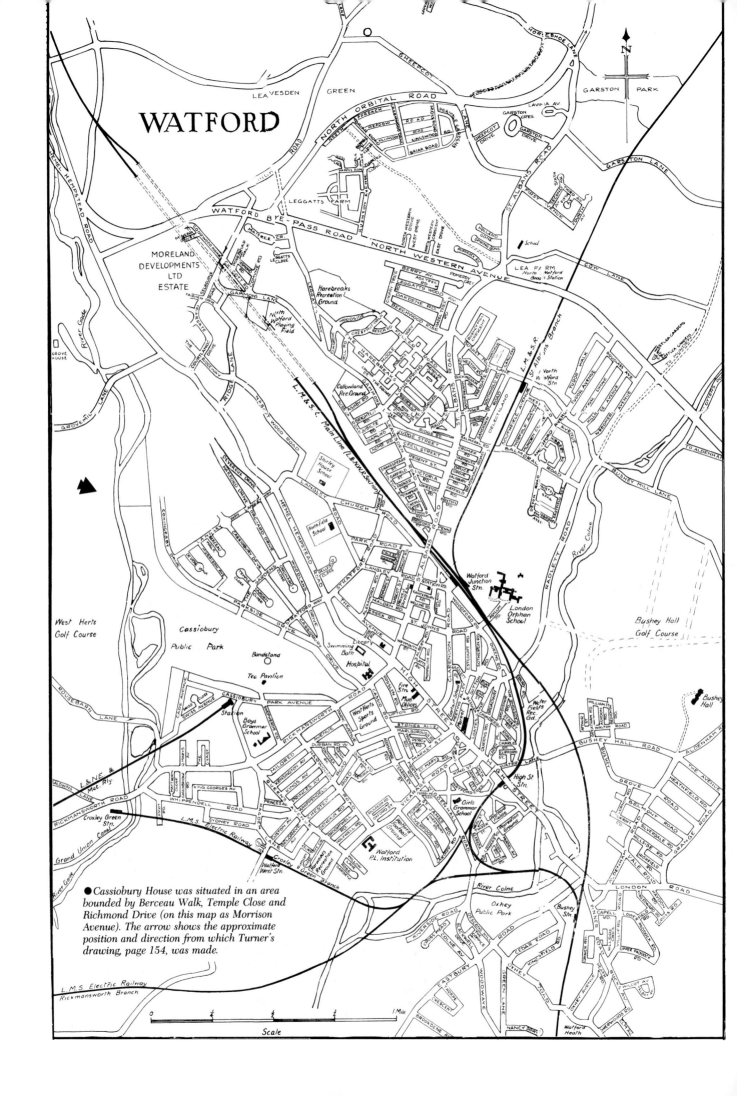

WATFORD

● Cassiobury House was situated in an area bounded by Berceau Walk, Temple Close and Richmond Drive (on this map as Morrison Avenue). The arrow shows the approximate position and direction from which Turner's drawing, page 154, was made.

Scale

0   ¼   ½   ¾   1 Mile

... the New Town Hall, ... busy hive of war production? ...

On the left is a map of Watford of 1938; little road or house building took place during the war years so the map is substantially valid for 1946. Not long after the map was produced and printed, a German plane well-equipped with aerial photographic equipment flew over the town and took the above photograph.

With the aid of the map, roads and estates may be easily identified; the older parts of the town being dark and stained in contrast to the Harebreaks, the Knutsford and Tudor estates looking very new indeed.

The heading reads 'War Photograph No. 446 M 141, latitude and longitude plus magnetic deviation in mid 1938 and 'Nachtrage'—supplement or postscript—date of 24th May 1939. The main heading refers to Watford, Electricity power generating station.

The 1946 "Watford Observer" story:

Watford's escape is the more remarkable when it is now possible to reveal that the new Town Hall was not an administrative building, but the busy hive of war electrical equipment production.

This mistake might have been very costly to the town—in lives, disorganisation and financially.

PERFECT PROOF

For the benefit of those who doubt this gross mistake we reproduce a photograph of Watford taken by the Germans on May 24, 1939—a little more than three months before war was declared. This photograph was filed with thousands of other aerial photos of towns and villages of England in a Luftwaffe library at Lubeck, North Germany—used at one time by the crack "Luftwaffe 26 Gruppe." It was probably taken by a German passenger plane. Further aerial views of Watford were taken in August, 1941, and similarly filed.

The survey reproduced shows in black relief the Town Hall and the area between the Public Library and extending down St. Albans-road. This area was marked "A" and labelled to indicate electric equipment works.

If this map was used it may have been responsible for the dropping in 1940 and 1941 of oil bombs, incendiaries and high explosives in the High-street, Queen's-road and Harebreaks areas.

WO September, 1946

Councillor J. Wright, Mayor, in the carriage, in St. Albans Road.

The procession, from the High Street, via Market Street and Cassio Road, to the Park.

Victory celebrations, June 1946

Legless Hero Opens Carnival

When Group Captain Bader arrived, in a grey civilian suit, early in the afternoon, he was met by the Mayor, who escorted the legless hero to the platform and introduced him to the cheering crowd.

By coming to Watford on such a great day, said the Mayor, Group Captain Bader had done Watford high honour. They were privileged to have with them a man whose deeds had made his reputation international.

Declaring the afternoon session of the carnival fair open, Group Captain Bader said with a smile: "In spite of the nice things the Mayor has said about me, I would rather face anything than be facing you chaps on this rostrum.

"Nevertheless, I am very pleased to come to Watford, for Ald. Timberlake has been writing to me and telling me quite a lot about your show.

"I see that in 1943 you made a record 'high' for your hospital of £4,000. To-day I hope the organisers will go one better and squeeze out of you at least £4,001."

The Carnival Queen, Miss Betty Saunders, called upon everyone to enjoy themselves, and reinforced Group Captain Bader's appeal on behalf of the hospital.

WHP June, 1946

Whitsun Downpour

NOT even so impressive a combination as Victory Day and the Whitsun Carnival in aid of Watford Peace Memorial Hospital could produce a day of "flaming June" for the double event, although everything else was organised with the utmost efficiency.

After Group Captain Douglas Bader, "the legless wonder," had opened the Victory Day fete not even the torrential rain could separate holidaymakers from their revels.

Climatically, it was the same sad story on Monday. The gymkhana, highlight of the Whitsun carnival, suffered quick switches from sunshine to shower, but evening brought more settled weather, and thousands of visitors ploughed through the mud in search of pleasure—and found it, according to their varying tastes.

Children had a Victory concession. They were admitted free to the carnival and provided with tickets which were passports to the swings, roundabouts and other attractions.

Promptly at 10 a.m. Watford's Victory parade and carnaval procession moved off from Harebreaks, watched by crowds which thickly lined the four-mile route to Cassiobury Park.

Colourful and impressive came two open landaus, each drawn by a pair of prancing greys. The first bore the Mayor of Watford, Councillor J. Wright, in his red robes and glistening chain of office, together with the Mayoress, the Deputy Mayor, Councillor Mrs. Emily Beall, and the Town Clerk.

In the second landau travelled the Carnival Queen, Miss Betty Saunders, and her attendants, each carrying a gorgeous bouquet.

Round the two carriages rode six outriders—four girls and two men—smartly dressed in military style costume.

After travelling down St. Albans-road into Station-road and Queen's-road, the procession turned into High-street where the excited crowds were thicker than ever. The long column turned into Market-st. and proceeded by way of Cassio-road, Whippendell-road, Harwoods-road, Rickmansworth-road and Shepherd's-road into the side entrance of Cassiobury Park.

WHP June, 1946

Whit Monday gymkhana.

Council Workers Shocking Harvest

HALF A LOAF and 13 mouldy hunks of bread were the chief exhibits at Watford's "Battle of Bread" Exhibition, which opened yesterday at the Kingham Hall, St. John's-road.

They had been found by refuse collectors while clearing dustbins in one small sector of Watford on Saturday, and are typical of the shocking waste which is taking place in many parts of the borough every day, it is stated.

Mr. F. C. Sage, the Borough Engineer, told the "Post" yesterday that a special check had been made by his inspectors in the past few weeks and bread, potatoes, green vegetables and other waste food were often found in the van-loads of refuse.

It was hoped Ald. H. J. Bridger, local Food Executive Officer, would tell the Ministry of Food that Watford did not want bread rationing, If it was inevitable, that would be that, but if it was to be averted, the best means would be by avoiding any single scrap of waste.

Mrs. Gordon Spencer, a Ministry of Food speaker, outlined the causes of the present world food shortages, and the terrible effects it was having in the large Continental towns.

In the House of Commons Mr. John Freeman, Watford's M.P., asked the Minister of Food whether he was in a position to make a further announcement about the likelihood of bread rationing.

Mr. Strachey replied that consultations with the bakery trade and others concerned were taking place, but if there were the slightest risk of grave consequences by not rationing bread, then unquestionably the decision would be to ration. Nothing had occurred since his previous statement on May 31 to make the introduction of bread rationing appear less likely.

WHP June, 1946

£150 Fines on Dairymen

FINES totalling £150 were imposed on a 73-years-old farmer, of Coldharbour Farm, Bushey, and his son-in-law, of the same address, for selling more milk than the permit allowed.

Mr. T. Anderson Davies, prosecuting, said the farmer was the proprietor, and his son-in-law the manager of a farm where a dairy business was carried on. A permit issued to the farmer on March 3, 1946, allowed him to sell 517 gallons of milk a week. For the five weeks from March 2 he sold weekly 676⅜, 673⅜, 676⅜, 721⅜, and 693⅛ gallons.

From these sales he had made a total illicit profit of £37 8s. 8d. This position was discovered by an Inspector who examined the records at the farm.

Mr. Neild, for defendants, said the farmer had a farm of 180 acres, partly dairy and partly arable. He was 73 years of age and in poor health, and had never concerned himself with the milk records, which he left to the care of his wife.

His wife was also in poor health, and at the time of the visit by the Inspector the books were being kept by Thomas.

Some of the milk which was sold was produced on the farm, and the necessary amount was made up by buying from a wholesaler. When the farmer was producing more milk, supplies should have been cut down from the wholesaler immediately. That was where the omission had occurred. The books were available for the Inspector to look at any time.

WHP July, 1946

Progress on Housing Sites

MEMBERS of Watford Housing Committee, anxious to see the progress in the town's housing drive, travelled round the various housing sites on Thursday afternoon last week. The party was conducted by Mr. F. C. Sage (Borough Engineer).

The first site to be visited was at Riverside-road, where 44 permanent houses are to be built. Work had begun on 40 of these, and ten were nearly completed.

It was explained by Mr. Sage that difficulty had been experienced here with regard to access roads. Special roads had had to be built, and the materials had been brought to the site without damage. The installation of electrical work was proceeding in some of the houses.

The idea was to keep a certain uniformity throughout, which was being done by using the same type of bricks, and a feature of these houses was the new type of concrete roofing tiles which were being used on all the houses.

The cost of the houses would be about £1,200 each, with some additional costs. This figure would not include the price of the land.

There were four old cottages, which would be pulled down when the tenants could be rehoused in the new houses now being built. These cottages were the last of the "back-to-back" type in Watford, and some of the families had been living there for over 50 years.

There were seven contractors working on the site, and on one particular block of houses there were eight carpenter trainees and eight brick-layer trainees from the Government Training Centre, with two instructors working. In all there were about 125 men working on the project.

The Committee members inspected some of the houses, and expressed their satisfaction with the work.

The next site to be inspected was at Leavesden Green on the Watford bypass. Here it is planned to erect 200 permanent houses, of which half have been started. The foundations have been dug, and in some cases building up to a height of three or four feet has been reached. It was stated that there were already 300,000 bricks on the site.

The last of the sites to be visited was at Garston Park, off the St. Albans-road, where it is planned to build 280 houses. Here they have been busy cutting roadways, and the foundations of a few of the houses have been laid.

Altogether nearly 600 houses are being built in Watford by the Watford Borough Council at the moment.

WO October, 1946

£2,000,000 Herts Project

An Act of Parliament in 1937 gave the Colne Valley Sewerage Board the authority, by the Colne Valley Sewage Disposal Act, to construct a disposal works which would take the place of 24 small works all over the county. With their new scheme in mind they started a year later, but were forced to stop at the outbreak of war.

In May of this year, with the help of 165 German prisoners, they restarted.

"By 1948," Mr. E. A. Williams, deputy clerk of the Board, told our reporter, "we shall have finished the job."

"People may think that sewage is a distasteful subject, but it is all very necessary. In days not so long ago, when refuse was run into the fields and ploughed in to fertilise the ground for next year's crops, it was a distasteful thing."

WO December, 1946

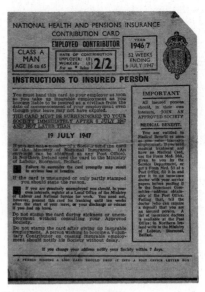

Man's insurance card, 1947.

--- CUT THIS OUT AND KEEP IT AS A GUIDE ---

How to get your new Ration Book

WATFORD BOROUGH

NAMES BEGINNING:	WHEN TO GO:	WHERE TO GO:
S — Z	Thursday, July 3 & Friday, July 4	Small Town Hall, entrance side leading to Car Park from Rickmansworth-road, Monday to Friday, 9 a.m. to 5 p.m.

WATFORD RURAL DISTRICT

ABBOTS LANGLEY and RADLETT SUB-OFFICES will be closed for normal procedure from June 7 until further notice.
Saturday, July 5, 13, Upton-road, Watford.
Thursday, July 3 & 4, Carpenders Park, Church Hall.
Tuesday, July 8, Letchmore Heath, Village Hall.

RICKMANSWORTH

RICKMANSWORTH DEPOT, THE BURY, BURY LANE, RICKMANSWORTH
Thursday, July 3 and Friday, July 4.
10 a.m. — 1 p.m. 2.15 p.m. to 5.15 p.m.

CHORLEYWOOD

CHORLEYWOOD DEPOT, CHORLEYWOOD HOUSE
Thursday, July 3 and Friday, July 4, 2 p.m. to 5 p.m.

WHAT TO DO

1 Fill up page 4 of your present ration book and leave it in the book.

2 Take your ration book and identity card to the distribution centre. (If your identity card does not bear your right address or if you have lost it or it is in a very bad condition, go to the Food Office instead.)

3 If you hold a green ration book as an *expectant mother* and you have to produce a fresh medical certificate to the Food Office before 20th July, you can get your new ration books at the same time.

4 If you hold a *temporary identity card* and have to renew it at the Food Office before 20th July, you can get your new ration book at the same time.

Food Facts will tell you what to do after you get your new Ration Book

MINISTRY  OF FOOD

235

Despite years of rationing, children were healthy and well-fed.

Station Road/Langley Road/St. Albans Road. Corner shop is Fisher's.   1947

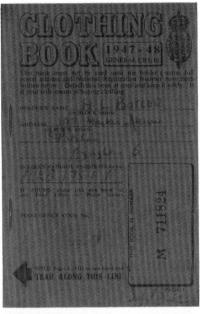

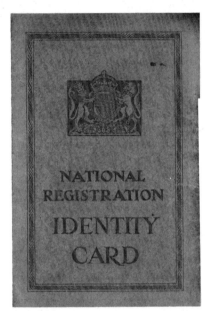

"NO" To Squatters

IN a test case yesterday, Watford Furnished Houses Rent Tribunal decided it has no jurisdiction to hear applications from squatters occupying huts at Langley Way Camp for reductions in the 9s. a week rents they pay to Watford Corporation.

Reason was that the huts, comprising a former U.S. Army camp, now belong to the Crown. Said the Tribunal Chairman, Mr. W. R. L. Trickett: "After carefully examining the legal issues, we have arrived at the conclusion that we should not assume power to give a decision or make an order against the Crown, or against the local authority as managing agents of the Crown."

"It is settled law," Mr. Trickett explained, "that the Crown is not bound by a statute unless specifically mentioned in it, or is by necessary inference brought within its terms.

"We must decline to take a step which would in effect disturb the administrative and financial arrangement obtaining between the local authority and the Government."

WHP May, 1947

Knowing the round, the horse would instinctively make for each stop, pause, and then make for the next.

A battery of 40 high speed Letterpress machines at Odhams. Odhams (Watford) Ltd was started in 1936 to print many titles previously printed by Sun Printers. Production included not only magazines but a wide range and variety of hard-back books.

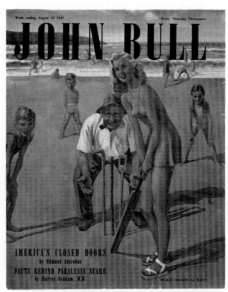

'John Bull', the people's crusader, a counterpart to 'Picture Post'. 'John Bull' carried more articles, less photographs, and had more reader-involvement in correspondence.

Answers at Housing Exhibition

WHEN it is my turn for a house, what will it be like? Will it be easy to manage, and keep clean? Will it have any "gadgets"? These are probably just a few of the questions the Mrs. Jones, Mrs. Smiths and Mrs. Browns, who make up the waiting list of 3,773 applicants for houses in Watford have been asking themselves.

They had the opportunity of finding out the answers to some of their queries at Watford Housing Exhibition last week, where main interest of women visitors was centred on the complete house, constructed on the middle of the ballroom floor in the Town Hall.

This house was exactly similar to one of the types of permanent prefabricated houses Watford Corporation is building on its sites.

This was no empty shell, but a fully furnished home, such as newly-weds, and couples sharing homes or living in rooms must often have dreamed of. Nothing had been forgotten. There were flowers in the vases, the clocks were ticking, and in the wonderland kitchen, there were all the necessary pots and pans, and even packets of cleaning materials.

In the past kitchens have been treated as the "Cinderella" room of the house. Whether the women members of the Watford Housing Committee have brought their influence to bear or not, I don't know, but one thing is certain: in Watford houses of the future, that will definitely be a thing of the past, and the kitchen will take its rightful place, as one of the most important home features.

Nothing has been forgotten which will make for easy running. Ample window space ensures maximum light and air, and correct placing of commodious cupboard units, and a refrigerator, leaves plenty of room to work, without wasting unnecessary energy.

One typical housewife, who was looking over the model, spent most of her time in the kitchen. "I think it's wonderful," she told me as she opened and inspected cupboards, pleased with everything she saw.

WHP April, 1947

Planning Minister's Visit

It was an astute move on the part of Watford Corporation to invite the Minister of Town and Country Planning to open the Housing Exhibition in Watford on Wednesday, but what a lack of imagination was shown by the organisers in the lay-out of the Town Hall by making no accommodation for the Press. With a visit of a Minister of an important Government Department one would have thought such provision would have been among the priorities. From an echoing microphone reporting was almost a game of chance, and we feel sure our readers will understand that any brevity in our record is due to the absence of Press arrangements.

Mr. Lewis Silkin did not disclose his mind on the vexed question of County Borough status, except, perhaps, in his emphasis that the development of Watford must be considered in relation to the whole of Hertfordshire. While he had praise for the enthusiasm shown regarding housing schemes and the enterprise in recent planning, Mr. Silkin could not forego a tilt at Watford's "untidy and sprawling" growth.

The new Planning Bill, he considers, will smooth the way for Local Authorities by its compensation provisions. Alderman Simmons was in agreement with the Minister when he deprecated Watford becoming a "second London." Watford has its own community outlook, and has no desire either to ape, or be swallowed up in, the Metropolis.

As to the Exhibition, various contractors display their wares, a most interesting stand being that depicting the work of the Government trainees. The Exhibition remains open until tomorrow evening.

WO April, 1947

Harder Work Prescription

THRILLER of the year—The Economic Survey for 1947—weighs the nation's resources and finds them seriously wanting. The facts of Britain's parlous state should now be apparent to the least politically minded. The Survey's prescription: harder work, less inefficiency and more co-operation, has still to be swallowed in factory and home.

Meanwhile the labour position shows every sign of deteriorating in the coming months, due in no small part to the raising of the school-leaving age, and the continuance of conscription.

In countless factories, however, thousands of youngsters who could be productively employed are spending one or more years at the start of apprenticeships doing little of value and learning less.

Apprenticeship, as enforced at present, is a relic of the past. It is so much deadwood, and needs drastic pruning.

The Government is showing the way ahead with its Training Schools for ex-Service men, of which in Watford there is an excellent example for the building trade. The scheme might well be extended.

Leaving school at 15, children will be better adapted to intensive courses in their chosen professions, which could be fitted in before they are conscripted. On demobilisation a short "refresher" would fit them for an immediately active place in industry. Thus the short-term loss of an extra year in the classroom will be even more outweighed by the long-term gain.

Industrial backwoodsmen and trade union mandarins, in pondering this, might at the same time remember Mr. Attlee's words: "Everything will depend on the willing co-operation and determined efforts of all sections of the population."

WHP May, 1947

The years of intensive troop movements have passed; the Junction Station with a stripped-out canopy roof looks tired, tatty and careworn. There's not yet enough labour and materials to start 'facelifting'. In mid-1947 the lamp posts still have war-time black-out bands of white. *p.129, 311, 342/3*

Trademan's 22 Offences

COMPLAINTS by a housewife of being over-charged when buying fish from Ankers, Ltd., High-street, Watford, were received by a Minis-try of Food inspector the day after he had discovered 21 other offences by the same firm of selling fish without statements of price or weight.

This was stated at Watford Court when on Tuesday, the proprietor, Allen Anker, described as "one of the old original tradesmen of the town," pleaded guilty to all the offences and was fined £45 with five guineas costs.

Mr. T. Anderson Davies, prosecuting, des-cribed how the inspector had seen the van delivering fish in Hempstead-road on February 21. He examined the tickets and found that none showed the weight or price.

He went to the shop in High-street, and the record books produced gave no indication of the prices per lb. or weights delivered.

"By a strange coincidence," said Mr. Davies, "the inspector was visited by a Mrs. Morris, of Aldenham, who complained of being over-charged by the same firm."

Mrs. Morris had been charged 4s. 8d. for 4lbs. of cod by Herbert Edwards, the manager. Later, the same day she want into another branch of Ankers in Lower High-street, and for the same type of purhase was charged 10d. per lb.

When Mrs. Morris told the assistant of the discrepancy, he advised her to go back and reclaim the excess.

While sympathising with the difficulties of shopkeepers these days, Mr. Davies said the need for the regulation was self-evident. People must be protected from overcharging.

WHP June, 1947

Town's Industrial Exhibition

WATFORD—sleepy market town at the close of the last century—has taken its place in the forefront of provincial industrialism. Four de-cades of managerial drive and workers' crafts-manship put it there on Thursday, when the curtain was raised on the borough's own indus-trial exhibition, destination of overseas visitors and the shop window of the town's producing prowess.

Born from informal discussions between manu-facturers and the Town Council, the project brought from factory bench and technician's shop a sweeping, inspiring survey of the diversity of Watford's industry and wrote a new page in the history of Britain's industrial life, for never before has a town the size of Watford put its goods before the world.

This week—after busy workmen had won their fight against time to get over 60 stands ready by zero hour—the Town Hall has been the rendez-vous of British and overseas buyers. They saw what was described at an inaugural luncheon on Thursday as the results of the team work of local industry, and came prepared to negotiate large orders with local firms.

WHP June, 1947

David Greenhill—Master Printer . . .

Colour Barrier

In 1890 a Mr. Andre started a small business which specialised in half-tone engraving at Bushey, then took in his two nephews Wallace and Arthur Sleigh.

In 1895 Cassells bought the firm of Andre and Sleigh and built the premises in Bushey Hall-road, later acquired by Ellams and burned down, where a new building stands today, for the adventure into colour work.

"Arthur Sleigh took me into his confidence," Mr. Palmer recalls. "I was the only one besides himself and his brother who took part in the experiment because they did not want anybody to know about it until such time as they had made it a success."

By 1896 they had come to be able to produce the three primary colours—yellow, red and blue. After further efforts they managed to blend in black with the work to give depth and a finishing touch.

"It was a very difficult job in those days," said Mr. Palmer. Negatives were very poor and it was a long time before we could get screens and filters to pick out the colours.

"Precision was the most important factor because otherwise the four blocks overlapped and made a sort of blurred pattern. And we had to leave the colour from each block a whole day to dry instead of running on each colour while wet as nowadays."

The great year of triumph was 1899. By that time the pioneers had brought the new process to the practical printing stage.

"We took on small printing orders," recalled Mr. Palmer "which would probably amount to about 5,000 in those days because there were hardly any printing machines able to print colour work on account of precision, or register. But the makers soon began to improve the machines altogether."

The first machine which satisfied the requirements of colour half-tone was the Miehle.

In 1913 Mr. Edward Hunter bought the firm of Andre and Sleigh from Cassells and it has become the world famous Sun Engraving Company.

In the early 1900's there was a number of colour printers in the town, chief of these being Messrs. Bemrose Dalziel, of North Watford, Andre and Sleigh—a first rate process house and one of the first of its kind—and the Mempes Printing and Engraving Company in Whippendell-road.

At that time there was in Watford a brilliant young engineer who had already made his mark with Bemrose Dalziel. His name was David Greenhill, a name which afterwards became synonymous with the "Sun."

In 1909 the famous printing house of Cassells, owners of Andre and Sleigh, formed a new company known as Bushey Colour Press and young David Greenhill was appointed manager. He also became assistant manager of Andre and Sleigh and subsequently the whole of the process works of the two companies came under his supervision and management.

A printing exhibition in London in the Spring of 1914 brought about the first moves that led to the birth of Sun Printers Limited. Some fine quality colour work was shown at the exhibition by Andre and Sleigh and Mr. Edward Hunter, chairman of the Anglo Engraving Company, who were also exhibiting, realised that under Mr. David Greenhill's management Andre and Sleigh were likely to be keen rivals with his own firm competing for quality work.

Mr. Hunter started negotiations for the take-over by Anglo Engraving of Andre and Sleigh and the subsidiary company of Bushey Colour Press, and after several meetings this was arranged for August 1, three days before the outbreak of World War 1.

With the outbreak of war in 1914 the British Government recalled the gold coinage and Mr. Greenhill, by now recognised as an expert in printing, was called in for consultation by the Treasury and asked to act in an advisory capacity in the printing of treasury notes.

He soon found that it was easy to forge the first monochrome attempts at paper currency and between 1914 and 1916 he took an active part in the experiments to produce a banknote that would not be easy to forge.

With this end in view he linked up with another Watford printing house, Waterlow Brothers and Layton—afterwards to become Waterlow and Sons Ltd, (Milton Street, North Watford).

Often David Greenhill worked right through the night at his home to perfect a note that could not be copied and after many setbacks the answer was found in a combination of the three major printing processes—letterpress, lithography and gravure—which neither colour filters nor other photographic methods could successfully copy.

Waterlow's got the contract for printing the new notes, and it was the part played by Anglo Engraving Company in developing the notes that lifted them to a prosperous establishment able, in 1918, to take over the Mempes Printing and Engraving Company.

On this amalgamation the four companies, Andre and Sleigh, Bushey Colour Press, Anglo-Engraving Company and the Mempes Press, were renamed the Sun Engraving Company, with Mr. David Greenhill as a director and general manager.

It was not long before Mr. David Greenhill introduced the printing of periodicals.

Mr. David Greenhill's nephew, Mr. Gordon Greenhill, was appointed managing director of the new Rembrandt works in Whippendell-road.

One of the earliest and perhaps largest orders he undertook at this time was the reproduction of a series of Poster Stamps in photogravure for St. Dunstan's, using a series of bright single colours to give variety to a monotone production.

There was not at that time a suitable photo-gravure machine in existence which could be adapted for such a formidable job.

Under his guidance one of the Sun machines was subsequently converted to print two colours on one side of the paper with monotone on the reverse to test the possibilities of printing colour work on a rotary press from a reel of paper.

Many of the experts considered such an undertaking was not practical, but Sun went ahead with an inset to a large publication and cylinders were etched for two colours to print from a reel.

The experiment proved a great success and resulted in a demand for this class of work far greater than the facilities Sun Engraving had to offer.

Having overcome the difficulties for two colour printing, Mr. Greenhill turned his thoughts towards three or even four colours on each side of the paper by rotary printing.

An English firm of engineers was approached to build a small machine to print four colours on one side of the paper and one colour on the reverse.

They refused to accept responsibility for making a machine they did not believe would work. Undaunted, Mr. Greenhill and Mr. J. A. Hughes, another director, went to Germany to try and get engineers there to build the rotary they needed for the Sun.

Again they were unsuccessful. They failed to convince the Germans that such a machine was a practical proposition and had to return to England empty handed.

David Greenhill did not lose faith in his idea and eventually he persuaded the firm of Messrs. John Wood, of Ramsbotham, to build the machine.

Even they would not guarantee that it would be capable of four colour printing and said it was up to Mr. Greenhill to make it work.

As Sun were the experimenters, they were prepared to take the risk and work on the machine pushed ahead.

The great day arrived when it was installed at Watford and trial runs showed that very little adjustment was needed to produce sheets printed in four colour one side with monotone on the reverse.

David Greenhill's brainchild had become a reality. He had produced the first colour sheet printed by Rotary Gravure.

This machine was the prototype from which many more were built and incorporated with larger machines so that complete magazines with pages interspersed throughout could be produced.

WHP July, 1957

Soon after The Engraving Co. established itself at Watford, David felt it important to introduce periodicals, which from a trading point of view was sound judgment as it established a regular turnover. A start was made with *The Draper's Organizer*, a weekly letterpress magazine which included a number of 4-colour illustrations. This development, however, made a great difference to the working conditions in the factory because it was not possible to produce such a book in a normal working week. Day and night work had to be introduced which has continued ever since, and this has enabled the firm to offer a service to its many clients which has been second-to-none in the printing trade. Before long other letterpress periodicals were undertaken and the department was kept very busy.

Nor was the expansion limited to the main factory. In 1932 an interest had been taken in Rembrandt Photogravure Ltd., a firm previously mentioned. In 1934 this firm was acquired by The Sun Engraving Company and it moved from Norwood to Watford where it continued to prosper until 1940 when World War II made it inevitable to close it down owing to the necessity for transferring the men to war work or the fighting services.

Although the development of special photo-gravure machinery was quite outstanding, David nevertheless had an equal interest in the machinery needed for other departments. Mr. B. B. Bausch was the supply agent for the "Albert-Frankenthal" machines in London, and apart from some photogravure machines made by this firm in Germany, David wished to discuss the making of a special twin-type of Letterpress Rotary in order to print economically *Weldon Ladies' Journal*. After many alterations and additions to the plans prepared, Herr Kurt Ganss came over from Germany to help reach a decision on the final specification.

David initialled the final plan and notes which Herr Ganss and Mr. Bausch took to 'the Chief' in London, who confirmed the order for the machine, which owing to its twin-character and the necessarily large number of guide-rollers,

239

turner bars and spindles, gave the delivery-end of the machine a harp-like appearance, and the "Albert" designers and engineers always referred to this machine as the "Greenhill Harp."

Mr. Bausch and Herr Ganss met David over a period of many years between the two wars to discuss machines that for one reason or another British firms at the time seemed reluctant to make.

David saw many changes in Germany between the years 1921 to 1937, and his comments on what he saw were of great interest. The essential fact stands out that orders went to Germany only because most British firms seemed more interested in repeating standard machines than experimenting with the new ideas which David and Mr. C. F. Cook discussed at length together, and which the German firms were enterprising enough to interpret into blueprints and finally machines which gave the particular performance required.

In the early nineteen-twenties David first became interested in estate development. Sixteen acres of land were purchased at Garston, and the fifty houses eventually built there were the commencement of all development of Watford north of Harebreaks estate. The land had a frontage to St. Albans-road, and David was anxious to preserve the fine trees bordering the road, and in addition arranged tree planting along Garston Drive and Garston Crescent, which were constructed to serve the estate.

David formed the company known as Watford Ideal Homes Ltd., of which his wife's cousin, Mr. R. Scott Willis was first secretary, becoming director in 1935.

The earliest of the new buildings had been the Clock House, adjoining Messrs. Bucks Restaurant in High Street, Watford, in 1923, and this provided shops offices and garages. "Rutherglen," which had remained unsold when the family moved to Gade House, was converted into three flats. The next venture was more ambitious, as in 1934 he built a block of shops and offices to the designs of Mr. Hubert Lidbetter, F.R.I.B.A., and Mr. Henry Colbeck, F.R.I.B.A., on a site at the crossroads, Watford, opposite to the site on which was later built Watford's new Town Hall. This building was the cause of a good deal of anxiety, as it was a little distance from the main shopping centre, and for some time it was probably more of a liability than an asset. The site of Faircross House had been that of the house and garden of David's old friend Dr. Herbert Hall, who told him he wished to sell this, and wondered what price he should ask for the property. David realized that Watford was developing so fast that ultimately the value of the site would appreciate, and named a figure that he felt Dr. Hall should obtain. However, no buyer came forward, and David decided to offer to buy at the figure he himself proposed.

Faircross House eventually became a reasonable investment, particularly since the building of the new Town Hall has brought added activity to the immediate neighbourhood.

David's last building venture before the war was the building of a block of flats in Clarendon Road, Watford, on the site of a large semi-detached house known as "Grantchester" standing in a good-sized garden. This house was demolished and on the site the block of flats known as Grantchester Court was erected to the designs of his son-in-law architect, Mr. John Howard Leech, F.R.I.B.A. This block of flats proved a great success, and a drawing of them was exhibited at The Royal Academy Exhibition in 1938.

Some of the heaviest responsibilities came about through people asking his advice and help and then perhaps lacking the courage and capital to carry out the recommendations made. David had such confidence that his proposals were sound, that he found himself offering to make himself responsible for the necessary reorganization. To the family's amazement and concern (they felt he had more than enough responsibility in his printing career), they found that he had become involved in the affairs of a large drapery store, and later in a large farming estate, comprising four farms, three at least in a serious state of neglect. David, whatever project he undertook, realized the importance of "key" men, and by appointing Mr. E. A. Corp of The Sun Engraving Company as secretary of the drapery store, and asking his advice on all the aspects of costs and expenditure on his various other enterprises, found he had not only a dependable associate, but a good friend and colleague, in whom he could confide many of his purely personal and private affairs.

Nineteen thirty-nine was the peak year for The Sun Engraving Company Ltd., who were printing and dispatching more than 1,500 tons of printed matter each week. The staff had grown to over 2,000 and was always a problem because of the highly specialized character of the work. These figures give some impression of the magnitude of the firm's efforts, and in order to accomplish the required output it was necessary for the factory hours to be continuous from 12 o'clock midnight on Sunday until 10 o'clock the following Saturday night. Below is a list of some of the most popular publications which were produced by the company:

Ladies' Journal, Film Pictorial, Woman's Own, Good Taste, Weldons Bazaar of Children's Fashions, Mother and Home, Good Gardening, Passing Show, Picturegoer, Weekly Illustrated, Pictorial Education, Farmer's Weekly, Mickey Mouse, Silver Star, Cavalcade, Everybody's, Picture Post, Supplement to Weekly Times, Vogue, Vogue Pattern Book, Vogue Knitting Book, Housewife, Country life, Christmas Pie, Summer Pie, Nursing Mirror, Pearson's Magazine, Today, Insets and Covers to *Radio Times.*

The weekly publications at one time had a total circulation of over 6,250,000. The monthly magazines totalled 2,600,000 and the quarterly and special editions amounted to approximately 6,000,000 copies. David had more than a cursory knowledge of all this work. Indeed, he would discuss the details with his executives, who had a great respect for his unbounded knowledge.

The volume of printed work had now reached enormous proportions and it was difficult to imagine that the output of the Works could be increased to an appreciable extent. The Company was seriously considering expansion by building to meet the increasing demands, when one of the largest publishers with whom The Sun Engraving Company had a great reputation announced that they were building a photogravure factory of their own and would be taking away and themselves printing various publications. Although there had been rumours and the blow was not entirely unexpected, it caused much anxiety. The Company, if it were to make progress, had to replace this work very quickly.

There were two new publishers with whom David was in close contact, and it soon became evident that if contracts could be secured from them, these would more than compensate the firm for the loss of the other publications. Before the last periodical of the old publishers was taken away The Sun Engraving Company was in the throes of preparing the new publications, one of

which was *Picture Post*. In all the negotiations it was suggested that *Picture Post* would start at approximately 375,000 and fall back to 250,000 or 300,000 copies per week, but everybody was hopelessly wrong in this conjecture. Instead of falling after the first issue of 450,000 the second week's issue reached a total of 750,000 copies per week, and the number continued to rise rapidly until a total of 1,750,000 copies per week had been reached with a total of 104 pages per week.

Of all the work David handled, *Picture Post* was the finest achievement in photogravure, and the most remarkable example of his powers of organization, made possible by his ability to work as the leader of a team of specialists who shared his enthusiasm in this undertaking.

Although the purpose was not known until much later, it was about this time that The Sun Engraving Company Ltd. began to do the experimental work on a vital stage of the Atomic Bomb Development. It began with an interview between David's colleague—Mr. Noel Hunter—and an official of the Metals Division of Imperial Chemical Industries Limited; this firm was engaged on special work and thought the experience of The Sun Engraving Company might be used or adapted to assist them.

The production of the newspapers was, perhaps, unique; it started shortly after the Invasion of Normandy and continued seven days a week until May 1945. Formes were received at 5 a.m., stereos cast, and on machine by 8 a.m.; presses were running by 8.30 and 1,500,000 newspapers were delivered by 2 p.m. These newspapers (whose editors were Germans) contained the latest and most accurate information for the German soldier, and they were packed into special fused containers for delivery by the R.A.F. and the U.S.A.A.F. to the German Army by 5 p.m.

The firm's effort, the tempo of which constantly grew, kept pace with the steadily increasing demand, until even its enormous capacity was taxed to the limit. Taxed, but never beaten, as the staff worked long hours. Some men were recalled from munitions and from the Forces, and every means possible was used to maintain this important work. The work for the Political Intelligence Department alone totalled 1,848,000,000 leaflets, many in four colours, weighed 4,400 tons and used 250 tons of ink.

The Sun Engraving Company's Engineering Department was constantly used to boost production in other factories and, particularly, those of high priority and in short supply. This breaking-up of bottle-necks meant that the plant and staff were being constantly changed and adjusted to meet a varying demand; nevertheless, the record is impressive:

679,000 bearings for Bren-gun carriers.
525 main-drive gears for Matilda tanks.
500 sprocket wheels for Matilda tanks.
975 stub axles for Hamilcar Gliders (including the prototype).
420,000 fuse timing rings for A.A. shells.
180,000 various parts for bulldozers, excavators and tanks, from screw bolts to major components.

Much of the work was of a very difficult and specialized nature, and its success was a tribute to the high degree of accuracy achieved by the Company's Engineer—Mr. Donald Berry.

Early in 1942 the Company was approached by the Admiralty Signal Establishment to assist in making practical application of a scheme to improve inter-ship radio communication. The idea was that should a ship be in action the Signal Officer should have for his use a chart from

. . . the 'Bible of the Invasion of Europe by the Allied Forces' . . .

which, with the aid of a code, he could determine what frequency of wavelength to use.

The work was of great operational importance and of the utmost urgency. Speed was essential, for the U-boat war was at its height, and yet the idea was a new one and production of its type had no precedent. Furthermore, a completely new set of charts was required each month and in time to distribute to all the thousands of ships at sea, in every ocean of the world. How could this idea be committed to paper and be illustrated in such a way that ships' crews could easily understand and apply the knowledge under conditions which would permit no errors and with no loss of time? The firm's staff, artists and production chiefs under David got down to this problem and devised a method of illustration and production which was completely satisfactory and thoroughly practical. The production of these charts, a most exacting task, was continued for five years, and was later extended to include every Allied ship throughout the oceans of the world.

About the autumn of 1943, the Air Ministry, on the advice of His Majesty's Stationery Office, contacted David about some highly secret work which ultimately proved to be the most exciting that had been undertaken. It was of the highest importance and had to be conducted under conditions of absolute secrecy and urgency. It was, in fact, the "bible" of the Invasion of Europe by the Allied Forces. The whole of the coast of France and Normandy had been photographed from the air and these photographs pieced together by experts. Vast areas were to be reproduced in the finest detail and thousands of copies printed and bound into book form for the use of the British Invasion Forces. So excellent were the results achieved that the Americans abandoned their own effort and the British scheme extended to cover all Forces.

The work was obviously of a highly confidential nature, and every production department had an area screened off; entrances were guarded and plates and copy transported between departments in locked containers. David contracted to produce 60 units of a certain size per week; at the production peak this was extended to equal 480 of the original units. The work was of the highest possible quality, combining fine engraving and good printing. It was probably the largest process engraving order ever placed, comprising the etching of over 600,000 square inches of 175 screen plates, over 70,000 hand engravings of lettering and diagrams, also the make-ready and printing of over 1,300 separate sheets, 14,000,000 hand-folds and 27,000,000 hand collations. Individual books weighed up to 7½ pounds, and to cover the operations up to and after "D" Day to the Rhine, 37 individual volumes were produced. The first work in the interest of security was called "Boxes."

After the invasion, as the Allied Forces swept eastward, so the demand for more and more production became increasingly insistent. The next work was called "Cases," and made practical the gigantic strategic operations of Bomber Command and the American 8th Army Air Force. "Kartons" followed—covering tactical targets and ground operations in Holland, Belgium and France, not covered by the "Boxes" series. Finally "Pakkets," code name for a further series covering the operations on the Rhine, the Ems and the Elbe rivers and also the Southern Redoubt on the Danube.

The tempo of work increased day by day as the campaign developed, and as demands appeared more impossible, so the response of the staff kept pace. The machine-room staff worked for forty-three Saturdays out of fifty-two in addition to late

working on every day of the week. Girls in the warehouse worked for thirty weeks without a single day off.

David had shown qualities of leadership, organization and improvisation which have seldom been equalled, and had inspired his managers and staff to very great efforts. This period was a great strain on him, but he rarely lost the ability to look with confidence to the future, and time and again his mind would turn to plans for peacetime production and development. As early as 1941 he had asked for development plans and reports from his senior executives. His interest in the reduced periodicals never lapsed, and the work produced during the war years under extreme difficulty was of good quality.

It is not possible adequately to express the appreciation he and his co-directors felt for their staff, who spared nothing in effort, and put in long hours in order to meet every call for greater production required to meet the demands for special work for the Air Ministry, the Ministry of Information, the Political Intelligence Department and the Stationery Office. Certainly the whole staff made a contribution of which they might be justly proud, to do their part, whether serving in the Forces, or doing urgent war work in the factory at home.

David Greenhill died in 1947 after a short illness.

State-Owned Hospital

AFTER nearly a quarter of a century of fine service to the community as a voluntary institution, Watford Peace Memorial Hospital will, next year, under the National Health Act, become State-owned.

In the interim, the Board of Management is disposing of the hospital's free assets. The money is to be used for the benefit of the hospital, prior to nationalisation, in the firm conviction that "a bird in the hand is worth two in the bush."

It will go mainly to meet the cost of extensions now in hand, and for repairs that were held up by lack of labour and materials during the war. Watford and district residents, whose generosity provided the money, will, no doubt, endorse the action of the Board of Management.

Under nationalisation, incentive for voluntary effort, which it is the joy of many people to give to their local hospital, will presmuably disappear. But if the reorganisation will result in better salaries and conditions for hospital staffs, it will have achieved something really useful.

Nursing is a noble profession, but it is, generally, not well paid. Small wonder that only those who love nursing are prepared to devote their lives to it.

WO October, 1947

Diesels To The Rescue

AMONG 80 large firms in Watford Electricity Undertaking's area are now operating load transfer schemes, some have introduced staggered hours, others have begun night shifts and over 30 have installed auxiliary diesel or steam generating plant.

Reduction of the load by 33⅓ per cent between 7 a.m. and 7 p.m. is compulsory by a Government directive which came into force this month.

Because of certain essential services and continuous processes which must be exempt it will

be necessary, to attain an over-all 33⅓ per cent transfer, for industry in the Watford area to reduce daytime consumption by 40 per cent.

Help in arranging this is contained in a pamphlet just issued by the Town's Electricity Committee, ten thousand copies of which are being distributed to local managements and workers.

It suggests that daytime use of electricity can be reduced by installing alternative types of factory heating or the transfer of machinery test running to night-time.

Firms have found that workers have readily co-operated in the new arrangements, Mr. F. W. Berringer, Watford district officer for the Board of Trade, told the "Post." "Both have shown a sympathetic appreciation of the position."

"So serious is the need that it is not a case of hoping Watford's scheme will work—it has got to work. Otherwise nothing can prevent indiscriminate power cuts which will mean interruption or loss of production, and create unemployment."

WHP October, 1947

Oxhey Place Town Is Born

AT 3.30p.m. yesterday, Mr. and Mrs. W. A. Caldwell, formerly of Paddington, crossed the threshold of 50, Hayling-road, on the new L.C.C. Oxhey estate, and became the first inhabitants of a new town.

They had just been presented with the key by the Rt. Hon. Lady Nathan, chairman of the L.C.C., who said the estate represented "a fine example of democratic planning to meet imminent means."

Lady Nathan made particular reference to the modern kitchens of the houses, which she described as "ideal workshops for the housewives."

They are four-roomed cottages, without parlour, but with kitchens large enough to dine in.

Kitchen fittings and cupboard accommodation provide for perambulators, fuel and tools. Ground and first floors each have a lavatory, and a constant supply of hot water is provided from the stove in the living room, which gives off background heating by means of ducts to two of the bedrooms. One bedroom is fitted with an electric fire, and the other two have points for fires. The linen cupboard is warmed by a hot water cylinder.

Typical of the foresight of the designers is the "one pipe" drainage system, which not only saves cast ironwork, but, being inside the house, is protected in frosty weather. Ample window space gives all the rooms a bright and cheery appearance.

These are the houses in which will live the first of an estimated 14,000 population, when the programme of 3,950 houses is completed.

WHP November, 1947

241

... *Princess Elizabeth weds* ...

We Wish Them Happiness

TO-DAY we celebrate the marriage of Princess Elizabeth.

From the hearts of all of us springs the hope that her romance may be one of long and unbroken happiness.

Princess Elizabeth holds a place of particular affection in the hearts of Watfordians. We shall not soon forget her youthful grace, vitality and charm, so abundantly evidenced when she visited the Hertfordshire Show in Cassiobury Park last year. Sincerely we trust that the Heir to the Throne may renew her contact with South-West Hertfordshire, and this time not alone.

Our thoughts to-day are particularly of two young, sublimely happy people. But as the memory of this great day recedes into history, the Crown which one day the Princess will wear remains for us the emblem of stability, of unity, of continuity. It is a reminder of the principles and traditions which are the bedrock of our British way of life.

It symbolises our faith in our destiny, for which we fought on in Britain when all the odds were against us. Yet it was not the people of these islands who stood alone. Throughout the Commonwealth and Empire, men and women rallied unhesitatingly to the cause. To them, too, the Crown is an unshakable emblem, and to its high service the Princess brings not only her own devotion, but our affectionate loyalty.

WHP November, 1947

☆☆☆☆☆☆☆☆☆☆☆☆☆☆☆

Cycle Theft Epidemic—No Petrol

REMOVAL of basic petrol has increased the demand for bicycles, and an epidemic of cycle stealing has broken out in Watford. During the past week eight cycles have 'disappeared' from this district.

WHP October, 1947

Sirens To Warn You

Air raid sirens are to be used in Watford as à last-minute warning of impending electricity cuts.

This decision was reached following complaints from industrialists that the cuts came so suddenly that they had no time to close down their machines or to prepare other methods of lighting.

Mr. A. W. Barham, chief engineer of the Borough Electricity Undertaking, told the "Post" that if the public also co-operates when they hear the sirens, the duration of the cuts will be substantially reduced.

Even with this method of notification, industrialists will have to move quickly as there will be only minutes, possibly seconds, to spare, as Watford electricity undertaking has no greater warning.

WHP November, 1947

Overpriced Elastic!

PLEADING that he had lent his stall in Watford Market to a friend in order to repay a debt, Nanigopal Nandi, of Charlotte-street, W.1. was dismissed by Watford magistrates on Tuesday, when summoned for selling elastic at an excessive price and failing to display a price notice at his stall on July 8.

Mr. W. W. Dalziel, for the Board of Trade, said that Mr. Gover, a Board inspector, bought two yards of elastic from Nandi's stall for 10d. The controlled price for this elastic—six stranded, flat grade—was 1½d. per yard. Nandi was not at the stall at the time, and Mr. Grover was attended to by Abdur Mohamid Asind Rauf.

WHP December, 1947

●*At £22 3s. 10d (including 30% Purchase Tax), this radio cost the equivalent of 5 weeks work to purchase. The 1987 comparative cost would be approximately £366! For a 'reverse' comparison a 1987 portable mains/battery radio, mono but with VHF, at approx. £20, would have been 90p (18/-) at 1947 prices.*

Future of Langleybury

Further representations to the Ministry for the requisition of Langlebury mansion for housing are to be made by Watford Rural Council.

Herts County Council want the house as a secondary school and seven flats.

Chairman of the Rural Council, Mr. G. Follet told the Council on Tuesday there was strong objection to children having to cycle along dangerous roads from Abbots Langley and Bedmond. Watford Corporation was developing the district and there would be an increase of 500 children. Schools were being promised but it was doubtful when they would materialise. Schools should be going up at the same time as houses so that children go to schools "fit and proper, not hovels."

Mr. H. J. Harvey said the Council's proposal "looked rather like obstruction." It would be better to have a conference than to ask one Ministry to oppose the efforts of another.

The Clerk pointed out it was up to the Ministries to decide to which authority they would give way.

WO January, 1948

New Industrial Developments

HINTS of proposed new developments in and around Watford were given at a Public Inquiry held at the Town Hall on Tuesday. They included, apart from the already announced development of 'Kytes' as a paraplegic settlement, the zoning of Lea Farm for industrial purposes and the acquisition of the majority of the land there by Shell-Mex for research laboratories.

Another proposed development referred to was the use of Garston Manor and estate for agricultural research laboratories and a new secondary school.

The Inquiry conducted by a Ministry Inspector (Mr. S. G. Bulstrode) followed Watford Corporation's application to acquire by compulsory purchase 76 acres of land at Hillside, Hunton Bridge, for a new housing site. The objectors were the land owner, Mrs. V. Fisher; the lessee, Mrs. Lawson; and the farming tenant, a Mr. Norman. Mr. F. Thelfall, a Hunton Bridge resident, also registered an objection.

Watford Corporation's case was presented by Mr. H. I. Willis, and was based on the need for immediate acquisition of additional housing sites to enable contractors to carry on when work finished on the present sites. It was submitted that the Corporation had other sites, but these lacked roads and services, features which commended Hillside as an estate which could be developed speedily.

The Hillside estate, it was considered, had high amenity value and was in close proximity to the Abbots Garden estate now being developed. Provision for development there had been made in the Abercrombie Plan.

Although it was regrettable that agricultural land should be swallowed up, it was inevitable that there would always be hardship to someone, and in this case, the Ministry of Agriculture had not seen fit to over-ride a proposal to develop the estate.

WO January, 1948

St. Albans Road looking towards the town. On the left, the Police Station; after the Police Station, Penn Road, shops, Barclay's Bank, the 'Queen's Arms' and Railway Cottages. Just over the bridge the 'Railway Arms'. On the right, Leavesden Road and the 'Stag'.   *p.345 b.*   **1949**

St. Albans Road, 'Railway Arms' on the left and Church Road to the right.   *p347 c*   **1949**

Whitsun Carnival procession, Scammell Mechanical Horse, float entered by Premier Coaches

... and Benskin's real horses. Station Road.   1949

"Old Town Hall" site

COUNCILLORS protested vigorously when they were asked to approve important proposals for the disposal of 14, High-street—the 'old town hall'—because they had had no opportunity of seeing them until arriving for Monday's Watford Council meeting. The Mayor, Ald. H. Coates, agreed to a five-minute adjournment to enable members to study them.

Eventually the Council accepted the proposals, chief of which was that Herts County Council should receive 12½ per cent. of the proceeds of the sale or lease, the remaining 87½ per cent. going to Watford Borough. A batch of tenders is being considered.

A report of the Acquisition and Disposal of Land Committee emphasised that the site, on which stands the Old Council Offices as well as the Fire Station and Ambulance Station now occupied by the County Council as fire and ambulance authority, should be sold or leased as a whole.

If it proves possible for development to be carried out on Watford Corporation's portion of the property before the County Council vacate their portion, this may be undertaken as a "first instalment" of the general development.

The County Council is to be asked to agree to erect a new Fire and Ambulance Station on another site "at the first available opportunity." While continuing to use the present site, they are being asked to concentrate their services in a smaller area of the property.

The Committee's chairman, Ald. H. J. Bridger, said "These tenders have now been opened, but I am not going to tell you the amounts offered because we are waiting for a report from our agents as to which, in their opinion, is the best to accept. The final decision will rest with the Council, but there is more to it than just the disposal of the land. There are several other important considerations."

Explaining how the County Council came to have a 12½ per cent. interest in the land, Ald. Bridger said they were entitled to a proportion in accordance with the amount of the site held by the National Fire Service in 1939.

"We hope to be able to lease the ground on quite favourable terms. But it must be realised that it may be three, four or even up to 10 years before the Corporation will gain revenue because of the considerable building restrictions in force just now. For the time being, therefore, the lessees would only pay a peppercorn rent."

WHP September, 1948

Waste Paper Needed

IN every load of garbage valuable paper is mixed up with waste, and although the workmen salvage clean cartons and bottles, etc., they cannot be expected to sort out each piece of paper when fresh loads are continually arriving. In any case, once soiled its value is decreased.

If only each householder would scrupulously put aside, tied in a neat bundle, every piece of paper when the dustman calls it would save everybody a lot of trouble.

If housewives would watch the unloading of waste paper at the Tolpits-lane tip they would not ask dustmen to do an impossible job, but would make it easy for them.

Watford's paper collections show a steady increase over the past years, however (in 1945-46 421 tons were saved, in 1946-47 455 tons, and in 1947-48 507 tons in 11 months). A marked increase in paper collection since the new campaign has been shown, but there is still room for improvement.

WO March, 1948

Clarendon Road looking towards the Junction. Congregational Church on the left.   *p.352 bl*

Clarendon Arms Hotel, (built 1860, listed Grade II, 1975), bus terminus for routes 142 to Kilburn, and 158 to Ruislip and Harrow.

p.343 t

The Parade, High Street. Upton Road to the right.

p.153 b   **1949**

St. Albans Road, counterpart to photo on p.243. The Plaza cinema was built onto and around the original 'Clarendon Hotel', of which part may be seen between the hoarding and cinema facade, in 1912. The cinema was first named 'Coliseum'; a change was made in 1930 from silent to sound and the cinema was renamed the 'New Plaza' in 1936.   *p.269 t, 347 t.*   April 1950

Clarendon Road looking towards the High Street. Gates on the left are of the foot entrance to the Drill Hall.   *p.172 b, 312 c.*   1949

The 'Mansion House' was built by Sir Robert Carey, the Earl of Monmouth, and was used by his widow as the Dower House until her death in 1640. The grounds were extensive, joining with those of Watford House and extending to beyond the railway. The house was divided in 1771 and altered in 1830; the south house being named 'The Platts' and the north 'Monmouth House'.

Both were successfully converted in 1928 to business premises, retaining the name Monmouth House.

Above, the Pond. *p.92 bl, 355 tr*

Spy in the Sky

AN allegation that the outside wall of a brick building in St. Albans-road, Watford, had been treated with some material in order that it should not appear new was made by the Town Clerk (Mr. A. Norman Schofield) in the Watford Magistrates Court on Tuesday.

Mr. Schofield was prosecuting for the Watford Corporation in the case against a haulage contractor and builder, who denied that he was in the process of constructing a building without having the authority required by the Defence (General) Regularions, 1939.

In his opening summary of the prosecution's case, Mr. Schofield said that in March of this year a building inspector of the Corporation noticed that a building was in proces of erection in St. Albans-road. On checking it was found that no plans had been submitted. It was also ascertained that no licence had been issued by the Ministry of Works for the building, which was estimated to have cost £269 0s. 8d.

"It is our contention that this building has been erected within recent months," went on Mr. Schofield. "I believe it is the intention of the defence to show this building was, in fact, begun at a date prior to that mentioned in the Defence Regulations. We have taken the trouble to obtain from a Government department copies of an aerial photograph of this site taken in 1946; we have here an expert on aerial map-reading who, I hope, will prove that these buildings were not there in 1946."

In fact, the aerial photograph was not shown to the Bench, it being held that it was not admissible evidence, there being no witness to prove the time and date at which it was taken, or that it was, in fact, a photograph of the area concerned.

After the Bench had considered the case, the Chairman (Mr. Gordon Ross) said: "We accept the evidence that this work began before the material date, and although there was an alteration in the scheme, there was no alteration to the actual building." In these circumstances, he said, the charge would be dismissed.

WHP September, 1948

Seven Cinemas—(1948)

North Watford Odeon
The Plaza (North Watford)
Odeon (by the Pond)
Gaumont (the Parade)
Carlton (Clarendon Road)
Regal (King Street)
Empire (Merton Road)

Clarendon Road, counterpart to that on the preceding page. *p.122 t*

Gaumont, the Parade. Sunday programmes were special 'one-day'; there was a choice of seven cinemas. *p.203 t, 336 tr*

Maze of new roads, and partly-made roads necessitated this totem-pole signpost. In the background is the 'target' scoreboard showing the number of houses scheduled and the total actually completed in the preceding week, together with running total to date.

Prestwick Road shops built but not all occupied, roads unmade—a reflection of pre-1930 days.   1949

After long anticipation, a happy moving-in day for one family.

South Oxhey.   August 1949

With very few shops yet built, the Watford Co-op Society provided a regular calling service of greengrocery, meats and groceries.

South Oxhey—moving-in day

I was about four or five when we moved to Oxhey. I remember the moving van, something like alongside but more boxy; it took two days. The kerbs were ever so high, but I was small. The house wasn't finished and if you know where to look you can still see the wheel marks of my three-wheeled trike from where I went gaily through the wet cement.

The station is interesting; my mother used to tell me of my parent's visit of inspection. We lived in Bethnal Green and coming from Broad Street was no problem—she handled my pram OK. When she got to Carpenders Park Station to go back she couldn't see any way to get across the track. It was so long ago—a porter said "Can I help you, Madam?"; "I want to get back to London, how do I get across?" "I'll help you" was the reply, and the porter carried the pram and me across the track; my mother had to walk the boards. You can see, in the photograph (p.251) where the white-edge line has been worn away. A year or two later they must have built the footbridge. Life at South Oxhey was bad for the first few years; the roads were just being laid out; they weren't made, nothing seemed finished and it was miles to walk to the few shops. We had a horse and cart delivering to our part.

Recollections 1987

Evidence of appreciation of lighted shops after years of blackout. Inflation, though not yet serious, has meant that Woolworth's have had their '3d. and 6d. Stores' sign removed. (Nothing over 2½p.) Fluorescent lamps in use; the old not yet removed. *p.325 t* 1949

Mayor Gets "Switched On"

THE Mayor of Watford, Cllr. F. H. Vince, pressed a switch on Monday night, and in Watford Lower High-street the new fluorescent street lighting system blazed forth. It was greeted enthusiastically by the spectators lining the pavements, for a new milestone in the town's progress had been reached.

WHP June, 1949

Milk Five Days Old

MOST of the milk sold in Watford is anything up to five days old and may have been pasteurised twice. This was said by Mr. K. H. Marsden, Watford deputy Senior Sanitary Inspector, when a deputation from the Public Health Department on Wednesday addressed Watford Trades Council on food hygiene.

A member had complained that milk delivered to him in the mornings was 48 hours old and was

"off" by tea-time. "It seems," he said, "that the surplus milk is taken back to the milk people and dished out next day."

Mr. Marsden said most of the milk sold in Watford came from large distributive companies and was anything up to five days old.

It may come from the West Country or Bedfordshire. The milk is collected from the farms, taken to a collecting centre and pasteurised. It then comes by road tanker or rail to London and the surrounding towns, is pasteurised again and stored in a refrigerator for 10 to 15 hours. The milk is then delivered.

"There is nothing we can do about it," said Mr. Marsden. New milk regulations came into force in 1949 prior to which it was an offence to pasteurise milk more than once.

The Government recognised that it was impossible to enforce this law and amended it.

WHP August, 1950

High Street, corner of entrance to Church Yard. *p.333 c*

Queens Road looking to the High Street. Dog-leg turn into King Street was the source of constant traffic snarls. *p.276 cr*

Traditional Remembrance Sunday. Two-minute silence and short service outside the Peace Memorial Hospital, by the Salvation Army. *p.163 b, 322 tr.*

249

. . . like sheep to market?

. . . but a butcher's wry reminder of the meat ration at 8d. (per person, per week). (About 3p. 1987 value approx. 43p.)

New Hope In Lower High Street

FOR far too long there has been a lot of airy talk about the widening of Watford's Lower High-street, but out of the evidence at a public enquiry on Friday emerges the hope that a start will be made in about six months' time.

It will probably not be a very spectacular beginning. The proposal is to build two new factories 20 feet back from the new highway, which will have an over-all width of 64 feet, and will include 10-foot footways on either side. If not a spectacular start, it will at least give an impression of the shape of things to come.

How long it will be thereafter that the face of Lower High-street is completely changed is a matter of conjecture. To give a date for completion would, as the Borough Engineer puts it, be an entry into the realm of prophecy.

WHP July, 1950

Penalising The Press

WATFORD is the most renowned printing town in the country, and those thousands of craftsman who have added lustre to its reputation must be viewing with some misgivings the announcement that the stocks of newsprint have fallen so low that a return to war-time newspapers is a distinct possibility.

How long will it be, they must be wondering, before the periodicals and magazines, which Watford produces by the million every week, will also sustain a cut?

The Government, in addition to standing indicted for neglect in allowing the newsprint situation so sadly to deteriorate, may find itself accused of an assault on the freedon of the Press, to which it pays so much lip service in the intervals between condemnation by certain Ministers.

If, as is being alleged in some quarters, the newsprint famine has been deliberately engineered, is it fair that hundreds of independent local newspapers should be penalised along with the Party organs from out of Fleet-street, which are anathema to touchy Ministers?

WHP July, 1950

"Fly-Bomb" Memorial

Witnessed by only a few members of the public, the stone erected at North Watford Cemetery in memory of the 40 people from the Sandringham-road area who lost their lives when the flying bomb fell in North Watford in July, 1944, was dedicated on Friday by the Rev. E. D. P. Kelsey, Vicar of Christ Church.

He was accompanied by the Mayor, Cllr. Mrs. M. E. Bridger, and members of Watford Town Council. The ceremony was simple to an almost Spartan degree. There was no unveiling, no wreath-laying, no hymn-singing, no flowers.

Mr. Kelsey recalled two things which stood out in his mind from the day on which the bomb fell. First was the noise of the missile. Soon afterwards there was a second noise—the sound of first aid squads and neighbours hastening to help the stricken. It was an enduring impression, exemplifying the eventual triumph of right over evil.

While the stone is a memorial to the 40 who lost their lives, it bears the names only of the 12 victims who are buried nearby in the Cemetery.

WHP August, 1950

Tandon Motor Cycles; for a short while were assembled and manufactured at Colne Way, North Watford. Unfortunately the enterprise did not last long

owing to difficulty in obtaining Villiers engines and competition from the new BSA Bantam (among others).

Carpenders Park Station before being completely rebuilt to deal with increased local demand; Bakerloo electric train from Watford Junction to Elephant and Castle waiting the clear to proceed. Story, p.248.   1949

£90,000 Railway Station

WORK on a £90,000 railway station at Carpenders Park will be started as soon as possible, state British Railways.

The present station was opened in 1914 as a halt to serve Oxhey golf course, but since St. Meryl housing estate was developed in 1935, and more recently the L.C.C. commenced building at Oxhey, railway facilities have been inadequate. British Railways said that any temporary relief by platform widening was out of the question, because of the nearness of the steam main lines.

They believed that a completely new station was the only solution.

Approval for the new station follows continual agitation from Carpenders Park Community Association.

The two housing estates on either side of the line will be connected by a 12ft. wide subway, from which another another subway will serve the island platform. Besides the usual station accommodation there will be space for 200 passengers' bicycles.

Central heating will also be installed.

The new platform, 450ft long with provision for any necessary future extension to 600ft., will stand immediately south of the present station.

WO June, 1951

Council Wins Churchyard Fight

CANON Reginald James, "a parishioner of Watford for 81 years," has lost his fight to prevent the old parish churchyard being converted into a garden of remembrance, but has gained the safeguards he sought against its becoming "a picnic ground."

The local authority desired to improve the town, and it had been inspired by the Festival of Britain to improve the churchyard along with other sites.

The Council had submitted its proposals to the St. Albans Diocesan Advisory Committee, but the committee rejected them unanimously.

A hint of things to come was given by the Town Clerk when he said the Mother Church of the town was entitled to any improvements that might be made in the vicinity.

It was the intention of the local authority, in the not too distant future, to remove the shops fronting the High-street, which at present obstructed the view of the Parish Church from the High-street.

Vicar of Watford, Canon A. St. John Thorpe, told the Court that he and his churchwardens had requested the Council to take over the maintenance of the old burial ground in 1943.

WHP June, 1951

Herts Population Rise

HERTFORDSHIRE is now the home of more than half as many people again as in 1931—by far the largest percentage increase of any county in England and Wales. Over a third of this new population live in that area of the county of which Watford is the hub, and where the population has risen by nearly 90,000 to within sight of the quarter-million mark in the same 20 years.

Of the 43¾ million population of England and Wales, one in about 70 are in Hertfordshire, and one in less than 200 are in the above-mentioned West Herts area, stretching from Tring to Bushey and from Chorleywood to Elstree, which forms the main circulation area of the "West Herts and Watford Observer."

These interesting facts and those which follow emerge from the Registrar-General's preliminary report (which, he says, are unlikely to show any material discrepancy) on last April's census, just published by H.M. Stationery Office.

WO July, 1951

Twenty years ahead . . .

A Peep Into the Future!

Next week, at Watford Public Library, the public of Watford and Bushey will be able to see some of the results of careful, painstaking work on the part of the planners of County Hall, and what development is outlined for the Watford corner of the county in the years to come.

There, in easy-to-read graphs and maps, will be the main conclusions of the 192-page bound volume which is the analysis of the County Development Plan, a 1951 version of the Domesday Book in detail and scope.

How Watford must change to suit the times, yet still retain its best features, is shown. Suggestions include:—

HOUSING: About 6,400 houses to be built, 1,200 at Woodside, Hillside and Kytes estates and other sites between 1951 and 1953; 2,100 at Cow-lane, the Sewage Farm, etc., between 1953 and 1958; 3,100 at various sites and at Bushey between 1958 and 1973.

SHOPS: 60 new ones—20 (1953-58) and 40 (1958-73) at Cow-lane and the Sewage Farm.

SCHOOLS: 12 new ones, i.e., Woodside and North Watford, (1953-53); Cow-lane, Woodside, Gammons-lane (primary, infants), North Watford (R.C.), Cassiobridge Farm, Gammons-lane (primary), Gisbourne House (primary, infants), and Sewage Farm (secondary) (1958-73).

INDUSTRY: Set aside are 100 acres, mostly on the Cassiobridge Sewage Farm and the Station Estate, Radlett-road (1953-73).

ROADS: In addition to the main improvements the major proposals are—Horseshoe-lane, diversion to new junction with North Orbital-road (1958-73);

Radlett-road, new junctions with the Watford Bypass and Queen's-road (1958-73);

North Orbital-road, extension beyond Hunton Bridge to Rickmansworth (1958-73);

Birmingham Radial-road, a new trunk road leaving the Watford Bypass north of Hartspring-lane (1958-73);

Aylesbury Radial-road, a new trunk road bypassing Watford to the West.

The last of these proposals is not likely to be carried out during the next 20 years unless the economic conditions change considerably.

Other projects: a new fire station in Whippendell-road; a police station in Leavesden High-road; a telephone exchange in Stones-alley, Market-street; an extension to the gasworks in the High-street; and the new T.A. drill hall on the Sewage Farm. Car parks, open spaces and other items are also contained in detail in the full report.

WO February, 1952

Watford Store's £250,000 Fusion

A quarter of a million pounds was involved in recent negotiations which led to James Cawdell and Co. Ltd., the private company operating the town's biggest store, amalgamating with Macowards Ltd., which owns all its ordinary shares.

Under its new title of James Cawdell and Co. Ltd.,—in which Mr. Robin Mugford, O.B.E., who was for many years managing director of the old company, will continue in that capacity—the company has absorbed Pocock's of Brighton, Dawson's of Sidcup and Macowards of Tunbridge Wells.

On January 1st last year the Legal and General Assurance Co. Ltd. bought for £260,000 the whole of the freehold store and arcade at Watford, which in February the Society leased to Macowards for 99 years at an annual rental of £13,500.

WHP (July, 1950)

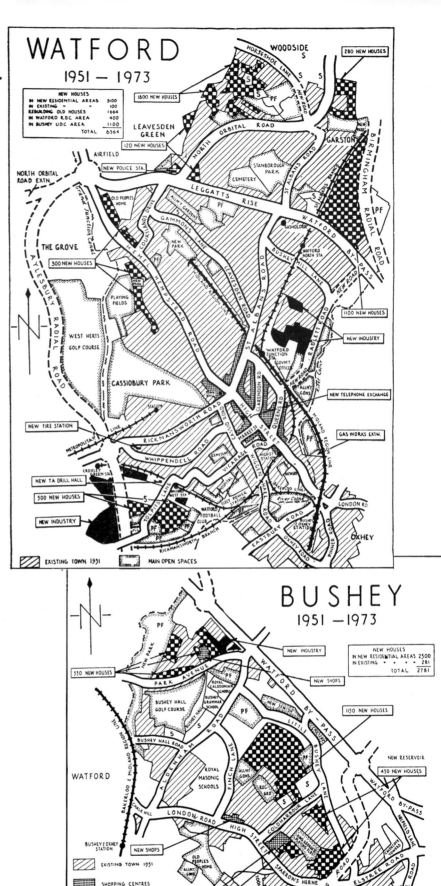

Most plans would be carried out, notable exceptions, the Aylesbury Radial Road is cancelled/deferred, and Radlett Road not much improved.

Nylon Smuggling at Watford

LARGE-SCALE smuggling and evasion of import and export prohibitions on nylon stockings and currency were revealed in a case, which sounded something like an American gangster thriller, to Watford Magistrates Court on Tuesday. There were seven charges preferred against an American citizen, and an Englishman was sent to prison for carrying nylons with intent to evade Customs duty.

T. C. Fry, Jun., the American, of Sandringham-road, Watford, was charged with dealing in nine dozen pairs of nylons with intent to evade duty in April; dealing in 108 pairs of nylons with intent to evade duty in April; dealing in nylons at Brize Norton, Oxfordshire, with intent to defraud on duty for 72 pairs between February and April; dealing in 72 pairs of nylons with intent to evade import prohibition; attempting at Ruislip to evade duty on 120 pairs of nylons with intent to evade the import prohibitions; and in March, contrary to export prohibitions, sending 35 £1 notes out of the country.

Fry pleaded guilty to all the charges. He was represented by Mr. Donaldson.

WO June, 1951

The scene as Market Street traders count the cost of lost business whilst the street is remade. *p.353 tr*

Market Street Traders Losses

WATFORD Market-street traders, who met on Thursday to share their "considerable alarm" at the losses they have sustained through the thoroughfare being closed to traffic, wondered whether they could get compensation from the Corporation, enough to pay for fluorescent street lighting!

Their chairman, Mr. Russell Thomas, sen., said the Corporation had first to complete installing the new lighting for the whole length of High-street, and after that in St. Albans-road, and the question arose whether Market-street traders would be willing to raise the money for lighting their own street. He understood the Corporation were willing to erect the standards, but the rest of the work would cost £475.

Mr. Russell Thomas said that about 30 of the 70 traders in the street had expressed their readiness to help pay for the lighting, but if the others did not come in the scheme might have to be dropped.

A trader then said he knew of a comparable case to the Market-street closing where the traders claimed compensation from the local authority—and got it.

"Rebate on the rates would pay for the cost of lighting," commented the Chairman.

WO September, 1951

Mayor Councillor Mrs. Bridger pressing the button to start the press printing the 1951 Festival of Britain 'Watford, a Pictorial Record', Rembrandt House. 1951

Watford Market Links On View

IN an effort to bring Watford industry and achievement to the notice of the world, and also to strengthen the links between the Commonwealth and the United States of America, Watford and District Industrial Exhibition opened with a flourish yesterday.

Industries, both large and small, had got together, and the result of their efforts was an exhibition unsurpassed in the history of the town. It remains open until June 27.

Crowds gathered at the Town Hall to welcome Commander Douglas Fairbanks, who opened the exhibition.

WO June, 1951

Duchess of Kent at Watford

WATFORD Town Hall entrance was thronged with people on Wednesday afternoon, eager to welcome the Duchess of Kent as she stepped from her car and waved her hand before going on a tour of Watford's Industrial Exhibition.

Her Royal Highness, wearing a lime crepe de chine dress, white hat and shoes, and carrying a white handbag, was received by the Lord Lieutenant of the County (Viscount Hampden), the Mayor and Mayoress (Councillor and Mrs. L. E. Haines), the Town Clerk (Mr. A. N. Schofield) and Mr. G. R. Barclay and Mr. C. R. Greenhill (chairman and vice-chairman of the Exhibition Committee).

WO June 1951

15,000 Visitors to Exhibition

WATFORD Industrial Exhibition closed at 9 o'clock on Wednesday shortly after the 15,000th visitor had paid to enter.

Although attendance at the commencement two weeks previously was not good, it had improved daily, and large numbers were passing through the gates during the last three days.

Many thousands of pounds worth of export orders have been placed, including dollar export and sterling convertible export orders from South Africa, Australia, Indonesia, Portugal, etc. One transformer, ordered as a result of the exhibition, will cost the purchaser over £5,000.

Hundreds of inquiries have been received from potential buyers, and many young people from Watford and the surrounding district have reviewed the various employments that will be open to them locally upon their leaving school.

WO June, 1951

Douglas Fairbanks Jnr., KBE., DSC., American Ambassador, shortly after opening the Watford and District Industrial Exhibition, Thursday June 14th. Here with Mayor and Mayoress, Councillor and Mrs. L. E. Haines.

Duchess of Kent being received by Viscount Hampden, Lord Lieutenant of the County, at the 1951 Industrial Exhibition at the Town Hall.

103 Years—Four Clerks

OFFICIALLY welcomed at his first Council meeting on Monday, Watford's fifth Town Clerk in 103 years, Mr. Gordon Hamer Hall, has been busy at work this week picking up the threads of his new job.

"I've spent most of the time in the Town Hall, and haven't been able to go out meeting many people," he declared to the "West Herts and Watford Observer," "but I've been delighted at the warm welcome I have received. I have been very much interested in the diversity of industry in the town. It is a fine shopping centre, and the Town Hall is magnificent—I don't think I have seen anything to equal it in my career in local government.

At the moment the new Town Clerk, like many a Watfordian, is looking for somewhere to live. He has two sons, Richard and Christopher, aged 12 and five, and they will probably be going to school in the district soon. Mr. Hall came to Watford from Ilford.

WO February, 1952

Keep Death off the Bypass

FOURTEEN Bypass firms, Watford Trades Council, and Leavesden Green and North Watford residents' organisations were represented at a meeting on Wednesday when the Watford Bypass Industrial and Residential Road Safety Committee was formed.

To keep death and injury off the busy and often fog-ridden bypass, the new committee decided to strive for a dual carriage-way for motorists, special tracks for the thousands of cyclists who use the road daily, safer crossings for pedestrians and better lighting for all.

A subway, fencing and pram-ramp at Leggatts-way, and a flashing red light suspended above the bypass at Cox's Corner (Hartspring-lane) pending a traffic roundabout at that point, were other suggestions, but by a majority it was decided not to press for a speed limit.

Formation of the committee was prompted by the recent fatal by-pass accident to an employee of Cox and Co. while he was cycling home. The firm's senior trade union representative, Mr. W. Slade, is chairman, and assistant personnel manager Mr. Frank Hampton, is secretary of the new association.

The latter quoted bypass accident figures which he described as "a black record which must be eliminated."

WHP March, 1952

Only the Best for Preservation

WATFORD Town and Country Planning and Plans Committee disagree with three of the buildings that the Ministry of Town and Country Planning suggest should be preserved in Watford as buildings of special architectural or historic interest.

The buildings concerned are Nos. 96 and 98, High-street, and No. 4, New-street. Objections will be made to the Ministry through the County Council, and the whole matter will be thrashed out before final decisions are reached.

Mr. F. C. Sage, the Borough Engineer, told the "Post" this week: "Just because a building is old it doesn't necessarily mean it's worth preserving. The buildings in the High-street, though old, have been spoilt by modern shop fronts.

We don't think these are worth preserving, and they are in the way of desirable improvements in the High-street and adjoining areas, so we have got to object to them," said Mr. Sage.

WHP March, 1952

Friday Market Starts

Last week, for the first time in its 24 years "under cover" history, Watford Market opened on a Friday, in addition to the usual Tuesday and Saturday. This will continue for a trial 12 months.

About 70 new traders had stalls, presumably in place of regular Tuesday-and-Saturday holders, who were trading elsewhere.

Among the "regulars" who supported, however unwillingly, the first Friday opening was Mr. E. Evett, greengrocer and fruiterer, and secretary of the Market Stallholders' Association.

He said that trade was not so brisk as it was usually on the regular opening days.

"If it keeps going for the year, the Friday market will be a success," he said. "But, quite frankly, I don't think it will keep going for a year," he added.

Said Mrs. Alice Canning, of 442 Gammons-lane Watford, "I think the Friday opening is a good idea, because the Market isn't so crowded as it is on a Saturday.

"Another thing is that we live a bus ride away from the market and it is a job to get on the buses on Saturdays; they, too, are so crowded.

"I shall certainly be here regularly on Fridays."

Mrs. Constance Rolph, of Regent-street, Watford, said that she thought the Friday market was a good idea because it was less crowded than on a Saturday.

"On Saturday, too, I have my family at home, and have the midday meal to prepare, so I shall continue to come here on Fridays."

WO October, 1952

Flats in the Centre of Town?

HERTS County Council had their own reasons for wanting Watford to close its housing list and stop expanding, hinted Watford Borough Councillors at their meeting on Monday. One way of keeping the list open was by building blocks of flats when the centre of the town was redeveloped, they suggested. A proposal mooted by Herts County Council that Watford's housing list should be closed was referred to the Housing Committee for further discussion and report.

Alderman Horwood commented: "I think to some extent the County Council are trying to lead us out into the wilderness on this matter, and we should not take the lead."

Councillor Amey said he proposed reference back because closure of the list would be doing a great number of people a great disservice and wrong.

"It will mean that people who have been on the housing list for two years or more—two years and 11 months even—will not be able to be considered for a house," he said.

Seconding, Councillor Harris suggested: "While not wishing to pick any quarrel with the County Council," that the Borough Council was responsible for the government of the town.

"I think that the County Council do not want to see Watford grow, and I would suggest that we all know the reason for it," he said.

Supporting reference back, but for different reasons, Councillor Baxter said that closing the list was in the best interests of the people of the Borough. If they had nowhere to put people, they should not accept them on a list.

"When we have built up the whole of Watford we still shall not have dealt with all the cases on our housing list," he said. To add to it was giving promises they could not keep.

"The County Council should indicate to us where these people can be placed on a list, and not be put under handicap because they live in Watford," he said.

WHP December, 1952

Duchess of Kent takes a keen interest in block-pulls from a proofing press on the Sun Printers stand. Right: the Duke of Edinburgh during a visit to the Building Research Station, Garston. *WO*

5½ Hours' Stay

LIKE most other people, the Duke of Edinburgh comes up against ordinary every-day problems which, though unimportant, arouse curiosity from time to time.

One of these problems was solved for the Duke by Mr. A. E. S. Wise during his visit to the Building Research Station at Garston on Monday.

Prince Philip had been taken into the experimental plumbing section, and was observing the flow of water through glass waste pipes when he asked Mr. Wise, the scientist in charge there, "Have you found what happens to make such a terrible noise when you are running the bath water away very quickly?"

Mr. Wise replied that they had, and ex-plained, "It is the vortex drawing air into the flow."

The Duke's next stop was in the pre-stressed concrete section, where he stepped on to a pre-stressed concrete plank, springing it up and down under his weight to test its strength.

He next observed the effects of pressure being applied to a half-scale model concrete wall, and eventually saw the wall crack and crumble under tremendous pressure. In the same department, modern photo elastic methods of studying the strength of concrete were demonstrated and explained.

WO May, 1952

Free Flights From Leavesden

THOUSANDS of visitors came along to Leaves-den Aerodrome on Saturday afternoon for the De Havilland Engine Co. Ltd.'s sports and open day, and the first thing they did was to make a bee-line for the notice boards to see if their programme number qualified them for a free flight.

While these flights were being made in a two-engined blue and white "De Hav. Dove," Sir Geoffrey and Lady De Havilland flew in from Hatfield in a stylish red and white "Heron," a four-engined version of the "Dove."

WHP (June, 1953)

Open Day at Leavesden Aerodrome; De Havillands factories in the background still wearing wartime camouflage paint. 1951

255

Water Lane, site of Aubon's decorated butcher's shop of 50 year's previous, just before road widening. The lane had existed as a main entrance and exit to the Hamlet of Watford from Aldenham and Radlett for hundreds of years.
p.73, 328 b

The New Garden

WHETHER or not St. Mary's Churchyard was a suitable site for Watford's Memorial Garden of Remembrance to the Fallen of World War II is a controversial matter which this column has no wish to reopen.

But now that the Garden has been completed, even those who opposed the scheme must surely concede congratulations to the Corporation and to the Parks Superintendent, Mr. L. Ellis, and his staff upon the most agreeable result.

Inviting and gay with the first flush of spring flowers, it is as though the trim new lawns of this delightful oasis have spread a lush carpet over what has been a desolate, neglected nook for decades past.

The conversion has been carried out not only with an eye for beauty, but with skill, for there has been a perfect blend of churchyard, memorial and garden which will mellow not only into usefulness, but into greater charm.

The Memorial Garden of Remembrance is sheltered from the High-street. It is, indeed, the restful, dignified haven from the thronged main thoroughfare the sponsers had in mind. Now it is incumbent upon the public of Watford and all who use this sanctuary to see that it is maintained as such.

WO April, 1952

Holywell's Murky Past

IT IS not the intention of the Corporation to retain the unsalubrious title, "Sewage Farm," for the housing estate mentioned in the plan. "Holywell Estate" is the distinctly more prepossesing name chosen by the Council.

Holywell House is still the property of the Council, though the famous herd of Wessex Saddlebacks which they owned at Holywell Farm has now been disposed of. These prize pigs were exported to many countries in the world, earning laurels for the then farm bailiff (Mr. F. Farquharson) and the Borough.

Controlled tipping has taken place for years at Tolpits-lane, and this area has now been practically levelled off. Eventually it will become playing fields. The Council now use Radlett-road for tipping, and are engaged in gradually raising the level of the ground, which is low-lying and in danger of flooding from the Colne.

By the way, experts made 100 per cent certain that the Holywell estate area is healthy. Some of the earth is being removed for top-soil elsewhere. What is left should be ideal for gardeners, they declare.

WO January, 1952

High Street and Water Lane junction; old-style timber construction of 159 (Simmon's, hairdressers), and 159a (Zip Cleaners), can be seen. Wilson's,

drapery store, remains and today is the 'island site' of Hammond's Music Store.
p.73

1952 rail disaster at Harrow Station when the Perth-London Express crashed into stationary local train; followed by a London-Manchester Express ploughing into the wreckage. There were 112 people killed, of which some 37 came from the Watford area.   October 1952

Harrow Crash

Watford and West Herts has been shockingly hit by Wednesday's triple train crash at Harrow Station.

Just before 8 p.m. last night, with the total death roll creeping relentlessly into the hundred mark, it was known that about a quarter of them were from local homes.

At 8 p.m. yesterday actual figures were: 19 from Watford, most of them from the North part of the town; Hemel Hempstead two: Tring two; and one each from Croxley Green and Kings Langley.

Many of the dead were teenagers.

In addition, anxious Watford families had reported seven persons missing. Approximately two-thirds of the sixty injured in the Watford and West Herts district are Watford residents.

WHP October, 1952

Mayor Visits Bereaved

THE Mayor of Watford (Alderman L. C. Johnson) visited 13 of the bereaved families yesterday morning. He expressed to the relatives his personal sympathy, and that of the people of the Borough. "I felt it would be a far better thing to do than to merely sign a letter," he said.

The Mayor explained that he asked the relatives if there was anything the Town Hall could do to assist in the way of giving either legal or financial assistance to tide them over immediate difficulties. So far, he said, no assistance had been requested.

The Mayor was accompanied by his secretary (Mr. P. E. Judge) and the Deputy Town Clerk (Mr. G. Salter Davies) who was prepared to give what legal advice he could.

WHP October, 1952

Planning Permission delay

One of the "most serious and alarming reports that has ever come before the Housing Committee" was how Housing Committee Chairman Councillor White described delays in the development of Kytes and Holywell Estates, speaking at Watford Town Council on Monday.

The Borough Engineer reported that delay in obtaining planning consent meant "there would be a temporary slackening off in the completion of houses."

He also drew the Committee's attention to the delays attributable to the present practice of issuing separate authorisations for steel and timber allocations.

This, he felt, could be ameliorated by the Ministry of Housing and Local Government authorising local authorities to issue timber and steel allocations within specified limits.

The Committee regretted the delay in obtaining town planning approval to the development of Kytes and Holywell, particularly in view of the repercussions of the provision of dwelling houses.

The Committee recommended that a request be addressed to the Ministry of Housing and Local Government for authority to issue within specified limits both timber and steel authorisations.

Councillor White said they had run across serious trouble over a long period with the Herts County Council over the Kytes estate. Negotiations had proceeded since July, 1951.

"We still haven't got planning permission for that estate, and it has caused delay in the housing programme, as near as can be estimated, of four months," he said.

They would feel the effect of that in nine to twelve months' time.

"Nothing will stop the hold-up in houses coming off the stocks in that time," he declared.

"In spite of not having formal consent we are proceeding with the Kytes estate," he said. "If they are going to pull the houses down afterwards. let them come and do it."

Councillors Edwards and Amey added their concern. The latter declared that of whatever political complexion they were, all councillors were deeply concerned with housing.

"I feel that the Herts County Council and the Planning Officer in particular are doing this Council a very great disservice," he said.

"This has been dragging on and on for months and months without the Borough Engineer getting anywhere at all ... I think we should send the strongest possible protest to County Hall about the delays which will be caused."

WO October, 1952

Black Market in Sweets

WHEN two Ministry of Food officials saw a Watford man offering chocolates for sale from the boot of a car outside a public house, they hit on a black market trail which ended in Watford Magistrates Court on Tuesday. There, fines totalling £1,795 10s., plus 86 guineas costs, were imposed on ten defendants in respect of 84 charges involving nearly a quarter of a million personal points worth of sweets.

The "centre of the web of a system of illicit trading of very considerable substance," said Mr. B. M. Stephenson, prosecuting for the Ministry of Food, admitted 43 charges of supplying various retailers with a total of 212,562 points value in sweets, contrary to the Rationing Order, between October and August.

WHP November, 1952

257

Wiggenhall Road, with power station in the background.

Lower High Street outside the bus garage and gas works.   *p.105 tr*

Watford and St. Albans gas works, lower High Street.

Woodman's Yard (at one time was known as Orchard Yard).

Water Lane; field on the right (one-time venue for travelling amusement fairs) would later be the site for George Stephenson College.   *p.354 c*

Harrow Rail Crash

Automatic control of a warning type might have prevented, or mitigated, the Harrow triple train crash on October 8, states Lieut.-Colonel G. R. S. Wilson, Chief Inspecting Officer of Railways, Ministry of Transport, in his report of over 30,000 words published yesterday, of the disaster which cost 112—many of them Watford —lives.

Lieut.-Colonel Wilson also found that District Relief Signalman A. G. Armitage, of Harrow No. 1 Box, "should be exonerated from all responsibility for the accident."

The accident, the second worst in the history of Britain's railways, happened just after 8.15 a.m. The 8.15 p.m. Perth to Euston express, running late "at 50-60 miles per hour," in a patch of fog, passed the Colour Light Distance Signal at Caution and two Semaphore signals at danger, and crashed into the back of the 7.31 a.m. Tring to Euston "Local."

The "double-headed" 8 a.m. London to Liverpool and Manchester express, which was approaching "at not less than 60 miles per hour," crashed into the wreckage.

WO June, 1953

Must They Use This Back Street Hole?

INTO the 'Post' bag the other day came a very thoughtful letter from commercial photographer, Mr. J. B. Nunn, about Watford's register office. "A back street hole," he calls it, and suggests a move from Church-street to the Town Hall.

Mr. Nunn writes: "One of Watford's depressing aspects is the dingy Registrar's office in Church-street. Many marriages are solemnised there and there are difficulties for car-hire drivers in finding parking space and for photographers in finding a background other than a dirty brick wall or the graveyard. And the drabness of the surroundings does not in any way add dignity to a wedding. In fact the Registrar's office looks just like a back street hole.

"Would it not be possible to find suitable rooms at the Town Hall for the Registrar's Office? A register office wedding held at the Town Hall would give a far more pleasant atmosphere than at the present premises. Yours, etc.,

J. B. Nunn."

A good point, Mr. Nunn. And we can add a detail or two. Look at all those cars in our photograph. How on earth do the photographers manage to take anything at all? Not much room there for a wedding group.

Background? There's that "dirty brick wall." Or perhaps a few cheerful gravestones? Well, if you wait until summer to get married the foliage on the trees to the left of the Office will hide the sheds in the background. That improves things a little.

In the past photographers dodged their headache by posing their groups in front of the nearby parish church. Quite understandably the Vicar, Canon St. John Thorpe, has said "No" to that.

Why not take photographs at the reception? Often there is not a suitable outdoor setting there either. And an indoor photograph is not quite the same. Anyway, why shouldn't the happy couple have their on-the-spot group for the family album?

The office is controlled by the county council. It has been at this old school building since December 1936 and there have been no previous complaints, an official told the "Post." Inside the building is quite presentable and there are hundreds of weddings there every year. Of course it is no good complaining about photographs or taxis to the officials there. The accommodation is a county council matter.

The Town Hall? Certainly a much better spot for the couple, the photographers, the taximen

Visit to Odhams, by the Duchess of Gloucester with her two sons, Prince William and Prince Richard, to see production of Coronation Souvenir Programme.

Watford Registrar's Office, Church Street, one-time National School. Buildings in background were workhouse of the mid 1700's.

and everybody concerned. But the Registrar's Office is no concern of the Borough Council. Anyway, there is no spare office space at the Town Hall, the 'Post' is informed by new Town Clerk, Mr. G. Hamer Hall. And there is not a suitable entrance for wedding parties. Obviously they could not block up the main hall. But if the county council approaches the borough council on this point it would, of course, be considered, says Mr. Hall.

Certainly, thinks the "Post" someone should look into Mr. Nunn's comments. Those hundreds of couples each year deserve better than the present squalid surroundings for the big day of their lives. At least in a town with Watford's good name for public amenities.

WHP March, 1953

Coronation,
June 1953 . . .

For the eagerly-awaited Coronation everyone had to get, or get to, a television set. And to celebrate, street parties were held wherever there was enough enthusiasm to organise one. The town's buildings were garlanded, and bunting, portraits and loyal greetings abounded on shops, civic buildings and homes.

The souvenir issue of the 'Picture Post' (raised to 64 pages) had enticing adverts of 'things to come'. Agfa was advertising colour print film but for the average camera-owner it was 120/620 and 127 black and white roll films. What little colour was available was 35mm Kodachrome.

Cover of the 'Picture Post' Coronation Souvenir Issue.

Proclamation announcing Princess Elizabeth as the future Queen Elizabeth, (top) by the Deputy Town Crier in St. Albans Road, outside the Midland Bank, and (below) at the Town Hall.   February 1952

Two youngsters of the Church Road street party group, (opposite).

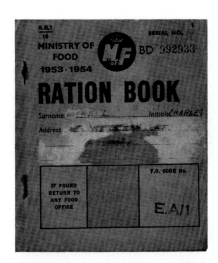

● *In the 1953 ration book, above, coupons for sugar, bacon, fats and meat were cancelled (used). Cheese and tea coupons were unused.*

Cawdell's store decorated overall.   p.98, 335 b

Coronation Crowds Missing

In historic Cassiobury Park, once the estate of the Earls of Essex, holders of the title of Elizabeth I's famous favourite, preparations had been made for loyal Watford subjects of Elizabeth II to make merry in honour of their young Queen, who had been crowned only a few hours earlier.

But at the time the celebrations were due to start, many Watfordians apparently preferred to sit by their TV or radio sets while the great State procession threaded its way through London rather than brave the elements and weave their frozen way to the local park.

Nevertheless, a bright new Union Jack flew bravely in the centre of the festivity arenas, and, despite the cold and wet, sportsmen and sportswomen were limbering up for running track events.

An early arrival was the Mayor (Alderman A. G. Dillingham), who strolled round with his gold chain of office hung over a warm overcoat, and the few policemen had capes over their shoulders as if on mid-winter patrol. The Deputy Mayor and Mayoress (Alderman and Mrs. L. C. Johnson) and the Town Clerk (Mr. Gordon H. Hall) were also among the sparse gathering.

The attendance was so small that even in the beer tent, where loyal toasts might reasonably have been drunk in plenty, there were more assistants on the service side of the bar than customers on the other.

WHP June 1953

● *Television has not yet taken over from the cinema—and the cinema has added advantage of colour, which television lacks. Here, local school children are taken to see the film of the Coronation.*

Situations Vacant

The engagement of persons answering these advertisements must be made through a Local Office of the Ministry of Labour or a Scheduled Employment Agency if the applicant is a man aged 18-64 inclusive, or a women aged 18-59 inclusive, unless he or she, or the employment is excepted from the provisions of the Notification of Vacancies Order 1952.

WO June, 1953

Street party group, Church Road.

North Watford Odeon; 'A Queen is Crowned'.   p.198

The 'Green Man', decorated. *p.81*

Rolling out the barrel from Benskin's cooperage; there's a young man inside who has just completed serving his apprenticeship.

Lunch time entertainment outside the 'One Bell'. *p.334 tr*

Benskin House, built in 1785 by Edward Dawson, later to be Benskin's Brewery offices, now Watford Museum. *p.312 b*

Watford's 'C' Division Women's Section is increased to nine; WPC Rafter on traffic control duty, April 1953.

Cromer Road, North Watford; a 1929 MG is the only car parked in the road, such is the shortage of cars. 1953

American forces left Bushey Hall at the end of the war—and return to aid defence of Western Europe—32nd A.A.A. Brigade.

Empire Youth Sunday Parade passing Town Hall.

Road or Beauty Spot?

"The planners may wish to surround Watford by a green belt. Let us not be surrounded by a tarmac girdle."

So declared Watford Town Clerk, Mr. Gordon H. Hall, voicing Watford's objections to the proposed Aylesbury radial road, at the opening session of the County Development inquiry at the Small Town Hall on Monday.

He told the Inspector, Mr. R. B. Walker: "The reason for our objection is that we consider the present line of the proposed road, as shown on the County Development Plan, would involve what we consider the desecration of this beautiful woodland, and we consider it would be to the very serious detriment of the amenities of our district, and also the enjoyment of many people from all walks of life, and from all parts of the county."

Mr. F. P. Boyce, deputy clerk to the Herts County Council, outlined the Council's view.

"It remains to emphasis that this is not a plan for all time, it is rather a prediction of the future in general limited for the next 20 years; a principal exception to that limitation being the trunk roads. The Plan has made that prediction with the first five of the 20 years particularly in mind. It is important that those who are concerned with this inquiry should remember that this Plan must be the subject of revision at five-yearly intervals, or more frequently if occasion demands." And:

"The County Council regard the preservation of the Hertfordshire section of the Metropolitan Green Belt, the Green Belt proposals shown on the plan, as the primary defence of the county against the continued spread of suburbia, and of fundamental importance."

The inquiry is expected to last into the New Year.

Mr. Hall said that he was pleased to hear from the Inspector that the Minister would be giving the town's representations most careful consideration, and declared:

"If the Ministry of Transport do proceed with the proposals on their present line, I think I can promise them unmitigated opposition at every stage."

He told the Inspector that a few hundred yards from the hall where they were sitting was the entrance to the park, where Watfordians and others could walk for miles without thinking that they were near an urban area. It was this that would be disturbed by the proposed road.

"When negotiating for the purchase we had support from all hands. We had the Council unanimous on the proposal, and support from ratepayers' organisations and individuals. There was not one voice that said we should not purchase this land," he declared, adding: "We obtained a contribution to the cost of it, not only from the Herts County Council, whose Development Plan this is, but also from the London County Council."

He produced the sealed deed relating to the purchase, and read the clause which stated that the land should be maintained and managed by the Corporation as an open space "for the public use for ever."

WO December, 1953

Shooting for 'House in the Square' by the lock in Cassiobury Park; starring Ann Blyth and Tyrone Power. Released in 1951.

p.114 tl

263

Arrival of Grammar School Girls at Town Hall Assembly Hall; celebration of 250th year of founding of Dame Fuller's Free School. The boys have already arrived.

After meeting the Mayor, Alderman E. C. Amey, Mr. L. Ellis (Parks Superintendent) and other officials connected with the new Woodside running track, HRH the Duke of Edinburgh chats with a lively group of schoolgirls.
1955

Schools' 250 Years of History

In 1704, the year of Blenheim and the taking of Gibraltar, a school was built not far from the Parish Church of St. Mary, Watford. Inscribed over its doorway were the words: "Anno Dni, 1704. This Free School was built and endowed for the teaching of poor children at the proper cost of Mrs. Elizabeth Fuller of Watford Place" . . .

From this modest building, with its 40 boys and 20 girls, the first pupils, grew Watford Grammar Schools for Boys and Girls, who this week celebrate the 250th anniversary of their foundation.

The story of their remarkable growth, fully justifying the schools' motto—"Sperate Parati," or "Prepared with hope"—is told in a fascinating commemorative history of the schools, which has been produced by Miss M. Sweeney and Mr. W. G. Hughes, who are members of their teaching staff.

Until her death in 1709, Mrs. Fuller herself supervised the affairs of the school, making provision in her will for its running after her demise.

40 shillings were laid out yearly for the purchase of wood and coals to be burned in winter. 20 shillings was paid annually to the Minister of Watford for preaching a sermon on May 1. 20 of the most deserving boys were to receive grey cloth coats with broad brass buttons and bands, and each boy was to receive a new grey bonnet. If the revenues extended so far, the girls were to be clothed with linsey-wolsey gowns of the same colour as the boys' coats, Holland bands, quoives, or head-dresses, and blue aprons.

The last stage in the schools' history culminated in the building of the present girls' school, which was taken over in 1907, and the opening of the boys' school, in Rickmansworth-road (once again performed by Lord Clarendon) in 1912.

WO 1954

Death of Former Mayor

WE regret to record the death on Tuesday night at his Cassio-road home of one of the best-known, best-respected men in Watford—Mr. Thomas Rubython Clark, retired builder and former Mayor, Alderman, "Father" of the Council, and lay preacher. A widower for some years, he leaves two daughters.

Mr. Clark, who was 86 at the time of his death, came to Watford as a small boy, and his long years of devoted public service will probably be best remembered through the reconstruction of the Borough's highways.

With the slogan "Vote for Clark and better roads" he was elected in 1910 to the old Watford Urban District Council. He became its chairman in 1916, and again from April to November, 1922, when he was succeeded by the Charter Mayor of the Borough, Lord Clarendon.

In was in 1921 that Mr. Clark was elected chairman of the Council's Highways Committee, in which capacity he gave the Borough unstinted service. Elected Alderman in 1922, he was elected Mayor of the Borough in November, 1925, and Councillor Bickerton justly observed: "If you want to see a monument to Alderman Clark, look at the roads."

In 1943 Alderman Clark was admitted an honorary Freeman of the Borough as, in the words of Councillor (now Alderman) Harry Horwood, speaking at the ceremony, one who had "devoted a lifetime of service to his fellow townspeople."

Mr. Clark had been a member of the old War Tribunal and for some eight years was chairman of the local Burial Board.

As a builder he was concerned in erecting much local residential and other property too numerous to detail.

WO November, 1955

Lord Clarendon

Fire Brigade exhibition at the Drill Hall, Clarendon Road. June 1951.   *p.172 t*

Death of Lord Clarendon

LESS than three months after a bronze statuette of a Boy Scout was passed by him to the 1st Abbots Langley Scout Group in memory of his son, the Earl of Clarendon, last remaining Freeman of Watford, died on Tuesday at his London home at the age of 78.

The Grove, the mansion now used as offices by London Midland Region of British Railways, was once the Earl's seat. Part of Lees Wood on the estate was given by Lord Clarendon to the 1st South West Herts and 2/1st South West Herts Scouts as a camping site in memory of his elder son, George Lord Hyde, who was killed in a shooting accident in South Africa.

In appreciation of his great assistance in obtaining for Watford a charter of incorporation, and for his services as the new Borough's first Mayor, the Town Council in 1928 presented him with his portrait in oils. This is now hung in the Town Hall.

He was made Freeman of the Borough in 1924. Following the recent death of Mr. T. Clark, he was the last surviving Freeman.

WHP December, 1955

The "City" in Watford

OUR Borough Engineer, Mr. F. C. Sage, interested the experts at a national conference on housing and town planning with an idea he would like to see incorporated in The Design For Watford. It is a simple plan, just the establishment of a Threadneedle-street in the heart of the town.

But it is a good plan, and if it impressed outsiders with its simplicity, it will delight the citizens as a sound and very natural development of the business usage that has already taken control of the Clarendon-road, Station-road area.

That stretch is already a wing of the city. It is the administrative centre of many large firms and industries. But because they occupy the old houses, a lot of valuable space is lost.

By tearing down those old buildings, Clarendon-road rebuilt could easily provide office accommodation for many thousands of white collar workers who now suffer the daily strap-hanging routine to London E.C. and so could play a big part in decentralising the City offices.

We could also help relieve the burden of

London Transport by employing here our neighbours from Harrow and Wembley.

Watford is not the only place that could help in this way but Watford is our interest. And, of course, Mr. Sage's design for Clarendon-road would bring in so much extra money to the rates without creating a new housing problem.

WHP November, 1956

Beehive Flats

Large blocks of flats in city centres were compared to beehives by Mr. F. C. Sage, Watford Borough Engineer, addressing the National Conference of the Town and Country Planning Association in London on Friday.

"I am not sure that a man housed in a beehive won't tend to become a bee—very efficient, very much like his fellow, and quite soulless."

Mr. Sage, speaking during a discussion on housing densities, said he believed that in the large cities of Central Europe where housing took place in that way, it had proved to be the breeding ground of Communism.

Mr. Sage said he lived in a hamlet and would not like to go back to living in town, for there were two very great disadvantages in flat life in the centres of cities—smoke and noise.

"Until you tackle these two basic disadvantages, flat life in town will never be very popular."

WO December, 1956

Beehive Flats

I FEEL that the brief report in the issue of the "Watford Observer" of December 7, upon remarks which I made at a recent Planning Conference, are likely to give an impression I did not mean to convey.

It is true I stated that I preferred living in a hamlet but also stated that my daughter, who is a medical student at one of the large London hospitals, was practically obliged to live in town in a flat and thus within the small compass of one family the desirability for both house and flat accommodation was manifest. The clear inference was that a need for both types of dwelling was likely to be even more manifest in the larger "family" of a town.

The protagonist for flats in this session of the

Conference was Mr. Sergei Kadleigh, well known as the designer of "High Paddington," a huge block of buildings intended to be built over railway lines in the neighbourhood of Paddington, and containing not only flat dwellings but also shops and commercial premises on a vast scale. The project might truly be described as a Tower Town. It would be possible for anyone living in such a block to pass his whole life therein without the necessity of leaving it at all.

I felt that such an existence, cut off from all contact with the countryside which God had given us, was not the type of life to be encouraged in our own country.

It was to this building that I applied the name "Beehive" and not to the usual type of flat block, excellent examples of which have been included in many recent schemes in this country.—F. C. Sage, Borough Engineer, Watford.

WO December, 1956

North Sea Gas

For some time gas has been obtained from wells drilled in the North Sea, near Norway. This gas is piped to both Holland and Norway where it provides a cheap and clean alternative to coal gas. This gas field is too far from Britain and so benefits are not available here.

VII

"Why don't they do something?"

The memory of the stagnant, unrewarding, wearisome postwar years had faded. Door-to-door salesmen were offering water softeners and carpeting, Hoover were offering their washing machines and steam irons on hire-purchase. The prewar kitchen was hardly big enough to accommodate a refrigerator.

The housing programme was well under way but by no means complete. Almost all the sites shown in the plan on page 251 had been built or were in the course of construction; Kytes, Garston, Woodside, Hillside, Meriden, Hempstead Road, Holywell and Bushey.

The plans of 1937/39 for the St. Albans By-Pass (p.187) were in advanced planning stages, paradoxically given the designation M1.

The immediate postwar years were frustrating but the next few years were anything but that.

Watford, however, still had a mainly Victorian road system with prewar parking facilities and an ever-increasing population. The traffic flow of work-days was severely disrupted by the numerous narrow and awkward road junctions; King Street/Queens Road, Market Street/High Street, Clarendon Road/High Street, Upton Road/High Street, Cassio Road/Rickmansworth Road, Derby Road/Queens Road, Vicarage Road/Merton Road/Wiggenhall Road, etc. Then, as now, car parking and its attendant problems worsened at weekends. The burning question on everyone's mind was "Why don't they do something?" No matter the cost to the environment, the motor car must be given space.

With this in mind planning had taken place during the preceding years including a vehicle count between April and September 1954. This estimated future traffic flows, destinations, numbers and where parked.

The conclusions, together with land use recommendations, were published in 1956.

Among suggestions for car parks were: Church Street, 120; High Street Station forecourt, 10; Crown Passage, 20; Carey Place, 260; Meeting Alley (Roger's Timber-yard site), 330; rear of Clements, 130; rear of old YMCA in Clarendon Road, 130; Junction Station (Hotel garden), 40. These proposed car parks would give additional space for about 1000 cars. The number parked 'on-street' on a normal week-day was in the region of 750.

An exit into Rosslyn Road was proposed to ease the bottleneck of entrance and exit from Shrubbery Car Park into the High Street.

Although this plan was more in the nature of a survey, recommendations for minor works were included. It also contained the basic concept for the relief Road (Beechen Grove) and the framework for Exchange Road.

Well before the plan was published shops built

opposite the Town Hall were set back at a curve, to follow the future road line.

At this time cars were still not freely available and so the pressure was bearable, but within a very few years car ownership became widespread. The road which could have saved Watford from the carve-up which was to follow in the early sixties — the Maple Cross to Hunton Bridge link — was obstructed at planning stages by environmentalists not resident in or near Watford, and then by lack of funds, owing to unexpected difficulties discovered on the projected route. That all traffic from the west (Slough) had to travel through Watford, meant constant jams at the Town Hall roundabout. There was no way this traffic could be routed elsewhere; but traffic north and south, along the High Street to and from Hempstead Road — and suffering the hold-ups in the High Street — could be diverted along new 'relief' roads which could be fairly easily built, and this was the plan proposed.

But before the 'master' plan could be put into operation, chaos dictated earlier measures and these came in 1962.

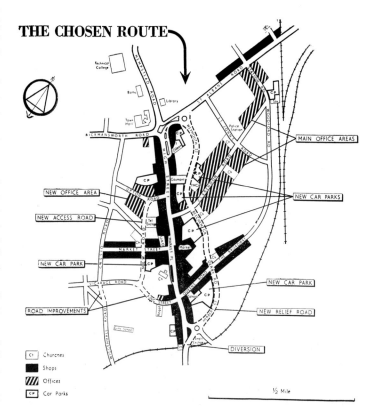

THE CHOSEN ROUTE

St. Albans Road railway bridge, Church Road is still accessible from St. Albans Road, the North Watford Plaza still exists. The railway coalyards are busy and the railway motive power is still the steam locomotive. The Junction platforms have the covered walkway and stairs linking them to the Callowland entrance. The engine sheds are just north of the platforms and the old 'station-master's' house is alongside. The industrial site is Watford's oldest after the Silk Mill and Carey Place with Cassiobury Mills (Turners) being established in the 1870's. At the time of this photograph Cassiobury Mill housed Fishburn Printing Ink, McCaskey Registers, Petroflex Tubing; at the extreme right is Ilford's 'Apem' Works.

New Road Through Watford

THE 'new look' scheme for the central Watford area has reached the embryo stage.

A draft plan, submitted by the Herts County Council, received the formal approval of Watford Town Council at its meeting on Monday night. Chairman of the Town and Country Planning Committee, Councillor H. Buckingham, described it as "the most important development — in the physical sense—since the acquisition of Cassiobury Park."

The most outstanding feature of the plan is the provision of a 72ft relief road which will take through traffic completely off the High-street between the High-street Station and the Town Hall.

Asked for details of actual property affected, the Borough Engineer (Mr. F. C. Sage) told the "Watford Observer" that the majority of houses in **Herbert-street** would have to go and some would be affected in **Clifford-street** and **Charles-street**.

In **Derby-road**, the School, the Tabernacle and Standard Range premises would be unaffected, although the other side of the road would not be. The shops on the **Queen's-road** corners, for example, came into the line of the new road, and **Horton's Garage** would be affected to a consid-

erable extent. Further along, **Beechen Grove Schoolroom** would make its contribution, but it was after the crossing of **Clarendon-road** that the majority of residential dwellings would eventually come down. Hardest hit would be **Weymouth-street**, the whole of one side of which comes out, but a number of properties would be affected in **Monmouth-road, Platts-avenue**, and **Albert-road.**

Although it is hoped to proceed with the implementation of the scheme as soon as possible, some of the projects have been designed so to fit in with likely development or re-development that a co-ordinated scheme of public and private improvement is possible.

In moving approval of the draft plan, Councillor Buckingham said he was sure it was something for which they had all been waiting long. He recalled that it had been talked about for at least ten years and said, "It must be the most important development, in the physical sense, of our town since the happy day when we decided to acquire Cassiobury park."

The Councillor referred to the forthcoming exhibition and said that sometime during February both the County officers and their own officers would be pleased to meet representatives of local organisations as a body in order to explain the proposals in detail.

Finally Councillor Buckingham emphasised, "These are draft proposals only." At the proper time ample arrangements would be made for the hearing of objections, he said and added, "It must not be presumed it is a fait accompli. There is a lot of machinery to be gone through yet."

WO February, 1957

Mayor's Fund Over £300

Delight has been brought to 700 poor and needy folk of Watford this week who have received gifts—mainly food parcels and vouchers from the Mayor's Christmas Appeal fund.

At the week-end the fund topped the £300 mark and by Monday had reached £307 5s. 9d.

WHP January, 1957

Composite panorama of the Parade opposite the Town Hall; No. 1 St. Albans Road on the left-hand side. First phase of the new shops at the corner of St. Albans Road are built but not yet let; second phase, turning the corner to follow line of planned relief-road not yet started.　　　c1957

No Subsidy for £9+ Tenants

MORE than 96 per cent of Watford Council house tenants interviewed during the past 12 months have an income of over £9 a week.

This was disclosed to the Borough Council on Monday night, when the Labour Group attempted to get the rate subsidy for housing raised from £30,000 to £35,500. It was defeated by 21 votes to 19.

Cllr. T. D. Bathurst said that he felt the tenants could afford to pay a little more. It was significant that of the number of tenants they had interviewed during the past 12 months 96.1 per cent had an income exceeding £9 a week.

Tenants of council houses were not expected to pay more than one-seventh of their income. They had 4,611 houses, and some 3,476 were available on this basis to people with £9 or less a week.

In a report on the rents of council houses the Borough Treasurer reported that the additional amount to be raised from the tenants was £21,000, and it was recommended that the rents of council houses should be increased. The suggested figures are nil to 1s 9d. a week for pre-war houses (average increase 10d.) nil to 3s. 6d. per week for post-war houses (average 2s. 2d.)

WHP January, 1957

Petrol Situation is Grave

WATFORD can expect more sackings if the petrol muddle continues.

After nearly a month of rationing, local firms which depend on petrol for production and distribution are realising just how much those coupons will mean to them and how much the shortage is hitting at the foundations of industry.

Commenting on the situation at the annual luncheon meeting of the Watford Manufacturers' Association at the Small Town Hall on Monday, the retiring chairman, Mr. Kenneth McKell, of Penfold Wire Fencing Ltd. said:

"The effect of petrol and fuel rationing, although expected to be fairly severe, is, in many instances, proving to be grossly inequitable in its effects on industry. In some directions unemployment is already threatened and unless some urgent action is taken to relax or redistribute some of the restrictions there is little doubt that it must become more widespread.

Factories cannot continue to work unless they receive their raw materials, frequently, according to their processes, to the dictates of a strict programme sequence, nor can they continue to produce goods if they cannot despatch them from the factory.

WHP January, 1957

Books on Wheels

WATFORD has a mobile public library. Whether we can afford it just now or not, and in spite of continuous Conservative opposition, it is here.

Can we afford it? The people living on the edge of the town provide the answer. Every reader in Watford is now within a mile of a book, and this has been achieved, with the mobile bookshelves covering four districts, at the cost of one branch library.

Remember this, too. The mobile library brings Watford privileges other towns have enjoyed for years. It has long been talked about here, but was not included in the borough estimates until this financial year, and the order was placed in April.

Now it is in service Mr. R. C. Sayell, the librarian, says it is the finest he has seen in London or other counties. Watford can take full credit for it. The Trailer was built by Alfred Walker, coach builders, of Loates-lane, on a Scammell chassis. It is of the caravan type and will be towed to the sites by a Scammell mechanical horse driven by an employee of the Highways Dept.

There is one more point. This service will provide the evidence the Council needs before siting the additional branch libraries that will ultimately be necessary.

WHP January, 1957

More Room For Motorists

MOTORISTS will be interested to note that new car parks, scattered strategically throughout the Borough, will provide room for about 1,000 cars.

For comparison, the number of cars parked in the streets in the central area on a normal weekday is about 750.

WHP February, 1957

Benskin's Merger

WATFORD and the area served by Benskin's Watford Brewery will continue to get Benskin's beer if the take-over by Burton brewers Ind Coope and Allsopp is confirmed.

This is disclosed in a letter from Chairman and Managing Director of Benskin's, Mr. W. Kilkenny, recommending shareholders to accept the terms for the merger offered by Ind Coope.

The terms of the offer—now in the hands of shareholders—are that Ind Coope shall take over the entire share capital of Benskin's in exchange for the issue of shares credited as fully paid by Ind Coope on the basis of eight Ordinary 5s. shares for every £1 Ordinary stock unit in Benskin's.

WO February, 1957

Beechen Grove Baptist Church; Beechen Grove car park to the left, later, Charter Place.　　　*p.320 r, 352 t*

King Street Maternity

SINCE 1948 the local Hospital Management Committees have been at constant war with the Regional Boards, who are boss, fighting for no more than an adequate hospital service. In most of these formative issues it has been not so much what you want as what we can afford.

There is no such reason to back the Board's latest argument with Watford.

They have conceded our need for more maternity beds. They had to. Mothers leave King-street too soon, others are being sent to Hemel Hempstead because King-street is so crowded. So something has to be done.

Watford points to land which the committee own at Shrodells and wants to build there for the mothers. The Board say they should extend by buying the property they need in King-street. We suggest to the Board that if they knew more of the King-street story they would not argue with the local people who know local problems as well as local needs.

King-street is going to be no place for more maternity beds. It will soon be a really busy traffic thoroughfare. There are more reasons than the availability of land why the hospital should be extended along the Shrodells back-water. And the Board will be well advised to climb down and re-erect their ladders there.

WHP February, 1957

Watford's "Mainz Week"

Plans are afoot to run a "Mainz Week" in Watford later this year, Cllr. E. C. Amey announced on Monday when he spoke to Watford chamber of Commerce about the aims of the new Mainz-Watford Society.

He said an approach would be made to the Chamber and to Watford traders to run a "Mainz Week." Wine merchants would, if interested, be able to make a good show of the Rhine wines made in Mainz.

WHP March, 1957

Cameras—now available

In the early years following the war there were no imports of cameras except for a few for 'essential' use. For the average user they were non-existent and ranges of improved models, used in the rest of the world, were unknown in this country.

As restrictions were gradually eased by mid 1950's imports were permitted of cameras which cost not more than £5 ex-works. With import duty, wholesale and dealer margins, plus Purchase Tax, the price became £25 in the shop. By 1956-58 very limited numbers of more expensive cameras became available for general sale, and in 1959 import restrictions were completely relaxed. Japanese cameras, still basically in a period of intense development, with rather more innovation than the German models (whose designs were tailored around between-lens shutters) started a new 'single-lens-reflex era'. In the same manner that German inventiveness had earlier proved more popular than British offerings, so the Japanese would eventually oust the Germans from world markets.

St. Albans Road; beyond the railings, to the right, the Railway Cottages. Across the road, the 'Plaza' cinema demolished.   *p.246 t, 347 t*   **1957**

In the intervening years little has changed (from p.243); the pedestrian crossings are now 'zebras', motor-cyclists are still in carefree days when crash helmets are not obligatory and Church Road is still open to add to work-day traffic snarls.   *p.243 b, 347 c*

High Street, Garner's on Clarendon Road Corner.   *p.122, 316 t, 336 c*

269

Russell Lodge, corner of Longspring/St. Albans Road. Demolished. Site owned by Benskin's who wanted to develop it as shops with flats over, but for which planning permission was not granted. Site now used as a car park.   *p.136 t*

Hunton Bridge of 1957 still has an air of rusticality at weekends. The road to the right is 'Old Mill Lane', the early original lane from Watford to Hunton Bridge village, at which point it took a left turn, over the canal bridge and a right turn just before the church, to continue towards Kings Langley. The stretch in continuance of the A41 By-Pass to Langleybury Church is comparatively modern, (c1920's).

Families On Emigration Trail

DOZENS of families from all over South west Herts are selling-up and hitting the Empire and Commonwealth trail.

And many of the emigration inquiries made through the last weeks have been from skilled Watford technicians.

Said Mrs. Russell, who has been handling the bookings for transatlantic air and sea passages at Pickford's Travel Agency in Clarendon-road: "None of them seem to have any personal dislike for Watford. The majority of them are in good employment, good trades. They are fairly highly-paid workers.

"Their main reason for going is for the sake of the children."

A typical couple who confirmed this outlook were Mr. and Mrs. Ralph Kenny, of 17, Albans-view, Watford. A fitter at Scammell Lorries, Mr. Kenny declared: "At school I twice passed for special places at High School, but my parents just couldn't afford to send me.

"If my children," he said, pointing to seven-years-old Ralph junior and the toddlers, Theresa (3) and Lynn (2) "are bright they would automatically get a University education in Canada."

WHP February, 1957

Goodbye Watford

HIT by petrol rationing, a North Watford decorator and his brother-in-law, an Abbots Langley carpenter, left this country on Tuesday to try their luck in Canada.

And they are not the only people caught up in the emigration "snowball." The previous day, two middle-aged residents of Leggatts Wood-avenue emigrated to Canada and another family man whose parents live in that road is off to Toronto in a few months' time.

A young couple from the Kingswood area might go to Canada soon and a 27-years-old Abbots Langley man is going out in June to make a new home for his hairdresser wife.

WHP March, 1957

● *Twelve years after war's end and there are now enough second-hand cars to warrant a special advertising feature to coincide with the traditional Whitsuntide Bank Holiday. The number of used car dealers in Watford was not great (not all are included in this feature) and it was not unexpected that one would have to travel to local surrounding towns to seek a wider variety.*

A new Registrar's Office is due to open in Clarendon Road but in the meantime local couples who wed at the Registrar's Office, and want photographs, are inevitably obliged to use part of the Parish Church forecourt. Not because they require a 'church' background but because

Almondswick—the old and first National School of 1841.

parked cars take up free space. This 'snap' inadvertently had church; the groups had railings and tombstones . . . Mr. and Mrs. A. Power.

Watford Example

"WATFORD stands out as an example to other towns." These words were spoken by Mr. Timothy Rootes, a member of the famous Rootes family who have built up a nationwide organisation in the motor car trade, so his praise is worthy of respect.

He was addressing a large audience at the opening of the new £50,000 showrooms built by Watford Motor Co. in the High-street and stated that figures proved our town to be one of the most wealthy areas in Great Britain.

The company opened in Lamb Yard, its present site, in July, 1921. And now it is one of the biggest motor engineering firms in the whole county. The staff is 40-strong and facilities are available for body-building, for painting and for welding, together with machine shops for any comprehensive work.

WHP July, 1957

Lamb Yard; Three Tuns.

The Regiment

"GENTLEMEN, the Regiment." That will still be the toast, for though the county regiment will disappear with the merging of the Bedfs. and Herts and the Essex Regiments, the spirit will never die.

The Hertfordshire Regiment (T.A.) will in the true sense of the word become the county regiment.

These are two of the considered opinions of members of the Bedfs. and Herts Old Comrades Association whose hearts are full of pride for their old regiment and who have the battle honours of the 16th Regiment of Foot at their fingertips.

The new regiment will join the Royal Norfolks and Suffolks, the Lincolns and Northamptonshire Regiment to form the East Anglian Brigade.

The amalgamation of the Bedfs. and Herts. and the Essex Regiment is expected to take place well before the date envisaged.

In a Special Order of the Day, Lieut.-Gen. Sir Reginald F. S. Denning, Colonel of the Regiment, intimates that the Regimental Depot at Kempston will cease to exist as a training establishment.

"It is felt," he adds, "that the presence of a Regimental Headquarters will preserve the full regimental spirit, help our Old Comrades to cling closer together and continue to bring aid to members of the Regiment who may be in need."

And from Hertford, Brigadier J. A. Longmore says he would like to make it clear that none of the Territorial units are affected by the reorganisation.

The Hertfordshire Yeomanry Artillery, the Hertfordshire Regiment, The Hertfordshire Company R.A.S.C., the Provost Detachment and the Hertfordshire Company W.R.A.C. will continue their tasks and titles unchanged.

They have recently reverted to a wholly voluntary basis, and in the few months that have elapsed since this was introduced they have gone a long way to recapture the pre-war corporate and comradely spirit which can only be achieved among genuine volunteers.

The 16th Regiment of Foot was formed in 1688 at Reading, and in its early years had such battle honours as Namur, Steinkirk, Blenheim (1704), Ramillies (1706), Oudenarde (1708) and Malplaquet (1709). Because of its service as Marines during the attempt to capture Cathagena in South America in 1740 the Regiment is entitled to play Rule Britannia in addition to its Regimental March.

It was in 1809 when the Regiment assumed the title of Bedfordshire and in 1881 the 1st and 2nd Battalions were affiliated to the Bedfordshire and Hertfordshire Militia.

During the Indian Campaign the Regiment added Chitral to its battle honours and this was followed quickly by South Africa, Mons, Ypres, Loos, Somme, Gaza, and Palestine.

Casualties during the First World War were 18,000 with 336 officers and 5,745 N.C.O.'s and men killed. Nine Victoria Crosses were gained.

In 1919 the title was changed to Bedfordshire and Hertfordshire to create a closer link between the regiment and the two counties.

The Second World War brought a crop of battle honours starting with Dunkirk(1940), N. W. Europe (1940), Tobruk (1941), Tobruk Sortie, Bel Hamed (the only infantry regiment to gain this honour), Tunis N. Africa (1941-43), Cassino, Trafimene Line, Italy (1944-45), Athens, Greece (1944-45), Singapore Island, Malaya (1942), Chindits (1944), Burma (1944).

The Hertfordshire Regiment T.A. during this war gained honours at the Normandy Landing, N.W. Europe, Montorsoli, Gothic Line, Monte Gameraldi, Monte Ce Co, Monte Grand, and Italy (1944-45).

With such a record behind them how can the spirit fail? Or as the Old Comrades say, "What's in a name?" And already they are devising badges for the new Brigade. Favourite at the moment is a simple laurel wreath with "East Anglia" scrolled across it.

WHP August, 1957

Picture Post, the decline, 1950-1957

" As the war went on, *Picture Post* got thinner and thinner as the paper shortage got more and more severe. Stories which had previously been spread over four or six pages were now restricted to two or three. War pictures took up more and more of the available space. In consequence my earnings, still based on the extent of my contributions, and still at the original rates, dropped considerably. I had to look for work outside *Picture Post*, and I ventured into a new sphere when I accepted assignments for *Harper's Bazaar*.

While I was, on the one hand, very glad to have been able to continue working during the war, apart from one short interruption, it has to be said, on the other hand, that the Hulton Press had taken full advantage of the fact that I was an alien in a foreign country. I had to accept what was offered me, hand over all my negatives—something I had never done before—and accept payment below my usual rate. Meanwhile the publishing house and the paper were flourishing, and the proprietor was able to turn Hulton Press into a public company, at great profit. I was determined not to continue in this way, and refused to accept a new contract similar to the old one. So, when the war was over, and after seven years, I left *Picture Post*.

For the next few years, I was not attached to any paper, and indeed took very few photographs; my interest switched to a different sphere, in a sense going back to my early days as a student of painting and the history of art. It was from this background that I had first stumbled, as it were, into photography.

I now conceived the idea of a book on the history of lithography. Only Pennell's, published in 1898, existed, and I spent many months scrutinising the print collection in the British Museum.

This most pleasant occupation was interrupted in the autumn of 1948. *Picture Post* had again started to publish a four-page colour section every week. I was asked if I would be willing to take some colour pictures for the magazine, since the Editor was not satisfied with what he was getting from the *Picture Post* staff. The management accepted the terms I put forward, and this approach led to two years of happy co-operation with Tom Hopkinson.

From then on, I did not look back. I travelled all over Europe, collecting colour essays, and usually adding some black-and-white pictures as well. I tried everything, and found no task too difficult, even those things which it seemed must be impossible to photograph on 35mm Kodachrome. Something never done before was a sunset at Whistler's Corner in London, in December 1948, with all the glowing colour in the sky and water. Another picture not attempted before was a Canonisation in St. Peter's, Rome, with Pope Pius XII.

In 1950 I went on a journey for several months to the West Indies and to British Guiana. *Picture Post* planned a colour feature about conditions in these colonies, and about the election of the first Parliament in Trinidad. My relationship with Tom Hopkinson had been most friendly, and this last period of co-operation had been very fruitful.

It was now about to come to a sudden end. When I reached the Myrtle Bank Hotel in Kingston, Jamaica, amongst the mail waiting for me was one from the Editor:

London, November 8, 1950
My dear Hans—
When you receive this letter, I will no longer be editor of *Picture Post* as I have been relieved of my post by Edward Hulton. We had an argument about a story with photographs which our men in Korea had sent back, which I wanted to publish, and which Hulton rejected . . .

I have talked to my successor, Ted Castle, and he wishes you to continue your journey as planned, to Cuba and Florida . . .

He will write to you himself . . .

All the best wishes to you both,
Yours, Tom

I was completely stunned. This was the beginning of the end. I had left London early in October. The editor and I had such a good understanding, that we had not troubled to renew my contract, due to expire in November when I would be travelling in Jamaica. Throughout the journey I had assumed that it would automatically be renewed.

The new editor, later to become Lord Castle, had other ideas. When I returned to London in January, my retainer was stopped, and I was told 'We don't need your work from this journey, as we are going to stop publishing in colour.' I would not accept this treatment, and went to Court to fight it. I had to wait two years before the case was heard in the High Court. After five days, I won a substantial sum in damages, and costs, and it was pleasant to hear Mr. Justice Streatfield say 'It was obvious that the plaintiff was a man of the utmost skill as a photographer, and he was described as the best colour photographer in the country.' The *Times* published a full report of the case. Hulton Press did not appeal.

No paper can stand losing its experienced editor and its experienced contributors at the same moment, as well as trying to change the form and style of the magazine at the same time. Playing down to the masses does not always pay. Though *Picture Post* lingered on for another six years, under a variety of editors, it was its old self only in name. It had none of the convincing vigour of the early years; one could sense sickness and death approaching. The increased importance of television may have had something to do with it, but other magazines managed to survive, and even flourish, for many years. The right people in the right place could have overcome the difficulties; but they had been sacked, for which the publishers had to pay a heavy price.

Tom Hopkinson

When the news of this disagreement got around, most of the editorial staff wished to resign. I was against this, considering the paper's future much more important than that of any individual. Finally almost everyone agreed to stay on, provided Mr. Hulton would guarantee that the paper's policy would remain unchanged. As earnest of this the staff insisted that Ted Castle, the assistant editor, should take over. Ted, who had intended to resign, finally accepted, since without the assurance of his presence, the rest were not prepared to stay. He was given a guarantee of six month's tenure, during which time he did his utmost to maintain the paper's continuity.

His replacement directly the six months were up inaugurated a succession of short periods of rule, in which a wide variety of talents were called upon. Men from management, advertising, from newspapers and magazines followed each other in rapid sequence, or at times exercised their influence simultaneously. Some, no doubt had excellent plans for the paper, but none survived long enough to arrest a general decline. The company's net profits, which had been £209,097 in 1949, amounted in 1952 to less than £15,000.

Some extraordinary managerial decisions contributed to this result. Nothing on a magazine requires more delicate handling than a change of price. *Picture Post*, however, was put up in price from 4d. to 5d. in August 1951, and again, only four months later in December, from 5d. to 6d. 'These increases', the annual report observes, 'had a very adverse effect upon circulation', and in August 1952 the price was put back once more to 4d. In the following year 'considerable improvement' was reported, and in 1955-6 imposing new offices, to be known as Hulton House, were under construction in Fleet Street, though the Chairman foresaw in his report for 1956 that 'the next year or so may prove difficult'.

His forecast was correct. In 1957 the net profit for the year was £11,383, and at the end of the financial year the Chairman reported: 'In May 1957, your directors decided that publication of *Picture Post* must cease, so that the financial position of your company might be fully protected . . .' In 1959 Hulton Press was bought up by Odhams Press, which in due course was taken over by the mammoth International Publishing Corporation.

Why did *Picture Post* fail? In a television interview after its death, the proprietor, Edward Hulton, attributed the collapse to television. Television was certainly bound to affect such a magazine in two ways. It would tend to draw advertising away. And, by showing news events on film, sometimes while they are actually happening, it robs picture magazines of what had been one of their biggest assets—the attraction of a news-story told in a sequence of pictures.

The many magazines which have successfully weathered the storm roused by the coming of television have all done so by making considerable alterations in their style. They dig deeper into subjects than they used to, going in for more argument and controversy. Pictorially they exploit colour, and they plan and contrive to secure the single dramatic shot—the picture which sums up a story or an issue—instead of relying on the sequence of 'picture series'. But such modifications were made slowly and cautiously, so as not to upset the general balance or give the reader the uneasy feeling—so destructive of all confidence —that the paper doesn't really know what it is trying to do.

With *Picture Post* the opposite was the case. A succession of editors—each anxious to arrest the landslide in sales and advertising but none staying long enough to establish a real character for the magazine—imposed dramatic changes. Stories appeared which were better suited to certain Sunday newspapers and, when these did not draw readers, there would be a serious number or two. But the frivolous or sensational stories had destroyed confidence in the magazine's good faith. "

Scammell's, in Tolpits Lane, have several times extended their works and are here in relative isolation before the building of the new Victoria S.M. School, 1962, and new housing nearby.

Only two Scammell '100-tonners' were built but their fame helped build Scammell's reputation. Photographed in St. Albans c1952.

● Scammell's survived pre-war depression by building more durable and more innovative commercial vehicles. During the last war their transporters were praised on all battle fronts and their mechanical horses played an essential part in the war effort. Post-war, demand for military contracts dwindled and politicising about the fate of the road haulage industry left Scammell's, for the first time, in a weakened state. The result was a merger in 1955 with Leyland in which Scammell would retain their identity. Within a few years considerable eminence in the sphere of heavy-duty vehicles had been regained. The mechanical horse had earlier been replaced by an improved version—the Scarab—but by the mid 1960's production had ceased.

The 'Contractor' range was introduced in 1964 and comprised seven models including recovery, heavy haulage, and road train (162.5 tonnes).

Numbers 212-206 High Street. The 'Fox', closed, Tividale Tools to its left, and to the right, Benskin's. *p.171 tr*

Pollard's, No. 242 High Street. Watford Town Mission Hall and, outside the picture, to the right, used to be Court No. 18.

Riverside path between Wiggenhall Road and Bushey Arches, Lower High Street, through Oxhey Park. War time defence pill-box not yet removed!

The original water main was laid in 1868 and the neck of a hydrant branch was covered and sealed during road reconstruction in 1921. Heat and vibration had caused it to fracture, fortunately, on a Wednesday afternoon, when 'early closing day' was strictly observed and little traffic was about. *p.92 t, 313 t   1957*

Town Mission to Close

ALMOST 101 years to the month after it was founded, Watford Town Mission, in the Lower High-street, is to close because of poor attendance.

When the Mission was started in October, 1856, that part of Watford was a poor and populous area. The only nearby school was the "Ragged School" in Ballards Building, which was filled to overflowing with poor children from the neighbourhood. It was from the school and from the alleys and back streets that the Mission drew its congregations, and with their disappearance the attendances at all services and Sunday School has dwindled.

WO December, 1957

Print Problems

Many firms have set up their own office printing departments, mainly for economic and convenience reasons. Although in a few instances recognised trade union labour is used, others use their existing office staff, and virtually encroach not only on trade work, but on the right of print unions to supply the labour which would normally be their prerogative. This piracy applies to some firms within the Watford areas, and could make serious inroads into the small printers' business.

The Hertfordshire County Council have been reported as operating machines with considerable saving in costs, as no doubt do other organisations and firms. This is not because of wages within the printing trade pricing the work out, but simply because with the nature of the printing equipment, under a company's direct control work can be produced faster and in exactly the desired quantities.

With offset litho equipment there is little make-ready. A plate can be in position and the machine running in a matter of minutes; an order could be made for several thousand forms and delivered in a few hours: a considerable saving in time, materials and cost.

Although some of the machines are capable of producing complicated multi-coloured work, the principal purpose of office printing machinery is for duplicating and the production of stationery such as letter headings, technical data and specification sheets, direct mail advertising literature and the hundred-and-one forms it appears necessary to have for business purposes today.

However, this trade is not standing still. Some machines can now be purchased with automatic feeding, and capable of producing good quality work for brochures, etc., and still require very little training to handle them.

The potential danger to the small printer needs no emphasis.

WHP September, 1957

High Street, 219-225. Left, frontage of Sedgwick's old brewery acquired by Benskin's, right W. Wren & Sons leather and saddlery.

High Street, 225-231 (Dumbelton's, butchers), opposite Watford Field Road.
p.75

Benskin's Watford Brewery; the walled garden is of the 'Railway Tavern', 184 High Street, now rebuilt as sheltered homes for the elderly.   *p.313 t, 330 tr*

High Street, cleaning up debris after minor accident (below).

A minor accident between a bus and a light van holds up traffic for some time—and gives us a chance to see a part of the olden street 'populated'.   *p.331 tl*

'Island' site of Nos. 100-96, entrance to Church Street blocked, then Nos. 94 & 94a.
s.53   c.1958

From the other view, 94 & 94a, Eastman's, butchers, No. 92.
s.53, p.324b
c1958

White Hart and Steabben's, Nos. 174-178.

The 'King's Arms', No. 130, opened in 1852 in what was the former gate-lodge to Watford Place. Demolished in 1961.
p.333 tr   1961

Lower High Street, photographed from a point just alongside Tividale Tools (No.208). Opposite High Street Station may be seen the jutting-out shop with

'DER' sign (No. 179). Beyond the foreground lamp post and to the left of it, the 'Three Tuns'.
p.271 b.

The 'King's Head', rebuilt at around the turn of the century, but here facing demolition before being redeveloped as shop premises. *p.57 t, 334 c.* 1961

Kingham's, wholesale and retail grocers, established 1790, shows no sign that the business will shortly close. Archway past the lamp-post is Red Lion Passage to the Market. *p.92 br, 97 t, 136 cr, 291 b*

Cassiobury home has link with past

IN a secluded part of Watford's Cassiobury Estate, in Richmond-drive to be precise, stands Cassiobury Court. Today it is an Old People's Home, housing about 30 residents, and staffed by four people, including the Matron, Mrs. A. M. Faulkner.

Also, the Court has seen service as a riding school and a dairy, but it is of most interest to historians, for once it housed the stables belonging to the old Cassiobury House (demolished in 1927).

Cassiobury House was begun in the reign of Henry VIII, and since then various alterations and additions had been made to the building. During the alterations attention was paid to the beautifying of the surrounding countryside, and this resulted in avenues of limes, oak, hornbeam and conifers. No wonder, then, that space was allotted for a riding stable. The present Cassiobury Park, which cuts like a wedge into the town, leads into open, unspoiled countryside. In those days, therefore, rides must have been extremely pleasant for the residents at Cassiobury (the Essex family), and others who had reason to visit the land that was once the domain of the British King, Cassivelaunus (54 B.C.), who was on his way to meet Cæsar's invading forces.

The outside, castellated walls of Cassiobury Court are the original ones, as can be said of the wooden beams in the writing room, dining room and lounge. Mrs. Faulkner explained that before she and her cook, Mrs. M. Asbury, started the home seven years ago, the present dining room was a builder's dump.

Now passers-by are impressed by the Court's tidy garden, and the building's clean appearance. Entrance is by way of a high gateway, leading into a courtyard. One wing has been rebuilt. The interior immediately suggests comfort, and attractiveness of rooms is furthered by well-designed rural murals.

WO November, 1958

Purchase Tax

Purchase Tax, introduced early in the last war, has varied considerably over the years. At rates varying from 25 to 100%, and different rates for 'ordinary' and 'luxury' goods, it was subject to change at almost every budget. In the 1958 budget the previously high 60% luxury rate was reduced to 30%. A £23 6s. 2d. camera became £20 0s. 9d. and a roll of black and white film was reduced to 2/10d. from 3/4d. Purchase Tax was continued until 1976.

Text of the Scroll presented by the Borough of Watford to the Regiment:

BOROUGH OF WATFORD

To Lieutenant-General Sir Reginald F. S. Denning, KBE, CB, Colonel, the Officers, Warrant Officers, Non-Commissioned Officers & Men of the 3rd East Anglian Regiment (16th/44th Foot).

GREETINGS

We, the Mayor, Aldermen, & Burgesses in the BOROUGH OF WATFORD in the County of Hertford acting by the Council, proud of the gallant and distinguished record and glorious traditions of the Bedfordshire and Hertfordshire Regiment (16th Foot) through Loyal and Devoted service to our Sovereign and County since its formation in 1688 *and* being desirous of acknowledging the close and cordial association between our Borough and the Regiment in which so many of our townsmen have served with pride and distinction *and* wishing to honour the occasion of the recent amalgamation of the Bedfordshire and Hertfordshire Regiment with their valiant comrades in arms the Essex Regiment to form the 3rd East Anglian Regiment (16th/44th Foot) *Do hereby Confer* upon the 3rd East Anglian Regiment (16th/44th Foot) the Freedom of Entry into the Borough and the privilege honour and distinction of marching through the streets of the Borough on all ceremonial occasions with colours flying, bands playing, drums beating and bayonets fixed.

The Corporate Seal of the Mayor Alderman and Burgesses of the Borough of Watford was hereunto affixed this fourth day of July 1959 in the presence of

Mayor   Thomas F. Harris

Town Clerk Gordon H. Hall

Troops in Rickmansworth Road whilst exercising the Freedom of the Borough to mark their return, in 1962, from a tour of duty in Singapore and the Far East, and change of name to 'Royal Anglian' Regiment. On the saluting dais the Mayor, Alderman J. R. Hicks. 1962

Council Chamber, Council meeting. Mayor Alderman A. Dillingham speaking. In company with Edward C. Amey (Mayor 1955/6, 1981/2, 1982/3) and

Hubert Buckingham, he was admitted Freeman of the Borough on 19th July 1976.

Whippendell Saved from Radial Road

VICTORY has come to Watford Council and local organisations who protested against the plan to drive the Aylesbury Radial-road through Whippendell Woods.

The Minister of Housing, Mr. Henry Brooke, has, in effect, told the County Council to "think again," and has deleted the project.

In general, he approves the County Development Plan, and states that the upholding of the Green Belt in Hertfordshire is a prime objective.

Of the Aylesbury Radial-road, the route of which was condemned as vandalism by Watfordians, he says:

"Although there is evidence of need for the section of this road proposed between Pinner and Hunton Bridge, the amount of traffic that would use it is uncertain, and much would depend on the effect of other roads proposals yet to be carried out.

"In view of the serious effect of this proposal on Whippendell Woods and the golf course at Watford, the Minister has come to the conclusion that further consideration must be given to this road, and he has, therefore, deleted the section between Cassio Bridge and the proposed North Orbital-road near Hunton Bridge.

"If at a future date the County Council wish to make further proposals, whether on the same or different lines, the Minister will consider them on their merits at the time."

WO December, 1958

Woodside Stadium in its early days.

Little Nascot, No. 1 St. Albans Road; before demolition for road improvements.
p.185 t

Watford Public Library before 1st-floor extensions to both wings.   1960

Watford's New High Street

THE face of Watford is changing rapidly. During the next year bigger changes still are likely to take place. These will follow the pattern of making Watford streets more attractive, wider and safer.

Three prominent "land marks" will go. Halsey House and the Fire Station in High-street and the old Brewery in St. Albans-road. Two streets will also disappear for a car park.

Already No. 1 St. Albans-road is on its way down to dust. What will become of this site is a matter of conjecture. In his mayoral speech in 1955 Ald. E. C. Amey broached the question of the council developing it as a citizens' theatre with a parade of offices and shops.

The Borough Council have considered its development, but there is no immediate plan before them as to what is likely to be done.

Once the building is down the gardens fronting St. Albans-road will be extended round the corner into Hempstead-road. Certain buildings at the back will be retained for the Parks Department and The Avenue car park will be left until something concrete is forthcoming.

Work is also to begin soon on the demolition of the Old Brewery in St. Albans-road and this site will be developed by Hille Ltd. with the erection of six shops which will be set back in line with the North Watford Post Office.

This development will allow a widening of the bottleneck at this point and construction of a wider pavement but whether the County Council will consider a plan for further development of this part of Watford is a matter of conjecture. There is no doubt the area is ripe for it.

A new railway bridge is to replace the present St. Albans-road one but the news at present is that it will be no wider.

WHP May, 1959

"New Look" for High-street

BLOCK up the very heart of Watford High-street. Block up the High-street entrances to Queen's-road and King-street. Force all through traffic into a clock-wise stream on a central Watford "rim" road.

In these drastic measures the Borough Engineer, Mr. F. C. Sage, sees the only chance of preventing the central shopping area of Watford from becoming completely choked in the next few years.

In these measures he sees the only possibility of enabling Watford to face competition from Hempstead's modern New Town and retain its popularity as a shopping centre and continue to enjoy prosperity.

Designed to create safer and more comfortable conditions for pedestrians and to reduce

Here is the proposed interim plan for the High-street.

congestion by increasing ease of traffic flow without increasing its general running speed, the scheme—it will cost £80,000—has been presented to the Highways Committee. So has an interim scheme costing £29,000, which can be put into operation very much more speedily.

WHP October, 1959

The lower two-thirds of this photograph shows the site of the 1914-18 HM No. 1 Powder Factory, now the Balmoral Factory Estate. During the building of Devon and Tavistock Roads many were the cartridge cases turned up in the digging. At the top right is British Moulded Hose, bounding Delectaland to Bushey Mill Lane. The BMH building and Balmoral Road Bridge can be easily identified. *p.139, 150, 288*

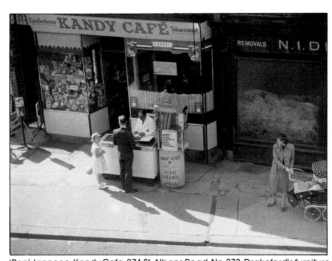

'Pop' Jannece, Kandy Cafe, 271 St. Albans Road, No. 273, Drakeford's furniture shop, closed. Both premises later to become corner site offices to the 'Evening Echo' newspaper. 1960

Late stage in the rebuilding of Balmoral Road rail bridge. 1960

The rail bridges in the area, from Kings Langley to Bushey are all original, designed to accommodate horse and cart on a narrow road. Tom's Lane, Hunton Bridge Hill, Radlett Road, Water Lane, are virtually unchanged from 1837.

Balmoral Road bridge, from 1858, a dangerous bottleneck to a road carrying through-traffic, and serving a residential and industrial estate, is at last being widened. 1960

Progress on Balmoral Bridge

AT last the long-awaited new Balmoral-road, Watford railway bridge is taking shape.

Work is now well in progress, and on Sunday, May 10, the old brick arch—for so long a danger spot for pedestrians and a traffic bottleneck— will be demolished and the new steel girder bridge rolled into position.

This will enable the local highway authority to widen the 12ft. road at this point to 45ft.

But in order that they may enjoy this very much needed improvement, the public must suffer some temporary inconvenience. For a time the road will be closed at this point and the rail service on this stretch of the Watford-St. Albans Branch Line suspended.

The Watford Council has made a temporary closing order and Balmoral-road, between the easterly side of Bradshaw-road and the westerly side of Southfield-avenue will be closed to vehicular traffic between May 4-14 and May 19-25.

Also, whilst work is being carried out on the bridge itself on May 10, train services between Watford Junction and Watford North will be withdrawn and replaced by special buses which will depart approximately five minutes earlier than would the normal trains.

The new bridge is being constructed by British Railways for Watford Corporation.

When this is completed and the old bridge demolished, the Council will arrange to carry out the necessary road works which include the major operation of lowering the road under the bridge. This is likely to take some months.

"While road work is in progress we will make what arrangements we can to insure the least possible interference with the public," declared Deputy Borough Engineer, Mr. C. H. French, this week.

WHP May, 1959

For Sewerage Read Drainage

ON May 14 the Colne Valley Sewerage Board ceased to exist—in name at any rate. Since that date its official title has been, by Act of Parliament, the West Hertfordshire Main Drainage Authority.

And in case you think this is just one more example of the trend among local and public authorities to go in for euphemistic titles, let me assure you this is not the case. The rat-catcher has become the rodent operative. The Sanitary Inspector is now the Public Health Officer.

But the Sewerage Board change is not like these. There is a very good reason for it, and it has been under consideration for some time. Due to the similarity in names there has been considerable confusion in the past between the Sewerage Board, the Colne Valley Water Company and the Colne Valley Urban District in Yorkshire, and from time to time this has led to mix-ups in correspondence.

Members of the Board will not be informed, officially, of the new name until their next meeting on June 12, but it became effective on May 14 immediately upon the promulgation of the Order.

WHP May, 1959

Churchyard Dig

RIGHT next to the roar of Watford's busy High-street traffic they have been digging up the past in no small way. Where the old houses stood at the end of Church-street they made a large hole.

And there they found five old wells. One of them, a large stone-lined well was uncovered to reveal that it was three feet six inches in circumference. And it went down 36 feet for certain, although it may have gone down still more.

It was bone dry and the brickwork was bound together with lime.

Mr. R. G. Woodfield, foreman in charge on the site, where shops will soon start to spring up, told our reporter that the well was a terrific job to knock in.

The well seems to point to a substantial building having been on the site, probably before the erection of the parish church, thinks Mr. E. J. Rogers of Oxhey-avenue, Oxhey.

Skulls as well as many powdered bones have been found by the footpaths behind the High-street shops. As this was obviously the limits of the churchyard in olden times, no inquest on the remains will be necessary.

WHP May, 1959

Last Cattle Market

ON the last Tuesday of 1959 there were more cattle than usual, as well as pigs, sheep and calves on offer, and competition was keen.

In 1890, the market came into the hands of the late Mr. W. Hurst Flint, of Messrs. Humbert and Flint, then to the late Mr. C. H. Halsey, till Mr. Hodgson took over in 1936. Watford Corporation now holds the Charter rights.

Watford market continued a busy and important venue for many years, but the Ministry of Food took over control of slaughtering during the war, and by the end of the war Watford had only two slaughter-houses left. At the same time Watford was progressively growing more urbanised and less agricultural, with the loss of farmland to the Hemel Hempstead New Town and other surrounding development.

So, with "the writing on the wall," Mr. Hodgson reluctantly made his decision to close the Watford market, but the goodwill of its business will be transferred to Mr. Hodgson's bigger market at St. Albans, which has been covered, provided with a car park and improved in various ways.

WHP December, 1959

At the time of taking this photograph, 'old Watford' still existed along the High Street, beyond the Station and almost to the site of the old mill. There still existed a number of grocers, butchers and, (here), a greengrocer (Meyers) and fishmonger (Mac Fisheries).   p.329 b.   1960

Mayor Explains High-street Scheme

COMPLAINTS about the council redevelopment down Watford High-street are answered by the Mayor, Ald. T. F. Harris, in a statement to the "Post" yesterday.

He writes:

I should like to clear up a misunderstanding which appears to exist in the minds of some people regarding the rebuilding of these premises.

I have heard it suggested that the Corporation, having acquired these properties for road widening purposes, are allowing the developers to rebuild to the old line. This is not so.

In fact the carriageway is being widened by 7 feet to 30 feet at the junction with the Market Place and, in addition, along the whole of the frontage a pavement 15 feet wide is being provided in substitution for the old pavement which at places, was as narrow as 5 feet in width.

The new pavement width to be provided is exactly the same as we ask other developers to provide on redevelopment.

WHP March, 1960

● *This refers to the block of buildings in front of the Parish Church, No. 92 to 100, and although the Corporation are correct in stating the footpath-width, the upper storeys of the building overhang and do not present a sympathetic appearance. In keeping with the 'old' line of Church Street which opened onto the High Street, an open walk-through is provided between No. 92 and 94. The Council's plan of June 1951 to 'remove' the shops (which the Council owned) was forgotten.*   p.324

£2 Million Idea

AT its next meeting the Watford Town and Country Planning and Plans Committee can expect a planning application before them which could radically change the face of Watford.

The proposal to develop a 12-acre "shoppers'

world" in Lower High-street is being put forward by the Blackpool firm of R. H. O. Hills, Ltd., retail store proprietors.

It is reported this week that negotiations have been completed to buy the site from Benskins, subject to Hills obtaining planning permission for their project. It is believed that the contract price for the sale of the land is about £200,000, and that the whole project will cost £2 million.

The site, which is on the opposite side of the High-street from Benskins, extends on the High-street frontage from the Watford Motor Company down as far as the old mill. It takes in all the land behind that frontage and over the river extends as far as Water-lane, including what is at present an undeveloped field.

WHP May, 1960

The Ever-rising Tide

To a degree there is, even as the flood of cars, lorries, buses and scooters mounts in an ever-rising tide.

Soon the representatives of Watford will be making their own tortuous way out of town to see the Minister of Transport with two resolutions strongly supported by the most important traffic meeting that Watford has held in years.

Mr. Marples should cut the cackle and ease the traffic. And while he is on the subject, despite what adverse figures his statisticians may try to dig up, he should be made to realise how important it is for the North Orbital-road from Hunton Bridge to join the Denham By-pass, a link so vital between east and west, a main artery flowing from the M.1.

WHP May, 1960

The ABC restaurant has been closed and a firm offering hardware and fancy goods come and gone—the shop would later be William's furniture store and, much later, Ponderosa, back to an eating house. The 'new building' next door was once the site of Tucker's Garage.   p.327 t   1960

Queens Road looking towards Derby Road. On the right, the glass show-case windows of H. W. Beall's drapery and millinery store. *p.340 t* 1960

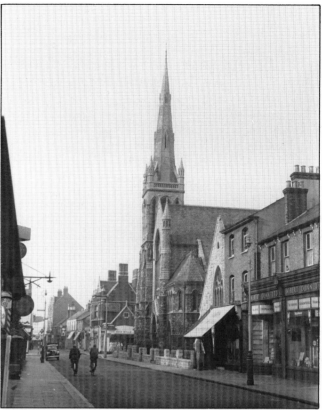

Queens Road looking towards High Street. On the right, Albert Dunn, Wallpaper and Paint, retail and trade, and Carr's second-hand books and antiques. The Methodist Church, the Wesleyan of 1889, soon to be demolished. *p.340 bl*

Meriden Tower Blocks

THIS is an impressive picture, you will all agree, and if I asked you where, it is hardly likely you would place the scene behind Watford by-pass on the Meriden Council Estate. But I tell you it could be.

The Borough Council are just now weighing up the possibilities of projecting four 12-storey blocks of flats on the northern sky-line, and if they do, as they most likely will, we must all be prepared for something like this.

The flats that will be built on stilts over the central car park will be only half this height. They're six storeys.

The dwarf-the-neighbours business block in Clarendon-road will be nine storeys.

So these at Meriden are way up there on their own.

Do not make the mistake of taking this scheme for granted. Not just yet anyway.

I go no further than to say I would like to see the picture in bricks and mortar. I may only add that I am encouraged to be optimistic about that possibility by the Town Hall interest in the preliminary plans prepared by Mr. F. C. Sage, the Borough Engineer and Surveyor.

They could have turned down those first plans on the spot, but they did not do that.

They were interested enough to want to know something of the cost, and they ordered sketches to be prepared.

We have months to wait, several at least, but the result will be worth it.

I know 2,000 families who think so for certain. They are the people on the council waiting list for houses. The projected flats, four blocks of them, each 12 storeys high, will provide homes for 144 families. And that's a whole lot more than could be accommodated in houses built on the same site.

WHP July, 1960

High Street, corner of Loates Lane, Peacock's printing works and the 'Watford Observer' offices, No. 101.   *p.333 c & b*   **1960**

Beat group outside the Chef Restaurant . . .

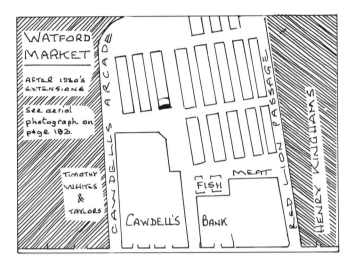

WATFORD MARKET

AFTER 1920's EXTENSIONS

See aerial photograph on page 182.

TIMOTHY WHITES & TAYLORS

CAWDELL'S ARCADE

CAWDELL'S

FISH

MEAT

BANK

RED LION PASSAGE

HENRY KINGHAMS

Watford Market, space to browse and shop.

. . . provide music for the dancers.   1960

The Whitsun Carnival procession has passed the roundabout and the resultant traffic jam on all four roads presents a temporarily insoluble problem.

Students' Rag Day, St. Albans Road opposite the Avenue; road to the right is Weymouth Street (later to be demolished to make way for the 'Eastern relief road'. *p.185 t*

The Odeon Cinema. *p.175 tr, 192 c.*

Hille House, St. Albans Road 1961; only Barclays Bank in occupation as yet. (In a country-wide reduction of numbers of unprofitable branches, the branch of Barclays was among those closed in January 1987.)

Fire Station Closes

THE name's the same, the faces are the same, and the telephone number is the same. But that is where the similarity ends. For as from 14.30 hours yesterday, Watford Fire and Ambulance moved, after 60 years, from Watford High-street, to its brand new £80,000 Station at the junction of Rickmansworth and Whippendell-roads.

The bells for fire and ambulance will ring out no more from Watford High-street.

Instead it will be life in the ultra-modern, twin block station, with its 83-foot radio mast towering above, revolving around the watch room round a three-sided control console with rows of telephone switches, bells, buzzers, warning lights, factory alarm systems, and an impressive red emergency phone. The whole thing looks for all the world like the control room of a nuclear power station.

WHP February, 1961

Watford's Parking Solution

A bold multi-storey car park plan to save Watford from committing commercial suicide —"the inevitable fate of a town which fails to solve its parking problems"—was presented to Watford Town Council by the Borough Engineer (Mr. F. C. Sage) on Monday.

The plan looks way into the future—to the time when, it is estimated, parking facilities will be required for 3,500 vehicles.

It provides for meter street parking for 500 cars, surface car parks (possibly metered) for 642 cars, and multi-storey facilities for 1,996 vehicles.

Suggested sites for the multi-storey parks are the Central car park (Beechen-grove), at Carey-place, in Church-street and at the Shrubbery car park.

The fact remains that our roads are becoming so conjested that they can no longer be used as free car parks," Mr. Sage told the members.

WO January, 1961

Rear of the 'One Bell' and Public Conveniences; site of the old workhouse, in use as a 'temporary' car park pending construction of the Church Street multi-storey car park. In the background, Almondswick, Registrar's Office, also in the background are barns on the same site as shown in the 1771 plan. *p.20*

Changing Face of Watford

THERE are three more "pubs with no beer'—to borrow the words of a popular song—in Central Watford at the moment.

They are the three old "locals"—"The Greyhound," "The New Inn," King-street, and "King's Head" in Market Place—which closed their doors when the new "Robert Peel" was officially opened last week.

"The New Inn," meeting place of Watford and District Darts League, and A.E.U. branch, and other organisations, was at one time associated with Healey's Brewery, situated in George-street on the site of Pickford's depository, which was absorbed by Benskin's at the end of the last century.

Closing of "The King's Head" means that several organisations, including the Buffaloes, Watford Cine Society, another A.E.U. branch, and the local chess club have had to find alternative meeting places. It has been noted for its catering and, in particular, for "Kaye Aitch Night," which was introduced by a former manager for the serving of chicken in the rough.

WO April, 1961

King Street looking towards the High Street. The old Police Station on the right before being converted into the 'Robert Peel' public house. 1962

St. Albans Road, Nos. 108-124, Railway Cottages.   *p.345 b*

St. Albans Road, No. 102, the ex 'Railway Arms' closed pending demolition, next to the Bridle Path by the railway. 1839 to 1959.   1961

Buck—Best in Catering

ONE of Watford's oldest family businesses—P. Buck, Ltd., has an impressive history of continual success and expansion. Next week another piece of history, perhaps the most significant in the 92 years of the firm's existence, will be made when the spacious new building in Exchange-road is opened.

The story of Buck's is not only one of business triumph, behind there is also a fascinating personal story of four generations of a family who have worked hard to bring the firm to its present eminent position as the county's leading caterers.

It was in 1868 that an enterprising couple, Mr. and Mrs. Philip Buck, set up shop as cooks, caterers and confectioners at 48, High-street. No new business, particularly of this type, can be established without devoted work, but Mr. and Mrs. Buck were soon rewarded with success.

Within four years of the opening this small shop was already inadequate, so, in 1872 the adjoining shop at 50, High-street, was acquired. A double front was put in and the whole facade of the buildings given a face lift.

More building was again in hand in 1889 when a model kitchen and bakeries were added.

WHP June, 1961

For Sale!

The old police station site in St. Albans-road, Watford—at present used to house homeless families—is to be sold by Herts County Council. Part of the sale price will be used for the acquisition of other properties for the purpose of the homeless families scheme.

WO August, 1961

Barclays Bank, No. 128; the 'Queen's Arms', No. 126 and the Railway Cottages demolished; the new stretch of widened road open to traffic.   *p.345 b*

High Street, No. 101, corner of Loates Lane, C. H. Peacock's printing office and works in course of clearance for rebuilding.   *p.333 b*

Traffic diverted to the new road alongside allows rebuilding of old bridge to proceed.

More shops

In 1951 plans were announced for the building of some 6,400 new homes plus associated schools and industrial sites.

Apart from the M1 (1959) and Aylesbury Radial Road (scotched) there were no plans for town centre development of new shops or of road relief, but road outline changes came in a draft plan in 1956.

In the meantime, the shopping facilities were, with minor exceptions, little better than pre-war, i.e. 17 years out-dated.

As remarked on page 232, the consumer-goods shortage persisted and so the stores coped; but when the goods gradually became more readily available the space to sell and buy appeared woefully inadequate. In the latter part of the 1950's numerous plans were conceived, applied for, and passed and in 1959, 1960 and 1961 demolition and rebuilding was commonplace and extensive.

Concurrent with these individual works (Woodlands Parade, Gade House, 100 High Street (Island Site) 'Spread Eagle' site, British Home Stores, Littlewoods, plus revamps for Woolworths, Clements and Cawdells) plans to develop the Benskin's Lower High Street site were announced (1960). The subject of an extensive enquiry, the Minister of Housing and Local Government vetoed the Benskin's Shopper's World proposal as 'unsuitable' remarking that the site should be used for 'housing and industrial use' as per the development plan.

This plan was put on ice to resurface 25 years later as the 'Tesco' project.

At the time the Benskin enquiry was concluding (January 1962), more plans were announced, this time for Queens Road, High Street and Derby Road sites—MARS.

They came to nothing but the announcement blighted Queens Road for many years until Littlewoods extended and Sainsbury's built a food store upon the old Library/Technical School site.

In 1961/2, goods to buy, luxuries previously hard to come by, and new stores and shops, clean, modern and well lighted, drove out of mind the sweeping away of the older buildings.

The start of the 'swinging sixties' saw changes other than the moralistic freedoms; the rebuilt shops were on existing sites, and for a short while longer the shape of the town—one long street—remained.

Watford's worst fire for many years, at the factory of British Moulded Hose Co. in Bushey Mill Lane. Thirteen fire stations in Herts, Middx, Bucks and Beds sent 15 appliances and 70 firemen to deal with the blaze. The factory is that built in 1921/22 by the Watford Manufacturing Company and is adjoining the Vi-Cocoa factory which was gutted in 1903. In the BMH blaze the smoke was seen from twenty miles away; there were no casualties.
June, 1961

All that remains of No. 14 High Street, the old Council Offices, are the entrance steps; the fire station is in course of demolition. Beyond what is now the Gade House site is 'Exchange Road' (previously Upton Road). Wren's have moved from 46 High Street and next door, Buck's have moved from Nos. 48-52 High Street. In the site being cleared may be seen the old air-raid shelter/warden's post.

p.88, 123 t

Chop-Shop in the High Street

WE often hear talk about the changing face of Watford High-street. Do we ever pause to really consider the extent of those changes over the past ten years or so?

There remains little more than the railway arches and gas works at one end, the Pond at the other, and the Parish Church in the centre, to identify it with the main thoroughfare that was Watford's in the early twenties.

Demolition and reconstruction work in the central area of the town has been gradually gathering momentum in recent years, and today the town centre must surely be undergoing more changes than at any other time in its history.

How many old Watfordians returning to the borough would recognise it from any of the views obtained by an "Observer" cameraman in a recent pictorial survey of the High-street?

Only the other day a lady travelling into the town on a coach was overheard to remark to her friend, "I wonder what building we will find they have started pulling down today?"

Starting a journey down the High-street from the roundabout, we find ourselves completely surrounded by buildings which were non-existent when Watford received its Charter in 1922, and the extension to the parade of shops on the St. Albans-road corner has only taken place in recent years.

The pond, of course, has been a feature of the town since its earliest days: the Odeon (first called the Plaza) was the first large cinema to be built in the High-street, and the nearby Monmouth House will be remembered by some of the oldest inhabitants, although several of the shops it encompasses have brought many changes to its general appearance.

It is the opposite stretch of the High-street (or The Parade as it is generally known at this point) that has either undergone or is undergoing the greatest change in recent years. Now nearing completion on the site of the original Halsey House, home of the Watford Conservative Club, is a vast new block of modern shops and offices matching in design the neighbouring block which stands on the site of the old residence known as The Woodlands.

Moving further down we pass what remains of the old Watford Fire Station and, looking across the site of 14 High-street from which the affairs of the borough were conducted before the war, we get an unusual view of Exchange-road (formerly Upton Road). This in itself would only be familiar to those who have known the town in recent months and, when the new traffic scheme is put into operation, it will form the northern outlet from the western relief road.

Continuing our journey we see few shops which have escaped vast structural alterations at some time or other since the war. An outstanding exception is, perhaps, the building which "houses" a jeweller's, newsagent's and an old world restaurant, which is reputed to be over 300 years old.

In the Market-place there still remains the "Rose and Crown" to remind us of days gone by, but the once nearby "Spreadeagle" has disappeared to make way for a modern shop, and the "King's Head" is destined for destruction very shortly. On our left the opening leading to the central car park is another new feature which was preceded by demolition work, and as we pass into the narrow section of the High-street, our attention is attracted by another new block of shops with its vista view of the parish church and the new car park opposite.

On the left are two more gaping "wounds" where, until recently, stood the premises of Kingham's and C. H. Peacock Ltd., both flourishing concerns—now moved to premises elsewhere—which still bear the names of the old Watford families.

The widened Water-lane turning (now nearing completion) will soon bring through traffic off the eastern relief road, and this brings us to Lower High-street which, though still, perhaps, the "Cinderella" of the town, has seen remarkable improvements and changes of late. The old mill, which stood a derelict eye-sore for many years following destruction by fire, has been replaced by a used car business with fountains playing in the foreground, and several similar business and modern garage premises have helped to bring a "new look" to the area.

But all this is but a drop in the ocean of alterations and developments still in the offing.

Four multi-storey car parks, a street meter parking system, a vast shopping area on the old brewery site—all these are "on the books" to complete the transformation of the small market town that was Watford at the turn of the century.

WO July, 1961

Moss Motors, Hempstead road, Volkswagen dealers.

St. Albans Road, Nos. 86-76   p.347 c   1960

St. Albans Road, towards Langley Road.

Mr. Clore Buys High Street Property

FINANCIER Mr. Charles Clore has entered the property market at Watford.

He has bought one of the few remaining old properties in High-street, the shops and cafe, Nos. 22 to 26. The price paid is given at £35,000.

The property includes the small newsagent's shop of Stan Pike, the double-fronted shop of D. Jackson jeweller, and the Brass Lantern restaurant.

This old Tudor property, one of the most picturesque in Watford, has six years of its lease to run and at present under the lease is understood to bring in a rental of just under £20 a week.

The restaurant has been well preserved and contains many of its original fittings and oak beams, as well as the oven, though this is not used and is merely one of the many attractions.

The jewellery firm of Dan Jackson was established in 1876 and was taken over from that well-known Watford figure, the late Mr. B. S. Morse. It was extended a few years ago when the shop next door became vacant.

The property belonged to Mrs. Boyle, another well-known Watford personality, of 1, Upton-road, Watford, where she has lived for many years.

WHP August, 1961

Youth Centre Progress

PREPARATORY and foundation work on the site of the new Y.M.C.A. Youth Centre is already well advanced—another indication of the changing face of Watford.

And, this week, Mr. H. D. Praat (chairman of the Watford Youth Centre Appeals Committee) told the "Observer":

"Following upon the announcement that a building contract has been signed for the new Y.M.C.A. Youth Club and Hostel, we are pleased to announce a gift of £4,750 from the Emile Wertheimer Trust to meet the cost of the new dining-room, its furnishings and equipment.

"Mr. Emile Wertheimer, an American, came to London in the early 'twenties and played a prominent part in the exhibiting and distribution of films. He died in 1954, whereupon the administration of his fortune became the responsibility of Trustees under the Emile Wertheimer Trust."

WO September, 1961

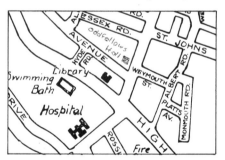

St. Albans Road, the 'Oddfellows Hall', opposite Weymouth Street.   p.347 b

St. Albans Road, Tucker's Garage to the left. Tucker's, before taking over the Nascot Motor Works of Otto Brookman, were situated at 135 High Street.
    p.347 b

Clarendon Road; stamp-vending machine outside the GPO Sorting Office, prior to GPO's removal to Balmoral Road in 1964.

Watford Carnival, fun fair in Cassiobury Park; reminder of the rides and prices.

Shoppers Dream Fading?

Will Watford's dream of a shoppers' paradise be shattered when the Borough Council meet to-morrow night? It could well be.

Through the long summer months the people whose responsibility it is to plan the future of our town, have been tackling what must surely be the biggest problem that has ever confronted them.

It was in October last year the Council first talked of the plans of R. H. O. Hills Ltd., the Blackpool firm, to build what some termed a paradise for shoppers off the Lower High-street.

And the members gave an initial blessing to the proposals,providing matters like road improvements, siting of buildings, car parking, loading facilities and the culverting of streams could be ironed out satisfactorily with the developers.

But industry was alarmed. The feeling was that such a huge development would drain too much labour away for staffing purposes. A Ministry of Housing and Local Government Inquiry was called for. But in calling for it, the Borough Council still let it be known that it smiled somewhat benevolently on the scheme.

But further thoughts came to their mind. This shoppers' paradise would have to tie up with the widening of the High-street, and the construction of a new roundabout. Car parking plans would have to be satisfactory. So would the provisions for the delivery of goods.

There was also a new theme, residential accommodation for at least 90 flats.

Talks went on throughout July. Out of them came the formula for a self-contained pedestrian shopping centre on American lines, covering seven-and-a-half acres and giving parking space for about a thousand cars to start with.

But it was also underlined that the Council had a plan of its own for the present central shopping area to be provided with relief roads to enclose it, and car parks for 3,500 cars. This present shopping space in the heart of Watford is increasing steadily to 28 acres.

Then came the million-dollar question. Did the 26 per cent increase in shopping floor space, provided by the proposed new shopping centre, reflect the true additional shopping potential of the area?

Would the potential turnover of the new shopping centre be matched by a comparable increase in the total turnover of the central area by attracting more people to the town?

Would the success of the new shopping centre come at the expense of the present shops to a large extent? The experts called in, thought it would. The setting up of a new centre to compete against the old shopping centre must be examined much more critically, they said. Of course the central area plan could be revised to bring the shopper's paradise into that plan. But this appeared neither desirable nor practicable.

So the experts have recommended that the Borough Council should oppose this proposed paradise for shoppers. As a place apart, although only a couple of hundred yards, from the present shopping centre, it would weaken, rather than reinforce the present centre.

Say the experts—this is a most interesting experiment in shopping in this country, given suitable conditions. But Watford, apparently, is not the place. Our interests could be best served by expanding the shopping centre within the proposed relief roads.

And so tomorrow night the Special Town Planning Committee will recommend the Council to have a change of heart, despite the earlier enthusiasm expressed for the plan of R. H. O. Hills, the official view now is that the development would not be in the best interests of the Borough of Watford and should not be allowed.

WHP September, 1961

Shop-Shape and Watford Fashion

THE good people of Watford are only just beginning to realise how lovingly the eyes of Britain's retailers linger on a town where the men in the main local industry (printing) average £1,275 a year, and the unemployment rate rests at a minimal 0.4 per cent.

No sooner did Mr. Leslie Goldberg's R. H. O. Hills group apply for permission to erect a £2 million, 12-acre "Shopper's World" on the old Benskin's Brewery site at what is at present distinctly the wrong end of the High Street, than Mr. Arron Lermon and Mr. Saul Magrill, of Macowards, revealed that they had been negotiating for two years to put up something exactly similar on a seven-acre site right in the town centre.

They already own Cawdells, the rambling store which winds its way across a key half-acre, backed by the local market and a string of Corporation property in fairly urgent need of redevelopment, and they have the full backing of Mr. Walter Flack, the Murrayfield millionaire who now runs the shop side of the Cotton-Clore City Centre set-up.

While Hills and Macowards growl, two other groups are acting. The Watford Co-op, in partnership with the Jacobson brothers' fast-moving Montague Burton chain, are spending £500,000 in the New Year to put a store on the old fire station site, and Clements, a local business, are spending another £500,000 to double their present size.

The only trouble is, Watford is already one colossal traffic jam during shopping hours. So what happens when it becomes the most heavily-shopped high street in the country?

Sunday Times November, 1962

Passage between left-hand building and the hoarding is Red Lion Passage, leading to the market. The cleared site was that of Henry Kingham's; rebuilding is for British Home Stores.   *p.277 tr*

New, purpose-built branch of Westminster Bank. Necessity for anti-bandit screens and metal grills had not yet arisen. Banking transactions were still negotiated at the open counter. 1961

Opening of the Bank's drive-in facility, Watford's first drive-in bank; Westminster, Station Road. 1961

New Way Out of Clarendon Road

IF the man-in-the-street in Watford does not appear to know quite where he is going at the present, then he can possibly be forgiven.

The biggest changes that this town has ever known are coming on to the stocks.

Last week we had the probe into the "Shoppers' World" off the Lower High-street. Then came the Eastern Relief Road inquiry. And around the corner is the plan to cut the High-street in two in order to try to solve the traffic chaos.

Back to the Eastern Relief Road, the plan for which has just been probed for a couple of days.

The blue-print envisages a three-roundabout plan—an extension of the Town Hall round-about to Weymouth-street, another down Clarendon-road and a third at Water-lane, plus, of course, demolitions and upheavals.

But at the inquiry, Clarendon-road businesses threatened by demolition produced a new way out. Shift the Clarendon-road roundabout to open ground behind the Gaumont Cinema and Clements and take from it a one-way street to the High-street, opposite Exchange (once Upton) road.

This, they claim, would lengthen the shopping precinct in the High-street as far as Exchange-road, make Clarendon-road into two additional shopping precincts, divided by the relief road cutting through. Traffic lights would control the flow of traffic across the High-street. All this would ease the flow into Clarendon-road. It would mean demolition in the High-street. But it would save premises in Clarendon-road.

Better for the traffic, maybe. But it was reck-oned that costs would go up by between £100,000 and £150,000. For High-street frontage commands £2,500 a foot, compared with about £500 in Clarendon-road. And an extra road would have to be built.

Those who shape the future of Watford will look into the new idea. It could even be that a start will eventually be made to both ends of the relief road while the debate continues about the contours of its middle regions.

But one thing seems certain. The relief road must go through—whichever way it eventually goes.

Obviously, some drastic surgery is needed to unclog the traffic arteries of the Borough, before we succumb to vehicular thrombosis.

But when the Town Hall's scalpels have carved out new channels for the traffic to flow freely, will it, after all, be a case of: "Operation successful, patient dead?"

By next year, we will have one vehicle to every five persons in Britain. By 1985, one for every two people. In 1960, there were 9,000,000 vehicles licensed. In 1970, there will be 17,000,000 in 1980, 25,000,000, in 1990, 30,000,000.

Not only that, but the average yearly mileage of each vehicle on the road is also growing. In fact, even the rate by which this mileage is increasing is believed to be still going up

WHP November, 1961

Expansion Plans for Watford Stores

On the heels of the £2 million "Shoppers' World" project for Lower High-street comes news this week of other big developments planned for Watford's central shopping area.

Clements and the Watford and Harrow Co-operative Society each have £2 million schemes, and Montague Burton Ltd. and Cawdells also plan to expand, although in Cawdells' case planning permission has not yet been sought.

The Co-op and Montague Burton Ltd. are jointly to develop the ex-fire station site in the High-street. They have offered the site free to the Corporation as a car park until Christmas shopping is over.

Director Mr. H. V. Hornsby, giving evidence at the "Shoppers' World" inquiry on Friday, said the project would start "in the next few weeks."

The first stage, he said, would add 40,000 square feet of floor space and parking for 110 cars. There would be roof as well as ground level parking space.

The second stage would increase floor space by another 10,000 square feet.

WO November, 1961

Bandstand, Cassiobury Park, later to be dismantled and eventually re-sited in the precinct next to the Central Library. Now listed, Grade II structure.

Peace Memorial Group, now re-sited next to Public (side) entrance to Town Hall. Now 'listed' for preservation.

Park Gates, Rickmansworth Road. Out of the picture to the right, were the 'Essex' almshouses.   *p.86, 338 bl*

Imperial Way

Imperial Way is extended by a new road called Colonial Way to Radlett Road and most of the 16 sites have been taken. Among them are Messrs. Keens, Dennison Manufacturing, T. Walls & Sons, British American Optical and McKay Transport. Five sites are vacant.

WHP November, 1961

University Post For Mr. Rée

Watford Boys' Grammar School is to lose its popular headmaster.

It was officially announced this week that 47-year-old Mr. Harry Alfred Rée has been appointed the Professor of Education at the new York University.

Mr. Rée came to the Watford Grammar School at Easter, 1951, upon the retirement of Mr. Percy Bolton. He was previously at Bradford Grammar School, where he was senior science master, and before that had taught at Beckenham and Penge County School.

While serving as a captain in the Intelligence Corps during the war, Mr. Rée parachuted into France, and, as a "French civilian," he helped to organise the Resistance Movement. Later he returned to this country to continue organisation of the Movement and to supervise the dropping of necessary supplies.

It was in recognition of this service that he was awarded the D.S.O., and O.B.E. and the French Croix de Guerre.

Since he has been in Watford Mr. Rée has frequently taken part in broadcasts on education, and has written widely on the subject.

Both Mr. Rée and his wife have taken an active interest in the work of the Watford Marriage Guidance Council.

WO December, 1961

Blizzard

The last day of 1961 and the first few of 1962 saw many falls of heavy snow driven by northerly winds. The town on the Monday morning presented a deserted air as people faced unaccustomed difficulties in travelling. Along the Parade by MacFisheries, Garners and to Clements, the snow was piled some two or three feet high upon the edge of the pavement, leaving just a narrow snow-bound passage for passers-by.

Film, 'Around Watford', 1961-62

Mail Held Up

Mr. A. K. Smith, Head Postmaster, said at the sorting office in Clarendon Road that normal mail had been cleared after the Union of Postal Workers' work-to-rule. But there was an accumulation of what was called 'deferred matter'.

Bad weather conditions and staff shortages meant that the strength was 60 staff short out of 200.

WHP January, 1962

Winter 1961/62's cold spell; the 385A broken down and temporarily abandoned outside Clements; old Council Office and Fire Station site cleared and work started on the building of Gade House in the background.   *p.336 b*

... *Croydon of North London* ... *MARS* ...

New £380,000 College on Stilts

THE new South-West Herts College of Further Education has been designed as a college on stilts. This is because the £380,000 college is to be built on a four-acre site in Water-lane, Watford, where danger from flooding from the nearby Hillfield Brook has to be considered.

In 1947 the site was flooded to a depth of four feet, and in 1960 it was also flooded to a lesser extent.

The centre block will be raised on stilts which will be both a safeguard against flood danger and also give under-cover parking space.

The architects of the County Architect's Department, under Mr. G. C. Fardell, who have designed the college, have based their space allowance for parking on the needs which have had to be met at Watford Technical College, where parking has presented a considerable problem. They have provided parking space for 176 cars and 100 motor-cycles.

The college, which will house 1,040 students in the first instalment, will have workshops, science laboratories, 19 classrooms, a library, drawing offices, a dining room, kitchen, gymnasium and hall. It will have oil-fired central heating.

It is expected to be built by 1965.

WHP January, 1962

MARS!

THE face of Central Watford will change drastically during the next five to seven years. By that time it is hoped that the Borough will have become the Croydon of North London.

Situated as it is on the perimeter of the Greater London Council it has a great potential. Planners have seen this potential.

First there is the Shoppers' World on which a public inquiry has just ended. This £2,000,000 scheme will result in the redevelopment of Lower High-street.

Now comes the redevelopment of the area between Queens-road and Water-lane, extending back to the Eastern Relief road. This is a £3,000,000 scheme the Watford Borough Council will discuss at the February meeting.

Featured in the possibilities of the new scheme is a first-class hotel with assembly rooms behind.

On the other side, under a six- or seven-storey car park, a ten-pin bowling alley is planned.

Another feature will be a pedestrian precinct from High-street near the corner of Water-lane.

The scheme, aptly called 'The Mars Scheme," is being sponsored by Cubitt London Properties, Ltd. The architects are H. G. Huckle and partners. It will mean the redevelopment of nearly 7½ acres extending along Queens-road to the Eastern Relief road and will include Albert-street and Carey-place, both of which will vanish completely.

The area.   the redevelopment goes forward, will be dominated by an 11-storey central tower block of 130 flats with garages for the tenants underneath the block.

For the shoppers there will be a multi-storey car park. Access will be by the Eastern Relief road to the car park, from where the people will enter the pedestrian precinct to visit the shops. There will be a rear service access to all the shops.

Another feature will be the provision of overhead walkways.

Cubitts also have in mind a ten-pin bowling alley for the scheme under the multi-storey car park, which will accommodate at the start 600 cars.

The Company already own a considerable number of properties in Queens-road and are actively negotiating for others in Queens-road, fronting, and in the rear of High-street.

They have suggested that their holdings and the Corporation's holdings should be merged and the whole area redeveloped comprehensively.

The first phase, it is suggested, should take into account the pattern of acquisitions and take in the construction of the multi-storey car park and the Queens-road shops from Derby-road to, but not including, the College of Further Education.

It is also suggested that the Borough Council could to some extent control the development, as Cubitts would be willing to sell their freeholds to the Corporation subject to them being given a long lease at a ground rent calculated on an agreed percentage of the total cost to the Corporation of the purchase of their interests and the Corporation's interests.

The Company also proposes that such ground rent should be reviewed every 25 years. One of the suggestions is that the Company should build the multi-storey car park and sub-lease it to the Corporation, who would thus have absolute control of parking.

The surveyors, Rogers, Chapman and Thomas, have asked the Borough Council whether the scheme would be acceptable in principle, and have intimated they would be prepared to appear before the appropriate committee for further discussion.

The Borough Council have sought the views of the Corporation's consultants, Hillier, Parker, May and Rowden, and it is these views that the Property Committee will consider and pass on to the Borough Council for the February meeting.

WHP January, 1962

'Skyscraper' Staff Move In

"MELTON HOUSE"—the new Clarendon-road "skyscraper" office block—is now partially occupied.

Three hundred members of the staff of the Revenue Section of the Accountants' Department, British Railways, last weekend vacated the seven huts they have occupied at The Grove since 1939 and moved into the first five floors of this nine-storey building.

Standing 92ft. high, "Melton House" is now the tallest building in Watford. The title was originally held by the British Moulded Hose factory (84ft.) followed by the telephone exchange (75ft.).

Other departments of British Railways are to occupy the remainder of the building, and it is expected that all will be in occupation by June. They are: District Engineers (from St. Pancras), Superannuation Funds Office, and a small section of the Welfare Department.

In charge of the 300 already installed is Mr. J. Carr (Revenue Accountant), who said this week: "After the old life-expired huts where we had to put on hats and coats to visit the next department, this is a very acceptable change.

It is wonderful to be able to move around in complete comfort and in such clean surroundings."

WO February, 1962

Fine New School For Holywell

The huge Victoria Secondary Modern School in Tolpits-lane is nearing completion. It sprawls over several acres on a site opposite Scammell Lorries' factory, and is a necessary corollary to the Holywell Industrial Estate.

WHP April, 1962

● *(later Westfield Girls' School)*

Watford Cine Society

Formation of a cine society was mooted during early 1958 and a preliminary meeting was held on July 8th, '58. Founder members were Roger Moon, Alan Campbell, Roger Nicholls and Bob Nunn. Alan Campbell was declared first Chairman and the first meeting was held on Monday September 1st and thereafter fortnightly on Mondays. This pattern continued during the winter of 1958/59 and weekly meetings started in September 1959—the meeting places moving from the free School Hall to 14a High Street (which is now the site of Gade House).

At an early date public shows were aimed at to bolster funds. The first show, in 1958, was at St. Mary's Church Hall and a 'Ten Best' show. Ices were served in the interval! 16mm projectors used were Bell & Howell and Debrie. From this it was decided to make up a mixed programme and so the first Film Festival was held at the Town Hall on 19th November 1959. This included two Society productions, both on 16mm with striped sound. Unfortunately the hired arc projector could not cope with the edge stripe and sound 'wild' tape was run—the sync. being not too bad! The 2nd Festival was again a mixed programme with one Society 16mm film included. At the 3rd Festival the 1959 'Ten Best' programme was shown together with the innovation of telling the audience that at the end of the show a special short 8mm show would be shown at the side of the hall as an 'experiment'; would those who wished to stay, please do so?

The audience stayed—the picture quality was good (Eumig with 6ft screen), and in fact better than the 16mm films because trouble was experienced with the borrowed projector and, sad to relate, the 'home made' 8mm films were voted better entertainment than the 16mm 'Ten Best'!

So the decision was made. All future public shows would be of the members' own work and the first all-8mm show was in 1962. Eumig projectors have been used at each showing and the screen size is now 8ft.

In the meantime the Society's meeting places have included the 'King's Head' (now demolished); the 'Green Man'; 'Hertfordshire Arms'; British Legion Hall Croxley Green (never to be forgotten by those who attended during the bitter winter!).

JBN, Cine Society History

VIII

The Changes Start

The access roads of King Street, Queens Road, Market Street, Upton Road and Clarendon road were all so narrow that a queue of just a few cars at each junction created a 'jam'. When added to the 'through' traffic which used the High Street — cars, buses, lorries, and the delivery vehicles stopped outside shops and stores, the result was chaos.

The plan announced in 1959 suggested blocking up the High Street and introducing a simple one-way ring-road. During the early part of Spring 1962 an apparently endless number of new traffic signs were erected and covered until the great day. The Sunday dawned fine and teams of workmen were busy painting new road direction signs, uncovering the new and removing some of the old. Traffic lights had to be altered. It was not long before the change had been made — and the local residents who had been up and about watching with great interest now had the sight of bewildered motorists finding that they could no longer travel their accustomed routes. For example, it was no longer possible to travel from King Street across the High Street to Queens Road; King Street was now one-way leading from the High Street.

Good humoured patience was much in evidence and by the end of the day the system was established.

As a temporary measure the Plan succeeded in easing some High Street traffic flow, although bus passengers had to learn new stops and there were unexpected problems at the Clarendon Road crossing, and between there and Upton Road.

Lower High Street and the Parade/Pond stretch were little changed.

Two years later the 'Draft Plan 1956' was re-introduced as the updated and new '1964 Draft Plan'.

In the meantime through traffic did not have to face the congested stretch of road between Market Place and Water Lane.

The High Street, Watford's backbone from time immemorial, had been broken at Market Street and Clarendon Road corners.

'D-DAY' IS ON MAY 20!

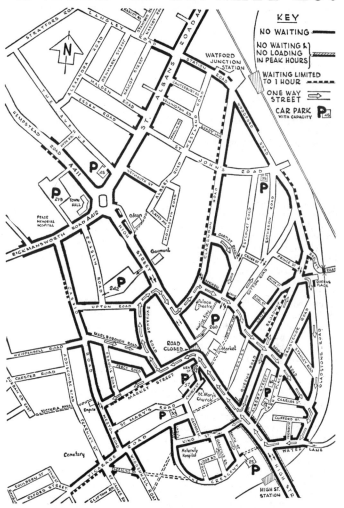

Clarendon Road, outside the Palace Theatre, direction-sign painting for the ▶ new system. *p.336 c*

295

Sunday 20th May, 1962. Contractors have not yet finished painting and placing new road signs; but the road is blocked and the new system working. A new era has started. *p.80*

Fluoride Opponents Still 'Anti'

SINCE fluorides have been added to Watford's water supply, the number of three-year-old children completely free from tooth decay has barely doubled. But despite the encouraging statistics revealed this week in the Ministry report on fluoridation studies in the United Kingdom, opponents of fluoridation remain unmoved.

Schoolmaster Mr. H. B. Foxwell, of St. Albans-road, Watford, who led the local attack against the experiment, still collects all his water from outside the borough. And he says he will continue to do so.

After reading the findings, he said this week: "This is just what we expected. There probably is some apparent benefit, but it does cause mottling, and the benefit may be of short duration."

Of the medical reports of no harmful effects, Mr. Foxwell said: "We know people who have made complaints to the Town Hall about stomach trouble following fluoridation, but these have been brushed aside.

"In one family I call on, three generations were affected. These things build up in our systems. Some people develop mysterious diseases, but we can never really put it down to fluoride.

"I am inclined to think something makes the 'soil' suitable for reception of the germs."

Mr. Foxwell said it was now believed that toothpaste with fluoride added was proving equally beneficial. This being so, fluoridation of the water was no longer necessary, and the actual "intake" could be reduced, he said.

As regards the statistics he declared: "They talk about a 50 per cent improvement at the age of five. I believe the average at that age was two decayed teeth per child, so for the sake of one tooth, they are taking away everyone's liberty to enjoy pure water."

The average number of decayed, missing and filled teeth was 66 per cent less at the age of three years, 57 per cent less at four years and 50 per cent less at five years.

WHP July, 1962

Shirley House College Plans

WORK on providing the new College of Further Education, proposed for the controversial Shirley House site in Watford, has been suspended—because of an unexpected legal complication dating back nearly 100 years.

Discovery of the snag has forced Herts County Council to send out some 300 registered letters to local residents asking if they would object to the lifting of the ban that this ancient covenant imposes on the erection of certain types of buildings on the site.

The covenant was signed in 1865.

It forbids the building of "a public house, inn, beer shop or other shop or for any purpose of sale trade, manufacture or business or public establishment of for any purposes whatsoever which may in anywise be a nuisance to the neighbourhood or to the owner or occupier of any land adjacent..." without the previous consent of the owners, their heirs or assigns.

WO October, 1963

Derby Road prior to widening.

Water Lane widened in readiness . . . *p.256, 328 b*

Counterpart to the 'snow' scene on p.293 showing the Gade House site on the right, just part the entrance to the Shrubberies car park.   *p.322 b*   1962

Graves Dug Up

HIDDEN from view by high screens, men are at work exhuming the remains of Baptist worthies who were buried in Beechen Grove Churchyard, Watford, over 200 years ago.

The screens, made of sacking nailed to wooden staves, were put up following complaints that the macabre work could be seen by people on the upper deck of buses in Beechen Grove.

Mr. Bernard Cunningham, from St. Albans, said he and his men might find some gold rings or bracelets.

"There are 15 graves marked by stones, but there are also a lot unmarked. Some will be six feet deep, some 10 feet," he said.

The oldest grave dated from 1721, he said, the last was dated 1861.

The removal of the remains and gravestones is being done by the Corporation to provide an addition to Beechen grove car park in time for the Christmas shopping rush. The Council bought the old Schoolroom and adjoining buriel ground for about £17,000 early this year and promoted an Act of Parliament for permission to remove the graves.

No officials of the church or members of the public objected to the Council's move when it was advertised.

The Rev. Irwin Barnes, Minister of Beechen Grove Baptist Church said it had not yet been decided what to do about the headstones, some of which are now undecipherable.

The graveyard was the original burial ground for Baptist dissenters in Watford, but there have been no burials there for over 100 years now.

WHP October, 1963

As is usual with 'one-way' systems, they very soon become 'race-tracks', for once in a car most drivers give way only to another car. And if all are going in the same direction there's little to cause problems . . . is there?

The corner of Clarendon Road became a nightmare to pedestrians. Themselves not over-used to waiting for the pedestrian traffic lights to give the go-ahead, at this point they quickly learned that, although the lights were in their favour to walk across, they were dis-regarded by many motorists . . . in this photograph the pedestrians have the 'clear' but almost each face is apprehensive and one couple are still standing waiting . . .

He's just the age to notice, and wonder what will happen if he dares to reach up and press the button! Corner of Clarendon Road, pedestrian-controlled traffic lights.   1962

297

Watford Junction, engine sheds; in the background, Fishburn's at Cassiobury Mills.

Platform 12, the St. Albans line.   1963

Last puffs of steam

Given the bad state of roads the horse and cart was the accepted form of local carriage although being rapidly replaced by motor vans and lorries. Steam trains were supreme countrywide and the network of rail extensive. Scammell's, by developing the three-wheel 'Mechanical Horse' and trailer, sounded the death knell of city-based horse traffic.

In 1921, to effect working economies, the old individual railways were merged into four regional groups of LMS, LNER, GWR and SR. They continued to lose business and revenue up to the last war; these losses paved the way for nationalisation in 1948, into British Rail.

In 1955 British Rail had a locomotive stock of some 19,000 steam engines— but diesel and electric locomotives were more efficient and modernisation plans were introduced. By the time the London Midland Region was electrified in 1966, the stock of steam locomotives had been reduced to 7000. The networks of works sidings had long since been disused and most taken up.

Bushey Arches Facelift

THE secret of modern bridge building is pre-planning—and evidence of how essential this is was apparent during Saturday night and Sunday as the new bridge at Bushey Arches was placed on the reinforced concrete trestles that had been prepared for it.

Three weeks ago the old part of the bridge was removed. Officially it was known as the "second widening," for it was the second addition to the original bridge that Robert Stevenson, son of the famous George, had erected.

This second widening was started in 1871 and by coincidence the contractor who signed the plans on August 28 of that year was himself a Stevenson.

This old bridge had a girder of 208 feet; it rested on concrete filled cast-iron columns that weighed nearly 30 tons.

The new bridge has been designed completely by British Railways. The designing engineer is Mr. C. F. Bonnett, of Berkhamsted.

WO October, 1963

400 New Kitchens

HOUSEWIVES living in Watford Borough Council houses are due for a big surprise—a Council scheme has started to give them modern, well-appointed kitchens and a hot water supply.

Apart from the houses modernised some two years ago, and the 80 houses in Riverside-road and Rose-gardens where work is now in progress, the Council plans to install "dream kitchens" in a further 396 dwellings.

"And this is just a start," a spokesman at the Town Hall told the "Post." "We will be considering what we can do for other council houses once this plan is well under way."

The houses under the modernisation plan are spread out as follows: 80 in Thorpe-crescent; 122 in Crossmead and Colne-avenue; 124 in Chilcott-road, Comyn-road, Desmond-road, Rosebriar-walk and Courtlands-drive; and 70 in Gammons-lane, Leggatts-way and Elm-grove.

Work on the Thorpe-crescent houses is due to start after Christmas. Crossmead and Colne-avenue will be dealt with shortly, and the other areas will be treated later.

"This is the first two-year modernisation programme," the Town Hall spokesman said. "Others will follow."

The scheme centres on the kitchens.

Bathrooms will be moved to give more floor space where possible—the baths themselves will be of modern squared-end style. Lavatories will be separate, and the coal cellars will be abolished.

Instead concrete coal bunkers will be built outside the kitchens, in the back gardens, but adjacent to the house walls.

Floors will be tiled, new sinks—the white sinks of the advertisements—will be provided and modern wall units and work-tops will be installed.

But perhaps the most important thing, from the householders' point of view, is the knowledge that modern boilers will be put into the kitchens —to supply hot water to sink, bath and newly fitted wash-hand basins—and hot water tanks put into the first floor bedrooms will be fitted into new airing and linen cupboards.

Front gardens will be separated from the pavement with new cement block walls and metal gates, and fences separating back gardens are to be replaced by plastic-covered wire fences.

In the living rooms, modern grates, capable of utilising smokeless fuels, are to be installed.

WHP November, 1963

Rise of Odhams

In the 27 years since building in Watford the firm has several times extended. The factory employs over 2,700 people and produces over 7,000,000 magazines per week. Following intensive research and development the introduction of pre-printed colour in national newspapers was accomplished in collaboration with Odhams Press Ltd.

WO Centenary Issue, 1963

Tributes to President Kennedy

WATFORD and district has this week been grieving with the rest of the world over the assassination of President Kennedy.

Special prayers have been said in churches and tributes have been spoken at all sorts of functions, from bazaars to a golf club dinner.

WHP November, 1963

Banks to Computerise

A LINE of strange figures typed on the bottom of a cheque in magnetic ink marks a revolution in local banking—the Westminster Bank has brought electronic accounting to Watford, the first town outside London to join in what the bank hopes will be a nation-wide computerlink among its branches.

The Watford Junction branch was the first to come into the scheme, 14 days ago. Last week the High-street branch switched over, and, from this morning (Thursday) the Cross Roads branch, at the Parade, joins in.

In addition to going over to computing procedures, the Watford banks are trying out a new system—the three branches will operate from a single set of machines at the Watford Junction office.

The single line of figures printed across the bottom of personal cheques is the secret of the new system. It is a method that will reduce the time necessary to maintain individual accounts, no matter how active they are, and at the same time will relieve staff for other duties.

Though thousands of pounds have been spent on the new machinery required and on the training of operators, it is the everyday telephone that supplies the key link between Watford and the Central Computer System at the Bank's offices in Lothbury, London.

WHP December, 1963

Eight phase, 20-year plan . . . link road to West Watford . . .

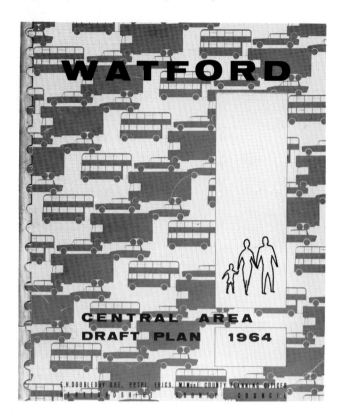

Church Street car park finished and in use.

Following the 1956 Central Area draft plan, minor road improvements were carried out and in the meantime Hertfordshire County Council and Watford Borough Council had held 'informal' discussions on the shape the town should take. A new draft plan was published.

With the assistance of Chartered Surveyors and Estate Agents, Messrs. Hillier, Parker, May and Rowden, detailed analysis of shopping space and useage was made. Plans were made to turn Clarendon Road into an 'office' centre to save Watford residents travelling to London. It also had the effect of attracting outside workers into the area. Plans were similarly made for designation of factory and industrial areas.

Labelled a 'Draft Plan' this informal document carried detailed suggestions for a completely new system of roads, including a simple one-way ring road to provide access to the centre; an Eastern relief road; improvements to St. Albans Road and Rickmansworth Road which included a 'flyover' at a new junction at Weymouth Street; an underpass at Cassio Road; a major junction system to link with the M1, a new road linking the southern end of the High Street with West Watford, and the eventual closing of the greater part of the High Street to vehicular traffic. And at a later date the traffic flow was to be reversed in the system.

Regarding traffic density, the 1956 premise of a 75% increase in 20 years was reached within 8 years. The forecast was amended to 150% increase by 1980, i.e. 2½ times 1959 level. The report commented that increase in vehicle usage 'will not cease at 1980 but will continue until a saturation point is reached in the year 2010.'

A number of shopping-site proposals were noted. The 'Central Car Park site' took place and became known as Charter Place. The site bounded by High Street, Queens Road and the proposed Eastern Relief Road became known as the 'Mars' site.

Arising from these various proposals was the question of whether the demand would be sufficient for the extra sales space created, and whether staff would be available, as, in the meantime, a number of established stores had already carried out substantial extensions.

Among the comments on the 'office survey' was noted the danger of 'reverse commuting' into Watford if the building of office blocks was not curtailed, and that those people who did so would eventually want to live in Watford.

The proposals put forward were designed to meet traffic requirements in 1980 and would have in general reached a limiting capacity and, to use the phraseology of the Buchanan Report, 'it is expected that the town centre will have reached its limit of accessibility'.

At the end of the Draft Report were listed the various phases for carrying out the works.

Phase 1 included Shrubberies car park, Charter Place, St. Mary's car park, and redevelopment of Queens Road for shopping.

Phase 2 was a new traffic gyratory system (Vicarage Road).

Phase 3, Cassio Road, Town Hall flyover (changed to underpass) and first stage of the Eastern relief road.

Phase 4, West Watford Link.

Phase 5, completion of Eastern relief road. Mars site (not done); and commencement of residential development opposite High Street Station (not done).

Phase 6, third section of Eastern relief road to link with M1 connection, and to link with West Watford; redevelopment of Smith Street and Granville Road/King Street.

Phase 7, dual carriageway in Clarendon Road between Beechen Grove and St. Johns Road.

Phase 8, redevelopment of St. Albans Road/Langley Road, Park/Church Road/Nascot Road/Stamford Road, for residential use with some neighbourhood shops.

Market Place. Fisher's has gone, the 'island' site SMC to Maddox (p.272) replaced by a new concrete and glass structure. Across the road Henry Kingham's, grocers for nearly two hundred years, now gone, and on the site British Home Stores with an extension in progress. Through-traffic is now banned and vehicle access is restricted to service to shops, and buses to and through Market Street. All major stores have undergone major internal reconstruction to comply with recent fire-regulations whereby stairways and lifts must be separated from main store area. *p.97t, 98, 324 b   1966/7*

Palace Theatre

The Palace Theatre, Watford and Hertford-shire's only live theatre, has, after a long and chequered history since its start in 1908, become a Civic Trust—a Theatre Trust supported by the Borough Council. The policy is to present straight plays, musicals and revues as part of a season of fortnightly runs.

Electrification

From March 1967 the suburban services be-tween Watford Junction, Bletchley, Rugby and Birmingham will be operated by new four-car electric multiple-unit trains. Each train will have seating for 19 first-class and 319 second-class passengers. Two units can be coupled together to form an eight-car train. The frequent service to and from Euston will be either non-stop or calling at Harrow.

Watford Official Guide

Compulsory Purchase Confirmed

THE Minister of Housing and Local Govern-ment has confirmed the Compulsory Purchase Order of the Watford Borough Council for 280, 282, and 284 High-street, Watford. The land, according to the Council, is needed for road improvement.

The order covers approximately 580 square yards of land and includes a motor-cycle engin-eer's, a cafe and a tobacconist's.

The public inquiry was held on May 7 when it was stated for the council that the dwellings were unfit for human habitation, and part of the land was needed for proposed road improvements. In the meantime it would be used as a car park.

WO August, 1963

Gade House

Gade House was officially opened on 28th January 1965.

George Stephenson College

The new college 'on stilts' in Water Lane has many departments installed; completion is ex-pected in 1966.

Princess Margaret at Palace Theatre

Princess Margaret and the Earl of Snowden paid an unheralded surprise visit to the Palace Theatre, May 19th, to see a performance of 'Macbeth'.

WO May, 1965

More car space

Clement's car park, holding 350 cars, is now in use.

WO May, 1965

Steam power has served the railways well for 120 years. Railways were already losing traditional business to road hauliers. Steam was relatively inefficient, labour-intensive and no longer viable in an emerging technological age. For a number of years diesel power had been appraised after trials as a transitional alternative before the introduction of an electrification scheme on heavily-worked routes. Electrification of the London-Birmingham section was not completed until 1966/7 and contributed to a delay in rebuilding the St. Albans Road bridge.

Water Lane 'temporary' bridge is not yet built; on the right, just above centre, is Benskin's Brewery. The two courses of the river are plainly discernible with Sedgwick's Brewery buildings upon one bank. At the top left corner the gas works are on one side of the High Street and the Watford Engineering Works on the other. Photographed in 1965 by Aerofilms Ltd, not long after the railway was electrified.

Few out-door events would be complete without an ice-cream barrow of either Grillo's or Cerasale's in attendance; Grillo's premises on the corner of Sutton Road. *p.348 bl*

Derby Road, Sutton Road, Baptist Sunday School, Wilk's, cycle repairers; now the site of Sutton Road multi-storey car park. The Sunday School building housed the Watford School of Music during the years 1957 to 1967 before the School of Music moved to its present home in Nascot Wood Road. *p.348 bl*

The Queen Mother, as Colonel-in-Chief of the Royal Anglian Regiment, asked to visit and inspect territorials and cadets of the 1st Battalion Beds and Herts Regiment. Here she meets Gordon H. Hall, Town Clerk; after inspecting the troops in the park she took the salute in Rickmansworth Road where the privilege of Freedom of Entry was exercised. She later visited the new Drill Hall in Tolpits Lane. July 3rd 1965.

Beaten—But Gloriously

BEATEN 3-1 but not humiliated. This can be Watford's proud boast after they gave their all at Liverpool last night. In the end, their determination, courage and skills did not prove enough to baulk the Liverpool maestros. But their plucky and spirited fight will long be remembered by the warm-hearted Mersey-siders.

Watford took the field to loud applause from a capacity 54,000 crowd some 15 minutes before the kick-off. Gates were shut 30 minutes before the start. Furphy's men jogged up to the Kop end and waved to the seething mass of heaving fans. It was a gesture that was highly appreciated.

WHP February, 1967

'Rag' Van For Meals on Wheels

WATFORD College of Technology students on Saturday handed over to Watford Women's Royal Voluntary Service the meals on wheels van which was bought with money raised during 1967 Rag Week.

Chairman of the Rag Committee, Mr. Ian Tarr, of 149 George Street, Berkhamsted, also presented a cheque for over £200 to provide holidays next year for old people.

Later, the students entertained about 70 elderly men and women to tea at the Central Darby and Joan Club and gave each of them a gift of chocolates and cigarettes.

WHP July, 1967

£1¼M. Bid For Wemco

A £1,250,000 takeover bid is being made for the Watford Electric and Manufacturing Company Limited.

The bid is being made by the British subsidiary of Harvey Hubbell, the American electrical wiring accessory giant whose sales last year were over 40-million dollars.

Full details of the cash offer have only just been received by WEMCO and the board is to consider the bid in conjunction with its financial advisors, S. G. Warburg and Company within the next week.

Last week, WEMCO shares rose by 1s 10½d. to 9s. 1½d. on the Stock Exchange, and some observers are wondering if a counter offer will come from within the United Kingdom.

The offer, which the WEMCO board had little to say about this week, is for the Whippendell Road, Watford, factory and the subsidiary company in Northampton.

Altogether, about 650 men are employed, but Managing Director Mr. R. G. Smith seemed confident this week that a take-over would not mean any loss of jobs.

WHP July, 1967

Postal Codes

BY next year it is expected Watford will be one of the towns on the new "Postal Code" system of mail delivery.

Every house and business in the area will have its own individual code to enable more speedy and efficient sorting and delivery of mail.

The system has been successfully tried in some parts of the country already and Watford is one of the towns to be included in the next stage.

By 1969 it is hoped that 70 per cent of all addresses will be coded. This is a mammoth task since there are about 17,000,000 in the country.

In Watford, too, it is a huge task, and something of an uphill one at this stage.

A team of experts started work back in February and have spent months poring over maps and studying the present postal system. They have great trouble even finding some houses, because they don't have numbers and the new owners often change the fancy names.

Help with this sort of problem often comes from the rates office.

The system at present in operation in some towns is for the first three letters of the town's name to be used in conjunction with three other figures and letters.

Thus an address in Watford may have a code like WAT2EF.

WHP July, 1967

WEMCO premises in Whippendell Road, (joint first prize winner, with Benskins, for Coronation industrial premises decoration, 1953).

... £54,000 proposal to resite ancient lodge ...

The Park Gates looking towards Rickmansworth Road. The usually immaculate flower beds just inside the gates were a source of pride and pleasure and a welcome entrance to the park.

Council House Sale

THE Tory plan to sell council houses to sitting tenants was given the go-ahead, in the face of Labour opposition, at Monday's Watford Borough Council meeting.

But the burning question of how much the houses will cost to buy remained speculative. One Labour member claimed that with rates and other expenses, purchasers would be faced with outgoings of over £9 a week for a £4,500 house on a 95 per cent mortgage.

But Councillor John Charman, Chairman of the Housing Committee and "author" of the scheme, said if a tenant wished to buy a £4,000 house on a 30-year mortgage from the housing revenue account, he would be asked to put down a minimum 5 per cent deposit (£200). With interest at 7 per cent in the £, it would cost the purchaser £4 4s. 7d net for the mortgage repayments. In addition, there would be rates, insurance and repairs.

"Nobody denies this," he declared, "but even adding that lot on, it is a long way from the £8 and £9 a week we have had bandied about tonight."

Ald. Amey said he imagined the only houses that could be sold for £4,000 were those at Harebreaks. "None of the post-war houses could be sold at this price," he added.

Councillor Peter Wilson (Conservative) said the idea had captured the imagination of some of the tenants. It should be made clear it was an optional scheme. They were not depriving people on the waiting list. "The people who will want to buy their council houses are people who would remain tenants anyway so long as they remain in Watford."

WHP July, 1967

Park Gates

WATFORD's 19th century Tudor Lodge at Cassiobury Park gates, Rickmansworth Road, is likely to be resited and rebuilt as a cafeteria.

Watford Borough Council is to be recommended on Monday to approve a scheme which is estimated to cost £54,000. As well as the cafeteria, it will include new public conveniences and a shelter.

It is hoped that the cost will be met by Government grants. If these are not forthcoming, it has been suggested that the council should pay for the work.

The site on which the lodge now stands is required for road improvements, but because of the historical and architectural interest of the building, the Ministry of Housing is against its demolition.

To be re-erected with the same external appearance but adapted inside, the lodge would have to be dismantled brick by brick. Investigations show that the cost of dismantling and rebuilding the lodge with the necessary survey and adaptations would amount to £35,000.

It is impossible, the council's investigators say, to determine in advance how much material could be salvaged and how much would have to be replaced.

Consideration has also been given to three other alternatives for the Rickmansworth Road frontage. They include a simple landscaping scheme costing £15,000; a shelter, refreshment kiosk, conveniences and store at £20,000, and a pergola type building with cafeteria, store and conveniences at between £20,000 and £50,000.

WHP August, 1967

Unions Fail in Cox Closure

"IT now appears inevitable that the manufacture of car seats and tubular furniture will finish at Cox of Watford's factory", Mr. Roger Horner, Divisional Organiser of the Amalgamated Engineering Union told the "Post" this week.

This was the outcome of a meeting on Monday between union officials and directors of Raleigh Industries, which recently took over Cox.

The meeting has been requested by the unions to ask Raleigh's to reconsider their decision to transfer the activities of the Watford factory to the Midlands.

However, the Raleigh directors said they had considered for a long time retaining work at Watford, but their extensive research had led them to only one conclusion, that it was impossible on economic grounds, to do so.

District officials and senior shop stewards of the Boilermakers Union, the Transport and General Workers Union, the Amalgamated Engineering Union and the National Union of Furniture Trade Operatives, were present, with a senior shop steward of the Electrical Trades Union.

The best hope now, Mr. Horner said, appeared to be for some other manufacturer, who would retain as many of the staff as possible, to take over the Cox factory premises.

Union leaders intended to meet trades unionist Members of Parliament and Mr. Raphael Tuck, M.P. for Watford, in the near future, and this possibility would no doubt be raised then.

WHP August, 1967

. . . four-bedroomed Harebreaks house £3,800-£4,000 . . .

1965 TA Centre to be Sold

WATFORD'S Territorial Army Centre, Tolpits Lane, shows, in the words of Coun. E. O. Collyer, "extreme bad planning," "incompetence" and "wasteful spending."

It was, he said at Monday night's town council meeting, a gross misuse of the taxpayers' money.

Coun. Collyers' outburst resulted from a report by the Territorial and Auxiliary Forces' Association that the centre is to be put up for sale by public auction. The property was offered to the council but they have no use for it.

The building, Coun. Collyer protested, was only built in 1965 and the cost was "fantastic—many thousands of pounds." It was a case, he said, of the "Government wielding a big stick and saying 'don't do as I do, do as I say."

WHP July, 1967

Watford Census Results

THE picture of an affluent Watford and District, with thousands of two-car families, emerges from the Sample Census taken in April last year. The results were published on Tuesday.

But as well as affluence, there is also a less prosperous side to life in this part of Herts.

The census reveals nine homes in the borough and in Bushey, six in Rickmansworth and 21 in Watford Rural District that are without flush lavatories.

And one in 10 homes in the borough still have no hot water tap and nine per cent. no fixed bath. Thirteen out of every 100 homes have an outdoor lavatory only.

There are more people with cars than without in Bushey, Rickmansworth and Watford Rural. In Watford the position is reversed, and there are also comparatively fewer two-car families in the borough than in the other three areas.

In the borough, nearly every other family— 12,650 out of 25,200—has no car. Over 10,000 of them have one car and 1,660 have two or more cars.

Most homes in Watford borough, Bushey and Rickmansworth are owner-occupied. Those in the borough number 13,760 compared to the 9,360 rented homes. In Bushey about two thirds of the homes are owner-occupied.

At Rickmansworth there are 5,940 owner-occupied and 2,630 rented homes. In Watford Rural District there are more rented homes— 8,790 compared to the 6,520 that are owned by the people who live in them. Caravans number 10 in the borough, 20 in Rickmansworth, 120 at Bushey and 310 in the rural district.

Women outnumber men in Watford. Out of a total population of 75,960, there are over 39,000 women and over 36,000 men.

Over 66,000 of the people in Watford were born in England and over 72,000 of them in the British Isles. Nearly 56,000 are natives of the South-East. The Irish form the next largest group with people from the North coming a close second. The Welsh outnumber the Scots by a short head. There are nearly 1,700 people from Commonwealth countries, Colonies and Protectorates.

These are the figures operating a year last April. The census shows that the population in Herts has risen by over 8 per cent since 1961 and now stands at over 832,000. There are proportionately fewer people over 55 in Herts than in England and Wales as a whole.

WHP August, 1967

What Your Council House is Worth

These are the types of council homes Watford Borough Council is prepared to sell.

The three-bedroom 'semi' at Garston Park would cost £5,000 to £5,250. Four-bedroom Harebreaks house, £3,800 to £4,000. Three-bedroom Harebreaks house £3,600 to £3,750. Two-bedroom Meriden house £4,000 to £4,250.

WHP August, 1967

Dispelling a Myth

SHRODELLS Wing of Watford General Hospital is the place where they take old people. The geriatrics. Men and women with most of their life behind them and death very much in front of them.

Not a very nice place. Or so it would appear to those who have never entered its doors, or appreciate the work that goes on there.

This week, West Herts Hospital Management Committee, invited the "Post" to tour the wing, to ask questions, to find out the truth.

The invitation followed allegations that the conditions in which geriatrics exist nationally, is a scandal.

The "Post," representing the interests of the public, carried out its investigation. It toured the wards, and spoke to the patients.

What did he find? Helplessness, yes. And pathos, and lingering silence. But it also found the great majority of men and women geriatrics had a zest for what life remained. There was courage and humour in the wards.

Above all, it found a dedicated hospital staff striving hard to make life worth living for the people who desperately depend on them.

The fact that the hospital authorities invited the Press to see conditions for themselves, does not mean the authorities have suddenly decided to reveal all.

The public has always had the opportunity to see inside Shrodells, because it is, after all, a hospital, with usual hospital visiting times.

But because a reporter was given the opportunity to question and look, with the eyes of a trained observer, does prove that the hospital has nothing to hide.

The invitation has given us an opportunity of dispelling the myth in some people's minds that Shrodells is a communal death house, full of the dispirited, and uncaring and the uncared for.

WHP August, 1967

Spitfire Scandal

THE Battle of Britain never really got as far as Watford. Dog-fights in the sky were so rare as to be practically non-existent, no enemy plane crashed anywhere near the town during the whole battle, and—compared to the hammering that neighbouring London got—Watford's quota of bombs was a mere handful.

But, 27 years ago this week, adjectives such as "apathetic" and "scandalous" were part of Watford's household vocabulary. They were not directed at the apparent lack of action. They were directed at Watford's attempt to buy a Spitfire.

This plan, enthusiastically announced in July, 1940, by the Mayor, Alderman, L. H. Andrews, was for the people of Watford to raise the cost of a £5,000 Spitfire by donation to a fund. The plane was to be emblazoned with the Borough coat of arms and flown, if possible, by a Watford pilot.

At the time, the "Post" said: "It is anticipated that the idea will so grip the imagination of the townspeople that the fund will be completed by the end of August."

In fact, by the time the £5,000 had been raised, the year was 1941 and the Battle of Britain had been won. Meanwhile, other towns had taken up the idea. Wisbech, for instance, with one third of Watford's population, had bought its Spitfire in less than a month—a fact which did not go unnoticed in Watford.

Hardly one of the dark, desperate days of September, 1940, passed without angry comments being aimed at Watford's inability to raise enough money for a single Spitfire. Controversy over the town's alleged meanness came to a head when a Rickmansworth firm said it would give £10 to the fund—but only if at least nine other firms promised to do the same.

WHP September 1967

Chaos Continues!

PLANS for the critically-needed North Orbital Road, intended as a relief for the M1 traffic flowing through Rickmansworth and Watford, have once again been shelved. The Ministry of transport has announced that there is now no hope whatsoever that construction will be able to start in 1970, as originally planned.

This means that local car-using residents will now probably have to face at least five more years of mounting chaos on the already overworked A412 between Maple Cross and North Watford.

In a letter to Mr. Gilbert Longden, M.P. for S. W. Herts, the Parliamentary Secretary to the Minister of Transport, Mr. Neil Carmichael, says that due to "ground contours" on the North Orbital's proposed route, the estimated cost had risen from the original £1-million to at least £2½ million.

"All this means that the programming of the scheme has to be reconsidered," writes Mr. Carmichael. "We will press on as fast as we can, but at present, when there are still so many uncertainties, I cannot indicate when a revised scheme will start."

The news will come as a massive blow to all those who use the A412 to get to and from work. Already this year, there have been several instances of four-mile traffic jams, and rush-hour progress is often so slow in some parts that it is literally quicker to walk.

WHP October, 1967

No North Sea Gas until 1971

WATFORD gas users will have to wait until after 1971 for North Sea gas, the natural rather than the present manufactured gas.

Eastern Gas plans to convert all its customers to North Sea gas on a progressive programme over a period of years.

The changeover is to start in April 1968 in the Hitchin, Baldock and Letchworth districts and will spread in the first year to Cambridge and parts of Norfolk.

The whole country is expected to take between seven to ten years to complete.

All appliances will need a different type of burner for natural gas and the conversion work to be carried out in each household by Gas Board contractors takes a number of days to complete. More essential appliances, say the Gas Board, will be done on the first day.

And the advantages to natural gas? It will be safer, cleaner and in the long run cheaper, say the Gas Board.

WHP October, 1967

Queens Road. In the distance the Technical School is being demolished, following a disastrous fire, to make way for a new Sainsbury's supermarket. The Literary Institute was founded in 1874 as a Library and School of Science and Art. It survived as such until the (Central) Library was opened in 1928. On the right Trewin's has expanded and the 'Queen's Pantry' (No. 32); Johnson Bros. Dyers (No. 34); Singer Sewing Machines (No. 36); and Duke's (No. 38) have gone. Maitland's, jewellers, at No. 40, remain (they later moved across to No. 41 before moving, in March, 1987, to premises on the Parade).

p.211, 341 t

Lean Years Nearly Gone

AFTER nearly seven years of steady decline, Queens Road in Watford will soon become a busy shopping centre.

A row of twelve shops which have lain idle for the past few years, has now been completely renovated and two are expected to be open before Christmas.

On the opposite side of the road, Littlewoods are preparing a new development which will continue their frontage from the High Street round into Queens Road.

The shut-down of the twelve shops started seven years ago when Cubitt (London) Properties planned a joint re-development scheme with Watford Corporation. The scheme fell through, however.

The two shops which have already been taken will be occupied by specialist food concerns. Shopfitting is underway in one.

The other ten shops, all of which have been completely rebuilt within the existing shells, are the subject of negotiation.

The proposed Littlewood development has encouraged interest from furniture, catering, electrical equipment and supermarket concerns.

Trewin Bros., part of the John Lewis organisation, which has lasted out the depression, re-developed their Queens Road premises two years ago.

A Civic Trust type operation to brighten up the exteriors of the group of twelve shops is further planned.

WHP November, 1967

Hempstead Road. Typical of the daily morning and evening traffic converging on the roundabout at Watford, now quite unsuitable for handling ever-increasing traffic volumes.

p.110 t, 176 c, 322 tl   **1968**

Coach Owners to Fight

SOUTH West Herts coach operators were preparing this week to do battle with Barbara Castle over her plans to take-over private coach companies.

At a meeting on Monday, coach operators from Watford and other areas of S.W. Herts formed themselves into a committee with Mr. Gordon Hewitt of Premier Coaches, Watford, at the head. This committee will co-ordinate with committees now being formed in North Herts, Bucks and other adjoining areas.

Through the Passenger Vehicle Operators' Association, who are organising the opposition to the Ministry of Transport plan, the South West Herts committee will liaise with coach operators all over the country.

Mr. Leslie Withey, of Knightswood Coaches, Watford, a member of the new committee, said: "We know we have no hope of preventing the Bill. What we want to do is force amendments.

"I don't think it will have an immediate effect, but in the long term we could lose our businesses," he said.

Mr. Withey claims that the nationalised operation would result in less satisfactory service to the public.

"Without the element of competition you won't get 100 per cent service," he said.

WHP December, 1967

We're Proud of Our Role–Music Head

AS the lilting music of Schubert's "Shepherd on the Rock" drifted softly around the new concert room—once a school gymnasium—Watford School of Music's new premises in Nascot Wood Road became officially operational on Thursday afternoon.

The opening ceremony was performed by Mr. Claude C. Barker, Chairman of Herts County Council, which took over the school in 1955 at the request of the governing body. The new premises are in the extended and modernised ex-Gartlett School.

The Principal of the school, Mr. Kenneth Leaper, spoke of how the school was founded in 1880 as a result of a musical society inaugurated two years earlier by the Rev. Newton Price, Vicar of Oxhey, who brought teachers from London to train his 60-strong choir.

"Today, thanks to the foresight of the local authority, we now have this beautiful house," said Mr. Leaper, who is the third principal this century.

"Our primary aim is to try and give the best possible individual instruction, then opportunities for musical merry-making in groups under professional instruction. Now we must look forward to more expansion.

"The school is proud of the role it has played in the past and looks forward to the increased demands in the future," Mr. Leaper concluded.

WHP 1967

New Gas

At last conversion is at hand; in many older homes the old original gas pipes are being replaced with new high-density yellow plastic pipes. Gas fires, cookers, water heaters, are all being fitted with new burners. The change-over to natural gas is not far away, and the days of the old gas works are numbered.

BOROUGH OF WATFORD

THE HIGHWAYS ACT, 1959
THE ROAD TRAFFIC REGULATION ACT, 1967
and
THE ACQUISITION OF LAND (AUTHORISATION
PROCEDURE) ACT, 1946

NOTICE IS HEREBY GIVEN that the Minister of Transport in exercise of the powers conferred on him by the above-mentioned Acts on the 20th day of September 1968, confirmed with one modification a compulsory purchase order entitled the Borough of Watford (Central Area Phase III) Compulsory Purchase Order 1967 submitted by The Mayor Aldermen and Burgesses of the Borough of Watford acting by the Council of the said Borough. The order as confirmed provides for the purchase for the purpose of carrying out the Highway and Car Parking proposals of the Borough of Watford Central Area Redevelopment Phase III the details of which proposals are more particularly specified in the first schedule thereto of the land described in the schedule hereto.

A copy of the order as confirmed by the Minister and of the map (comprising seven sheets) referred to therein have been deposited at the Town Clerk's Offices, Town Hall, Watford and may be seen there at all reasonable hours.

The order as confirmed becomes operative on the date on which this notice is first published, but if application is made to the High Court under paragraph 15 of the First Schedule to the Acquisition of Land (Authorisation Procedure) Act, 1946, within a period of six weeks from that date by any person agrieved by the order the court may, by interim order, suspend the operation of the order either generally or in so far as it affects any property of the applicant, and may, if satisfied that the authorisation granted by the order is not empowered to be granted or that the interests of the applicant have been substantially prejudiced by any requirement of the said Schedule or of any regulation made thereunder not having been compiled with, quash the order either generally or in so far as it affects any property of the applicant.

SCHEDULE

Land comprised in the order as confirmed.

Albert Road: Complete property:—No. 10.

The Avenue: Complete properties:—Nos. 10, 17, 21, 27. Part of gardens Nos. 22, 31. Private roadway leading off The Avenue between Nos. 4 and 6.

Cassiobury Drive: Part of garden:—No. 1.

Cassiobury Park Avenue: Part of gardens:—Nos. 1, 2.

Cassio Road: Part of West Herts Sports Ground.

Clarendon Road: Complete properties:—Nos. 23, 27, 29 Part of gardens and/or forecourts:—31, 33, 35, Part of car park at rear of No. 33. Accessway:—No. 35. Part of land rear of Y.M.C.A.:—No 37. Part of land at rear of Nos. 41 and 43.

Essex Road: Complete property:—No. 2. Part of garden:—No. 4.

Hempstead Road: Complete properties:—Nos. 14, 18, 25, 28 and 29 otherwise The Dog Inn. Part of gardens:—Nos. 76, 78, 81, 83. Part of vacant land adjoining No 90. Land between Nos. 20 and 22 and garages at rear thereof.

Hyde Road: Complete property:—No. 8.

Monmouth Road: Complete properties:—Nos. 27, 29

The Parade, High Street: Part property: No. 115 Part of car park to Clements Department Store at Nos. 23/33 and at the rear of No. 41.

Platts Avenue: Land adjoining and used as part of the garden of No. 2. Air raid shelter and vacant land at rear No. 2 known as part of the Monmouth Arms Site

Rickmansworth Road: Complete properties:—Nos. 8, 10. Part forecourts and/or gardens:—Nos. 3/5, 7, 11 35, Halsey Masonic Hall.

St. Albans Road: Complete properties:—No. 6 otherwise Old Berkeley Hunt Public House, Oddfellows Hall, No. 5 otherwise Tuckers Garage, Nos 7, 9 13/13A, 27, 50, 54, 56, 58, 60, 62, 64, 66, 74/74A. Part properties:—Nos. 8, 10, 11/11A/11C. 20, 22, 70. Part of gardens and/or forecourts: Nos. 12, 14, 16, 18 and Ace of "Herts" Garage, 24, 35, 37, 39, 41, 43, 45

Station Road: Complete property:—No. 29.

Stratford Way: Part of garden:—No. 9.

Upton Road: Part of gardens. Nos 30, 33.

Weymouth Street: Complete properties:—Nos 12, 16, 17, 26, 27, 29, 30, 31, 38.

DATED the 10th day of October, 1968.

GORDON H HALL
Town Clerk.

The Penny Drops

THE traditional British penny becomes redundant in February next year with the advent of decimal currency—it has grown old like human beings.

Although it will remain legal tender until 1973, its purchasing power will by that time be virtually nil.

WHP May, 1970

Trouble Again at Odhams

A DISPUTE between electricians and management at Odhams printers on Sunday led to a stoppage of work in the machine room of the production department.

"There was a difficulty between the management and the ETU chapel," said a spokesman.

The dispute arose over the number of electricians to be engaged to do overtime work in the production department on Sunday.

As a result four presses were still throughout the day. It is not known whether the trouble will recur next Sunday.

It is understood that fewer electricians were required to do overtime work on Sunday than usual, and the men objected.

WHP May, 1970

Comedy of Errors

IT WAS JUST one of those nights when everything that can possibly go wrong went wrong for the 25 members of the Watford and District Branch of the Royal Air Forces Association.

There they all were in the Escourt Tavern, Escourt Road, Watford, on Wednesday night, waiting to be presented with the Ivor Calverley Cup, which is awarded annually to the Branch in Hertfordshire which returns the greatest percentage increase in the Wings Collection over the previous year.

It was the first time the Watford and District Branch had won it. The members were at the pub for 8.00 p.m. ready for the presentation. Everyone was waiting for Mr. Mike Pierce, Herts Region Secretary, who lives in Hemel Hempstead, to turn up, for he had the coveted cup.

Actually, he didn't arrive until 9.30. What had happened was that he had driven from Hemel Hempstead and parked his car in the car park in Escourt Road.

It was there that he discovered that he'd left the most important thing at home—the cup!

So back he travelled to Hemel Hempstead, picked up the cup and drove back towards Watford down the M1 motorway. Unfortunately he ran out of petrol . . .

"The whole night was just one glorious comedy of errors", said Mr. Ted Parrish, Chairman of the Watford and District Branch. "Everything that could go wrong went wrong.

"Thank goodness we were in a pub. I hate to think what would have happened if we'd been standing around drinking tea."

WHP May 1970

... the last 'Post' ...

... the Gate goes ...

WATFORD POST

135 THE PARADE, WATFORD. Tel. 26045

No. 4306   Thursday, May 21, 1970   6d.

Postage on this issue 4d.

Founded in 1887, some 24 years after the Watford Observer, and at a time when many of the town's inhabitants were less educated than they are today, the West Herts Post achieved, in its early years, an empathy with a readership more 'working class' than the farming and professional classes who were the the 'Observer's' original readers. This distinction can be easily seen in the late 1800's/early 1900's W.H.P.'s by the amount of 'small-shopkeeper' type of advertisements carried.

Published first from 42 High Street a change of ownership took place in 1919 and the Watford Newsletter was bought and incorporated into the title. Upon a move to Carey Place new machinery was installed and the innovation made, in September 1919, of clearing the front page of advertisements and putting news in its stead. Perhaps because, in those days, a paper without the solid appearance of advertisements on the front page looked less than successful, it reverted to 'style' after one year.

In 1941, when news of the town's activities during the war was important, the Post again cleared the front page of advertisements, at the same time halving the page size and increasing the number of pages. A brighter and more readable paper was the result and the Post grew in popularity and status.

During the late 1960's a further change crept in whereby news stories were shortened to little more than 'bare bones' with catchy headlines. In November 1967 Thompson Regional Newspapers published the 'Evening Echo'—a daily paper based in Hemel Hempstead—and so the 'Observer' and 'Post' faced the competition of a new, bright daily paper produced by more modern methods than the older papers had at their command.

Without warning, after issue No. 4306 dated May 21st 1970, the retitled 'Watford Post' ceased publication. Home Counties Newspapers Ltd. of Luton (name changed from Gibbs and Bamforth Ltd.) had withdrawn from the Watford area.

Upon closure, all photographs, plates and films negatives of people, places and happenings, made during the 'Post's' existence, were discarded without trace.

'Just a piece of Victoriana; what did it mean?'

Perhaps these were the thoughts of some of the Council when the time came to make a decision on what to do about the gates.

The gates were, by now, obstructing the plan to ease the Rickmansworth Road and roundabout traffic congestion. As the Council owned the property it was not published in the list of properties affected. It was only a few years previously that plans were printed showing the various alternatives, and that the gates could be demolished would appear unthinkable, but with astonishing rapidity the pick-axes struck.

True, there was no longer a mansion for the gates to give entrance to. But since the struggles to buy the parkland for Watford, at the early part of the century, Watfordians had accepted its acquisition with pride, and realised that the Council of the time had done a 'proper job' in completing the purchase.

Perhaps, as a fitting mark of the carefree days of the 'swinging sixties' (during which so much of the old was so swiftly swept away) few people thought the gates worth keeping.

Nevertheless, it was a fitting entrance to a place of great natural beauty and it was deeply felt as an act of vandalism that they were demolished.

The aftermath is that the remains of the Peace Memorial Hospital, now that the hospital has moved to the General Hospital in Vicarage Road, are equally under threat. But public outcry has been such that efforts are being made to incorporate the original front into the future new buildings, and in April 1987, it is conjectured that the Peace Memorial group of statuary (opposite the Library) may be moved to near its original site.

...YMCA...new 175 study/bedroom block...

If you haven't a bathroom or toilet...

WATFORD, like many other towns, is entering the 1970s with a significant proportion of 19th Century housing. Most of it is capable of being improved, and we want to help..." These are the words of Watford's Chief Public Health Inspector, Mr. K. Marsden.

For the Watford Borough Council **does** want to help and to see better housing in the town.

And now, under the 1969 Housing Act, the Council can help more than ever before. Grants —of up to £1,000—are now available to house-owners to bring their accommodation up to date, provided that application is made to the Council and approved by them *before the works are commenced.*

Grants for improvement have been available since 1949, but until now many people who qualified for them have been too disinterested or unaware of their rights to apply.

While the Council is eager to assist, the house-owner must also show willing, of course, In no case can the amount of the grant exceed half the approved expense of the improvement works, which may include some incidental works of repair and replacement. This means that the applicant must find the other half himself.

But even here the Council can help. If an owner feels he cannot meet his half of the bill, the Council can, at its discretion, make a loan to cover this on mortgage. Grants are not available, however, for doing repairs only, or for replacing derelict or worn out appliances.

WOT June, 1970

Pumphouse

A BRAVE new venture in amateur theatre and arts in Watford and district will be hoping for a financial boost from a play which is being staged from October 4 to 7 at St. John's Hall.

The venture is the Pumphouse Theatre and Arts Centre, and the play "No, No, Nanette."

The Pumphouse Theatre and Arts Centre consists today of a Victorian pumphouse in Local Board Road, and a band of enthusiasts dreaming of a permanent amateur auditorium and studio facilities for Watford—and of the £15,000 or so needed to get the scheme really moving.

Among its current assets are some old seats, salvaged from a demolished theatre, and some offers of volunteer labour in the renovation work.

Plans are already under way for monthly fund-raising activities.

The Pumphouse has been leased by the Borough Council, and the original group interested in setting up the centre has been joined by the former South-West Herts Drama Council, which was formed about 20 years ago with the intention of achieving a similar objective.

Among the activities which the South-West Herts Drama Council carried out in the district is the annual Drama Festival, which will continue under the Pumphouse Theatre umbrella.

WOT September, 1972

Multi-million Scheme Starts Soon

IN something like three years' time, in place of the Central Car Park in Beechen Grove, there will be a massive shopping complex which should place Watford even more firmly in the top league of the country's shopping centres.

The new scheme—which will cost over £5 million—is centred around the overall plan for expanding and "pedestrianising" the shopping centre. The new project, which extends from the rear of the Palace Theatre to Red Lion Yard, and from Beechen Grove to the rear of the High Street's shops, will have underground servicing facilities for all its shops, and will allow rear service access to the existing shops on the north side of the High Street between Clarendon Road and the Midland Bank.

Demolition work is due to start this summer, and the excavation for the basement service areas will start in the autumn.

Under the scheme, the market will move into a new market hall with all sorts of new facilities for the market traders. One link with the past will remain; stallholders will continue to 'serve from the front' in the time-honoured manner.

Social needs have not been forgotten. The YMCA will have a new 175 study/bedroom block and in addition provision will be made for a restaurant, lounges and dining rooms, a gymnasium, squash courts, sauna and plunge bath facilities, and a conference room. All these facilities will be run by the YMCA, but will be available for the public as well as their own members.

Above part of the shopping complex will be four car-parking decks with spaces for 800 cars. The car park will be served by lifts and stair-cases, and traffic direction to vacant parking spaces will be electronically controlled.

The entire site is being developed by Watford Borough Council, and the co-ordination work is being carried out by the Director of Technical Services, Mr. R. H. Brand. Consultant Architects are Messrs. Ley Colbeck & Partners, Consultant Engineers Messrs. Ove Arup & Partners, Consultant Quantity Surveyors, Messrs. Pritchard, Williams & Hunt, and Consultant Surveyors, Messrs. Hillier, Parker, May & Rowden.

WOT May, 1973

Better Traffic System

NEARLY ten years ago, plans were set before Watford Borough Council which were to alter the entire face of the town centre of Watford as it then existed. The plans dealt with the Central Area Highway Proposals, considered at the time to be almost revolutionary.

Watford of the future was to be created in eight phases. Today, three phases have been practically completed and we look forward to the summer of 1975 when the next step will begin.

Phase four—a relief road for West Watford—has been placed on ice awaiting a re-appraisal, but phase five is "all systems go" at present.

It is interesting to note, however, that at a time when the critics declare that we are "sacrificing everything for the motor car," Watford's shopping areas are gradually being rid of vehicles. Cast your mind back to the days of the two-way major road traffic in the High Street, and you will soon see the benefit that is already being enjoyed. Add to that the proposed greatly improved facilities in the High Street, Queen's Road and King Street areas and Watford joins some of the country's new towns and cities as a safe and pleasant place in which to shop.

Bus passengers also have not been forgotten and special arrangements will be made at the junction of the ring road with the High Street. At this point buses alone will be given access to allow people to get as near the shops as possible.

The town of tomorrow is taking shape. The progress is gradual and occasionally inconvenient. But the end product will benefit pedestrian, and motorist, resident and visitor alike.

WOT September, 1973

Phase 3, construction of the Town Hall underpass in progress.   1971

Cut and cover method of underpass construction, main contractors are Costain, (builders of the Town Hall in 1938/9).   *p.347 b*

Watford covered Market. The rear, from Red Lion Yard/Beechen Grove approach.

The box collectors

The market approach hasn't changed much since it was opened in 1928, except for the roof. The barrows, rubbish and bric-a-brac . . .

What has gone though, from the early 1930s, are the several families who would arrive in the evening around 8 o'clock, before closing time and wait along the Red Lion Passage wall.

With home-made two or four wheeled barrows they'd be waiting for the traders to pack up—and then they'd be round collecting the apple and orange boxes. The wet, smelly, fish boxes they'd leave until last as make-weight if the evening's collection had not been good.

The youngsters would be under the stalls as soon as possible for there'd be fruit thrown down there. True, the apples would be bruised, and the oranges soft in spots, but the bad parts could be cut out. And who knows, under one of the sweet stalls perhaps they could find a few toffees and dream of finding a complete box left behind!

The parents would doubtless be on the lookout for last-minute food bargains; it was the era when a joint of beef for a family could be bought late on a Saturday evening at Fisher's, across the Market Place, for around a shilling.

The wood? That, after carting home, breaking up, removing nails and wire, would be sawn, chopped, bundled into firewood and sold to supplement a meagre income.

Recollections, 1987

Kept Going in the Gloom

DESPITE the harsh restrictions imposed on industry by the energy crisis, most local firms have so far managed to avoid laying off workers on any large scale.

"We have not heard of any firms having to close altogether yet. In fact, some small firms are getting more work done in their permitted three days work than they usually do."

WATFORD industry and commerce were shivering their way into the New Year this week as the nation's energy crises began to bite locally.

Some firms, mostly those with small labour forces, were planning to lay-off employees because of the three-day working week.

The shopping world of Watford was adjusting itself to trading without heat or lighting for part of each day.

January, 1974

Road Toll Falls

ROAD accident figures for Herts have shown an expected reduction since the introduction of the 50 m.p.h. speed limit on December 8.

It is, however, impossible to say whether the drop can be attributed wholly to the reduction in speed when there has also been a fall in the number of vehicles using the roads.

Comparative figures issued by Herts police for the period December 7 to 31 in 1972 and 1973 showed fewer accidents, fewer deaths and fewer injuries last year.

WO January, 1974

Market Moves

THE Central Car Park Redevelopment Scheme between Beechen Grove and the High Street covers the area now occupied by the present market. This means that, whilst work is in progress, it must have another home until the scheme is completed.

The new temporary site is on the ground floor of the Shrubbery Car Park. It will open for trading on the weekend of March 29-30. All the usual stalls as well as a snack bar will be under cover. You will be able to shop in comfort, even in wet weather, and park the car nearby.

WOT March, 1974

Charter Place on Schedule

WATFORD'S biggest single redevelopment ever—the Charter Place Project between High Street and Beechen Grove—is back on schedule.

The three-day working week, steel shortages and other local difficulties combined to upset the programme of work. These problems have all been overcome, however, and the help of good weather has enabled the contractors to get back on target.

WOT October, 1974

Pump House Success

AFTER just one full year in operation, the Pump House Theatre and Arts Centre in Local Board Road has reached an exciting turning point.

In the past 12 months three full-length plays and two one-act play festivals have been staged. During the same period the centre has launched three club activities meeting once a week: Folk, theatre and jazz. These have enjoyed a remarkable season, collecting between them over two thousand members.

This means that in order to allow nightly events to prosper—and at the same time, to allow stage presentations a full week's run—there is a need for a second auditorium with its own bar, entrance, cloakrooms and so forth.

WOT October, 1974

Queens Road, Ansells, No. 46; Grevilles Studios, once the Crown Post Office, 1886-1932, No. 48. Although Greville's had warning that a move would, at some date, be necessary, the eventual request was at very short notice. Such that they regrettably had to leave behind, to destruction, their vast collection of photographic plates, which, as their business took over from W. Coles, may have contained valuable early pictures.

Queens Road, looking towards the High Street.   *p.211, 341 t*

Queens Road, Derby Road pedestrian underpass during construction.   *p.340 cr*

Shopper's Paradise Regained!

THE opening of the Charter Place Development means that Watford will be an even greater attraction for shoppers this Christmas.

Although there will be 800 additional car parking spaces at Charter Place, parking and traffic conditions will still be difficult in the Town Centre and to ease the problem and free "park and ride service" will again run on Saturdays between the Junction Station (British Rail Car Park) and the Town Centre.

The service is provided by the Borough Council, with a contribution from the Hertfordshire County Council.

Last year on nine Saturdays the service carried over 32,000 passengers to and from the Town Centre. It provided free car parking at the Junction Station for about 1,000 cars on each day, even though the car park was never more than two-thirds full. It also provided a free service for rail passengers arriving at the Junction Station. The service operated so well, thanks to the co-operation of British Rail and London Country, that it will be repeated this year, without modification, on the nine Saturdays prior to Christmas (October 23 until December 18 inclusive).

WOT November, 1976

Designer's Museum Drawings

IN 1975 Watford Borough Council acquired the Benskins Brewery site. Part of that site is a very fine building, fronting the High Street.

As this building is listed as a building of particular historical and architectural importance, the Council felt that its most appropriate use would be as a museum.

It is intended to open the interior of the building and to restore it, as closely as possible, to its original state.

To assist in our aims the Borough Council has appointed Mr. Richard Daynes, FSIA, as consultant designer. Mr. Daynes is one of the country's foremost museum designers and his work over the last few years has helped to revolutionise museum displays.

WOT August, 1979

Flats on Slope a Challenge

HANDOVER is expected any day of the Caractacas Cottage scheme, one of the most exciting and unusual developments the Borough Council has tackled for some time. These 82 flats have been built for us by Barratt Developments (Contracting) Ltd on a sloping site which proved a difficult challenge to our architects.

The flats and maisonettes have all been designed to take account of the slope and to give the tenants a relatively uninterrupted view of the Colne Valley. For example, the ground floor maisonettes were built with the living room at first floor so that best use can be made of the available view.

Two other projects have started this year. On the Kytes Estate a mixed development of houses and elderly persons' flats is being built by John Laing Construction Ltd and should be completed by January 1982.

Right in the heart of town a start has also been made on a further development of flats for the elderly—the George Street site of 29 flats for elderly persons plus a flat for the resident warden. This development is due to take 18 months and should be completed by Spring 1982.

WOT December, 1980

Purchase Tax/VAT

Purchase Tax (see p.277) was abolished in 1976 and VAT introduced in its place. The first rates were 8% and 12½%; these were increased to one rate of 15% in June 1979.

Early morning—waiting for transport to work. 1980

Frustration, no trains, strike. 1982

During week days the newspaper kiosk is busy . . . 1983

. . . but closed on Sundays; newspapers sold outside.

Evening; steady stream of collector's cars to pick up returning workers.

p.76 tr, 129 t, 238, 342 t 1977

Phase 5, second section of ring road across the High Street, adjacent to High Street Station.

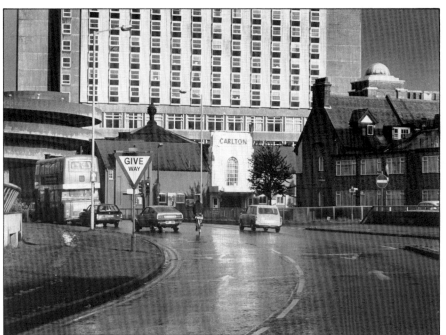

The Carlton cinema dwarfed by the YMCA block at Charter Place.   1980

Facelift for Palace

AT THE beginning of May the Palace Theatre is to have its first major facelift for many years. The work is expected to take six months to complete.

The council has agreed to carry out work necessary to improve safety standards. For example, the whole of the electrical installations are to be renewed and improvement made to exit facilities for both artistes and patrons.

At the same time, the opportunity is being taken to improve the level of comfort including the renewal of seating to both ground floor and circle and by improving the layout of ground floor seating. New carpeting is also to be fitted.

Clare Ferraby, the country's leading theatre designer, has created a new decor for the Palace.

The large majority of costs will come from the appeal funds. The borough council has agreed to fund the "licensing" works (rewiring, etc.) which will cost about £75,000. The refurbishment costs of about £125,000 are to be met by the theatre trust from the proceeds of the appeal.

WOT April, 1981

Lower High Street; Benskin House is now Watford Museum. As part of the once-thriving community the buildings to the left extended further forwards when they were shops, and included grocers, tobacconists, etc.

The old High Street is in front of the station and where the group of youngsters is. Demolished to make way for the ring road (upon which the young lad is walking) were, next to the station, No. 182, the Ford Garage, originally Wilkinsons and then Norman Reeves, No. 180 the 'White Hart' and Nos. 174, 176 and 178 of Steabben's men's outfitters.   *p.109 t, 274 b, 276 cl*

Museum Opens to Public

WATFORD Museum opened to the public on Saturday, March 14. A cavalcade of historic vehicles came down the High Street and was headed by the Benskins Dray carrying the guests of honour, the Mayor of Watford and Terry Scott. The Watford-born actor made a very amusing speech and unveiled a plaque. He later spent a long time in the Museum, signing autographs and chatting to the visitors.

Almost 1,000 people came into the Museum on the opening day, and in the following week a further 1,300 people visited the Museum. Apart from the permanent displays, there is also an exhibition in the picture gallery of portraits that will be on view for several months.

WOT April, 1981

Linear Park Plans Soon

THE Borough Council will shortly be publishing its Linear Park Plan for the Colne Valley in Watford.

Many people and organisations have been consulted on the plan and the proposals and policies it contains should help to increase access and recreational use of the valley, while also improving the environment and making provision for the retention of wildlife.

Measures proposed in the plan include tree planting, river clearance, footpath improvement, signposting, and so on. Longer term ideas include the creation of a continuous footpath along the valley, the creation of a cycle route and the consideration of appropriate uses for the various sites in the valley.

The Borough Council will take the initiative in carrying out the proposals as part of a three-year programme and has allocated finance to enable work to be started. In addition, it will invite other interested groups and organisations to play their part.

Two projects on which a start has already been made are:

The clearance of the River Colne; During the past two or three months, the Borough Council has, with the help of labour from Watford Community Service Scheme, organised the clearance of rubbish from the river, particularly in Oxhey Park.

The creation of a continuous riverside walk; This walk will mostly use public rights of way and will follow the Rivers Colne and Ver for much of its route. Yellow and blue path signs have already been provided along the route between Lower High Street and Bushey Mill Lane. The path was officially opened on August 1, 1981 and free leaflets describing the walk will soon be available.

WOT August, 1981

Promotion

After 3 years in Division 2 and previous year in Division 3, Watford FC finally won promotion to the First Division in 1982.

New Development Brings Jobs

THE next few years will see significant amounts of industrial developments on the western edge of the town and in adjoining Croxley area in Three Rivers District.

The Borough Council has entered into partnership arrangements with the Carroll Group of Companies to secure a first-class extension to the Holywell Industrial Estate, which has been re-named Watford Business Park.

The aim is to provide high-class accommodation for industry, including new high technology industries, and warehousing space. It is also envisaged that the existing Holywell Estate will be the subject of a concerted effort of environmental improvements to bring it into the '80s.

The extension of the Business Park will not only bring jobs to the town but increase the Borough Council's rental income, enabling it to cushion rate increases.

The Council is also maintaining an interest in other developments in the area. These include aims to secure the redevelopment of the former Sun Printers ink factory site, which has been derelict for many years, and the redevelopment of the former Cassio Photographic Paper Company site, the premises of which have been demolished.

WOT December, 1983

John Dickinson & Co. Croxley Mills, manufacturers of noted 'Croxley' brand fine papers.   c1960

THE FINAL Echo

No 2295   Wednesday, November 16, 1983   12p

The Evening Echo *was established in 1967 by Thomson Regional Newspapers Ltd., Mark Road, Hemel Hempstead. Using new printing technology the wage and cost structure negotiated by the print unions at the outset was far higher than warranted. Success in first years meant costs could be met but later periods of recession meant drastic cuts in advertising—particularly of situations vacant, upon which the* Evening Echo *largely depended—and huge losses of £2,000,000 in 1981/2 and £1,000,000 in 1982/3 could not continue.*

When the West Herts Post *closed the final issue carried no special announcement; there was just no more. The* Evening Echo, *in contrast, provided a retrospect of their brief 16-year span.*

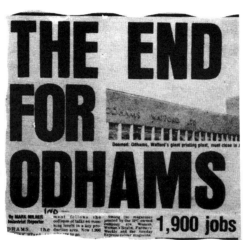

1983: End of an era and the largest job loss in the history of Watford. Odhams print works, one of the leading print houses in Europe for nearly half a century, closed.

Knighthood for M.P. Raphael

OCTOBER, 1980: Arise Sir Raphael! Watford's MP for 15 years on the day he got his knighthood. One of the best constituency MPs of his day, Sir Raphael Tuck served the town selflessly. His kindliness and sincerity transcended political barriers.

In November, 1980, Sir Raphael was made a freeman of the Borough of Watford, the town he loved and where he made his final home. Earlier this year Watford council decided to name five streets after him or some aspect of his life. He died in 1982.

EE November, 1983

'Junket' Jibe Over Councillors' Trip

WATFORD Council's ruling Labour group has been accused of "junketing" on the rates.

Tories are angry about a two-day visit to Sheffield to discuss twin-links with Russia.

Deputy Conservative leader, Councillor Robert Gordon, said it was no surprise they were rushing off to the 'Kremlin of the north' for the junket.

He told the full council meeting: "It is precisely expenditure of this type that compels the Government to take action before the Red Flag flies over our town hall."

Three Labour councillors will be going to the twinning seminar organised by the Socialist-controlled Sheffield City Council. Each will be entitled to claim attendance, travelling and subsistence allowances.

Councillor Arthur Reynolds, one of the delegates, denied they were Left-wing extremists or that the visit would be all wine, women and song.

"The idea is to find out how other towns are conducting their relationships with the Soviet Union," he said.

Labour leader, Councillor Fred Hodgson, accused the Tories of being hypocritical by supporting attendance at a West European twinning conference previously.

He added: "If you ever get control it would be the Stars and Stripes flying over the town hall."

Post Echo, final issue, 16 November 1983

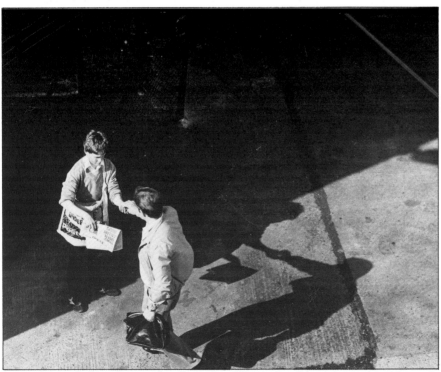

Evening Echo relied heavily upon 'location' sales each evening. This was one such. Entrance to Fishburn's, St. Albans Road.   6th July, 1982

Boys Brigade Centenary Year, 1983. This march went through the town to the Museum, where a special BB display was mounted.

Printing

If one picks up an old Guide to Watford the comment may be noticed that 'Watford is a print town; the largest in the country, possibly all Europe'. It is a statement believed today by many but is no longer true for, although modern society consumes ever more printed material, Watford's share of large-scale printing has dwindled to a mere fraction of that of its heyday. It is not that the earlier magazines have been replaced by television, for colour supplements, mail order catalogues and the like have provided possible alternative business.

The roots of print's downfall may lie in the days of its early success. Sun Engraving and Sun Printers in the years before the last war were ahead of their time with quality rotary gravure colour printing. There was no shortage of customers requiring their services. The war reduced the demand for printing in general as paper shortages continued and even worsened in the post-war years.

When paper became freely available again, there was still a huge demand for the products of Sun and Odhams. During the years of paper shortage, technology in Germany and the USA had caught up with and surpassed that in use in the Watford factories. An artificial printing boom in the late 1950's and early 1960's camouflaged later problems. Customers wanted colour printing; equipment was getting outdated; extra effort was needed to meet deadlines.

Unions were the first to appreciate that in the short term higher wages could easily be obtained from the employer by the threat of strike action with a consequential loss of production and late or non delivery. Management succumbed to these pressures. The increased costs had to be passed on to the customers who then turned to other print centres in the country that would only too willingly handle the work. Watford's position was threatened unless costs could be reduced to the extent they again became competitive. The years of escalating costs accepted by customers, with little alternative, had passed. To attempt to reduce costs, managements took the logical step of seeking to introduce new techniques and machinery which could be manned by fewer staff; a step bitterly fought by unions. The result was that machines were either over-manned, still continuing with high costs, or shut down.

Watford was acknowledged as a town of 'high wages of the printers'. In 1963, the Daily Mirror intended to start a colour supplement. Union branches circularised every print business, large and small, within a large area announcing that Odhams needed staff. With the attraction of high wages, the reputation of easy work loads and plenty of overtime, they had soon recruited and met their requirements. Scores of smaller businesses lost skilled and vital machine minders and other staff in the exodus, being unable, in commercial and jobbing print, to equal the high payments.

At this time, 1963, the workforce of Odhams and Sun numbered some 3,500 each.

The Mirror supplement failed; Odhams became, over the years, plagued with strikes. Resulting from one closure of many weeks a Royal Commission was held. The finding suggested that 'management and union should attempt to better cooperate'.

A loss-making situation followed, making eventual closure inevitable.

At Sun Printers the trend of lower cost printing was quite clearly noted. Gravure produced high quality but took longer in preparation, and was more expensive. The Sun staff took immense pride in their achievements and, when the proposition was made to install the cheaper web-offset, the union's stance was that no members should suffer. In other words, the cheaper process should be, once again, overmanned and therefore, non-competitive. Multiplicity of unions meant quite severe and pronounced 'demarcation' problems. Web-offset was not installed at that time.

The years from the mid-1960's were traumatic for managements, unions and staff and it was not until very recent years that amalgamations started and demarcation restrictions eased.

The damage had long been done; large print orders were placed elsewhere in this country and abroad.

Odhams closed in 1983 and merged with Sun and at the new Odhams/Sun co-operation led to reduced manning levels and more competitive lower unit costs. The Odhams/Sun workforce totals just over 700; they face the future with confidence.

New Sainsbury's Store

The recent start on the new Sainsbury's store on the Monmouth Arms site is the product of several years planning and negotiations by the Council.

The development has been made possible by the Council initiating in 1979 the compulsory purchase of the land not already in their ownership.

Interestingly, the whole site had been in the ownership of the late Mr. Cox in the 1920s but he had sold off land from time to time, and by 1979 there were 15 different owners of parts of the site. Clearly, only the Council could hope to bring the site back into single ownership so that it could be developed as a whole.

It was expected that Tesco would be the Council's tenants, but after prolonged negotiations they withdrew in 1980. Fortunately, the Council had taken the precaution of requiring a very substantial deposit which, before its eventual repayment, earned thousands of pounds in interest. This helped the Council take the courageous decision to press ahead with acquiring the site, even though there was no longer a definite developer in view.

By 1982, the national retailing situation had improved sufficiently for the Council to have detailed negotiations with a development company and Sainsburys, leading to an initial agreement in March this year, again supported by a substantial payment.

Since then, the developers have successfully agreed to buy the Odeon cinema from Ranks. This has enlarged the site to give a better-designed store, and four unit shops fronting The Parade, with a snooker hall above.

The promotion by the Council of this development reinforces the town's shopping facilities, adds to the available car parking, improves rear servicing and, not least, aids the rate fund by the payment made by Sainsburys for the site.

WOT December, 1983

End of an Era as Odeon Goes

The Council has decided to recommend that the new public highway serving the rear of numbers 47-115 The Parade and the Sainsbury's Store, be named "Gaumont Approach" —the Odeon was formerly named the "Gaumont".

WOT December, 1984

Screen 1, the mainscreen projectors.

The 'Circle'.   17th October, 1983

Clarendon Road Corner, 1984; shops in 'run-down' phase prior to site re-development.

p.336 c

Radlett Road council dwellings, in early stages of construction, summer 1984.

St. Albans Road, prior to dual-carriageway to Leavesden Road junction.

p.345 b

Well Done!

Even if the football club did not win the Cup their reception by the people of Watford could not have been warmer.

On Sunday May 20 Watford's Charter Place was crammed full and was a blaze of yellow and red.

The Borough Council was delighted to join with the people of Watford in saying "Well Done Lads—We Are Proud Of You".

The Wembley final with Everton (which Everton won 2-0) was described as the Friendly Final. In Watford the day after will be recalled as the happy homecoming.

WOT June, 1984

Sub Post Office to Close

Watford's Head Postmaster, Mr. R. H. Staines recently announced that he intends to close the New Town Sub Post Office in Langley Road, Watford.

WOT December, 1984

Council Unveils New Estate

WATFORD Borough Council's Radlett Road housing estate was officially opened by Lady Monica Tuck on Friday 19th July 1985.

In her speech officially opening the estate, Lady Tuck thanked the Borough Council for marking the town's great affection for her late husband by naming the main roads on the estate after him.

The Mayor then proposed a vote of thanks to Lady Tuck and said "The residents of Watford must give thanks to Sir Raphael Tuck, our Member of Parliament for so many years, to whom the town owes a great debt of honour."

She then complimented the speed and efficiency with which the contractors, Croudace Limited, had carried out the work so far on the estate. From the start in April 1983 the first properties were handed over in July 1984. The estate was going a long way to relieve the pressure on the Borough Council's housing list, she said.

More than 300 additional homes are to be built on the site, which should be completed by March 1988. The northern section of the estate is now complete with 80 houses—69 of which are already occupied, and 93 flats, of which 33 are occupied. The final two blocks on this section are complete but have not yet been officially handed over.

WOT August, 1985

Cassiobury Park, Watford Carnival fun fair.

River Colne, Oxhey Park.

Cassiobury Park, Watford Carnival fun fair.

Cassiobury Park, River Gade.

Palace Theatre's Cash Crisis

WATFORD'S Palace Theatre, probably the most successful regional theatre in the Country, is again facing a cash crisis.

Its principal funding bodies, the Borough Council and the Arts Council, are both being hit hard by Government restrictions on public spending and are unlikely to be in a position to increase their grants significantly.

Despite its superb record of attendances—audiences have averaged over 90 per cent for the past four years—subsidy has failed to keep pace with inflation.

However, a recent meeting of the Watford Civic Theatre Trust heard of a surprise of £4,000 from Equity, the Actors' Union, from a special fund. As a result of this, the Theatre Trust have decided to give serious consideration to continuing with its May production, which was in danger of having to be cancelled.

The Theatre is now launching an appeal to the business community for further sponsorship to ensure the May production proceeds.

Arthur Reynolds, Chairman of the Trust, said "that the Arts Council had appealed for other local authorities to match their grant pound for pound. Here in Watford the Borough contributes £148,700 and the Arts Council £79,810. If only they would match us pound for pound!"

The Theatre normally closes down during the summer period. Some profitable use for the Theatre during this period is being considered.

WOT February, 1985

Sedgwick's original steamer, Knebworth Steam Engine Rally.   1986

Dredging the river Gade, Cassiobury Park.

Leggatt's School—teacher-parent evening.   1980

Grange Park School—action meeting.   1984

Success of Link Town Ventures

IT IS obvious from his letter in the Watford Observer (March 9) that Mr. Stanley Sharpe is woefully ignorant of the many activities resulting from Watford being twinned with Nanterre and Mainz.

Over the years there have been exchanges between school children, basketball, volleyball, football, tennis and athletic teams, church groups particularly of young people, school orchestras, choirs, townswomens' guilds, scouts, apprentices and business studies students, to name only a few.

Most exchanges are on the basis that visitors stay in the homes of families in the host towns and this very much concerns the "ordinary people" mentioned by Mr. Sharpe.

We often have inquiries from our link towns for accommodation for individuals who wish to come to Watford for a holiday, or for children wishing to improve their English by staying in a family. If Mr. Sharpe is able to provide hospitality in this way it would be greatly appreciated.
—Councillor Arthur Reynolds, Chairman, Link Advisory Committee.

WO March, 1984

Alcohol Advice

MR WALTER WARD draws attention to a dilemma faced by magistrates, police, medical practitioners, social workers and indeed, the whole of society. How does one deal with the anti-social behaviour of a person drugged with alcohol?

Very often, at the time of the offence, it may truly be said that the individual is no more responsible for his actions than one anaesthetised for surgery.

Mr. Ward says that it is the individual's duty to keep his drinking under control. That is true, so why do some professional men and women, as well as many less able folk, allow themselves to drink too much?

The Alcohol Advice Centre at 120 Exchange Road, Watford (telephone Watford 21037) offers both information and help with individual problems. The office is open from 10 am until 2 pm Monday to Friday for information, and during those hours appointments may be made to meet experienced counsellors with whom problems may be discussed freely and in confidence.

Private interviews can be arranged during the day or evening and the service is free. For many, just the opportunity to talk to an impartial listener is a great relief in itself and frequently a course of counselling together with the counsellor's support had led to the drink and associated problems being solved.

WO March, 1984

Grange Park

SINCE the new proposals for the closure of Grange Park, Leggatts and William Penn schools have been announced, many reasons are, and will be given, as to why the above schools should stay open.

But while the fight goes on, please give some thought to the children who will have to try to maintain a high standard of work in a very unsettled atmosphere.

Most of the children, whether or not they show it, must be feeling as if their own little world is falling apart.

Is it not bad enough that we as a nation cannot guarantee them a job after all their studying? We are also unable to promise them that their schooling will be uninterrupted. Will the powers-that-be please remember statistics don't have feelings, but children do!—Mrs. G. A. Siggery, Maytree Crescent, Watford.

WO March, 1984

Leggatts School

IF THERE have to be cuts in Local Authority spending why does our next generation have to suffer so much, especially these days when a good education is vital, more so than when we as parents were at school.

First you say our children will be forced to go out of school in order to obtain lunch, now you tell us that the children of North Watford are going to be forced to travel miles out of their way in order to get to school.

Is nobody concerned for the pupil who, being uprooted from his school, his friends and security of surroundings, may never be able to recover from the changes and which may inevitably cause poorer exam and school results than may well have been.

Why pick on Leggatts Way School, when Central Watford and Bushey are well supplied with schools. Leggatts is the only school supplying the residential area of North Watford, the nearest school being four miles away.

Leggatts School has been the choice of many parents over the years and that of my husband and I, because of its extremely good record, also because of its close proximity to our homes.

The grounds for sports use are excellent. The very important and much enjoyed after-school activities (including Saturday mornings) would have to be omitted from our sons' schooling because of having to catch buses in order to get home. My sons chose Leggatts because they do not want to have to travel far to school. The school they want to go to is on our doorstep. It seems to me parental choice is simply a meaningless word these days.

In a few years' time the authorities will be reopening these schools or having to rebuild because of the increasing numbers of school-aged children.

There simply must be other alternatives. We are not prepared to lose our local school. Our school is important to us.—Mr and Mrs. J. P. Rackley, Maytree Crescent, Watford.

WO March, 1984

● *Falling school rolls necessitated closure, or merger, of some schools. Plans in 1982/3 to merge Bushey Hall School (co-ed) and Grange Park (boys) were resisted. As part of a 'package' of changes the propositions went to appeal and were dismissed. Undaunted, Herts County Council tried again, this time proposing to close William Penn, Rickmansworth; Leggatt's, North Watford; and Grange Park, Bushey. As before the proposals were bitterly contested and much effort was expended by head teachers, staff, pupils and parents in campaigning, protesting, fund-raising and petitioning. Leggatt's case rested upon badly sited alternatives; Grange Park that no alternative school places existed and that to close the boys' school restricted parents right to choose. The closure plans were not well formulated; parents worried that pupils would be left on dying sites; Herts County Council and 'new school' head teachers assured anxious parents that this would not be so.*

In the event, closure orders were confirmed in the summer of 1985 and the pupils left on 'dying' sites. The closure co-incided with a long-drawn-out campaign of 'industrial action'—disruptive tactics—by teaching staff in protest over pay and conditions, and despite the best efforts of some long standing dedicated staff the pupils did not receive the care and education that should have been theirs.

Grange Park boys' numbers dwindled from around 350 of September 1985 to around 135 in July 1987. Full integration with Queens School had not taken place and in the face of knowledge that Grange Park site was to be used for Bushey Hall School the remaining boys were intensely aggrieved at the treatment they had received. An attempt at integration was made two weeks before the end of the school year (when many boys had left) and had "nothing to do with rumours that an end-of-term demonstration of dissatisfaction was planned".

Bob Nunn, ex-Chairman,
Grange Park Association

Grange Park School wind band.   1984

Leggatt's School production of 'Smike'.   1981

Educated English

If you are reading this in some remote part of the world, and there is a one in ten chance that you are, you are not going to believe a word of what follows.

It seems that Her Majesty's Inspectors for Schools (HMIs)—a body of men and women who plainly no longer strike the terror they once did into the heart of teacher and pupil—are getting a bit concerned about what children in England are being taught about the English language. So they fired off a pamphlet aimed at teachers outlining what they thought the little ones, from age five to age sixteen, should be taught about their mother tongue.

Here is the eyebrow raiser. So fierce was the response from teachers that the HMIs have had to redraft their contentious ideas.

No longer do they suggest that a child of eleven should know the difference between a vowel and a consonant. Altogether too demanding they now think, to suggest that the same kid might have been told by their teachers that in a sentence there is often a subject and a verb, and that it is a good idea if they agree.

No awareness of different tenses, by the end of a child's primary education, will be looked for.

In the face of considerable criticism from teachers the hapless HMIs, intuitive spoilsports every one of them, have dropped from their original list of high attainment for eleven-year-olds a knowledge of the rules of spelling, the functions of the main parts of speech, and the ability to tell the difference between statements, questions, commands and exclamations.

The HMIs are not the only ones in the education business who are bothered. They say that a consultation exercise they have conducted over the past eighteen months has shown that there is substantial agreement that children should learn something about their language and how it works. But even this modest concession to learning doesn't get anywhere, for no one can agree what it should be. With the result, maintain the HMIs, that many pupils are taught nothing about how language works as a system.

Readers in the UK have long suspected it.

British Printer, August 1986

Schools must teach 3 Rs

TEACHERS are to be forced to give all pupils a thorough grounding in the three Rs, Education Secretary Kenneth Baker announced yesterday.

He spelled out details of a national curriculum which will expect every child in England and Wales to reach an acceptable standard in English and maths.

Mr. Baker said it was an unacceptable fact but many children's basic education suffered 'through the accident of where they happen to go to school. His proposals would bring them into line with the Continent, where nationally-set curricula are followed.

"The aim is to raise standards of achievements in our schools," he said. "Many already offer such a curriculum, though not always to all their pupils. But many offer something far less."

The intention, he said was to ensure that pupils received a basic education which would stretch their talents and prepare them for the world of work. "This can be guaranteed only if it is required and enforceable by law."

Mr. Baker stressed that schools should also set aside time for music, art and sport.

The Education Secretary said he would not enforce the national curriculum without consulting teachers' unions, education authorities and other groups and arriving at 'a broad national consensus'.

Daily Mail April, 1987

Watford Boys' Grammar School

IX

Into a future

During 1962, 25 years ago, comprehensive plans were laid before the council for development of land behind Queens Road and the High Street. The scheme was called 'Mars'. Proposed by surveyors Rogers, Chapman and Thomas, the Council invited the views of the advisors, surveyors and estate agents Hillier, Parker, May and Rowden. The verdict was that the time was not then ripe for such a huge expansion of shopping area, as, in the meantime, established stores had extended.

The Queens Road shops were blighted and years passed before revitalisation occurred.

In 1986, the 'Mars'plan was re-introduced to the public, concurrent with the plans for the 'Tesco site', the 'M1 link road' and the 'West Watford link road'.

During the early 1970's, with immense pressure upon the town, Charter Place was conceived and built. At a time when money was short, some corners had to be cut and the eventual result was perhaps not quite to the standard expected. It is a project, the first of its kind in the Borough, which has not stood well the test of time; it is announced that, after only fifteen years, it is to be 'revamped'. It is a term which will mean physical and financial chaos to traders who have invested years of effort. 'Mars', not yet constructed, is also stated to have a life of 10-15 years before revamping.

The letter from M. Paterson, on page 325, may well indicate latent desires and anticipations; in the high value units — with consquent high rates — will these desires become reality?

The North Watford Odhams site is redeveloped and now includes South-West Hert's first hypermarket; the 'business parks' at West Watford are well on the way to completion and the lettings offer a diverse and challenging spread of modern industry to those seeking employment. The thrusting pace of 'selling the town', so evident 80 years ago, still continues . . .

From page 322 the photographs show the High Street from Town Hall to Bushey Arches, then return. Next follows Rickmansworth Road, Queens Road, the Junction, St. Albans Road. The sequence carries on with Charter Place, Parish Church, West Watford and other scenes around the town which have seen major changes.

The original frontage of 1890 is being retained during and after reconstruction of the bank building.   p. 59t

Part of Charter Place;a 15-year life span 'before revamping' is suggested.

Rembrandt House, Whippendell Road, started about 80-years previously as Neilsen's Watch Factory, enlarged and became the home of North's Magneto's. North, in turn, suffered in the 1928-30 depression and went into liquidation, the premises becoming that of Rembrandt Photogravure Ltd. in 1934. Following, Hazell, Watson & Viney merger with Sun Printers, a 'pruning operation'

By contrast, the rear of Computer & Systems Engineering PLC (CASE), Caxton Way, one of the larger 'new-technology' industries.

resulted in closure in c1960 when the building was converted and sub-let in small- and medium-sized industrial units.

Jobs need skilled workers

HIGH technology industries currently flocking to Watford might decide to go elsewhere unless the town can provide skilled workers for jobs.

That is the warning in a blueprint report for Watford Borough Council on what the next ten years has in store for employers and employees alike.

The report, meant as a discussion document, says the number of people working in Watford has fallen from 54,460 in 1966 to 42,120 in 1981 with the decline in traditional industries, including printing and publishing. New high technology and computer firms are stepping in to take over, and local schools, colleges and government and private agencies, together with the borough council, should take note of their training needs, the report says.

"If the skill shortage in Watford persists, potential new firms may decide to locate elsewhere," states the report.

The Employment Topic Paper, which will be used when changes are made to the Watford Local Plan, accepts that the new industries are being located on purpose-built business sites in the borough, such as the Watford Business Park and WENTA Business Centre.

But the report warns that businessmen should be encouraged to develop older industrial sites in the borough. This should be helped by the completion of the M25 which has already improved access to Watford.

"Employment generation in the towns adjoining the M25 is difficult to predict, but it is highly probable that there will be increased demand for space for high technology, warehousing and light industry," says the topic paper.

"Completion of the M25 is likely to intensify pressure for office development in Watford."

But the borough council looks set to keep a close eye on the number of applications to build

offices in the town as it does not believe it would provide many jobs for Watford's unemployed.

Without controls, Watford leader Fred Hodgson said, Watford was not alone in not having enough workers skilled to suit high technology and computer industries.

"Almost every town in the country is likely to be in the same position. If you look at the high-tech industry the demand does exceed the supply. I know that from my own industry and areas connected with the computer business.

"The majority of those on the dole in Watford are unskilled or semi-skilled. Office blocks may solve some of the unemployment problems, but only on a short-term basis," he added.

WO July 1986

G. W. Jones' factory in Whippendell Road (L/H side) still stands as part of 'Sun Engraving' though the incorporation of Odhams has meant a name change. The small hump-back bridges (p.117) have twice been widened and a large roundabout connects Rickmansworth Road and Whippendell Road with the Watford and Croxley Business Parks.

Hempstead Road, looking towards the Town. The old road was little wider than the space between the trees. *p.110 b, 305 b*

Two minute's silence by two old comrades; Remembrance Sunday, November, 1985, at the Peace Memorial alongside the Town Hall. *p.163b*

Drop in Property Values?

Dear Sir,

THERE is a more serious side to Mr. Cowin's amusing letter (Watford Observer, December 5) and that is the effect on existing High Street shops if uncontrolled development of out-of-town shopping centres is permitted in South West Hertfordshire.

The completion of the M25 has brought no less than five applications for major shopping developments within Watford's catchment area.

Furthermore, there is the fallacy that surrounding every potential "green field" site there is a large untapped reserve of consumer spending power waiting to be put into the new shopping centre as soon as it opens its gates.

But little additional turnover is created—it is trade diverted from somewhere else—from local corner shops or from existing High Street department stores. And when trade drifts away from the traditional shopping areas jobs are lost, rateable values drop, services decline and town centres die.

The regeneration of the twilight area of Watford's Lower High street, under the umbrella of Mars 1, may appear a laudable project, but are we not merely relocating the shopping centre 400 yards back down the High Street and will not any increase in rates revenue from the new centre be counter-balanced by a corresponding drop in property values in the upper High Street?.

R. E. H. Edmonds, The Parade, Watford.

WO February, 1986

Proving town has a heart!

Dear Sir,

IF THE Mars 1 development of Watford is to take place, there must be a commitment to reopen the roads in The Parade and upper High Street.

People can then see that a town exists; that it has a heart; that there is easy accessibility to a first-class theatre, places of entertainment and restaurants.

It must not continue to be a place which is alive with shoppers during the day and completely dead at night.

If this scheme and other superstore developments are allowed to proceed without consideration to public amenities, then Watford, which geographically has probably the greatest potential of any town in the country, would just become another large clinical shopping centre.

S. Lipman, Gordon Hudson & Co., The Parade, Watford.

WO April, 1986

A winter Sunday allows the view to be seen (see p.292); later in the year the trees in foliage obscure all but the pavement. *p.88, 289, 297 t*

View from the 'fly-over' connecting Exchange Road with Beechen Grove; Boys Brigade marchers receding into the distance.   *p.153 b, 245 b*   Nov. 1983

The Market Place, early May 1987, 124 years on from the view on page 45.   *p. 164b*

(above) This is the nearest modern match to the drawing of 1832 (p.21). Despite the 155 intervening years, the site outline remains although the premises and their tenants have changed several times.

(Left) Rose & Crown corner, Market Street. By concidence the bus is in almost the same position as the mid-20's photograph (p.170 b)   *p.66, 170 b*

(Below) On the right, where the lady is walking, the passage through to the church; on the left H. Samuel (No. 89) shows well the original building line almost to the road. It's a Sunday morning and the road sweepers have swiftly cleaned through the town; there's no sign left of the Saturday debris.

Create a clean, bright shopping centre

Dear Sir,

HOW pleasing it is that the shabby area to the south of Queens Road in Watford is to be developed.

What a wonderful opportunity our council has to redeem itself and see that a shopping area that is bright, clean and attractive is created.

We don't all want another noisy Brent Cross, nor even less another grey and soulless Charter Place, but a precinct that is a pleasure and relaxation to be in.

Do please let provision be made with affordable rents for arcades of small individual shopkeepers with their crafts and specialised merchandise. Not just the big multiples.

Please make ample car parking easily accessible so that our roads are not clogged by traffic, and please create an area of beauty of which Watford can at last be proud.

M. Paterson.

WO April, 1986

Sunshine Carnival record

JUBILANT organisers have announced an all-time record collection of more than £1,000 as part of this year's Bank Holiday carnival in Watford.

The news follows several disastrous years in which dismal weather forced the three-day event into the red, ruining organisers' hopes of raising money for local charities.

Now it looks as though this weekend's dry, sunny weather may have broken the run of bad luck for the Cassiobury Park extravaganza.

WO May, 1986

Victoria School goes

ANOTHER of Watford's landmarks bites the dust this week as bulldozers move in to knock down the old Victoria School in Addiscombe Road.

The site is being cleared to make way for the construction of the new Chater Junior School.

Built in 1897, it began its life as Fearnley Street School and was one of the first "board schools" of the period.

Previously all schools were private or church run until boards of elected local representatives were set up in each town to provide publicly-owned education for all.

In 1959 a decision was taken by the school governors to move the then named Victoria School to a new site in Tolpits Lane.

By 1963 the Addiscombe Road buildings were out of use and the new Tolpits Lane site was renamed Westfield School. Westfield School later became an all-girls school and the boy pupils were moved to Grange Park School in Bushey.

Although no longer a school, the Addiscombe Road buildings were back in use in August 1979 when they became a temporary police station while the present Watford station was being rebuilt. It remained the house of the law for 18 months.

WO May, 1986

A November Saturday; for a surprise comparison, see pages 111 b and 129 t.　　　*p.135 br*

Banks have been 'closed Saturdays' for many years (though there is a gradual tendency for several main-branch banks to re-open on Saturday mornings for limited services). The greatest revolution of the 1980's has been widespread acceptance of 'plastic credit cards' and 'cash-point' services—the latter being cash-dispensing machines, for which this queue is waiting at Nat. West.

Woolworth's, King Street, and Barclays Bank (p.125). Barclays shortly after turning to 12-hour seven-day self-service via electronically-controlled service points. Access is gained only by utilising special 'magnetic key-card'. The first bank to be fully automated.　　　*p.121 t, 125 t,c*　　1986

King Street looking across to Queens Road. This view in 1985; Sainsbury's supermarket has transferred to a new site behind Monmouth House, a move which inevitably draws trade away from Queens Road although Trewins and the small shops still attract many shoppers. Two years later, May 1987 virtually all shops are closing pending imminent demolition to accomodate the MARS project. The imposing facade of Ketts (built in 1913 for Boots) is to be retained as an entrance to the new shopping conurbation.   *p.152 r*

16th-century houses go for new shops

ONE of Watford's oldest houses will be demolished to make way for a £100-million shopping complex because "it doesn't fit in with" the developer's plans.

Number 1a Carey Place is a timber-framed Grade II listed building dating from the 1600's and is superceded only slightly in age by number 22 the High Street—a restaurant and a jeweller's.

St. Mary's Parish Church is the only building with parts which pre-date both.

The Mars 1 development means the flattening of almost all buildings bounded by Queens Road, Beechen Grove and the bottom end of Watford High Street.

This week the developer's intentions to erect large shops, a shopping mall and a "food court" in the area have been branded as "unimaginative" by a leading conservationalist who says the architects must alter their plans to suit the existing scene.

"The architects are not the slightest bit interested in the retention, preservation and refurbishment of this important listed building," says Stephen Castle, a member of a national architectural interest group and writer of a reference book called "Timber Framed Buildings in Watford."

"Their statement that the building is a sad and much modified version of the original and contributes nothing to the townscape of Watford is utter nonsense."

Mr. Castle says the right solution would be to expose the timber framing of No 1a and the adjacent Nos 137 to 139 the High Street for conversion to an attractive period restaurant and pub.

Backing the alternative plans local archaeological society spokesman Tony Rawlins says a pub would be a good answer to the problem.

"You can't just sweep listed buildings away. A good solution would be a pub or some other integral part of the development.

"I am opposed to its removal. It is a fine 16th-century building indicating what the alleys and courts of Watford once looked like."

The developers plan to take the backs off many of the shops in the bottom part of the High Street so that the old frontages, some of which date from the early 17th-century, are retained, although they would act as doorways to large stores and not be individual shops as now.

But developers Capital and Counties say nobody in Watford cares or even knows about No 1a's historic structure (it is a hairdresser's shop) and making it into a pub doesn't fit in with their re-development plans.

"We have offered to take it apart and erect it elsewhere, perhaps as a sports pavilion," said C&C's Anne Forster. "But as no site has been identified we have had to apply for demolition."

The council looks unlikely to provide an alternative site. Development and planning committee chairman Les Cox says he's "not bothered about the building".

WO May, 1986

Destruction

Dear Sir,

YOUR generous coverage, in the Watford Observer of May 16, of the proposed demolition of listed 16th- and 17th-century buildings in Watford's historic High Street/Carey Place is greatly appreciated by those who are concerned about the retention of Watford's architectural heritage.

Nos 129-131, 133-135, 137-139 and 141 High Street and No 1A Carey Place were listed as Grade II in January 1983, as part of the Department of the Environment's resurvey of Watford's historic buildings to survive in the town. The DoE resurvey was prompted by the appalling wholesale destruction of the majority of Watford's historic buildings in the period 1950-1979.

This current application envisages not only the unnecessary demolition of the 16th-century No 1A Carey Place, but also the removal of the earliest part of No 137 High Street, which dates from c.1614—viz the mural depicting the Stuart Coat of Arms (Royal Arms of James I) removed to Watford Museum.

As No 1A Carey Place and No 137 High Street are statutorily listed buildings they cannot be demolished without the consent of the Secretary of State for the Environment. It is important to mention to Watfordians that sufficient representations to the Secretary of State, on this and other aspects of the proposed Mars development, may persuade him to hold a public inquiry.

In 17 years spent recording and campaigning for the preservation of Watford's historic buildings, I have received nothing but support from Watfordians.

Generally speaking they have mourned the passing of Cassiobury, Cassiobury Park Gates, numerous historic public houses and also the replacement of the traditional brick and timber-framed buildings of Watford's historic town centre with concrete muck-heaps! The only opposition I have witnessed has originated from Watford Town Hall!

Stephen A. Castle, member of the Vernacular Architecture Group.   *WO May, 1986*

Between Thoms and Water Lane are some of the few remaining old shop buildings, one dating from c1614. By May 1987 most are empty, derelict and awaiting their fate; meanwhile, a few are still trading.

p.282 b

Urban environment important

Dear Sir,

IN YOUR report on the proposed Mars development and its impact on the few remaining historical buildings from Watford's past, you quote the chairman of the Council Development Control Committee as stating: "Anyone wanting to preserve No 1A (Carey Place) must be in cloud cuckoo land."

His, and apparently his Committee's attitude to our report appears to directly contradict the policies of the Labour Party in Hertfordshire, who want to give more support for conservation and listed buildings.

Many of us in the Labour Party do feel that it is important to preserve the heritage of ordinary people, rather than destroy or demolish everything for the greater glory and profit of big business and the land speculators.

The apparent desire of the council to raze much of the remaining Watford tradition to the ground is in sharp contrast to their expressed policies of opposition to development in the green belt.

A pleasant urban environment is as important as the countryside. The popularity of tourist centres such as Chester or York, where the old towns have been preserved, is an indication that people do value the older buildings, and are willing to be involved in their preservation.

The developer's proposals for the High Street frontage would leave little more than a sham shell of Watford's history.

Surely pride in our town should not only be measured in the square footage of commercial and office development, but also in the way of life of ordinary Watford people in the past, as illustrated by these older buildings, which I believe should be preserved.

County Councillor Dr. John Dore, Watford.

WO May, 1986

The west side of the High Street is not under threat; No. 146 (Hot Bread) was formerly site of the once notorious 'Nag's Head' pub, which, by subscriptions raised by the Parish Church, later, c1834, became site for the 'National' infants' school. The Church Lands Charity sold the premises for £3,100 in 1920.

The 'One Crown' is the Town's oldest surviving pub, dating from 16th century. It is a listed building. Next to it, 'Live Wire', No. 158, is 17th century, remodelled 18th century; it too, is a listed building. By its side is Crown Passage, an ancient right of way giving access to Watford Fields.

Mars 1 plan angers local historian

A LOCAL historian, angry over Watford Borough Council's plans to demolish listed buildings as part of the MARS 1 town centre redevelopment, has accused the council of not preserving historic architecture.

Archaeologist Mr. Stephen Castle, a member of the Vernacular Architecture Group, said that the plans will add to the loss of the town's historic buildings from the 1950's onwards.

Renewing his earlier attack, he laid the blame squarely on the shoulders of the local authorities. "It has to be the attitude of local councillors.

"To my mind the council has not been compromised—it has been demolition all the way with one or two exceptions," said Mr. Castle.

But as Mr. Castle gave his view and Three Rivers Council delivered its observations on the scheme, noting the loss of listed buildings, the chairman of the Borough's Development and planning Committee described at least one listed building earmarked for demolition as "an eyesore" and said he didn't care about the views of Three Rivers.

"My distinct impression is that other planning authorities in Herts seem very, very concerned about historic buildings and go to great lengths to ensure their preservation, and it seems quite clear to me that over the last 20 years or so Watford has done quite the opposite," said Mr. Castle.

He said that the resurvey of listed buildings by the Department of the Environment was deliberately brought forward because of the losses. "That was a conscious response to the appalling destruction of historic buildings in the town between the 1950s and 1979," he said.

Among the losses he noted were the Leather-sellers Arms, High Street, dating from at least the seventeenth century, the sixteenth century Swan, the seventeenth century White Hart close to High Street Station, and the sixteenth century Eight Bells.

"We are talking about dozens and dozens of buildings, some listed grade two, others not listed," he said.

Turning to Lower High Street, he said: "With the exception of Frogmore House and the Benskin Mansion and the adjacent coach house and some small Georgian houses in a sadly dilapidated state, nothing has survived.

"That area which was once rich in historic buildings has been pretty well annihilated," said Mr. Castle.

Last week Three Rivers Council considered the MARS 1 proposals.

The Planning Committee noted the loss of listed buildings, thanking Watford for the consultation. Three Rivers' main concern was the impact of additional traffic at Bushey Arches, themselves listed.

WO June, 1986

In this segment of old buildings, Farr Bedford, No. 172a, dates from 1680-1720, and Crystal Harvest Wholefoods, No. 172, dates from the 17th century. Both buildings are listed Grade II.

Rethink over plans for Mars 1 site

DEVELOPERS involved in the Mars 1 scheme in Watford have bowed to public pressure and submitted a new plan under which most of the listed buildings earlier set to disappear will be retained.

A spokesman for Watford Borough Council said that two previous plans from joint developers Capital and Counties PLC and Sun Alliance Assurance had been withdrawn and that under the new one most of the listed buildings would be retained "with modifications".

The new plans involve improvement and refurbishment of the front range of buildings at numbers 129-151 High Street and 1A Carey Place. The rear sections would however be removed under the new scheme.

Number 1A Carey Place has been described by conservationists as including features now unique to buildings in Watford, and the new plans follow only weeks after the chairman of the Watford Borough Council Development and Planning Committee described one listed building as "an eyesore".

In the meantime, shopkeepers with premises earmarked for demolition to make way for the Mars 1 development have been given a stay of execution.

Developers Capital and Counties confirmed this week that the bulldozers are unlikely to start in October as originally planned and the land agents have given shopkeepers an option to extend their lease until March 1987.

WO June, 1986

Keystone of arch over wagonway to No. 145 (William Hill) bears initials 'WH' and the date 1786.

Rear of, *right:* 137, *left:* 141 High Street.   1987

Water Lane; derelict cottages and Hammond's Music Shop; announced early 1987 that the site is to be redeveloped.

p.73, 256

Carey Place from the High Street; the old West Herts Post's printing office and works.

William Hill, No. 145, may have been c1790, the 'Boot'. To many Watfordians it will be remembered as 'Allen Ankers' and 'MacFisheries', both fishmongers. The 1786-dated building is listed Grade II.

Carey Place

Carey Place was a narrow road which ran from the High Street, from between numbers 135 and 137, to Derby Road at a point almost opposite Grosvenor Road. It was so named by a Mr. Carey who, it is stated, came to Watford to work as a plasterer on the old Beechen Grove Chapel. The road was unusual in that the numbering was consecutive rather than odd one side, even the other. The building, above, was built for the West Herts Post in 1919/20; prior to that the site had an interesting history.

In the early 1800's the Petty Sessions were held in a room at the old Essex Arms Hotel in the High Street; then, for some years, both the Petty Sessions and County Court were held in

the POST old building until the Court in King Street was built (c1854).

In 1870 records state that the Literary Institute had been the centre of educational influence for 16 years, following the removal of the Court from the premises.

In 1871 Mr. Stephen Camp broached the subject of establishing a Public Library and Reading Room with the result that Mr. Thomas Clutterbuck presented land in Queens Road and public subscriptions of £3000 enabled the building to be erected, and opened in October 1874.

The then disused Carey Place premises became, firstly, a Primitive Methodist Chapel around 1884 (Minister Rev. W. Holland) and

then headquarters for the Salvation Army before they moved to their new Citadel in St. St. Mary's Road.

Before the buildings were demolished they were last used by Messrs. Christmas & Co. for their coach-building business.

Meanwhile, the (West Herts) Post had been published from 42 High Street; upon demolition and clearance of the once Police Court, School, Library, Chapel, a new building was erected and the Post started publishing in it in 1920; it continued as such until the Post moved to Luton; a number of printers were subsequently housed in it and the locality including Hills & Lacey; Hudson & Stracey; Charles Straker and Wetherby.

Shop 'without a fascia' (No. 129) was opened by Jonathan Chater in 1834. Upon the death of the founder the business was carried on by his two sons, Edward M. and Mathew T. Chater. Edward was keenly interested in education and was for many years Chairman of the old Watford School Board. To commemorate his name Chater School was named after him. The business passed, in 1911, to D. W. R. & A. W. Barker. 'Chater's' moved to Queens Road in 1954, the shop being sold to a firm of radio and television dealers. The premises, late 17th century, are listed Grade II, as are Nos. 131, 133, 135, 137, 141, 143, 145, 149 and 151.

p.96 t

High Street Station. The left-hand track was of the original single-line to Rickmansworth, opened 1862.

Sheltered houses next to the Station. The Watford Borough Council, in developing the Benskin's Brewery site for housing acceded to the developer's request to site these houses on the High Street where the elderly inhabitants 'could watch the passers-by and traffic and not feel forgotten'.

Site of the 'Three Tuns' public house.   p.271 b

High Street homes for the elderly

THE first sheltered flats for sale to the elderly at 30 per cent less than the market value are now nearing completion in Watford Lower High Street between the Museum and the railway station.

They should be ready for occupation in February of next year and Watford Council, which has the right to nominate 50 per cent of the purchasers, is currently carrying out a "trawl" to establish how many of the initial inquirers are keen to pursue matters.

Warden Housing Association, a registered housing association, is building 35 flats, including one for a warden, and hopes to be able to issue brochures to people on the waiting list early in 1987.

At current prices the one bedroom flats for two people are valued at around £43,000 and the two-bedroomed flats for three people at £49,000. If sold today they would sell for £30,100 and £34,300 but there will have been a rise in price by the time the flats do go on the market.

Service charges to cover the cost of the warden and so on will be an additional cost to purchasers but Mr. Hugh Arthur, the association's development executive at Ruislip, said they are a non-profit-making body and service charges are kept as low as possible. There have been plenty of inquiries about the flats and he is confident the Watford scheme will be extremely successful.

WO July, 1986

Billboard on the left is approximate position of the once-important Watford Town Mill; at time of writing the future of the area is dependent upon the outcome of 'M1 Link Road' enquiries.   p.93 tl, 162

High Street, Nos. 212, 214, listed Grade II in 1983. *p.93 t*

Local Board Road; Pump House at the end was once the town water-pumping station, part used in pre-war days as Tividale Iron Foundry—a number of whose cast-iron man-hole covers and road gratings may be found around the town.

Kwik-Fit exhaust centre was once the Monaco Garage; just past that the entrance to the old bus garage (before transfer to Garston c1950).

Compare with the drawing on page 33; right-hand part of the building was once the 'King William'.

Just past 'Sewfine' was the original 'Wheatsheaf' dating back to c1750. Rebuilt further back from the road 1930. *p.178*

Looking through Bushey Arches, once the Toll Gate.

On the right, the 'Hit or Miss' public house.

In the centre of the picture is the used-car site of Glenne Motors just a few weeks before its closure for development of the 'Tesco site'. Glenne Motors site was that of the Watford Mill, p.162.

Glenne Motors, High Street, see above.

Council job adverts row

NEW council advertising could attract sex perverts, say some Watford councillors.

They are opposing moves to change the wording on council ads for jobs, fearing they may attract people who are not "welcome" in the area.

The matter was raised at Monday night's management committee meeting, but after a heated debate, was deferred.

With present advertising, the wording used is "Watford Borough Council is an Equal Opportunities Employer."

But to bring it in to line with other authorities, the suggested change is: "Watford Borough Council welcomes applications regardless of sex, race, colour, ethnic or national origin, sexual orientation, disability or marital status."

Tory leader Councillor Alistair Allan said it was unnecessary to specify peculiarities. He was among a number of councillors who thought the ad might attract the wrong people. "Would someone who enjoys sex with children be welcome here?" he asked.

Labour's vice-chairman Councillor John Watts said: "There are some people I wouldn't welcome job applications from."

Tory Councillor Mrs. Ann Wightman added that she didn't want "people with quirky ideas playing with children.

But Labour Councillor Mike Jackson reminded others that sexual orientation was not a criminal offence. He said the wording was a good idea and should be adopted.

"It's a proper use of words spelling out what we mean by equal opportunity employers."

Councillor Allan also criticised the wording of an advertisement for staff at an old people's home, Mardale, in Stratford Road, Watford, run by the London Borough of Brent authority.

The ad said Brent is an equal opportunity employer and applications were welcome from "candidates irrespective of race, nationality, ethnic or national origins, age, marital status or gender, and from lesbians and gay men and disabled persons."

Councillor Allan said: "I think it is totally wrong to identify groups like that in an advertisement. It is possibly encouraging people who we might say are not normal, to apply for jobs."

WO October, 1986

High Street, the once Vicarage gardens and Ellis cycle makers sites.   *p.111 t*

The junction of King Street and Queens Road with High Street, which, to the north, is now a service road only.

D.I.Y. Observer

NEWSPAPER production at the Watford Observer and Free Observer has stepped smartly into the 20th-century and made a little bit of history in the process.

The Observer has become the first weekly newspaper house in the country to go direct input with full co-operation from the unions involved.

The transition from typewritten stories to single-keying on computer over recent weeks means that stories written directly on to computers by editorial staff, and advertisements from the tele-ads department, are sent directly to the photosetters, without further keying by the production department.

Much of last week's Watford Observer and this week's Free Observer have been produced by the new method and today's paper, including the article you are reading now, has been single-keyed by journalists.

The change-over means that typewriters have been replaced by high-tech equipment and production facilities, leaving the field open for the area's leading local newspaper to expand its operation in South West Hertfordshire.

The Observer's C. H. Peacock group of newspapers has already launched two new titles in the past year, in St. Albans and Potters Bar. Reduced overheads and swifter production methods invite even more ambitious projects, which could include the launch of an evening newspaper.

Following the signing of the Observer's new tech agreement, which has been negotiated at length by the National Graphical Association and National Union of Journalists, C. H. Peacock Managing Director Mr. Tony Greenan said: "Single keying has the effect of reducing the break-even point for publication. Now we can think about an evening. But our research is only just beginning.

"I cannot tell you whether it will be a paid-for or a free paper or how much investment will be needed—that would be anticipating the viability study."

WO May, 1986

Loates Lane, between Manfield and and Freeman Hardy Willis, was once a main track to places east of Watford hamlet. Future development may envelope this historic lane.   *p.84, 129 b*

Just this side of Marks and Spencer's is a much-altered three-storey Georgian town house, No. 97. It was the house and shop of Mr. David Downer where his son Frederick started his photographic career. Premises to the rear, No. 3 Loates Lane, later became Frederick's studio and, later still, the 'Watford Engraving Company Limited'. The property is listed Grade II.   *p.96 b*

Ratners No. 92; Millets, ex-'King's Head', No. 86, 88.

One Bell, 90 High Street.

Market Place; redevelopment of this stretch has retained both sites and approximate sizes of buildings as changes have occurred. The 'closed' shop was Dixon's (electrical goods) before their move along the road to Buck's /Palmer's premises. Shortly after this photograph, Finlay's closed.

Market Place pedestrian precinct.

p. 261t

Fisher's building still stands but the Rose & Crown Hotel has been replaced by a Boot's store, itself replacing Timothy Whites and Taylors (which used to be opposite) after moving from the corner of Queens Road.

Market Street corner, comparison to the early bus of 1906.   *p.117*

Charter Place facelift

A CONFIDENTIAL report has recommended Charter Place shopping precinct be refurbished by Mars 1 developers Capital and Counties who are part South African owned.

The outdated appearance of Charter Place will look even worse against Mars 1 when it is built and Watford Council's original plans were for another developer to undertake a revamp which is likely to cost about £20-million.

But it is understood that a report which consultants Hillier Parker have written for the council recommends Capital and Counties undertake the work and take over the precinct's management.

The report has gone before two council committees which have been held in private. A decision is due to be made at a full council meeting on November 10.

The Chairman of Watford Council's Development and Planning Committee and Mars 1 Special Committee said there are "a number of options" open to them over Charter Place but he denounced calls to shun Capital and Counties because of their South African connections.

"We are forbidden to speculate on whether the refurbishers will be Capital and Counties or someone similar but it is our duty to look at the best deal for ratepayers," he said.

"A bank loan to the council for £20-million would mean us taking all the risks and a colossal debt for ratepayers.

WO October, 1986

Life of MARS 1

THE £100-million MARS 1 shopping complex will have to be revamped within 15 years, the chairman of the special committee on the development admitted this week.

Councillor Les Cox said Watford Council was considering options on the refurbishment of Charter Place which would be too costly for the council to carry out on its own.

"We have to accept that we, like other authorities, have to re-vamp precincts every so often. We are looking at 10 to 15 years life for any centre," he said.

WO October, 1986

● *Charter Place market has more than 300 stalls of 6ft length. They are let on a daily basis, singly or in multiples, at a rent of £10 per 6ft per market day. There are also fifteen special-purpose fish and meat stalls.*

At the turn of the century stall rent in the market place was 4d. and in 1928 5/-. (s.170)

Entrance to Charter Place, left, from the High Street.

Palmers, ex-Bucks of p.54—Supersnaps of this photograph is the yard entrance of 1872; the Wimpy, by twist of fate, a modern eating house, in place of Buck's ballroom and restaurant. (Court 6, Edlin's Yard.)   *p.54, 193*

When the Gaumont was built Buck's garage, on this site, was moved to the rear. This parade of shops is built on what was more or less the Gaumont/Odeon forecourt.   *p. 203t*

Palace Theatre among the best

THE WAY has been paved to develop Watford Place Theatre's reputation as one of the most innovative and exciting repertory theatres in the country says civic theatre trust chairman Veronica Conlon.

In the 1985/6 annual report she notes that attendances have been extremely good for both new plays and international ones, with Toys in the Attic even playing a Sunday performance.

Councillor Conlon has taken over as chairman following the death of Councillor Arthur Reynolds last summer.

"The Palace Theatre's already high reputation has been reinforced both locally and nationally through extremely good press and other media coverage and is seen to be one of the most exciting theatres in the country," Councillor Conlon states in the report.

The theatre received £148,000 subsidy from Watford Borough Council and £101,500 from the Arts Council during the year. Other money came from Watford Parish Council (£300) and Hertsmere Borough Council (£250).

WO October, 1986

The old single-storey shops on the corner of Clarendon Road have given way to a large new complex of shops.   *p. 316t*

End of concrete . . .

Clarendon Road Corner has been untidy and under-developed ever since Dr. Brett's estate was sold; now the corner is developed. With an excess of trees and street furniture in the old road it may be thought that the street is over-cluttered; be that as it may, there is no shadow of doubt that the new structure continues the improvements which have taken place during the past few years.

For many years one-storey shops occupied the corner. Now the new structure, designed to be in accord with current architectural fashion and identifiable with trends already apparent in the 1930's, blends in well with adjacent buildings. This is also true of four new development in Clarendon Road, the Court House, Station Road, and the new block of shops on the Gaumont/Odeon site. Two smaller office blocks in the Bridle Path area are similarly brick clad. The Junction Station, though not brick-faced, is sympathetically faced in warm-coloured pre-cast cladding.

In the distance, Upton Road, now renamed Exchange Road, crosses the pedestrian precinct by means of a flyover.   *p. 91, 128*

The pond: gone is the horse and cart access, gone are the railings which once complete enclosed it. On the left Cakebread Robey's ironmongery had given way to 'The Oliver', in turn closed and refitting. A 'super-loo' beyond the Pond, right-hand side.   *p.127*

Twin-town mayors made freemen

THE MAYORS of Watford's twin towns in France and Germany were made Freemen of the Borough on Saturday in a ceremony that was marred by controversy over a defeated Labour proposal to include jailed South African Nelson Mandela.

The freeman-making ceremony opened to the pop song "I want to know what love is" played by the Civic Organist.

The Chief Executive read the Resolution passed by Watford Council on August 18 admitting Herr Jockel Fuchs, Mayor of the German town of Mainz, to Honourary Freeman.

Council Leader Fred Hodgson said Herr Fuchs had supported the aims of the town friendship movement for the 21 years that he had been Mayor.

"Herr Fuchs is Mainz's second most famous son," he said. "In a town survey he came second only to Gutenburg."

Mr. Hodgson said the twinning of both towns has displayed 30 years of friendship which was forged in difficult times following the war, and Mainz has been a centre of the peace movement in Germany since.

Herr Fuchs then assumed his robe, signed the Freeman's Roll and received a casket containing a scroll bearing the Resolution.

In his response, Herr Fuchs paid tribute to Edward Amey, the Watford mayor who made the first contacts with Herr Fuchs' predecessor in a Mainz wine-cellar in 1955, a meeting that led to the link being made a year later.

He referred to the appropriateness of the twinning. Both were printing towns, Mainz being where Johannes Gutenburg invented moveable type.

"I am proud of the great honour accorded to me. It is not just for me but for all the people of Mainz and I should like to extend greetings to all

the citizens of our twin town Watford," he said.

Councillor John Watts then welcomed Monsieur Yves Saudmont, Mayor of the French town Nanterre, praising his enthusiasm and determination for the twinning movement.

In his response Monsieur Saudmont said 25 years after its creation the link was in "very good health."

Mr. Saudmont paid tribute to the late Councillor Arthur Reynolds and finished by saying: "Long life to Watford, long life to the friendship between Watford and Nanterre."

The ceremony ended with the Macebearer taking the Mace, after which the company was played out to the same tune—a favourite of Watford Mayor Paul Harrison.

WO October, 1986

A few minutes before 11 am, Rememberance Sunday, November 1985   *p.47 c, 190 b, 194*

Closed and derelict before demolition, only the original central block of the Peace Memorial Hospital remains at the time of writing, while its ultimate fate continues to be debated. Having served the community well for over 60 years, the site and buildings were inadequate for future needs. *p.163 t*

Goodbye Peace

The Peace Memorial Hospital, Rickmansworth Road, was reduced to brick and rubble as it was demolished to make way for a long-stay geriatric hospital. The buildings had been empty since May 1985 when the hospital services were transferred to the Shrodells site.

WO March, 1986

Proud of our new hospital

Dear Sir,

I WAS sorry to see the letter from an old Watfordian in last week's paper, where she deprecated the loss of the old Watford Peace Memorial Hospital. I wonder if she ever worked or stayed there as a patient.

I, for one, am most grateful for the new wing at Shrodells. It may look like an air terminal but then it has to cater for so many of us.

Having the misfortune to fall ill recently I had occasion to use the Watford Hospital service. I found it excellent. All my appointments were kept to time and I was met with great civility and cheerfulness at every port of call.

My stay in the Flaunden Ward was an education in how nursing should be. Nothing was too much trouble. There were many serious cases there but everyone was given the utmost attention. I don't think you could do better anywhere.

Six patients to a ward section was very spacious. (How many to a ward at the Peace?) We had the radio service, the papers and people to do our shopping. We had visits from the vicar and the priest. We also had the most wonderful food which was always good and hot. The soups were really something special.

Though I met many patients in the new Shrodells who had stayed at the Peace on previous hospitalisations not one would like to go back there. We were all too delighted with our luck.

Though it is often pleasant to look back on old times we do tend to gloss over the bad things that happened. I hope the lady will never be ill but I would advise her to stay where she is.

There are many good things about Watford and the Shrodells is one of them.

Jeffrey Higgins, Bushey.

WO October, 1986

U.S. twin town

WATFORD NOW has a twin town in the United States.

Wilmington, Delaware, became the town's fourth twin when Mayor, Councillor Paul Harrison, put pen to paper to sign the agreement.

The historic agreement was signed before the annual Mayor's Reception at the Town Hall, Watford. Appropriately, our colonial cousins were guests of honour at the celebration supper.

For good measure, representatives from the Russian Embassy were also among the guests, representing the people of Novgorod, Watford's twin-town behind the Iron Curtain.

Watford is also twinned with Mainz, Germany and Nanterre, France.

The theme of the evening's speeches was the twinning issue and international understanding and peace.

Before Mr. Harrison spoke, the Wilmington delegation had already expressed their views of the importance of the twinning agreement and of the strong similarities and relationships between the two towns.

WO October, 1986

Gentleman crossing the northbound carriageway of Rickmansworth Road stands in the approximate position of the Park Gates. *p.86*

Corner of Shepherds Road. *p.86*

338

Scene of traffic jams for years, this sign heralds false optimism—there is no four-lane continuation, the St. Albans route is a three mile detour; the direction London M1 misleading. The reality is the jam at North Watford's bottleneck by Leavesden Road—mercifully lessened upon the opening of the M25.

p.86 b, 185 b

Help!

A RECORD 34,500 people sought help at Watford Citizens' Advice Bureau last year, including a staggering 4,361—28 per cent up on the previous year—inquiring about social security.

According to their annual report, Watford CAB staff saw clients at the rate of 137 a day or 21 each hour or one every three minutes.

The report just published shows that in addition to inquiries related to social services there were 3,709 concerned with employment and 2,991 came under the family and personal heading.

Carol Firman, deputy organiser, in her report says the main problem clients are experiencing in the area of social security is severe delay in assessment and progression of claims by the Department of Health and Social Security.

Far from being a temporary situation it appears to be worsening by the day causing considerable distress to claimants.

WO November, 1986

Cassiobridge Lodge, Gade Avenue.   *p.86*

Traffic peace a welcome relief

A HUGE sigh of relief is being breathed by residents of Garston's traffic-choked Kingswood estate following the opening of part of the M25 motorway last Friday.

They say life close to the congested A405 has been unbearable during the last year and are only thankful that the motorway has opened before one of their children is killed.

Forced to put up with a constant trail of high-speed cars and lorries during the many months of construction work, they have also been sickened by noise and fumes.

But now the opening of the new five-mile motorway stretch between Micklefield Green and Bricket Wood has left the A405 virtually empty of vehicles.

"You could say that a weight has been lifted from our shoulders," said Kingswood resident Mrs. Jean James.

Neighbour Mr. Laurant Parent of Meadow Road, who narrowly avoided a serious car accident on the A405 three months ago, said: "The traffic used to be shocking but the other day I went across for my usual walk and it was like a ghost town."

Mr. Fred Lambert, caretaker of Kingsway Junior School, said: "The road was like a race track and every child was in danger every minute of the day. The cars used to do speeds of 70 and 80 mph but you could almost push a pram down the middle of the road now."

Acting Sgt. Peter Brooks of Watford traffic police said the new motorway stretch was busy but accident-free, the only trouble-spots being at the northbound interchange with the M1 and at the eastern margin of the new section at Bricket Wood.

"The A405 is a ghost road by comparison. It has been virtually dead," he added.

Problems faced by people living on the Kingswood estate were particularly severe because of the area's location sandwiched between the A405 and the busy St. Albans Road, with access to and from their homes almost impossible during peak traffic hours.

WO October, 1986

Scammell seal huge MoD order

WORKERS at troubled Watford truck builder Scammell have got a £120m Christmas cracker from the army.

Just two weeks after the Leyland specialist vehicle maker announced 100 redundancies and short-time working in the face of falling orders the Defence Ministry has awarded them a massive order for 1,500 ammunition carriers.

"It's the best Christmas present we could have," said one Scammell worker, summing up the jubilation of the work-force.

WO November, 1986

Scammells to close

NEWS Of the Scammell closure has been received with surprise and anger by workers and union chiefs who dismiss claims made by Watford MP Tristan Garel-Jones that there are enough jobs in the town to cope with the 650 redundancies.

The mood outside the factory gates was pessimistic this week, with many workers fearing the Leyland-Daf merger would mean the end of their working lives.

"For the ordinary man working on the shop floor who is semi-skilled it is going to be very difficult to find work in this area," said chassis frame driller Andy Stevens.

"It's disgusting. We thought we were going to be saved," said rectification fitter John Bisley. "There are some men who have been made redundant recently and they have applied for jobs and they can't find work."

The decision was also attacked by Peter Sweeting, joint shop steward for hourly-paid workers at the plant, who said it was nonsense to suggest that men who had been building trucks for 30 or 40 years would find new jobs in Watford.

WO February, 1987

Queens Road 'A5'—old site of Mr. Morley's Post Office; next door Sainsbury's supermarket—old Technical School/Library/School of Music.   p.112 tr, 152 r, 283 tl

Queens Road, shops opposite Trewins, in the year of trading before closure for MARS site development.   1986

Queens Road pedestrian underpass.

Queens Road, looking to Watford, across road, Allied Carpets, site of former Wesleyan Congregational Church.   p.180 tl

One-time horse-trough at the junction of Queens and Sutton road, dedicated to the memory of soldiers of the district who died in the Boer War (1899-1902). Erected by Mrs. W. R. Woolrych, of Croxley House, in 1903.

Queens Road; in the distance, Sainsbury's occupying the old Library/School of Music/Technical School site. On the right, Maitland's early premises, No. 40, still remains between the extended Trewin's.

p. 112tr, 305t

Queens Road

Queens Road (first called Queen's-street) was opened up c1861/62 leading towards the railway station, but for more than ten years went no further than Loates Lane (modern junction with Radlett Road). A narrow but very busy thoroughfare, this short stretch (previous page, top), has, on the right, housed a Post Office, Mr. Peacock's printing office from which was published the first Watford Observer in 1863, and a few doors along, the purpose-built Library and School of Science and Art (1874) (p.112). The library lasted until 1928 when it was moved to its present position. The old library buildings then became the 'Technical School'.

Vandals' Paradise

QUEENS Road pedestrian precinct, once a busy and thriving Watford shopping area, has become a desert of boarded-up windows, graffiti and torn posters, as traders have closed up and moved out in preparation for the Mars 1 shopping-development.

Michael Clewer, who runs one of the four remaining businesses, is preparing to follow suit. However, 12 years after opening in Queens Road, he is leaving with a bad taste in the mouth.

In keeping with other remaining businesses, we've had our shop windows smashed by mindless hooligans," he explains.

On two nights in early July, vandals smashed the windows of County Bedrooms, Abbey National Building Society and Habitat. On the first occasion, seven store-front windows belonging to Trewin Brothers, part of the John Lewis Group, were attacked.

There is general agreement among the four remaining businesses in Queens Road that one solution would be an increased police presence at night.

A police spokesman comments: "Queens Road is patrolled regularly during the night. However, we are undermanned and given the resources available to us, putting additional officers on duty would mean neglecting other streets."

Mr Clewer feels that crimes of this type are not connected with drunkenness. "In the case of Abbey National, there was insufficient time to have new glass fitted before the criminals struck again," he says.

The total damage inflicted on the four premises was in the region of £6,000.

Focus July, 1987

Queens Road, 'turned round' house behind lamp is No. 163, identifies picture on page 148. Demolished a few months after this photograph for development of six 1-bedroomed flats.

Trade Union Hall, Woodford Road. Built 1931; turned into a billiard/snooker hall. 1986

Watford Junction, the new station is finished, offices complete and to let.

p.76 t, 311

Toilets priority for BR planners

Dear Sir,

RECENT history informs us that there were once open sewers to be seen in the streets of cities and towns in this country, but thankfully this unhealthy and offensive state of affairs no longer exists.

This may indeed be true for the streets of Britain but it is regretably not true for British Railways. Surely it is time that it was!

The stretch of line which is of particular concern to me, as a commuter, is the line between Watford Junction and Euston, which is particularly "unpleasant" on the approach to and even into the station itself.

Never mind Advanced Passenger Trains; how about civilised passenger toilets?

R. S. Dodwell, Abbots Langley.

WO February, 1986

Who's in Charge on the Buses?

THE Government is proposing to make the most significant change in 50 years to the way public transport is run and financed in this country.

The proposals which were published in the transport Bill in February of this year are complex and their implications far reaching. From the reaction by local authorities, public transport operators and passenger representatives they have also proved to be controversial. In brief the Bill proposes:

● To deregulate public transport by abolishing the licensing of bus services. In future anybody with the appropriate driving licence and observing certain minimum safety standards will be able to run a bus service wherever and whenever he or she pleases.

● To privatise the National Bus Company and to break it up into smaller companies. This will almost certainly affect the largest operator in the Watford area, London Country Bus Services Ltd.

● To introduce competitive tendering for all subsidised bus services and to prevent the payment of subsidy in any other way. All but two local routes in Watford receive some element of subsidy from the ratepayers to ensure the present level of service.

WOT 1985

Green is go

GREEN double-decker buses will replace the red ones currently operating on London Regional Transport's 142 bus route from Brent Cross to Watford from Saturday, June 21. The change follows London Country Buses taking over the route on contract.

WO June, 1986

Watford Junction, the new station under construction, June 1985

142 Bus terminus in Woodford Road. Last 'red' bus 21st June, 1986.

Old station building adjacent to Woodford Road has been cleared and turned into mini-car park and mini-bus stop/station.

New stock on the electric line to Euston, against the background of the new station building, the offices now let as the Headquarters of Ford- Iveco.

Departure time for a north-bound Inter-City train.

Track maintenance, August 1986, lengths of rail replaced and re-welded. North of Watford Junction.

In the background, ex-Cassiobury Mills, now Fishburns; across the tracks of the railway, the old station master's house, derelict.   1985

'Winos', hazard to users of St. Albans Road pedestrian underpass.   1984

Salters Almshouses, Church Road.   *p.46*   1985

Cassio College, once the site of Shirley House School.   1985

Terrace Gardens, one of the oldest roads of early Watford of the 1840's.   1982

Service entrances to Homebase, petrol stations and Fishburns are the cause of frequent accidents.   1986

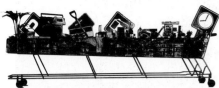

Fishburn plans to quit Watford

A move is in the offing for Fishburn Printing Inks, Watford. And while nothing has been settled yet, Fishburn is looking closely at two sites, one in the north and one in Sussex.

'We have been investigating the possibility of a move for some time,' says Paul Covell, head of oil inks sales, 'We looked at alternatives like Milton Keynes and others, but there's no decision yet.'

The company is waiting for approval of development plans from BASF's board before pressing on. When Fishburn bought Croda last year, it had planned to redevelop Croda's nearby Harefield site. But Fishburn was itself the victim of a takeover by BASF, and the plans fell through.

Printing World June, 1987

One of the earliest industrial sites—Cassiobury Mills, once a large and thriving sawmills and builder's merchants—Turner's, manufacturing croquet sets, cricket bails and wickets; house and building timberware; through a wide variety of uses and for around 50 years, Fishburn Printing Inks, recently absorbed by BASF Inks and Coatings. Behind Fishburn's, the Junction Station; tall building to the right, Star House, Clarendon Road.   1986

Fishburn looks to the West

Favoured spot for Fishburn when it moves from Watford is Slinford in Gloucestershire *(sic)*. This has the advantage over the other possibilities because parent group BASF already has a site there.

The decision is not expected until the end of the year, and any move would not take place until three years after that.

Printing World July, 1987

Odhams ready for summer

Work is nearing completion on the first presses being installed at Odhams, Watford for the printing of the Daily Mirror.

A team of German engineers from MAN Roland are working round the clock on the installation of three two-unit Colorman 35s, printing on a 1.6 metre web. Sources within the factory say that the fitting will be completed in about two weeks, with a little longer needed for setting the electronic controls. Experimental print runs will commence in four weeks.

Printing World June, 1987

St. Albans Road, left-hand side, ex-site of Police Station—p.243; Fishburn's warehouse c1970; New Hertford House, No. 96 c1965; Fishburn's offices replacing Railway Cottages, c1965. In the distance, Dean Park Hotel. On the right, Leavesden Road, the 'Stag' and the 'Leviathan'. *p.243 t, 287 c, 316 b,* 1986

The Guard/sentry hut on the Balmoral Estate, once the sentry point to the munitions works.

Sandown Road, looking towards what was once the premises of Vi-Cocoa.
p.101 br

St. Albans Road, remaining buildings of 'Red Lion' Well's Brewery, behind Hille House.

St Albans Road, Dean Park Hotel (renamed from Caledonian); Nos. 26 & 24 alongside sold and pending hotel redevelopment.

Modern counterpart to turn-of-century photograph on page 103, the parades of buildings to the railway bridge are little changed.

At the extreme left, the 'Chosen' car sales office-- once part of the original 1837 station building. The tyre and exhaust centre, closed, was once site of the North Watford Coliseum/Plaza and upon this site was the first Clarendon Hotel.

Watford's Chinese Takeaway

WATFORD made a triumphant return to Vicarage Road yesterday from China with club secretary Eddie Plumley declaring: "That was the best tour we've been on."

The Hornets crowned a magnificent two-week stay in China by winning the Great Wall Cup, defeating the China National side 2-0 after extra-time in the final at the Shanghai Stadium.

The tour was a personal triumph for striker Luther Blissett who scored five goals en route to the final and was presented with the leading marksmans award. Young Gary Porter also collected an award after being voted the player of the tournament.

The Hornets finished the five-match campaign unbeaten and goalkeeper Steve Sherwood did not concede a goal. "He was not voted the goalkeeper of the tournament which amazed us," said Plumley, "so Elton bought a trophy of his own to present to Steve."

WO June, 1987

St. Albans Road.

p.243 b, 269 c, 290 tr

Town Hall underpass; eight-lane road relieves traffic at the Town Hall crossroads but not at lower Rickmansworth Road or in North Watford. Since the opening of the M25 this road is lightly used in the daytime. The plan for relief road from near the North Watford Plaza site to A405 has yet to mature.

p.157tr, 308br

Modern counterpart to the 'Firewatchers' on page 222. The 'Spread Eagle', 'King's Head', Cawdell's, Kingham's -- all gone. In the place of Kingham's is British Home Stores and of Cawdell's, Charter Place of which the concrete roof occupies the foreground. In the distance, left of centre, the pair of chimneys is of the electricity generating station; right of centre is the Watford General Hospital.

Charter Place ground-level mall.

Charter Place Market, where a stall rent can exceed £13,000 pa.

Sutton Road multi-storey car park.

George Street, sheltered homes for the elderly

p. 302t

A stone's throw from the Market Place stands the Parish Church, centre of the town's life and activities for hundreds of years. Few traces of earlier life remain; the tree at the extreme right marks the spot of the 'Fire Engine House' and first National School, later Almondswick when it was the office of the Registry of Births, Marriages and Deaths; opposite the entrance to the Church once stood the workhouse; beyond the Church at the righthand side may be seen the Free School and next to it the offices which replaced St. Mary's Church Hall.   p.53

Smaller buses travel further

A new minibus service will link Watford town centre, Holywell estate and the Radlett Road estate.

The W10 route will have a more frequent service using the smaller buses.

There will be another new service bringing workers at Watford Business Park to and from the town centre at lunchtime.

The slight revamp is part of the new system currently coming into force with the county council appointing operators to loss-making routes by competitive tender.

WO October, 1986

£250,000 repairs

ONE of Watford's oldest buildings is to be restored at a cost of quarter of a million pounds.

Watford Parish Church is one of only two Grade 1 listed buildings in Watford but a survey last year revealed the roof and organ of St. Mary's needs extensive restoration, which will cost £250,000.

Already parishioners have committed themselves to £140,000 and the balance will come from public fund-raising events.

The building has stood in the centre of Watford for more than seven centuries, and although maintenance and general repairs have been carried out over the years, this will be a major restoration project.

Some of the roof's oak timbers are infested with death watch beetle, parapet stonework in the tower has begun to crumble, and parts of the old lead roof have had to be replaced. In the north transept some of the roof timbers have sagged causing the supporting walls to bow outwards.

Already steel pins have been resin-grouted into the timber joints to prevent further movement and to do this, most of the 2,440 organ pipes have had to be removed. The organ, containing parts dating back to 1871, has to be cleaned and rewired.

WO March, 1987

The Essex Chapel 1986; the family tombs long since removed and the Chapel in regular use.   p.115 bl

New Street, formerly entrance to Ballard's Buildings.   p.161

The 'Stanley Rous' grandstand in last stages of construction.   1986   The 'Cottage Hospital', Vicarage Road.   p. 54

Sir Stanley Rous

LOYALTY is a rare quality in the modern game of football, but Sir Stanley Rous was one of the sport's greatest ever servants.

Right up to his death last week at the age of 91, Sir Stanley's passion for soccer was as strong as ever, taking him across the world to the World Cup Finals in Mexico.

That he should still have been travelling the globe with youthful enthusiasm is a tribute to the man who began his career as a master at Watford Grammar School and finished as Honoury Life President of FIFA.

He was born the son of a Suffolk grocer in April 1895 and was later educated at Exeter University, but it was in Watford that his career in soccer began.

While working in Watford, Sir Stanley was recommended to become a linesman on the Football League list by a director of QPR.

He soon graduated to the job of referee and in 1934 achieved the honour of refereeing an FA Cup Final—the first one at Wembley.

A week later he was secretary of the FA and his influence on the national game began to take shape. He redrafted the rules of football, which were promptly adopted and not altered again until 1966, and he devised the diagonal system of refereeing which is still used today. He also organised the first international referees' course and became a founder member of UEFA.

In 1943 Sir Stanley took over at the FA, but his interest in the development of international refereeing and in youth soccer remained undiminished.

Sir Stanley's amazing career was crowned in 1962 by his appointment as president of FIFA, the governing body of international football.

He continued to serve football and wherever he travelled was respected and admired for his integrity and sense of fair play.

Six years ago he became a vice-president of Watford Football Club and was a regular spectator at Vicarage Road.

WO June, 1986

In a brief ceremony on Saturday, Watford FC Chairman Elton John unveiled a plaque naming the new stand "The Sir Stanley Rous Grandstand" after the club's former vice-president and famous football administrator, who died during the summer.

WO October, 1986

Hospital's computers speed it up

STAFF at Watford General Hospital will no longer have to rifle through files in cupboards and cabinets to get the vital information they need on patients.

Manual systems have been replaced with new computer arrangements, said David Kemsley, South West Hertfordshire Health Authority. The new technology will mean a fair amount of procedural change within the hospital.

Medical information on patients will be obtainable at the press of a button. "It is going to be much easier to identify whether a patient has been in hospital before, and where his notes are." Mr. Kemsley said.

New technology is being implemented across the board within the region, and Watford is among the first half dozen hospitals to be provided with it.

For a couple of years until the system was switched on in May, it was unofficially in use so that staff could get accustomed to it.

Accuracy has improved over manual indexes, and maintenance is easier. There is improved staff productivity, and the changes involved for all patients when a general practitioner moves can be recorded automatically, with higher speed and accuracy.

Also in the planning stage is a system that will reduce the time patients have to wait for attention. A pilot scheme using one clinic should start in early December.

WO June, 1986

£1m appeal

HARD on the heels of the Baby Watch campaign launched at the maternity unit two weeks ago to raise up to £250,000 for new updated equipment, Watford General Hospital will be appealing for a massive £1m in January for another project.

The hospital wants a Computerised Tomography Scanner—a machine which uses X-rays linked to a computer to put cross-sections of a patient's body onto a television screen—and the £1m will cover the cost of the equipment and provide enough money to invest for future running costs.

In the last year about 600 of Watford General Hospital's patients have had scans at Mount Vernon or Northwick Park Hospitals and according to a report which will be before Friday's meeting of the South West Hertfordshire Health Authority, as many as 1,000 more could have benefited from this equipment.

WO October, 1986

How "Shrodells" Got Its Name

Sir,—I am told that the numerous references to Shrodells in your columns this week is causing considerable comment and curiosity among those of your readers who are ignorant of the origin of this charming old name, and I am glad to be able to enlighten them.

When working at my history of the Parish Church, I came across an ancient list of "gardens, meads, etc., in Watford Town" and among them I saw Shrodells. As this word is not recorded in any dialect dictionary, nor in any collection of archaic words, we may safely regard it as having belonged exlusively to Watford, and it was undoubtedly associated with the adjacent woods of Whippendell.

When I was asked to suggest a name for 60, Vicarage-road (something descriptive of that locality in olden days), I was glad to recall Shrodells from the echoes of the past; and it is pleasant to know that this long-forgotten name will survive among the annals of Watford when many other links with the past have been completely destroyed.

Yours, etc.,
HELEN RUDD

WHP (April, 1932)

Desirability

"I leave Luton at about 7 to 7.15 and if I get to work by 9 o'clock I am lucky. There's a holdup, usually, at Junction 9—the Redbourn turn off—but no matter which way—and I must have tried all permutations—there's no easy way to get here.

"Move? I'd love to, but the house prices are way beyond my reach; going home isn't so bad—it takes an average of three-quarters of an hour."

Shop worker, 4th December, 1986

"The Junction's new then, what was there before, how did people get to London? I'm new here; only been here a month, just moved from London you see. I like it—Watford's nice and interesting, not crowded."

Lady misdirected by bus driver, 4th December, 1986

A sense of peace pervades what once was a scene of despair as 'down and outs' and the needy were obliged to turn to the workhouse for help. No. 60 Vicarage Road.   1986

Bradford Wing—geriatric unit of Shrodell's.

Ninety-nine years ago the state of St. Andrew's district footpaths was a cause of complaint (p.63). Youngsters, if they trip and fall, are rarely hurt. It is the elderly who, as always, are at risk, particularly in wet and windy weather. Closure of Langley Road Post Office necessitates 'Nascot Village' residents facing such hazards, which are by no means confined to this stretch of path. A slip or fall can result in hospital treatment for fractures or broken bones.

Watford's new General Hospital in Vicarage Road adjoining the Shrodell's site and extending to Willow Lane. In the foreground of the new building is the old 'H' block of Shrodell's.   1986

Beechen Grove, YMCA in background. The road is to an approximate line of Derby Road, passing over the demolished site of Grevilles, ex-Post Office, and the position of photograph of Mail Coach.

p.64

Estcourt Road, in the distance the YMCA residential block at Charter Place.

Clarendon Road, from left to right, Melton House, Star House, Nos. 73 and 75.

Clarendon Road, looking towards the Junction. p. 244b

Exchange Road, in the distance the Holy Rood Church and on the right, in Cambridge Road, the Watford Islamic Mosque.

Merton Road, Empire/ABC cinema, renamed Cannon shortly after the photograph was taken.

Market Street

p.253 t

Business is booming

WORK has started on two new complexes at the Watford Business Park.

The Carroll Group of Companies, in partnership with Watford Borough Council, has begun its latest phase of construction work to develop Centre Two and Centre Three.

The development is scheduled to be completed by the end of March next year, expecting to attract a square foot rent of more than £5.

The two buildings will be the latest addition to Carroll's £30-million business park. Centre Four was opened earlier this year by the then Mayor of Watford Mrs. Irene Tunstall Dunn.

Centre Four—two industrial units of 12,400 square feet each—has now been fully let. The first unit was taken by Horsell Graphic Industries which deals in the storage and distribution of printing equipment such as ink and paper.

The second building has now become headquarters for the rapidly expanding company Maxon Europe.

Maxon, originally based in Tolpits Lane, specialises in the manufacture of telecommuni-

cations equipment such as radio-pagers and short wave radios.

Letting agents Stimpsons are confident that the two new phases of the business park will be just as popular as Centre Four.

"The demand for this area is tremendous. Primarily it is because of the M25 but the site is also close to Watford and in an area which is becoming very established.

"The road links are also excellent," said Stimpsons' Mr. Mike Peters.

WO December, 1986

Postmen on strike

A STRIKE by post office workers at the main sorting office in Watford caused havoc for people all over Hertfordshire this week.

No post was delivered or sorted from Tuesday morning and thousands of firms were deprived of vital letters as boxes were sealed up throuhout the area.

More than 700 workers from the Union of

Communications Workers walked out of the main sorting office in Ascot Road on Tuesday. They were led by the early shift at 7 am but afternoon and late shift workers joined them later along with cleaning and catering staff.

A spokesmen for the UCW said workers all over the country were entitled to the bonus but local management had told them they did not have the authority to give it.

Mr. Brownfield admitted that there had been a huge increase in letters dealt with by Watford since the sorting office at Welwyn Garden City was closed last year but 140 new staff had also been taken on, he said.

"The letters we are dealing with have virtually doubled but our bonuses haven't. It is all to do with over-staffing. Members should not be penalised for what is the management's fault," said a union spokesman.

WO March 1987

Early stages of 'industrial unit' construction at the Croxley Centre.

1986

'Five Arches', to the left, beyond the arch was once Watford's public bathing place until closure in 1936. Through these arches was projected in 1928 a new road to connect the then new By-pass with the High Street.

p.34, 121b, 174b

Water Lane, the George Stephenson College on the right.

p.105b, 258b

We want M1 Link constructed soon

Dear Sir,

MAY I correct what would appear to be a contradictory statement on the M1 Link road in last Friday's Watford Observer.

Watford Labour party, and its representatives on the Borough Council, have fully supported, and have pressed vigorously, for the early construction of this road.

As chairman of the Highways committee I have always been aware of the full backing of the Watford Labour Party, not to mention that of both Watford and Bushey Conservatives.

The road when constructed is expected to bring reduced traffic flows in Aldenham Road and St. Albans Road, and to return Gladstone Road to a quiet residential street again. Tudor Ward, Central Ward and, indeed, the Aldenham Road area of Bushey North will all receive improved environmental conditions.

There is no doubt that the road will have an impact on the so-called Colne Valley, but with the construction will come the opportunity for the introduction of the long-awaited Linear Park and, who knows, perhaps Councillor Colne can be constructive and persuade his council to tidy up the derelict land between the river and Park Avenue/Greatham Road.

Councillor L. T. Hughes, Chairman, Highways Committee, Watford Borough Council.

WO February, 1987

February 1987; for the second year, plans of the proposed M1 link road and the West Watford link are on view so that the public may express opinions. George Stephenson College.

Watford's main listed buildings

Jackson, Jeweller's, The Parade.   *p.91*

Monmouth House, The Parade.   *p.92 bl*

Little Cassiobury, Hempstead Road.

Frogmore House, High Street.

The 'Free School' building.

The Bedford Almshouses, Church Street.

Part of the 1837 Railway Station buildings, St Albans Road.

355

In the letters and packet sorting section two lines of operators are 'coding' the letters so that subsequent sorting may be mechanical. In the background are bays and racks for hand sorting of packets.

p.121

The miracle of the Post

Not long after the turn of the century a lady wrote on a postcard, "as the day is fine I will see you outside this building this afternoon." Within two or three hours it would have been delivered and the appointment kept. Of course, the address, at St. Johns Road, was quite near the sorting office in Queens Road. The new streets off Leavesden Road were not yet all built and most of the Bradshaw and Sandringham area was green fields, in other words the catchment and delivery area was small.

Today, at the Watford sorting office a fleet of vans and lorries help pick up and deliver, not a few thousand, not twenty or thirty thousand, but a staggering half-million letters PER DAY. To help deal with this amount such items as date cancelling are conveyor belt automatic; more than 20 highly skilled operators scan addresses at a rate of some 2,000 per hour, and 'code' the envelopes so that further sorting, into areas right down to a postman's round, is as automatic as possible.

Lack of postcode makes more manual attention necessary as do odd-sized envelopes. Letters and packets are despatch-timed to connect with mail trains; parcels are handled by road trunker services. To maintain legal driving times containers are taken to 'swap' points, the outward bound drivers do a 'container swap' at this halfway point and return with an 'inward' load.

To deliver letters and small packets some 120 roundsmen cover the Watford area.

The Ascot Road sorting office is one of 30 Parcel Concentration Offices in the UK and is responsible for all parcels posted and delivered in Hertfordshire. Watford depot's average weekly total of parcels processed is 160,000. The staff numbers around 900; the transport fleet numbers some 250 vehicles, from small vans to 40ft articulated trailers.

To deal efficiently with the flood of letters and parcels, ebbing and flowing every day, demands a highly complex and efficient organisation.

Mr. Morley, Postmaster of a Victorian era, would surely gaze with wondering eyes were he able to return . . .

First-class mail has priority and the 'dot-coded' envelopes are electronically sorted into 150 out-going destinations. Later, these machines will be used to sort incoming mail for local destinations.

Parcels are almost completely untouched by hand. Emptied from collection containers, parcels are fed by conveyor belt to the sorting point where they are faced address up.

The parcels are sorted electronically, travelling upon an endless belt of tipable platforms . . .

. . . until being tipped into a chute leading to a destination container. July, 1987

Colne Springs

The Celts are usually accorded blame for introducing Iron Age man to real ale. For two thousand years he diligently perfected the art of brewing in the home. By the seventeenth century many innkeepers had set up their own operation on the premises for direct sale. The earliest known large scale common brewer, selling to other public houses in Watford, was Nicholas Colbourne (died 1630). His nephew continued until 1662.

The first John Dyson was the son of a maltster and grandson of a miller-baker. He commenced brewing in Dyson's Yard, off New Street, in about 1750. He was succeeded by a son and a grandson of the same name, and the second John Dyson bought a mansion with attached grounds at 194 High Street, and moved his brewery behind it in 1812. The house had been built by a Londoner, Edward Dawson, for his wife, in 1775. The third John Dyson extended the brewery and by his time the family owned or rented a large number of pubs in the district. This last John Dyson was a bachelor, and his executors sold the brewery, by then called Cannon Brewery, to Joseph Benskin, a retired London publican in partnership with Mr. Bradley, a Watford draper in 1867. Later Bradley dropped out, and after Joseph's death his widow carried on. Later still Benskin's became a limited company, and at the turn of the century rebuilt their premises on a far grander scale. In 1897 Benskin's bought Groome's of Kings Langley. In 1898 they bought Healey's. In 1923 they bought their long-time rival, Sedgwick's. In 1957 they were themselves bought by Ind Coope, and they in turn were part of Allied Lyons by 1963. The name "Benskin" has recently been revived, but the beer comes from Romford. The badge is a pennant.

Samuel Smith, miller at the Grove, in partnership with Robert Shackell, a distiller, bought a disused malthouse and yard at 223 Watford High Street in 1753. Here he started brewing and began to buy up pubs in the district as outlets. When he died his son William continued, but sold out to George Whittingstall, son of a Hitchin miller, in 1790. On George's death in 1822 his brewery went to a cousin, Edmund Fearnley, a cattle dealer, who assumed the surname of Whittingstall. His son George sold the business in 1862 to W. F. Sedgwick, of a local farming family. The brewery was now known as Watford Brewery. Robert Ashby was the manager until 1890 when he retired to be a developer of working class estates in Watford. In 1927 their buildings were converted to maltings and demolished by 1966.

In 1763 Thomas Meadows, a Watford corn dealer, in partnership with Thomas Clutterbuck snr., land agent to the Earl of Essex, bought a small brewery on Stanmore Common. The business expanded under further Clutterbucks, and they had another brewhouse at Hunton Bridge. The business, with 83 pubs, was sold to Cannon Brewery, Clerkenwell, in 1923. In 1930 it merged with Taylor Walker. Ind Coope bought them in 1960. The old brewery still stands on Stanmore Hill.

c1750 Stephen Salter was brewing in Rickmansworth. He was followed by his nephew Samuel who died in 1829, providing free beer in his will! Salter had a partner, Job Woodman of Watford. Another partner, Thomas Fellowes then ran the brewery with William Capel. It continued, as a public company, until 1924 when it and its 76 pubs were bought by Cannon of Clerkenwell. Demolished.

The Groome brewery was started by the Goodwin family in 1720. In 1768 it passed to Thomas Groome. The brewery with 32 pubs was bought by Benskin's in 1897. It was in Kings Langley. A malting remains as a parish room.

Samuel Roate commenced brewing in about 1845 near Watford old railway station, at 147 St. Albans Road, on the corner of the later Church Road. By 1874 Fred Cocks had the business, by then called Victoria Brewery. In 1891 Healey's bought it and brewing ceased. The house remains but the brewhouse has been demolished.

Joseph Healey, a Londoner, was for many years the manager of Whittingstalls. His son George set up in Watford as a grocer and wine merchant, after acting as brewer's clerk to George Whittingstall. It was his son Charles who bought the stable block of the former Watford Place estate in George Street and King Street, and converted it to a brewery in 1852. Colonel Charles Healey sold out to Benskin's in 1898 for a seat on the board. He was son of the founder, who died prematurely in 1863. As Colonel Charles was only 7 at the time his mother ran the business for many years. It was called King Street Brewery. The badge was a primrose.

Ralph Thorpe was a Lincolnshire farmer who settled here in 1889. He bought land in St. Albans Road, and opened his brewery for business in 1890. In 1913 the small brewery was greatly extended, its plant and methods were the most up-to-date in the area. He had acquired 20 pubs by 1925. In 1951 it was bought by Benskin's. Some of the buildings still stand. It was known as Wells Brewery because of the deep wells in the chalk subsoil. The trade mark was a red lion, so sometimes it was called Red Lion Brewery.

Watford lost its reputation as a 'brewing' town, the processes perfected throughout the centuries and the expertise acquired by generations of employees. This labour-intensive industry, like so many others, had become a victim of the age of rationalisation.

An account of the licensed houses closed prior to 1900

The information for this exhaustive account has been drawn from several sources. They are, (1) The survey of Watford Manor in 1605. (2) The return of 1756 billeting facilities for men and horses. (3) The Manorial Records of Watford Manor. (4) Various deeds especially those of the former Sedgwick Brewery. (5) Early directories from 1792 until 1829. These documents are in Herts County Record Office, Guildhall Library, Watford Central Library, Public Record Office Kew, etc. I have also used the findings of the Watford Archaeological Society. In the period for which this information is valid, Watford was governed by the parish vestry and, to a decreasing extent, by the Manorial Court Leet which appointed constables for the 'hamlets' into which the parish was divided. These were Town Hamlet, Cassio Hamlet, Leavesden Hamlet, and Oxhey Hamlet. The High Street was not yet numbered, but I shall use for convenience the numbers given by 1871 and largely still in use today.

Artichoke, later **Hart.** c.1730-c.1800.
This was in a building lately occupied by the Oliver, and before that by Cakebread Robey, whose mock-Tudor showroom superseded the original 18th century house, on the west side of the Pond. A mug from this house is in the museum. In 1756 the landlord was John Crickmore, and there was room for billeting one soldier and stabling two horses.

Six Bells, 100 High Street. c.1700-c.1750.
Little is known of this house, except that it was closed by 1750 when the church peal was increased from six to eight.

Three Horseshoes. 110 High Street.
Even less is known of this which may have been merely the trade sign of the smith who is known to have lived there in the early 18th century. Afterwards it was a private house, later used as a shop. It is now Importers' Coffee Shop.

Maltsters Arms, 120 High Street, 1859-1880
It belonged to the almshouses and was kept by Will Norris. Demolished.

Nags Head, 146 High Street, c.1750-1821.
Now Oscar's coffee and bread shop. In 1756 kept by Edward London who accommodated two men and no horses. In the years up to 1821 when it closed to become the Church Infant School it was kept by Will Kemp, said by Williams to have received bodysnatchers' parcels and to have sent them on to London by carrier. Owned by the Parish Church.

Crooked Billet or **Duke of Cumberland, 164 High Street,** c.1700-c.1800.
Now occupied by Carousel. In 1756 John Doggett had it with room for one guest. It was owned by the parish church and later became a shop.

Tun Inn, 196 High Street, c.1600-c.1740.
It is mentioned in an old deed and after being converted to private use was bought in 1773 by the mother-in-law of Edmund Dawson. Demolished and the present museum (Benskin House) built on the site in 1775.

The Anchor, 272 High Street, c.1750-c.1815.
In 1756 Jane Burren billeted one man. This inn was revived as a beerhouse in the latter part of the 19th century. According to Williams's History John Savigny (who owned it till his death in 1808), of Frogmore House, frequented this inn and composed a rhyme for its signboard.

Combes Beerhouse.
In 1878 was attached to Tidcombes Iron Foundry, Lower High Street. Charles Lovers, tenant.

Duke William or **Dukes Head, 253 High Street,** c.1750-1800.
Now part of Ausden's premises. In 1756 Rachel Butcher had room for two men and two horses.

Fleur de Lys, 101 High Street.
No information at all about this house now occupied by Manfields Shoes.

It may not have held a licence. In 1824 Stewart Marjoribanks presented it to the Morrison Trust as a home for the parish church Lecturer or Curate, having demolished the old Lecturer's House near the churchyard.

Saracens Head, 85 High Street, c.1550-1780.
Now beneath the British Home Stores. In 1756 had room for two men and eight horses, John Harding landlord. It became a private house, and late in the 19th century the shop of Henry Kingham, grocer extraordinary. Here in 1744 a mercenary soldier stabbed a local lad in a quarrel about a girl and was almost lynched.

Chequers, 73 High Street, c.1700-1865.
Now the Midland Bank. In 1756 John Powell put up two men, and two horses in the yard, (now Charter Place). Thomas Cole kept it from 1820 to 1850. Salters.

Bull or **Bullshead, 61 High Street,** c.1680-1772.
Now Burton's Tailors. It was bought in 1772 by James Rogers, Senior, ironmonger, father of the Rose and Crown landlord, and converted to a shop (Rogers and Gowlett). In 1731 it was owned by the Runnington family. In 1756 Will James had room for two men and ten horses. The long side yard is now part of the widened Meeting Alley.

Fighting Cocks, Water Lane. c.1750-1856.
This was kept in 1750 by William George but had no accommodation.

Chequers, Waterdell, c.1750-1900.
Will Neale had it from 1840. It was a Salter's House.

The Railway Hotel or **Old Clarendon Arms, St. Albans Road.**
Was in the yard of the old railway station from 1838 until 1858, when the station was transferred. It belonged to Calvert and Co., of Furneaux Pelham, and was kept by, first Mary Howard, and then John Laws.

The Jolly Sawyers.
Stood on the site of St. Huberts Lodge, 61 Church Road. It belonged to a Mr. Wright, and was kept by Tom Barrett, a sawyer, in 1849. In 1854 it was demolished.

Leavesden Beerhouse.
Of which the site is unknown, existed briefly in the 1840s and early 50s.

Little Oxhey Lane Beerhouse c.1840-55.
Kept by Mary Lawrence and James Gregory, farmers, in Storey's or Tooke's Farm, later S. Oxhey Library.

Ganders Ash Beerhouse c.1840-1880.
Was kept by Mervyn Dollamore.

Samuel Roate's Beerhouse.
From c.1850, 147 St. Albans Road in a building erected by Roate, a brewer. It remained a brewery with off sales until c.1896. Later called Victoria Brewery under F. Cocks. (Now a flower shop.)

Swan, 223 High Street.
This house was founded by Sam Smith, brewer, on his brewery premises in 1753, and closed by George Whittingstall in c.1800 and the name transferred to the Hole in the Wall opposite. In 1756 Richard Harding was the landlord with room for one guest. Demolished.

Nags Head.
Somewhere between 171 and 223 High Street in 1691. (Possibly 177 or 195 High Street, both mediaeval merchant houses demolished for road works.) (Could have been the later Three Tuns.)

Cross, later **Boot, 145 High Street,** c.1750-1820.
In 1756 as the Cross was kept by Ruth Doggett with accommodation for two men. By 1800 it was renamed Boot. Now William Hill, bookmakers.

Swan, 113 High Street, c.1660-1730.
Now the National Westminster Bank. This inn was bought by Thomas Hobson, and passed to his widow Dame Fuller, who placed a rent charge of £4 annually on it to support her Free School. It was run by the Brockett family. Later it became a shop.

Three early inns have not been located. The **Christopher** was owned by John Anderson or Potter in 1605. In 1662 Nicholas Colborne, Brewer, left an inn called the **Cock** near the market in his will, and in 1731 the Will of Will Runnington, landlord of the George, refers to the **Royal Oak.**

These are some of the inns or public houses in Watford Parish founded before 1830.

An Alphabetical Check List of Watford Pubs Existing Since 1900

1. **The Anchor** 272 High Street. On the site of an earlier Blue Anchor. Belonged to W. Lewin and Sedgwicks. 1850-1957. Demolished. Originally a common lodging house.
2. **The Angel** 253 High Street. Salters of Rickmansworth c.1750-1903. Demolished.
3. **The Arches** formerly Railway Tavern, Chalk Hill. Clutterbucks of Stanmore. 1857-1973. Known often as Luckett's after the family which kept it for over 90 years. Demolished to create the roundabout.
4. † **The Badger** Gossamers, Meriden Estate. 1961-.
5. † **The Beaver** Courtlands Drive. 1963-.
6. † **The Bedford Arms** Langley Road. 1869-.
7. **The Brewers Arms** 233 High Street. Kept originally by a brewer's servant. 1839-1911. Demolished.
8. **The Clarendon Hotel** Station Road. Belonged to Brewsters. Is now Benskin's Office. 1862-1976.
9. **The Coachmakers Arms** 30 High Street. Started by George Ware, a coachmaker. 1850-. It was rebuilt and enlarged and in 1985 became a Wine Bar, now unoccupied.
10. **The Compasses** 68 High Street. Smiths were the original brewers. When it was partly demolished in 1888 a fifteenth century window was discovered, still in the wall by the Post Office. c.1725-1966. Rebuilt.
11. **The Cricketers Arms** Watford Fields. It was first called the Masons Arms after the first landlord, a mason. 1859-1967. Demolished.
12. **The Crown** St. Albans Road, Garston. Whittingstalls Brewery. c.1790-1980. Rebuilt as Calendars Licensed Restaurant, Allied-Lyons.
13. **The Crystal Palace** 121 High Street. This tiny beerhouse doubled as a greengrocer's under the Rosson family who kept it for most of its life. Dysons Brewery. 1854-1908. Demolished.
14. † **The Dean Park Hotel** St. Albans Road. Formerly called the Caledonian Hotel. Modern building. 1969-.
15. **The Dog** Hempstead Road. Smith's Brewery. A former haycarters' pub. 1720-1969. Demolished and now the car park for Watford College students.
16. **The Duke of Edinburgh** 2, Aldenham Road. Originally the Colliers Arms. Healey's Brewery. 1860-1965.
17. **Eight Bells** 111 High Street. Started as the Barley Mow. Sam Smith, brewer, bought it in 1753. The yard was rented from the former Swan next door (now the Natwest Bank). 1725-1954. John Kilby had it for many years. Demolished.
18. **The Essex Arms** 69 High Street. In private ownership for many years but latterly Salters of Rickmansworth. Watford's leading inn and posting house for hundreds of years. The corn-exchange was a 19th century adjunct. 15th century-1930 when it was bought and demolished by James Cawdell to extend his drapery. It was the White Hart until c.1780.
19. † **The Essex Arms** Langley Way, Cassiobury Park. An old name on a new site. 1975-.
20. † **The Estcourt Arms** St. Johns Road. 1869-. named after the previous owner of this part of Watford (The Estcourt Estate).
21. † **The Estcourt Tavern** Estcourt Road. 1869-. This road was originally called Beechen Grove from Grove Circus as far as Clarendon Road. Most of it is now called Gartlet Road, after a defunct girls' school.
22. **The Fox** 206 High Street. 1854-1956 and demolished. The alley at the side was once called Rising Sun Alley after an inn which much earlier occupied the same site as the Fox beerhouse, and is not to be confused with the Rising Sun Beerhouse at 232 High Street.
23. **The George Inn** 91 High Street. Smith's Brewery. 15th century-1935. This was one of the three leading inns of Watford. It had a galleried yard. Demolished.
24. † **The Golden Lion** Estcourt Road. 1869-.
25. **The Green Man** 60 High Street, Clutterbuck's. c.1730-1975. Demolished. This was not a coaching or posting inn, but leased out gigs and small vehicles to private users.
26. **The Greyhound** 8 King Street. Owned by Bradshaws. Built in 1852 on Watford Place Estate and closed in 1961 and demolished. Originally called The Freetrader.
27. **The Hammer in Hand** Leavesden High Road. Was at the corner of Hunter's Lane. Originally a smithy kept by the Mallord family. Demolished in 1960.
28. † **The Hammer in Hand** Ganders Ash. 1961-. An old name on a new site.
29. † **The Happy Hour** Eastbury Road. A large pub on the edge of town. 1958-.
30. † **The Hare** High Road, Leavesden. Originally a farmhouse. Rebuilt. Long kept by the Downer family. Whittingstalls. c.1790-.
31. † **The Haydon Arms** Upper Paddock Road. Sedgwicks. 1862-. The name is taken from the nearby Haydon Hill. Recently threatened with closure.
32. † **The Hertfordshire Arms** St. Albans Road. Benskins. This was the first new pub built in Watford since the late 19th century, for the new estates developed by Ashby and Brightman had 'no alcohol' covenants written into the deeds. A large neo-Georgian house, with a music licence. 1935-
33. † **The Highwayman** Tolpits Lane. Nearly opposite West Watford Station to serve the new estates and factories. 1959-.
34. † **The Hit or Miss** 274 High Street. Started in c.1850 as the Carpenter's Arms by G. Clarke, a carpenter, but changed quickly to its present name, a kind of joke about whether prospective customers could find it. It was also a common lodging house. Rebuilt this century. 1850-.

35. **The Hollybush** 228 High Street. A small beerhouse from 1850-1903. Demolished.
36. † **The Horns** Hempstead Road. Clutterbucks. 1740-. Like the Dog it was a call for haycarters. Rebuilt at the turn of this century.
37. **The Jolly Anglers** 286 High Street. Started in 1860 by Healey's Brewery on or near the site of an earlier pub of the same name. Closed in 1964 and demolished.
38. **The Jolly Gardeners,** St. Albans Road, on the corner of West Street. Built by John West who gave his name to the street. 1850-1958. Demolished.
39. **The Joseph Benskin** 68 High Street. Installed in the old Compasses building in 1974 and closed in 1980.
40. **The Kings Arms** 130 High street. Opened in 1852 in the former gatelodge of Watford Place. Groomes of Kings Langley. 1852-1961. Demolished.
41. **The Kings Head** 86 High Street. Dysons. c.1600-1961. Demolished.
42. **The King William** 319 High Street. Dysons. c.1840-1959. Kept by the Lonnon family for many years. The building still stands by Bushey Arches. This pub, like those of the so-called Oxhey Village, was in Bushey Parish until the 1890s.
43. **The Lamb** 201 High Street. Healeys. 1854-1902. Demolished.
44. **The Leathersellers Arms** 235 High Street. Dysons. c.1680-1960. From 1820 to 1840 John Tookey, the landlord, was Watford's exciseman. Demolished.
45. † **The Leviathan Steamer** St. Albans Road. Built by Henry Parsons, a St. Albans brewer, in 1839, and named after the whole class of new transatlantic steam-assisted vessels, such as the British Queen, then disputing the 'Blue Riband'. 1839-.
46. † **The Load of Hay** Watford Heath. In a cottage on manorial waste. c.1840-.
47. **The Malden Hotel** Station Road. Inde Coope. 1865-1973. Demolished.
48. **The Merton Arms** Merton Road. Later an off-licence, but no longer. c.1890-1938.
49. † **The Nascot Arms** Stamford Road. 1869-.
50. **The New Inn** King Street. Healeys. Attached to Healey's Brewery buildings.1852-1961. Demolished to widen King Street.
51. † **The Oddfellows Arms** Fearnley Street. Benskins. 1869-. Once kept by Barnabas Mendham whose family also had the Jolly Gardeners.
53. **The Old Berkely Hunt** St. Albans Road. This was on the corner of Weymouth Street opposite the Oddfellows Hall. 1869-1969. Demolished for the roundabout.
53. **The Oliver** by the Pond. Berni Inns. In Cakebread Robey's old mock-Tudor building from 1971 until 1985. It was a licensed restaurant with bars, and by sheer chance occupied the site of the 18th century Artichoke.
54. † **The One Bell** 90 High Street, beneath the Church Tower. This is the oldest existing licence of present-day Watford pubs, but the structure is turn of the century. Smiths. c.1660-.
55. † **The One Crown** 156 High Street. Dysons. If the One Bell has the oldest licence the One Crown occupies the oldest building, dating in part to the 16th century. The first landlord was Jeremiah Friend, who then owned the building. 1750-.
56. † **The Pennant** Station Road. Benskins. Started in 1978 in the former stables of the Clarendon Hotel, built in 1860. Named after Benskin's trademark.
57. **The Prince of Wales** 78 Villiers Road. Benskins. c.1868-1955.
58. **The Queens Arms** St. Albans Road. Dysons. Opposite the old railway station. Demolished to widen the bridge. 1839-1958
59. **The Queens Arms** Queens Road. Sedgwicks. Originally belonged to John Kilby, former landlord of the Eight Bells. 1862-1968. Demolished.
60. † **The Railway Arms** Aldenham Road. c.1858-. Dysons. The Lonnon family held it.
61. **The Railway Arms** St. Albans Road. Dysons. By the railway bridge opposite the old station. 1839-1958. Demolished to widen the bridge.
62. **The Railway Tavern** 184 High Street. Dysons. Originally a nameless beerhouse it acquired its name when the Rickmansworth branch was built. 1854-1974. Demolished.
63. **The Red Lion** Red Lion Passage (or 81 High Street). Healeys. This was a very old pub, originally called the White Horse, and later the Plough. c.1600-1905. Demolished.
64. † **The Red Lion** Colney Butts (Vicarage Road). Dysons. This was a smallholding called Coney Butts (Rabbit Strips) till 1800 when inherited by the Dysons. 1800-. Rebuilt c.1898.
65. † **The Rifle Volunteer** 36 Villiers Road. Clutterbucks. c.1857-. Named after a local Volunteer Regiment.
66. **The Rising Sun** 232 High Street. A tiny beerhouse. 1854-1905. Demolished.
67. **The Rose and Crown** 72 High Street. Vied with the Essex Arms and the George as Watford's leading inn. A stop for coaches with good stabling. Several times rebuilt. c.15th century-1968. James Rogers, landlord, who died in 1831, was of enormous size. Demolished.
68. † **The Rose and Crown** 9 Market Street. A new pub with no connection with the old inn except propinquity. 1968.-

69. † **The Royal Oak** Watford Heath. Like the Load of Hay built on manorial waste. c.1860-.
70. † **Shakers Wine Bar** Market Street. Recent.
71. † **The Sir Robert Peel** King Street. Opened in 1961 in the former Police Station and cells.
71. † **The Southern Cross Hotel** Langley Road. Originally run by Australians. It is in converted houses and has bars. 1968-.
73. **The Spread Eagle** 82 High Street. Clutterbucks. An early thrift club was held here, and it was often in trouble for making too much noise in the early days. c.1750-1958. Demolished.
74. † **The Stag** St. Albans Road Originally the Bricklayers Arms, and later the Queens Bays. Dysons. 1850-. Partly rebuilt.
75. † **The Swan** 216 High Street. Whittingstalls. This pub was rebuilt in the 1930s and moved back from its street frontage. In 1984 it became Shades Wine Bar. Until 1800 it was called the Hole in the Wall. c.1750-.
76. † **The Tantivy** Queens Road. Built by Fred Sedgwick in 1873 to celebrate his revived Tantivy Coach to London. Then renamed Victoria Tavern until recently reverting to the original name. 1873-.
77. **The Three Crowns** 160 High Street. Dysons. This was one of Watford's oldest pubs. It started life as the Bull, and later became the Crown. In 1750 it became the Three Crowns. The building and sign bracket remain. c.1600-1958.
78. † **The Three Horseshoes** Garston. Originally a smithy. Rebuilt. c.1750-.
79. **The Three Tuns** 205 High Street. This inn belonged to the first John Dyson. It closed in 1974. Demolished.
80. † **The Tudor Tavern** Bushey Mill Lane. In a mock-Tudor building on Rice Brothers' Tudor Estate. 1943-.
81. † **The Verulam Arms** or **Hotel** Station Road. Dysons. 1860-1957. Demolished.
82. † **The Verulam Arms** St. Albans Road. A new site for an older name. 1957-.
83. † **The Victoria** Chalk Hill. Salters. c.1858-.
84. † **The Villiers Arms** 108 Villiers Road. c.1866-.
85. † **The Wellington Arms** Woodford Road. 1869-.
86. † **The Wheatsheaf** Oxhey. Built by the site of the Toll house of the Turnpike Trust at Bushey Arches. Salters. It was a little low building with a garden at the rear where strolling actors performed. Rebuilt. c.1750-.
87. **The White Hart** 180 High Street. This very old pub in an equally ancient building was demolished in 1974 to make way for the Ring Road. It was originally called the Maidenhead. Salters. c.1600-1974.
88. † **The White Lion** St. Albans Road. Weller and Co. 1850-. Partly rebuilt recently when the yard was filled in.
89. **The Woodman** 25 Red Lion Yard. Healeys. Moved from its earlier position of 25 Grove Circus in 1900. 1860-1968. Demolished.
90. † **Blakes Free House** 92-96 Queens Road. Recent.

All the above pubs are in Watford Borough, but the following are or were in Watford Rural Parish and are now in Three Rivers District.

1. † **The Broadwalk** formerly The Pheasant, Bridlington Road, S. Oxhey. 1961-.
2. † **The Cart and Horses** Commonwood. 1840-.
3. † **The Clarendon Arms** Chandlers Cross. Clutterbucks. 1840-.
4. † **The Dick Whittington** Prestwick Road, S. Oxhey. 1957-.
5. † **The Grapevine** Prestwick Road, S. Oxhey. 1967.
6. † **The Jet** Hayling Road, S. Oxhey. 1959-.
7. † **The Partridge** The Mead, Carpenders Park. 1969-.
8. **The Rose and Crown** Bucks Hill. Groomes. c.1800-1964. Building remains.
9. **The True Blue** Bucks Hill. Salters. c.1770-1914. Building remains.

† These premises are still licensed bars.

The original brewers have been mentioned where known.

E. J. Chapman, B.A. (Hons.)

Our heritage

The Secretary of State for the Environment is required to compile "lists" of buildings of special architectural merit or historic interest. The administration of local and national conservation policies is, or should be, based on the lists which are themselves constantly under revision.

The guidelines observed by the Department of the Environment presume all buildings erected before the 17th century in original or near original condition are automatically listed. The majority of the buildings of the 18th century and up to 1840 qualify on a selection basis. For the period between 1840 and 1914 the usually applied yardstick may be defined as the "principal works of principal architects."

Due consideration is also given to buildings and structures that may be associated with our social and economic history. The "historic" factor may be defined as involving "known characters and recorded events". Then there is the all-embracing "group value" in the form of a terrace, square or village green.

In the selection process a qualifying building or structure will be graded and listed in the following manner:

Grade 1—of very special merit

Grade II*—of highest general grading deserving special attention

Grade II—of considerable importance and accorded to the majority of buildings.

The protection provided by current legislation offers safeguards only against unauthorised demolition and may be abused. A building is not necessarily sacrosanct because it is 'listed'.

Listed Buildings

Address	Grade	Date Listed	Address	Grade	Date Listed
1A Carey Place	II	7.1.83	Nat. Westminster Bank, 58 High Street	II	4.3.74
14 Chalk Hill	II	4.8.75	Lloyds Bank, 63-65 High Street	II	17.6.80
St. Andrew's Church, Church Road	II	7.1.83	Midland Bank, 73 High Street	II	25.10.77
Gates to, and Salters Almshouses, Church Road	II and II	7.1.83	97 High Street	II	7.1.83
Nos. 1-8 Bedford Almshouses Church Street	II	26.8.52	129-131 High Street	II	7.1.83
St. Mary's Church (Parish), Church St. (off High St.)	I	26.8.52	133-135 High Street	II	7.1.83
Monuments in St. Mary's Churchyard	II	7.1.83	137 High Street	II	7.1.83
Free School, Church St.	II*	26.8.52	141 High Street	II	7.1.83
Beechen Grove Baptist Church, Clarendon Road	II	12.9.80	145 High Street	II	7.1.83
Palace Theatre, Clarendon Road	II	14.7.82	149-151 High Street	II	7.1.83
Baptist Tabernacle, Derby Road	II	7.1.83	The One Crown P.H., 156 High Street	II	7.1.83
Watford Central Primary School, Derby Road	II	7.1.83	158 High Street	II	7.1.83
St. Michael's Church, Durban Road	II	7.1.83	160 High Street	II	7.1.83
St. Matthew's Church, Eastbury Road	II	7.1.83	166-168 High Street	II	7.1.83
Holyrood House, Exchange Road	II	7.1.83	172 High Street	II	15.9.83
Cassio Bridge Lodge 67 Gade Avenue	II	7.1.83	172A High Street	II	18.9.82
Russell's, Greenbank Road	II	24.8.79	Watford Museum 194-196 High Street	II	26.8.52
Canal Bridge, 200m N of Grove Mill (BWB) Grove Mill Lane	II	15.11.73	198 High Street	II	23.1.73
Heath Farm Court (formerly Heath Farm House), Grove Mill Lane	II	26.8.52	200-202-202A High Street	II	23.1.73
Canal Cottage, Grove Mill Lane	II	7.1.83	Iron railings in front of former Benskins Brewery Site	II	23.1.73
Dower House (ex Grove Mill House) Grove Mill Lane	II	26.8.52	Nos. 212-214 High Street	II	7.1.83
Little Cassiobury (H.C.C. Education Office), Hempstead Road	II*	26.8.52	Frogmore House, High Street*	II	26.8.52
Garden Cottage, 129 Hempstead Road	II	7.1.83	Bushey Arches Railway Viaduct, Lower High Street	II	7.1.83
Tollgate Lodge, 235 Hempstead Road	II	7.1.83	All Saints Church, Leavesden, Horseshoe Lane	II	7.1.83
South Lodge, Hempstead Road	II	7.1.83	The Bandstand by Town Hall, The Parade	II	7.1.83
Manor House, 79-87 High Road, Leavesden	II	7.1.83	The War Memorial by the Town Hall	II	7.1.83
Watford Place, 27 King Street	II	26.8.52	Former Holy Rood R.C. School, Percy Road	II	7.1.83
Kytes House, Kytes Drive and Outbuilding to North of Kytes House	II	7.1.83	Former Convent of St. Vincent, Percy Road	II	15.9.83
Holy Rood R.C. Church, Market Street	I	12.9.80	Cassiobury Court, Richmond Drive	II	7.1.83
Govt. Buildings, (former London Orphan Asylum) and Chapel, Orphanage Road	II	7.1.83	Watford Boys' Grammar School Rickmansworth Road	II	7.1.83
(Jacksons) 14-16 The Parade	II	7.1.83	Master's House, Watford Boys' Grammar School, Rickmansworth Road	II	7.1.83
Monmouth House, 85-89 The Parade	II	25.11.77	The Old Station House, 147A St. Albans Road	II	20.2.79
91, 93, 95 The Parade	II	7.1.83	Benskins House (former Clarendon Hotel) Station Road	II	12.9.75
Nat. Westminster Bank, 151-153 The Parade	II	7.1.83	Watford Railway Tunnels, South entrance to West Tunnel	II	7.1.83
			St. John's Church, Sutton Road	II	7.1.83
			Shrodells Wing (former Watford Union Workhouse), Vicarage Road	II	15.9.82
			Five Arches Railway Viaduct 200m N. of Water Lane	II	7.1.83

Last days of the Odeon; closed and the removal vans taking away projection equipment, etc.

p.247 b 17th October, 1983

Cinemas

The first film exhibition at Watford was part of a circus programme at the Clarendon Hall (formerly Agricultural Hall), Beechen Grove, on Monday 8th March 1897. Lantern lectures were already abundant, and in January 1898, on three successive evenings, a Lumiere Brothers Cinematograph was exhibited at the Library (Queens Road). The 'films' shown had a short running time of approximately 60 seconds and comprised scenes of everyday movement—passing trains, processions, etc.

J & R Ellis, of 122 High Street, advertised animated pictures and magic lantern shows before 1900.

Touring showmen visited the Clarendon Hall during the early years of the century, and W. F. Jury's Imperial Bioscope Company made the greatest contribution here with regular seasons from 1905 to 1910. W. F. Jury was an early cinematograph entrepreneur in that he 'rented' film from his stock of some 100,000! He later organised films in connection with the 1914-18 war, became director of Cinema Propaganda for the Ministry of Information, and was Knighted in 1918.

The Palace Theatre, opened in 1908, presented short excerpts of animated pictures. In 1909 Edward and Harold Downer formed Bipics Limited, established in the Conservative Hall, while the Kinetic Picture Company opened in the Corn Exchange. By this time the programmes and content had lengthened and improved, and a 2-hour show, admission 3d. or 6d., was normal.

In May 1911 the Cinema Palace was opened in the High Street, next to (present) Barclay's Bank (corner of King Street), as the town's first purpose-built cinema.

First of the 'long-term' cinemas was the Electric Coliseum, St. Albans Road, opened in October 1912. It went 'sound' in June 1930, changed its name to New Plaza in December 1936, and closed in July 1954.

The Empire in Merton Road opened in November 1913, went sound in August 1930, twin-screened in August 1980, renamed ABC in May 1985, Cannon in August 1986.

The Central Hall in King Street opened in December 1913, went sound and renamed Regal in September 1929, changed to Essoldo in 1955, and closed for bingo conversion in November 1968.

The Clarendon Road Skating Rink conversion opened as the Super cinema in February 1921. Renamed Carlton in August 1930, and closed in July 1980.

The first building of the super cinema era was the Plaza by the Pond, opened in April 1929. It was taken over by the Odeon circuit and renamed in October 1936, closed in November 1963, and was demolished to make way for a ground-floor supermarket and Top Rank Suite.

The Gaumont opened in May 1937, renamed Odeon in September 1964 after closure of the original Odeon just along the road, went three-screen in June 1974, and was still trading profitably in 1983 when the site was sold for redevelopment.

The Odeon, North Watford was the final cinema to open in November 1937 and, with a short life, closed to become a supermarket in May 1959.

CHAIRMEN OF THE LOCAL BOARD
AND URBAN DISTRICT COUNCIL

Local Board

Charles W. Moore	1850 to 1872
Henry Catlin	1872 to 1873
Charles Francis Humbert	1873 to 1884
Lt.-Col. Copeland	1884 to 1884
Edward John Slinn	1885 to 1895

Urban District Council

Edward John Slinn	1895 to 1896
Walter Tidboald Coles	1896 to 1897
Charles Pryor Ayres	1897 to 1898
Joseph Clemson Benskin	1898 to 1899
Albert Edward Pridmore	1899 to 1900
George Potter Neele	1900 to 1901
Francis Fisher	1901 to 1903
Edward Kingham	1903 to 1904
Ralph Alfred Thorpe	1904 to 1906
George Longley	1906 to 1907
Sydney J. Ellis	1907 to 1908
John Andrews	1908 to 1909
Ralph Alfred Thorpe	1909 to 1910
Septimus George Mobbs	1910 to 1911
Ralph Alfred Thorpe	1911 to 1912
Joseph Southam	1912 to 1913
Walter Francis Goodrich	1913 to 1915
Charles Alfred Solomons	1915 to 1916
Thomas Rubython Clark	1916 to 1917
Ralph Alfred Thorpe	1917 to 1919
Frederick Hunt Gorle	1919 to 1920
George Longley	1920 to 1921
Henry Belcher Watkins	1921 to 1922
Thomas Rubython Clark	April to Nov., 1922

MAYORS OF WATFORD

The Rt. Hon. The Earl of Clarendon	1922 to 1923
Alderman Ralph Alfred Thorpe	1923 to 1925
Alderman Henry Belcher Watkins	1925 to 1926
Alderman Thomas Rubython Clark	1926 to 1927
Alderman Thomas Rushton	1927 to 1928
Councillor Francis Joseph Bache Hemming	1928 to 1929
Alderman Mrs. Amelia Florence Broad	1929 to 1930 (April)
Alderman Francis Joseph Bache Hemming	(April to Nov.) 1930
Alderman Frederick William Jeffs	1930 to 1931
Alderman William Bickerton	1931 to 1932
Councillor Joseph Evans	1932 to 1933
Councillor Charles Edward Griffin	1933 to 1934
Alderman Henry Jules Bridger	1934 to 1935
Councillor Ernest Charles Last	1935 to 1936
Alderman Henry Coates	1936 to 1937
Councillor Thomas Rigby Taylor	1937 to 1938
Councillor Harry Horwood	1938 to 1939
Alderman Lewin Halsey Andrews	1939 to 1940
Councillor Ernest James Baxter	1940 to 1941
Councillor Wilfred Harry Price	1941 to 1942
Alderman Thomas Herbert Simmons	1942 to 1943
Councillor Mrs. Martha Ann Ward	1943 to 1944
Alderman Herbert Waterman Beall	1944
Councillor Mrs. Emily Gertrude Beall	1944 to 1945
Councillor James Wright	1945 to 1946
Councillor Ransley William North	1946 to 1947
Alderman Henry Coates	1947 to 1949
Councillor Frederick Harold Vince	1949 to 1950
Alderman Mrs. Mary Edith Bridger	1950 to 1951
Councillor Laurence Edgar Haines	1951 to 1952
Alderman Leonard Charles Johnson	1952 to 1953
Alderman Albert George Dillingham	1953 to 1954
Alderman John Davies	1954 to 1955
Alderman Edward Cecil Amey	1955 to 1956
Councillor Albert Abbott	1956 to 1957
Alderman Harry Horwood	1957 to 1958
Councillor Reginald William Gamble	1958 to 1959
Alderman Thomas Frederick Harris	1959 to 1960
Alderman Ernest Henry Harrowell	1960 to 1961
Alderman John Richard Hicks	1961 to 1962
Alderman Henry William Lodder	1962 to 1963
Alderman George Wilfred Knox	1963 to 1964

Alderman Arthur Reynolds	1964 to 1965
Councillor Leslie Cyril Wright	1965 to 1966
Alderman Finlay Mackenzie	1966 to 1967
Councillor Miss Doris Mary Scawen	1967 to 1968
Alderman Alec Leonard Merrifield	1968 to 1969
Alderman J. Stanley Oliver	1969 to 1970
Councillor Ronald W. Jackson	1970 to 1971
Alderman Mrs. Mary Dodd	1971 to 1972
Alderman Robert J. Caton	1972 to 1973
Councillor Roger S. Horner	1973 to 1974
Councillor William G. Everett	1974 to 1975
Councillor Harry Price	1975 to 1976
Councillor Derrick Coleshill	1976 to 1977
Councillor Alan W. Bonney	1977 to 1978
Councillor Samuel I. Deakin	1978 to 1979
Councillor Norman H. Tyrwhitt	1979 to 1980
Councillor Sidney G. Reynolds	1980 to 1981
Councillor Edward Cecil Amey, O.B.E.	1981 to 1982
Councillor Edward Cecil Amey, O.B.E.	1982 to 1983
Councillor Geoffrey R. Greenstreet, A.I.I.M., M.I.P.D.M.	1983 to 1984
Councillor Mrs. M. I. Hughes	1984 to 1985
Councillor Mrs. I. Tunstall Dunn	1985 to 1986
Councillor Paul Harrison	1986 to 1987
Councillor Les Hughes	1987 to 1988
Councillor P. A. Allan	1988 to

HONORARY FREEMEN OF THE BOROUGH

The Rt. Hon. George Herbert Hyde Villiers, Earl of Clarendon. (Admitted 28th July, 1924) (deceased).

Alderman Ralph Alfred Thorpe. (Admitted 22nd June, 1927) (deceased).

The Rt. Hon. Lord Hemingford. (Admitted 22nd March, 1943) (deceased).

Alderman Thomas Rubython Clark. (Admitted 22nd March, 1943) (deceased).

Mr. Wm. Hudson. (Admitted 22nd March 1943) (deceased).

Ernest James Baxter, O.B.E., J.P., (Admitted 1st September, 1959) (deceased).

Harry Horwood, Esq., O.B.E., J.P., (Admitted 1st September, 1959) (deceased).

Edward C. Amey, O.B.E. (Admitted 19th July, 1976) (deceased).

Hubert Buckingham Esq. (Admitted 19th July, 1976) (deceased).

Albert G. Dillingham, Esq. (Admitted 19th July 1976)

Sir Raphael Tuck, B.SC.,(ECON), M.A., LL.M. (Admitted 15th November 1980) (deceased).

FREEDOM OF ENTRY

On the 5th July, 1959, the 3rd East Anglian Regiment (16th/44th Foot) were granted the privilege, honour and distinction of marching through the streets of the Borough on all ceremonial occasions with colours flying, bands playing, drums beating and bayonets fixed.

On the 26th May, 1983, this privilege, honour and distinction was formally extended to the 3rd Battalion (Bedfordshire, Hertfordshire and Essex) of the Royal Anglian Regiment as successors to the 3rd East Anglian Regiment (16th/44th Foot).

CLERKS OF THE LOCAL BOARD AND
URBAN DISTRICT COUNCIL

John Sedgwick	1850 to 1882
Henry Morten Turner	1882 to 1910
William Hudson	1910 to 1922

TOWN CLERKS OF WATFORD
1922 to 1974

William Hudson	1922 to 1940
Alfred Norman Schofield	1940 to 1953
Gordon Hamer Hall	1953 to 1974

CHIEF EXECUTIVE AND TOWN CLERK
OF WATFORD

Robert Bruce McMillan	1974 to

INDEX

*Page numbers set **bold** refer to illustrations*

Comparative Values

To convert an 1880 price to 1987 value, multiply by the 1880 figure, e.g. an 1880 wage of 30/- (£1.50) x 48.7 would be £73.05.

To convert a 1987 price to suit an earlier period divide by the appropriate year value. e.g. a 1987 car, at £4,800, would be £154.83 in 1937 or £580.41 in 1967. These figures apply to consumers' expenditure; house prices at time of writing exceed normal inflation rates.

1860	45.5	1919	23.9	1957	10.9
1880	48.7	1927	28.2	1967	8.27
1900	56.0	1937	31.0	1977	2.9
1914	51.2	1947	16.6	1987	1.0

Based upon UK purchasing power and prices index
1860, 150; 1928, 100; 1949, 50; 1972, 20.1; 1977. 7.9; 1987, 3.3 (estimated)

SUBSCRIBERS TO THE
SLIP CASE EDITION

°Albert G. Dillingham,
  (Freeman of Watford)
°Lady Monica Tuck
°Councillor Les Hughes,
  (Mayor of Watford, 1987-)
°Councillor Paul Harrison,
  (Mayor of Watford, 1986-87)
  Watford's Link Towns:
    °Mainz
    °Nanterre
    °Novgorod
    °Wilmington
    °Pesaro
°A. J. Greenan, (Managing Director, Watford Observer)
°David Wynne Jones, (Editor, Watford Observer, 1983-1987)
°Richard Greville
°Harry Williamson
°Stephen Moore, (Librarian, Watford Central Library)
°Joan Saunders
°Ted and Peggy Parrish
°George Lorimer
°Edgar Chapman, B.A. (Hons)
°Linda V. Nunn
°Colin A. Pascoe
°Watford Central Library (10 copies)
  °*Presentation copies*

Elizabeth Attwood
Margaret Marshall
Pat Wesley and the late Joe Wesley
Roland and Ethel Warburton
Dick Leach
Dorothy and Ken Bedford
Major and Mrs. D. O. Tedstone
Mr. A. Bishop, Miss J. E. Bishop, Miss J. Bishop
Jeff and Irene Fox
James Darvill and Son (2 copies)
Robert and Lesley Dunlop
Maria Jeffreys
Dennis R. Hubbard
Michael K. Neighbour
Mr. and Mrs. Grant Longman
Irene Tunstall Dunn,
  (Mayor of Watford 1985-86)
John S. Ausden
Raymond M. Janes
Mrs. Susan Birch
Mr. and Mrs. Kenneth McDonald
Derek Russell
R. D. Humphreys
Mrs. Betty Simpson
C. G. Albon
James G. Connolly
F. E. Lewis and H. Lewis
Geraldine and Colin Siggery
Mary and Joan Wicks
Christopher and Nancy Wicks

Donald and Margaret Wicks
Martin Alan Betts
George and Yvonne Buckingham
Bill and Joan Nash
Mr. and Mrs. J. E. Tomlinson
Elizabeth N. R. Waddell
Robert J. Waddell
Colin S. Waddell
R. J. and S. Packwood
Norman and Valerie Sutton
Peter Hagger
Norman Lane Materials Ltd.
Mrs. C. P. Brightman
Laing Properties (U.K.) Ltd.
Allied Irish Banks PLC
K. H. Challis
John E. Gower
Michael Pritchard
Alan and Lesley Pritchard
Ken and Jean Walker
Eric Lewis and Ruth Starer
Mr. and Mrs. K. P. Bone
Hammonds of Watford (2 copies)
Viking Autos Limited (3 copies)
Mr. and Mrs. R. W. J. Proctor
David Conway
Ann E. Hayes
Stuart R. Gumbiner, M.Sc.(Econ)., F.Inst.D.
Arnold & Co.
Erith building Supplies
Knutsford J.M.I. School (Chairman of Governors (1987) A. Dillingham)
Mr. and Mrs. E. Kirtley
Peter K. H. Eames
Olive and Jack Norwood
The Central Primary School
R. G. Lewis
R. F. Johnson, J.P., B.V.Sc., M.R.C.V.S.
Mabel George
Peter C. Smith
John Gregory
Barclays Bank PLC, Watford
Marks & Spencer PLC, Watford
Proffitt & Gough
L. A. Franklin & Son (Transport Services)
Weller Hill Hubble (2 copies)
R. E. H. Edmonds
D. Jackson
G. Clout
Lina and Ivor Lane
Donald James Lane
H. L. Wicks
Ken and Rose McNamar.
R. C. Wallis
David R. Pygram
Michael Billingham, R.D.
Marbaix Lapointe Ltd.
Miss M. Baxter
Colin and Rose-mary Lancaster
Watford Grammar School for Girls
H. Smith
Grange Park School Bushey

Jean and Paul Price, J.P.
Geraldine Ann Robertson and David George Robertson
G. M. Reeve
Sarah and Euan Grant
Geoffrey Law
Frederick and Maura Pigram
Mr. and Mrs. D. E. Harper
A. J. E. Gibbons
A. G. Biswell
Samson Accounting
A. J. Seems
J. Wheeler
W. Wise & Son
M. J. and N. G. J. Passey
Mrs. Betty King
BPCC Odhams-Sun Printers Ltd. (2 copies)
Russell MacDonald
Matthew MacDonald
Watford Field J.M. School
Mrs. V. Meekins
Mrs. J. Battersby
R. P. A. and S. M. Canfield
Mr. A. Hobbs and Mrs. F. A. Hobbs
B. Johnson
Mrs. A. Johnson
Victor and Christine Randell
James and Doreen Gatesman
H. R. Peyto
Mr. P. H. Field
A. J and A. F. Rayner
E. May Reeve
Terence John Hearnden
Janet and Gordon Stewart (Sift Ltd)
Mary and Charles Gue and Family
Brian James Wall
James W. N. and Catherine M. Stratford
John and Marion Evans
Ron and Pauline Sharples
Michael Delderfield, Kaye Delderfield
Philip Delderfield, Karen Delderfield
Geoffrey Watkins
Roy and June Nash
John and Evelyn Hiscock
B. Boden
Mr. and Mrs. Ronald Watson
Josephine M. Bodimeade
Ronald Bentley
Barbara Edwina Collier
Peter Markwell
Fred and Joan Walker
J. W. Derbyshire (3 copies)
Mr. and Mrs. A. E. Morgan
P. L. Jakeman Carpets
Barbara and Tony Izasars
Dulcie and John Wilson
Mr. and Mrs. Frank Procter
F. G. Green
Mr. and Mrs. C. R. Brooks
Laurie Elvin
Miss. R. G. Reed
Alec Howarth

Subscribers 1 to 180

Pat and Derek Lander
Roger J. Grimmond
Sheila and Peter Hall
Ray Jefferson
Michael Bonsor
Janice Evans
Barbara J. Van Der Velden
Lawton Prior & Mecklenburgh
M. B. Kennett
W. Donovan
Mrs. Kathleen Grace
E. Weatherly
E. J. Petty
Frederick B. Coates
Gary Kemp
Margaret Birch (née Houlding)
Ursula and Derek Lodge
Watford Launderers and Cleaners Ltd.
Brian Dilks
Jean and Eric Groome
Brian, Mark and Matthew Cornwell
Patricia and Christopher King
H. E. and N. A. Croft
John and Kathleen Cassidy
Wesley Richard Ward
Jean S. Cherry, R.J.Dip. 1987
Mr. and Mrs. K. Pine
Martin G. Ware
Mr. and Mrs. P. Layman
Mr. and Mrs. P. W. Rumball
Dr. M. R. Buckton
Joan and Robert Pettitt
Doris Bettle
Alan Geoffrey Saunders
C. A. Shakeshaft
Cyril and Gladys Broome
F. Dowse
K. J. and M. E. Willis
Pauline Ffitch
John A. Bridgewater
Mr. and Mrs. P. J. Harland
Mr. and Mrs. E. W. Mann
Ray Boscher
Ben Sheward
George and Nancy Cross
Aga and Arthur Tuffin
Geoffrey Lewis
Richard and Kathleen Crawford
Robert and Marianne Harry
Peter Frank Hill
V. L. Pemberton
Margaret and Colin Willis
Don F. Roberts
Ray Coles and Annie Finding
June and Frank Armstrong
Margaret Waring/Walter Waring
Denise and David Rees
Steve Peck
Mr. and Mrs. R. H. Castle
Miss. S. Kemp
Charles Rawlinson
Frank S. Montague

Mr. and Mrs. W. F. R. Dell
Sheila and Ashley Patel
Lorraine Matthews
Joyce Wood
Herbert B. Hawkins
Sandra Thirtle and Tony Cook
R. J. Fox
J. V. Woodward
Mr. and Mrs. G. T. Maguire
Alec L. Merrifield
Simon and Wendy
Carol Ederle
Beatrice M. Smith
E. H. Cummings
Culverhouse, Alan, Sylvia and Martin
Dorothy and Dennis Woodward
Nurdin and Peacock Ltd.
Cassio College Library
N. C. Whelan
Arthur H. Green, I.S.O., C.St.J.
Harry J. Jones
Kenneth Francis W. Fayers
Mr. and Mrs. D. Heath
Robert and Maureen Howe
Frank Cordery
Albert and Kathleen Treadwell
Gil and Bob Harris
Mr. R. and Mrs. D. E. Bradshaw
Frederick O'Mahoney
Unity Freda Robinson
Anthony, Anke, Sonja and Larsen Rivers
Mrs. Charlotte Anne Cahill
Mr. and Mrs. A. R. Walker
Councillor Ian G. Brown (2 copies)
Frank and Dorcas Reed
Shirley Neale
David Mapp
Mr. E. J. and Mrs. G. E. Hawkins
Kevin Cann (Avatar Publishing)
Hertfordshire Old Peoples Homes Ltd.
  Cassiobury Court, Richmond Drive
Hertfordshire Old Peoples Homes Ltd.
  Montrose, Langley Road
Dr. T. Stanley
Mrs. Judith Eadie
Peter W. Amos
Jerry D. Amos
Bruce and Brenda Clark
David and Ann Hopkirk
Ken and Barbara Frost
Mrs. Dorothy Margaret Blackwood
James Griffin
Mr. and Mrs. Dennis Bradbury
Richard E. Higgins
J. K. Farmer
E. Kennedy
Alan Ruston
Alan Ford
Anthony Keeling
Lesley Leak, Katy Holdich
Brenda Valarie McLaughlin
Joyce Neighbour

Paul and Lynne Jackson
Franklin Family
Mrs. V. G. Hall/Mr. A. H. Hall
T. W. Mullaney
Mr. C. F. How/Mrs. G. M. How
Edward Patrick Osborne
P. K. Emery
Don Dunham
Clare Dunham
S. E. Connor (Locksmiths) Ltd. (2 copies)
Geoffrey and Jennifer Stead
Zed Scuitt
R. G. Braybrooke
W. J. and J. E. Crouch
Mr. and Mrs. A. J. Jones
Jack and Margaret Davies
John and Pamela Pipe
G. H. Rentell
Ronald Charles Spooner
Leonard Cobbett
R. J. and C. A. Middleton
J. E. Harris
Christine Jane Orchard
Peter Middleton
C. J. Keeble
Peter M. Jefferies
Roger and Margaret Waterton
Richard Andrews
Jimmy and Marion Smyth
C. J. Keniston/R. W. James
R. E. Oakley/J. M. Oakley
Michael A. Ottaway
Mrs. P. E. Dolling
John V. Tapster
Mr. and Mrs. D. Reeves
Mr. and Mrs. J. N. Sainsbury
G. W. Pamment
P. Heffer
Stephen H. Black
Rose and Gordon Thomas
Julia and John Milligan
E. and S. Knowles
Alwyn James Rickett
Mr. and Mrs. David Harrison
Walter and Hilda Gilks
Bruce E. Wooton
R. D. Grillo
Kathleen Glen
Roger H. Culverhouse
Winty and Peter King
Shirley M. Ramsay
Elizabeth A. Leach
Nicholas P. King
Ted Reynolds
R. L. F. Saunders
Peter and Jean Groves
Dennis and Shirley Mead
William and Florence Doherty
Philip C. Rayner
Tony and Pat Harris
Mr. and Mrs. C. Winter
Elinor and Jennifer Mann (2 copies)

Mr. and Mrs. A. C. Trebble
Thomas and Mary Sawyer
J. G. Innes
Olive and Arthur Blatchford
Mr. B. B. Brown
Neil Spratling
Investors in Industry plc ("3i")
Kathryn Ann Dunscombe
Mrs. Joy Bentley
John and Thelma Boxall
Patricia Goodrich
Derek Perkins and Pauline Ann Perkins
Richard and Vivienne Steer
Mr. and Mrs. B. F. Baxter
Winifred Petty and Family
Gordon Norwood
Shirley and Brian
Geoff and Adela Edwards
Eric C. Oakins
Rodney Hale
John Hurrell
J. P. Ahern
Beverley and David Everhart
Ruth Dodds (née Bennewith)
John Bennewith
Miss Jenny Spencer
Miss Ann Hastings
Mr. W. R. Hall and Mrs. J. M. Hall
Carl Wadham and Betty Wadham
B. M. Kellond
Helen Susan Lewis
Heidi Jayne Lewis
Phaik Geok Goh
Charles E. S. Parsons
John Barry Cox
Mr. and Mrs. W. F. Lee
Imprint Reprographic Services
Ivor Buckingham
Christopher William Munday
Christopher John Canfield
Dave and Mandy Jones
S. D. and M. G. Westrope
Alan David Wootton
Kenneth Bunce and Ira Bunce
Rod, Ann, Richard and Katrina Nicholas
Philip and Teresa Akers
Audrey Adams
Tom, Lattie and Kevin Cahill
Joan and Reg Williams
Mr. and Mrs. J. Osborne
Carmine Volpe
Mrs. E. R. Chappell
Miss Angela Louise Hagger
Ronald Francis Tamplin
Don and Zoe Porter
Mr. and Mrs. A. Pearce
Mr. and Mrs. John Challis
Mrs. Gwen Pike (née Norton)
David Miller
B. N. Franklin
Mrs. Edna A. L. Clifton, M.B.E.
Stanley A. Parker

Syd and Margaret Hawkins
Mr. and Mrs. K. Daniels
Paula Wiggins (née Revell)
E. K. B. Austin, Managing Director,
   A. C. Fincken & Co. Ltd.
Premier-Albanian Coaches
Allsorts (5 copies)
Alec Q. Smith, M.A., J.P.
James Stirling
Mr. and Mrs. D. H. S. Conner
Mr. and Mrs. L. W. D. Levinson
Dr. D. I. Ruffett
John and Sheila Clark
Janet M. Clark
K. Oakins
Ernest W. Long
J. Taylor
John S. Ball
Robin K. Jefferis
David Jones
John and Jean Donald
Mrs. Marjorie Joan Waterton
Don and Mary Perfect
Michael G. Beaumont
Colin and Janet Angela Lines
Les J. Carpenter
Douglas Carroll
Colin Robinson
Alec and Diane Uezzell
Mr. and Mrs. W. F. Griffith
Mr. and Mrs. J. K. Douglas
G. H. and S. G. Coster
Emma and Joe Bannister
Mr. H. A. French and Mrs. S. M. French
David, Helen, Shelley and
   Damien Silver
Albert and Barbara Bunce
B. A. Tanswell
Robert S. Reynolds
Denise Lutener/Ian Harrison
A. Lambert
Henry Gayler
Keith A. C./Jean M. Curry
M. J. King
Alan S. Atkinson
Stephen Woodard
Suzette Robson
Mike and Alison Makin
William James Rogers
Brian Markham
Patricia and Bryan Bass
Fredrick Laver
Benjamin James Taylor
David Robertson
Kenneth T. Ford and Daphne M. Ford
Pat Snoxell
Thomas A. L. Culverhouse
Jonathan Head
Richard M. W. White
Eric Tofield
Basil Kenneth and Ivy Hilda Elliott
John and Margaret Pounce

Leonard W. Baldwin
W. T. Boroughs Coachworks
John E. McClaran/Anthony Paul
   McClaran
Brenda M. Smith
R. G. Hollingdale
Mr. and Mrs. T. D. Hollingdale
Mr. and Mrs. E. A. G. Hollingdale
J. W. Sargent
L. W. Batute
P. R. Lancaster
Doug Garrod
Sally A. Lessiter
Mr. and Mrs. V. B. Crookes
Miss Ann Burrow
J. F. and S. A. Tilbury
Herbert and Eileen Barham
Jackie and Bob Sharp
Mr. and Mrs. B. Preece
Neville and Toni Price
William Graham and Molly Graham
E. and K. Courtney
Mr. and Mrs. R. G. Harvey
M. A. T. Tearle
K. Carpenter
J. V. and S. J. Weatherly
R. G. Dunscombe
Charles Martin
Edward and Janet Wells
Evelyn Cook
H. R. Brookes/Marie Brookes
Kenneth Stephen Upson
Eric G. North
Michael and Diane Hill
Brendan Garvey
A. A. Fisher Ltd.
James D. O. Thomas
Bert and Mary Fishenden
Betty Masterson (née Myers)
J. B. Cummings
John and Pamela Pratley
B. G. A. Wiggs
David and Julie Sparks
Ian Donlan Gransby
Jim and June Gerred
Linda G. Barrett
Colin and Lesley Adams
Philip Anthony and Carol Swann
Mrs. I. M. Nash
William and Jeanne Stormont
Gordon and Joan Pinder
The Day Family
The Speed Family
L. W. Andrews
Winifred Redrup
Frederick Child
J. and J. Crampton
Rowland J. Spurr
Anthony Evans
Jack J. Smith
Martyn and Joan Ausden, celebrating
   50 years marriage, 11 September, 1987

Lynn Dean (née Toms)
David Nicholas Robert Johnson
Edith E. E. Dawson
Cyril Goss
R. Foskett
Brian Seems/David Birch
John Cayford
J. G. Wheeler
D. F. and V. J. Bailey
Herbert Lister for Homemanor House
Pamela Gaitskell
Hilda Anthony
John and Cecilia Power
Joan and Frank Randall
Betty and Fred Goodfellow
Peter and Jean Spivey
Frances Susan Beauchamp
Christoher Beauchamp
Mrs. Ethel Sears (3 copies)
Ronald Henry and Doreen Joyce Hawes
William Edgar Hancock
Miss. H. A. Scott
Richard George Gravestock B.Sc.
George Gravestock B.E.M.
Susan O'Sullivan
B. N. D. Wood
R. M. Godman
Roadmaster Services Ltd.
P. A. Craig
Norman and Freda Roshier
Francis K. Farquharson
Margaret and Ivan Hollins
Harold Jordan
T. H. and H. R. McCloud
Mr. and Mrs. A. J. Syred
Theo. E. B. Pratt, Dorothy Pratt
　(née Hammick)
D. R. Digby
Peter N. Croston
Watford Chamber of Commerce
　and Industry
Jean and Ken Saunders
Kathleen Joan Pittman
W. J. B. Brown—B. B. Installations
Watford Fire Station
1st Watford Central Scout Group
Martyn Groves
P. E. Gabbitass
A. J. Gabbitass
Raymond Penrose
Nicola and James William Element
Jean and Richard Machin, Margaret,
　Mollie and Mary
Arthur George Gibson/Doreen Joan
　Gibson
Beryl Rod
Margaret W. Rhodes, (Headmistress,
　Watford Girls' Grammar School, 1973-87)
Mrs. Mary Nunn
Doris Collier and the late Reg Collier
Linda Collier
Brian Collier
Tony and Christine Paddington

Jock and Irene Learmonth
Ken and Sandra Hayes
Graham and Ann Learmonth
Alan and Robbie Nunn
Ron and Edie Nunn
Molly Derby
Alan and Janet Power
Lily and Bill Page (ex Blaw Knox)
John and Linda Page, Helen and David
Terry and Barbara Page, Christopher
　and Elizabeth
Mr. and Mrs. Power
Barbara Pascoe and the late Roy Pascoe
Mike and Rosemary Pascoe
Pete and Sue Pascoe
Jean Barton
Malcolm and Joy Waller
Mike and Jo Dellow
Master Gary John Thackham
Sam Gardiner
Frederick John Cox
A. D. Grace
D. W. Bradley
J. W. and J. A. Morgan
Mr. and Mrs. Dennis A. Viccars
Dorothy M. Mathews
John W. Reeves
Robert Hopkins
Brian J. Fox
Denise Coppock
Derrick Arthur Smith
K. C. and Mrs. S. Norman
G. V. Davenport
J. G. Davenport
James R. Pughe
Mr. and Mrs. T. G. Stevens
Gordon E. Lines
V. L. Dowse
K. R. Dixon
Mr. and Mrs. Arthur J. Fox
Edward Allenby Smith
Janet Ann Wesson
Mr. and Mrs. R. L. Dunsford
Jack Bass
Denis and Freda Jackson
Russell Latimer
Keith Warren
Kevin Anthony
Mr. and Mrs. Kenneth Knee
Eric T. Finerty, F.L.A.
Mr. Albert Vincent/Mrs. G. M. Vincent
M. McNicholl
C. Musk
Julie and Glyn Franks
Ronald S. Pearse
E. P. Lumley
John Sargant
Peter Tapping
Emory Clayton Collier
D. S. Newlyn
Mrs. L. C. Woollard
The Anstee Family

Olive Dorothy May Evans
Jean Mills
S. W. R. Brazier
Mark V. Noades
David J. Noades
John Byford
W. R. Hope
Paul, Sally, Dawn and Sarah Fishwick
Peter W. Booth, A.R.I.C.S.
Colin C. Bullimore
Ronald Peers
Nemo and Michelina Ermini
Topaz Hair & Beauty (prop. P. D'Urso)
Gordon E. French
Valerie A. Owen
Christine S. E. Chance
Rodric Jones
Mr. and Mrs. S. Bell
Derek R. Creasey, Joan M. Creasey
Ian S. Creasey, Kim Deary
Michael, Fiona and Rebecca Royal
F. E. J. Hicks
Miss June Clarke
David Johnson
Brenda, Dennis and Curtis Langston
Ron and Thelma Outrim
Vincent R. Tucker
Joan Enid Gunton (née Mounter)
Walter S. Brett
C. F. Trumper/F. A. Trumper
Mr. and Mrs. R. M. Tabor
D. A. Noades
Robert J. W. Snelling
David John Hughes
Amy Rebecca, born 2nd July 1987, to
　Peter William and Isobel Green
Anne Gayfer
C. Wilcox
John Keable, B.Eng., and
　Mrs. Denise Keable
Bernard and Dorothy Woodward
Doreen and Robert Wood,
　32nd anniversary, 9th July, 1987

Ron and Margery Cook
James D. Kent and Jane D. Young
John Michael Nicholas
C. Baldwin
Mr. A. E. and Mrs. G. W. Durrant
Mr. Norman Lane and Mrs. Alex Lane
John Dale Whiting
Russell and Gillian Crowson
Dr. and Mrs. A. K. Huggins
Keith Burberry Cook
Clifford E. Groves
Sylvia and Jim Norwood
Europa Trucks (Herts) Ltd
Sheila J. Day
Peter and Elaine Elespe
Dorothy W. Smith
B. G. K. Shilleto
Mr. and Mrs. Charles Poxon
Michael S. Bacon

J. R. Wakelin and Trish Wilkinson
Joyce Wakelin
Circe Virginia Allen
Mr. and Mrs. C. Heath
Nellie Grace
Adrian Robin Cottingham
C. F. Albon
Eveline and Harold Parsons
Joseph H. and David G. Wiggs
Mr. and Mrs. G. B. Hillier
Mr. and Mrs. A. R. Oliver
Nellie, Douglas and Jean Giddings
Connie, Bill, David and
    Edward Gallagher
Alan and Joan Gransby
John Anthony Redrup
P. G. Birch
Pamela Hedges
I. C. and S. M. Pankhurst
J. Goodman
Caldon of Watford Ltd. (2 copies)
Eleanor Macmillan
Jean and George Beeston
Joan and Dorothy Attwood
Mrs. M. K. Bishop
H. C. Sawyer
Tessa Miles
Bryan and Brenda Adlam (2 copies)
Autoturn Engineering
Michael Suter
Barrie Suter
John Hamperl
Mrs. V. Slevin
Sydney R. Cross
Frances Brenda Worlidge
Christine and Michael Howse
Beryl and Douglas Gilbert
Brian John Arnold
Mrs. Maria Blackburn and Sam N. F.
    Blackburn
Ray and Ann Swann
Gerald Hodges
Mrs. Queenie Rose Wood (née Baker)
Peter James Vincent/Joyce Vincent
H. Hall
John F. Bates
Alfred Stobart and Margaret Stobart
Christopher Horne
Kathleen and James Wilson
Roy and Marjorie Warwick
Mr. and Mrs. E. J. Voller
Chrichton and Judith Limbert
Vera Bergmanis
Mrs. J. A. Hilton/Mr. F. W. Hilton
Shaw & Kilburn Ltd.
David Gigney and Ann Davis
K. W. Cox (2 copies)
Brynley and Josephine East
Robert A. Wade
W. F. Meredith
H. D. Parslow
Royal Caledonian Schools

Linda Pressland
Gordon H. Hall, LL.B.,
    (Town Clerk, 1953-1974)
Anthony Ronald Harding
Keith Anthony Hall
Mr. and Mrs. E. J. Brady and Family
Mr. and Mrs. C. Turner/Mrs. A. M.
    Schutt and Family
Michael and Annjo Droog-Hayes
O. Grant
Ann and Ed. Martin
Mrs. Elsie Revely (née Bone)
Ernest Gerald Latham
Ted Jones
L. V. Liberty
Edgar D. W. Matthews
Ronald A. J. Pine
George Stanger
Paul and Annette Holman
Mrs. J. F. Hawthorn (née Wright)
Peter R. Sampson
Mary and Juan Gonzalez
Connelly Engineering and Building
    Services
The Incorporated West Herts Golf Club
Mr. A. J. Gussin/Mrs. L. A. Gussin
Edith Bines
Hazel Mary South
Alan Milton
C. Hagger and Son, Plumbers
Mr. and Mrs. Lionel G. Tomlin
Barbara Daphne Joan Hickman
Rex and Iris Nicholls
E. S. Moss Ltd.
Geoffrey Thompson
David and Gloria Fawcett
Stephen John Bone
Thomas William Bone
Wallington Fabian & White, incorporating
    James Smith & Co.
Kingswood Roofing
Mr. A. E. C. Clarke/Mrs. D. P. Broomfield
    (Chief Supervisor B.T., Rtd.)
Donald Vincent Rayner
Amanda Jane Powell
John, Linda, Amanda and Justin Bishop
Mrs. M. Gregory
Christine Johnson
G. R. Brown
Esmé and Gawan Vesey
Anthony J. Southern
Paul Martin Davies
Judith Anne Davies
Yvonne and Jim Upwood
Sheila and Steve Upwood
Ruth and Ray Upwood
Yvette and Mark Waldock
Maurice Smith
Sean and Anne Flynn
Derek and Margaret Perks
Phil and Shann Madsen and Family
Mr. and Mrs. L. Staton

Mr. and Mrs. J. S. Bone
Frederick and Peggy Read
Mark Sheldrake
Ernest Ronald Kingaby
G. J. R. Tricker
Mollie and Peter G. Lambourne
James T. Leah
Garry, Geraldine and Elizabeth Rimmer
Pete and Pat Bates
Laurence G. Nobes
Frank Dainton
Peter and Pamela Hussey
Fireman William Frank Perry,
    (Watford Fire Station)
Fireman Hugh Patterson Marshall,
    (Watford Fire Station)
Pat and Ron Dillingham
Audrey and Harvey Jaquest
John Barton Guy
Enid and Bryan Probet
Allen and Edna Nuttall
Councillor John Watts
Harry Smith, (Borough Treasurer,
    1944 to 1971)
Mrs. B. Harris
J. Stanley Oliver
Cllr. Veronica Conlon/
    Cllr. David Barnes
Norman Hugh and
    Mavis Beulah Tyrwhitt
Mr. and Mrs. W. T. H. Price
Mrs. Arthur Reynolds
Mrs. Winifred Horner
    (Mayoress, 1973-74)
Jean Mary Knapp
Dr. W. Eric Wightman/Cllr. Mrs. Ann
    Wightman
Frank Furness
Mr. and Mrs. E. J. Owens
Vera Camfield and Dora Camfield
Malcolm Holmes
Michael J. Galan/Susan E. Galan
Elaine and David Sands
Mrs. Maud V. Wickham (Waverly, Iowa,
    USA)
Mrs. Pamela J. Pease (Caledonia, N.Y., U.S.A.)
Robert Ian Neilson Gordon
Leslie John Barrell
Bill and Sheila Lead
Leroy Daley
Eric Pearce
Sheila B. Murray
David and Valerie Blair
Jenny Collier
Thomas and Margaret Davies
    (née Picton)
Mr. and Mrs. R. S. Allen-Smith
E. T. Jamieson
Philip G. and Freda M. Greenstreet
Kathleen and Gillian Todd
Mollie and Coleen Males
Co-operative Bank Plc.
Jean and Brian Paling

Brian L. Wicks
Edward Mills
Christopher John Mills
Mark Patrick Mills
Walter T. Cooper
Ray and Joyce Buksh
Graham and Anne Parker
Nigel Markwick
Mr. J. W. Taylor and Mrs. D. O. Taylor
P. G. and J. H. Jenkins
Sue Hicks
Alan Batchelor
Lionel F. Wise
Owen C. Vaughan
Mr. and Mrs. R. C. B. Cannard
M. H. and V. E. Jeeves
Miss Dorothy Hearn
Graham and Valerie Scott
Ann Stangroome/Stephen Stangroome
M. G. Fowler
John Armstrong Benning
Cyril Pelling/Audrey Pelling
Geoffrey Ian and Eileen Patricia Molson
P. Farnham
Paul Tear
William Frederick Thomas, J.P., and
    Rita Lily Thomas
Barbara and Ken Harrison
Irene and Thomas Wilkinson
Rosina Smale
Georgina and Barry Watts (2 copies)
Brian and Marianne Billing
William and Mary Eley
George and June Boarder
Edward A. and Ivy Martin
Andrew L. Turton and Annice Turton
Benjamin Lewis Cooper
Charis L. Beaton
Alexander J. Beaton
Ron and Barbara Davis
Paul J. Davis
William and Mary Wood
Mr. and Mrs. W. Hodgkiss
M. D. Perry
Alan Albert Allaway
Fred Richards
Kenneth Eric Martindale
Peter G. Ausden
The Library, Hatfield Polytechnic,
    Wall Hall
G. R. Greenstreet
Cllr. and Mrs. P. Kiely
L. A. Lorimer
A. E. Lorimer
Ray and Peggy Reynolds
Andrew Finnigan
N. C. Hamilton
Cynthia Orchard
Patrick J. Lucas
Yvette

Denise Warnes
Mr. C. Sheate and Mrs. C. M. Sheate
Joan Backhouse
Florence E. Wilkins
Frank and Di Hoeksma
E. A. Sutherns
G. A. Starkey
Ian Colley
Arthur and Carole Garman
Anne Beard
Stephen Hemsworth
Michael and Juliet Hart
Mrs. K. Cheshire
Bryan Hughes
Mr. and Mrs. P. J. Carpenter and
    Masters M. C. and R. G. Carpenter
Mr. and Mrs. A. G. Martin
Mr. and Mrs. J. Ireland
Sabat's of Abbots
Evelyn Cooper
Mick Wade
Nigel Wade
Mr. and Mrs. K. J. Gee
Steve Ayres
Lesley E. Hurley
R. A. C. Avery
David Richard Humphrys
John Morris
Mary Gubby
Brian Gregory
Mrs. Joyce Sharp
Miss J. M. Birch
M. Furness
Bernard G. Kent
Derek C. Piggott
Joan and Terry Burkett
Victor Alexander McDougall
Richard and Julie Martin
James B. Richards
G. C. Bourne
Eric Ford
Mrs. D. Q. Ellis
A. K. Child
Hatchards (10 copies)
Allan Humphris
Mrs. Josephine Whitmill
Mr. and Mrs. Michael D. H. Hill
D. L. Findell
Roger and Marilyn Bourne
Parsons Paper Ltd.
Mrs. D. S. Nash
John James Childs
John P. Bedborough
Maureen Ballam
Frank Maynard and Jane Anne T.
    Anderson
Rex and Lesley Darlow
Andrew and Gaye Gunton
Juliette and Maurice, Graham and
    Roger Jones

Mr. and Mrs. Gibsone
George and Monica Lakey
Margaret L. Marsden
D. Gahan
D. R. Gahan
P. Mitchell
Peter M. Cole/Isabel M. Cole
E. and J. Griffin
Mrs. D. P. Cross
Christopher and Mary Newson
M. R. Cooper and M. A. Fowke
Margaret Gwynedd Clarke
Physics For You Tutorial Agency
G. Gussefeld, F.R.S.C.
Gordon James Floyd
Mr. and Mrs. D. F. Inns
The Orchard School
Cassiobury Junior School
W. J. Elbourn
Tudor and Marian Marshall
R. Evans
Miss Amanda Carol Challis
James Bradley
Frank Phillips
Les and Yvonne Morgan
Mr. and Mrs. N. Blake
Doug Marriott
Parmiter's School
Anthony Moss
Colin Rickard
Mr. and Mrs. I. Pigram
John Edward Cooper
A. Tronnolone
M. Joan Ming
V. N. Lyford
Elaine and Derek Allen
Mr. and Mrs. Brian V. Maisey
John S. Burnett/Laurie B. Harwood
V. M. Richardson
Richard Stevens
Chris Johnson
Mrs. E. Close
Mr. M. Parkins
Frank Childs
Ron and Audrey Middleton
Black Horse Agencies—Stimpsons
Michael John Smith
Field Search Services
Heather M. Smith
Mr. and Mrs. H. Hedge
Mrs. Janet Love Miller
R. E. Grange
Polychrome
Mrs. Mavis Lewis
Keith F. G. Debenham
C. H. L. Nickless
Gary and Christine Grimley
Colin A. Pascoe (Grange Park School,
    1982-1987)

*The Subscribers' List for the Slip Case Edition opened on June 1st 1987, and
closed on July 22nd 1987. 1055 subscriptions were placed, the balance to
1100 being presentation and complimentary copies. In addition 200 copies
were requested for Civic Presentation use by the Watford Borough Council.*

Acknowledgements

As "The Book of Watford" is essentially an account of the past 100 and more years my main source of information has been the local newspapers. Selected items were photographed and re-typeset in the style and manner of the original – which accounts for the spelling differences as, e.g., Callow Land and Callowland.

To link these excerpts and provide extra background material I have been fortunate to have had the services of Ted Parrish, George Lorimer and Edgar Chapman—all well-known writers who have contributed extensively to magazines and newspapers articles of local interest. Edgar Chapman's speciality has been early history and history of brewing and pubs; he also drew my attention to many useful items I would otherwise have missed. Ted Parrish contributed much material on early history and background to social history to modern times. George Lorimer, in taking on the task of proof reading the whole, added helpful comments and observations throughout. He also, with Ivor Buckingham, provided material for the section on cinemas. Finally, David Johnson compiled the index.

In addition to excerpts from local newspapers I am grateful for permission to publish extracts from several books, and to have found others useful for reference. I was pleased to have had the extended loan of a copy of Britton's "Cassiobury", and the typescript of W. R. Saunders' "History of Watford". I am indebted to Major T. D. Sainsbury for permission to publish extracts from "Medals and Awards", and to Roger Culverhouse for assistance on matters dealing with the history of the Fire Brigade, and to the District Head Postmaster, D. E. Brownfield, for permission to photograph the sorting office in Ascot Road.

As changes to the town are continuing at a rapid pace, and many readers may not have visited Watford for a number of years, the end section includes a collection of photographs taken especially to up-date and help locate many of the earlier and long-since-gone places. It is hoped that they will provide reference to researchers in years to come.

As so many illustrations have been used in the book I have been at pains to make sure that they are reproduced as well, or better, than would be expected. To this end the half-tone screens used are considerably finer than is normal. As page layout changed frequently during the planning stages many of the negatives were made more than once and I have to thank Colin Pascoe who, as a school-leaver, served an 'apprenticeship' at a task of what, at times, seemed endless and of daunting magnitude; the quality of the reproductions is testimony to his perseverance.

The collection of illustrations in the Reference Library has been added to over many years and in a period of conservation many photographs have been remounted but, unfortunately, the author's name, if known, has not been carried forward.

The earliest positively dated photograph is by Frederick Downer of the Wedding Day procession, 10th March 1863 (p.45). His, and his sons work spans a period to 1919.

From about 1888 until 1926 William Coles rivalled Downer in quantity and quality; his business passed into ownership of Theodore Greville and many of his original negatives still exist.

Whitford Anderson was an architect who extensively photographed Hertfordshire's towns and villages; his record of Watford spans 1895 to c1905. Jesse and Percy Landon, between 1895 to c1929 added views, as did Albert Warren (1902-1914).

A professional studio which produced town views was Couper Mathews, later Gregg Couper, c1906 to c1960. Mr. F. H. Haines was a gifted amateur, associated with the Camera Club, c1905-1920; he made many views of the town. George Bolton contributed much material from c1922 to c1939.

Greville Studios, c1935-1943, were under contract to provide photographs for the Watford Observer; many negatives of this period survive, in particular their 'war-time' series. Next on the scene is Harry Williamson who worked first for the West Herts Post and then for the Watford Observer and his work spans the years 1944 to c1956. His negatives made for the West Herts Post are lost but those for the Watford Observer survive.

It is due to the courtesy extended by the Watford Observer that I was able to research early years of their collection, and to use any felt to be of interest.

A number of prints are by members of the Watford Camera Club, but carry no names, and also used are a number of 'anonymous' prints.

I am aware that many collections of old postcards exist, and I have been pleased to have used several donated by well-wishers. (The Watford Museum is also building an illustrations collection but, at the time of work on this book, the collection was not fully catalogued or easily available for reference, but should be a rich source of material, in due course, for future researchers.)

In many instances, copies have been made from newspaper prints, the originals having long since been lost.

The following list of illustration credits is sequential. (ex) *indicates an exception on that page listed.*

Frontispiece and p.154, views of Cassiobury by J. W. M. Turner, from Britton's 'Cassiobury', c1837, as are the line drawing to title page and page 13 (courtesy Keith Seabrook).

Albert Dillingham's portrait, Gregg Couper.

Photographs of Parish Register pages by George Bolton.

Line drawings by Charles Healey and Alfred Macdonald.

Railway drawings p.31, 33, Bourne.

Railway drawings p.32, 34, 35, The Heale Bequest, Camden Library.

p.40, probably by Frederick Downer, perhaps as trial exposure for his 'great-day' group, on p.45.

Frederick Downer (and, later, Sons)
p.46, 47 (ex c) 53, 55, 64b, 67 (reproduced from Watford Illustrated), 74, 76tl, 78, 79, 82, 84t, 88, 96t, 101, 111b, 112tr, 115tr, rt; 118, 119 and 120 (ex b) from Goodrich's 'Guide to Watford'; 121c. The following from 'Watford Illustrated': 130-134 and 135b; 135tl. From 'Watford Illustrated': 136 (ex top). 145, 148b.

Not known, or reference in doubt: 48, 49, 54, 56, 57, 59, 61, 63, 70, 75, 76tr, 81, 84b, 87, 99tr, 100, 104tr, 107br, 121t & b, 109b, 111, 113, 114, 115tl, 116, 117, 124, 126, 129t, 136t, 139bc, 147, 148t, 149, 152t, 160c & b, 163t, 165, 169, 171, 175, 179, 180, 181, 190t, 237, 271b, 273br, 278b, 302t & b, 307, 309.

Portrait of Henry Williams, p.57, from an original painting, courtesy Peter King.

Negatives which may be by W. Coles: 57t, 58, 64c, 65, 66, 73, 90, 98, 108, 109t, 110, 112t, 123b, 127, 164b, 166, 167, 170b.

W. Coles: 60, 89, 94, 99b, 105, 106t, 112b, 123t, 137, 138, 139t & br, 140, 144, 168. (Photograph p.89 courtesy of S.O. Middleton, H.C.C. Fire Brigade, Watford.)

Whitford Anderson: 80, 91, 92, 93 (ex t & cl) 94, 99c.

Albert Warren: 86 (Cassiobridge Common); 96b, 104tl.

Negatives which may be by F. H. Haines: 97, 115bl, 121bl, 122b, 135r.c, 160t, 161.

Reproduced from newspapers: 99tl (WO), 156tl, 162t, 163c (Daily Sketch); 174b (WO); 192c & b, 214b (WHP); 217tl (WHP); 218 (WHP); 233 (WO); 259b (WHP); 283b (WHP).

Miscellaneous: 100, 148t, 149b—prints loaned by Mrs. Jenkins; 129—postcard loaned by George Lorimer; 141tl—postcard loaned by Lesley Dunlop; 153t—print loaned by Dennis Hubbard/R. Greville; Pubs, pages 171, 173, 174 and 176—prints loaned by John Ausden; 218tl—print loaned by R. Nicholls.

From Postcards: 103, 104, 107bl, 125b, 129b, 141, 143, 157b, 170tl, 231c.

John Cullen: 104b; Jesse Landon: 106

Central Aerophoto Co: 150, 151.

George Bolton: 152b, 156, 159, 176t & c, 177 t & b, 178, 179t, 185t, 190b.

Frith Bros Ltd: 153b, 155; Otto Brookman: 157tl & c, 184tl.

Gregg Couper: 163b, 184tl, 185b, 186t, 192t, 268t.

Aerofilms Ltd: 158, 164t, 183, 301.

Greville Studios: 170tr, 172, 189, 191, 193, 194, 195, 198-213, 214t, 215, 216, 217tr, 218 219-221 (most in their capacity as 'official photographer' to the Watford Observer).

Harry Williamson: 224, 225, 251t & b, 234 (all WHP); 250t, 253, 254-256, 258, 259t, 260bl, 261 t & b, 262 (ex bl), 263, 264t, 265t, 273bl, (all WO).

Author: 236, 238, 243-249, 250b, 251, 260tl, br, 261c, 262br, 268b, 269, 271tl, 274c & b, 275 c & b, 276 cr, b, 277 tl, b, 278t, 279r, 280b, 281, 282-285, 286t, 288, 290, 291t, 292-297, 299, 300, 303, 305, 308, 310-361.

Keystone Press Agency: 257; The Observer: 265c.

Tempest, Cardiff, 267, 273, 280t.

Watford Camera Club: 270tl, 274t, 275t, 276t & cr, 277tr, 286b.

Raymond Nunn: 270tr, Graphic Photos: 271tr, 279tl, 302c.

Watford Observer: 286c, 287bl, 289, 291b.

Ray Munday: 298; Colin Pascoe: 342br.

Main source and references:
Kelly's Directories 1949, 1970.
Man With Camera Felix H. Mann, Secker & Warburg.
Railway Motor Buses and Bus Services 1902-1933 Vol 1, John Cummings.
The Years Between, the National Story, R. J. Crawley, D. R. MacGregor, F. D. Simpson.
History of Watford, Henry Williams.
Original typescript of *History of Watford*, W. R. Saunders by courtesy of his daughter, Joan Saunders.
Watford Central Area Draft Plan 1956, and *1964*, E. H. Doubleday, OBE, PPTPI, FRICS, MIMunE, County Planning Officer, Herts County Council.
Cassiobury, Britton, small paper version, (courtesy Keith Seabrook).
Street and Place Names in Watford Alan W. Ball.
Hertfordshire Photographers 1839-1939, Bill Smith and Michael Pritchard
David Greenhill, Master Printer Miriam Leech.
World Trucks—Scammell Pat Kennett.
Metro Railway, London's Metropolitan Railway Alan A. Jackson.
The Story of Hertfordshire Police The Letchworth Press.
The London & Birmingham Railway Thomas Roscoe (c1840).
Shopping in Victorian Watford.
Hertfordshire Illustrated Review 1894.

Newspapers:	
The Watford Observer	Watford Illustrated
West Herts Post	Watford Our Town
Watford Newsletter	Focus
	Evening Echo

Errata

p.144   Caption. Wrong photograph (photograph used is of celebrations for King George V's Coronation).

Addendum

p.157   Caption, centre photograph. Tucker Bros. took over the business of Brookman's on 2nd November, 1953.

p.282   Caption, top. Allen Anker, fishmonger, transferred their business to MacFisheries 27th July, 1953.

p.273   Caption. Small pic, Scammell's 100-tonner—date *should be* January 1951. (The load a 70-ton 660hp diesel-electric loco en-route to the South Bank for the 1951 Festival, and thence for export to Tasmania).

Typeset by L. V. Nunn; artwork, negatives, plates and original printing – Pageprint (Watford) Ltd. Film assembly by CN Graphics, Amersham and binding by Dorstel Press Ltd, Harlow.
Soft-cover edition 1992 printed by B & H Printing Services Ltd, Watford.

Supplement to
The Book of Watford

Harlequin Food Court and Phase II opened, 1991

Mars 1 to Harlequin

The 'Mars' project started just after *'The Book of Watford'* was published; the Queens Road properties had been in a devitalised state for many years.

The changes in Watford during the past decade have been profound and the Council are currently exploring yet more with the just-announced 'Watford Regeneration and Economic Forum.' The *'Book of Watford, II'* deals specifically with the decade or so; this 'Mars' supplement, an abridged excerpt, is designed to up-date 'The Book of Watford' with part of the Harlequin story.

MARS 1

When I started photography my choice of chemicals was simple – Johnsons; they were a few pennies cheaper than Kodak and, more important, gave instructions for different brands of film whereas Kodak only mentioned their own. Though, from time to time, I used other makes Johnsons could always be found in my darkroom.

The time of founding can be traced back to 1743 when young John Johnson started an apprenticeship as a goldsmith; out of apprenticeship he later started his own business in the profession of Assayer and one of his two sons, Charles, started work in Hatton Garden as a refiner, laying the foundations of the well-know Johnson Mathey. During the time of Fox Talbot, 1850s, Johnson and Sons made chemical salts of gold and silver which were needed for Talbot's new process – beginning their long association with photography.

During the Great War (1914-18) Britain was in need of chemicals not previously made in this country and a factory was built in Hendon where chemical manufacture was started. Johnson and Sons, later Johnsons of Hendon Ltd, continued making photographic chemicals, and a wide range of darkroom accessories, measures, dishes, trimmers and dryers, etc. After the WWII Johnsons took on distribution of photographic products which I, then in retail trade, stocked and sold; these included the well respected Voigtlander cameras and Eumig cine cameras and projectors. (The latter caused an especial stir when in the mid 1950s they introduced the P8 8mm film projector with 12v 100w lamp giving a brighter picture than their previous model with a 210v 500w lamp).

A family firm, they fell to a targeted acquisition by a company called Hestair. Manufacture of raw chemicals ceased and Johnsons moved to Radlett; the chemical side of business (which had stopped in 1972) was sold in 1974 to a new company, Photo Technology Ltd, and I was invited to handle their launch advertising and literature production – the latter until we finally closed in 1990.

What, you may rightly wonder, has this to do with Watford?

Hestair Ltd were not interested in the chemical business; rather they introduced a new phrase to relish – 'asset stripping' – it transpired that they had eyes on the land upon which the factory was based. It was cleared, and redeveloped into what we know as 'Brent Cross'.

In subsequent years 'going to Brent Cross' meant a shopping experience the like of which most of us had never met, ample and convenient car parks; for those who did not wish to go by car there were regular, and special, bus services.

Doubtless the impact would have given a fresh urgency to bringing forward the 'Mars' plans but there will be very few who can recall the weekly 'West Herts Post' let alone an issue in January 1962 which carried a story of a project which 'would change dramatically the face of Watford within the next five to seven years'. Perhaps the general public may be forgiven for their lack of interest, for how many times has something been announced, to be forgotten within days and not to resurface until perhaps decades later?

With a headline of MARS! the story told of a forthcoming February Council meeting at which would be discussed the projected plans for redeveloping the area between Queens Road and Water Lane into a shopping complex.

To cost £3,000,000, the possibilities included:
• first-class hotel with assembly rooms behind
• a ten-pin bowling alley
• an eleven-storey central tower block of 130 flats with garages for the tenants underneath the block.

Sponsored by Cubitt London Properties Ltd they suggested that ground rents be reviewed every 25 years; that they should build the multi-storey car park and sub-lease it to the Borough who would then have 'absolute control over parking'. The 7½ acre redevelopment scheme would include Carey Place and Albert Road which would disappear completely. The Borough Council, it was stated, had sought the views of the Corporation's consultants, Hillier, Parker, May and Rowden and it was their views that the Property Committee would be considering.

The scheme fell through though the name stuck. Years passed; steam power on the railway gave way to electric; manual accounting at the banks gave way to computer-power; shops in Queens Road were refurbished and given a new lease of life. Town gas (from coal) gave way to natural

Text excerpts and research

The text excerpts used are as originally printed except that some may have been shortened owing to lack of space; the original sense and meaning is unaltered. Letters, when used, are used uncut as published.

All items acknowledge the source, and month, of publication, and so no problem should arise if and when researchers wish to consult or refer to the originals.

Any student wishing to photocopy photographs in this supplement for scholastic projects may do so with the sole exception of the aerial photograph (pages 4/5) which is the copyright of Aerofilms Ltd. If any copy is made of photograph or text the photograph should be acknowledged to *The Book of Watford* and the text to the newspaper concerned – WO for *Watford Observer;* F Obs for *Free Observer* and the *Review.*

"Here lies the remains of dwellings and premises which were once Albert Street, Carey Place, Charles Street and Clifford Street, much of Derby Road, some High Street premises, as well as the shops of Queens Road between Derby Road and High Street."

gas and our coinage went decimal. The Beatles and the swinging sixties evolved into only slightly more staid 70s. Watford lost most of its cinemas, found the High Street cut about and broken, lost the 'West Herts Post', and the Park Gates, and, almost as unthinkable, lost Odhams as well!

The old market went as did Cawdells and after what seemed an interminable period of time Charter Place shopping centre – 'Shoppers Paradise' – finally opened at about the same time as Brent Cross. But a 'Brent Cross' it was not.

The Mars plan had not, however, been forgotten. Developers and Watford Borough Council were biding their time; buying pockets and parcels of land against the day when action could begin. And, sure enough, in the early days of 1986 – 24 years on – the plans resurfaced.

The cost had increased by 43 times to about £130,000,000.

A knowledgeable town trader ventured to state that there should be a commitment to revitalise the Parade and top end of the town; Councillors argued about what type of entrance it should have . . .

Behind the scenes, in Council, there were deeper rumblings. Although the council was well aware that the complex would close in the evenings – no night life – they wanted what had been originally promised; entertainment of some sort, and a swimming pool was settled upon, though hardly 'evening entertainment.' Councillors wanted it within the complex; the developers knew it would not be viable to mix shops and swimming and wanted it separated.

Council had land across the road – Benskin's old site – and although zoned for industry (and changed to housing) it was found that this would be an apposite place to build a swimming complex to be funded by payment from Mars' developers. But Capital and Counties would pay only £500,000 in lieu of the complex space promised; the Borough's ratepayers would have to stump up the projected balance of £4,500,00 needed and when finally finished Watford Springs was stated to have cost £10,000,000.

The first issue of the revamped Watford Our Town

(October 1990) put the matter of cost rather quaintly; "the whole complex when complete will have cost the Council only 12 per cent more than it cost taxpayers to construct just one mile of the M25 motorway" – the inference being that the Government took money from *taxpayers* for part of a road, but that, in Watford, the *Council* paid for a swimming complex.

The housing which was to have been built upon the Benskin site was instead built upon the old Isolation Hospital site in Tolpits Lane.

The internal wrangling had split the local Labour group into two factions one half trying to insist upon leisure within the Centre (despite the unsuitable mix) on the altruistic idea of forcing the centre to stay open 'so that there was life after closing time', the others recognising that, despite the cost, a purpose designed and built swimming complex made better sense, albeit at a hugely increased cost.

The matter dragged on with plans being shown, and concerned Watford Fields residents protesting, until Councillor Vince Muspratt told the meeting that 'the complex had to be finished by March 1990 or it would never be built; Government restrictions upon spending mean that after that date the money will not be available and the much needed modern swimming pool will not be built.'

'Watford Springs' opened much later than expected and, it is stated, with considerable structural problems in its wake and unresolved; though a popular venue of its type it does nothing for Watford's evening life (which was the original intention) such as would have been achieved if a leisure complex such as Woodside's Warner Cinema had been built upon the site.

As it happens, and not by any design of Watford's Council, the town does have in Harlequin an asset which is in some ways unique. Other towns in the country too have 'shopping centres'; Harlequin stands very high on design comparison – other centres may be converted large department stores – and the ancestry cannot be hidden; even worse, some may be built out of town where shoppers forsake the

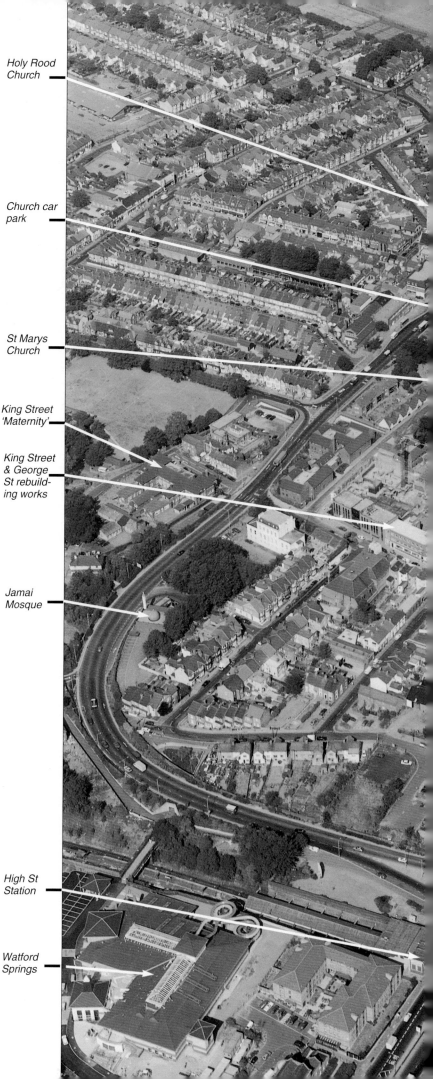

Holy Rood
Church

Church car
park

St Marys
Church

King Street
'Maternity'

King Street
& George
St rebuild-
ing works

Jamai
Mosque

High St
Station

Watford
Springs

traditional town-centre shops with even more dire results than we have seen in Watford. Originally Watford wanted to build its centre further down the High Street where land could be more easily acquired. County Council vetoed the plans as ' making the shopping spread out too far' and so we have a centre which is actually in the town.

An item in an issue during September 1986 of the *Review* showed some of the questions which would have to be solved; the Mars plans introduced to council members quickly threw up the thorny problem of the development which long since promised 'entertainment facilities' but which, when the crunch came, could not be incorporated within the structure as envis-aged by the planners who were more con-cerned with providing an efficient shopping centre with as much car parking space as possible. A sensible comment that the ques-tion about 'public transport' being looked at seemed to have got lost.

Mars one scheme gets a green light

A MASSIVE new development which will jolt Watford's shopping centre into the 21st century has been approved by Watford councillors. They gave the green light to the transformation of the Mars one site at a meeting of the development and planning committee on Tuesday night. Members were told that a number of "minor" problems such as landscaping, lack of light to flats and effect on listed buildings in the High Street had been over-come during negotiations between council officers and the developers.

The plan is to construct a five level shopper's paradise on land between Charter Place and the Hammonds triangle site at the southern end of the

In this aerial photograph the first phase of Harlequin is substantially on the way to completion but in Queen's Road Trewins is still trading and awaiting the readiness of their new store within Harlequin.
At about the centre of the picture may be seen the new dome which adorns the Harlequin's High Street entrance.
To its left may be seen the white scar indi-cating the rebuilding of the Woolworths site and substantial works from the High Street to George Street.

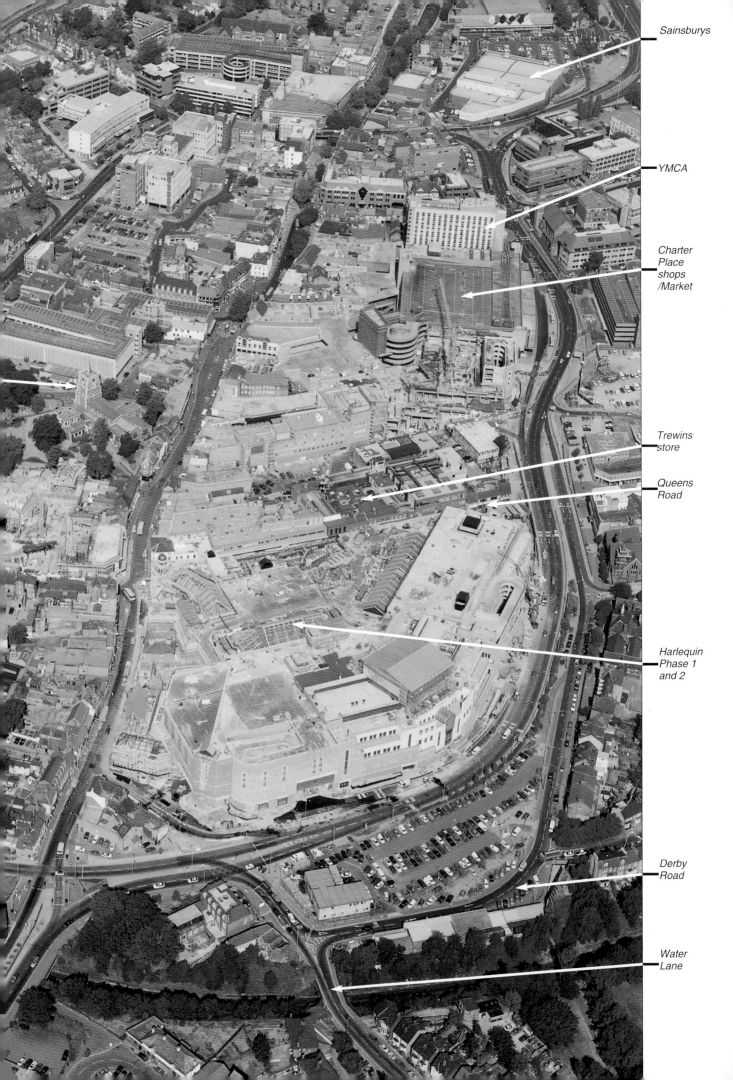

Sainsburys

YMCA

Charter
Place
shops
/Market

Trewins
store

Queens
Road

Harlequin
Phase 1
and 2

Derby
Road

Water
Lane

November 1988: the whole area cleared and for a time Derby Road can be seen by those working on the site. The depth below ground level is necessary to house the vast and complex underground unloading bays which service Harlequin's sales units.

High Street. It will provide 662,000 sq ft of shopping floor space and involve the relocation and extension of Trewins and an enlargement of both Marks and Spencer and British Home Stores. The entire development will be covered and closed at night and covered walkways will link the whole development with Charter Place.

The council are to enter into legally binding agreements to ensure that the scheme incorporates a leisure facility though exactly what form it will take has not been decided. Creche facilities are also to be included. The main stumbling block on Tuesday night proved to be what type of main entrance the shopping complex should have on the corner of Queens Road and the High Street where Ketts stands.

After a lengthy debate it was decided that planning approval be given for the scheme with an entrance that retains the upper part of the distinctive Ketts domes. Councillor Mike Jackson told the committee: "The developers have made a number of improvements for the better since the application first came before us. "But I would like to ensure that parking bays for the disabled are incorporated into the scheme."

On the question of the Ketts Building councillor Bill Everett described it as "an abortion" and urged members to "get rid of it." but he was in a minority when it came to the final vote. One group who are not happy with the scheme are members of the National Trades Union Council. They wrote a strong letter to committee members complaining of a lack of public consultation and said that even councillors got scant details of the plan.

Secretary Dennis McGrath wrote: "We are also concerned about the airey-fairey unconfirmed and uncommitted nature of the provision of any leisure facilities for the people of Watford."

After the meeting he said that the trades council feared a minor interest development

such as was included in the Monmouth Arms site – the last large parcel of land to be developed in the town. He said that the council had also failed to look at the question of public transport in the development though after reading his letter councillors agreed to pass the comments on to the bus services sub-committee for consideration.

Review September 1986

An energetic committee, headed by Joyce Stevenson, the Council's Development Control Officer, looked into myriad details of design, access, decor, safety and contributed greatly to the eventual outcome. But the 'leisure provision' threat had not gone:

Mars 1 changes considered

Mars 1, the Watford town centre shopping complex which could start early next year, has undergone changes in the past year of planning discussions.

Its appearance now is less of a Moorish Casbah, Watford borough councillors were told when they studied drawings and a model showing major extensions to Marks and Spencer, British Home Stores and Littlewoods. One member of the Development Control sub-committee, Councillor Geoffrey Greenstreet, said some of the new development looked as if it were designed to replace Cawdells, a former Watford department store. "It is in that style" he remarked.

The past year has been spent negotiating a whole host of details of what is the largest and most important development this town has seen in generations, said Mrs Joy Stevenson, the borough council's development control officer, at the Wednesday meeting.

Floorspace has increased marginally, large retail units have decreased from four to three and small to medium units have increased from 103 to 121.

But councillors are not happy with a cut in some of the tree planting, aimed at softening the look of the massive complex.

And they do not want the lunge pool and other leisure facilities which will be provided at the Queen's Road-Beechen Grove end of the site to be cut off from the shopping centre. For operational reasons the developers are unwilling to connect the two uses.

"This is something I would wish to see taken up later on," said Councillor Martin Rainsford.

WO, November 1987

Upon the completion of the M25 a triangle of 'spare' land was formed near Bricket Wood; dubbed the 'Golden Triangle' it was targeted for a shopping complex development but, upon public inquiry was squashed as infringing green-belt land. One threat to Mars had been lifted but another loomed, at Aldenham, where the old LPTB Bus Overhaul Garages site was to be redeveloped – a shopping complex was projected, but the proposal was defeated:

Town faces trade threat

WATFORD stands to lose millions of pounds worth of trade and some of the biggest retailers lined up for its £100 million Mars 1 shopping complex.

Both business and council chiefs admitted this week that the town is under siege as retail wars are raging all around the borough.

A solitary figure enjoying a few minutes of warm sunlight and perhaps oblivious to the import of the site behind his back.

With the Natwest Bank on the corner of Queens Road acting as a landmark among the High Street boarded up frontages, construction work carries on apace.

The planned rosy future for Watford as a booming regional shopping centre will be in serious jeopardy if a similar project at nearby Elstree is approved, Watford's Assistant Planning Director Peter Kerr warned.

As well as losing an estimated £10.1 million in trade from durable goods in 1996, it is anticipated that major retailers will abandon Watford's Brent Cross-style development for the alternative site at Aldenham Bus Works.

Watford Borough Council made strong objections to Slough Estates plans for a retail development on the A41 at a public inquiry last week. "The Aldenham proposal presents a serious risk to Watford in terms of trade loss and the fact that retailers will find it just as easy to locate in Aldenham," said Mr Kerr.

Final details of the Mars 1 scheme were hammered out at Watford's Development Control Sub-committee on Wednesday night. Development is expected to be underway by the end of 1988. Watford Chamber of Commerce president Mike King spelt out the bleak future for Watford if the Aldenham project goes ahead. "Watford is under siege at the moment and it will destroy the town centre as we know it. We are vehemently opposed to Aldenham," said Mr King.

Another big concern already familiar to large-scale employers in Watford is staff recruitment. Mr Kerr's evidence at the inquiry included a statement from Clements personnel director outlining manpower problems. Other traders in Watford, in particular Asda and Tesco, are known to be experiencing difficulties in filling vacancies.

WO, May 1988

Roger Hillier was a tireless campaigner against both Mars and the M1 Link who, after the completion of Harlequin, left Watford. His reference

to 'purchasing cabbages in the High Street' was more than thirty years out of date as even by 1958 there were few greengrocers in the High Street; most greengrocery being bought in the Market or from more local greengrocery shops to be found in the town before they, in turn, lost business to supermarkets and closed:

Mars One leaves town 'no scope'

A SCATHING attack has been levelled at the Mars One scheme by a Watford resident who claims that it will leave no scope for "life after dark in central Watford."

Giving evidence at this week's public inquiry into aspects of the project to rebuild a key section of the shopping centre Mr Roger Hillier also lodged objections to the threatened increase in traffic the scheme would attract and the loss of valuable town centre housing. To put it bluntly "what is in it for the residents of central Watford?" demanded Mr Hillier, of Gladstone Road.

"Watford already has more shoe shops than the average person needed, but it is impossible to buy a cabbage in the High Street," he claimed. "I am not sure that Mars One will remedy this shortfall," he remarked.

The key to his case was the question of whether or not Mars One relied on the proposed road linking the town centre with the M1 going ahead. Mr Hillier is a fierce campaigner against the link road, which was recently debated in detail during an eight-week public inquiry, which ended shortly before Christmas. Watford council told this week's hearing, held at the Town Hall, that the M1 link was not a vital part of the Mars One

project. "Of course, the M1 link assists the scheme but it's not essential to it," said Mr John Taylor, counsel acting for Watford Borough Council.

But Mr Hillier quoted evidence given by Watford Borough Council at the link road inquiry which stated that the Mars One scheme would be in jeopardy without the M1 Link Road, and he claimed that the council had considered them to be "interconnected schemes."

WO, January 1988

Breaking the ground for shopping complex

WORKMEN started up their bulldozers this week as clearance work began to pave the way for the £100 million shopping city which will change the face of Watford.

The Mars 1 development took its first steps forward as contractors set to work on the now closed Clifford Street car park site. More than 400 workmen will play their part over the next three-and-a-half years in building 130 shops, stores and a food court on the 10 acre site.

WO, September 1988

The choosing of the name 'Harlequin' proved to be very apt and brought the airy-fairy 'Mars project' down to earth.

But before the work had started another outcry was raised concerning the impending destruction of some of Watford's few remaining listed character buildings; the start was delayed and many fronts and shells saved and incorporated into the High Street frontage:

At the extreme left the view looks towards the Food Court and the entrance mall. Phase II has been open for some while and Phase III is anticipated soon. About half of the shops are let and visitors are split between 'sightseers' and shoppers.

New name for Mars 1 complex

WATFORD'S multi-million pound shopping complex – previously known Mars 1 – is to be called the Harlequin Centre. The name was chosen by a panel of judges after more than 250 people responded to a competition to name the shopping centre.

The winning name was sent in by Mrs Moyra Castle of Bushey who won a £500 shopping voucher to be spent at Trewin's, which is to be one of the major outlets in the redeveloped centre. The panel of judges was made up of representatives from the development partnership of Capital and Counties, Sun Alliance Insurance Group and Watford Borough Council.

The competition suggested that a local or regional name might be appropriate but the panel was attracted to the name Harlequin, because it "reflects the exciting and attractive image of a modern shopping centre."

The judges were impressed with the number of entries they received and with the amount of research into the history of Watford.

They were particularly impressed with the efforts of youngsters from Central Primary School who launched a full-scale project on the centre. Mrs Castle suggested the winning name after hearing it being used as the new name for the British Rail line from Euston to Watford.

WO, December 1988

Harlequin Centre work right on target

WORK on the £100 million plus Harlequin Centre is on target with the first phase due to be opened in September of next year.

During the whole of the construction period it is estimated that about 600 men will be at work on the site at any one time. To make sure that the operation is completed on time nine large tower cranes are strategically placed so materials and equipment can be quickly moved around the site. Heavy vehicles delivering to the centre's shops will use a basement service road in order to keep commercial traffic and shoppers' cars separate.

The first phase, which includes 41 shops and the new store for Trewins, is due to open in September, 1990. Above it will be 600 parking places in a five-storey car park. Phase two will follow shortly after in Spring 1991, with 49 shops and a further 900 parking spaces.

WO, June 1989

The disappearance of the entire Carey Place complex and associated streets raised misgivings with some, but as the area had been systematically cleared over the previous ten to twenty years no-one bothered very much:

A community has been lost

I READ the article on the wonderful new shopping centre the town will have but wasn't there among the statistics about the number of bricks, etc., used, the number of houses that were pulled down?

In fact, a small community was lost.

I hope the profit from this venture salves the consciences of those who ordered it - or will it? - J. W. N. S, Sutton Road, Watford.

WO, August 1990

Underground servicing of shops and stores, here part of Charter Place complex, takes delivery vehicles out of the main street.

The panorama of about 275° looks towards the Queens Car Park entrance and, in the far distance, leads towards the blocked off approach to Phase III which is still under construction.   *1992*

Harlequin centre poised to open for business

CUSTOMERS will be flooding into the Harlequin Centre next week when the first store of the multi million pound shopping complex opens for trading.

By Christmas 40 new stores will have opened in the Brent Cross-style shopping mall which is costing in the region of £120 million. The new Trewins store will be the biggest in the 11-acre shopping centre with 200,000 sq ft of shopping and storage space, doubling the floor space at its Queen's Road site. Trewins has been trading in Watford for more than a century. It started as a tiny drapery business owned by a Mr Matthews in the late 1870s but quickly grew.

In 1880 Arthur Trewin took over the store and by 1913 he had been joined by his brother Henry and had expanded to three shops in Queen's Road. After the Great War, Trewins was bought by Selfridges and was then one of 16 stores acquired by John Lewis Partnership in 1940. The present site in Queen's Road was rebuilt in 1965 but the store remained, until now, the smallest in the John Lewis chain.

When the last customers leaves the branch on Saturday evening Trewins staff will have to move the entire enterprise, lock, stock and barrel, before the re-opening on Wednesday morning. Much of the stock, such as mannequins, videos, pots and pans, will be taken on foot along Queen's Road to the new store.

WO, August 1990

Bus services were unaltered, but ring road traffic and bus lanes were altered to aid traffic flow; with entrance and exit from the Palace car park crossing the flows problems arose:

Not everyone has own transport

IN your July 27 issue you gave information regarding the Harlequin Centre, and the number of parking spaces, but no mention of bus services to there.

I do hope that the organisers of this development have not forgotten that there are still many people who do not have their own transport and have to rely on the bus service.

Unreliable as it is, we do get there – eventually! - R. B, Meadow Road, Kingswood.

WO, August 1990

Upon the Gartlett Road car park (flat land) was built the Edward Hyde offices; the Shrubberies Car Park was renamed Gade; the two new ones being called Kings and Queens respectively:

Car park in six letters

LONG names of town centre car parks are proving to be a mouthful for the designers of new sign posts for the revamped Watford shopping centre. Councillors are now being asked to con-

sider new names of no more than six letters, which can be fitted on road signs once the Mars 1 redevelopment is finished.

But in accepting that shorter names would be needed, councillors decided to reject some of the ideas put forward at the meeting.

These included Gart for the Gartlet Road car park, Cassio instead of Hempstead Road, Ross instead of Shrubbery, Church instead of Church Street, Palace instead of Charter Place, Sutton for the Sutton Road car park and Queens for the Mars A and B, among others.

The shorter names are needed because of the restricted width of the new signs which are

Moselle's move into Harlequin was one of the earlier.

Upon completion of Phase 1 Trewins moved home and their store in Queens Road finally closed.

Fitting of plate glass windows to the left of Harlequin's High Street entrance; December 1990.

to be positioned in the town centre and approach roads. The signs will direct drivers to the eight car parks and attempt to give information such as whether they are short or long stay car parks, closed or open.

WO, August 1987

Phase II completed on time

PHASE II of Watford's £100 million plus Harlequin Centre has been completed on programme by the P&O company Bovis Construction Ltd. The shopping centre, which occupies a ten-acre site in the town centre, will eventually provide 700,000 square feet of retail accommodation in 150 units. The basement provides lorry access to the shops.

There are upper and lower malls running the full length of the centre from the High Street to Charter Place, under a glazed atrium at roof level.

The five levels of car-parking above the shops are served by three street entrances and an underpass, also being built by Bovis Construction, which will link directly with the M1 slip road.

The £40 million final stage is due for completion in June next year and is being built on the site of the old Trewins store. Demolition could not start until the Trewin operation had been transferred to its 200,000 square feet store in the Harlequin Centre.

This store was completed four weeks ahead of schedule and enabled Trewins to begin trading there last August. The first phase was 100 per cent let and the second phase is already 50% let.

W O June 28 1991

Centre opens — and that's final

MORE than four years of hard labour and planning finally came to fruition on Tuesday, when the third and final phase of the Harlequin centre was opened. Flanked by a leaping, twirling Harlequin and brass band and watched by eager shoppers, Watford Mayor Councillor Peter Kiely revealed the plaque and declared the centre open.

A carnival-like atmosphere then filled the aisles of the two-floor mall with masks, balloons and flowers festooning staff and shoppers alike. Dominating the Watford skyline for miles around, the Harlequin Centre stretches from Queen's Road around the back of the High Street, linking up with Charter Place. Hailed as the major regional shopping centre for North London and the Home Counties, it boasts almost 150 shops and stores, both local, national and international.

But traditional shoppers also have High Street favourites like British Home Stores, Marks and Spencer and Littlewoods, linking up to the mall. Other stores expected to open in the near future include Hennes, Mothercare, Dixons and Miss Selfridge.

The completion of the centre marks a dream which started almost 30 years ago, although the first of nearly four million bricks were only laid in 1988. Trewins was the first store to open as Phase One in August 1990.

Phase Two was completed in June last year, with the third and final phase completed on Tuesday. Managing directors of Capital and Counties and Sun Alliance Group Properties proudly declared that all deadlines had been met exactly to the day.

WO, June 19 1992

The opening of Phase II saw many desertions from the High Street including the showrooms of British Gas and Eastern Electricity. Elderly people who bussed into the town centre to pay their bills – and perhaps collect a prescription from Boots – found that all three had gone and they had to trek down the High Street to an alien place:

What future for shops?

SHOPKEEPERS in The Parade fear that soaring rates and rents will force up to half of them to close within the next six months.

That's the claim being made by one retailer who says the Harlequin Centre has created a Catch 22 situation for small businesses in other parts of Watford. Austin Rockman, who runs Sarnies Sandwich Bar in The Parade, says business has been lost to the Harlequin Centre but retailers like himself could not afford to move to the centre as the rents are so high. "I believe that we will see up to 50 per cent of traders moving out of The Parade within the next six months because they just cannot afford to pay the business rates and the rents. Trade has dropped off a lot since the Harlequin Centre opened and somebody has to do something about it soon or The Parade will be dead before the year is out.

"I have had to apply to the council to extend my opening hours just to try and keep the money coming in. I don't want to have to work 12 hour days but I haven't got any choice. If things don't improve soon I will seriously have to consider closing down altogether. It's getting that bad," said Mr Rockman.

According to figures obtained by Mr Rockman from estate agents trying to lease units, the cost of a 218 sq ft shop space in the

September 1990 and three pleased-looking workmen pause for a memento photograph near a unit reserved for Moselle (next to Evans).

At about the same time Moselle's on the Parade are holding a 're-location sale'.

Harlequin Centre is £31,000 a year with a well positioned 233 sq ft unit available for £43,000. There's no way businesses like mine could be able to afford those sort of prices but at the same time trade is so bad where we are we can't afford not to move," he added.

Brian Sykes, chairman of Watford Chamber of Commerce and Industry said the chamber was aware of the problem of The Parade.

"I have heard a number of such stories recently. To be honest there is very little that can be done in the short term but we are working closely in conjunction with other bodies like the council with a town centre enhancement scheme which aims to make the whole shopping area more attractive to shoppers. My vice-chairman Robert Baldry, who is manager of the Harlequin Centre, is about to launch a major advertising campaign, and has offered to help businesses by offering publicity on the back of his campaign."

He added that leaflets on what else is on offer in the town centre will be handed out to Harlequin Centre shoppers to bring them into other parts of the town.

Review, June 1992

1992/3 were perhaps the worst years for the High Street so many closures having taken place and replaced, albeit very temporarily, by swag shops, with many letters, some of which not entirely in favour of Harlequin, written to the local press:

We love the Harlequin

REFERRING to the various letters and articles in the Watford Observer criticising the development of Watford, and in particular the Harlequin Centre, I thought I should write to assure you that many people including my

family and myself, think a most wonderful job is being done.

Of course we remember the old country town that Watford used to be, the cattle market, the High Street outside Cawdells with two-way traffic and parked cars. It seems incredible now, but there were not so many cars then, were there?

In the 1950s I worked at the Ever Ready factory in Lower High Street and there were 120 of us with just three cars.

Now I work in a factory in Leavesden with 96 people who come in more than 90 cars. That is an indication of the changes that have taken place in our lifestyles and we congratulate the council on keeping up with them.

We love the Harlequin Centre and look forward to the next phase. We feel very pleased that we live in such a progressive area and we thank the planners for that.

F and G B, Duncan Way, Bushey.

WO, June 1992

A tale of two shopping complexes

TWO shopping complexes within the same catchment area having widely different fortunes are illustrated by The Harlequin Centre, Watford, and The Galleria, Hatfield.

Hatfield's American-style shopping mall was looking forward to a better future after chartered accountants Grant Thornton was appointed receivers on Monday, with the shopping complex owing secured and unsecured lenders about £160 million.

The Galleria's financial problems originated from a combination of a £60 million overrun in the original £90 million construction budget. Adding to this was an 18 month delay in the original 21 month building timetable and operational problems due to the failure to complete the complex to its original specifications.

Banks and other secured lenders are owed £130 million, the Carroll Foundation itself is currently owed some £30 million in unsecured debt and writs exceeding £50 million have, been issued against a number of parties involved in the design and construction of The Galleria.

Watford Retail Group chairman Mr David Hignett said The Harlequin Centre and The Galleria are within the same catchment area and The Harlequin Centre might benefit from The Galleria's problems. He added: "However, I think the impact would only be minimal because The Galleria has never traded successfully."

A Capital and Counties spokesman said a main difference between the two projects was that The Harlequin Centre has a sound financial base and construction contracts were completed on time or ahead of schedule.

WO, September 1992

Naturally, upon its opening, many photographers wanted to try their hand at capturing images of the new centre – only to be astonished on being told by security men that 'photography was not allowed.' An enquiry elicited a reply that some shopkeepers did not want their shop fronts photographed and perhaps published in their trade's magazines when they had a new, and innovative shop-front design:

Exclusive images for stores in the centre

SHOPPERS will be forgiven for not recognising well-known stores in the Harlequin Centre. For many have been designed exclusive to Watford 150 – and may not be seen anywhere else in the country.

Harlequin, like any department store, is open at set times; there is no flexibility for traders to open at hours to suit either themselves or particular trade needs. Until Sunday opening was permitted (July 1995) Harlequin remained tantalisingly closed with shutters at Queens Road and Charter Place entrances (Queens Road, above).

Signage within Harlequin is clear, legible and easily visible; but the direction finder was most used, in the early days, until familiarity began to assert itself.

Mr Jonathan Rawnsley, senior manager of the Harlequin project explained the centre and the retailers worked together to come up with exciting and individual shop fronts for the centre.

He said: "We said to all the retailers you can do your usual shop front if you want but how about doing something different. It just makes it more exciting and interesting, not just the same old thing over and over again."

Richards has steered clear of its conventional shop image and introduced real changes both inside and out, with different colours, marble floor, and spacious interior with plush changing rooms. Ravel has also undergone major changes with Harlequin-like lettering on the shop front and revamped displays.

"People in Watford are going to be extremely proud of this centre," Mr Rawnsley said.

WO, June 1992

Woolworths closed and did not reappear in the town under their old guise but, as part of the Kingfisher Group, closed their B & Q warehouse at Lower High Street and re-opened larger as the 'Depot':

The wonder of Woolies that was

THE WOOLWORTH store in Watford High Street closes on Saturday after more than 70 years service in the town.

It is not known whether management at the company's head office plan to open up another shop in the area. They are said to be looking at a number of sites. A company spokesman said: "This is part of the development programme that is going on at the moment. Decisions are going to be made that are best for the customer and for the employees."

"Five million pounds is being spent on re-equipping the chain. It is Woolworth's dream to have a shop on every single high street in every single town. Staff have been offered the option of either a transfer to any company within Kingfisher PLC, the conglomerate that owns Woolworths, or redundancy pay.

The majority have taken redundancy pay. The run-up to the closing down has seen feverish activity with the shop opening on Sundays." Morale amongst staff has been low since Christmas.

One member of staff, Mr Jonathan Steeden, said: "Staff reaction to the closure has been very depressing. A lot of us take pride in the shop and seeing it in such a mess is horrible. "I think we will all be relieved when it's over because it has been hideous since Christmas,

we have had no respite."

The shop was opened on May 13, 1916. It was the 68th to be opened in a chain that now has 785 outlets.

WO, January 1990

The legacy of the town's planners who, in the 1960's, proposed that the ring road, when completed should have its traffic flow reversed, came to roost. If the logic was correct that traffic travelling in an anti-clockwise direction would permit passengers to alight from buses into the centre, and that cars could enter and exit car parks from the

The legend 'all enquiries' on a sign board affixed to premises frequently indicates a 're-development potential'.

12

If the seats are occupied when one most needs a rest there's always the Food Court a short distance away where a variety of snacks and beverages may be had.

High gloss and cleanliness is a feature of Harlequin which is taken for granted – and is in marked contrast to the drab High Street; though sometimes the cool fresh air of the 'outside' can be very welcome!

natural, inside, slow lane, it proved impractical in the long run. The Palace car park, being among the first built, has crossed-over entrance and exits which blocked traffic flow. Lane-changing brought chaos to the system resulting in gridlocks.

Upon the opening of the M1 link a drastic rethink was applied and over a short period of time road markings were changed to allow traffic to flow more freely than hitherto.

Police helpless as campaign brings chaos

"A TRAFFIC blockade" was how Watford Police described the snarl-up at the centre of town last Friday. Chief Inspector Vic Botterill said: "We had over 250 calls on Friday night. The place was choc-a-block and Beechen Grove was at a complete halt.

"The problem is that Watford is a successful town in trading terms, but it has a road system which just doesn't support it.

"The roads don't service the sheer weight of traffic. Some people were attempting to park, some people were trying to get off the road system; some people were just going round and round, the end result was chaos.

"One woman phoned us in tears she didn't know the system and had been around six times without getting off; in fact, one of the big problems was the number of motorists who were unfamiliar with the area."

He said that Watford's commercial success was a double-edged sword. The Harlequin Centre continued to attract thousands of shoppers into the town in the run up to Christmas and its successful advertising campaign had proved a great draw.

"The thing is, the campaign is set to continue, so more and more people will be coming into Watford,' said Inspector Botterill.

He added: "The official line is that we are doing all we can to service a road system that was not built for a successful trading town. Nothing can be done in policing terms. It is a challenge for everyone. Of course its easy to say that the planners should have thought about at, but it's too late now."

He suggested that a "traffic-watch" office should be set up in the Harlequin centre to advise potential shoppers on the road and parking situation. "Even a recorded message, updated every half hour or so would be useful," he said.

"We must advise people that if they are coming to Watford they are going to have to deal with the situation. We would appeal for them to use public transport, trains, wherever possible. If you are coming to shop here from outside the district, let the train take the strain, not the ring-road." said Inspector Botterill.

WO, October 1992

Harlequin is not to blame

HARLEQUIN boss Bob Baldry has hit back at claims that the pre-Christmas town centre gridlocks were the shopping centre's fault.

He pointed to figures showing more cars parked in the town centre car parks in January than in the pre-Christmas rush. "The figures certainly seem to show the blame is not entirely at our door, they vindicate what we've been saying all along," he said. Car parking hit an all-time high on Saturday, January 23, when 14,139 cars squeezed into the seven town centre car parks.

The Saturday before Christmas, December 19, had the largest pre-festivities total with 13,569 cars parked. "I think the situation is that there is less tension now than in the pre-Christmas period and drivers are being more considerate towards one another " Bob said.

"And perhaps the pre-Christmas problems have taught people a lesson or two.

"I still don't think we have sufficient car parking space in town but we are pleased with the way we are dealing with it at the moment." The increase in cars coming into town is great news for the town's retailers.

"Not only are they coming in in good numbers, but they seem to be spending as well," Bob added.

F Obs, March 1993

Bricks laid to perfection

LOVE it or hate it, Watford's giant shopping centre – dubbed the "theatre of shopping" by its owners – has caught the eye of judges in a national building design competition. More than three million bricks, in first class condition and laid to perfection, helped make the Harlequin Centre the South East regional winner of the 1993 Brick Development Association (BDA) Quality Brickwork Awards. It was chosen from more than 300 building projects spread throughout the United Kingdom and Northern Ireland, and received one of the 13 regional awards in the annual competition.

Just about everyone involved with the Harlequin Centre, previously known as the MARS 1 contract, got a share in the honours.

Certificates were awarded to Chapman Taylor, architects of the centre, Bovis Construction and Ben Barrett and Son, building contractors, and to the owners of the centre, Capital and Counties, Sun Alliance and Watford Borough Council.

Judges considered ten key areas of the building work, including straightness of courses, alignment of wall faces, cleanliness of faces and finishing and match of mortar joints.

WO July 1993

In the wake of the work on the Harlequin site it came as little surprise that, towards the end of 1989, it was announced that Woolworths were to close. Closure took place in January 1990, the store demolished and the site joined the general activity of rebuilding which included the old Vicarage, premises in King Street and Pickfords warehouse on the corner of King Street/George Street.

If Harlequin was a major project for the town to absorb what of the rest of the town during the four years of building Harlequin?

In Kingswood there were years of bitter wrangling over the decision to close the Golf Range and build a leisure park; from the futuristic drawings it was christened the 'Horrordome'. Nearer to the town centre the building of the Watford Springs was dogged with delays and acrimonious arguments which caused a rift in the Watford Labour Party.

There were proposals to Municipalise the West Herts Golf Course – which were defeated; the Council lost money on direct labour projects and in 1993 were forced to announce a package of cuts including closing the Town Hall's Assembly Halls provoking an enormous outcry resulting in their continuance until handed over to a private firm to run as the 'Colosseum'.

Finally the Peace Memorial saw work started in turning into a very long delayed Hospice. The M1 link – taking the route proposed in 1928 – opened in 1993, following which some thought was given to Watford's road direction marks so that traffic, at last, was sensibly 'laned' to avoid the clogged car parks and enable it to turn off for West Watford, etc.

Rolls-Royce closed and precipitated arguments as to the future of Leavesden Aerodrome which developers see as a fantastic opportunity to make a pile of money; – but many nearby residents would prefer to see much of the land restored to its original purchase use as playing fields. Scammells closed and plans announced for part of the site to be a business park but, instead, 457 homes were built and £350,000 donated by the developers for 'improving the rail link from West Watford'.

A patch of playing field at Courtlands Drive was appropriated to housing as was a patch in Ridge Lane. Chiswell Wire, in Sandown Road closed and developed into housing. Bushey Hall School site was developed into housing. George Stephenson College was closed and demolished; developers want to turn the site into a retail warehouse park. Reeds School site, Orphanage Road, was developed with three large hi-tech office blocks and nearly 300 homes; the Odhams-Sun site in Whippendell Road is to be redeveloped; approaches were made by developers who wish to build a retail warehouse park.

Tolpits Lane was extensively developed into the Metro Centre and Wolsey Park. Two retail warehouse parks were created at Lower High Street (by, coincidentally, the same developers as involved in the Kingswood Leisure Park scheme) and a road Gyratory system built to encircle them and connect with the M1 Link; to get from Bushey Arches by car one has to cross the old High Street three times in the process.

The developers renamed the Bushey Arches area as 'Watford Arches.' Three large office blocks were finished in Clarendon Road, and sites cleared for three more.

Fishburns closed in 1990 and after five years the site was cleared for development into a retail warehouse park; Sainsbury's (who wanted a supermarket on Odhams site long before ASDA arrived) finally got a supermarket opposite Odhams. Watford General Hospital entered into cooperative partnership with Mount Vernon.

A notice appeared that the West Herts Sports Ground may be under threat of sale (for development) but nothing has so far happened; an application from some West Watford residents for a cricket pitch in Cassiobury Park was agreed by Council; this was feared to spell doom to the Annual Horse Show which would be precluded from having the horse rings on the part appropriated to the cricket outfields.

Hard upon the heels of the shops whose tenants had moved into Harlequin (or ceased business due to the recession) came a new phenomenon; that of many shops being taken on apparently short lets and selling a wide variety of plastic, housewares and clothing at cheap prices. The stores quickly earned the title of 'swag shops.' Above, left, corner of New Street; right, Gordon Scott's ex-shoe shop.

One may be forgiven a wry smile if, upon asking what extra transport facilities have been arranged to cope with this extra influx of business one learns that the answer is exactly nil. But as congestion looms heavily around the corner the exhortation is to cut down using one car; there is no sign of the projected West Watford Link which would give huge relief to Vicarage Road, Hospital services and West Watford Residents although in September 1996 improved access to Watford and Croxley Business Parks was finally provided.

An outcry was caused about the 'state of the town' following the exodus of so many local traders and their replacement by scruffy, untidy and raucous 'swag shops', and the swift decline of the upper parade. The council's answer was to permit the only trades willing and able to take occupancy and the result has been a number of licensed premises opened, following which there has been a spate of shop window breakings and advertisement display unit wreckings, and many shops obliged to install metal shop blinds for after shop hour protection.

No provision has been made within the town to replace the loss of small industrial units . . .

As will be seen from this list there have been immense changes which have happened to – some will say afflicted – Watford during the past few years, with yet more to follow.

This supplement, to update your copy of The Book of Watford by reference to Watford's most important recent change, is an abridged part of the Mars 1 story from *'The Book of Watford, II'* a book which details the major changes of the past thirty-five or so years.

A major part of this new book is a colour pictorial record of the High Street from end to end, both sides, (nearly two and a half miles) reproduced on a scale of approximately 1:250 over 62 pages, together with comment and many older comparison photographs.

Another major part is the publication in it of the entire work of John Britton's 1837 book *'Cassiobury'* (first time ever) with all original plates in colour, plus, of course, many aspects of modern Cassiobury.

The frustration of gridlock; during this minor occasion it was possible to walk from Beechen Grove around to the flyover passing stationary cars on the way. 1993

Supplement to
The Book of Watford

J B Nunn, Malden Road, Watford. Text excerpts by courtesy of Westminster Press Ltd and the Review Newspaper Group. Photograph on page 4/5 by Aerofilms Ltd. Colour Separations by Riverside Reproductions Ltd, printing by Moorland Printers Ltd, Watford. 1996.

Supplement to
The Book of Watford
Price £2.95 when sold separately.